RESIDENTIAL & LIGHT COMMERCIAL CONSTRUCTION STANDARDS

*Compiled from the
Nation's Major Building Codes,
Recognized Trade Custom
& Industry Standards*

RESIDENTIAL & LIGHT COMMERCIAL CONSTRUCTION STANDARDS

Compiled from the
Nation's Major Building Codes,
Recognized Trade Custom
& Industry Standards

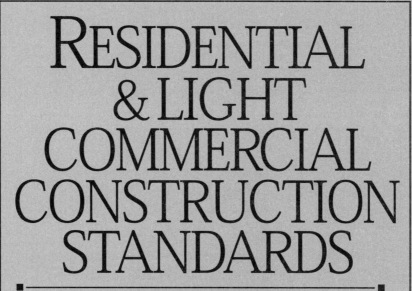

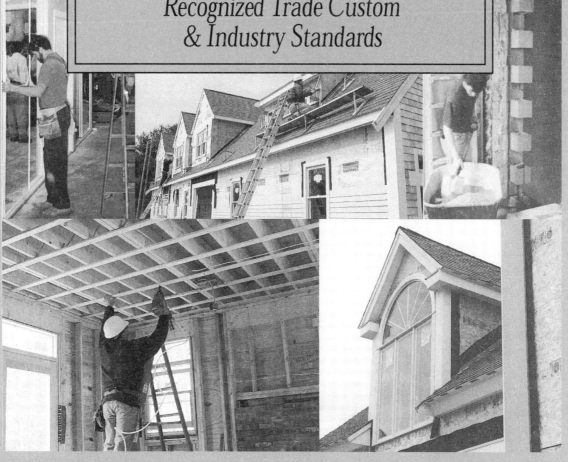

Copyright 1998

R.S. Means Company, Inc.
Construction Publishers & Consultants
Construction Plaza
63 Smiths Lane
Kingston, MA 02364-0800
(781) 585-7880

The editors for this book were Mary Greene, manager, Reference Books; Robin MacFarlane, manuscript editor; Marla Marek, copy editor; and Howard M. Chandler, Senior Engineer/Editor. The production manager was Michael Kokernak. Composition was by Paula Reale-Camelio and Erin Terry. The art director was Helen A. Marcella. The book and cover were designed by Norman R. Forgit. Blueprint background on the cover is courtesy of Matthew Doheny, E.M. Doheny Associates, Duxbury, MA.

Printed in the United States of America

10 9 8 7 6 5 4

Library of Congress Cataloging in Publication Data

ISBN 0-87629-499-9

TABLE OF CONTENTS

See the beginning of each chapter for a detailed listing of contents. In addition to the topics listed below, every chapter includes Common Defect Allegations and a listing of professional associations.

PREFACE

The concept for this book began with a group of California construction defect analysts who, in the course of their work in claims litigation, collected a tremendous amount of data to help define construction quality standards. Their ongoing efforts to compile and maintain a current library of information from a range of authoritative sources convinced them that having this kind of data collected in one convenient resource would be a boon not only to defect analysts and insurance personnel, but for contractors and subcontractors, engineers, architects, and owners. Having quick access to reliable standards would enable users to answer questions directly and avoid costly errors and disputes. The result is fewer sources of conflict among all the parties involved in a project, and a much better chance for a job that meets code, quality, and schedule expectations.

At the National Association of Home Builders 1997 Builders Show, a group of contractors, leaders in both their industry and NAHB, came together to help outline the book's contents. These individuals, listed in the Acknowledgments (see "About the Editors"), provided the direction the book needed to ensure its usefulness to contractors and other members of the project team. Some of these NAHB members, most of whom are Trustees of the Commercial Builders Council, went on to play a major role in the book's development as editors. R.S. Means editors brought their own practical experience as contractors and engineers to this project, and directed and organized much of the research.

The Introduction explains the parts of the book and how to find what you need. It includes some examples of situations in which the book can be used to solve common problems. The last item before Chapter 1 is a brief explanation of current and evolving building codes.

DISCLAIMER

This book is a collection of information from a variety of published sources, both print and electronic, together with comments from the editors based on their own experience. Sources include model building code organizations, related testing and standards organizations, trade associations, commercial publishers, and a few product manufacturers. Presentation of this information is not intended to suggest that there are no other sources, nor that these are the legal requirement or standard for every location. Other accepted standards may be found on any of these topics. Product manufacturers can provide additional information and instructions, and other publications may provide more detail or a different perspective on some installations. Manufacturers' warranty requirements should always be followed. In all cases, users of the book should consult their local codes and building practices. The editors have made their best effort to ensure that the information from the model codes, standards organizations, and professional associations is current as of this book's printing. Users are urged to check with these organizations to ensure that they are referring to the latest available information at any given time.

Users of the book should apply their own judgment based on professional experience with the construction installations described, or obtain guidance from a professional with expertise on the subject(s). Users are also advised to refer, as necessary, to the excerpted sources in their entirety for a more complete understanding of a topic, and to consult the organizations listed at the beginning of each chapter for further information if needed. Many of the construction systems covered in the book are addressed by excerpts from several sources. The focus, coverage and specific recommendations may differ from one source to another. The purpose of including these different versions is to provide as complete a perspective as possible.

Note that the editors' comments (printed in white type in blue boxes throughout the book) represent these individuals' own experience in the field and are not intended to signify building code requirements or other standards. The editors have applied diligence and judgment in locating and using reliable sources for the information included in the book. However, neither R.S. Means Company, Inc. nor the editors make any express or implied warranty or guarantee in connection with the content of the information contained in this book, including the accuracy, correctness, value, sufficiency, or completeness of the data, methods and other information contained herein. R.S. Means makes no express or implied warranty of merchantability or fitness for a particular purpose, nor does it have any liability to any customer or third party for any loss, expense, or damage including consequential, incidental, special or punitive damages, including lost profits or lost revenue, caused directly or indirectly by any error or omission, or arising out of, or in connection with, the information contained herein.

Certain organizations that have provided excerpts in this book have their own precautionary statements regarding use of their information. These statements appear in the bibliography with the listing of the organizations' publications.

Illustrations shown in the book are provided to assist users in understanding the construction systems. These graphics may not include all requirements for a system, product, or unit, and may not represent the only acceptable method.

Note that a few pages of published material from manufacturers are included in order to demonstrate installation methods. These references are not intended as an endorsement of any product or manufacturer. By the same token, the First Source product information Web site connection for readers of this book is offered as an information tool only, and does not imply endorsement of the products or manufacturers.

ACKNOWLEDGMENTS

Assembling this book required the input, efforts and cooperation of a team of experts, including a number of organizations. The editors selected the materials excerpted from other sources, and added their own "Comments" based on years of experience in the field and as instructors. The editors — contractors, engineers, an architect and a former building inspection official among them — are listed in the "About the Editors" section of these acknowledgments. Several other individuals who contributed their time and efforts in reviewing and helping to shape the book from its initial stages are listed below.

The earliest drafts of the book were reviewed by Ray Caruso, Wayne DelPico, and Buzz Artiano. Mr. Caruso is Vice President of Operations for the F.N. Thompson Company in Charlotte, North Carolina, a general contracting firm. Mr. DelPico is Vice President of Comprehensive Development Corporation in Hingham, Massachusetts and an instructor at Northeastern University's Construction Management department, as well as the author of *Plan Reading & Material Takeoff*. Mr. Artiano is a residential and light commercial restoration contractor from southeastern Massachusetts and an active member of NAHB.

Key input in the development of the book came from a number of individuals, all of whom are active members of the National Association of Home Builders Commercial Builders Council: Cliff Schilling, a residential and light commercial and remodeling contractor from Portland, Oregon, and past president of the NAHB Commercial Builders Council; George Goudreau, Jr., a commercial developer from Cleveland, Ohio; Dale Gruber, a residential and light commercial contractor from Minnesota; Robert Ross, Vice President of Ross Construction, a residential, commercial and industrial contracting firm in Kalispell, Montana; Fred Dallenbach, a residential and light commercial builder in Louisville, Kentucky and former Chairman of the Commercial Builders Council; and Jim Quinly, a residential custom builder in Kansas City and former Chairman of NAHB's Remodelors Council.

We would also like to acknowledge the input of Jesse Page on the concrete and paving chapters. Jesse is a civil engineer with 15 years experience as a construction project manager and estimator, and is currently the editor of several cost books and a seminar instructor for R.S. Means. Keeping the manuscript organized through its many reviews and revisions and obtaining permissions were major undertakings in the preparation of this book. These tasks were deftly handled by Robin MacFarlane.

Marla Marek copyedited and organized Chapters 14-16. Linda Messersmith, Operations Director of Architects First Source, developed an Internet link for users of this publication to a customized directory of building products and manufacturers.

We are grateful to the model code organizations, professional trade associations, product manufacturer institutes, and publishers who allowed us to reproduce their materials. Each source is identified where it is quoted in the book. The bibliography at the end of this book lists all of these sources by chapter. Contact information for these organizations is provided in the chapter introductions. (Code contact listings are included in "Understanding Building Codes & Other Standards," preceding Chapter 1.)

About the Editors

Don Reynolds has more than 30 years experience in construction as a residential and commercial builder and a construction defects analyst. He is a licensed contractor and insurance adjuster, and is currently Senior Estimator at Ninteman Construction Company, a firm that specializes in medium and high rise buildings, condominiums, and concrete parking structures. Don is also president of Inland Property Consultants in San Diego, California, a firm that performs construction defect analysis, interprets building code, and provides expert witness testimony in litigation. Don has been a speaker at the National Association of Home Builders' annual Builders Show, on the topic of defining and achieving quality in construction, and avoiding defects. He is a member of the International Conference of Building Officials (ICBO).

Dale Peterson has been the owner of Peterson Construction Company in Little Falls, Minnesota, for over 25 years. In addition to performing new and remodeling construction jobs, both residential and commercial, Mr. Peterson serves as a "Construction Expert" in mediation and arbitration cases. He is an active member of the National Association of Home Builders, and a trustee of that organization's Commercial Builders Council. He also serves as the director of the Builders Association of Minnesota. Despite the growth and diversification of his business, Mr. Peterson continues to work in the field with his employees to ensure the quality for which his firm is known.

Jim Watanabe is President of JW Inc., a construction and construction management company in Honolulu, Hawaii. His work focuses primarily on light commercial projects. Mr. Watanabe is active in the National Association of Home Builders, serving as chairman of its Commercial Builders Council and former area vice president and Executive Committee member. He is also a member and former president of the Hawaii Building Industry Association, and has been honored by that organization as "Builder of the Year" three times.

Dennis Fong is a general contractor in California, with over 20 years experience in residential and commercial construction. Mr. Fong also performs construction analysis for insurance companies for litigation claims.

Howard Chandler, Senior Engineer/Editor at R.S. Means Company, is the editor of Means' *Residential* and *Repair & Remodeling Cost Data* books and instructor for Means' estimating seminar series. Mr. Chandler has spent more than 25 years in the construction industry, as the owner of a residential construction company and manager of field operations for a firm specializing in commercial, industrial, and institutional construction. Mr. Chandler has taught construction technology and management as Director of Education for the Massachusetts/Rhode Island Associated Builders and Contractors and at the Wentworth Institute of Technology, and has presented programs for the Appraisal Institute, the National Association of Home Builders (NAHB), and the National Association for Women in Construction, among other organizations. He is an active member of NAHB, currently on the national board of its Commercial Builders Council, and is a member of the Associated Schools of Construction.

Andrew Fleming, a licensed Master Plumber, Journeyman Plumber and Gas Fitter, has more than 25 years experience in plumbing, as a practitioner, inspector, and instructor. As a Master Plumber, Mr. Fleming performed all phases of plumbing, heating, and gas fitting in residential, commercial and industrial locations. He is a former plumbing and gas inspector for the city of Medford, Massachusetts, and has for the past eight years taught plumbing and gas fitting to apprentices and journeymen studying to obtain state licensure. He currently provides training, technical support and quality control and ensures code compliance of work performed by trade partners with his firm, ServiceEdge Partners, Inc. in Burlington, Massachusetts. Mr. Fleming is on the Board of Directors of the New England Association of Plumbing, Gas, and Mechanical Inspectors, where he served as Vice President for six years. He is on the Board of State Examiners of Plumbers and Gas Fitters, and Chairman of their Modular Home and Special Code committees.

Keith Everhart is a construction analyst for Golden Eagle Insurance Corporation. He performs investigations of residential construction defect allegations throughout California and Arizona; reviews building code interpretations, plans, and specifications; and determines "duty owed" based on industry standards and trade custom. Keith has over 30 years experience as a general contractor, building homes and managing commercial projects including schools and libraries, malls, parking garages, movie theaters, and hospital remodels. Keith is a past president of the Builders Association of Greater Nevada, a chapter of the National Association of Home Builders.

Raymond Arms, P.E., is a registered professional engineer with over 30 years experience in design, construction, contracting and failure analysis. He is registered in seven states, including California and Florida, where he designs electrical and HVAC systems for commercial and institutional buildings and performs failure analysis and construction defect analysis. He is a member of NFPA, ASHRAE, and the Southern Building Code Congress International (SBCCI).

Keith J. Reynolds is a general contractor who has built projects throughout the states of California, Arizona, and Texas. Mr. Reynolds performs both remodeling and new construction work, both residential and commercial, including shopping centers, with a specialty in banks and ADA modifications.

William Jorgensen is a contractor, construction analyst and estimator with over 20 years experience in residential, commercial, and institutional construction, and a specialty in concrete, framing and detailing in earthquake zones. As a construction analyst, he has sought fairness in identifying legitimate deficiencies by researching and presenting industry standards for items that are often not defined in the building codes. Mr. Jorgensen is currently Vice President of Quality and Loss Control for CNA Commercial Insurance Company's Building Assurance Center.

William H. Rowe III, AIA, PE is a principal of his own design and engineering firm in Boston. His work has involved a tremendous range of new and retrofit construction projects, including residential, institutional and commercial buildings. Mr. Rowe is a frequent lecturer at universities, including Harvard and the Rhode Island School of Design. He is the author of HVAC: *Design Criteria, Options, Selection* and a contributing author to other publications on mechanical design, facilities management, and property management.

John Moylan is a former editor of Means' *Mechanical Cost Data*, and is currently a cost consultant to R.S. Means Company. Prior to his tenure at Means, Mr. Moylan was a partner in a plumbing contracting company for more than 15 years.

John Chiang, P.E., is a registered professional engineer with over 15 years experience in electrical design and construction. His projects have included hotels, apartments, and medical and office buildings. Mr. Chiang is the editor of *Means Electrical Estimating Methods*, *Electrical Cost Data* and *Electrical Change Order Cost Data*.

Mary Greene, manager of R.S. Means' Reference Book publishing program, has edited more than 50 publications on topics geared mostly to contractors, architects, engineers, and facility managers. Under her guidance, a major focus of this program has been and continues to be working with leaders in the field to address the most needed topics in a practical, accessible format.

INTRODUCTION

Purpose of the Book

This book is a resource for anyone concerned with quality in residential or light commercial building construction projects. It is a compilation of current standards that define quality in construction. Its purpose is to give contractors and others one-stop access to information that will help resolve or avoid disputes, set a quality level for subcontractors or employees, and answer client questions with authority. It is based on building code requirements, and the educational materials developed by leading professional associations, product manufacturer institutes, and other recognized experts.

There are several ways to assess and interpret quality in building construction — including meeting safety and warranty requirements, aesthetic criteria, and other details of craftsmanship that contribute to the integrity and longevity of the structure. A fundamental measure of quality is adherence to the standards established by building codes, whose purpose is to protect life and property. Another definition of quality is the recommendations of institutes representing building product manufacturers. Their guidelines are distributed through publications and electronic products, on the Internet and in training sessions and videos. These recommendations, based on field and laboratory research, are often linked to warranties on the materials used. Quality standards are also set forth by professional associations that serve as advocates for contractors and design professionals. One of the ways these organizations serve their members is by developing and distributing educational materials on current and correct construction methods. Finally, there are the respected and experienced craftsmen, many of whom have taught courses and contributed to or authored books that convey quality in construction. The books they have written are often used in college-level and vocational schools to set a standard for the practice of residential and light commercial building construction.

To provide the most complete and balanced picture, the editors have drawn on as many of the above sources as practical in this book. In the process, they have reviewed scores of the most current publications, Web sites, and other materials. They have excerpted, with permission, key definitions of standards to create a one-stop overview of what contractors, owners, architects, building officials, and insurers should expect in the houses and light commercial structures they build, inhabit, design, inspect and insure.

How the Book Is Organized

This book is organized into 16 chapters. The Table of Contents at the beginning of this book lists chapter titles and the major topics within each chapter. Each chapter has its own "mini" Table of Contents, with more detailed listings. Throughout the book, the editors will refer you to related information in other chapters. Note that colored type and boxed text are used to clearly distinguish between building code excerpts, other industry standards, and the editors' commentary.

In addition to the list of contents, each chapter contains:

- **Common Defect Allegations:** Items to watch out for that are frequent targets of disputes.

- **Introduction & Professional Associations:** Background on the topic and a list of authoritative resources to contact if you need more detailed information that exceeds the scope of this book. These listings include phone numbers, addresses and Web sites. (We have made every effort to ensure that this information is current at the time of the book's printing. However, changes are inevitable, within organizations and particularly on the Internet. These contacts are, at the least, a reliable starting point.)

- **Model Building Code:** Always in blue lettering, these excerpts have been selected to give an overview of code requirements for various construction installations. UBC, CABO, and the Uniform Mechanical, Electrical and Plumbing codes are referenced to show how a construction installation is addressed by building codes, but users of the book will want to consult their own local codes for specific requirements in their own localities. Code excerpts in the chapters are always introduced by name, publication year, and code section number. In some cases, code sections may include references to further details or exceptions within the code book that we have not included in this publication due to space limitations and our focus on providing an overview. We have tried, in these cases, to summarize or note the topic of such references so you will know whether it is likely to be relevant to your question or problem. See "Understanding Building Codes" later in this section for an explanation of the various codes and how they apply (and relate to one another) in different parts of the country.

- **Industry Standards:** Recommendations, requirements and tolerances for construction installations from professional associations, product manufacturers' institutes, and respected published references. Often these resources provide more specific requirements for quality and finished appearance than do the building codes, since codes are focused primarily on ensuring the safety of the building occupants. In some cases, the recommendations of one Industry Standard authority may differ from another. Some may put forth more explicit, detailed or stringent requirements or tolerances than others. Our purpose is to provide users with as complete a perspective as possible, based on reliable information from the leading authoritative sources. (Note: The National Association of Home Builders' Residential Construction Performance Guidelines is a significant standard in this category that we were unable to excerpt in this book due to that organization's reprint policy. We did, however, note topics that are addressed by the NAHB publication.)

- **Comments:** Always appearing in white type within blue boxes, "Comments" are practical observations from the editors, respected construction professionals, based on their own experience and knowledge of various regions. A few items are covered primarily in the form of Comments. This occurs when there are no building code requirements on that topic and/or there are few available published standards for that type of installation.

In addition to the 16 chapters, there is a bibliography at the end of the book, with a complete list of the reference sources excerpted throughout the book.

- **Internet Link to Product Information:** www.rsmeans.com/prodsupp/rlstand.html

A customized link and directory for the *First Source Online* Product Information Web site. Once code and industry standards are known, products (whether or not they have been specifically identified by an architect or engineer in the project documents) need to be located, particularly non-"stock" items that may need to be tracked down. *First Source Online* is the most comprehensive listing of building product manufacturers available. It includes manufacturers' addresses, telephone numbers, trade names, and regional identification, with illustrated product descriptions. You can also link to the manufacturers' Web sites directly from the First Source site.

Note: Connecting to the First Source listing does not imply the editors' or publisher's endorsement of any of the listed products or manufacturers. The site connection is provided as an additional information resource.

Applying the Information

Following are a few examples of the many ways this resource can be applied to resolve or prevent a problem. Having readily available, authoritative information answers questions directly so that disputes and costly errors can be avoided. This helps reduce adversarial relations among all the parties involved in a project, and fosters a job that meets code, quality, and schedule expectations.

Example # 1

The model building codes that apply to various regions of the country are very similar in their basic requirements. (See "Understanding Building Codes" later in this section.) This book, with its building code excerpts (primarily from UBC and the *One- and Two-Family Dwelling Code* [ICC]), allows you to quickly and easily identify the aspects of a construction system that are addressed by building codes, and shows you the format and language in which you are likely to find that item in your own local code. For example, a question arises on correct standards for installation of a roofing system. Finding the answer in a code book may require prior knowledge of the subject as well as familiarity with the code format and organization. Chapter 8 of this book shows the main issues and requirements addressed by the model codes and other experts for the roof system in question. This information is easy to find, as it is clearly organized by type of roof installation. While you must still comply with your local building code and the project documents, this book gives you both the basic requirements and some tools to help you navigate any building code.

Chapter 8 is also full of supporting information including the recommendations of authorities like the National Roofing Contractors Association, guidance from respected construction publications, and practical comments from experienced contractors. If you require very detailed information beyond what is covered in the book, the chapter provides contact information, including Web site addresses and phone numbers, to contact your preferred source.

Example #2

A residential contractor is having to hire subcontractors to perform specialty concrete work for a light commercial job. While the contractor is confident in his firm's ability to build the project per plans and specifications, neither he nor his superintendent are experienced with this type of construction. Using Chapter 2 of this book as a reference enables the contractor and his superintendent to resolve any quality issues that come up, and to head off problems such as cracking, puddling, and cold joints. Not only is this information a helpful tool for preconstruction meetings with subcontractors, but it will be used during construction to clearly communicate quality standards and expectations.

Example #3

The owners of a new home complain to the contractor that they can hear the sound of plumbing in the bathrooms from the adjoining rooms. The contractor explains how he installed insulation in the interior partition walls to reduce sound transmission, but that it is impossible to completely muffle the sound. In Chapter 7, "Insulation and Vapor Retarders," the section on Soundproofing states that while "you cannot expect to make any walls in the house truly soundproof, you can effectively cut down the transmission of sound ... (using) a number of approaches (including) filling the interior partition wall with batts of R-11 unfaced fiberglass insulation or rigid foam rated at around R-11. If you want to make the wall even more soundproof, double the drywall on each side of the wall." While these are indicated as acceptable solutions, the reference also notes that the "best" technique uses 2x6 top and bottom plates, with staggered 2x4 wall studs, weaving insulation between the studs, then installing double layers of drywall on each side of the wall. In the example scenario, the contractor has used what industry standards would consider a reasonable approach to reduce sound transmission. Contractors might want to offer homeowners a choice of these options, spelling out differences in their associated costs. (Note: The "Common Defect Allegations" at the beginning of Chapter 14 offer a plumbing solution to the noise problem.)

Example #4

A general contractor has been hired to perform interior build-out work for a corporate library. Based on previous experience with similar projects, the contractor has submitted an estimate based on shelving and units that are more costly than the client had anticipated. Using wider units and thinner shelving material would decrease the cost significantly, but increase the likelihood of shelf deflection (bowing and sagging) and, consequently, customer dissatisfaction. Using the American Woodwork Institute reference table on shelf deflection in Chapter 6, the contractor can provide the owner with a clear and authoritative explanation of his recommendation.

These examples are a small sampling of the many uses contractors, engineers, architects, owners and others have described for this book. The primary intent of this publication is to make key information available for quick reference, thereby reducing errors and disputes and increasing project quality.

Understanding Building Codes & Other Standards

While up to four different levels of building code (federal, state, local and model) may apply to a project, these various requirements are normally identified within the local building code or by the local zoning board. In designing and building a project, the contractor and architect (and sometimes owner) consult local building code requirements and may discuss them with the local building department personnel.

Federal Codes address issues such as land use and environmental requirements. This category may include protection of historic properties and wetland protection. Federal codes are not involved in most residential and light commercial projects.

State Codes, enforced by local building officials, address life safety issues in areas such as fire protection and mechanical and electrical requirements. State codes may also cover environmental issues.

Local Codes are based on *model codes* established by the national organizations listed below, and may include additional requirements for your location. For example, local codes may specify setback and drainage requirements, maximum roof height, and minimum lot size. Local codes are typically enforced by the city building inspector and county zoning board.

Model Codes are established by national organizations for adoption by states within the regions they address. In this book, we have included excerpts from model building codes (primarily the UBC and CABO) to demonstrate what is commonly required by model codes for various construction installations. The other two model codes differ on some points, based on differences in regional practice. Model Codes include BOCA National Codes, ICBO Uniform Codes (including UBC), SBCCI Standard Codes, and the One & Two Family Dwelling Code. The first three apply to specific regions of the country; the fourth incorporates material on residential construction only from the other three and is applicable nationally. While the model code organizations update and modify their respective codes annually, most government agencies adopt the revisions every three years. The BOCA, ICBO, and SBCCI codes are in the process of being unified into one code called the *International Building Code*. Following is an overview of the model code organizations and the codes each produces.

The Three Major Model Code Organizations

The three organizations who write most of the code each publish a model building code. These are the Building Officials and Code Administrators International (BOCA), the International Conference of Building Officials (ICBO), and the Southern Building Code Congress International (SBCCI). BOCA's *National Building Code* applies to the northern states from the Mississippi to the East Coast. ICBO's *Uniform Building Code* (UBC) applies generally to the area from the West Coast to the Mississippi. The *Standard Building Code* (SBC), published by the SBCCI, addresses the southern Atlantic states, extending west through Texas.

These three code organizations share a common format, though specific provisions of the codes differ on certain items. Also, the UBC maintains design and material standards within the code, whereas the SBC and the NBC reference other consensus documents for those kinds of standards. (This is one reason why the editors chose to include UBC excerpts in this book.)

In addition to the *National Building Code*, BOCA also produces: the *National Mechanical Code*, the *National Plumbing Code* (*& Provisions Applicable to Detached 1 & 2 Family Dwellings*), the *National Fire Prevention Code*, and the *National Private Sewage Disposal Code*. The ICBO publishes not only the *Uniform Building Code* (UBC), but also the *Uniform Mechanical Code*, *Uniform Fire Code*, and many specialty codes on issues such as building conservation and abatement of dangerous buildings. The International Association of Plumbing and Mechanical Officials (IAPMO) publishes the *Uniform Plumbing Code*. In addition to the *Standard Building Code*, the SBCCI also publishes the *Standard Mechanical Code*, the *Standard Gas Code*, and the *Standard for Hurricane Resistant Residential Construction*, among others.

CABO: One & Two Family Dwelling Code

The fourth major code, which addresses residential construction only, is the *One and Two Family Dwelling Code* (OTFDC). This code, along with the *Model Energy Code*, has been maintained by CABO (Council of American Building Officials) through the 1997 amendments. The 1998 *International One- and Two-Family Dwelling Code* (IOTFDC), developed and maintained by the International Code Council, replaces this document and incorporates the former CABO code. The IOTFDC is applicable nationwide and covers residential new construction, remodeling, repair, use, occupancy and maintenance of detached one- and two-family dwellings and single-family townhouses not more than three stories high. Referencing standards from the other major model codes, it includes design data, and specifies building elements' dimensions, thereby reducing the need for an engineer in standard design and construction.

The International Building Code (IBC) — One Unified Code for the Year 2000

The International Code Council (ICC) was formed in 1994 by the three major model code organizations — BOCA, ICBO, and SBCCI — with the purpose of creating one national code by the year 2000 that covers building, mechanical, plumbing, and fire protection. (*The National Electrical Code®* will continue to be maintained by the National Fire Protection Association.) So far, the ICC has published the *International Plumbing Code*, *International Mechanical Code*, *International Fuel Gas Code*, *International Property Maintenance Code*, *International Zoning Code*, and the *International Private Sewage Disposal Code*. (In support of the ICC and the developing *International Building Code*, BOCA, ICBO and SBCCI are referring to ICC codes on plumbing, mechanical and sewage.) ICC has taken responsibility for maintaining the *International One- and Two-Family Dwelling Code* (formerly CABO) as well.

The 1997 UBC, excerpted in this book, should be the final version of this code, which will be merged with the ICC by the year 2000. The final version of the SBC was also published in 1997. The BOCA code will be updated and published again in 1999, a final version before the release of the IBC. While the ICC will include aspects of the three major model codes in the IBC, it will continue to reference consensus-approved standards prepared by committees consisting of producers, consumers, general interest and regulatory members.

Code-Related Standards

Building codes often reference standards, such as NFPA, ASTM, and ADA, which provide specific technical installation requirements for a particular system. For example, the building code specifies where a fire suppression system must be installed within a building, and also specifies that the system must comply with the *National Electrical Code®* (published by NFPA). This standard is referenced in all of the model codes, and is enforced in every state as part of the electrical requirement.

The Americans with Disabilities Act (ADA), also referenced in the building codes, is a federal civil rights law requiring building accessibility for people with disabilities. It applies to new construction for buildings with public accommodations or commercial use. Several states have adopted the ADA Act Guidelines as a code requirement (some with amendments).

Factory Mutual, Underwriters Laboratories (UL), and the American National Standards Institute (ANSI) are also referenced in building codes. Factory Mutual is a property loss prevention service. It offers testing and listing of construction systems, such as fire-resistance ratings on doors and other components, and wind resistance for roofing materials. Underwriters Laboratories also tests and lists construction systems and components for qualities such as fire and wind resistance. UL also has listings for electrical equipment and products.

The National Institute of Standards and Technology (NIST) conducts research on building materials which helps to provide guidance for building codes. The Federal Emergency Management Administration (FEMA) provides guidance related to flood management and disaster preparedness, and advises on related building code issues.

Contact Information

Following is a list of code and related organizations, with phone numbers and Internet Web sites.

International Conference of Building Officials (ICBO)
5360 Workman Mill Road
Whittier, CA 90601
Telephone: 800-284-4406
www.icbo.org

Southern Building Code Congress International, Inc. (SBCCI)
900 Montclair Road
Birmingham, AL 35213
Telephone: 205-591-1853
www.sbcci.org

Building Officials and Code Administrators International Inc. (BOCA)
4051 West Flossmoor Road
Country Club Hills, IL 60478
Telephone: 708-799-2300
www.bocai.org

International Code Council (ICC)
5203 Leesburg Pike
Suite 708
Falls Church, VA 22041
Telephone: 703-931-4533
www.intlcode.org

Americans with Disabilities Act
U.S. Department of Justice
Telephone: 800-514-0301
www.usdoj.gov/crt/ada/adahom1.htm
or the ADA Technical Assistance Center
Telephone: 800-949-4232

American National Standards Institute (ANSI)
11 West 42nd Street
New York, NY 10036
Telephone: 212-642-4900
www.ansi.org

American Society of Testing and Materials (ASTM)
100 Barr Harbor Drive
West Conshohocken, PA 19428-2959
Telephone: 610-832-9500
www.astm.org

Factory Mutual Engineering Corporation
1151 Boston-Providence Turnpike
P.O. Box 9102
Norwood, MA 02062
Telephone: 781-762-4300
www.factorymutual.com

Federal Emergency Management Administration (FEMA)
500 C Street, SW
Washington, DC 20472
Telephone: 202-566-1600
www.fema.gov

National Fire Protection Association (NFPA)
1 Batterymarch Park
P.O. Box 9101
Quincy, MA 02269-9101
Telephone: 617-770-3000
www.nfpa.org

National Institute of Standards and Technology (NIST)
Public Inquiries Unit
Building 101, Room A903
Gaithersburg, MD 20899
Telephone: 301-975-NIST
www.nist.gov

Underwriters Laboratories, Inc. (UL)
333 Pfingsten Road
Northbrook, IL 60062
Telephone: 847-272-8800
www.ul.com

CHAPTER 1 ASPHALT PAVING

Table of Contents

*Text in blue print indicates excerpts from model building code(s). "Comments"
(in solid blue boxes) were written by the editors, based on their own experience.*

**For building product information, use this book's special
Internet gateway to thousands of manufacturers:
www.rsmeans.com/prodsupp/rlstand.html**

CHAPTER 1

ASPHALT PAVING

Common Defect Allegations

- *Movement of the subgrade is the major cause of asphalt pavement failure. Water is the major cause of subgrade movement, beyond poor compaction. The cross slope should be such that there is no water ponding on the surface. Water should be directed away from buildings and paved surfaces.*

- *Ordinarily we experience defect claims on asphalt that include cracking, settling, and alligatoring. Sometimes problems are caused by improper installation, but usually they result from lack of maintenance, or the system has simply run the length of its Normal Useful Life. Traditional maintenance requires that the surface be recoated regularly with a slurry seal or fresh oil and sand to reduce the evaporation of resins from the integral adhesives within the product. The insurance industry assigns the Normal Useful Life of various products to establish depreciation schedules. The recognized industry Normal Useful Life of asphalt paving is 10 years. Therefore asphalt paving that shows deterioration at 9 years and 10 months is quite ordinary, and not a compensable claim.*

Introduction

Often there is no written residential standard that clarifies trade custom or defines deficiencies commonly found in defect claims. In the case of asphalt paving on private land (driveways rather than street paving), standard building codes typically do not address installation. There are, however, some industry standards that are helpful.

This chapter presents these industry standards, in addition to the editors' comments on good practice, which is based on experience in residential asphalt construction and light commercial paving.

The following checklist may be helpful as you review the site in preparation for starting the project.

Site cleaning _____

Soil type _____

Subgrade moisture conditioning_____

Subgrade compaction _____

Drainage_____

Vehicle weight _____

Asphalt mix design _____

Weather extremes _____

Local code _____

Local custom _____

Edgings_____

Special Considerations _____

_____

The following resources may be useful for locating additional information on asphalt paving.

National Asphalt Pavement Association
5100 Forbes Blvd.
Lanham, MD 20706-4413
Telephone: 301-731-4748
www.hotmix.org

Association of Asphalt Paving Technologists
1983 Sloan Place
St. Paul, MN 55117
Telephone: 612-293-9188

The Asphalt Handbook
Asphalt Institute
P.O. Box 14055
Lexington, KY 40512-4053
Telephone: 606-288-4960
www.asphaltinstitute.org
The Asphalt Institute produces educational materials to help ensure the proper use of asphalt. The organization offers several publications, including "Model Specifications for Small Paving Jobs" (CL-2).

See Chapter 2 for information on concrete slabs, finishes, and paving, including tolerances, defects, and deterioration.

Ed. Note: Comments and recommendations within this chapter are not intended as a definitive resource for construction activities. For building projects, contractors must rely on the project documents and any applicable code requirements pertaining to their own particular locations.

Subgrade Preparation

Comments

While there are no recognized national standards for residential driveway subgrade preparation, the following guidelines are recommended good practice.

Frequently, private asphalt driveways are placed on native soil. Consideration must be made as to soil type. Among the least desirable soil types is expansive clay, and preferable types include crushed stone. When expansive clay is encountered, an aggregate base material might be used to separate the subgrade and the asphalt. Asphalt pavement is considered flexible; however, it will fail with subgrade movement. In simple terms, the best base is a granular material that will allow water to perk away from the asphalt without expanding or contracting. Design criteria should allow for slope to divert water away from buildings and paved surfaces without ponding, usually requiring a horizontal surface slope of 1/4" per foot or more.

Subgrade compaction helps support and strengthen the pavement. The thinner pavements commonly used on private driveways require that the subgrade be compact. While compaction and moisture testing is optimal, it is not usually performed on private driveways. Often, project specifications require that weed killer be applied on the subgrade prior to installing the base course.

One cause of bumps and dips in the pavement is lack of smoothness in the subgrade. The grade should be shaped to drain, and should be as smooth as the asphalt pavement that will be placed on it.

In colder climates, water can freeze under the asphalt and expand, causing heaving and cracking. Occasionally, wood 2x edge forms are used at the pavement edges to achieve proper thickness and maintain specified grade. The edge forms should have full bearing on the grade to prevent the roller from driving them down and changing planned grade.

Layers

Industry Standards

Means Graphic Construction Standards
(R.S. Means Co., Inc.)

Asphalt pavements transfer and distribute traffic loads to the subgrade. For commercial applications, the pavement is typically made up of two layers of material, the wearing course and the base course. The wearing course consists of two layers: the thin surface course and the thicker binder course that bonds the surface course to the heavy base layer underneath. The base consists of one layer that varies in thickness, type of material, and design, according to the bearing value of the subgrade material. If the subgrade material has a low-bearing value, either the thickness or the flexural strength of the base must be increased to spread the load over a larger area. For residential driveways, typically only an asphalt wearing course, or asphalt with crushed stone base course would be used.

Increasing the flexural strength of the base course can be accomplished by mixing asphalt with the base material. The addition of the asphalt doubles the load-distributing ability of a conventional granular base. For unstable soils, a layer of geotextile stabilization fabric can be added between the base and the subgrade. This fabric not only adds tensile strength to the base, it also prevents the subgrade material from pumping up and contaminating the base when the different layers are being installed. This method is sometimes used for light commercial projects. For commercial applications, granular base courses usually range from 6" to 18" in thickness.

Asphalt Pavement for Commercial Applications

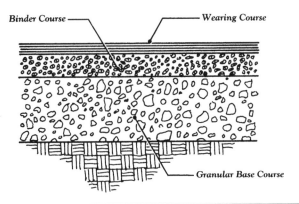

R.S. Means Co., Inc., *Means Graphic Construction Standards*

Figure 1.1

Asphalt Placement

Comments

There are no recognized national standards for asphalt placement. However, the following guidelines are recommended good practice.

Do not begin placing asphalt when the atmospheric temperature is below 40°. Never place asphalt on frozen ground.

Asphalt for paving is a mixture of various aggregate sizes and asphalt oil. This mixture is heated and hauled to the job site in open dump trucks. The mix for private driveways and parking lots is usually finer (no coarse aggregates) than for streets. This makes the surface smoother, with a finer texture. Ideally, you should know what temperature the asphalt should be when it arrives at the site. This information can be obtained from the plant. It is best to check the load in the truck with a thermometer. Experience has shown that an excessive amount of blue smoke will rise from a too-hot mix. If the mix is too cold, it will appear too stiff, and the large aggregate will not be fully coated with asphalt. If the mix levels off in the truck, the contractor has a good indication that there is too much asphalt in the mix. Asphalt is stiff enough when it remains in a pile or heaped in the truck. When there is too little asphalt oil, the mixture will have a brownish color and appear dull. Watch for nonuniform mixture.

Prior to placing the asphalt, all concrete and asphalt edges should be coated with tack coat, or emulsified asphalt diluted with water. The tack coat allows the pavement to bond with other materials, helping to seal out water.

Sometimes, residential driveways are too confined and too small to permit the use of a mechanical spreading machine. When this situation occurs, the asphalt mix is dumped on the grade in piles. The piles should be spotted, so workers who are spreading the mix by hand do not walk on the material. If they should step on it, the footprints should be raked out to the full depth of the course. The hand placing should not include casting or throwing the material. An asphalt, or lute, rake should be used to spread material placed in piles by shovels.

The mixture should be placed to the depth of the final thickness—plus 1/4" per 1" inch of depth—to allow for compaction.

Design

Industry Standards

Means Graphic Construction Standards
(R.S. Means Co., Inc.)

The thicknesses of the courses within the pavement vary with each layer, according to the intended use of the pavement and, as noted earlier for the base course, the bearing value of the subgrade. For example, pavement may contain a 1" surface course, a 2"–3" binder course, and a 5" or more base course. Standard commercial parking lot pavement may consist of 2-1/2" of wearing surface and 8" of granular base, while a residential driveway may consist of two 2-1/2"–3" wearing course with no binder course.

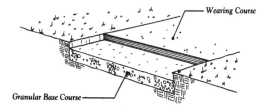

Bituminous Sidewalk or Driveway

R.S. Means Co., Inc., *Means Graphic Construction Standards*

Figure 1.2

Use a ride-on driven smooth wheel roller for compaction. Small, inaccessible areas can be compacted by a smooth plate vibrating compactor. Initial rolling should occur as soon as possible. This first pass rolling will provide the greatest compaction on the pavement. The drive wheel of the roller should always be forward in the direction of the paving. On very steep grades, this position may have to be reversed. Work from low side to high side for the initial and second passes. Final finish rolling to achieve a smooth surface should occur when the mix is hot but can barely be touched with the hand.

It is a common practice to use diesel oil to coat lute rakes, shovels, and compactors. This should be minimized as much as possible, because the distillate will damage the asphalt. Heating the shovels and lutes will work well to keep them clean.

If you should run short of paving mix and only need a small quantity to complete a job, you still have to order a ton of mix to keep it warm in transit. Long distances from the plant will require a larger quantity to keep warm. The plant dispatcher should be able to provide guidance on these issues.

Recommendations

National Asphalt Pavement Association
(NAPA Internet Web Site: www.hotmix.org)

Hot mix asphalt is a mixture of aggregate and liquid asphalt cement, combined at a hot mix plant. The advantages of hot mix asphalt include:

- Availability for use immediately after being placed and rolled, with no curing time
- Durability
- Ease of maintenance
- Conformance to varying terrain
- Flexibility (resistance to damage from freeze–thaw)

Asphalt can be mixed in different formulas for different textures and purposes, such as a driveway that also functions as a play area or basketball court.

Full-depth hot mix driveways (constructed of hot mix from the subgrade up, as compared to a stone base with an asphalt layer on top) are more resistant to freeze–thaw and drainage problems, since they provide greater uniform pavement strength and keep water out of the driveway base.

Correct drainage must be figured before installing a new driveway and any low or soft spots corrected. A soil sterilizer should be applied to prevent grass or weeds from germinating and growing up through the pavement at a later date.

When overlaying an existing asphalt driveway with a new one, it is important to first patch and correctly compact all holes and trouble spots. If the driveway has a gate, the gate may need to be rehung to adjust for the increased thickness. If there are surface boxes (for example, water valves) or drainage gratings in the driveway, they may need to be releveled. These items may or may not be covered by the asphalt contractor.

Full-Depth Asphalt Pavements for Private Driveways

Industry Standards

Asphalt Institute
(AI Internet Web Site: www.asphaltinstitute.org)

Drainage

Good drainage is important for pavement durability. It is desirable to blend the surface of the pavement to the contour of the existing ground so that the surface water runs over it or away from it in its natural course. In flat areas, the driveway should be sloped or crowned not less that 1/4 in./ft. (2 cm/m) so all surface water will drain off. Roof drainage from downspouts should, if feasible, be piped well away from the edge of the driveway. In some cases, pipe cross drains may be needed to take the water under the driveway. Water should not be allowed to stand at the edges.

Generally, an underdrain system is not required when the pavement is constructed by the Full-Depth asphalt method, even over poor soil or in certain other undesirable drainage conditions. However, an underdrain system may be required if the driveway pavement is constructed using an untreated gravel or crushed rock base.

Pavement Width

Primary consideration should be given to building a driveway of proper width. It should be no less than 8 ft (2.4 m), but 10 ft (3 m) is a more practical minimum width. If the driveway will be used for both pedestrians and automobiles a 12 ft (3.7 m) width should be considered.

It usually is desirable to preserve aesthetic objects such as trees and rocks. Also, to avoid unsightly cuts in hilly areas, driveways should conform to the terrain. Therefore, where the property will accommodate it, a curving driveway will be more attractive. A curved driveway needs to be wider in sharp curves.

Pavement Thickness

Full-Depth asphalt pavements for residential driveways should have a minimum of 4 in. (10 cm) compacted thickness on a properly prepared subgrade (see Subgrade Preparation, below). This minimum is sufficient for many years of service (automobiles and an occasional truck) if the driveway is properly constructed. However, if there is concern about foundation conditions, such as soft subgrade or an exceptional number of heavy vehicles using the pavement, it may be desirable to increase the thickness to 5 in. (13 cm), or under extreme conditions, 6 in. (15 cm).

Ed. Note: The Asphalt Institute offers further information on thickness design in two reports, "Full-Depth Asphalt Pavements for Parking Lots" and "Service Stations and Driveways."

Subgrade Preparation

Before construction begins, buried utility lines in the vicinity of the driveway should be located. If they are likely to be damaged during construction, they should be relocated or protected. The subgrade soil must serve as a working platform to support construction equipment, and it also must serve as the foundation for the pavement structure. Because it must be capable of carrying the loads transmitted to it from the pavement structure, it is most important that the subgrade be properly graded and adequately compacted.

After grading and compacting with a roller, the subgrade should be tested to determine if it will support the construction equipment. This is done by driving a heavily loaded truck over it and noting the deflections. If part of the subgrade shows pronounced deflection, this indicates that the soil has not been sufficiently rolled or that the soil-moisture content of the subgrade is too high. If additional rolling fails to correct the unstable condition, the soft areas should be removed and replaced with 2 or 3 in. (5–8 cm) of hot-mix asphalt. In some cases of extremely poor subgrade, it may be necessary to remove the upper portion of the subgrade and replace it with better material.

Where it is possible that weeds may grow in the subgrade soil, the subgrade should be treated with a non-toxic commercial sterilant prior to paving.

Composition of Paving Mixture

It is recommended that the asphalt paving mixture to be used be of a type locally and readily available. Typically this would be a state highway department mix used for residential streets. Because they are used extensively, these mixes are usually the least expensive. If such locally specified mixes are not available, it is advisable to use the American Society for Testing and Materials Standard Specification D351 5, "Hot-Mixed, Hot-Laid Asphalt Paving Mixtures." Mix Designations and Nominal Maximum Size of Aggregate, 1/2 in. (12.5 mm) or 3/8 in. (9.5 mm) are recommended.

Spreading the Mixture

The thick lift technique [placing in lifts of 4 or more in. (10 or more cm)] is in most instances satisfactory. However, if subgrade conditions or traffic loads necessitate thicknesses greater than 4 in. (10 cm), it is suggested that the asphalt be placed in two layers. In some cases it may also be necessary to place the mix in more than one layer to achieve desired smoothness. Three in. (8 cm) of base and 2 in. (5 cm) of surface mix or 4 in. (10 cm) of base and 2 in. (5 cm) of surface are suggested thickness combinations for 5 and 6 in. (13 and 15 cm) total thicknesses.

Small pavers are available but most asphalt paving machines in use today place widths ranging from 8 to 12 ft (2.4 to 3.7 m). Relatively sophisticated self-propelled pavers as well as simpler towed equipment have been successfully used for residential driveway construction.

Whenever possible, hand placement of the mixture should be avoided. However, where access to the driveway site is limited, hand placement may be the only feasible construction method. When the asphalt mixture is placed by hand, it is essential that forms be set at the edge of the driveway. These will ensure a neat edge and will minimize surface imperfections when used as a reference for a strikeoff board.

Weather Conditions

Weather conditions affect asphalt construction. To obtain the best results asphalt paving should be done in warm and dry weather.

Compaction

Compaction of asphalt pavement mixtures is one of the most important construction operations contributing to the proper performance of the completed pavement. That is why it is so important to have a properly prepared subgrade against which to compact the overlying pavement. A steel-wheeled tandem roller is generally used for this type of work. However, many other types of rollers, including small self-propelled vibrating rollers, can be used to obtain the required compaction.

Maintenance

It is not necessary to seal the surface of a newly-constructed asphalt concrete driveway. When the pavement is properly constructed, the driveway should afford many years of service before a thin application of asphalt emulsion driveway sealer containing mineral grit (available at hardware stores) becomes desirable to improve the surface texture and seal small cracks. But, if the pavement is not properly compacted during construction a surface sealer may be needed within two to four years.

CHAPTER
2 CONCRETE

Table of Contents

(continued on next page)

Text in blue print indicates excerpts from model building code(s). "Comments" (in solid blue boxes) were written by the editors, based on their own experience.

For building product information, use this book's special Internet gateway to thousands of manufacturers: www.rsmeans.com/prodsupp/rlstand.html

2 CONCRETE

Common Defect Allegations

- A frequent defect claim on foundations involves sulfate corrosion of reinforcing steel and/or the corrosive effects of sulfates on the concrete paste. These conditions usually are related to water accumulating around the foundation due to poor drainage. Code violations (such as soil or paving installed too close to the sill plate, or site grades with negative slope) are often associated with these claims.

When sulfates are discovered, they usually enter the concrete from clay type soils that are rich in sulfates. The water is the vehicle for the sulfate migration. Elimination of the water condition should stop any advancement of the chemicals.

Reinforcing steel can also corrode when foundations with high accumulations of water, in low sulfate soils, have a hot water circulating system underslab. Often the cold water line and the hot water line will act as electrode and diode, producing a galvanic action that deteriorates the wall thickness of the hot water line. The first sign of this failure is often a complaint of hot spots in the floor when walking barefoot on hard surfaces.

In some cases where chlorides are present and steel has developed chronic failure from corrosion, concrete has cracked from expansion. Calcium chloride should never be used to accelerate concrete setting in foundations, when steel is present.

The solution for the above conditions is, almost always, to eliminate the water source and redirect the water as a part of the remedy. This can be done using a variety of methods, the most common of which is a french drain or chimney drains. These percolating drain systems have a tendency to fill with silt and become inactive after years of discharging water. Therefore a filter wrap is recommended around the crushed rock to keep the perforated pipe open and working as long as possible. Often sump pumps are installed in existing basements to eliminate water.

- Another defect is honeycombing, where the aggregate shows through in what should be a smooth concrete foundation wall. Improper vibration is typically the cause.

- Cold joints are a defect caused when too much time elapses between placement of batches of concrete. The concrete has begun to harden when the next load is placed on top of it, and the two batches do not completely merge. A cold joint could allow moisture to penetrate the foundation wall.

- Flatwork surface pitting from shale is another defect. The shale is found in some quarries where aggregate is being mined. Shale is a hard sandstone, small pieces of which go through the separators and get batched into the concrete. Pops in the surface tend to occur about a week after the concrete has been poured as the shale gradually absorbs moisture and expands, breaking out a small portion of the slab above it.

- Another common claim is structural soil settlement, causing foundation cracking and vertical dislocation. Claims can involve post-tensioned slabs (slabs with steel rods and threaded ends tightened after the concrete setting), tilting, but not cracking. This happens along the crown of a slope, especially on expansive soil from slope creep. Slope creep usually results from the cycle of drying and wetting of the soil, with gravity creating a dynamic that results in all movement, expansion and contraction, down slope. The bank starts shifting downhill.

- Placing concrete in very hot or very cold weather can create structural problems. To avoid these problems, ready-mix plants can add ice or hot water to maintain the proper temperature during placement. Concrete placement in extreme temperature conditions should, however, be avoided if possible.

- Exposed reinforcing steel is another concrete foundation complaint. Steel ties should be broken off and the wall patched with appropriate mortar wherever the ties were broken off.

We address the allowable tolerances for concrete installations in other parts of this chapter. However, the acceptable tolerances for a structure following exposure to natural disasters is a much broader interpretation. For example, immediately after the Northridge, California earthquake, when many buildings were being condemned, some building officials adopted a standard of ±1" in 20 feet as straight *line livable level. This became a common criterion of acceptability. Many factors play into the formula. While the standard homeowners policy excludes most disasters, many people had no shelter and no financial ability to restore the structure.*

Introduction

Concrete has long been thought of as a relatively simple product that is permanent, needs no maintenance, and generally only fails due to an outside, unexpected force. New research and advanced testing has shown that concrete is, in fact, sensitive to many ordinary conditions, such as the effect of sulfates, chlorides, and salts that exist in soils and are transported through water migration. In some cases, a quarry will sell unwashed sands or crusher run (rock manufacturing byproducts) at reduced prices for fine grading under slab. Often these materials carry corrosives that will not show up in the soils report, but will become harmful if water migration develops. These chemicals can attack the cement paste and/or reinforcing, resulting in early concrete failure.

Most of the leading forensic engineers in the construction industry will agree that methods to prevent concrete failure are relatively inexpensive, compared to the cost and complexity of remedial cures. The prevention is usually as simple as raising the cement quantity in the mix to create a more dense product, placing at a lower slump (less water), and installing surface grading and subsurface drainage so that all accumulated water will perk or drain away from the concrete structure.

Another form of prevention, especially in clay soils, is to keep copper water lines either overhead in the building or completely wrapped underground to prevent the accelerated effects of galvanic action when acids or corrosives are present, especially on re-circulating lines.

For more detailed information on various concrete installation procedures and standards, contact:

American Concrete Institute (ACI)
ACI, International
38800 Country Club Drive
Farmington Hills, MI 48331
Telephone: 248-848-3700
ACI offers many publications on the details of correct concrete design and construction. Among these publications is *Troubleshooting Concrete Problems*, which describes how to avoid potential problems with fresh and hardened concrete.

NAHB Research Center
400 Prince George's Blvd.
Upper Marlboro, MD 20772-8731
Telephone: 800-638-8556
www.nahb.com
Also refer to sections 2–4, 2–5 through 2–10, 2–12, 2–14, 2–17 and 11–7 in the National Association of Home Builders' publication *Residential Construction Performance Guidelines* for more information on concrete construction standards.

Portland Cement Association
5420 Old Orchard Road
Skokie, IL 60077-1083
Telephone: 847-966-6200
www.portcement.org
The Portland Cement Association publishes many books on mix design, placement, and testing.

Other organizations that offer technical information on concrete construction are:

Concrete Reinforcing Steel Institute
933 North Plum Grove Road
Schaumburg, IL 60195
Telephone: 847-517-1200
www.crsi.org

National Concrete Masonry Association
2302 Horse Pen Road
Hemdon, VA 20171-3499
Telephone: 703-713-1910
www.ncma.org
NCMA offers publications that provide information on building code requirements for masonry structures, software, and educational programs for contractors, designers, and home owners.

Ed. Note: Comments and recommendations within this chapter are not intended as a definitive resource for construction activities. For building projects, contractors must rely on a copy of the project documents and applicable codes pertaining to their own particular locations.

Planning Concrete Construction

Comments

The concrete requirements for a project are found on the structural drawings, specifically the foundation plan and sections showing details of footings, walls, piers, and slabs. Concrete items may be indicated on other drawings as well, such as mechanical/electrical, which may specify box-outs for piping and conduit or equipment. Architectural drawings should indicate surface finish treatments. The specifications and drawings should provide information on the strength of the mix and any admixtures that might be required.

Most general contractors have the capacity to perform the work related to cast-in-place concrete using their own employees. However, there is an increasing number of specialty contractors who form, place, and finish concrete and may be used as subcontractors by the GC. Most cast-in-place concrete used on construction projects is ready-mixed, delivered to the construction site by special trucks, and then placed in the forms by one of several methods: by a chute directly into formwork, into a hopper for distribution by wheelbarrows and mechanical buggies, into buckets to be hoisted by a crane, or into a concrete pump and pushed through a portable pipeline.

Industry Standards

Plan Reading & Material Takeoff
(R.S. Means Co., Inc.)

While concrete has many applications in construction, its main function is as a structural component. Concrete has an extremely high *compressive strength*; that is, the ability to resist a crushing force, usually imposed by the weight of the structure it supports.

With water as a main ingredient, mixed concrete is greatly affected by temperature and weather extremes. When placing concrete in cold weather, the poured concrete must be protected against freezing. Concrete that freezes prior to curing will never achieve its full strength. Similarly, pouring concrete on hot, dry days may evaporate essential water used for the curing process before it has a chance to set. Both conditions should be avoided.

The following factors should be considered in planning concrete construction:

1. The strength of the mix, specified as the concrete's *compressive strength per square inch* after curing (e.g., 3000 psi, 4000 psi).

2. The use of additives that accelerate the time for reaching full strength. For example, High Early Strength Portland cement will achieve the same strength in 72 hours that other types normally achieve in 7 days.

3. The size and type of the coarse aggregate used in the batching; for example, gravel, peastone, stone, and/or local aggregates such as slag.

4. The percentage of air incorporated into the mix, in the form of tiny air bubbles. This is known as *air entrainment*. Air entrainment increases the concrete's workability and resistance to weathering and salts. The standard air entrainment is between 3% and 5% and is accomplished by the use of an additive included in the mix.

5. Chemicals added to the mix, such as calcium chloride, which acts as a drying agent and decreases setting time for pouring in cold weather. Other chemicals are available that increase the curing time.

6. The use of lightweight aggregates to reduce weight per CY. Materials such as perlite and vermiculite are the most common and add considerable cost per CY. They are used to reduce the weight of the concrete, thereby reducing the overall structural load.

Other considerations for planning, such as a requirement for hot water (common practice in cold climates during the winter months), may be related to localized batching practices, and should be reviewed on an individual basis.

As a result of significantly better quality control, the use of ready-mixed concrete has all but eliminated the job-site batching of concrete in any large quantity. *Ready-mixed concrete* refers to concrete that is batched at an off-site location, then transported to the site in mixers.

Comments

Residential concrete is often ordered and handled based on industry and regional standards. Seldom is a design mix requested. Rather, the contractor may be required to submit the strength of the mix, specified as the concrete's **compressive strength per inch** *after curing (e.g., 3000 psi, 3500 psi). Contractors engaged in light commercial, commercial and heavy construction often work with design mixes and are required to submit specific documentation to the architect or engineer from the ready-mix supplier identifying the characteristics of the cement, aggregate or any admixtures used in the mix to conform to the specification. In these circumstances, site testing and certification of proper placing and curing procedures may also be required.*

Freezing & Thawing Exposures

UBC — 1997

1904.2.1 Normal-weight and lightweight concrete exposed to freezing and thawing or deicing chemicals shall be air entrained with air content indicated in Table 19-A-1. Tolerance on air content as delivered shall be ± 1.5 percent. For specified compressive strength f'_c greater than 5,000 psi (34.47 MPa), reduction of air content indicated in Table 19-A-1 by 1.0 percent shall be permitted.

1904.2.2 Concrete that will be subjected to the exposures given in Table 19-A-2 shall conform to the corresponding maximum water-cementitious materials ratios and minimum specified concrete compressive strength requirements of that table. In addition, concrete that will be exposed to deicing chemicals shall conform to the limitations of Section 1904.2.3.

1904.2.3 For concrete exposed to deicing chemicals, the maximum weight of fly ash, other pozzolans, silica fume or slag that is included in the concrete shall not exceed the percentages of the total weight of cementitious materials given in Table 19-A-4.

Comments

Pozzolans are organic materials that are ground and used as additives to increase the workability of the mixture or as a water retainer.

ACI offers publications on cold and hot weather concreting. (See the Introduction for more on ACI.)

Deterioration, Damage & Defects

Industry Standards

Concrete Repair and Maintenance Illustrated
(R.S. Means Co., Inc.)

Concrete does not always behave as we would like; some of the undesirable behavior can be seen as disintegration, spalling, cracking, leakage, wear, deflection or settlement.

A variety of factors influence concrete behavior. These factors include: design, materials, construction, service loads, service conditions and exposure conditions. Most of the observed behaviors are a combination of these factors working together.

Causes & Effects of Concrete Problems

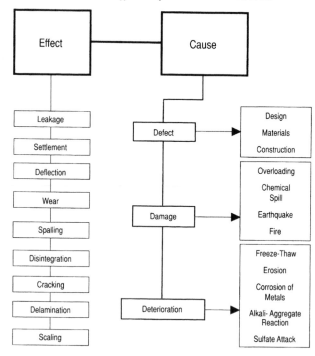

R.S. Means Co., Inc., *Concrete Repair and Maintenance Illustrated*

Figure 2.1

Industry Standards

Building Materials Technology, Structural Performance & Environmental Impact
(The McGraw-Hill Companies)

3.16 Building Problems Related to Concrete

In general it is true that the most dense and impermeable concrete is more durable and more resistant to a hostile environment. Quality concrete requires carefully graded sizes of aggregate, adequate proportion of cement, selection of the appropriate type of cement for the intended application, and proper curing.

Some of the common building problems related to concrete are listed here with their causes and suggestions for correction.

1. Sulfate deterioration of concrete is caused by moisture and sulfate salts in the soil that is in contact with concrete foundations, floor slabs, and walls. Type V sulfate-resisting cement is made for this purpose. To correct the problem (if the soil cannot be kept away from the concrete), better drainage might keep the soil dry and the salts in solid, not solution, form.

2. Efflorescence is the appearance of an unsightly fluffy white crust on the surface of walls. It is caused by salts in solution (in the concrete, the stone, or the bricks) moving to the surface of an interior or exterior wall. As the water evaporates from the salt solution in dry weather, a loose mass of white, powdery salts remains. The process of efflorescence slowly continues as the soluble salts are leached from the concrete by heavy rain entering the wall through joints or cracks. These soluble salts can come from admixtures, but most likely will come from poorly washed aggregates. Some relief from efflorescence can be gained by treating the surface of the wall with a water repellent and sealing all cracks and joints to keep out rain. If no cracks or pin holes are in the coating, these soluble salts should no longer be able to reach the surface.

3. Freeze-thaw cracks (forming in concrete in subfreezing weather) can be caused by concrete with a water/cement ratio that is too large. This can produce tiny crevices and voids around the aggregates, allowing penetration of water into the concrete by wind-driven rain. Tremendous forces, produced by the expansion of water as it freezes to form ice, cause spalls and cracks in the concrete. Prevention requires a better water/cement ratio and an examination of the admixtures if any were used.

   Correction requires waterproofing the surface of the concrete with a polymer-modified cement-based surface coating. Further protection could be gained by applying a protective coat of paint.

4. Corrosion of steel rebars can cause cracks and rust stains to appear in the concrete.

5. Leaks in concrete roofs or parking decks are due to water penetrating the surface. Although these surfaces should have been level, slightly raised in the middle, or slightly tilted toward the edge, rainwater often stands in pools. This water eventually penetrates into the concrete. Other cracks form from freezing and thawing or from heavy traffic on decks. Perhaps the parking deck is subjected to overloads and should have had better reinforcement. Perhaps expansion joints should have been used. Water leaks eventually form in the ceiling, with efflorescent salts showing in the cracks. A waterproof coating alone rarely works because the cracks continue to grow. A solution is to use epoxy in the clean cracks and to fill them with a flexible sealant material.

Cracks: Acceptable Tolerances and the Effects of Chlorides

Industry Standards
Concrete Repair and Maintenance Illustrated
(R.S. Means Co., Inc.)

Cracks and construction joints in concrete permit corrosive chemicals such as de-icing salts to enter the concrete and access embedded reinforcing steel. (See **Figure 2.2**.)

Steel corrosion may take place even in a high alkaline environment if chlorides are present. Chlorides are not consumed in the corrosion process, but instead act as catalysts to the process and remain in the concrete.

ACI 224R–90 presents the following table of tolerable crack widths in reinforced concrete:

Exposure Condition	Tolerance Crack Width	
	(In.)	(mm)
Dry air, protective	0.016	0.41
Humidity, moist air, soil	0.012	0.30
De-icing chemicals	0.007	0.18
Seawater and seawater spray; wetting and drying	0.006	0.15
Water-retaining structures*	0.004	0.10

*Excluding non-pressure pipes.

Note: 0.004 inches is equal to the width of a human hair. A crack of this width is almost unnoticeable unless the surface is wetted and allowed to dry.

The Corrosive Process

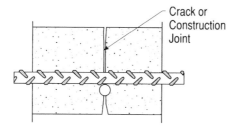

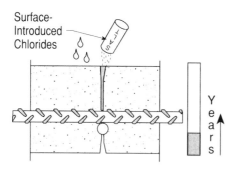

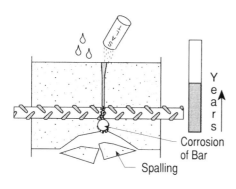

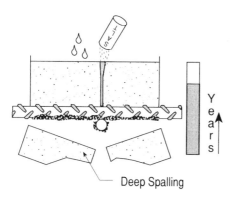

The corrosion process is progressive, beginning at the intersection of the crack with the reinforcing bar, then progressing along the bar.

R.S. Means Co., Inc., *Concrete Repair and Maintenance Illustrated*

Figure 2.2

Sulfate Exposure
UBC — 1997

1904.3.1 Concrete to be exposed to sulfate-containing solutions or soils shall conform to the requirements of Table 19-A-4 or shall be concrete made with a cement that provides sulfate resistance and that has a maximum water-cementitious materials ratio and minimum compressive strength set forth in Table 19-A-4.

1904.3.2 Calcium chloride as an admixture shall not be used in concrete to be exposed to severe or very severe sulfate-containing solutions, as defined in Table 19-A-4.

Industry Standards
Concrete Repair and Maintenance Illustrated
(R.S. Means Co., Inc.)

Sodium and calcium are the most common sulfates in soils, water and industrial processes. Magnesium sulfates are less common, but more destructive. Soils or waters containing these sulfates are often called "alkali" soils or waters.

All sulfates are potentially harmful to concrete. They react chemically with cement paste's hydrated lime and hydrated calcium aluminate. As a result of this reaction, solid products with volume greater than the products entering the reaction are formed. (See **Figure 2.3**.)

The formation of gypsum and ettringite expands, pressurizes and disrupts the paste. As a result, surface scaling and disintegration set in, followed by mass deterioration.

Sulfate resistance of the concrete is improved by a reduction in water-cement ratio and an adequate cement factor, with a low tricalcium aluminate and with proper air entrainment. With proper proportioning, silica fume (microsilica), fly ash and ground slag generally improve the resistance of concrete to sulfate attack, primarily by reducing the amount of reactive elements (such as calcium) needed for expansive sulfate reactions.

Effects of Sulfate on Concrete

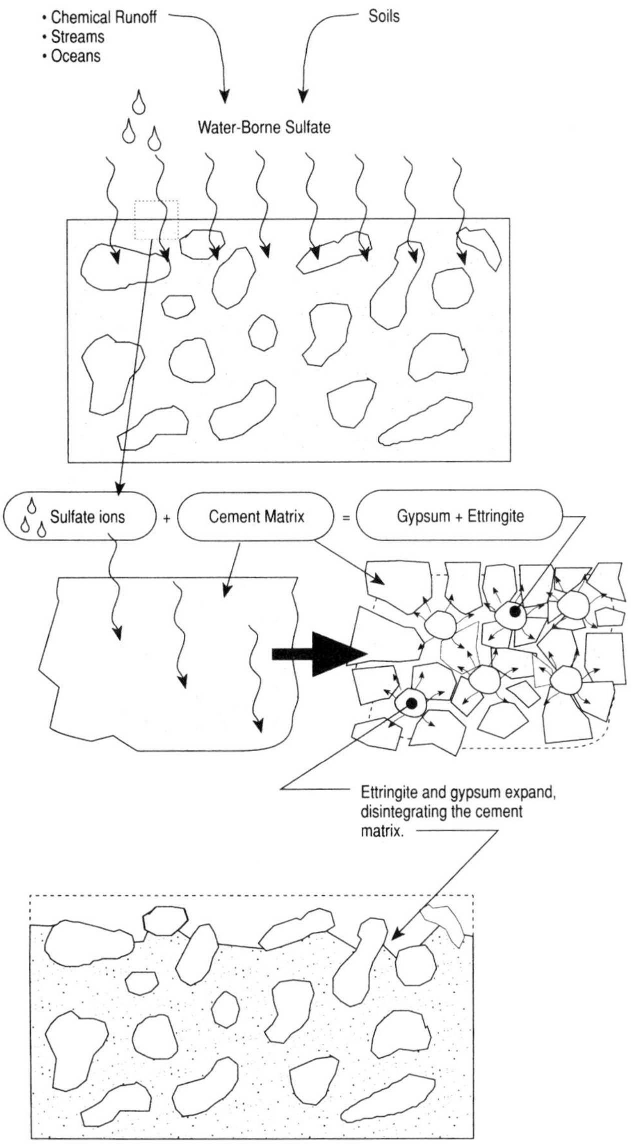

- Chemical Runoff
- Streams
- Oceans

Soils

Water-Borne Sulfate

Sulfate ions + Cement Matrix = Gypsum + Ettringite

Ettringite and gypsum expand, disintegrating the cement matrix.

R.S. Means Co., Inc., *Concrete Repair and Maintenance Illustrated*

Figure 2.3

Corrosion Protection of Reinforcement

UBC — 1997

1904.4.1 For corrosion protection of reinforcement in concrete, maximum water soluble chloride ion concentrations in hardened concrete at ages from 28 to 42 days contributed from the ingredients, including water, aggregates, cementitious materials and admixtures shall not exceed the limits of Table 19-A-5. When testing is performed to determine water soluble chloride ion content, test procedures shall conform to ASTM C 1218.

1904.4.2 If concrete with reinforcement will be exposed to chlorides from deicing chemicals, salt, salt water, brackish water, seawater or spray from these sources, requirements of Table 19-A-2 for water-cementitious materials ratio and concrete strength and the minimum concrete cover requirements of Section 1907.7 shall be satisfied. In addition, see Section 1918.14 for unbonded prestressed tendons.

Industry Standards
Concrete Repair and Maintenance Illustrated
(R.S. Means Co., Inc.)

Concrete is a high-alkalinity material. The pH of newly produced concrete is usually between 12 and 13. In this range of alkalinity, embedded steel is protected from corrosion by a passivating film bonded to the reinforcing bar surface. However, when the passivating film is disrupted, corrosion may take place.

Corrosion is an electrochemical process requiring an anode, a cathode, and an electrolyte. A moist concrete matrix forms an acceptable electrolyte, and the steel reinforcement provides the anode and cathode. Electrical current flows between the cathode and anode, and the reaction results in an increase in metal volume as the Fe (Iron) is oxidized into $Fe(OH)_2$ and $Fe(OH)_3$ and precipitates as FeO OH (rust color). Water and oxygen must be present for the reaction to take place. In good quality concrete, the corrosion rate will be very slow. Accelerated corrosion will take place if the pH (alkalinity) is lowered (carbonation) or if aggressive chemicals or dissimilar metals are introduced into the concrete. Other causes include stray electrical currents and concentration cells caused by an uneven chemical environment. (Clifton, J.R. *Predicting the Remaining Service Life of Concrete*, National Institute of Standards and Technology Report NISTIR 4712).

Industry Standards
Building Materials Technology, Structural Performance & Environmental Impact
(The McGraw-Hill Companies)

3.15.3 Rusting of Rebars in Concrete

As concrete ages, faulty design or improper curing results in inadequate drainage and in crack formation. Additional cracks result from the stresses of thermal expansion and contraction of the concrete.

Seepage of water into these cracks, half a millimeter in size or larger, carries dissolved oxygen and carbon dioxide into the concrete. This dissolved oxygen and the carbon dioxide are active in promoting corrosion. For example, oxygen maintains the alkalinity of the cathodic electrodes by its conversion to the hydroxide ion. This reaction keeps the pH at the cathodes at a high alkaline value. Dissolved carbon dioxide destroys the passivity of steel at the anodes by neutralizing the alkali in the hydrated cement and by releasing free chloride ions from calcium-chloride-containing cement (carbonation). Also, as water seeps through the cracks, it leaches out the soluble alkali from the concrete. As the pH of the concrete adjacent to the steel drops below 9, the protective film of ferrous oxide deteriorates and the passivity it once provided the steel surface is lost.

Pitting occurs at the anodes as iron dissolves to form ferrous ions. At the cathodes, oxygen and water are converted to hydroxide ions, which further increases the corrosion voltage. Thus the corrosion process is accelerated and serious structural deterioration occurs if further environmental exposure is not prevented.

Protecting Finishes from Chemical Damage
Industry Standards
Concrete Repair and Maintenance Illustrated
(R.S. Means Co., Inc.)

Aggressive chemical attack (liquid or gas) on concrete surfaces can be controlled by using chemically resistant materials in the concrete mix, or using surface-applied barrier coatings, membranes, or surfacing systems. Typical protection systems are listed in **Figure 2.4.**

Selecting Appropriate Surface Protection

Type of Surface Protection	Maximum Service Temperature °F/°C	Alkalies		Acids				Solvents		Bleach
				Inorganic	Organic					
		Strong	Weak		Weak	Moderate	Strong	Organic	Inorganic	
Epoxies	150/66	✔	✔		✔	✔		(1)	(1)	✔
Epoxy—Novolac	180/80	✔	✔	✔				✔(2)	✔(2)	
Furans	360/180	✔	✔	✔	✔	✔	✔	✔	✔	
Methacrylates (MMA)			✔		✔			✔(2)	✔(2)	
Polyesters	230/107		✔		✔	✔				✔
Potassium Silicates	2000/1093			✔(3)	✔	✔	✔	(1)	(1)	
Sulfur Cement	190/88			✔(4)	✔	✔				
Urethanes	150–250/66–122	✔	✔	✔(4)	✔	✔				✔
Vinyl Esters	220–250/104–127		✔	✔	✔	✔		✔	✔	
PVC		✔	✔	✔	✔	✔	✔			
Acid Brick	High			✔(3)	✔	✔	✔			
Carbon Brick		✔	✔	✔	✔	✔	✔			

(1) Resistant only to some solvents
(2) Moderate resistance to solvents
(3) Not resistant to Hydrofluoric Acid (HF)
(4) Moderate resistance to acids

Note: This table should be used as a guide only. Actual performance may differ depending on formulation.

R.S. Means Co., Inc., *Concrete Repair and Maintenance Illustrated*

Figure 2.4

Preventing Surface Defects

Comments

There are many causes for concrete surface defects. Some of the major defects, their causes, and the construction techniques that should be used to prevent them are described here. Many defects result from improper curing or errors in mixing or finishing.

Industry Standards

Concrete Repair and Maintenance Illustrated
(R.S. Means Co., Inc.)

Plastic Settlement (Subsidence) Cracking

Plastic settlements cracking is caused by the settlement of plastic concrete around fixed reinforcement, leaving a plastic tear above the bar and a possible void beneath the bar. The probability of cracking is a function of

1. Cover
2. Slump
3. Bar size

Settlement of plastic concrete is caused by

1. Low sand content and high water content
2. Large bars
3. Poor thermal insulation
4. Restraining settlement due to irregular shape
5. Excessive, uneven absorbency
6. Low humidity
7. Insufficient time between top-out of columns and placement of slab and beam
8. Insufficient vibration
9. Movement of formwork

Settlement (or Subsidence) Cracking

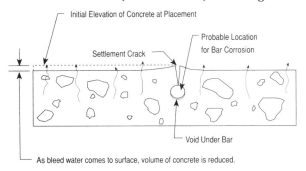

Probability of Subsidence Cracking (%)*

Cover	2″ Slump			3″ Slump			4″ Slump		
	#4	#5	#6	#4	#5	#6	#4	#5	#6
¾″	80.4	87.8	92.5	91.9	98.7	100	100	100	100
1″	60	71	78.1	73	83.4	89.9	85.2	94.7	100
1½″	18.6	34.5	45.6	31.1	47.7	58.9	44.2	61.1	72
2″	0	1.8	14.1	4.9	12.7	26.3	5.1	24.7	39

R.S. Means Co., Inc., *Concrete Repair and Maintenance Illustrated*

Figure 2.5

Plastic Shrinkage Cracking

Plastic shrinkage is caused by the rapid evaporation of mix water (not *bleed water*) while the concrete is in its plastic state and in the early stages of initial set. Shrinkage results in cracking when it produces tension stress greater than the stress capacity of the newly placed concrete. Plastic shrinkage cracking rarely fractures aggregate, but separates around the aggregate. Plastic shrinkage cracks may lead to points of thermal and dry shrinkage movement, intensifying the cracking.

Shrinkage Cracking

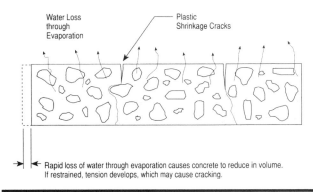

R.S. Means Co., Inc., *Concrete Repair and Maintenance Illustrated*

Figure 2.6

Industry Standards
Construction Principles, Materials, and Methods
(John Wiley & Sons, Inc.)

3.7.6.1 Scaling

Scaling is the breaking away of the hardened concrete surface of a slab to a depth of about 1/6 to 3/16 in. It usually occurs at an early age of the slab. Scaling of a slab might occur if it is subjected to cycles of freezing and thawing soon after the slab has been placed. A favorable temperature must be maintained long enough to prevent injury. Cycles of freezing and thawing and applications of de-icing salts on non-air-entrained concrete can also cause scaling. This is why air-entrained concrete is recommended for all severe exposure conditions.

Performing a finishing operation while free excess water or bleed water is on the surface causes segregation of the surface fines (sand and portland cement) and also brings a thin layer of neat portland cement, clay, and silt to the surface, leaving another layer of nearly clean, washed sand that is not bonded to the concrete under it. To prevent scaling from this cause, water should be allowed to evaporate from the surface or be forced to evaporate by fans or blower-type heaters, or it should be removed by dragging a rubber garden hose over the surface before finishing operations begin.

3.7.6.3 Dusting

Dusting is the appearance of a powdery material on the surface of a newly hardened concrete slab. An excess of harmful fines (clay or silt) in a concrete mix with the sand and portland cement at the surface can result in dusting. This condition emphasizes the need to use clean and well-graded coarse and fine aggregates.

Premature troweling and floating mix excess surface water with surface fines, weakening the portland cement paste. Troweling should be delayed until all free water and excess moisture have disappeared and concrete has started its initial set.

When carbon dioxide, as might be emitted from open portable fossil-fuel heaters and gasoline engines, comes into contact with the surface of plastic concrete, a reaction takes place that impairs proper hydration. Such fumes should be vented to the outside and sufficient fresh air ventilation provided.

Condensation sometimes occurs on a concrete surface before floating and troweling have been completed, usually in the spring and fall, when materials have become cold due to low night temperatures. If possible, this condition should be anticipated, and the concrete should be heated or at least hot water should be used for mixing. If this is impossible, blower type heaters should be used to lower the humidity directly over the slab, and fans should be used to increase air circulation. If heaters and fans are not available, windows and doors should be opened. When condensation is present, floating and initial troweling should be held to a minimum, and a concrete surface should not be given a second troweling.

Neat portland cement and mixtures of portland cement and fine sand should never be used as a dry-shake. Because condensation may occur for several hours while concrete is beginning to harden, emergency measures may have to be taken to finish a slab. A well-mixed dry mixture of 1 part portland cement and 1 part well-graded concrete sand may be evenly and lightly distributed over a concrete surface, if it is followed at once by troweling. There should be no second troweling, because additional condensation may take place after the first troweling.

Winter-protection heaters may lower the relative humidity around concrete excessively and inhibit proper hydration of the portland cement.

Water jackets should be placed on heaters to increase the relative humidity by evaporation, and moist curing methods should be employed. Heaters should be moved periodically so that no area will be subjected to an extreme or harmful amount of heat.

Proper curing for the correct length of time is essential. Concrete that is not cured properly will often be weak, and its surface will be easily worn by foot traffic.

Segregation
Industry Standards
Concrete Repair and Maintenance Illustrated
(R.S. Means Co., Inc.)

Segregation of concrete results in nonuniform distribution of its constituents. High slump mixes, incorrect methods of handling concrete, and over-vibration are causes of this problem. Segregation causes upper surfaces to have excessive paste and fines, and may have excessive water-cement ratio. The resultant concrete may lack acceptable durability.

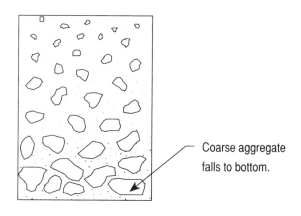

Coarse aggregate falls to bottom.

R.S. Means Co., Inc., *Concrete Repair and Maintenance Illustrated*

Figure 2.7

Cold Joints

Industry Standards

Concrete Repair and Maintenance Illustrated
(R.S. Means Co., Inc.)

Cold joints are places of discontinuity within a member where concrete may not tightly bond to itself. Cold joints may form between planned placements and within a placement. Some construction placement procedures require multiple lifts. A dam is a good example, as are tall walls. To achieve proper bond and water-tightness, the surface of hardened concrete must be free of dirt, debris, and *laitance*.

Proper cleaning and placement procedures sometimes are not followed or are very difficult to achieve. The result is a weak connection between placements that could result in weakness or leakage at a later date.

The other type of cold joint may occur within a planned placement if a part of the concrete in one placement sets, and then the reset of the concrete is placed on it. During the set, laitances form, providing for a weakened plane. Leakage may occur when the structure is put into service.

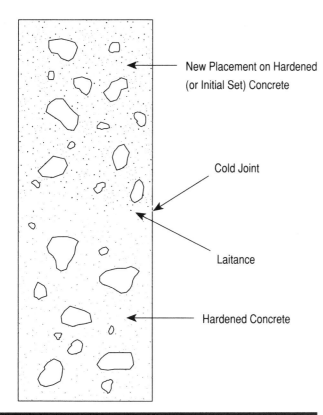

New Placement on Hardened (or Initial Set) Concrete

Cold Joint

Laitance

Hardened Concrete

R.S. Means Co., Inc., *Concrete Repair and Maintenance Illustrated*

Figure 2.8

Honeycomb and Rock Pockets

Industry Standards

Concrete Repair and Maintenance Illustrated
(R.S. Means Co., Inc.)

Honeycomb is a void left in concrete due to failure of the mortar to effectively fill the spaces among coarse aggregate particles. Rock pockets are generally severe conditions of honeycomb where an excessive volume of aggregate is found. (See **Figure 2.9**.)

Primary Causes of Honeycomb

Design of Members

- highly congested reinforcement
- narrow section
- internal interference
- reinforcement splices

Forms

- leaking at joints
- severe grout loss

Construction Conditions

- reinforcement too close to forms
- high temperature
- accessibility

Properties of Fresh Concrete

- insufficient fines
- low workability
- early stiffening
- excessive mixing
- aggregate that is too large

Placement

- excessive free-fall
- excessive travel in forms
- lift that is too high
- improper *tremie* or *drop chute*
- segregation

Consolidation

- vibrator too small
- frequency too low
- amplitude too small
- short immersion time
- excessive spacing between insertion
- inadequate penetration

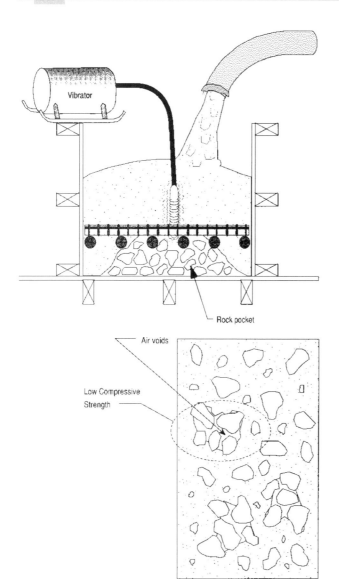

R.S. Means Co., Inc., *Concrete Repair and Maintenance Illustrated*

Figure 2.9

Water Penetration Prevention Measures

Industry Standards

Construction Principles, Materials, and Methods
(John Wiley & Sons, Inc.)

Mix Ratios & Curing Time

3.5.1.3 Impervious concrete requires a portland cement paste formulated to produce watertightness, or imperviousness. As with strength and durability, there is a direct link between the watertightness of a concrete and the relative quantities of water and portland cement in its mixture.

Tests show that the permeability or watertightness of a portland cement concrete depends on the amount of mixing water used in its water paste and the extent to which the chemical reactions between the portland cement and the water have progressed. The results of subjecting discs made with portland cement mortar, fine aggregate, and water to 20 psi water pressure are shown in **Figure 2.10**.

In these tests, mortar cured moist for seven days had no leakage when made with a water-cement ratio of 0.50, but there was considerable leakage with mortars made with the higher water-cement ratios. Also, in each case, leakage became less as the length of the curing period was increased. Mortar discs with a water-cement ratio of 0.80 leaked, even when moist-cured for a month.

Concrete Curing Time & Watertightness

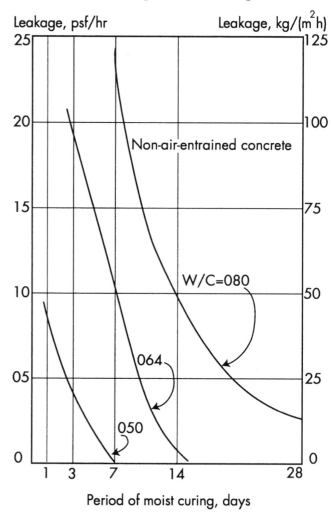

The effect of water-cement ratio on watertightness. Leakage is reduced as the water-cement ratio is decreased and the curing period is increased. Specimens were 1-in. x 6-in. (25-mm x 150-mm) mortar discs. Pressure was 20 psi (0.14 Mpa). Values are 48-hour averages.

Courtesy of Portland Cement Association

Figure 2.10

Air entrainment improves watertightness by allowing reduction of the water-cement ratio. To be watertight, concrete must be free from cracks and honeycombing.

As a result of testing and experience in the field, definite recommendations can be made regarding the maximum amount of mixing water that should be used for various construction applications.

Vapor Barriers

3.6.1.2 Slabs on Grade Subgrades should be trimmed to specified elevations, uniformly compacted, and moist when the concrete is placed. Except when a vapor retarder has been placed immediately below a slab, a moist subgrade is important to prevent too rapid extraction of water from the concrete when it is placed, especially in hot weather.

When a vapor retarder, waterproof membrane, or separator is not used, the bed to receive concrete should be moistened to minimize extraction of water from the concrete. However, at the time of placing, there should be no mud, soft spots, or free water standing where concrete will be placed.

The Portland Cement Association (PCA) recommends that a vapor retarder be placed under every concrete slab on grade where an impervious floor finish will be installed and in every other location where the passage of water vapor through a slab on grade is undesirable.

However, a vapor barrier placed in contact with the concrete will cause excess moisture in the concrete to bleed to the surface rather than downward, increasing the number of capillaries in the concrete and contributing to weakening the surface, more cracking, and higher permeability of the slab. Therefore, the PCA recommends that a vapor retarder not be placed directly beneath a slab, but rather covered by a 3-in.-thick layer of granular, self-draining material, such as sand.

When a vapor retarder is not used beneath a slab on grade, and a base course or fill is provided, a separator of building paper or other material that will withstand handling and construction traffic is sometimes installed. When such separators are used, they are usually installed between the base course or fill and the slab to prevent the fines or paste of plastic concrete from seeping down into the base course or fill. However, if such a separator is complete and impervious, it should not be placed directly in contact with the slab. If it is, it could act in the same way a vapor retarder often acts and contribute to warping (curling) of the slab and exacerbate drying shrinkage cracking.

Steel reinforcing, ductwork, heating pipes, and other items embedded in a slab should be set and supported at the proper elevation before concrete is placed.

Industry Standards
Concrete Repair and Maintenance Illustrated
(R.S. Means Co., Inc.)

Proper Slab Grading

Slabs requiring drainage for proper runoff need special attention. Drains should be at low, not high points. Proper slope-to-pitch for quick runoff is important to prevent deterioration and leakage within the structure. Standing water provides concrete with the potential for saturation, the worst condition for a freeze-thaw cycle. The quicker the water runs off the structure, the less leakage can occur through joints and cracks.

Incorrect Grading

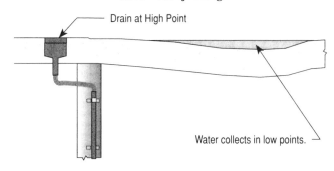
Drain at High Point

Water collects in low points.

R.S. Means Co., Inc., *Concrete Repair and Maintenance Illustrated*

Figure 2.11

Waterproofing & Dampproofing Foundations

Waterproofing
Industry Standards
Plan Reading & Material Takeoff
(R.S. Means Co., Inc.)

The purpose of waterproofing is to prevent the penetration of water through the exterior surfaces of the structure. Waterproofing is most often done below grade at the foundation level to prevent the transmission of water through the foundation walls or slab. When reading a set of drawings, care should be taken to determine the limits of waterproofing materials.

There are three basic classifications for waterproofing. The *integral* method involves the use of special additives mixed with concrete for use in poured foundations. *Membrane waterproofing* is the application of a waterproof membrane

Foundation Waterproofing

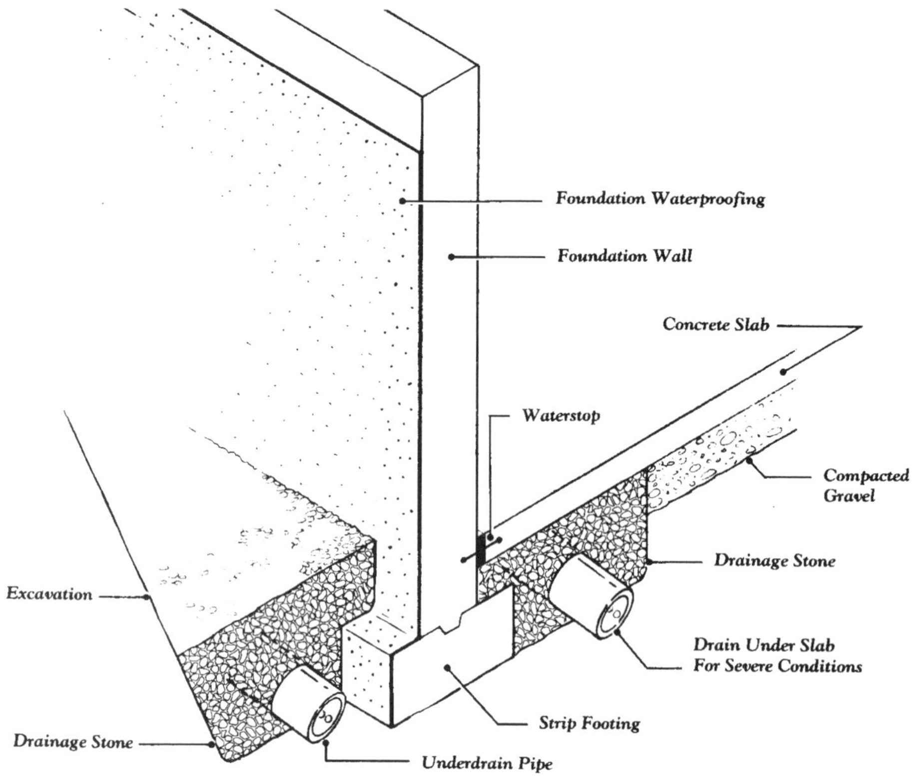

R.S. Means Co., Inc., *Means Graphic Construction Standards*
Figure 2.12

to the surface of the protected area. Finally, *metallic waterproofing* involves the use of a fine iron powder mixed with oxidizing agents applied to the surface area to be protected. The compound fills the pores of the concrete or masonry and, as the iron particles rust, they expand to form an impervious barrier to the migration of water.

Again, the specifications should be thoroughly reviewed for methods and products to be used.

Comments

For more detailed information on concrete waterproofing, consult ACI's Waterproofing the Building Envelope and Guide to the Use of Waterproofing, Dampproofing, Protective and Barrier Systems for Concrete.

Dampproofing Foundations

Dampproofing is typically applied to the foundation area below grade. It is not intended to resist water pressure and should not be confused with waterproofing. Dampproofing is used to prevent the penetration of moisture through the foundation wall in below-grade applications.

The most common methods of dampproofing include the application of a bituminous-based tar-like coating on the protected areas. The bituminous materials can be sprayed, painted, or troweled on, to provide a uniform coverage of the areas below grade. Another method involves the plastering of a cement-based mixture, called *parging*, over the surface area to be protected. Certain dampproofing products may require the application of a primer coat prior to the actual dampproofing application.

Industry Standards

Means Graphic Construction Standards
(R.S. Means Co., Inc.)

To be effective, foundation waterproofing requires a protective coating or covering on the exterior of the wall, a collecting underdrain, and porous backfill material to direct water to the underdrain. The protective coating may consist of bituminous coating applied by brush or spray, troweled on, asphalt protective board and mastic, or a membrane, an application of protective iron coating may also be used for waterproofing but requires an additional chipping of the concrete surface before installation.

The underdrain conduit should either be porous or contain openings to ensure collection of water. The conduit should be surrounded by coarse rock or gravel and laid with sufficient slope to direct the water to the collection area. The underdrain materials may be asbestos cement, bituminous fiber, corrugated metal (asphalt-coated), corrugated polyethylene corrugated tubing, porous concrete, vitrified clay, or PVC.

The porous backfill should extend up to a minimum depth below the final grade as required by site conditions. Where gravel or stone are uneconomical or unavailable, concrete block installed dry with spaced joints provides both protection for the waterproofing and a channel for excess water.

Comments

Normally the drain pipe is placed on the outside only of the foundation. In situations where the ground may become extremely wet, a drain pipe may also be placed on the inside of the foundation wall under the slab.

UBC— 1997

1402.4 Dampproofing Foundation Walls. Unless otherwise approved by the building official, foundation walls enclosing a basement below finished grade shall be dampproofed outside by approved methods and materials.

Testing Methods for Concrete Evaluation

Concrete Consistency/Slump Tests

Industry Standards

Construction Principles, Materials, and Methods (John Wiley & Sons, Inc.)

3.5.3.1 Slump Test

A slump test conforming with the requirements of ASTM Standard C 143 may be used as a rough measure of the consistency of concrete. This test is not a measure of workability, and it should not be used to compare mixes of entirely different proportions or that contain different kinds of aggregate. Any change in slump on the job indicates that changes have been made in grading or proportioning the aggregate or in water content. The mix should be corrected immediately to get the proper consistency by adjusting amounts and proportions of sand and coarse aggregate, care being taken not to change the total specified water-cement ratio.

In a slump test, a test specimen is made in a mold called a slump cone, which is made of 16-gauge galvanized metal. The base and the top are open. The mold is provided with foot pieces and handles.

For a slump test, a concrete sample is taken just before its batch is placed in the forms. A slump cone is placed on a flat surface, such as a smooth plank or a slab of concrete, held firmly in place by the tester standing on the foot pieces, and filled with concrete to about one-third its volume. Then the concrete is puddled with 25 strokes of a 5/8-in.-diameter rod about 24 in. long and bullet-pointed at the lower end. The filling is completed in two more layers, each about one-third the volume of the cone. Each new layer is rodded 25 times, with the rod penetrating into the underlying layer on each stroke. After the top layer has been rodded, it is struck off with a trowel so that the cone is filled completely. The cone is removed, by gently raising it vertically, immediately after the top layer has been struck off.

The slump of the concrete is measured immediately after the cone is removed. If the top of the slump pile is, for example, 5 in. below the top of the cone, the slump for that concrete is 5 in.

Comments

The old rule of using a 4" slump and a minimum mix design of 2,000 psi or 5 sacks will not get it done anymore. The new UBC code follows the ACI code, and it has very elaborate rules regarding pretesting of a mix design at varying slumps from the concrete ready mix producer. The code also provides minimums on testing when deliveries exceed 50 cubic yards.

In the 1997 UBC, there is a new section on Structural Plain Concrete (Section 1922), which applies only to Seismic Zones 0 and 1. Seismic Zones 2, 3 and 4 are excluded, except footings for buildings of Group R, Division 3 or Group U, Division 1 occupancy constructed in accordance with Table 18–1–C, and except for nonstructural slabs supported directly on the ground or by approved structural systems.

Investigation of Low-Strength Test Results

UBC — 1997

1905.6.4.1 If any strength test (see Section 1905.6.1.4) of laboratory-cured cylinders falls below specified values of f'_c by more than 500 psi (3.45 MPa) (see Section 1905.6.2.3, Item 2) or if tests of field-cured cylinders indicate deficiencies

Testing Methods for Concrete Evaluation

Mechanical Properties	Chemical Make-up	Physical Condition	External Manifistation (behavior)
Compressive Strength -Core testing (1) -Windsor probe (3) -Rebound hammer (2)	**Electro-chemical Activity** -Half cell potential (9) -Electrical resistivity (10)	**Uniformity** -Petrographic analysis (11) -Pulse velocity (4) -Windsor probe (3) -Rebound hammer (2) -Core testing (1)	**Cracks/spalls** -Hammer sounding -Infrared thermography -Impact echo -Pulse velocity (4) -Remote viewing (TV, borescope) -Exploratory removal
Quality of Concrete Ultrasonic pulse velocity(4)	**Carbonation Depth** -Acid based indicators (Phenolphthalein Solution) -Petrographic analysis (11) -X-ray diffraction -Infrared spectroscopy	**Air-Void System** (15)	**Deflections from Service Loads** -Load testing (ACI 437R) -Monitoring movements
Tensile Strength -Pull off testing -Splitting tensile strength (5)	**Alkali-Aggregate Reactions** -Petrographic analysis (11) -Uranyl (Uranium) Acetate fluorescence method	**Delaminations/voids** -Hammer sounding -Chain drag -Impact echo -Pulse velocity (4) -Exploratory removal -Remote viewing (TV, Borescope) -Infrared thermography	**Movements of Service/Exposure Conditions** -Load testing (ACI 437R) -Monitoring movements
Flexural Strength (6) (7)	**Chloride Content** (12) (13) (14)	**Location/Condition of Embedded Metals** -Pachometer -Radiography -Ground penetrating radar -Exploratory removal	**Leakage** -Visual observations -Infrared thermgraphy
Abrasion resistance (8)		**Water permeability**	**Temperature/moisture conditions** -Thermocouple -Thermometer
Bond Strength -Pull off testing		**Air permeability**	**External Geometry** -Visual observations
		Water absorption (19)	
		Frost & freeze-thaw resistance (16) (17)	
		Resistance to deicing salts (18)	

Note: Figures in parentheses denote number of standard test in Table A.

R.S. Means Co., Inc., *Concrete Repair and Maintenance Illustrated*

Figure 2.13

Standard Test Methods for Evaluating Concrete

STANDARD TEST METHODS FOR EVALUATING CONCRETE

NO.	DESIGNATION	TITLE
1	ASTM C 42	Obtaining and Testing Drilled Cores and Sawed Beams of Concrete
2	ASTM C 805	Rebound Number of Hardened Concrete
3	ASTM C 803	Penetration Resistance of Hardened Concrete
4	ASTM C 597	Pulse Velocity Through Concrete
5	ASTM C 496	Splitting Tensile Strength of Cylindrical Concrete Specimens
6	ASTM C 78	Flexural Strength of Concrete (Using Simple Beam with Third-Point Loading)
7	ASTM C 293	Flexural Strength of Concrete (Using Simple Beam with Center-Point Loading)
8	ASTM C 418	Abrasion Resistance of Concrete by Sandblasting
9	ASTM C 876	Half-Cell Potentials of Uncoated Reinforcing Steel in Concrete
10	ASTM D 3633	Electrical Resistivity of Membrane-Pavement Systems
11	ASTM C 856	Standard Practice for Petrographic Examination of Hardened Concrete
12	AASHTO T 259	Resistance of Concrete to Chloride Ion Penetration
13	AASHTO T 260	Sampling and Testing for Total Chloride Ion in Concrete and Concrete Raw Materials
14	AASHTO T 277	Rapid Determination of the Chloride Permeability of Concrete
15	ASTM C 457	Microscopical Determination of Parameters of the Air-Void System in Hardened Concrete
16	ASTM C 666	Resistance of Concrete to Rapid Freezing and Thawing
17	ASTM C 671	Critical Dilation of Concrete Specimens Subjected to Freezing
18	ASTM C 672	Scaling Resistance of Concrete Surfaces Exposed to Deicing Chemicals
19	ASTM C 642	Specific Gravity, Absorption, and Voids in Hardened Concrete

R.S. Means Co., Inc., *Concrete Repair and Maintenance Illustrated* [Table A]
Figure 2.14

in protection and curing (see Section 1905.6.3.4), steps shall be taken to ensure that load-carrying capacity of the structure is not jeopardized.

1905.6.4.4 Concrete in an area represented by core tests shall be considered structurally adequate if the average of three cores is equal to at least 85 percent of f'_c and if no single core is less than 75 percent of f'_c. Additional testing of cores

extracted from locations represented by erratic core strength results shall be permitted.

1905.6.4.5 If criteria of Section 1905.6.4.4 are not met, and if structural adequacy remains in doubt, the responsible authority shall be permitted to order a strength evaluation in accordance with Section 1920 for the questionable portion of the structure, or take other appropriate action.

ACI offers several publications on concrete testing. See this chapter's introduction for information on this organization.

1905.11 Curing.

1905.11.1 Concrete (other than high-early-strength) shall be maintained above 50°F (10.0°C) and in a moist condition for at least the first seven days after placement, except when cured in accordance with Section 1905.11.3.

1905.11.2 High-early-strength concrete shall be maintained above 50°F (10.0°C) and in a moist condition for at least the first three days, except when cured in accordance with Section 1905.11.3.

1905.11.3 Accelerated curing.

1905.11.3.1 Curing by high-pressure steam, steam at atmospheric pressure, heat and moisture or other accepted processes, may be employed to accelerate strength gain and reduce time of curing.

1905.11.3.2 Accelerated curing shall provide a compressive strength of the concrete at the load stage considered at least equal to required design strength at that load stage.

Concrete Admixtures

Comments

Admixtures are materials that are added to concrete to enhance certain properties for particular applications. Some types of admixtures include:

- fibrous reinforcing
- air entraining
- water reducing
- plasticizing
- quick setting
- corrosion inhibiting

Fibrous Reinforcing

Fibrous reinforcing is a synthetic fiber that promotes resistance in conditions in which high impact and abrasion are anticipated. It provides excellent secondary reinforcing and crack control. Fibrous reinforcing can be used in thin sections, pre-cast units, vaults, pipe, sidewalls, floor slabs, and similar applications. One and one-half pounds of fibrous reinforcing are used per cubic yard of concrete, and can be introduced with the aggregates or after all ingredients have been mixed.

Our experience with filament glass fiber strands added to the concrete or plaster mix has shown us, in a limited quantity of tests, that the fiber deteriorates from the Portland cement unless the material was chopped from a polypropylene source. Otherwise, the material leaves a hole in the concrete or plaster after three to five years. We do not yet have sufficient test results to determine the cause.

Air-Entraining Admixtures

Air entrainment can be achieved by adding an admixture to concrete or by using air-entraining Portland cement (see ASTM Standard C 150). Air-entraining admixtures introduce many air bubbles to the concrete, which results in better resistance to freezing and thawing in concrete slabs on grade. Air entrainment also enhances watertightness.

Water-Reducing Admixtures

This commonly used admixture is particularly appropriate when the mix design calls for a high-strength concrete.

Plasticizers

Plasticizers are used to create concrete that is extremely workable for high slump with the ability to flow for applications such as pumping. This admixture might be used for light commercial projects, for example, where concrete must be pumped to the second floor of a structure. Plasticizers are very useful for situations where a low-water cement ratio is desirable, along with a high degree of workability for ease of placement and consolidation. It is used for tremie concreting and other situations where high slumps are required.

Accelerators

This admixture promotes quick, high strength in concrete. It is available in chloride and non-chloride formula. (The non-chloride formula will not corrode reinforcing steel, metal decks or other metal components.)

Accelerators speed up the chemical reaction between Portland cement and water, and accelerates the formation of gel — the binder that bonds concrete aggregates. Accelerated gel formation shortens the concrete's setting time, which in turn offsets the slow-setting effects of cold weather, while helping to increase the strength of the concrete. Use of accelerators can also reduce concrete curing time, enabling forms to be removed earlier.

Joints

Industry Standards

Construction Principles, Materials, and Methods
(John Wiley & Sons, Inc.)

3.12 It is impossible to entirely prevent cracks in concrete, but good jointing practice will help reduce their number and encourage them to occur in more acceptable locations. Joints in concrete work permit movement and volume changes; the handling, placing, and finishing of conveniently sized areas; and the separation of independent elements. The types of joints required in concrete include control joints, construction joints, isolation and separation joints, and building expansion joints.

The amount of thermal movement in concrete can be calculated by using its approximate coefficient of expansion (and contraction) of 0.0000055 in./in./°F. For example, a 100-ft. length of unrestrained concrete would expand 0.66 in. in length for each 100°F rise in temperature. If the temperature were to drop 100°F, the same amount of contraction would occur. Concrete would be exposed to a 100°F rise in temperature if it were placed in the spring when the temperature was 50°F and then in the summer the temperature rose to 150°F.

Concrete shortens about 0.72 in./100 ft. while drying from its saturated condition at placing to an average hardened state, with a moisture content equilibrium with air at 50% relative humidity. This shrinkage slightly exceeds the expansion caused by such an extreme increase in temperature as 100°F. Furthermore, in most outdoor applications concrete reaches its maximum moisture content (and moisture expansion) during the season of low temperature (and thermal contraction). Thus, the volume changes due to moisture and temperature variations frequently tend to offset each other. There is, therefore, no need for expansion joints in most concrete associated with buildings. The common reference to expansion is misleading because it implies that an increase in size after placement must be allowed for. There may be rare instances, in very large structures and in highways or other large, paved surfaces, where extensive surfaces of concrete are subject to large temperature variations and sufficient expansion may occur to justify expansion joints. In most instances, however, concrete is at its greatest mass when it is placed.

Nevertheless, some practitioners in warm regions insist that expansion joints are needed and include them as a safety factor, especially in concrete paving.

Control Joints

3.12.1 As concrete sets or hardens, its excess mixing water is lost through evaporation and through hydration of the portland cement. This initial loss of water in the early life of a concrete section results in shrinkage that is of greater magnitude than any subsequent increase in the size of the hardened mass due to temperature or moisture content rise.

Shrinkage is inevitable as water eventually dries from freshly placed concrete, and consequently large areas can develop jagged, irregularly spaced shrinkage lines and cracks. If shrinkage is anticipated and joints installed to limit areas and control where cracking occurs, concrete work can be made more attractive, serviceable, and relatively free from unsightly and expected random cracking. Such joints are called control joints. These joints provide a break or a reduction in slab thickness and thus create a weakened section that encourages movement and cracking to occur at that location. When concrete shrinks, the cracks in these joints can open slightly, reducing the number of irregular and unsightly random cracks.

The maximum spacing between control joints depends on the concrete's thickness and shrinkage potential, the curing environment, and the absence or presence of distributed reinforcement. Control joints in sidewalks should be spaced at intervals generally equal to the width of the slab, but should not be more than 6 ft. apart. Joints in driveways should be spaced generally equal to the width of the slab, but never more than 20 ft. apart.

In large slab areas that do not contain structural reinforcement, control joints should be provided so that the slab is divided into approximately square panels, with a maximum spacing of 20 ft. The actual spacings depend on the slab's thickness. A rule of thumb for plain concrete slabs is that joint spacing in feet should not exceed two slab thicknesses in inches for unreinforced concrete made with coarse 3/4-in. maximum aggregate.

Thus, a 4-in.-thick plain slab would require control joints at intervals not to exceed 8 ft. In residential construction, such spacing usually permits the joints to be placed under partitions. Additional control joints should be provided at the juncture of slab intersections.

Control joints are unnecessary in a slab that is to receive a floor finish, such as resilient flooring or carpeting, because the flooring will cover unsightly cracking resulting from shrinkage. Also, control joints are usually unnecessary in structurally reinforced slabs.

Control joints can be made by sawing a groove in the hardened but not yet fully cured concrete, by using a power saw, or by installing a keyed joint. Sawed joints are provided by cutting approximately 1/8-in. wide grooves in the concrete to a depth equal to one-fourth the total slab thickness, but not less than 3/4 in., and at least equal to the maximum size of the aggregate. Tooled control joints should be of a similar minimum depth. If a slab is to be grooved only for decorative purposes, joints may be shallower. Tensile stresses generated will be relieved at a control joint, thus reducing the likelihood of cracks occurring where they might be objectionable.

On large concrete flat surfaces it may be more convenient to cut joints with an electric or gasoline-driven power saw fitted with an abrasive or diamond blade. Joints can be cut as soon as the concrete surface is firm enough not to be torn or damaged by the blade (within 4 to 12 hours) and before random shrinkage cracks can form in the slab.

Comments

Control joints are typically cut with a concrete saw on the day after the concrete is placed.

For more information on joints, it may be helpful to consult these ACI publications: Joints in Concrete Construction *and* Building Movements and Joints. *(See this chapter's introduction for ACI contact information.)*

Industry Standards
Plan Reading & Material Takeoff
(R.S. Means Co., Inc.)

A control joint is a formed, sawed, or tooled groove in a concrete surface. It is not uncommon to have a combination of three different methods of creating control joints on the same project. The first, *tooled joints,* is accomplished by the use of a hand-held tool, and is typically used for walkways. The grooves are cut perpendicular to the length of the walk at intervals of approximately 5' during the finishing process. The second method, *saw cutting,* is done after the surface is hardened, but before final strength of the concrete has been achieved. Saw cutting is done with a diamond blade set to a specific depth. Saw-cut control joints occur at column lines in large slabs. Finally, *formed control joints* are created by edge-forming areas to be poured at different times. (The slab is edge-formed in a checkerboard fashion and alternate squares are poured.) Formed joints are typically created at the intersection of a column's base and the surrounding slab. **Figure 2.15** shows a control joint at the base of a column.

Control Joint at Base of Column

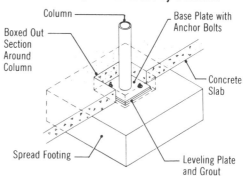

Column
Base Plate with Anchor Bolts
Boxed Out Section Around Column
Concrete Slab
Spread Footing
Leveling Plate and Grout

R.S. Means Co., Inc., *Plan Reading & Material Takeoff*

Figure 2.15

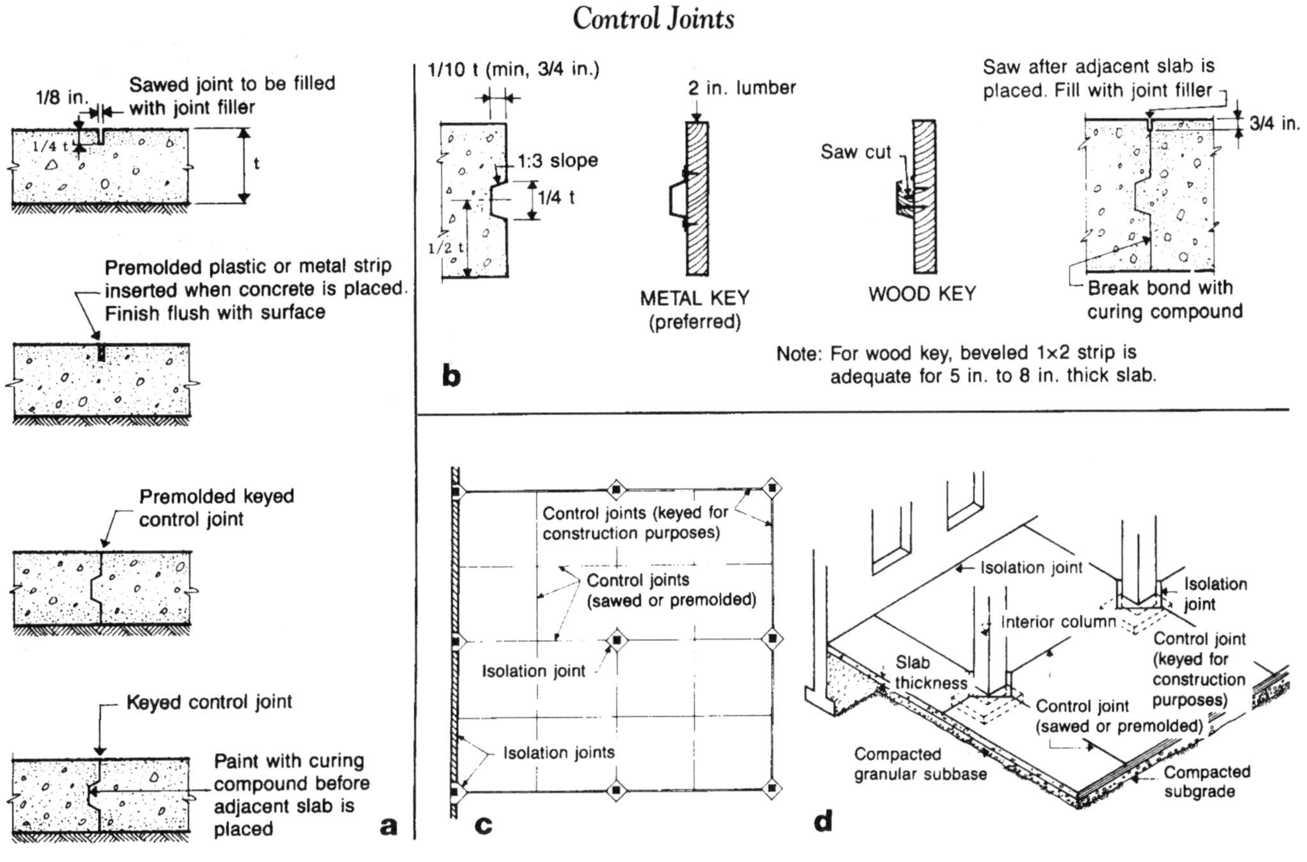

Control Joints

1/8 in.	Sawed joint to be filled with joint filler

Premolded plastic or metal strip inserted when concrete is placed. Finish flush with surface

Premolded keyed control joint

Keyed control joint

Paint with curing compound before adjacent slab is placed

1/10 t (min, 3/4 in.)
1:3 slope
1/4 t
1/2 t

2 in. lumber
Saw cut

METAL KEY (preferred)
WOOD KEY

Note: For wood key, beveled 1×2 strip is adequate for 5 in. to 8 in. thick slab.

Saw after adjacent slab is placed. Fill with joint filler
3/4 in.
Break bond with curing compound

Control joints (keyed for construction purposes)
Control joints (sawed or premolded)
Isolation joint
Isolation joints

Isolation joint
Isolation joint
Interior column
Slab thickness
Control joint (keyed for construction purposes)
Control joint (sawed or premolded)
Compacted granular subbase
Compacted subgrade

Courtesy of Portland Cement Association

Figure 2.16

Construction Joints

Industry Standards

Construction Principles, Materials, and Methods
(John Wiley & Sons, Inc.)

3.12.2 In large construction work, construction joints are necessary because it is not possible to handle, place, and finish a large area in one operation. When construction joints are installed, concrete can be conveniently and practically placed in several operations with no loss in the appearance or performance of the complete job. Although they may double as control or isolation joints, construction joints must allow no vertical movement in the completed floor and are thus often keyed joints.

Plastic or rubber waterstops are inserted in construction joints below grade and in other locations to prevent water penetration through a concrete structural element.

UBC — 1997

1906.4.1 Surface of concrete construction joints shall be cleaned and laitance removed.

1906.4.2 Immediately before new concrete is placed, all construction joints shall be wetted and standing water removed.

1906.4.3 Construction joints shall be so made and located as not to impair the strength of the structure. Provision shall be made for transfer of shear and other forces through construction joints. See Section 1911.7.9.

1906.4.4 Construction joints in floors shall be located within the middle third of spans of slabs, beams and girders. Joints in girders shall be offset a minimum distance of two times the width of intersecting beams.

1906.4.5 Beams, girders or slabs supported by columns or walls shall not be cast or erected until concrete in the vertical support members is no longer plastic.

1906.4.6 Beams, girders, haunches, drop panels and capitals shall be placed monolithically as part of a slab system, unless otherwise shown in design drawings or specifications.

Comments

Structural members such as steel beams may be embedded or cast into concrete to form a composite member. If a crack or construction joint intersects the top flange of the beam, corrosion may occur when moisture and corrosive salts are trapped against the beam. Corrosion on the top flange creates a jacking force on the concrete above. If the force is sufficient, delamination may occur, and the slab may separate from the beam.

Use of Premolded Joint Filler

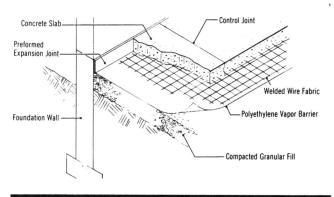

R.S. Means Co., Inc., *Plan Reading & Material Takeoff*

Figure 2.17

Isolation & Separation Joints

Industry Standards

Construction Principles, Materials, and Methods
(John Wiley & Sons, Inc.)

3.12.3 Isolation and separation joints often are necessary to separate concrete sections and to prevent the bonding of one concrete section with another or to separate a concrete section from another material or structural part so that one can move independently of the other. Isolation joints are sometimes called expansion joints.

Isolation and separation joints are usually formed by installing 1/8-in.-thick (or slightly thicker) asphalt-impregnated fiber sheets in floors at columns, footings, the junctures between floors and walls, and anywhere else that adjacent surfaces are required to move independently of each other.

Expansion Joints

Industry Standards

Plan Reading & Material Takeoff
(R.S. Means Co., Inc.)

Concrete, like other construction materials, expands and contracts with temperature changes. To allow for safe expansion and contraction without defects to the work, certain precautions must be taken during construction. For example, a premolded joint filler (which compresses as the concrete expands) allows room for expansion. These asphalt-impregnated fibrous boards come in a variety of widths, the most common of which are 4" and 6". Thicknesses are 3/8", 1/2", and 3/4".

Expansion joints typically occur at the perimeter of a concrete slab where it terminates at a masonry or concrete wall. **Figure 2.15** shows the use of a premolded joint filler at the perimeter of a slab that meets a foundation wall.

Industry Standards

Construction Principles, Materials, and Methods
(John Wiley & Sons, Inc.)

3.12.4 While expansion of the concrete itself is seldom a problem, expansion of an entire structure often requires the insertion of building expansion joints, which pass through both structural elements and finishes. Concrete that occurs at one of these types of joints must be interrupted. Various types of joints have been developed to cover such joints. In slabs and in walls, where water is likely to pass through a building expansion joint, waterstops are placed in the concrete.

Reinforcing Steel Placement

Industry Standards

Concrete Repair and Maintenance Illustrated
(R.S. Means Co., Inc.)

There are two important reasons to control the proper location of reinforcing steel in structures. First, reinforcing steel is placed in concrete to carry tensile loads, and if the steel is misplaced, the concrete may not be able to carry the tensile loads. Cantilevered slabs, and negative moment areas near columns pose particular risk. Second, reinforcing steel requires adequate concrete cover to protect it from *corrosion*. The alkalinity of the concrete is a natural corrosive inhibitor. If the concrete cover is inadequate, it will not provide the necessary long-term protection. Shifted reinforcing bar cages in walls or beams may also cause the reinforcing steel to lose proper cover.

American Concrete Institute (ACI)-Required Concrete Cover for Corrosion Protection	
Condition	Cover Required in. (mm)
Concrete deposited on the ground	3" (76)
Formed surfaces exposed to weather	
bars > #6	2" (51)
bars < #5	1.5" (38)
Formed surfaces not exposed to weather	
beams, girders, columns	1.5" (38)
slabs, walls, joists	
bars < #11	0.75" (19)
bars #14, #18	1.5" (38)

Ed. Note: Contact ACI for other reinforcement publications.

U.B.C. Field Inspection Workbook
[International Conference of Building Officials (ICBO)]

Surface Condition of Reinforcement

At the time of concrete placement, all reinforcing bars should be free of mud, oil, or other deleterious materials. Reinforcing bars with rust, mill scale, or a combination of both should be considered as satisfactory, provided the minimum dimensions, weight, and height of deformations of a hand-wire-brushed test specimen are not less than the applicable ASTM specification requirements.

Spacing of Reinforcement

The clear distance between parallel reinforcing bars in a layer should not be less than the nominal diameter of the bars, nor 1 in. Clear distance should also not be less than one and one-third times the nominal maximum size of the coarse aggregate, except if in the judgment of the Engineer, workability and methods of consolidation are such that concrete can be placed without honeycomb or voids.

Where parallel reinforcement is placed in two or more layers, the bars in the upper layers should be placed directly above those in the bottom layer with the clear distance between layers not less than 1 in.

Groups of parallel reinforcing bars bundled in contact, assumed to act as a unit, not more than four in any one bundle may be used only when stirrups or ties enclose the bundle. Bars larger than #11 should not be bundled in beams or girders. Individual bars in a bundle cut off within the span of flexural members should terminate at different points with at least 40 bar diameters stagger. Where spacing limitations and minimum clear cover are based on bar size, a unit of bundled bars should be treated as a single bar of a diameter derived from the equivalent total area.

Bar Identification Marks

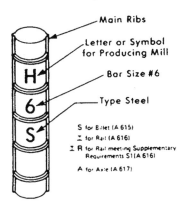

GRADE 40 AND 50

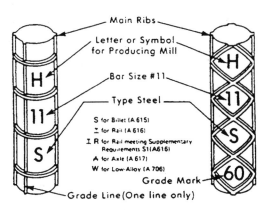

GRADE 60 AND A 706

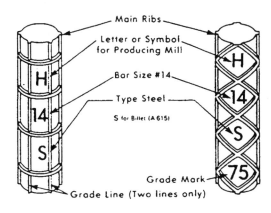

GRADE 75

Variations: Bar identification marks may be oriented as illustrated or rotated 90°. Grade numbers may be placed within separate consecutive deformation spaces.

Courtesy of ICBO, U.B.C. *Field Inspection Workbook* — 1997

Figure 2.18

ASTM STANDARD REINFORCING BARS

BAR SIZE DESIGNATION	NOMINAL AREA SQ. INCHES	NOMINAL WEIGHT POUNDS PER FT.	NOMINAL DIAMETER INCHES
#3	0.11	0.376	0.375
#4	0.20	0.668	0.500
#5	0.31	1.043	0.625
#6	0.44	1.502	0.750
#7	0.60	2.044	0.875
#8	0.79	2.670	1.000
#9	1.00	3.400	1.128
#10	1.27	4.303	1.270
#11	1.56	5.313	1.410
#14	2.25	7.65	1.693
#18	4.00	13.60	2.257

Current ASTM Specifications cover bar sizes #14 and #18 in A615 Grades 60 and 75 and in A706 only.

Copyright ASTM. Reprinted with permission.

Figure 2.19

In walls and slabs other than concrete joist construction, the principal reinforcement should not be spaced farther apart than three times the wall or slab thickness, nor more than 18 in.

In spirally reinforced and tied columns, the clear distance between longitudinal bars should not be less than one and one-half times the nominal bar diameter, nor 1-1/2 in. The clear distance limitation between bars should also apply to the clear distance between a contact lap splice and adjacent splices or bars.

Splices in Reinforcement

(a) **General.** Splicing of reinforcing bars should be either by lapping, welding, or by mechanical connections.

Splices of reinforcing bars should be made only as required or permitted on the design drawings or in the specifications, or as authorized by the Engineer. All welding should conform to the current edition of "Structural Welding Code — Reinforcing Steel" (AWS D1.4).

(b) **Lap Splices.** Lap splices of #14 and #18 bars should not be used, except in compression only to #11 and smaller bars.

Lap splices of bundled bars should be based on the lap splice length recommended for individual bars of the same size as the bars spliced, and such individual splices within the bundle should not overlap each other. The length of lap should be increased 20 percent for a 3-bar bundle and 33 percent for a 4-bar bundle.

Bar laps placed in contact should be securely wired together in such a manner as to maintain the alignment of the bars and to provide minimum clearances.

Bars spliced by noncontact lap splices in flexural members should not be spaced transversely farther a part than one-fifth the required length of lap nor 6 in.

(c) **Welded Splices.** A full welded splice is one in which the bars are butted and welded to develop in tension at least 125 percent of the specified yield strength of the bar.

(d) **Mechanical Connections.** Mechanical splice devices should be installed in accordance with the manufacturers' recommendations. A full mechanical connection is one in which the bars are connected to develop in tension or compression at least 125 percent of the specified yield strength of the bar.

Supports

Placing bars on layers of fresh concrete as the work progresses and adjusting bars during the placing of concrete should not be permitted.

Concrete Protection for Reinforcement

The following minimum concrete cover should be provided for reinforcing bars. For bundled bars, the minimum cover should be equal to the equivalent diameter of the bundle but need not be greater than 2 in.; except for concrete cast against and permanently exposed to earth, the minimum cover should be 3 in.

Welded Wire Reinforcement

Industry Standards

Wire Reinforcement Institute

Welded wire reinforcement is usually manufactured in 5' to 8' wide sheets and rolls. Sheets up to 12' wide are produced primarily for highway paving and precast components. Special widths can be furnished on request. Sheets can be provided up to 40' or more in length, but 12'-6", 15', 20' and 25' are the more common lengths for ease in shipping and placing. Pipe and standard building fabric are produced in roll form. Some standard building fabric is available in sheet form.

Wire sizes are available from W1.4-W45 and D4-D45. Other wire sizes are available and vary with individual manufacturers. The "W" for plan or "D" for deformed wire numbers are usually whole numbers. For a style designation of 12x12-D10xD10, the first set of numbers is the spacing of wires in inches for both the longitudinal and transverse directions, respectively. The second set is the cross-sectional areas of the respective wires in square inches multiplied by 100 (.10 sq. in. x 100 = 10, etc.). (See **Figure 2.20**.)

Common Styles of Sheet[2] Welded Wire Reinforcement

Style*	Wire Gauge	W[3] Numbers[4]	Weight (lbs/100 SF)
6x6	10/10	W1.4/W1.4[1]	21
6X6	8/8	W2.1/W2.1[1]	30
6X6	6/6	W2.9/W2.9[1]	42
6X6	4/4	W4/W4[1]	58
6X6	2/2	W5.4/W5.4	78
6X6	0/0	W7.4/W7.4	107
4X4	6/6	W2.9/W2.9[1]	62
4X4	4/4	W4/W4[1]	85
6X12	0/1	W7.4/W6.3	77

*Style numbers indicate spacing of wires in the reinforcement; 6x6, for example, has wires spaced at 6 inches on center both ways.

Notes:
1. Styles may be obtained in roll form.
2. Standard sheet sizes are 4x8, 8x12, 8x15, 8x20, 7x20, and 7x25.
3. W prefix is for plain wire. Wires may be deformed using prefix D.
4. The number following the prefix W identifies the cross-sectional are of wire in hundredths of a square inch.

Courtesy of Wire Reinforcement Institute

Figure 2.20

Spacings of longitudinal wires can vary from 2" to 16" (larger spacings are obtainable and vary with individual manufacturers). Transverse spacings are usually 4, 6, 8, 12, or 16". Wires can be cut flush or have overhangs on the sides of the welded wire. The ends will generally have overhangs of 1/2 the transverse spacing unless other multiples of the transverse spacing are requested, i.e., for 12" transverse spacing, 6" & 6" or 8" & 4" or 10" & 2", etc.

The more common or standard WWR styles are designated: 6x6-W1.4xW1.4, 6x6-W2.1xW2.1, 6x6-W2.9xW2.9, and 6x6-W4xW4. Heavier WWR styles utilizing wire diameters up to 1/2" (some manufacturers can exceed 1/2" diameter) can be used for structural applications.

The size and area of reinforcement required is specified by the engineer and depends on the slab thickness, the spacing of the construction and control joints, the type and density of the sub base, a friction factor for the sub-grade, and the yield strength of the welded wire. There are a number of design methods used when the WWR is used for strength in the reinforced concrete slab or structure.

The ACI Building Code (ACI-318) assigns a minimum yield strength (f_y) value of 60,000 psi to most steel reinforcing, but allows yield strengths up to 80,000 psi for many design applications.

Welded wire reinforcement can be used as ties and stirrups for column, beam and joist cage (confinement) reinforcement. WWR cage reinforcement is also used for concrete encased columns. The WWR supplier uses a welded wire bending machine to shape the materials into required configurations. The placing drawings will identify the location and details of the cage assemblies.

Placing

WWR rolls are unrolled, cut to proper length and turned over to prevent ends from curling. Flattening the material is best accomplished mechanically with a "Mesh Runner," which will provide the necessary flatness to achieve proper positioning. All WWR should be placed on support accessories to maintain the required position and cover as specified by the engineer.

Splices or laps, either structural or temperature/shrinkage types, should be specified by the engineer and in conformance with the ACI Building Code. Typically, structural laps for welded wire fabric are a minimum length of 6"+ overhangs for plain wire and 8" including overhangs for deformed wires. The Code requires that one or two cross wires, depending on type of wire, occur in structural laps of WWR. Deformed wire structural laps, when no cross wires are included in the splice region, are a minimum of 12". In areas of low stress, splice lengths can be reduced.

Note: Generally, splices for slabs on grade only need to lap sufficient lengths to obtain a flat and stable layer of reinforcement, a minimum of 2".

For slab on grade construction: With slab thicknesses less than 5", a single layer of welded wire is placed in the middle of the slab. For slabs 6" and greater, the top cover is 1/3 the depth of the slab.

When two layers are specified (usually over 8" thick), the top cover will be 1" to 2" depending on saw cuts (WWR is placed below the saw cuts). The bottom cover will be 1-1/2" min. on earth or 1" on vapor barriers. Support manufacturers produce concrete blocks or steel (coated and uncoated) and plastic chairs, bolsters, and WWF support accessories made specifically for either single layer or double layer reinforcing applications.

Placing WWR on appropriately spaced concrete blocks, steel or plastic supports with base plates and tying the WWR at laps is adequate to maintain its position during concrete placement. WWR should not be placed on the sub grade and pulled up during concrete placement. Following is a suggested guide for spacing support accessories:

Heavy WWR styles—W9 or D9 and larger	4'-6'*
Medium WWR styles—W5 or D5 to W8 or D8:	3'-4'
Light WWR styles—W4 or D4 or less	2'-3' or less*

* Spacing of supports for WWR with wires larger than W or D9 could possibly be increased over the spacings shown depending on the construction loads applied.

** Consider using additional rows of supports when large deflections or deformations occur — also spacing of supports may be increased provided supports are placed and properly positioned as concrete is needed.

Refer to ACI 318-95 for the ACI Building Code requirements for tension development lengths and tension lap splices of welded wire reinforcement. For additional information, see *Welded Wire Reinforcement Manual of Standard Practice* and *Structural Welded Wire Reinforcement Detailing Manual*, both published by the Wire Reinforcement Institute.

Accessories

Industry Standards

Construction Principles, Materials, and Methods
(John Wiley & Sons, Inc.)

3.4.3 Design and Replacement

Reinforcing steel should be designed, fabricated, and installed in accordance with the Concrete Reinforcing Steel Institute publication "Manual of Standard Practice." Other applicable documents are the American Welding Society publications AWS D1.4, "Structural Welding Code Reinforcing Steel" and "Connections in Reinforced Concrete Construction."

In most cases, reinforcing steel is fabricated in a mill or a shop according to shop drawings prepared by the fabricator from the structural engineer's drawings and approved by the structural engineer and the architect. The fabricated steel is bundled, tagged as to its location in the building, and delivered to the construction site. These bundles are delivered to their place in the building by hand or crane, where the reinforcement is wired to hold its place and alignment until the concrete has set. In some cases, sections of reinforcement, such as those for a column, are preassembled at the mill or the shop and delivered to the site in one piece. Such assemblies may also be preassembled at the site on the ground and lifted into place by crane.

Steel should be accurately positioned, secured to prevent its displacement during the placing of concrete, and cleaned of rust and foreign matter before concrete is placed against it. Steel should be protected from possible harm by fire and corrosion by a covering at least the thickness of concrete.

Welded wire fabric should be installed in the largest practicable length. Adjoining pieces should be lapped at least one full mesh and tied together with wire to prevent movement during concrete placement.

3.4.2.3 Accessories

Accessories are used with structural steel to support it in the forms and to make splices in it. Welded wire fabric in slabs on grade should be supported on similar devices having flat plates at their legs to prevent the legs from sinking into the slab base (sand plates). The common practice of supporting reinforcement in slabs on grade with pieces of concrete or concrete bricks is discouraged because concrete often does not adhere to such materials. This produces cracks, which

permits water to reach and rust the reinforcement, destroying its effectiveness. The plastic caps on the feet of the [wire bar] support devices are used when the underside of the slab will be exposed and in other locations to prevent the supports from rusting and transferring this rust to the reinforcement.

In beams, girders, walls, and slabs, when bar space is not at a premium, splices usually are made by overlapping the bars a prescribed number of bar diameters and tying them together with wire to keep them in place until the concrete has set. Sometimes, in columns when the space is limited, bars are butted end to end and connected with special devices made for the purpose or welded together.

Anchor Bolts

Comment

Anchor bolts are threaded, with right-angle bends embedded in poured concrete. They are provided for the future connection of steel columns, beams, or wood sill plates. They anchor that future work to the concrete. The size, quantity, spacing, and location of anchor bolts should be noted on the structural drawings. Often set by a surveying crew, anchor bolts are critical to the structure and must be located precisely.

UBC — 1997

1806.6 Foundation Plates or Sills. Wood plates or sills shall be bolted to the foundation or foundation wall. Steel bolts with a minimum nominal diameter of 1/2 inch (12.7 mm) shall be used in Seismic Zones 0 through 3. Steel bolts with a minimum nominal diameter of 5/8 inch (16 mm) shall be used in Seismic Zone 4. Bolts shall be embedded at least 7 inches (178 mm) into the concrete or masonry and shall be spaced not more than 6 feet (1829 mm) apart. There shall be a minimum of two bolts per piece with one bolt located not more than 12 inches (305 mm) or less than seven bolt diameter, from each end of the piece. A properly sized nut and washer shall be tightened on each bolt to the plate. Foundation plates and sills shall be the kind of wood specified in Section 2306.4.

1806.6.1 Additional Requirements in Seismic Zones 3 and 4. The following additional requirements shall apply in Seismic Zones 3 and 4.

1. Sill bolt diameter and spacing for three-story raised wood floor buildings shall be specifically designed.

2. Plate washers a minimum of 2 inch by 2 inch by 3/16 inch (51 mm by 51 mm by 4.8 mm) thick shall be used on each bolt.

1806.7 Seismic Zones 3 and 4. In Seismic Zones 3 and 4, horizontal reinforcement in accordance with Sections 1806.8.1 and 1806.8.2 shall be placed in continuous foundations to minimize differential settlement. Foundation reinforcement shall be provided with cover in accordance with Section 1907.7. 1.

Ed. Note: Refer to the Chapter 5, "Seismic Bracing" section, for more on seismic framing requirements.

1806.7.1 Foundations with stemwalls. Foundations with stemwalls shall be provided with a minimum of one No. 3 bar at the top of the wall and one No. 4 bar at the bottom of the footing.

1806.7.2 Slabs-on-ground with turned-down footings. Slabs-on-ground with turned-down footings shall have a minimum of one No. 4 bar at the top and bottom.

Exception: For slabs-on-ground cast monolithically with a footing, one No. 5 bar may be located at either the top or bottom.

Industry Standards

Construction Principles, Materials, and Methods
(John Wiley & Sons, Inc.)

3.11.3.5 Post-Tensioning

Tensile forces near the bottoms of loaded beams tend to pull the concrete apart, making it crack. Even when reinforcing steel is added, these cracks often are large enough to be seen. Such cracks can be eliminated altogether by placing the concrete in compression before an external load is applied. If enough compression is applied and held there, when a load is applied, the amount of compression will be lessened but will never disappear completely. Compressing the concrete in a beam will also permit it to carry the same loads with less concrete, making it lighter and less expensive.

Compression loads can be added to a beam by stretching the steel and locking it to the concrete at the ends. As the steel tries to return to its normal length, the resulting stress is transferred to the concrete. There are two procedures used to produce this result. Prestressing is done before concrete is placed around the steel. This process is best done under controlled conditions in a shop or a factory, because it is very expensive to do anywhere else. Prestressing is used almost exclusively in precast concrete work.

A process called post-tensioning is used to add permanent tension to the reinforcing steel in cast-in-place concrete and subsequently to place the concrete under compression. Essentially it is done using tendons, which are bundles of high strength, cold-drawn steel wire strands or steel bars. The tendons are coated with oil or placed in a steel tube to prevent bonding between the concrete and the tendons. The concrete is placed and permitted to cure. Generally, the tendons are fastened to one end of the beam and stretched from the other end using hydraulic jacks. When the desired amount of tension has been achieved, the jack end of the tendon is secured to the concrete, usually with a bearing plate of some sort. When the strands are very long, they must be stretched from both ends simultaneously to ensure uniform tensioning.

Tendons can be placed level, like conventional reinforcing bars. Post-tensioned beams are more efficient, however, if the tendons are placed in a shape that approximates the lines of tensile force in the beam. This is near the bottom of the beam in the center and sloping upward toward the top of the beam at the ends in a V-shape.

Post-tensioned beams tend to shorten due to elastic compression, shrinkage, and creep. These movements must be accommodated in the building design and construction. Adjacent elements that would be affected by these changes should be built after the post-tensioning has been completed, or they should be isolated from the post-tensioned unit. In addition, the amount of tension to be applied can sometimes be adjusted slightly upward to at least partially compensate for these movements.

Shotcrete

Comments

Gunite is similar to shotcrete, but uses mostly sand/ cement vs. shotcrete's combination of sand/cement/ aggregate.

UBC — 1997

1924.1 General. Shotcrete shall be defined as mortar or concrete pneumatically projected at high velocity onto a surface. Except as specified in this section, shotcrete shall conform to the regulations of this chapter for plain concrete or reinforced concrete.

1924.2 Proportions and Materials. Shotcrete proportions shall be selected that allow suitable placement procedures using the delivery equipment selected and shall result in finished in-place hardened shotcrete meeting the strength requirements of this code.

1924.3 Aggregate. Coarse aggregate, if used, shall not exceed 3/4 inch (19 mm).

1924.4 Reinforcement. The maximum size of reinforcement shall be No. 5 bars unless it can be demonstrated by preconstruction tests that adequate encasement of larger bars can be achieved. When No. 5 or smaller bars are used, there shall be a minimum clearance between parallel reinforcement bars of 2-1/2 inches (64 mm). When bars larger than No. 5 are permitted, there shall be a minimum clearance between parallel bars equal to six diameters of the bars used. When two curtains of steel are provided, the curtain nearest the nozzle shall have a minimum spacing equal to 12 bar diameters and the remaining curtain shall have a minimum spacing of six bar diameters.

Exception: Subject to the approval of the building official, reduced clearances may be used where it can be demonstrated by preconstruction tests that adequate encasement of the bars used in the design can be achieved. Lap splices in reinforcing bars shall be by the noncontact lap splice method with at least 2 inches (51 mm) clearance between bars. The building official may permit the use of contact lap splices when necessary for the support of the reinforcing, provided it can be demonstrated by means of preconstruction testing that adequate encasement of the bars at the splice can be achieved, and provided that the splices are placed so that a line through the center of the two spliced bars is perpendicular to the surface of the shotcrete work. Shotcrete shall not be applied to spirally tied columns.

1924.5 Preconstruction Tests. When required by the building official a test panel shall be shot, cured, cored or sawn, examined and tested prior to commencement of the project. The sample panel shall be representative of the project and simulate job conditions as closely as possible. The panel thickness and reinforcing shall reproduce the thickest and most congested area specified in the structural design. It shall be shot at the same angle, using the same nozzleman and with the same concrete mix design that will be used on the project.

1924.6 Rebound. Any rebound or accumulated loose aggregate shall be removed from the surfaces to be covered prior to placing the initial or any succeeding layers of shotcrete. Rebound shall not be reused as aggregate.

1924.7 Joints. Except where permitted herein, unfinished work shall not be allowed to stand for more than 30 minutes unless all edges are sloped to a thin edge. Before placing additional material adjacent to previously applied work, sloping and square edges shall be cleaned and wetted.

1924.8 Damage. In-place shotcrete which exhibits sags or sloughs, segregation, honeycombing, sand pockets or other obvious defects shall be removed and replaced. Shotcrete above sags and sloughs shall be removed and replaced while still plastic.

1924.9 Curing. During the curing periods specified herein, shotcrete shall be maintained above 40°F (4.4°C) and in moist condition. In initial curing, shotcrete shall be kept continuously moist for 24 hours after placement is complete. Final curing shall continue for seven days after shotcreting, for three days if high-early-strength cement is used, or until the specified strength is obtained. Final curing shall consist of a fog spray or an approved moisture-retaining cover or membrane. In sections of a depth in excess of 12 inches (305 mm), final curing shall be the same as that for initial curing.

1924.10 Strength Test. Strength test for shotcrete shall be made by an approved agency on specimens which are representative of work and which have been water soaked for at least 24 hours prior to testing. When the maximum size aggregate is larger than 3/8 inch (9.5 mm) or smaller, specimens shall consist of not less than three 2-inch-diameter (51 mm) cores or 2-inch (51 mm) cubes. Specimens shall be taken in accordance with one of the following:

1. **From the in-place work:** taken at least once each shift or less than one for each 50 cubic yards (38.2 m³) of shotcrete; or

2. **From test panels:** made not less than once each shift or not less than one for each 50 cubic yards (38.2 m³) of shotcrete placed. When the maximum size aggregate is larger than 3/8 inch (9.5 mm), the test panels shall have a minimum dimension of 18 inches by 18 inches (457 mm by 457 mm). When the maximum size aggregate is 3/8 inch (9.5 mm) or smaller, the test panels shall have a minimum dimension of 12 inches by 12 inches (305 mm by 305 mm). Panels shall be gunned in the same position

as the work, during the course of the work and by nozzlepersons doing the work. The condition under which the panels are cured shall be the same as the work.

The average of three cores from a single panel shall be equal to or exceed $0.85 f'_c$ with no single core less than $0.75 f'_c$. The average of three cubes taken from a single panel must equal or exceed f'_c with no individual cube less than $0.88 f'_c$. To check testing accuracy, locations represented by erratic core strengths may be retested.

1924.11 Inspections.

1924.11.1 During placement. When shotcrete is used for structural members, a special inspector is required by Section 1701.5, Item 12. The special inspector shall provide continuous inspection of the placement of the reinforcement and shotcreting and shall submit a statement indicating compliance with the plans and specifications.

1924.11.2 Visual examination for structural soundness of in-place shotcrete. Completed shotcrete work shall be checked visually for reinforcing bar embedment, voids, rock pockets, sand streaks and similar deficiencies by examining a minimum of three 3-inch (76 mm) cores taken from three areas chosen by the design engineer which represent the worst congestion of reinforcing bars occurring in the project. Extra reinforcing bars may be added to noncongested areas and cores may be taken from these areas. The cores shall be examined by the special inspector and a report submitted to the building official prior to final approval of the shotcrete.

Comments

ACI offers several publications on shotcreting, including specifications, application, and use. (See chapter introduction for more on ACI.)

Formwork

Industry Standards
Plan Reading & Material Takeoff
(R.S. Means Co., Inc.)

Because of its fluid-like consistency during placement, all cast-in-place concrete must be contained in some type of formwork. Formwork varies in size and composition, but is most often constructed from a wood facing applied over a steel or wood frame. Simpler forms, such as those used in forming a footing, may be no more than a plank anchored by stakes and straps.

Comments

Forms must not be allowed to warp or sag, and must be assembled tightly enough so that mortar cannot leak out. The project specifications indicate the duration that the forms should be left in place (typically 7 days for vertical forms and 28 days for support forms). Premature removal of forms (before the concrete has reached its proper strength) may result in compression and tension stresses, which cause cracking, deflection, and possible collapse.

Concrete foundation walls should be plumb and not bowed. Variances should not be more than approximately one inch in eight feet.

Forms must have a smooth interior surface, to provide a clean finish on the concrete. (If a textured finish is desired, forms may be lined with rubber – or other material – liners to achieve that effect.) Cracks between form sections should be avoided as they will result in ridges, or "fins," on the surface of the concrete. Removing these ridges can create problems such as rough surfaces and exposure of aggregate. Another problem occurs when some of the chamfer strips are left off the corners. Sharp corners tend to break off, leaving exposed aggregate. There should be no cracks in the finished wall large enough to allow water to penetrate the structure from the outside, nor should there be any cracks that contribute to bowing of the wall.

When forms are reused, they are oiled with a light oil, with the excess wiped off so the concrete will not be stained.

For more information on the construction standards for concrete formwork, see sections 2–11 through 2–21 in Residential Construction Performance Guidelines, published by National Association of Home Builders (Telephone: 800–368–5242).

ACI publishes Formwork for Concrete, a 500 page "bible" of the formwork industry.

Footing Forms

There are two main types of footings: *continuous strip footings*, on which walls will be erected, and *isolated spread footings*, which are used for supporting interior columns.

Strip Footings

To better distribute the load imposed by the structure, strip footings are wider than the walls they support. Strip footings follow the shape and perimeter of the wall. They are typically formed on both sides and braced on the top with temporary wood braces at 2' to 3' intervals. Bottoms of the footing are braced with a perforated metal strap at approximately 2' to 4' intervals. The forms used for footings are rough planking, similar to staging planks approximately 2" x 12", in varying lengths. Common sizes for footings are 20" to 36" in width by 12" to 18" in depth. The forms materials, with the exception of the perforated straps are reusable (see **Figure 2.21**).

Most strip footings remain constant in height. Because of the conditions of the soil after excavation, changes in elevation at the bottom of the footings may be required to ensure that the footing will rest on suitable soil. The contractor should note any changes in elevation that may require stepping the footings (see **Figure 2.22**).

Stepped Footings

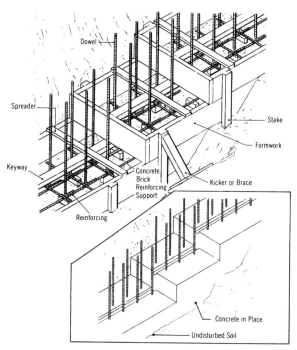

R.S. Means Co., Inc., *Plan Reading & Material Takeoff*
Figure 2.22

Strip Footings

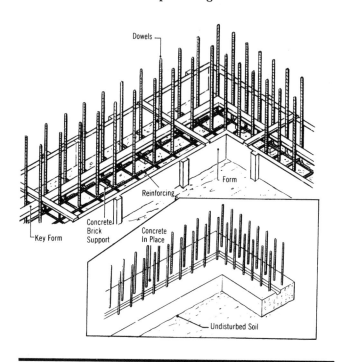

R.S. Means Co., Inc., *Plan Reading & Material Takeoff*
Figure 2.21

To reduce the lateral movement of the wall to be placed on the continuous strip footing, a small trough, called a *keyway*, is formed by using a tapered 2" x 4" embedded in the top surface of the wet concrete in the footing. **Figure 2.23** illustrates the keyway form and the resulting trough after the forms have been stripped.

Keyway Detail

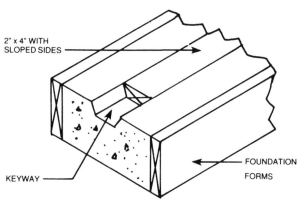

• The keyway in the footing is formed with a tapered 2 x 4 in. member.

Courtesy of Home Planners, LLC, 3275 W. Ina Rd., #110, Tucson, AZ 85741 (800-322-6797)
Figure 2.23

Spread Footings

Spread footings are isolated masses of concrete, often square or rectangular in shape, with thicknesses varying from 12" to 24". Their main purpose is to support point loads from the columns that rest on them. Their actual size is contingent upon the load carried and the soil's bearing capacity. A typical spread footing is shown in **Figure 2.24.**

The form material may be planks or panels, depending on the thickness of the footing. Footing forms are erected and braced in a manner similar to that used for strip footings.

Foundations with various-sized footings are typically listed in a footing schedule shown on the structural drawings. In addition, the spread footing may require the use of a template for embedded anchor bolts to support the column.

Foundation walls are formed by erecting and fastening modular panels side by side on top of the strip footing. Foundation wall formwork requires the "doubling up" of panels to create a narrow box to hold the concrete until it has hardened. The panels are held apart at a predetermined space using metal ties. This predetermined space is ultimately the thickness of the wall. **Figure 2.25** illustrates formwork for a typical wall.

Ties are usually spaced at 24" on center both horizontally and vertically, though they may require closer spacing for greater loads imposed by the wet cast-in-place concrete. In addition, the panels are braced on the exterior (against the hydrostatic pressure caused by the wet concrete) by a series of horizontal wood or metal braces known as *walers*.

In addition, the contractor must make provisions for coating the forms with a release agent to break the bond between the wood and the concrete during the curing process.

Spread Footings

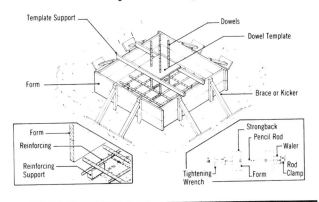

R.S. Means Co., Inc., *Plan Reading & Material Takeoff*

Figure 2.24

Foundation Wall

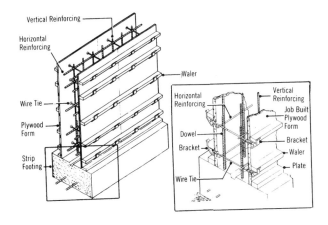

R.S. Means Co., Inc., *Plan Reading & Material Takeoff*

Figure 2.25

Walls and Piers

Concrete foundation walls are cast-in-place. Their function is to support the structure above. They are supported by footings and are mostly below grade. In a structure with a basement, foundation walls act to retain, or hold back, the outside soil.

A *pier* is a short column of plain or reinforced concrete used to support a concentrated load. Piers are used as components in foundation walls or as isolated, separate members.

Formwork for foundation walls is constructed of smooth wood sheathing applied to a 2" x 4" wood or steel frame. Formwork is built in modular sizes starting at approximately 8" in width and increasing to 16" widths in 2" increments. Larger panels for longer straight runs are in 24" and 48" widths. Standard panel heights are 48", 72", and 96".

Formwork for Grade Beams and Elevated Slabs

Grade beams are horizontal beams supported at the ends, as opposed to foundation walls that are supported by footings on the ground. The structure's load is carried along the grade beam and transmitted through the end supports (piers) to the soil below. Grade beams differ from wall formwork in that they sometimes require the forming of the bottom of the grade beam as well as the sides (see **Figure 2.26**). Custom-made or one-time-use forms may be required for certain applications.

Elevated cast-in-place slabs are often integrated with concrete beams, similar to grade beams. Formed horizontal areas require considerably more bracing to support the weight of the concrete they contain. **Figure 2.27** is an illustration of an elevated cast-in-place slab. Another type of elevated slab involves placement of concrete on corrugated metal decking supported by bar joists.

Edge Forms

The simplest type of form, called the edge form, is most commonly used to contain shallow pours of concrete for slab-on-grade, walks, or pads. Edge form materials are typically rough-grade lumber in the dimension required by the depth of the pour, such as 2" x 4", 2" x 6", 1" x 4". The actual edge form is held in place by wood or metal stakes, driven into the ground at spacing as needed to support the work and prevent bowing.

Elevated Slab

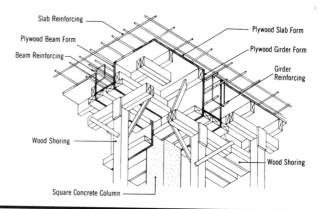

R.S. Means Co., Inc., *Plan Reading & Material Takeoff*

Figure 2.27

Piles & Caissons

Industry Standards

Construction Principles, Materials, and Methods
(John Wiley & Sons, Inc.)

3.9.2.2 Piles and Caissons

Piles and caissons are used as foundation support for buildings when the soil is not capable of supporting the loads that will be imposed by a building on spread foundations.

Driven Piles

Driven piles are column-like units that transmit loads through poor soil to rock or lower levels of soil that have adequate bearing capacity. In some regions, short piles are called piers. Piles serve the same purpose as footings in that they transmit loads to subbase strata capable of carrying the load. Piles usually are placed in clusters of two or more spaced from 30 to 48 in. on centers. This arrangement permits them to act together and produces a higher load-carrying capacity than can be achieved with isolated piles. The load capacities mentioned in this section are based on the piles being distributed in clusters. These load capacities are also the maximum permitted. Optimum load capacities are somewhat lower in each instance. Piles receive building loads from isolated columns and from grade beams by means of reinforced concrete pile caps. Pile caps are sometimes simply a widened section of a grade beam.

Pile foundations are either (1) *point bearing types*, which transmit loads to lower, stronger soil or rock through their points, or (2) *friction types*, which develop the necessary bearing capacity through surface friction between the pile and the ground.

Grade Beams

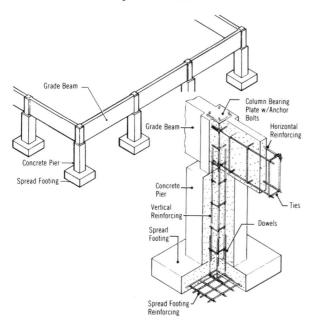

R.S. Means Co., Inc., *Plan Reading & Material Takeoff*

Figure 2.26

Piles are driven with heavy *hammers* in large machines called *pile drivers*. *Drop hammers* are simply raised and dropped on a pile by force of gravity. *Differential acting steam hammers* are rammed into the top of a pile by steam pressure or compressed air. Modern vibratory hammers and diesel-driven hammers are also used.

Friction piles are driven to a predetermined depth or resistance based on soil boring analysis and field tests. To verify the design analysis, test piles are usually driven and loaded before the remainder of the piles are driven. Point bearing piles are driven until additional blows of the hammer produce very little movement in the pile (*refusal*).

Piles may be made of wood, concrete, steel, or a combination (*composite*) of these. Timber piles have been used for at least 2000 years, probably longer. Some below-water timber piles beneath bridges in Europe are known to have remained in continuous service for more than 1000 years. These piles are, however, suitable only for relatively light loads (40 tons maximum) and must be treated with preservatives when they will extend above the water table. They are also limited in length to the effective height of the tree from which they are cut (45 to 65 ft.), because they cannot be spliced.

Steel piles may be H-shaped sections or pipes. H-shaped piles are heavy wide-flange sections varying in size from 8 to 14 in. in both depth and flange width. They can carry loads of from 50 to 200 tons each and may be as much as 150 ft. long. To produce such lengths, sections are welded together as they are being driven.

Steel-pipe piles are later filled with concrete. They are available in several types and shapes. These piles may be heavy-walled types, which can be driven directly, or thinner-walled types, which require a tight-fitting, heavy inner lining (*mandrel*) that is withdrawn before the concrete is placed. They may be smooth-walled or corrugated, round or fluted. Sizes range from 8 to 24 in. in diameter, and maximum load capacity ranges from 75 to 200 tons, depending on the type. Pipes with closed ends may be driven to as much as 120 ft. Other pipe piles are limited to about 80 ft., 10 to 54 in. across.

Precast concrete piles are either solid concrete or open cylinders that are later filled solid with concrete. They may be square, round, or octagonal in cross section. All precast concrete piles are reinforced, and most are also prestressed. Solid precast concrete piles with simple reinforcement can be up to 80 ft. long. This increases to 150 ft. for cylinder piles and up to 200 ft. when they are prestressed. Maximum capacity ranges from 100 tons for simple reinforced piles to as much as 500 tons for prestressed cylinder piles. Sizes vary from 10 to 54 in. across.

Composite piles are constructed in several configurations. Some have timber or concrete-filled steel-pipe lower sections and concrete-filled shell with mandrel upper sections. Others have H-shaped steel lower sections and precast concrete upper sections. Composite piles sometimes permit less expensive applications. For example, the combination of timber and concrete-filled steel shell permits the use of relatively inexpensive timber piles at much lower depths than is ordinarily possible (up to 150 ft.). A disadvantage of using composite piles is that their load carrying potential is limited to that of the lower of the two elements. For example, a composite pile of timber and concrete filled steel shell is limited to 40 tons, instead of the 75 to 80 tons the concrete-filled steel piles could carry.

Caissons

Caissons are concrete columns placed in auger-drilled or excavated holes. They serve the same purpose as piles. While some caissons are only 6 to 12 in. in diameter, most are much larger and capable of carrying heavy loads. They can reach as much as 6 ft. in diameter and carry 3500 tons or more. Caissons extend through unsatisfactory soil to a firm soil-bearing stratum or to bedrock. As a caisson hole is drilled or dug, a steel casing is lowered into it to keep the hole from caving in. This casing is raised and removed as the concrete is placed. Small, relatively short, and lightly loaded caissons, which are sometimes called *piers*, are frequently poured into cardboard or composition casings that are not removed as the concrete is placed.

Caissons come in four types: (1) *rock caissons* simply rest directly on solid rock; (2) *high-capacity rock caissons*, sometimes called *socket caissons*, rest in a socket cut into rock, thus supporting the load both by resting on the rock and by friction against the sides of the pocket (3) *hardpan* or *clay caissons* rest on a soil bearing stratum; and (4) *friction caissons*, sometimes called *cast-in-place piles*, are supported by the friction acting on the sides of the caisson, much as friction piles are supported.

Hardpan or clay caissons have either straight shafts or an enlarged base called a *bell*. Bells are produced by hand excavation or with a special device, a *belling bucket*, on the auger.

Concrete Slabs

Industry Standards
Construction Principles, Materials, and Methods
(John Wiley & Sons, Inc.)

3.7.1.4 Edging

When all bleed water and water sheen have left the surface and the concrete has started to stiffen, other finishing operations, such as edging, may be started. Edging rounds off the formed edge of a slab to prevent chipping or damage. An edger should be run back and forth until a finished edge is produced. All coarse aggregate particles should be covered, and the edger should not leave too deep an impression in the top of the slab. If it does, the indentation may be difficult to remove with subsequent finishing operations.

Usually, edging is not required for most interior slabs on grade; it is more commonly performed on sidewalks, driveways, and steps. An edger should not be used when a slab is to be finished with resilient flooring requiring a smooth, level subfloor. Edges at construction joints in the slab may be ground lightly with a silicon carbide stone to remove irregularities after the forms are stripped and before the adjacent slab is placed.

Comment

See also "Edge Forms" in the "Formwork" section earlier in this chapter.

3.7.1.5 Jointing

Except when joints will later be sawed, immediately following or during edging, premolded inserts are placed in concrete slabs to control cracking in the concrete due to shrinkage.

3.7.1 6 Floating

After edging and hand-jointing operations, a slab should be floated. Many variables, such as concrete temperature, air temperature, relative humidity, and wind, affect the process, making it difficult to set a definite time to begin floating. This knowledge comes only through job experience. In general, floating may be done when the water sheen has disappeared and the concrete will support the weight of the finisher.

The purpose of floating is fourfold: (1) to embed large aggregate just beneath the surface; (2) to remove slight imperfections, humps, and voids to produce a level or plane surface; (3) to consolidate mortar at the surface in preparation for other finishing operations; and (4) to open the surface to permit excess moisture to escape.

Magnesium floats should be used, especially on air-entrained concrete. Use of a metal float greatly reduces the amount of work required by the finisher because the float slides more readily over the concrete surface, has a good floating action, and forms a smoother surface texture than a wood float. A wood float tends to stick to and "tear" the concrete surface.

The marks left by edgers and jointers should be removed by floating, unless such marks are desired for decorative purposes. In that case, the edger or jointer should be rerun after the floating operation.

3.7.1.7 Troweling

Troweling is done on slabs that are to be left exposed or to receive thin finishes, such as resilient flooring, carpet, tile, or paint. When troweling is required, the surface should be steel-troweled immediately after floating. It is customary for a cement mason using hand tools to float and then steel-trowel an area before moving the knee boards. If necessary, tooled joints and edges should be rerun before and after troweling to maintain true lines, proper depths, and uniformity and to remove kinks.

The purpose of troweling is to produce a smooth, hard surface. For the first troweling, whether by power or by hand, the trowel blade must be kept as flat against the surface as possible. If tilted or pitched at too great an angle, an objectionable "washboard" or "chatter" surface will result. For the first troweling, a new trowel is not recommended. An older trowel that has been broken in can be worked quite flat without the edge digging into the concrete. The smoothness of a surface can be improved by timely additional trowelings. Intervals between successive trowelings will permit the concrete to increase its set. As the surface stiffens, each successive troweling should be made by a smaller-sized trowel tipped at a progressively higher angle so that sufficient pressure can be applied for proper finishing.

For exposed slabs, additional troweling increases the compaction of fines at the surface, giving greater density and better wear resistance. A second troweling is recommended even if the slab is to be finished with resilient flooring, because it results in closer surface tolerances and a better surface to receive the flooring.

3.7.1.8 Broom Finish

A steel-troweled concrete surface is very smooth. Unfortunately, such surfaces become quite slippery when wet. They can be slightly roughened to produce a nonslip surface by brushing or brooming them. A brushed surface is made by drawing a broom over the surface after steel troweling.

3.7.2 Finishing Air-Entrained Concrete Slabs

The microscopic air bubbles in air entrained concrete tend to hold the ingredients, including water, in suspension. This type of concrete requires less mixing water and still has good workability with the same slump. Since there is less water and it is held in suspension, little or no bleeding occurs. There is, therefore, no need to wait for the evaporation of free water from the surface, and floating and troweling can and should be started as soon as the slab can support the finisher and equipment. Many horizontal surface defects and failures are caused by performing finishing operations while bleed water or excess surface moisture is present. Therefore, better results are generally accomplished with air-entrained concrete.

As with regular concrete, if floating is done by hand, using a magnesium float is essential. A wood float drags and greatly increases the amount of work necessary to accomplish the same result.

If floating is done by power, the only major difference between the finishing procedures for air-entrained concrete and those for concrete that is not air entrained is that floating may be started sooner on air-entrained concrete.

3.7.3 Finishing Lightweight Structural Concrete Slabs

Finishing operations for slabs made with lightweight structural concrete containing coarse aggregates of expanded clay, shale, or slag vary somewhat from those used on slabs made with normal-weight concrete. When the surface of the concrete is worked, there is a tendency for the coarse lightweight aggregate rather than the mortar to rise to the surface. Lightweight concrete can be easily finished if the following precautions are observed: (1) the mix should be properly proportioned and not be over or undersanded in an attempt to meet unit weight requirements, and (2) finishing should not be started too early, and the concrete should not be overworked or overvibrated. A well-proportioned mix can generally be placed, struck off, leveled, and floated with less effort than is necessary for normal-weight concrete. Excessive leveling and floating are principal causes of finishing problems, because the heavier mortar is driven down and the coarse aggregate brought to the surface.

3.7.4 Special Slab Finishes

Due to the plastic quality of concrete, many surface finishes can be applied. The surface may be scored or tooled with a jointer in decorative and geometric patterns. Some of the more common special finishes are discussed here.

3.7.4 1 Exposed Aggregate

An exposed-aggregate surface often is chosen for any area where a special textural effect is desired. A surface that is ground and polished is suitable, especially for such places as entrances, interior terraces, and recreation rooms.

Selection of aggregates is so important that test panels should be made before the job is started. Colorful gravel aggregate that is quite uniform in gradation and in sizes ranging from 1/2 to 3/4 in. is recommended. Flat, sliver-shaped particles or aggregate less than 1/2 in. in diameter should be avoided, because they become dislodged during exposing operations. Exposing the aggregate used in ordinary concrete generally is unsatisfactory since a high percentage of coarse aggregates is not necessarily revealed.

A 5-1/2- to 6-sack concrete with a maximum slump of 3 in. should be used.

Comments

Variations in slab thickness will generally promote cracking through the artificial creation of weakened planes. The code addresses minimum thickness, however, a slab of uniform thickness has a better chance of deforming under load without cracking.

It is recommended that a slab-on-grade be poured so that the tolerance remain at plus or minus 1/2" of the recommended design thickness, as there is no practical way to pour heavy concrete on grade and hold a fine tolerance. This is then the definition of nominal thickness.

Slab Thickness

UBC — 1997

1909.5.3 Two-way construction (nonprestressed).

1909.5.3.1 This section shall govern the minimum thickness of slabs or other two-way construction designed in accordance with the provisions of Section 1913 and conforming with the requirements of Section 1913.6.1.2. The thickness of slabs without interior beams spanning between the supports on all sides shall satisfy the requirements of Section 1909.5.3.2 or 1909.5.3.4.

Thickness of slabs with beams spanning between the supports on all sides shall satisfy the requirements of Section 1909.5.3.3 or 1909.5.3.4.

1909.5.3.2 For slabs without interior beams spanning between the supports and having a ratio of long to short span not greater than 2, the minimum thickness shall be in accordance with the provisions of Table 19–C–3 and shall not be less than the following values:

Slabs without drop panels as defined in Sections 1913.3.7.1 and 1913.3.7.2 5 inches (127 mm).

Slabs with drop panels as defined in Sections 1913.3.7.1 and 1913.3.7.2 4 inches (102 mm).

Comments

The first process in concrete finishing is to place and consolidate the concrete. If it is a large rock mix (1" or larger), then tamping is required to move the rock away from the surface immediately after screeding and to raise the fine cement paste for later troweling.

ACI publishes several books on concrete slabs, including finishing, and surface defects (causes, prevention, repair). See this chapter's introduction for more on ACI.

Concrete Surfaces

Material Properties

Industry Standards

Concrete Repair and Maintenance Illustrated
(R.S. Means Co., Inc.)

*Ed. Note: See **Figures 2.28** and **2.29** on the following pages for desirable concrete properties and what to avoid. See also "Preventing Surface Defects," earlier in this chapter.*

Concrete Finishing

Industry Standards

Construction Principles, Materials, and Methods
(John Wiley & Sons, Inc.)

3.7.1.2 Screeding

The surface of newly placed concrete is struck off (*screed*) by moving a straightedge back and forth with a saw-like motion across the tops of the forms and screeds. If mechanical vibrating equipment is used in the striking-off process, the need for leveling may be eliminated. Whether boards, vibratory screeds, or roller screeds are used, a small amount of concrete always should be kept ahead of the straightedge to fill in low spots and maintain a plane surface.

3.7.1.3 Leveling

Leveling is the bringing of a concrete surface to true grade with enough mortar to produce the desired finish. After a concrete slab has been screeded, it should be immediately smoothed with a *darby* to level raised spots and fill depressions left after screeding. Long-handled floats, called *bull floats*, of either wood or metal, are sometimes used instead of darbies to smooth and level concrete surfaces. Because it is hard to produce surfaces in plane near the edges of a slab using bull floats, leveling with a darby is sometimes needed after the bull floating has been done.

Leveling is sometimes called darbying or bull floating, but this terminology requires that both terms be used or that the architect dictate the method to be used, which is inappropriate. In addition, the term *bull floating* confuses this activity with the later finishing step *floating*, which is an entirely different operation. The PCA in its literature and the AIA in its master guide specifications series, *Masterspec*, both use the broader term *leveling*.

The purpose of leveling is to eliminate the ridges and voids left by screeding. In addition, it should slightly embed the coarse aggregate, thus preparing the surface for the subsequent finishing operations of edging, jointing, floating, and troweling.

A slight stiffening of the concrete is necessary after leveling before further finishing operations are started. No subsequent operations should be performed until the concrete will sustain foot pressure with only about 1/4-in. indentation.

Pipes & Conduits in Concrete

UBC — 1997

1906.3 Conduits and Pipes Embedded in Concrete

1906.3.1 Conduits, pipes and sleeves of any material not harmful to concrete and within limitations of this subsection may be embedded in concrete with approval of the *building official*, provided they are not considered to replace structurally the displaced concrete.

1906.3.2 Conduits and pipes of aluminum shall not be embedded in structural concrete unless effectively coated or covered to prevent aluminum-concrete reaction or electrolytic action between aluminum and steel.

1906.3.3 Conduits, pipes and sleeves passing through a slab, wall or beam shall not impair significantly the strength of the construction.

1906.3.4 Conduits and pipes, with their fittings, embedded within a column shall not displace more than 4 percent of the area of cross section on which strength is calculated or which is required for fire protection.

1906.3.5 Except when plans for conduits and pipes are approved by the *building official*, conduits and pipes embedded within a slab, wall or beam (other than those merely passing through) shall satisfy the following:

1906.3.5.1 They shall not be larger in outside dimension than one-third the overall thickness of slab, wall or beam in which they are embedded.

1906.3.5.2 They shall be spaced not closer than three diameters or widths on center.

1906.3.5.3 They shall not impair significantly the strength of the construction.

1906.3.6 Conduits, pipes and sleeves may be considered as replacing structurally in compression the displaced concrete, provided:

1906.3.6.1 They are not exposed to rusting or other deterioration.

1906.3.6.2 They are of uncoated or galvanized iron or steel not thinner than standard Schedule 40 steel pipe.

1906.3.6.3 They have a nominal inside diameter not over 2 inches (51 mm) and are spaced not less than three diameters on centers.

External Loads/Concrete Material Properties

Goal (performance requirements)	Results if the wrong material is selected (undesirable response)		Look for these properties	Avoid these!
Moving liquids	Erosion of surface 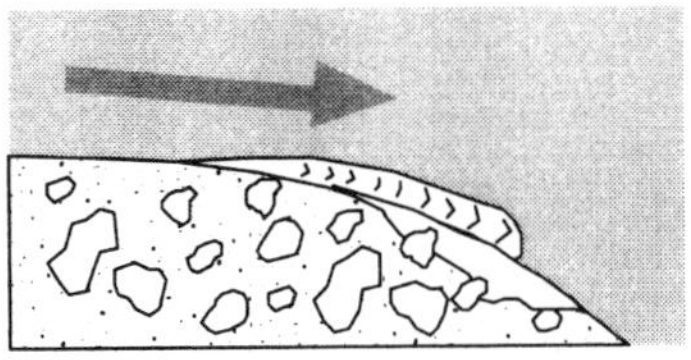		High density	Low density
			High compressive	Low compressive
			High tensile	Low tensile
Moving liquids and suspended solids			High density	Low density
			High compressive	Low compressive
	Erosion and abrasion of surfaces		High tensile	Low tensile
Vehicle wheels		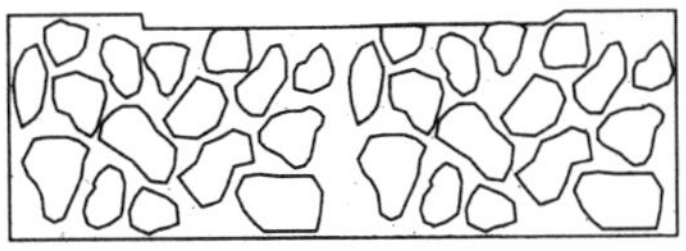 Abrasion damage to surface	High density, high compressive strength	Low density, low compressive strength
		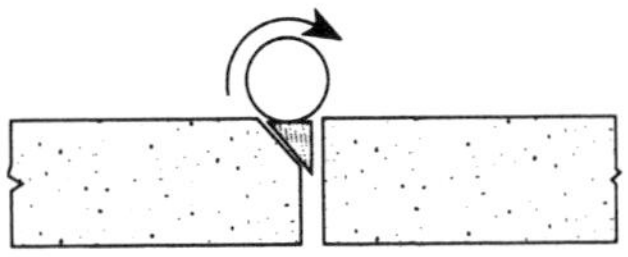 Edge spalling at joints	High compressive, tensile and bond strength, tensile anchorage into substrate	Low compressive, tensile and bond strength
Impact		Spalling	High tensile strength, internal tensile reinforcement	Low tensile strength
			High compressive strength	Low compressive strength
			Low modulus of elasticity	High modulus of elasticity
		Loss of bond	High bond strength, tensile anchorage into substrate	Low bond strength

R.S. Means Co., Inc., *Concrete Repair and Maintenance Illustrated*

Figure 2.28

Constructibility & Appearance Properties

	Goal (performance requirements)		Look for these properties	Avoid these!
Constructibility	Turn-around time 		Rapid strength gain	Slow strength gain
	Flowability 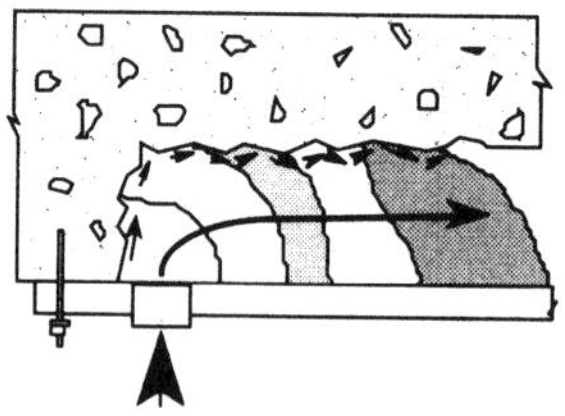		High slump	Low slump
			Small aggregate, fines, round shape	Large aggregate, angular shape, lack of fines
	Non sag 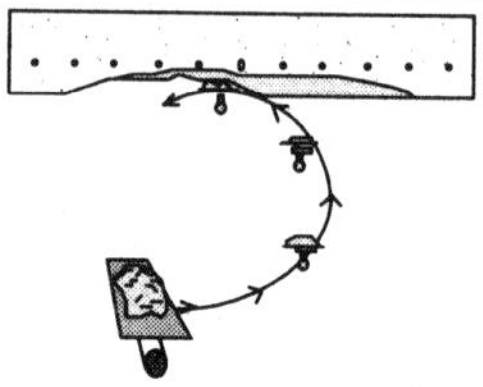		High internal cohesion, high adhesive grip	Low internal cohesion, low adhesive grip
	Forgiving **"Murphy's Law"**		Simple formulation, redundant	Complex formulation, dependent reactions

Goal (performance requirements)	Results if the wrong material is selected (undesirable response)	Look for these properties	Avoid these!
Appearance 	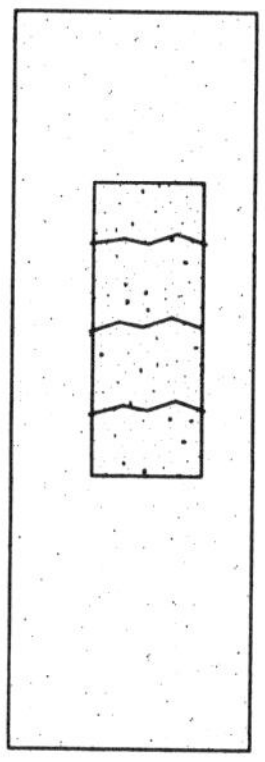 Cracking of surface from drying shrinkage*	Low drying shrinkage,* flexible surface membrane	High drying shrinkage*
	Cracking of surface in plastic stage	Low exotherm	High exotherm
		Low surface water loss during placement	High surface water loss during placement

*Refer to volume change affects included at the end of this section.

R.S. Means Co., Inc., *Concrete Repair and Maintenance Illustrated*

Figure 2.29

1906.3.7 Pipes and fittings shall be designed to resist effects of the material, pressure and temperature to which they will be subjected.

1906.3.8 No liquid, gas or vapor, except water not exceeding 90°F (32.2°C) or 50 psi (0.34 MPa) pressure, shall be placed in the pipes until the concrete has attained its design strength.

1906.3.9 In solid slabs, piping, unless it is used for radiant heating or snow melting, shall be placed between top and bottom reinforcement.

1906.3.10 Concrete cover for pipes, conduit and fittings shall not be less than 1-1/2 inches (38 mm) for concrete exposed to earth or weather, or less than 3/4 inch (19 mm) for concrete not exposed to weather or in contact with ground.

1906.3.11 Reinforcement with an area not less than 0.002 times the area of concrete section shall be provided normal to the piping.

1906.3.12 Piping and conduit shall be so fabricated and installed that cutting, bending or displacement of reinforcement from its proper location will not be required.

Buried Pipe
Industry Standards
Concrete Repair and Maintenance Illustrated
(R.S. Means Co., Inc.)

Buried pipes are loaded with surrounding backfill and overburden. Nonuniform loads surrounding the pipe may result in deformation of the pipe. Loads on top may exceed the load on the pipe's underside. The pipe is compressed in the vertical axis and bulges along the horizontal axis. Cracks may develop, forming hinges at three possible locations: the crown (top of pipe), and at the two spring line locations (side of pipe).

Effects of Nonuniform or Excessive Loads

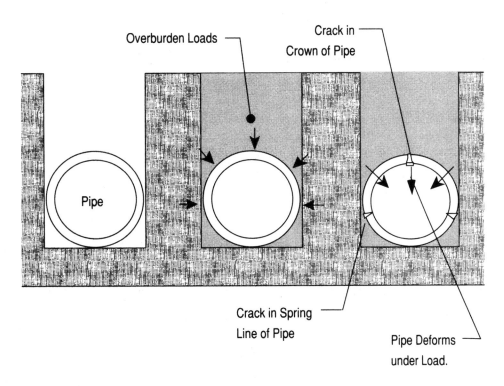

R.S. Means Co., Inc., *Concrete Repair and Maintenance Illustrated*

Figure 2.30

Allowable Tolerances

UBC — 1997

1806.5.5 Foundation elevation. On graded sites, the top of any exterior foundation shall extend above the elevation of the street gutter at point of discharge or the inlet of an approved drainage device a minimum of 12 inches (305 mm) plus 2 percent. The building official may approve alternate elevations, provided it can be demonstrated that required drainage to the point of discharge and away from the structure is provided at all locations on the site.

1003.2.6 Changes in elevation. All exterior elevation changes and interior elevation changes of 12 inches (305 mm) or more along the path of exit travel shall be made by steps, stairs or stairways conforming with the requirements of Section 1003.3.3.3 or ramps conforming with the requirements of Section 1003.3.4

1003.3.1.7 Landings at doors. Regardless of the occupant load served, landings shall have a width not less than the width of the door or the width of the stairway served, whichever is greater. Doors in the fully open position shall not reduce a required dimension by more than 7 inches (178 mm). Where a landing serves an occupant load of 50 or more, doors in any position shall not reduce the landing dimension to less than one-half its required width. Landings shall have a length measured in the direction of travel of not less than 44 inches (1118 mm).

Industry Standards

Concrete Repair and Maintenance Illustrated
(R.S. Means Co., Inc.)

Structural members that are cast out of tolerance pose aesthetic and structural problems. Members cast out of tolerance may have improper concrete cover and cross section, which may produce eccentric loading.

Tolerances for Formed Surfaces	
Variation from plumb	**in (mm)**
any 10' length	1/4" (6)
maximum entire length	1" (25)
Variations from level	
slab soffits 10' length	1/4" (6)
maximum entire length	3/4" (19)
Variations in cross section	
minus	1/4" (6)
plus	1/2" (13)

Structural Members Out of Tolerance

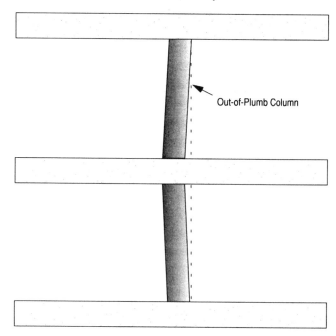

Out-of-Plumb Column

R.S. Means Co., Inc., *Concrete Repair and Maintenance Illustrated*

Figure 2.31

Comments

Concrete Paving Tolerance

The ACI Manual of Concrete Practice, *published by the American Concrete Institute, recommends a tolerance in concrete paving of ± 1/4" in 10' in all sideways measurements, and ± 1/8" when measuring parallel to the centerline of the concrete paving.*

Foundation Tolerances

The American Concrete Institute (ACI) and the American Society for Testing and Materials (ASTM) have developed a schedule to determine the **flatness** *tolerances separately from a level tolerance. (The term* **level** *is a comparison above or below a theoretical elevation plane (benchmark), and the term flatness is the differential within a 10' straightedge.) The allowance for level is ± 3/4" against the benchmark. The maximum allowance for flatness is ± 3/16" in 10'.* ACI *publishes Standard Tolerances for Concrete Construction, which includes tolerances shown in ACI documents.*

Ed. Note: See also "Cracks: Acceptable Tolerances and the Effects of Chlorides" earlier in this chapter.

CHAPTER 3

MASONRY

Table of Contents

(continued on next page)

Text in blue print indicates excerpts from model building code(s). "Comments" (in solid blue boxes) were written by the editors, based on their own experience.

For building product information, use this book's special Internet gateway to thousands of manufacturers: www.rsmeans.com/prodsupp/rlstand.html

Chapter 3

Masonry

Common Defect Allegations

- Many defect claims include a retaining wall movement allegation. Ordinarily there will be some observable deflection in a long straight wall, even during backfill. Usually high walls are required to be shored, prior to the backfilling activities, to reduce this distortion.

- Sometimes walls were improperly built. However, additional surcharges are often placed on the back of the wall in the form of either dead load improvements or the creation of an excessive live load where traffic of heavy vehicles impacts a previous design for a landscape wall. Sometimes a French drain is placed behind the wall with perforated pipe and crushed rock, and when the soil filters down through the gravel, it eventually fills the voids in the rock and plugs up the drainage, completely loading the wall with a new hydraulic static pressure. The proper method of creating a French drain is to use a filter fabric to filter out the silt, either around the perforated pipe with a sock, or preferably wrapping an envelope completely around the crushed rock. This is achieved by placing the filter fabric in the void before placing the gravel and the pipe, and then wrapping the fabric over the rock fill before the soil is placed.

- Occasionally, the "five foot to daylight" rule is violated. That rule basically states that the toe of the footing should be five feet from daylight (below ground) when the slope of the ground continues downward from this wall. First appearances are that the contractor built it wrong, although occasionally we find that the user of the property regraded the land in an attempt to create more usable pad area.

- *Wall cracks are generally considered tolerable to 1/4", as long as there is no dislocation of the plane of the wall and no vertical dislocation. Cracks should not be left open to the weather, but should be filled with an epoxy or expansive set grout and monitored for further movement with a crack gauge permanently mounted to either side of the crack and photographed for future analysis.*

- *Masonry-related claims for defects in construction often involve walls that are not laid up with precision. The basis of the disagreement usually lies in the contrast between hand-laid masonry and the exact measurement of synthetic panels, which actually can have an artificial appearance. In practical terms, building a wall involves a contractor's best judgment as well as variables between head joints, bed joints, and lead jambs. To the practitioner, the presence of variables among these elements is expected and adds to the attractiveness of hand-laid masonry. Determining the point at which an irregularity becomes a defect is a judgment that must be made by an experienced practitioner.*

Introduction

Our goal in this text is to clarify the standards of each trade, while noting deficiencies commonly stated in defect claims. We accomplish this by presenting code information, along with the recommendations of industry leaders. This section covers common masonry installations, such as block and brick walls, fireplaces, and retaining walls. Code requirements are interspersed with installation standards from the Masonry Institute, ASTM, and other industry authorities.

International Building Code Development

The development of the International Building Code (IBC) for the year 2000 will absorb many of the masonry standards defined regionally or by the Masonry Institute. The result will be a more comprehensive regulation that is much more definitive regarding applied methods of construction. The Masonry Alliance for Codes & Standards, a group of masonry industry representatives, is following the progress of the International Code Council to ensure proper incorporation of masonry provisions.

The following organizations may be helpful in providing more detailed information on masonry installations.

American Concrete Institute
38800 Country Club Drive
Farmington Hills, MI 48331
Telephone: 248-848-3700

Brick Industry Association (BIA)
11490 Commerce Park Drive
Reston, VA 20191
Telephone: 703-620-0010
www.bia.org

Marble Institute of America
30 Eden Alley, Suite 301
Columbus, OH 43215
Telephone: 614-228-6194
www.marble-institute.com
The Marble Institute offers information on standards of workmanship and suitable applications of stone products.

Masonry Institute of America (MIA)
2550 Beverly Boulevard
Los Angeles, CA 90057
Telephone: 213-388-0472
www.masonryinstitute.org

Masonry Alliance for Codes & Standards
(In NCMA office)
2302 Horse Pen Road
Herndon, VA 20171-3499
Telephone: 703-713-1900

National Concrete Masonry Association (NCMA)
2302 Horse Pen Road
Herndon, VA 20171
Telephone: 703-713-1900
www.ncma.org

Portland Cement Association
5420 Old Orchard Road
Skokie, IL 60077-1083
Telephone: 847-966-6200
www.portcement.org

Ed. Note: Comments and recommendations within this chapter are not intended as a definitive resource for construction activities. For building projects, contractors must rely on the project documents and applicable codes for their own particular locations.

Installation

Construction of Mortar Joints
UBC — 1997

2104.4.1 Mortar. The mortar shall be sufficiently plastic and units shall be placed with sufficient pressure to extrude mortar from the joint and produce a tight joint. Deep furrowing, which produces voids, shall not be used.

The initial bed joint thickness shall not be less than 1/4 inch (6 mm) or more than 1 inch (25 mm); subsequent bed joints shall not be less than 1/4 inch (6 mm) or more than 5/8 inch (16 mm) in thickness.

Grouting Procedure
UBC — 1997

2104.6.1 General conditions. Grouted masonry shall be constructed in such a manner that all elements of the masonry act together as a structural element.

Prior to grouting, the grout space shall be clean so that all spaces to be filled with grout do not contain mortar projections greater than 1/2 inch (12.7 mm), mortar droppings or other foreign material. Grout shall be placed so that all spaces designated to be grouted shall be filled with grout and the grout shall be confined to those specific spaces.

Grout materials and water content shall be controlled to provide adequate fluidity for placement without segregation of the constituents, and shall be mixed thoroughly.

The grouting of any section of wall shall be completed in one day with no interruptions greater than one hour.

Between grout pours, a horizontal construction joint shall be formed by stopping all wythes at the same elevation and with the grout stopping a minimum of 1-1/2 inches (38 mm) below a mortar joint, except at the top of the wall. Where bond beams occur, the grout pour shall be stopped a minimum of 1/2 inch (12.7 mm) below the top of the masonry.

Size and height limitations of the grout space or cell shall not be less than shown in Table 21-C. Higher grout pours or smaller cavity widths or cell size than shown in Table 21-C may be used when approved, if it is demonstrated that grout spaces will be properly filled.

Cleanouts shall be provided for all grout pours over 5 feet (1524 mm) in height.

Where required, cleanouts shall be provided in the bottom course at every vertical bar but shall not be spaced more than 32 inches (813 mm) on center for solidly grouted masonry. When cleanouts are required, they shall be sealed after inspection and before grouting.

Where cleanouts are not provided, special provisions must be made to keep the bottom properly filled.

2104.6.2 Construction requirements. Reinforcement shall be placed prior to grouting. Bolts shall be accurately set with templates or by approved equivalent means and held in place to prevent dislocation during grouting.

Segregation of the grout materials and damage to the masonry shall be avoided during the grouting process.

Grout shall be consolidated by mechanical vibration during placement before loss of plasticity in a manner to fill the grout space. Grout pours greater than 12 inches (300 mm) in height shall be reconsolidated by mechanical vibration to minimize voids due to water loss. Grout pours 12 inches (300 mm) or less in height shall be mechanically vibrated or puddled.

In nonstructural elements which do not exceed 8 feet (2440 mm) in height above the highest point of lateral support, including fireplaces and residential chimneys, mortar of pouring consistency may be substituted for grout when the masonry is constructed and grouted in pours of 12 inches (300 mm) or less in height.

In multiwythe grouted masonry, vertical barriers of masonry shall be built across the grout space the entire height of the grout pour and spaced not more than 30 feet (9144 mm) horizontally.

The grouting of any section of wall between barriers shall be completed in one day with no interruption longer than one hour.

Lateral Support
UBC — 1997

2109.5 Lateral Support. Masonry walls shall be laterally supported in either the horizontal or vertical direction not exceeding the intervals set forth in Table 21-O (see **Figure 3.1**). Lateral support shall be provided by cross walls, pilasters, buttresses or structural framing members horizontally, or by floors, roof or structural framing members vertically.

Except for parapet walls, the ratio of height to nominal thickness for cantilever walls shall not exceed 6 for solid masonry or 4 for hollow masonry.

Wall Lateral Support Requirements for Empirical Design of Masonry

CONSTRUCTION	MAXIMUM l/t or h/t
Bearing Walls	
Solid or solid grouted	20
All other	18
Nonbearing Walls	
Exterior	18
Interior	36

Courtesy of ICBO, UBC — 1997, [Table 21-0]

Figure 3.1

In computing the ratio for cavity walls, the value of thickness shall be the sums of the nominal thickness of the inner and outer wythes of the masonry. In walls composed of different classes of units and mortars, the ratio of height or length to thickness shall not exceed that allowed for the weakest of the combinations of units and mortar of which the member is composed.

Minimum Thickness
UBC — 1997

2109.6.1 General. The nominal thickness of masonry bearing walls in buildings more than one story in height shall not be less than 8 inches (203 mm). Solid masonry walls in one-story buildings may be of 6-inch nominal thickness when not over 9 feet (2743 mm) in height, provided that when gable construction is used, an additional 6 feet (1829 mm) is permitted to the peak of the gable.

Exception: The thickness of unreinforced grouted brick masonry walls may be 2 inches (51 mm) less than required by this section, but in no case less than 6 inches (152 mm).

2109.6.2 Variation in thickness. Where a change in thickness due to minimum thickness occurs between floor levels, the greater thickness shall be carried up to the higher floor level.

2109.6.3 Decrease in thickness. Where walls of masonry of hollow units or masonry-bonded hollow walls are decreased in thickness, a course or courses of solid masonry shall be constructed between the walls below and the thinner wall above, or special units or construction shall be used to transmit the loads from face shells or wythes to the walls below.

2109.6.4 Parapets. Parapet walls shall be at least 8 inches (203 mm) in thickness and their height shall not exceed three times their thickness. The parapet wall shall not be thinner than the wall below.

2109.10.3 Minimum thickness. The thickness of stone masonry bearing walls shall not be less than 16 inches (406 mm).

Use of Aluminum Equipment
UBC — 1997

2104.7 Aluminum Equipment. Grout shall not be handled nor pumped utilizing aluminum equipment unless it can be demonstrated with the materials and equipment to be used that there will be no deleterious effect on the strength of the grout.

Comments

When they come into contact, freshly mixed cement and aluminum tools produce a chemical reaction that weakens the eventual strength of the mortar or grout. Therefore, aluminum tools should not be used to place either of these mixtures.

Mortar Mixing
UBC — 1997

2103.3.1 General. Mortar shall consist of a mixture of cementitious materials and aggregate to which sufficient water and approved additives, if any, have been added to achieve a workable, plastic consistency.

2103.3.2 Selecting proportions. Mortar with specified proportions of ingredients that differ from the mortar proportions of Table 21-A may be approved for use when it is demonstrated by laboratory or field experience that this mortar with the specified proportions of ingredients, when combined with the masonry units to be used in the structure, will achieve the specified compressive strength f'_m. Water content shall be adjusted to provide proper workability under existing field conditions. When the proportion of ingredients is not specified, the proportions by mortar type shall be used as given in Table 21-A.

2104.1.2. All metal reinforcement shall be free from loose rust and other coatings that would inhibit reinforcing bond.

2104.1.6. The method of measuring materials for mortar and grout shall be such that proportions of the materials can be controlled.

2104.2.7. Mortar or grout mixed at the jobsite shall be mixed for a period of time not less than three minutes or more than 10 minutes in a mechanical mixer with the amount of water required to provide the desired workability. Hand mixing of small amounts of mortar is permitted. Mortar may be retempered. Mortar or grout which has hardened or stiffened due to hydration of the cement shall not be used. In no case shall mortar be used two and one-half hours, nor grout used one and one-half hours, after the initial mixing water has been added to the dry ingredients at the jobsite.

Exception: Dry mixes for mortar and grout which are blended in the factory and mixed at the jobsite shall be mixed in mechanical mixers until workable, but not to exceed 10 minutes.

Industry Standards
ASTM Material Specifications
(American Society of Testing and Materials)

Masonry Cement — ASTM C91 (Types M, S, or N)

Portland Cement — ASTM C150 (Types I, IA, II, IIA, III, or IIIA)

Blended hydraulic cement — ASTM C595 [Types IS, IS–A, IP, IP–A, I(PM)–A]*

Hydrated lime for masonry purposes — ASTM C207 (Types S, SA, N, or NA)**

Quicklime for structural uses (for lime putty) — ASTM C5

---

* Slag cement Types S or SA can also be used but only in property specifications.

** Types N and NA lime may be used only if tests or performance records show that these limes are not detrimental to the soundness of mortar.

Reinforcement Requirements Differ by Zone
UBC — 1997

Ed. Note: The UBC outlines specific reinforcement requirements that differ according to seismic zones in the United States. Buildings constructed in Zone 1 sustain the lowest risk, and those in Zone 4 have the highest risk. See the Seismic Zone Map in **Figure 3.2** *for an indication of seismic zones in the U.S.*

Comments

The code excerpts in the following sections demonstrate the importance of researching your area requirements prior to construction. They are not intended to provide sufficient information for actual construction.

Good construction supervision requires that a library of texts be present at the project site, including relevant code books, for handy reference when interpretation of proper construction techniques is necessary.

Stack Bond Joint Reinforcement
UBC — 1997

2106.1.5.4 Joint reinforcement. Prefabricated joint reinforcement for masonry walls shall have at least one cross wire of at least No. 9 gage steel for each 2 square feet (0.19 m²) of wall area. The vertical spacing of the joint reinforcement shall not exceed 16 inches (406 mm). The longitudinal wires shall be thoroughly embedded in the bed joint mortar. The joint reinforcement shall engage all wythes.

Where the space between tied wythes is solidly filled with grout or mortar, the allowable stresses and other provisions for masonry bonded walls shall apply. Where the space is not filled, tied walls shall conform to the allowable stress, lateral support, thickness (excluding cavity), height and tie requirements for cavity walls.

Concrete Abutting Masonry
UBC — 1997

2106.2.7.4 Concrete abutting structural masonry. Concrete abutting structural masonry, such as at starter courses or at wall intersections not designed as true separation joints, shall be roughened to a full amplitude of 1/16 inch (1.6 mm) and shall be bonded to the masonry in accordance with the requirements of this chapter as if it were masonry. Unless keys or proper reinforcement is provided, vertical joints as specified in Section 2106.1.4 shall be considered to be stack bond and the reinforcement as required for stack bond shall extend through the joint and be anchored into the concrete.

Reinforcement Placing
UBC — 1997

Working Stress Design—Seismic Zones 3 & 4

2104.5 Reinforcement Placing. Reinforcement details shall conform to the requirements of this chapter. Metal reinforcement shall be located in accordance with the plans and specifications.

Reinforcement shall be secured against displacement prior to grouting by wire positioners or other suitable devices at intervals not exceeding 200 bar diameters.

2107.2.2.1 Maximum reinforcement size. The maximum size of reinforcement shall be No. 11 bars. Maximum reinforcement area in cells shall be 6 percent of the cell area without splices and 12 percent of the cell area with splices.

Seismic Zone Map

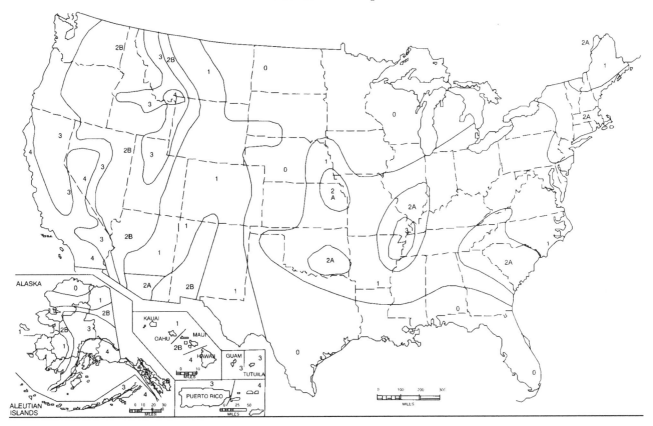

Figure 16-2 SEISMIC ZONE MAP OF THE UNITED STATES
For areas outside of the United States, see Appendix Chapter 16 (of the 1997 Uniform Building Code).

Courtesy of ICBO, UBC — 1997

Figure 3.2

Cover
UBC — 1997
2107.2.2.2 Cover. All reinforcing bars, except joint reinforcement, shall be completely embedded in mortar or grout and have a minimum cover, including the masonry unit, of at least 3/4 inch (19 mm), 1-1/2 inches (38 mm) of cover when the masonry is exposed to weather and 2 inches (51 mm) of cover when the masonry is exposed to soil.

Splices
UBC — 1997
2107.2.2.6 Splices. The amount of lap of lapped splices shall be sufficient to transfer the allowable stress of the reinforcement as specified in Sections 2106.3.4, 2107.2.2.3 and 2107.2.12. In no case shall the length of the lapped splice be less than 30 bar diameters for compression or 40 bar diameters for tension.

Welded or mechanical connections shall develop 125 percent of the specified yield strength of the bar in tension.

Exception: For compression bars in columns that are not part of the seismic-resisting system and are not subject to flexure, only the compressive strength need be developed.

When adjacent splices in grouted masonry are separated by 3 inches (76 mm) or less, the required lap length shall be increased 30 percent.

Exception: Where lap splices are staggered at least 24 bar diameters, no increase in lap length is required.

Anchorage for Shear
UBC — 1997
2106.3.5 Anchorage of shear reinforcement. Single, separate bars used as shear reinforcement shall be anchored at each end by one of the following methods:

1. Hooking tightly around the longitudinal reinforcement through 180 degrees.

2. Embedment above or below the mid-depth of the beam on the compression side a distance sufficient to develop the stress in the bar for plain or deformed bars.

3. By a standard hook, as defined in Section 2107.2.2.5, considered as developing 7,500 psi (52 MPa), plus embedment sufficient to develop the remainder of the stress to which the bar is subjected. The effective embedded length shall not be assumed to exceed the distance between the mid-depth of the beam and the tangent of the hook. The ends of bars forming a single U or multiple U stirrup shall be anchored by one of the methods set forth in Items 1 through 3 above or shall be bent through an angle of at least 90 degrees tightly around a longitudinal reinforcing bar not less in diameter than the stirrup bar, and shall project beyond the bend at least 12 stirrup diameters.

Comments

The masonry reinforcement information outlined in these UBC excerpts is so significant that it should appear on construction drawings as design criteria. In any case, during construction in seismic zones with high risk, the installer is bound by these rules. Commonly, defects occur at the corners in the placement of the vertical lap corner bars. These elements must be placed inside the corner bend of the horizontal bar when a single bar is placed in the bond beam block. This requires a machine bend that has a relatively sharp radius.

Similarly, retaining walls and restraining walls will differ as to the proper placement of the vertical bars, and the construction plans should clearly reflect the requirements. A retaining wall is based upon the footing that holds the vertical wall against the soil load; so the vertical steel rods should be placed at the back, or earth, side of the cell to stop rotation. A restraining wall is held at the bottom and the top by other structures. Therefore, the vertical rods should be placed away from the earth, or the front of the cell, where the wall may fail in the middle during tensile stress.

The loops or closed ends of simple U or multiple U stirrups shall be anchored by bending around the longitudinal reinforcement through an angle of at least 90 degrees and project beyond the end of the bend at least 12 stirrup diameters.

2106.3.6 Lateral ties. All longitudinal bars for columns shall be enclosed by lateral ties. Lateral support shall be provided to the longitudinal bars by the corner of a complete tie having an included angle of not more than 135 degrees or by a standard hook at the end of a tie. The corner bars shall

have such support provided by a complete tie enclosing the longitudinal bars. Alternate longitudinal bars shall have such lateral support provided by ties and no bar shall be farther than 6 inches (152 mm) from such laterally supported bar.

Anchor Bolts
UBC — 1997
2106.2.14.1 General. Bent bar anchor bolts shall have a hook with a 90-degree bend with an inside diameter of three bolt diameters, plus an extension of one and one half bolt diameters at the free end. Plate anchor bolts shall have a plate welded to the shank to provide anchorage equivalent to headed anchor bolts.

The effective embedment depth l_b for plate or headed anchor bolts shall be the length of embedment measured perpendicular from the surface of the masonry to the bearing surface of the plate or head of the anchorage, and l_b for bent bar anchors shall be the length of embedment measured perpendicular from the surface of the masonry to the bearing surface of the bent end minus one anchor bolt diameter. All bolts shall be grouted in place with at least 1 inch (25 mm) of grout between the bolt and the masonry, except that 1/4-inch-diameter (6.4 mm) bolts may be placed in bed joints which are at least 1/2 inch (12.7 mm) in thickness.

2106.2.14.2 Minimum edge distance. The minimum anchor bolt edge distance l_{be} measured from the edge of the masonry parallel with the anchor bolt to the surface of the anchor bolt shall be 1-1/2 inches (38 mm).

2106.2.14.3 Minimum embedment depth. The minimum embedment depth of anchor bolts l_b shall be four bolt diameters but not less than 2 inches (51 mm).

2106.2.14.4 Minimum spacing between bolts. The minimum center-to-center distance between anchor bolts shall be four bolt diameter.

Masonry Walls

Concrete Block Walls
Industry Standards
Means Graphic Construction Standards
(R.S. Means Co., Inc.)

Concrete blocks are among the most frequently used materials for constructing masonry walls and partitions because of their strength, versatility, and economy. They may be used for many different types of bearing and nonbearing wall structures, including foundation walls, exterior and interior bearing walls, infill panels, interior partitions, and fire walls. They may also function effectively as backup walls for composite and cavity-design wall structures with brick or other veneer facings.

Concrete blocks are manufactured in two types, solid and hollow, and in various strength ratings. If the cross-sectional area, exclusive of voids, is 75% or greater than the gross area of the block, then it is classified as "solid block." If the same area is below the 75% figure, then the block is classified as "hollow block." The strength of concrete block is determined by the compressive strength of the type of concrete used in its manufacture, or by the equivalent compressive strength, which is based on the gross area of the block, including voids.

There are several aggregates that can be used to manufacture lightweight blocks. These blocks can be identified by the weight of the concrete mixture used in their manufacture. Regular weight block is made from 125 lb. per cubic foot concrete (PCF), and lightweight block from 105 to 85 PCF concrete.

Care should be exercised when installing concrete block walls to prevent cracking caused by block shrinkage, temperature expansion and contraction, excessive stress in a particular area, or excessive moisture. The cracking can be controlled by selecting and installing blocks of the proper moisture content for the locality and by employing a sufficient amount of horizontal joint reinforcing. Cracking can also be controlled with vertical control joints, which are typically placed at intervals ranging from 20' to 40'. The spacing intervals of these control joints depend on the wall height and the amount of joint reinforcing used. Corners and openings generally require

control joints as well. Mortar joints throughout the wall should be made weather tight (to restrict moisture invasion) by being tooled and compressed into a concave shape.

Joint reinforcing and individual ties serve as important components of the various types of concrete block walls. Two types of joint reinforcing are available: the truss type and the ladder type. Because the truss type provides better load distribution, it is normally used in bearing walls. The ladder type is usually installed in light-duty walls that serve nonbearing functions. Both types of joint reinforcing may also be used to tie together the inner and outer wythes of composite or cavity-design walls. Corrugated strips, as well as Z-type, rectangular, and adjustable wall ties, may also be used for this purpose. Generally, one metal wall tie should be installed for each 4-1/2 square feet of veneer. Although both types of joint reinforcing may be used as ties, individual ties should not be used as joint reinforcing to control cracking.

Structural reinforcement is also commonly required in concrete block walls, especially in those that are load bearing. Deformed steel bars may be used as vertical reinforcement when grouted into the block voids, and as horizontal reinforcement when installed above openings and in bond beams. Horizontal and vertical bars may be grouted into the void normally used as the collar joint in a composite wall. Lintels should be installed to carry the weight of the wall above openings. Steel angles, built-up steel members, bond beams filled with steel bars and grout, and precast shapes may function as lintels.

Various methods may be employed for insulating concrete block walls. Rigid foam inserts or loose perlite can be used to fill the voids in the blocks of single wythe structures. Composite and single wythe walls can also be insulated by installing the insulating material between the furring strips for the interior wall facing. For cavity walls, rigid-board insulation may be attached within the cavity to the surface of the inner wythe.

Concrete Block Wall

Control Joint Backer Rods

Poured Insulation

Wire Strip Joint Reinforcing

Concrete Block

Control Joint Sealant

Comments

In some regions, termite treatment inside the cells is recommended to prevent termites from entering the structure.

For concrete block wall tolerance, see the end of this chapter. Also refer to sections 2–11, 2–12, and 2–13 in Residential Construction Performance Guidelines, *published by the National Association of Home Builders (Telephone: 1-800-368-5242).*

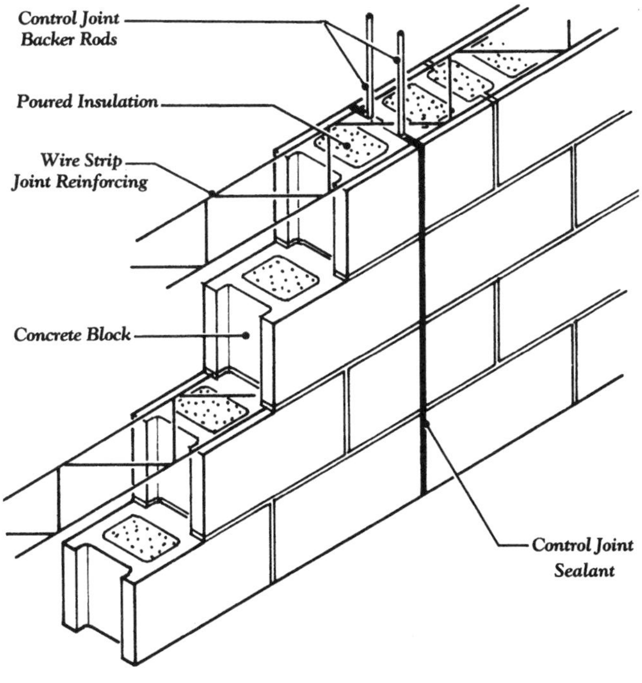

R.S. Means Co., Inc., *Means Graphic Construction Standards*

Figure 3.3

Brick Walls

Industry Standards

Means Graphic Construction Standards
(R.S. Means Co., Inc.)

Brick walls may function as bearing structures if the proper guidelines are followed for the type of brick, the type of mortar, and the reinforcement methods and materials. For example, brick units with a compressive strength between 2,000 and 14,000 psi, when installed with a mortar of commensurate compressive strength, produce a wall with a strength between 500 and 3,000 psi. Horizontal joint reinforcement can be placed within the wall to control shrinkage cracks and to tie the face wythe to the backup wythe in composite or cavity bearing wall systems. To provide resistance to lateral and flexural loads, bar reinforcement may be grouted vertically into the brick cores, or vertically and horizontally into the collar joint between two wythes of bearing wall.

Because brick walls are not waterproof, provisions must be made to limit the amount of water penetration through the exterior face. Flashing should be installed at the junction of walls and floors, as well as over and under openings. In cavity walls, the outside face of the backup wall or the insulation between the wythes should be waterproofed. Weep holes should be located above the flashing at brick shelves, relieving angles, and lintels to provide a means of escape for moisture that has penetrated the wall.

The most common size brick measures nominal 4" wide by 8" long, with heights of 2-2/3" (standard), 3-1/5" (engineer), 4" (economy), 5-1/3" (double), and 8" (square or panel). The next most commonly used size measures 4" in width by 12" in length, with heights of 2" (Roman), 2-2/3" (Norman), 3-1/5" (Norwegian), 4" (utility), 5-1/3" (triple), and 12" (square or panel). The heights of courses of brick may also vary slightly with the thickness requirements of mortar joints. For example, a 1/2" mortar joint requires a brick that is 1/16" thinner than does a 3/8" mortar joint to maintain the same modular coursing in the wall. Because the two apparent dimensions in any brick wall structure are its length and height, these two measurements are critical in determining the number of units of brick material to be used. Therefore, bricks with larger length and height dimensions are more economically installed because fewer of them have to be laid per square foot of wall area.

Comments

The Brick Industry Association provides technical notes on proper design and installation of structural and veneer brick walls. (See chapter introduction for telephone numbers and address.)

Glass Block

UBC — 1997

2110.1 General. Masonry of glass blocks may be used in nonload-bearing exterior or interior walls and in openings which might otherwise be filled with windows, either isolated or in continuous bands, provided the glass block panels have a minimum thickness of 3 inches (76 mm) at the mortar joint and the mortared surfaces of the blocks are treated for mortar bonding. Glass block may be solid or hollow and may contain inserts.

2110.2 Mortar Joints. Glass block shall be laid in Type S or N mortar. Both vertical and horizontal mortar joints shall be at least 1/4 inch (6 mm) and not more than 3/8 inch (9.5 mm) thick and shall be completely filled. All mortar contact surfaces shall be treated to ensure adhesion between mortar and glass.

2110.3 Lateral Support. Glass panels shall be laterally supported along each end of the panel. Lateral support shall be provided by panel anchors spaced not more than 16 inches (406 mm) on center or by channels. The lateral support shall be capable of resisting the horizontal design forces determined in Chapter 16 or a minimum of 200 pounds per lineal foot (2920 N per linear meter) of wall, whichever is greater. The connection shall accommodate movement requirements of Section 2110.6.

2110.4 Reinforcement. Glass block panels shall have joint reinforcement spaced not more than 16 inches (406 mm) on center and located in the mortar bed joint extending the entire length of the panel. A lapping of longitudinal wires for a minimum of 6 inches (152 mm) is required for joint reinforcement splices. Joint reinforcement shall also be placed in the bed joint immediately below and above openings in the panel. Joint reinforcement shall conform to UBC Standard 21-10, Part I. Joint reinforcement in exterior panels shall be hot-dip galvanized in accordance with UBC Standard 21-10, Part I.

2110.5 Size of Panels. Glass block panels for exterior walls shall not exceed 144 square feet (13.4 m²) of unsupported wall surface or 15 feet (4572 mm) in any dimension. For interior walls, glass block panels shall not exceed 250 square feet (23.2 m²) of unsupported area or 25 feet (7620 mm) in any dimension.

2110.6 Expansion Joints. Glass block shall be provided with expansion joints along the sides and top, and these joints shall have sufficient thickness to accommodate displacements of the supporting structure, but not less than 3/8 inch (9.5 mm). Expansion joints shall be entirely free of mortar and shall be filled with resilient material.

2110.7 Reuse of Units. Glass block units shall not be reused after being removed from an existing panel.

Fireplaces, Hearths & Chimneys

UBC — 1997

3102.4.4 Chimney offset. Masonry chimneys may be offset at a slope of not more than 4 units vertical in 24 units horizontal (16.7% slope), but not more than one third of the dimension of the chimney, in the direction of the offset. The slope of the transition from the fireplace to the chimney shall not exceed 2 units vertical in 1 unit horizontal (200% slope).

3102.4.5 Change in size or shape. Masonry chimneys shall not change in size or shape within 6 inches (152 mm) above or below any combustible floor, ceiling or roof component penetrated by the chimney.

3102.7.8 Clearance to combustible material. Combustible materials shall not be placed within 2 inches (51 mm) of fireplace, smoke chamber or chimney walls. Combustible material shall not be placed within 6 inches (152 mm) of the fireplace opening. No such combustible material within 12 inches (305 mm) of the fireplace opening shall project more than 1/8 inch (3.2 mm) for each 1-inch (25 mm) clearance from such opening.

No part of metal hoods used as part of a fireplace or barbecue shall be less than 18 inches (457 mm) from combustible material. This clearance may be reduced to the minimum requirements specified in the Mechanical Code.

3102.7.9 Areas of flues, throats and dampers. The throat shall be at least 8 inches (203 mm) above the fireplace opening and shall be at least 4 inches (102 mm) in depth. The net cross-sectional area of the flue and of the throat between the firebox and the smoke chamber of a fireplace shall not be less than that set forth in [UBC] Figure 31-1 or Table 31-A.

Metal dampers equivalent to not less than 0.097-inch (2.46 mm) (No. 12 carbon sheet metal gage) steel shall be installed. When fully opened, damper openings shall not be less than 90 percent of the required flue area.

3102.7.10 Lintel. Masonry over the fireplace opening shall be supported by a noncombustible lintel unless the masonry is self-supporting.

3102.7.11 Hearth. Masonry fireplaces shall be provided with a brick, concrete, stone or other approved noncombustible hearth slab. This slab shall not be less than 4 inches (102 mm) thick and shall be supported by noncombustible materials or reinforced to carry its own weight and all imposed loads.

Combustible forms and centering shall be removed.

3102.7.12 Hearth extensions. Hearths shall extend at least 16 inches (406 mm) from the front of, and at least 8 inches (203 mm) beyond each side of, the fireplace opening. Where the fireplace opening is 6 square feet (0.56 m²) or larger, the hearth extension shall extend at least 20 inches (508 mm) in front of, and at least 12 inches (305 mm) beyond each side of, the fireplace opening.

Except for fireplaces that open to the exterior of the building, the hearth slab shall be readily distinguishable from the surrounding or adjacent floor.

Ed. Note: See IOTFDC Table 1003.1 for a summary of requirements for masonry fireplaces and chimneys.

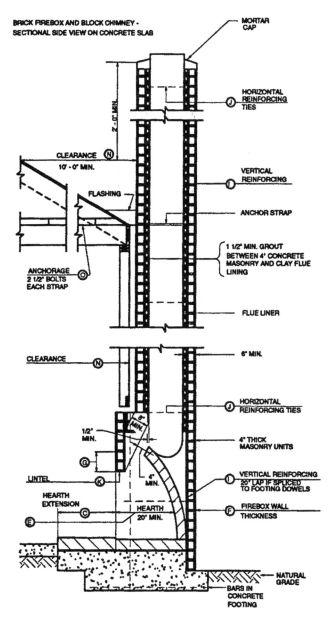

Courtesy of ICC, IOTFDC — 1998 (formerly CABO)[Detail from Figure 1003.1]

Figure 3.4

Fire Blocking

3102.7.13 Fire blocking. Fire blocking between chimneys and combustible construction shall meet the requirements specified in Section 708.

Placement of Fire Blocking

708.2.1.4. In openings around vents, pipes, ducts, chimneys, fireplaces and similar openings that afford a passage for fire at ceiling and floor levels, with noncombustible materials.

708.2.1.5. At openings between attic spaces and chimney chases for factory-built chimneys.

3102.3.7 Cleanouts. Cleanout openings shall be provided within 6 inches (152 mm) of the base of every masonry chimney.

3102.3.6 Height and termination. Every chimney shall extend above the roof and the highest elevation of any part of a building as shown in Table 31-B. For altitudes over 2,000 feet (610 m), the building official shall be consulted in determining the height of the chimney.

Comments

As a general rule, the height of a masonry chimney should be 2' above the highest building structure within a 10' radius. For altitudes over 2,000', the contractor must consult the area building official to determine the local requirements. Table 31-B in the UBC (Figure 13.5 in Chapter 13 of this book) is a schedule for chimney heights. Figure 13.6 (also in Chapter 13) provides UBC requirements for flue sizes.

2106.1.11 Reuse of masonry units. Masonry units may be reused when clean, whole and conforming to the other requirements of this section. All structural properties of masonry of reclaimed units shall be determined by approved test.

2110.7 Reuse of Units. Glass block units shall not be reused after being removed from an existing panel.

Industry Standards

Means Graphic Construction Standards
(R.S. Means Co., Inc.)

Masonry fireplaces are typically constructed of brick and block masonry units. (See **Figure 3.5.**) Because of the weight of the fireplace and chimney, a foundation of concrete block and/or cast-in-place concrete is required for support. The fire box consists of fire-resistant brick, while the hearth and face are of standard brick. Stone and tile are also used for these exterior surfaces. Accessories, such as clean-out doors, air vents and dampers complete the typical system.

Chimney types fall into two basic categories: masonry and prefabricated metal. Besides their use with fireplaces, chimneys are also required to vent exhaust gases from water heaters, furnaces, boilers and incinerators. Chimneys can be constructed within the building, on an outside wall, or as a freestanding structure. Foundation and intermediate support requirements will vary accordingly.

Masonry chimneys typically consist of a flue constructed from heat-resistant, refractory material, surrounded by a brick-framed exterior. Fire bricks and clay tiles are commonly used as refractory material. The weight of masonry chimneys is such that foundation support structures are also necessary. Both the chimney and the foundation should be sized according to the requirements of the specific installation.

Whether metal or masonry, all chimneys should extend at least 3' above the highest point at which they pass through or by the roof. Chimneys should also be at least 2' higher than any roof ridge within a 10' radius. For all chimney installations, it is important to use the appropriate material and to maintain the proper space requirements for installations.

Ed. Note: See Chapter 13, "Specialties," for more on prefabricated fireplaces.

Masonry Fireplace—Interior

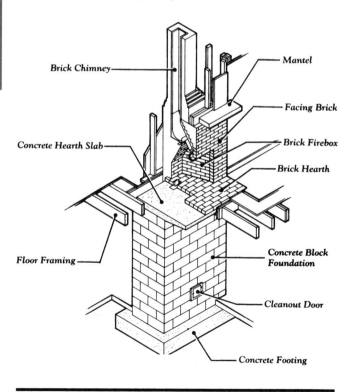

R.S. Means Co., Inc., *Means Graphic Construction Standards*

Figure 3.5

Prefabricated, Built-in Fireplace

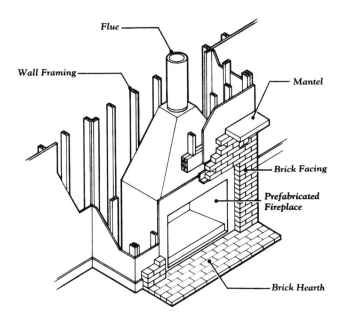

Flue
Wall Framing
Mantel
Brick Facing
Prefabricated Fireplace
Brick Hearth

Masonry Fireplace—Exterior

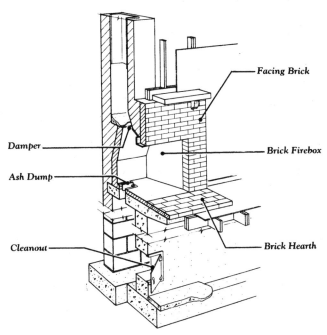

Facing Brick
Brick Firebox
Damper
Ash Dump
Brick Hearth
Cleanout

Masonry Chimney

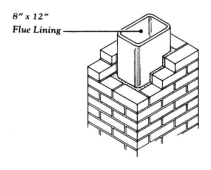

8" x 12"
Flue Lining

R.S. Means Co., Inc., *Means Graphic Construction Standards*

Figure 3.5 continued

Comments

The American Concrete Institute's Standard Practice for the Design and Construction of Reinforced Concrete Chimneys and Commentary *gives material, construction and design requirements for cast-in-place and precast reinforced concrete chimneys. (See the chapter introduction for ACI contact information.)*

Pipes & Conduits in Masonry

UBC — 1997

2106.1.9 Pipes and conduits embedded in masonry. Pipes or conduits shall not be embedded in any masonry in a manner that will reduce the capacity of the masonry to less than that necessary for required strength or required fire protection. Placement of pipes or conduits in unfilled cores of hollow-unit masonry shall not be considered as embedment.

Exceptions:

1. Rigid electric conduits may be embedded in structural masonry when their locations have been detailed on the approved plan.

2. Any pipe or conduit may pass vertically or horizontally through any masonry by means of a sleeve at least large enough to pass any hub or coupling on the pipeline. Such sleeves shall not be placed closer than three diameters, center to center, nor shall they unduly impair the strength of construction.

Retaining Walls

Industry Standards

Means Graphic Construction Standards
(R.S. Means Co., Inc.)

Masonry retaining walls may be constructed of block, brick, or stone.

Brick or block walls are usually placed on a concrete footing that acts as a leveling pad and distributes imposed loads to the subsoil. Both the wall and the footing may be reinforced. Voids in the masonry are usually filled with mortar or grout, and the wall capped with a suitable material. Solid masonry walls should include porous backfill against the back of the wall and weep holes or drainage piping to eliminate hydrostatic head.

Stone retaining walls may be constructed dry or mortar set with or without a suitable concrete footing. All masonry retaining walls should be placed a sufficient depth below grade to eliminate the danger of frost heave. Mortar set walls should include an adequate drainage system.

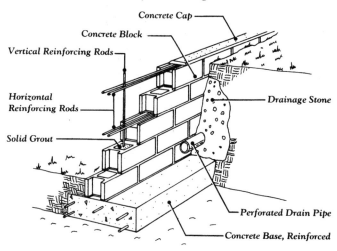

Masonry Retaining Wall

Concrete Cap
Concrete Block
Vertical Reinforcing Rods
Horizontal Reinforcing Rods
Solid Grout
Drainage Stone
Perforated Drain Pipe
Concrete Base, Reinforced

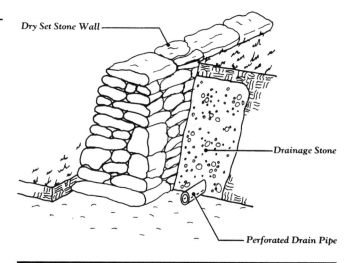

Stone Retaining Wall

Dry Set Stone Wall
Drainage Stone
Perforated Drain Pipe

R.S. Means Co., Inc., *Means Graphic Construction Standards*

Figure 3.6

Block Wall Tolerances

Industry Standards
ACI Manual of Concrete Practice
(American Concrete Institute)

Allowable Tolerances
American Concrete Institute (ACI) standards define both a total tolerance envelope within which the plane and edges of a wall must fall and relative alignment tolerances for adjacent elements and construction within a 10-ft (3-m) distance.

For top of wall alignment, the tolerance depends on whether the wall is exposed and whether it is a bearing surface. These are summarized below. All of the ACI tolerances apply to brick walls as well as concrete masonry walls and other types of masonry construction.

Top of Wall Alignment
Exposed	+/-1/2"
Not exposed	+/- 1"
Bearing surface	+/-1/2"
TOW Nonbearing	+/- 3/4"
Slope Alignment (Plumb)	+/-1/4" in 10'
Vertical Alignment (Plumb)	+/- 3/4" in total wall
Horizontal Alignment	+/-1/4" in 10'
Horizontal Alignment	+/- 1/2" in total wall

Comments
For more information on allowable tolerances in masonry construction, see Sections 4–2, and 4–38 through 4–42 in Residential Construction Performance Guidelines, *published by the National Association of Home Builders (Telephone: 1-800-368-5242).*

Paving

Industry Standards
Means Graphic Construction Standards
(R.S. Means Co., Inc.)

Both brick and stone may be set in a sand or concrete bed and grouted with mortar or watered and tamped sand. (See **Figure 3.7**.) Regardless of the type of bed material, the subbase must first be leveled and thoroughly compacted to prevent tracking and settling of the finished surface. Wire mesh reinforcing may be required in concrete beds that are large in area or subjected to heavy traffic.

Brick Sidewalk
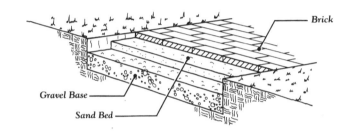

Plaza Brick Paving System
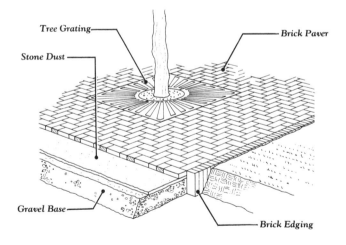

R.S. Means Co., Inc., *Means Graphic Construction Standards*

Figure 3.7

Brick Paving on Sand Bed

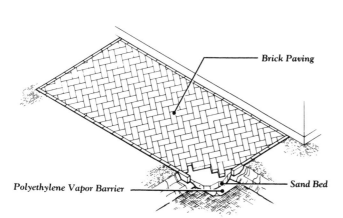

Stone Paving on Sand Bed

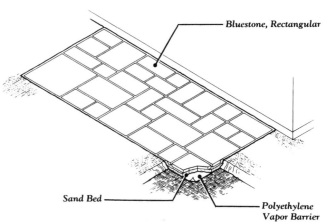

Brick Paving on Concrete Bed

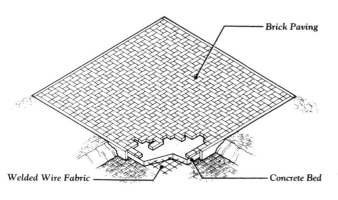

Stone Paving on Concrete Bed

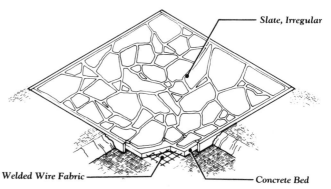

R.S. Means Co., Inc., *Means Graphic Construction Standards*

Figure 3.7 continued

Ed. Note: See Chapter 2 for concrete paving and Chapter 1 for asphalt paving.

CHAPTER 4

METAL FRAMING

Table of Contents

Text in blue print indicates excerpts from model building code(s). "Comments"
(in solid blue boxes) were written by the editors, based on their own experience.

For building product information, use this book's special
Internet gateway to thousands of manufacturers:
www.rsmeans.com/prodsupp/rlstand.html

METAL FRAMING

Common Defect Allegations

Light-gauge metal framing is not yet widely utilized in structural components. We therefore have seen few alleged failures. The one complaint that seems to reoccur is the lack of a tight fit between the stud and the channel in a load-bearing condition. The problem is caused by the fact that the track channel has a slight radius at the 90° angle, from when it was shaped during manufacture. Since a cut stud C-Channel has a sharp end, the stud channel does not make complete contact with the track channel. After the building has been standing awhile, it settles slightly, showing wrinkles in drywall tape and on EIFS synthetic exterior plaster systems.

The solution seems to be the same as in wood framing construction: load the building with roofing materials and stock as much of the interior weight as possible before placing wall finishes. Also, hydraulic jigs have been used to compress the studs in a site prefabrication of the walls and then lift the assembled wall to the erected location.

Introduction Use of metal components in residential construction is growing in the U.S., partly because of limited sources of timber. Metal makes a good building material for several reasons. Available scrap from recycled automobiles and construction activities makes metal inexpensive and plentiful. The components do not warp after installation, and the materials are not flammable or affected by termites or fungal attack. Buildings with metal structural framing can, however, suffer rust from prolonged exposure to moisture. Just like other structural materials, steel framing should not be exposed to moisture in wall cavities.

Light-gauge steel is the most common form of metal framing in residential and light commercial construction. Structural steel is also used in residential projects, such as girders to support floors. Structural steel and pre-engineered steel buildings are occasionally used for light commercial applications, but require extensive training and specialized equipment. While the UBC covers structural steel in their Chapter 22, that material is not included in this chapter since it is comprised primarily of technical design criteria and formulas, typically interpreted by the engineer who designs the installation. Structural steel framing is not addressed in the IOTFDC (formerly CABO).

There is a scarcity of skilled installers who know how to handle steel framing. Since there are few standard techniques accepted by building officials, all metal buildings must be engineered. Several professional associations offer guidelines.

The **American Iron and Steel Institute** can be reached at 1101 17th Street, N.W., Suite 1300, Washington, D.C. 20036-4700 (202-452-7100), by calling the Steel Home Hotline (1-800-79-STEEL), or by visiting the AISI Web site (**www.steel.org**). AISI offers a complete package of manuals, videos, and disks to aid in the design and construction process. The association has a Residential Advisory Group and offers guidelines, including framing details and fastener requirements. The Residential Advisory Group hosts five subcommittees that meet three times per year in conjunction with industry shows. These forums are attended by members who are steel producers, roll formers, builders, framers, engineers, architects, suppliers, manufacturers and industry representatives. For information about the group's newsletter and other materials, call the Washington, D.C. headquarters (202-452-7100).

AISI also offers a *Residential Steel Construction Directory, RG9801*, which lists companies that provide information on availability, distribution, prices, and technical assistance on steel products. The Steel Home Hotline provides a telephone link to structural engineers at the NAHB Research Center who are available to answer technical inquiries (1-800-79-STEEL, technical inquiry option 2).

The **American Zinc Association,** 1112 16th Street, N.W., Suite 240, Washington, D.C. 20036 (202-835-0164) may also be helpful.

Hawaii has the highest percentage of steel-framed home construction in the world. Cold Formed Steel Framing now accounts for 25–30% of all new housing starts in the state, and depending on the island, for 5–80% of metal roofing. Membership in the **Hawaii Steel Alliance** is open to home builders, framers, engineers, realtors, steel suppliers, roll formers, tool and fastener manufacturers, metal roofing manufacturers and college/university faculty. Tim Waite, of T.J. Waite & Associates, is the coordinator of the alliance. For more information , contact Mr. Waite by telephone at 808-486-3040 or by e-mail at bahaybakal@aol.com.

Ed. Note: Comments and recommendations within this chapter are not intended as a definitive resource for construction activities. For building projects, contractors must rely on the project documents and applicable codes for their particular locations.

Light-Gauge Steel Construction

Industry Standards

Means Graphic Construction Standards
(R.S. Means Co., Inc.)

Used for both light commercial and residential applications, light-gauge steel construction is a building system that utilizes galvanized steel studs for bearing walls and galvanzied C joists (single or double) for support of the floor system. (See **Figure 4.1** and **Figure 4.2.**) Decking may consist of plywood, steel slab form and concrete, steel deck and concrete, or precast concrete. Studs are also used as a backup system for preformed fascia of various materials. They allow for easy attachment and bracing to resist wind or earthquake forces.

Fastening is accomplished by using self-drilling screws or by welding. Plywood decks are fastened using screws or spiral shank nails. Adhesives may also be used in conjunction with screws or nails. When welds are used with galvanized members, weld areas should be touched up with a suitable paint.

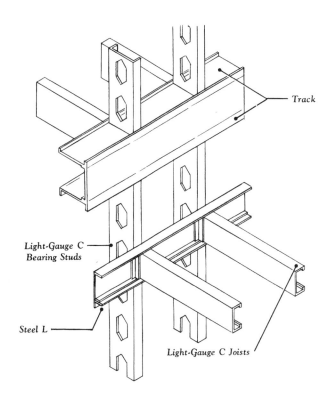

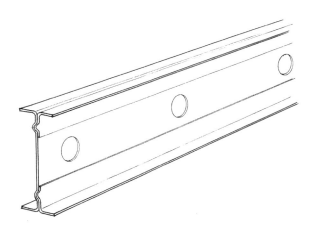

Light-Gauge Double Steel Joists

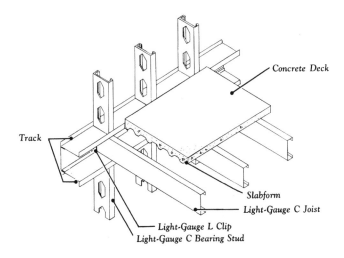

R.S. Means Co., Inc., *Means Graphic Construction Standards*

Figure 4.1

Light-Gauge Metal Framing — Walls

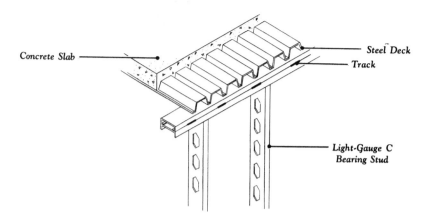

Concrete Slab

Steel Deck

Track

Light-Gauge C Bearing Stud

Floors, on Steel Beam

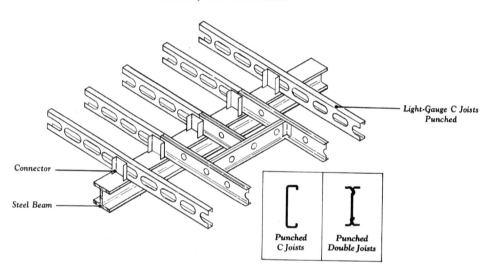

Light-Gauge C Joists Punched

Connector

Steel Beam

Punched C Joists

Punched Double Joists

With Plywood Deck

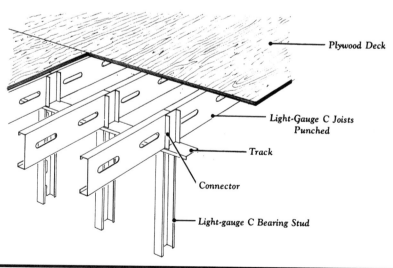

Plywood Deck

Light-Gauge C Joists Punched

Track

Connector

Light-gauge C Bearing Stud

R.S. Means Co., Inc., *Means Graphic Construction Standards*

Figure 4.2

Industry Standards

Gypsum Construction Handbook
(United States Gypsum Company)

Framing Components

It is important that light-gauge steel components such as steel studs and runners, furring channels and resilient channels be adequately protected against rusting in the warehouse and on the job site. In marine areas such as the Caribbean, Florida and the Gulf Coast, where salt air conditions exist with high humidity, components that offer increased protection against corrosion should be used.

Steel Studs and Runners

Studs and runners should be channel-type, roll-formed from corrosion resistant steel, and designed for quick screw attachment of facing materials. They are strong, non-load bearing components of interior partitions, ceilings and column fireproofing and as framing for exterior curtain wall systems. Heavier thickness members are used in load-bearing construction. Limited chaseways for electrical and plumbing services are provided by punchouts in the stud web. Matching runners for each stud size align and secure studs to floors and ceilings, also function as headers.

Available in various styles and widths outlined below:

Efficient, low-cost 25-ga. members for framing non-load bearing interior assemblies. Studs come in five widths—1-5/8", 2-1/2", 3-5/8", 4", 6"—and up to 20' lengths. Runners come in matching stud widths—10' lengths.

22-ga. studs and runners—Heavier gauge, stronger studs in four widths—2-1/2", 3-5/8", 4", 6"—and cut-to-order lengths, up to 20'. Runners come in matching stud widths—10' lengths.

20-ga. studs and runners—Heavier 20-ga. members used in framing interior assemblies requiring greater-strength studs and reinforcement for door frames. Also used in curtain wall assemblies. Studs available in 2-1/2", 3-5/8", 4", 6" widths—cut-to-order lengths up to 28'. Runners come in stud widths (with 1" unhemmed leg)—10' lengths.

Stiffened flange studs and runners—Used for framing load-bearing interior and exterior walls and non-load bearing curtain walls.

Partition Layout

Properly positioned partitions according to layout snap chalk lines at ceiling and floor. Be certain that partitions will be plumb. Where partitions occur parallel to and between joists, ladder blocking must be installed between ceiling joists.

Steel Framing

Steel stud framing for non-load bearing interior partitions is secured to floors and ceilings with runners fastened to the supporting structure.

Runner Installation

Securely attach runners:

1. To concrete and masonry—use stub nails, power-driven fasteners.
2. To foam-backed metal (max. 14-ga.) concrete inserts use FHA Type S-12 pan head screws.
3. To suspended ceilings use expandable hollow wall anchors or toggle bolts.
4. To wood framing—use 1/4" Type S oval head screws or 12d nails.

To all substrates, secure runners with fasteners located 2" from each end and spaced max. 24" o.c. Attach runner ends at door frames with two anchors when 3-piece frames are used. (One-piece frames should be supplied with welded-in-place floor anchor plates, pre-punched for two anchors into substrate.)

At partition corners, extend one runner to end of corner and butt or overlap other runner to it, allowing necessary clearance for gypsum panel thickness. Runners should not be mitered.

Stud Installation

Insert floor-to-ceiling steel studs between runners, twisting them into position. Position studs vertically, with open side facing in same direction and web punch-outs aligned properly, engaging floor and ceiling runners and spaced 16" or 24" o.c. max., as required. Proper alignment will provide for proper bracing, utility runs and prevention of stepped or uneven joint surfaces. Anchor all studs adjacent to door and borrowed light frames, partition intersections and corners to floor and ceiling runners. Intermediate partition studs should not be anchored to runners.

Backing

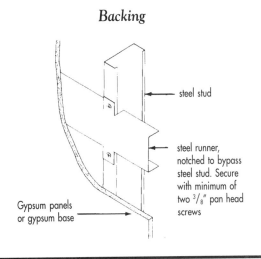

steel stud

steel runner, notched to bypass steel stud. Secure with minimum of two $^3/_8$" pan head screws

Gypsum panels or gypsum base

Courtesy of United States Gypsum Company, *Gypsum Construction Handbook*

Figure 4.3

Place studs in direct contact with all door frame jambs, abutting partitions, partition corners and existing construction elements. Grouting of door frames is always recommended and is required where heavy or oversize doors are used. Where a stud directly abuts an exterior wall and there is a possibility of condensation or water penetration through the wall, place a No. 15 asphalt felt strip between stud and wall surface.

Over metal doors and borrowed light frames, place a section of runner horizontally with a web-flange bent at each end. Secure runner to strut-studs with two screws in each bent web. At the location of vertical joints over the door frame header, position a cut-to-length stud extending to the ceiling runner.

Fasten together with two 3/8" Type S pan head screws in each flange or web. Locate each screw no more than 1" from ends of splice. Steel Studs may be conveniently spliced together when required. To splice two studs, nest one into the other forming a box section, to a depth of at least 8" and fasten with screws.

Curved Surfaces

Gypsum Panels and Gypsum Base can be formed to almost any cylindrically curved surface. Boards can be applied either dry or wet, depending on the radius of curvature desired. To prevent flat areas between framing, shorter bend radii require closer than normal stud and furring spacing.

Boards are horizontally applied, gently bent around the framing, and securely fastened to achieve the desired radius. When boards are applied dry, the minimum radius of curvature meets many applications. By thoroughly moistening the face or back paper prior to application, and replacing in the stack for at least one hour, the board may be bent to still shorter radius.

When the board dries thoroughly, it will regain its original hardness.

Installation of Curved Surfaces

Framing—Cut one leg and web of top and bottom steel runner at 2" intervals for the length of the arc. Allow 12" of uncut steel runners at each end of arc. Bend runners to uniform curve of desired radius (90 max., arc). To support the cut leg of runner, clinch a 1" x 25-ga. steel strip to inside of leg. Select the runner size to match the steel studs; for wood studs, use a 3-1/2" steel runner. Attach steel runners to structural elements at floor and ceiling with suitable fasteners as previously described.

Position studs vertically, with open side facing in same direction and engaging floor and ceiling runners. Begin and end each with a stud, and space intermediate studs equally as measured on outside of arc. Secure steel studs to runners with 3/8" Type S pan head screws; secure wood studs with suitable fasteners. On tangents, place studs 6" o.c., leaving last stud freestanding. Follow directions previously described for erecting balance of studs.

Panel Preparation—Select length and cut board to allow one unbroken panel to cover the curved surface and 12" tangents at each end. Outside panel must be longer than inside panels to compensate for additional radius contributed by the studs. Cutouts for electrical boxes are not recommended in curved surfaces unless they can be made after boards are installed and thoroughly dry. When wet board is required, evenly spray water on the surface which will be compressed when board is hung. Apply water with a conventional garden sprayer . Carefully stack boards with wet surfaces facing each other and cover stack with plastic sheet (polyethylene). Allow boards to set at least one hour before application.

Panel Application—Apply panels horizontally with the wrapped edge perpendicular to the studs. On the convex side of the partition, begin installation at one end of the curved surface and fasten panel to studs as it is wrapped around the curve. On the concave side of the partition, start fastening

Radius Walls

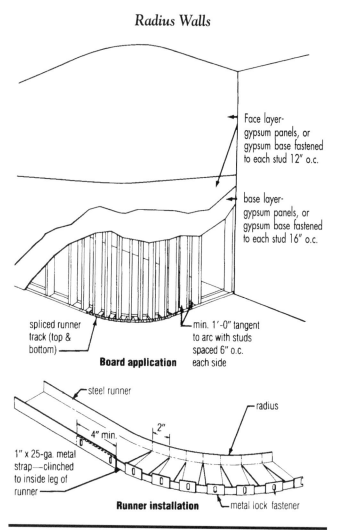

Face layer—gypsum panels, or gypsum base fastened to each stud 12" o.c.

base layer—gypsum panels, or gypsum base fastened to each stud 16" o.c.

spliced runner track (top & bottom)

min. 1'-0" tangent to arc with studs spaced 6" o.c. each side

Board application

steel runner

radius

4" min.

2"

1" x 25-ga. metal strap—clinched to inside leg of runner

Runner installation

metal lock fastener

Courtesy of United States Gypsum Company, *Gypsum Construction Handbook*

Figure 4.4

Screws

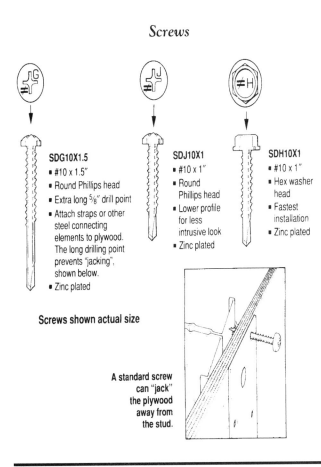

SDG10X1.5
- #10 x 1.5"
- Round Phillips head
- Extra long ⅝" drill point
- Attach straps or other steel connecting elements to plywood. The long drilling point prevents "jacking", shown below.
- Zinc plated

Screws shown actual size

SDJ10X1
- #10 x 1"
- Round Phillips head
- Lower profile for less intrusive look
- Zinc plated

SDH10X1
- #10 x 1"
- Hex washer head
- Fastest installation
- Zinc plated

A standard screw can "jack" the plywood away from the stud.

Figure 4.5

panel to the stud at the center of the curve and work outward to the ends of the panel. For single-layer panels, space screws 12" o.c. Use 1" Type S screws for steel studs and 1-1/4" type W screws for wood studs.

For double-layer application, apply base layer horizontally and fasten to stud with screws spaced 16" o.c. Center face layer panels over joints in the base layer and secure to studs with screws spaced 12" o.c. Use 1" Type S screws for base level and 1" Type S screws for face layer. Allow panels to dry completely (approx. 24 hrs under good drying conditions) before applying joint treatment.

Arches

Arches of any radii are easily faced with gypsum panels or base and finished with a joint system, or veneer plaster finish. Score or cut through back paper of panels at 1" intervals to make them flexible. The board should previously have been cut to desired width and length of arch.

After board has been applied to arch framing with nails or screws, apply tape reinforcement (Joint Tape for drywall panels or Tape Type P or S for plaster base).

Allowable Tolerances

Industry Standards
Handbook of Construction Tolerances
(The McGraw-Hill Companies)

The recommended tolerances from several sources are shown in **Figure 4.7**. Both the Metal Lath/Steel Framing Association (ML/SFA) and ASTM C1007 recommend that the plumbness and level of studs be within 1/960 of the span, or 1/8 in. in 10 ft (3.2 mm in 3048 mm). However, ASTM C1007 is for loadbearing studs only, while the ML/SFA specifications are for all metal studs. The 1/8 in. per 10 ft tolerance is consistent with the substrate requirements for other finish materials, such as some types of ceramic tile systems.

The Gypsum Association states that adjacent fastening surfaces of framing or furring should not vary by more than 1/8 in. (3.2 mm).

ASTM C754 requires that the spacing of studs and other framing members not vary by more than 1/8 in. (3.2 mm) from the required spacing and that the cumulative error not exceed the requirements of the gypsum wallboard. This is to ensure that the edge of a piece of gypsum board has sufficient bearing on half of a stud for fastening.

If the tolerances shown here are not required and specified, it is more likely that a +/- 1/4 in. (6-mm) tolerance will be observed in actual construction.

Metal Framing Connections

Tolerances

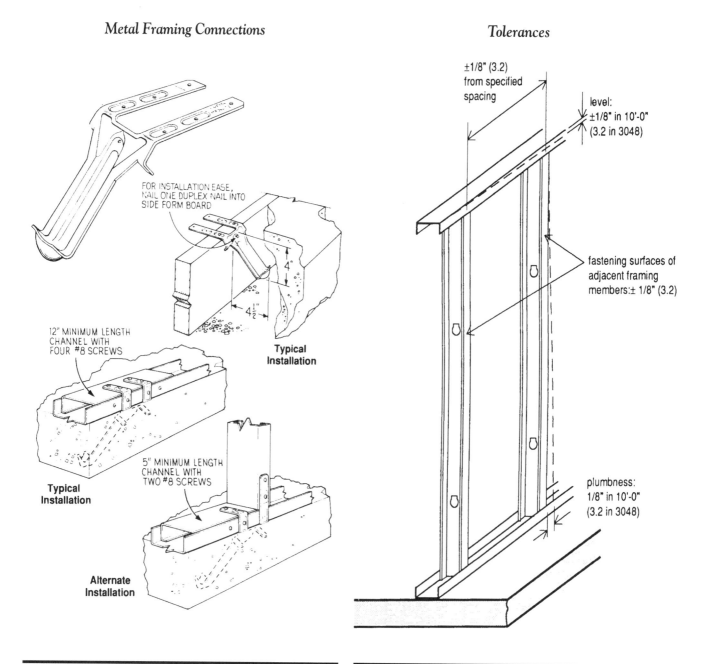

FOR INSTALLATION EASE, NAIL ONE DUPLEX NAIL INTO SIDE FORM BOARD

4"

4½"

Typical Installation

12" MINIMUM LENGTH CHANNEL WITH FOUR #8 SCREWS

Typical Installation

5" MINIMUM LENGTH CHANNEL WITH TWO #8 SCREWS

Alternate Installation

±1/8" (3.2) from specified spacing

level: ±1/8" in 10'-0" (3.2 in 3048)

fastening surfaces of adjacent framing members: ± 1/8" (3.2)

plumbness: 1/8" in 10'-0" (3.2 in 3048)

Courtesy of Simpson Strong-Tie Company, Inc., *Simpson Catalog on Light-Gauge Steel Construction, Catalog C–S96–R*

Figure 4.6

Courtesy of The McGraw-Hill Companies, *Handbook of Construction Tolerances*

Figure 4.7

Comments

The Simpson hardware in this chapter is shown only as an example of metal framing connections. A competent designer or architect must incorporate the hardware into the drawings as part of the overall design.

Seismic and Hurricane Ties

NOTE: Designed to provide wind and seismic ties for trusses and rafters, these ties may be used for general purposes, strongback attachments, and as all-purpose ties where one member crosses another.

MATERIAL: 18 gauge

FINISH: Galvanized. Selected products available in stainless steel or Z-MAX coating; see Corrosion-Resistant Connectors.

INSTALLATION: ■ Use all specified fasteners. See Screws, page 4.
- The S/H1 can be installed with flanges facing outwards (reverse of illustration #1). When installed inside a wall for truss applications.
- Ties are shipped in equal quantities of separate rights and lefts.
- S/H1 does not replace solid blocking.

MODEL NO.	FASTENERS			MAX ALLOWABLE LOADS		
	TO RAFTERS	TO PLATES	TO STUDS	UPLIFT (133)	LATERAL	
					F₁ (133)	F₂ (133)
S/H1	3- #10	2- #10	1- #10	330	100	115
S/H2	3- #10	—	3- #10	395	—	—
S/H2.5	4- #10	—	4- #10	415	90	125
S/H3	2- #10	2- #10	—	380	90	125

1. Loads have been increased 33% for wind or earthquake loading; no further increase allowed.

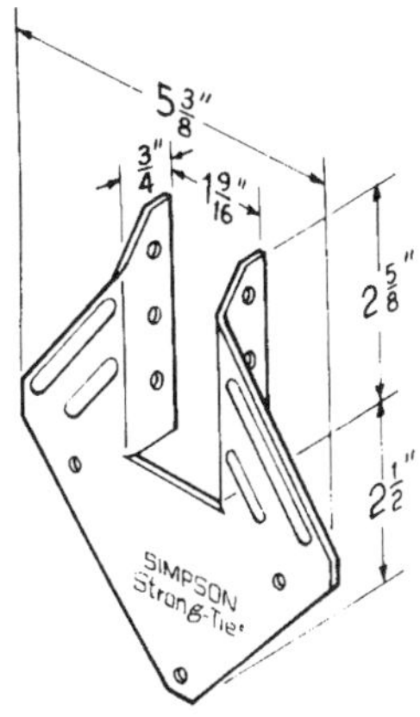

S/H1

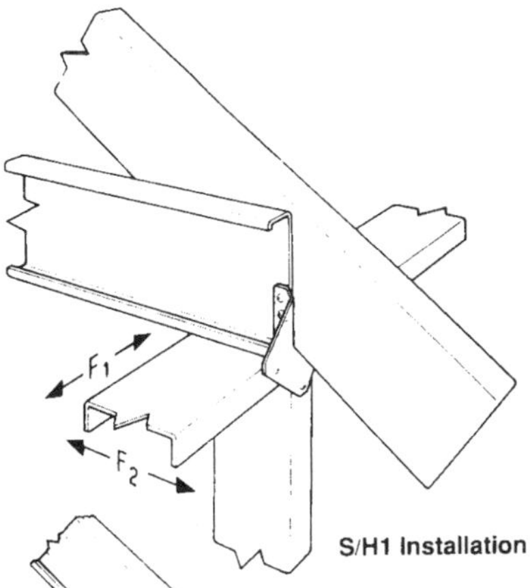

S/H1 Installation

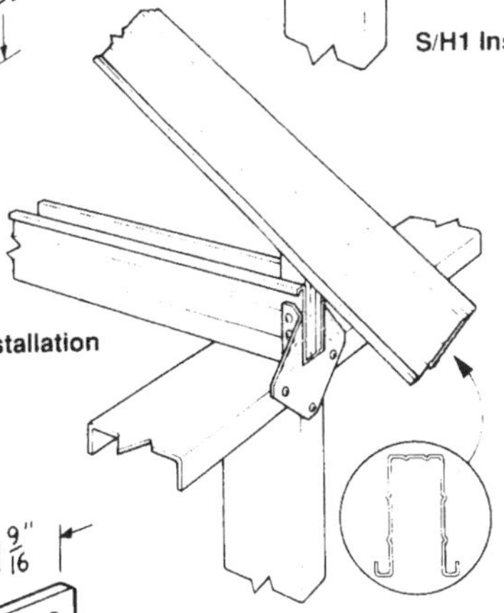

S/H1 Installation

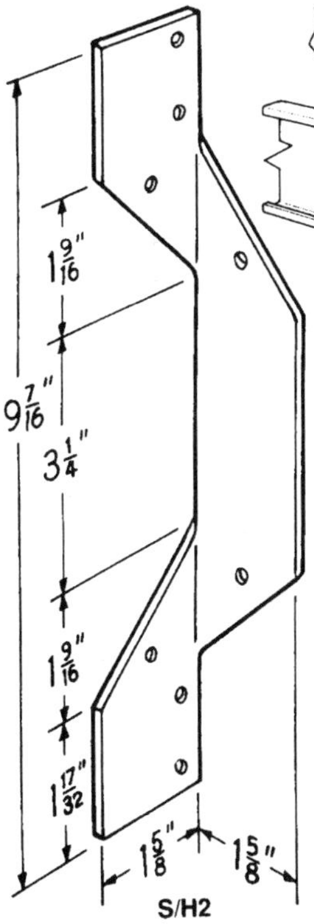

S/H2 Installation

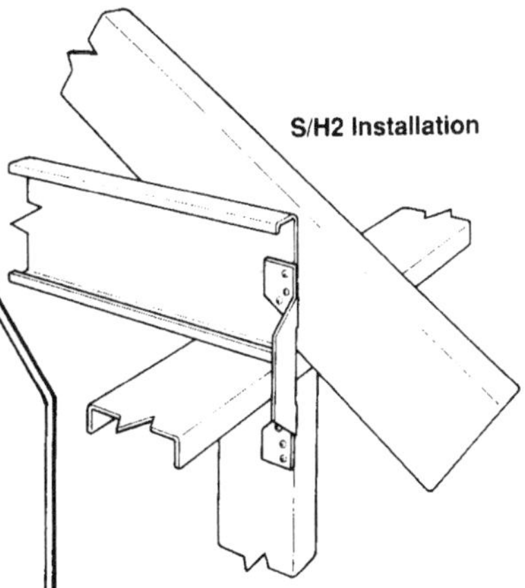

S/H2

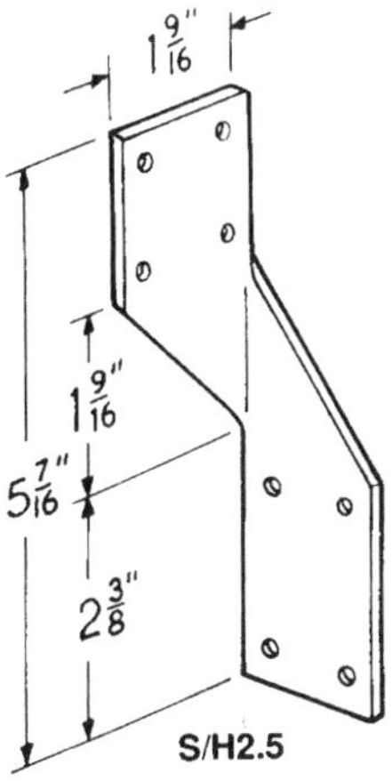

S/H2.5

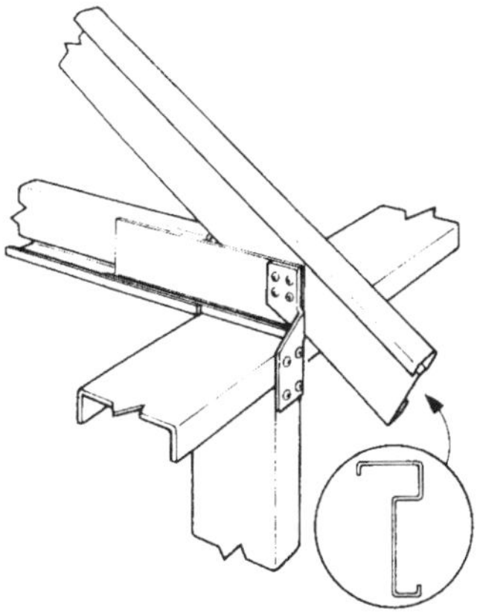

S/H2.5 Installation

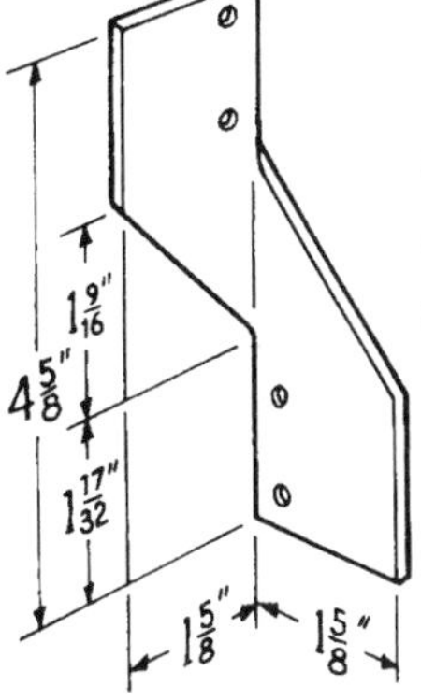

S/H3

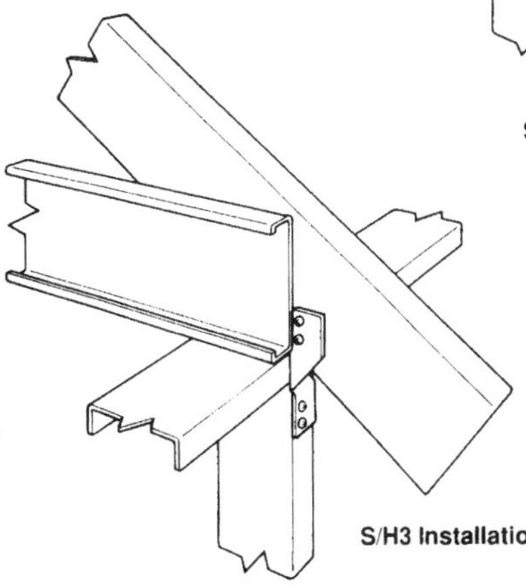

S/H3 Installation

Courtesy of Simpson Strong-Tie Company, Inc., *Simpson Catalog on Light-Gauge Steel Construction, Catalog C–S96–R*

Figure 4.8

Steel Framing Members

Industry Standards

Steelman's: How-To Guide and Resource Catalog for Residential Steel Framing
(American Iron and Steel Institute)

When selecting steel for framing, three primary variables should be considered: shape, thickness, and strength of the steel. Although many shapes of cold-formed steel are available, the most common in residential construction are the "C"-shape and the track. The "C" is used as a head and a stud, whereas the track is used like the top and bottom plates in wood construction (except most track is not capable of transferring vertical loads).

The "C"-shape consists of three parts: the web, flange, and lip. Care must be taken when selecting studs to ensure the dimensions are compatible with doors, windows, and other parts of the home. A 3-1/2 inch or 5-1/2 inch web (measured from the outside of the flanges) is consistent with today's lumber dimensions, although other sizes may be used but require additional attention at doors and windows. The flanges range from 1-1/2 inches to 1-5/8 inches, depending on the manufacturer and the type of stud.

The track section has a web and a flange, but does not have the lip that is present on the "C"-shape. This allows the "C" to fit into the track. Thus, the web of the track section is measured from the inside of the flanges. The flange of the track should be at least 1-1/4 inches to provide a surface for attaching gypsum-board, sheathing, and trim.

Other members that may be required for steel framing include flat straps and angles. Straps, which come in a variety of widths, are typically used for wall bracing and bridging.

Components of a "C"-Shaped Cold-Formed Steel Member

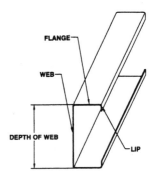

Cold-Formed Steel Track

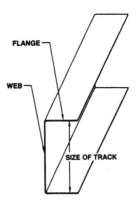

Table 1. Minimum Thickness of Cold-Formed Steel Members

Designation (mils)	Minimum Steel Thickness (inches)	Reference Gauge No.
18	0.018	25
27	0.027	22
33	0.033	20
43	0.043	18
54	0.054	16
68	0.068	14
97	0.097	12

Courtesy of American Iron and Steel Institute, *Steelman's: How-To Guide and Resource Catalog for Residential Steel Framing*

Figure 4.9

Angles are usually used for bulkheads and other specialty framing where a "C"-shape stud will not work.

Cold-formed steel members come in a variety of thicknesses, as shown in Table 1. More recently, the industry is beginning to adopt designations in mil thicknesses (inches x 1000) as shown in the first column of Table 1. The term "gauge" in the third column has been the traditional means to identify steel thickness. Note the minimum steel thickness (inches) for each designation. In addition to its thickness, the strength of a steel section is dependent on the size, shape, and yield strength of the steel. In the United States, most steel is designated as 33 ksi (kips per square inch) for 18 to 43 mil steel and 50 ksi for 54 mil and thicker.

Steel Framed Walls

Ed. Note: The following section refers to the 1995 CABO, with 1996/1997 amendments. This code has just been replaced by the International Code Council's International One- and Two-Family Dwelling Code (IOTFDC). See your local building department for the latest information.

Industry Standards

How to Design Steel Framed Walls
(American Iron and Steel Institute)

Thanks to the work of the American Iron and Steel Institute (AISI), the National Association of Home Builders (NAHB), and the U.S. Department of Housing and Urban Development (HUD), there are recent additions to the building code that allow architects, framers, builders, and even homeowners to do their own wall stud and floor joist design. Following is a step-by-step procedure for designing steel framed wall studs.

Step 1: Know Local Requirements. While many builders in rural areas have constructed steel framed homes without the use of a professional designer, most homes are not built in rural areas, and fall under the jurisdiction of local municipalities that have specific design requirements. If you are a first-time steel builder, or are designing in a new territory, make sure to check with all building agencies that may have jurisdiction. Find out exactly what drawings or sketches they need, what building code they use, and what loads they require for design.

Also, find out what individual or group will actually be coming out to your jobsite and inspecting your framing. If they don't know much about steel, it may be in your best interest to help teach them. See if you can get an industry representative, or manufacturer's sales representative to call on them, drop off some free literature, and answer some of their questions about light gauge steel framing. Making the building inspector's job easier can save you both time and money once your project is underway.

Step 2: Know the Loads and the Codes. Hopefully, your county or city has adopted the 96/97 Revisions to the 1995 CABO One- and Two-Family Dwelling Code. CABO stands for Council of American Building Officials, and their code is accepted in most areas of the country. Based on national standards, the local municipality has probably adopted the following for your city or county:

- wind speed;
- wind exposure category;
- seismic zone;
- ground snow load

You will need some or all of these values to go through the tables in steps 4 and 5. Section 301 of the CABO code has some charts and tables to give you a good idea of what these loads are. However, if you want to make sure everything is correct, ask an engineer or building inspector.

Step 3: Design within the Code Limits. The Prescriptive Method for Residential Cold-Formed Steel Framing [refers to the second edition of the Prescriptive Method printed August 1997] (AISI publication #RG-9713A) illustrates applicability limits in table 1.1 on page 2. If you are using the CABO code, this is summarized in section 603.1.1: Applicability Limits for Steel Wall Framing. Basically the structure must be less than 60' long, less than 36' wide, and 2 stories maximum. The maximum design wind speed is 90 mph—exposure C, or 100 mph—exposure B; the maximum ground snow load is 50 psf; and the allowable seismic zones are 0, 1, and 2.

Step 4: Design from the Top Down: Second Floor Walls. Table 603.3.2a (see **Figure 4.10**) in the CABO code covers either second-floor wall studs, or first-floor studs on a one-story building. Basically, the studs support only a roof and ceiling, and not the weight of floor joists or other floor loads. If you compare the values in this table to those in Table 603.3.2b (see **Figure 4.11**), you will see that a first-floor stud must be thicker or shorter to carry the same wind load as a second-floor stud.

For example, say you are designing an 8' wall with studs at 24" on center. Your building inspector has told you that you are in a 70 mph wind zone, exposure B, and you want to use 2 x 4 steel studs (3-1/2" x 1-5/8"). From the table, it says you can use a stud thickness of 33 mils (20 gauge). Notice if you had entered table 603.3.2b with these same values, a 43 mil (18 gauge) stud would be required. If you are using the Prescriptive Method [refers to the second edition of the Prescriptive Method printed August 1997], you will get the same values using Table 6.2 with a ground snow load of 50 psf.

Step 5: First-Floor Walls. First-floor walls are the same as second-floor walls, except you use a different table in the CABO code: Table 603.3.2b (see **Figure 4.11**). If you are designing a one-story building, you may skip this step, and move on to connection and bracing design. If you are using the Prescriptive Method [refers to the second edition of the

TABLE 603.3.2(2)
COLD-FORMED-STEEL STUD THICKNESS
Studs supporting roof and ceiling only
(One-story buildings or second floor of a two-story building) 33-kips-per-square-inch steel

WIND EXPOSURE		NOMINAL MEMBER SIZE	MEMBER SPACING (inches)	STUD THICKNESS[a,b] (mils)											
				8-foot walls				9-foot walls				10-foot walls			
				Building width[c] (feet)				Building width[c] (feet)				Building width[c] (feet)			
Exposure A/B	Exposure C			24	28	32	36	24	28	32	36	24	28	32	36
70 mph	—	2 × 4	16	33	33	33	33	33	33	33	33	33	33	33	33
			24	33	33	33	33	33	33	33	33	33	33	33	43
		2 × 6	16	33	33	33	33	33	33	33	33	33	33	33	33
			24	33	33	33	33	33	33	33	33	33	33	33	33
80 mph	70 mph	2 × 4	16	33	33	33	33	33	33	33	33	33	33	33	33
			24	33	33	33	33	33	33	43	43	43	43	43	43
		2 × 6	16	33	33	33	33	33	33	33	33	33	33	33	33
			24	33	33	33	33	33	33	33	33	33	33	33	33
90 mph	80 mph	2 × 4	16	33	33	33	33	33	33	33	33	33	33	33	33
			24	33	33	43	43	43	43	43	43	54	54	54	54
		2 × 6	16	33	33	33	33	33	33	33	33	33	33	33	33
			24	33	33	33	33	33	33	33	33	33	33	33	33
100 mph	90 mph	2 × 4	16	33	33	33	33	33	33	33	33	43	43	43	43
			24	43	43	43	43	54	54	54	54	68	68	68	68
		2 × 6	16	33	33	33	33	33	33	33	33	33	33	33	33
			24	33	33	33	33	33	33	33	33	33	33	43	43

For SI: 1 inch = 25.4 mm, 1 mil = 0.0254 mm, 1 foot = 304.8 mm, 1 mile per hour = 1.609 km/hr,
1 pound per square foot = 47.88 Pa, 1 kips per square inch = 6.894 MPa.
[a] Deflection criteria: L/240.
[b] Design load assumptions: Roof dead load is 12 psf; Ground snow load is 50 psf; Attic live load is 10 psf.
[c] Building width is in the direction of horizontal framing members supported by the wall studs.

Figure 4.10

Prescriptive Method printed August 1997], you may use Table 6.3 for 8' walls, Table 6.5 for 9' walls, and Table 6.7 for 10' walls. Note that using these tables with a 50 psf snow load and a building width of 36', you will get the same results as Table 603.3.2b.

Step 6: Connections and Bracing. The basic connection in a wall is screwing the stud to the track, and bolting or nailing the track to the foundation below. There are also special considerations for wind bracing or seismic design.

The data in the code is based on Prescriptive Method for Residential Cold-Formed Steel Framing. This is a two part publication from AISI, and you can order a copy by calling their residential steel home hotline at 1-800-79-STEEL. Part one is the actual code information (#RG-9713A), with many of the same tables and charts that are in CABO. Part two is the commentary (#RG-9713B), which has some really good design examples.

Most rollformers also have product data with several pages of span and load tables. By reading the footnotes, and paying careful attention to the nomenclature, you can get design information from these books. However, for the walls, the manufacturer's tables are listed in pounds per square foot rather than miles per hour. Making this conversion is not an easy matter, so be careful using these references rather than the code.

Construction Guidelines

Industry Standards
Low-Rise Construction Details and Guidelines
(American Iron and Steel Institute)

.1 FRAMING SYSTEM

.1.1 Axial load bearing members, including jamb studs and all members in built-up sections, should be installed seated squarely against the web portion of the top and bottom tracks.

.1.1.1 The maximum gap between the end of the stud and the web of the track should not exceed 0.063 inches (1.5mm).

TABLE 603.3.2(3)
COLD-FORMED-STEEL STUD THICKNESS
Studs supporting one floor, roof and ceiling
(First story of a two-story building) 33-kips-per-square-inch steel

WIND EXPOSURE		NOMINAL MEMBER SIZE	MEMBER SPACING (inches)	STUD THICKNESS[a,b] (mils)											
				8-foot walls				9-foot walls				10-foot walls			
				Building width[c] (feet)				Building width[c] (feet)				Building width[c] (feet)			
Exposure A/B	Exposure C			24	28	32	36	24	28	32	36	24	28	32	36
70 mph	—	2×4	16	33	33	33	33	33	33	33	33	33	33	43	43
			24	43	43	43	43	43	43	43	54	54	54	54	54
		2×6	16	33	33	33	33	33	33	33	33	33	33	33	33
			24	33	33	33	33	33	33	33	33	33	33	33	43
80 mph	70 mph	2×4	16	33	33	33	33	33	33	43	43	43	43	43	43
			24	43	43	54	54	54	54	54	54	54	68	68	68
		2×6	16	33	33	33	33	33	33	33	33	33	33	33	33
			24	33	33	33	43	33	33	33	43	33	43	43	43
90 mph	80 mph	2×4	16	33	33	43	43	43	43	43	43	43	43	54	54
			24	54	54	54	54	54	54	54	54	68	68	68	—
		2×6	16	33	33	33	33	33	33	33	33	33	33	33	33
			24	33	33	43	43	33	43	43	43	43	43	43	43
100 mph	90 mph	2×4	16	43	43	43	43	43	43	43	54	54	54	54	54
			24	54	68	68	68	68	68	68	68	—	—	—	—
		2×6	16	33	33	33	33	33	33	33	33	33	33	33	33
			24	43	43	43	43	43	43	43	43	43	54	54	54

For SI: 1 inch = 25.4 mm, 1 mil = 0.0254 mm, 1 foot = 304.8 mm, 1 mile per hour = 1.609 km/hr,
1 pound per square foot = 47.88 Pa, 1 kips per square inch = 6.894 MPa.
[a] Live load deflection criteria: L/240.
[b] Design load assumptions: Roof dead load is 12 psf; Second-floor live load is 30 psf; Second-floor dead load is 10 psf; Second-floor wall load is 10 psf; Ground snow load is 50 psf; Live load is 10 psf.
[c] Building width is in the direction of horizontal framing members supported by the wall studs.

Figure 4.11

.1.1.2 Cripple (or less than full-height) studs that are installed between an opening header and the bearing elevation of members above should be designed to transfer all axial loads from the members above to the header. These less than full-height members should also be seated squarely against the webs of the track.

.1.2 Bearing surfaces for joists, rafters, trusses, and the bottom track of axial load bearing walls should be uniform and level to assure full contact of the bearing flange or track web on the support over the required bearing and anchorage area.

Exception: Forces may be transferred through clip angles on sloped members such as roof rafters.

.1.2.1 A bearing material (i.e.: building paper, shims or grout) should be provided between the underside of the bottom steel track and the top of the foundation to provide a uniform bearing surface for the steel members.

.1.3 All axial load bearing members should be aligned vertically and transfer all loads to structural supports or foundations. This vertical alignment should also be maintained at floor/wall intersections.

Exception:

1. Where load carrying members do not align a load distribution member should be provided to transfer loads from joist bearing to axial load bearing studs.

2. Members may be added between the members at the specified spacing, to support members that are not in alignment. These added members should transfer loads into a continuous load path to a foundation or structural support.

.1.3.1 Where through continuity of axial load bearing walls cannot be maintained, due to an interruption by floor joists that are not aligned, short sections of joists, studs, track or added joist members, capable of transferring the loads, should be placed in alignment with the stud above. As an alternate, a small section of stud (a filler), with an axial capacity at least equal to the capacity of the stud above, is permitted to be used to transfer the loads.

.1.4 All framing members should be horizontally aligned, plumb and level, except where required to slope.

.1.5 Both flanges of studs should be attached to the top and bottom track with screws or an approved fastener.

Exception: Where slip joints are specified at the top track follow the detailing requirements for the slip joint.

.1.6 Splices in framing members should not be permitted.

Exception: Track members or tension members with designed slice connections.

.1.7 Additional framing members (i.e.: multiple studs or joists) may be needed as follows:

.1.7.1 Adjacent to openings as required by design. In lieu of additional members, an alternate member may be provided, with the required capacity, by increasing the steel thickness and/or flange width.

.1.7.2 At wall intersections and corners.

.1.7.3 Under joist supported partitions, parallel to the direction of the floor framing, where partition length exceeds one half of the joist span.

.1.8 The use of members with standard manufacturer's web punch-outs is usually acceptable. The location of these punch-outs should be coordinated with load, bracing and utility requirements.

.1.8.1 Web punch-outs or web openings should not be located at bearing points for studs, joists, rafters, and trusses without special reinforcement.

.1.8.2 Web openings should not exceed the dimension of the manufacturer's standard punch-out or the provisions in the AISI Specification without design analysis or reinforcement.

.2 Connections

.2.1 Utilize fasteners and fastener heads that are designed for the requirements of the connection. The substitution of screws, welds, bolts, powder actuated fasteners or pneumatically driven fasteners for the specified fastener in many cases can be considered acceptable. Each substitution should provide an equal or greater performance, and be approved by the designer.

.2.1.1 Penetration of screws through joined materials should not be less than 3 exposed threads.

.2.1.2 All weld should be completed by AWS D1.3 qualified welders experienced in welding sheet steel. Touch-up coatings damaged by the welding of exterior framing, and framing that separates rooms with large temperature or humidity differentials.

Comments

Touch-up is necessary because such conditions can cause moisture accumulation and rusting of exposed steel.

.2.1.3 Fasteners should be installed in accordance with manufacturer's recommendations.

.2.2 Multiple steel members designed as noncomposite can be connected together with one row of #10 screws at 16 inches (400mm) o.c. along the length of the member. Locate each row within 1 inch (25mm) from an adjacent flange. The fastener spacing for non-composite members less than 4 inches in depth may be revised to 24 inches (600mm) o.c.

.2.3 When approved by the designer, end connections for members 0.04 inches (1mm) or less in steel thickness, used for headers, sills, bracing, or blocking, may utilize the member web for the connection. Flanges can be coped or cut allowing bending of the web, as required, to form an angle for connection to supporting members.

.3 Bracing and Stiffeners

.3.1 Adequate bracing should be provided for all building systems until lateral stability systems (i.e.: shear walls or braced frames) have been installed and anchorage is complete.

.3.1.1 Adequate bracing is recommended for both chords or flanges of members until sheathing has been installed. Where Sheathing is applied to one side only, the required bracing should be permanently installed on the unsheathed face.

.3.1.2 Temporary bracing should be provided and left in place until work is permanently stabilized.

.3.2 Blocking may be a section of stud, joist or track which is the full depth of the framing member that is being blocked and should fit tightly between the members. Blocking should be anchored at each end.

.3.3 Bridging may consist of blocking, flat strapping, channel stock, or a proprietary bridging system. Bridging should be placed diagonally between opposite flanges of framing members or run flange to flange along the same face of the framing members.

.3.3.1 Bridging shall be anchored to each framing member.

.3.3.2 Wire tied bridging should not be permitted.

.3.3.3 Floor joist bridging may be spaced as follows, except where member design requires or will accommodate an alternate spacing:

Recommended Minimum Number of Rows of Bridging for Floor Joists	
Span, ft. (m)	Number of Rows
up to 14 (4.3)	1 row at mid-span
14 (4.3) to 20 (6.1)	2 rows at 1/3 points
20 (6.1) to 26 (7.9)	3 rows at 1/4 points

.3.4 End blocking or bridging for joists, rafters, and trusses is recommended over supports when bearing ends are not otherwise restrained from rotation.

.3.5 Web stiffeners should be provided, as determined by design, at bearing points and at points of concentrated loads.

.3.5.1 Web stiffeners can be a small stud, track or angle section designed to carry axial loads and cut to seat squarely against supports.

.3.5.2 Solid blocking or continuous track may be used in lieu of web stiffeners, when approved by the designer.

.4 MISCELLANEOUS

.4.1 All steel components and accessories in exterior walls, roofs, floors over crawl spaces, or in high humidity areas should be hot-dipped galvanized or aluminum-zinc coated. Co-polymer or cadmium coatings can also be used for fasteners.

.4.2 Back blocking for wall mounted assemblies should be made from flat stock or track or stud sections with flanges notched at the location of studs to allow for connections to the studs.

.4.3 It is recommended that steel framing members be cut with a saw or shear. Torch cutting of the ends of compression members in axial bearing connections is not recommended.

.4.4 Sheathing materials for shear walls or diaphragms should extend and be connected to chord members (i.e.: top and bottom wall track).

Design and Detailing General Considerations

Industry Standards

Low-Rise Construction Details and Guidelines

(American Iron and Steel Institute)

.A GENERAL

.A.1 The design of structural members and connections should be in accordance with the latest edition of the AISI Specification for the Design of Cold-Formed Steel Structural members or the Load and Resistance Factor Design Specification for Cold-Formed Steel Structural Members.

Exceptions:

1. The capacity and spacing of screws should be in accordance with the Center for Cold-Formed Steel Structures Technical Bulletin Vol. 2, No. 1 dated February 1993 or manufacturer's recommendations.

2. Pneumatically driven fasteners, powder actuated fasteners and expansion anchors should rely on manufacturer's or independent test data for design capacities and proper installation.

.A.2 Shear wall/diaphragm designs should be based on AISI Research Report CF 92-2 on the Shear Resistance of Walls with Steel Studs, American Plywood Report 154 dated July 1990, approved test results or rational engineering analysis.

.A.3 Refer to the **Residential Construction Guidelines** for additional guidelines that should be considered during design and detailing of cold-formed steel framing.

.B FRAMING

.B.1 All framing members should be spaced as required by design and as limited by the capabilities of the facing material.

.B.2 Material thickness for track or runners should be at least equal to the framing member thickness used for that framing assembly.

.B.3 Wall track should not be used to support any load, unless specifically designed for that purpose.

.B.4 Allowable tolerances for vertical alignment of webs supported on a track or track assembly should be based on the shear and bending capacity of the track or track assembly.

.B.5 Interior non-bearing partitions located under horizontal load carrying members (i.e.: joists, rafters, and trusses) should be evaluated for possible loads induced due to the deflection (dead and live load) of the horizontal members.

.B.6 Generally one member can be provided along the edge of openings for each member that is interrupted by the opening. As an alternative, members of greater thickness can be used to reduce the number of additional members.

.B.7 Construction adhesive or a gasket material between the top flange of floor joists and plywood flooring is recommended to reduce sound transmission.

.B.8 Solid blocking or continuous track may be used in lieu of web stiffeners, and should be designed to reinforce the member that is intended to support concentrated loads.

.C CONNECTIONS

.C.1 Material thickness and dimensions of clip angles or flat plates used for connections should be as required by design, but the thickness should be less than the supported member material thickness.

.C.2 Truss connections should be evaluated for shear, moment and axial forces due to the eccentricities of the connected members.

.C.3 Connections between multiple, ganged or built-up members and design of these members for composite action should be in accordance with the AISI Specification.

.C.4 The projection of screw heads used to connect steel framing members together under plywood, portland cement board or other rigid or brittle materials, may require back drilling of the board to allow a flush installation.

.D INSULATION AND MOISTURE PROTECTION

.D.1 A moisture barrier (i.e.: building paper), sealer and/or bearing material should be provided between the underside of the bottom track and the top of the foundation to create a thermal break, to prevent the migration of moisture through the joint, and to provide a uniform bearing surface.

.D.2 Insulation should fill the full dimension between member webs. In addition to providing insulation between framing members located in assemblies that separate climate controlled spaces from the exterior or nonclimate controlled spaces, the required insulation should be placed in all jambs, headers, doubled, and built-up members.

.D.3 The use of a thermal break or rigid insulation on the exterior face of framing can result in a significantly better thermal performance of the envelope, over adding additional insulation between the framing members. When a specific thermal performance is required, contact an engineer experienced in the evaluation of thermal building envelopes.

Steel Siding Support System

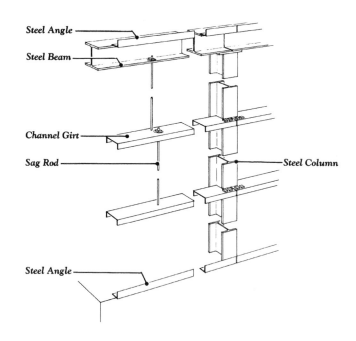

Channel Girt Connection

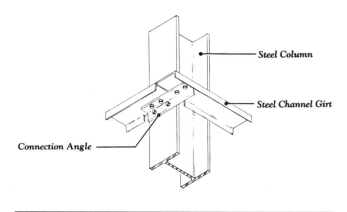

R.S. Means Co., Inc., *Means Graphic Construction Standards*

Figure 4.12

Steel Siding Zee Girt Connection

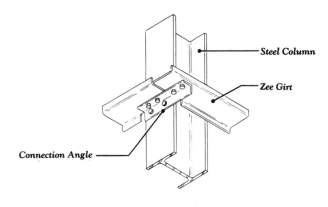

Steel Column

Zee Girt

Connection Angle

Steel Siding Girt Support

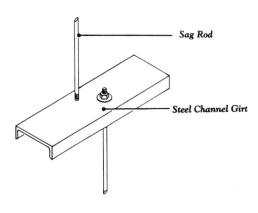

Sag Rod

Steel Channel Girt

Girt Connection

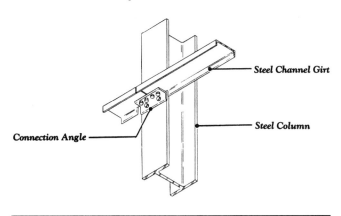

Steel Channel Girt

Steel Column

Connection Angle

R.S. Means Co., Inc., *Means Graphic Construction Standards*

Figure 4.13

Steel Siding Support

Industry Standards
Means Graphic Construction Standards
(R.S. Means Co., Inc.)

Steel siding support can be used as an alternate superstructure system in light commercial projects. Girts used to support aluminum, steel, or composition siding are usually channels with the stronger axis oriented horizontally to resist wind load. Bending or sagging is generally resisted by sag rods threaded at each end for connections and adjustment. When column spacing is greater than the allowable channel span, wind columns, or vertical members used to resist lateral loads, may be introduced. (See **Figure 4.12** and **Figure 4.13**).

Pre-Engineered Steel Buildings

Industry Standards
Means Graphic Construction Standards
(R.S. Means Co., Inc.)

Pre-engineered buildings, relatively low in construction cost, are used extensively for industrial, commercial, institutional, and recreational facilities. (See **Figure 4.14**).

Pre-engineered steel buildings are manufactured by many companies and are normally erected by franchised dealers. They are manufactured of pre-engineered components, which allow flexibility in the choice of configuration for one- or two-story buildings. Some systems are available with provisions for cranes, balconies, and mezzanines. There are four basic types: rigid frame, truss type, post and beam, and sloped beam. Roof pitches vary, but the most popular type is a low pitch of 1" in 12".

Eave heights are available in increments from 10' to 24'. Rigid-frame, clear-span buildings are manufactured in widths of 30' to 130', and tapered-beam, clear-span buildings in widths of 30' to 80'. Post and beam building widths, with one post at center, measure from 80' to 120'; with two posts, from 120' to 180', and with three posts, from 160' to 240'. Bay sizes are usually 20' to 24', but may be extended to 30'.

Roofs and sidewalls are normally covered with 26-gauge colored steel siding with various insulation options. Some manufacturers offer precast concrete and masonry siding options. Other options include eave overhangs, entrance canopies, end-wall overhangs, doors and windows, gutters and leaders, skylights, and roof vents.

Pre-Engineered Building

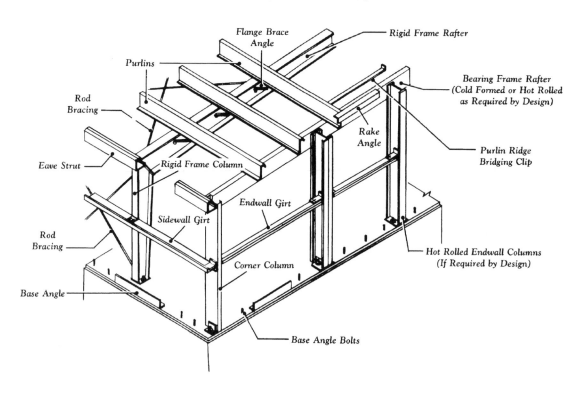

Flange Brace Angle

Rigid Frame Rafter

Purlins

Bearing Frame Rafter (Cold Formed or Hot Rolled as Required by Design)

Rod Bracing

Rake Angle

Eave Strut

Purlin Ridge Bridging Clip

Rigid Frame Column

Endwall Girt

Rod Bracing

Sidewall Girt

Hot Rolled Endwall Columns (If Required by Design)

Corner Column

Base Angle

Base Angle Bolts

Low Profile Rigid Frame

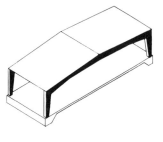

High Profile Rigid Frame

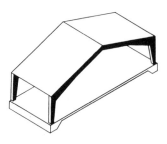

R.S. Means Co., Inc., *Means Graphic Construction Standards*

Figure 4.14

CHAPTER
5

WOOD FRAMING

Table of Contents

(continued on next page)

Text in blue print indicates excerpts from model building code(s). "Comments" (in solid blue boxes) were written by the editors, based on their own experience.

For building product information, use this book's special Internet gateway to thousands of manufacturers: www.rsmeans.com/prodsupp/rlstand.html

CHAPTER 5

WOOD FRAMING

Common Defect Allegations

Wood structural framing defects are a common and expensive claim on multiple- and single-family developments and custom homes. Framing is the basic skeleton of the structure, and repairs to the framing nearly always require removing finish materials. The destructive investigation of a less than 10-year-old structure will frequently result in the discovery of major framing deficiencies.

- A common complaint (particularly in multiple housing) is the lack of draft stops both in attics and, horizontally, in stacked party walls which are separated intentionally to prevent sound transmission. This item is commonly missed, very expensive to correct after the construction is complete, and is critical in stopping the advance of a ground floor fire.

- The most critical, and unfortunately one of the most frequent, deficiencies is the missing connectors to hold roof framing to the bearing walls. In zones with no seismic requirements and no wind load, it is not as critical a mistake. Because of the life safety issues and the extreme property damage caused by neglecting this attachment, we will address the following comments in terms of Seismic Zone 4 and hurricane design elements.

- Starting at the mudsill, there is a tendency for the framed wall to pull off of the bolted plate when the connection is strictly end nails spiked into the stud. Seismic and hurricane forces can simply pull the structure right up off of the wood plate. The positive connection that is usually called out on the plans involves clips or hold-downs that transfer the connection from the bolted sill plate through the framing to the top plate. Plywood shear is also called out on many walls. The code requires that when edge nailing is less than 3″ on center, all edges must be supported by 3x dimensional lumber. The reason for this is that the adjoining panel also must be nailed to the same member, and as the edge nailing gets closer than 3″ on each of the two panels, the 2x framing member will split and loose its nail-holding strength. For example, at 2-1/2" o.c., both of the adjoining sheets of plywood will be nailed into the same stud, spiking the wood on an average of every 1-1/4". This means that for any member, the edge-nailed studs, boundary blocking, sill plate or the top plate that will support two panel edges must all be 3x4 or 3x6. Caution: studs nailed through 3x material require a 20d nail due to the thickness of the plate.

- Mudsills with anchor bolts at close pattern will split the framing member under stress. Investigations of failures after the Northridge Earthquake in California revealed that 2x sill plate with anchor bolts at 16" o.c. often split right down the center.

- The plate line for the second story has the same potential pull-out of the spiked-end nails. The shear panel plywood often covers the floor joist of the second floor and stop. The upper wall shear starts at the second story plate. Therefore, the only connection between the two shear assemblies are spiked nails from the bottom plate to the floor joist. If this condition exists, it is imperative that metal straps are added to the exterior, or hold-downs are through-bolted, or some other code-approved metal clips are added to transfer a positive connection continuously through the joint.

- Roof-to-wall connections face the same dilemma. In ordinary framing, the roof rafter and joist or truss is simply toenailed onto the top plate. A positive blocking with metal clips all the way to the roof sheathing is required to resist high-wind load. In seismic or wind areas, check with your local building official for the minimum requirement.

- A common problem stems from the isolation of stair stringers from the wall to provide acoustic transfer. When the return air plenum uses a framed void in the vicinity of the stair assembly, the edges of the carpet can turn a black color (more noticeable on lighter shades of carpet). The black edge is from the return air being drawn through the carpet at the edges, which causes the carpet to act as a filter at that location. The solution is to pack backer rod foam or to caulk it solid with a nonhardening material such as silicone or PVC.

- Gypsum board installed in the stairwell will often develop a bead projecting out from the wall. This is due to lumber shrinkage with the tape joint beading out as the drywall closes the gap.

- Overdriven plywood nailing (driving the nail beyond the outer skin) is a common problem. Care should be taken to set the nail gun to just dimple the skin. Remember that nail pops result from lumber shrinkage; the nail itself usually does not move. Occasionally, when water leaks occur, the plywood will swell, lifting nails. However, most nail pops occur from the lumber drying out.

- It is imperative that the framer read and understand the plywood grade stamp. Carefully check the building plans for the required plywood grades. As noted in the text, some plywood panels now include a reference to "sized for spacing," which means the sheet is 1/8" shorter and 1/8" narrower to allow the edges and ends to be spaced in the event of reaction to moisture changes. We frequently see plywood panels that have expanded against each other so tightly that the edges actually swell and push out enough to crack stucco plaster. These panels were originally installed tight to each other, and a moisture increase caused them to swell and grow in size.

- Good framing practice requires that joists, beams, and headers be crowned up. We repeatedly see these members crowned down, and in some cases floor joists are crowned up and down alternately, making the floor roll like a roller coaster. Wall studs should also be crowned so that the wall will have a more uniform appearance, with all of the crowns in one direction.

The rules for mid-span joist and rafter blocking have changed with the 1997 UBC. Prior codes required midspan blocking on joists and rafters at intervals not exceeding 8', to stop rotation (collapse by folding over). With study and testing those guidelines were modified to a system that determines blocking requirements based on the width-to-height ratio of the joist, rafter or beam with consideration whether the top and/or bottom edges are held in line. The Code changes allow for the installation of joists, rafters, and beams without midspan blocks, if the ends are held in place and all of the supports that the joists or rafters bear upon are blocked. When we investigate allegations of framing errors, we frequently see blocks missing, improperly nailed, or at some other variance with the code. Most structural engineers address midspan blocking and/or alternate methods to prevent a "deck of cards" type collapse from rotation of the joist.

Introduction

Quality standards for wood framing can be defined in a number of ways that involve not only individual framing components, but the ways in which components are tied together to form a sound, aesthetically acceptable structure. A quality product must meet not only safety (building code) requirements and design specifications set forth in the project plans, but also standards of acceptable workmanship. Quality also means properly addressing regional issues, such as hurricane and seismic considerations, and other climate factors, such as provisions for special types of insulation.

This chapter is assembled in the order a house or light commercial project would be framed. Quality begins with the selection of the overall framing system and materials and understanding the effect and management of moisture, continues through the assembly of framing members, and ends with the supervision of work by other trades that may affect the soundness of the structure. A variety of sources have been referenced to convey accepted practices of workmanship, as well as guidelines for code requirements. While we have not covered every possible framing condition, we do address the subjects that are most commonly alleged in defect claims.

The following professional associations may be helpful in locating more information about wood framing standards:

APA—The Engineered Wood Association
(Formerly the American Plywood Association)
Box 11700
Tacoma, WA 98411
Telephone: 253-565-6600 or 800-838-9972
www.apawood.org
APA – The Engineered Wood Association is a nonprofit trade association whose member mills produce approximately 75 percent of the plywood and OSB manufactured in North America. The APA trademark is a symbol of the manufacturer's commitment to APA's program of quality inspection and testing.

American Wood Preservers Institute
2750 Prosperity Avenue, Suite 550
Fairfax, VA 22031
Telephone: 703-204-0500
www.awpi.org

American Society for Testing and Materials (ASTM)
100 Barr Harbor Drive
West Conshohocken, PA 19428-2959
Telephone: 610-832-9500
www.astm.org

NAHB Research Center
400 Prince George's Blvd.
Upper Marlboro, MD 20772-8731
Telephone: 800-638-8556
www.nahb.com

National Forest Products Association
1250 Connecticut Avenue, N.W., Suite 200
Washington, DC 20036-2603
Telephone: 202-463-2700

National Frame Builders Association (NFBA)
4840 West 15th Street, Suite 1000
Lawrence, KS 66049-3855
Telephone: 913-843-2444
www.postframe.org

Northeastern Lumber Manufacturers Association, Inc.
272 Turtle Road, P.O. Box 87A
Cumberland Center, ME 04021
Telephone: 207-829-6901

Southern Forest Products Association
P.O. Box 52468
New Orleans, LA 70152-2468
Telephone: 504-443-4464

Truss Plate Institute (TPI)
583 D'Onofrio Drive, Suite 200
Madison, WI 53719
Telephone: 608-833-5900

Western Wood Products Association
522 S.W. Fifth Avenue
Portland, OR 97204
Telephone: 503-224-3930
www.wwpa.org

Wood Truss Council of America (WTCA)
One WTCA Center
6425 Normandy Lane
Madison, WI 53719-1133
Telephone: 608-274-4849
www.woodtruss.com

Ed. Note: Comments and recommendations within this chapter are not intended as a definitive resource for construction activities. For building projects, contractors must rely on the project documents and any applicable code requirements pertaining to their own particular locations.

General Considerations

Lumber Grade Stamps

Comments

The grade stamp allows you to verify that the wood selected is appropriate for its intended use. Since grade stamps are usually located at one end of the product, experienced carpenters have learned to cut the opposite end, leaving the grade stamp intact for the building official to check.

The components of the Western Wood Products Association lumber grade stamp are defined in the graphic on the following page. Other agencies that designate standards for lumber include The Northeastern Lumber Manufacturers Assn., The Southern Pine Inspection Bureau, The Northern Hardwood and Pine Manufacturers Assn., The National Lumber Grades Authority, The Redwood Inspection Service, and The West Coast Lumber Inspection Bureau. The grading rules of these agencies have been approved by the Board of Review of the American Lumber Standards Committee and certified for conformance with U.S. Dept. of Commerce Voluntary Product Standard PS 20-70 ("American Softwood Lumber Standard").

Refer to the "Structural Sheathing" section later in this chapter for information on plywood stamp designations from APA — The Engineered Wood Association (formerly the American Plywood Association).

Industry Standards

Guide to Understanding WWPA Grade Stamps and Quality Control Identification
(Western Wood Products Association)

Integrity of the Grade Stamp

Western Wood Products Association is one of the largest associations of lumber manufacturers in the United States, representing sawmills in the 12 western states. The association's Quality Standards Department supervises lumber grading by maintaining a staff of lumber inspectors who regularly check the quality of mill production, including visual grade requirements of glued products and machine stress-rated lumber. (See **Figure 5.1.**)

The association's *Grading Rules for Western Lumber* establishes standards of size and levels of quality in conformance with the American Softwood Lumber Standard PS 20-94. The association is certified as a rules writing and inspection

agency by the Board of Review, American Lumber Standard Committee. The association is approved to provide mill supervisory services under its rules and the rules of the West Coast Lumber Inspection Bureau, the Redwood Inspection Service, the National Lumber Grades Authority for Canadian Lumber and the NGR portion of the Southern Pine Inspection Bureau Rules. In addition, WWPA is approved to supervise finger-jointed and machine stress-rated lumber.

Engineered Wood Products

Comments

OSB (oriented strand board) beams, joists, and sheathing are commonly used in residential and light commercial construction, and are referred to as "engineered wood products." They can be used in place of (or in conjunction with) typical framing lumber. The advantages of this material include: superior tensile and compressive strength, stability, the same workability as wood, and longer available lengths. The builder, designer and manufacturer's representative should work together to determine the appropriate application of these products for each structure.

See also "Wood Shrinkage," "Bored Holes & Notching," and "Wood Roof Trusses" later in this chapter, for further comments on engineered wood products.

Interpreting Grade Marks

Western Wood Products Association uses a set of marks to identify lumber graded under its supervision. The grade marks are stamped on the lumber and appear near the ends of the product. Most grade stamps, except those for rough lumber or heavy timbers, contain five basic elements. Lumber carrying the WWPA grade stamp will meet or exceed the performance and aesthetic standards set for each grade.

WWPA Grade Stamp

WWPA Certification Mark

(a) This symbol certifies association standards and is a registered trademark

Mill Identification Firm

(b) **12** Identifies the name brand, or assigned mill number. WWPA can be contacted to identify an individual mill whenever necessary.

Grade Designation

Provides grade name, number, or abbreviation.

Species Identification

Indicates species by individual species or species combination.

Condition of Seasoning

(e) **S-DRY** Indicates condition of seasoning at the time of surfacing: MC-15, KD-15 15% maximum moisture content; S-DRY, KD 19% maximum moisture content; S-GRN Over 19% moisture content (unseasoned)

Courtesy of Western Wood Products Association

Figure 5.1

Wood Shrinkage

UBC — 1997

2304.7 Shrinkage. Consideration shall be given in design to the possible effect of cross-grain dimensional changes considered vertically, which may occur in lumber fabricated in a green condition.

Section 2308 — Wall Framing

The framing of exterior and interior walls shall be in accordance with provisions specified in Division IV, unless a specific design is furnished.

Wood stud walls and bearing partitions shall not support more than two floors and a roof, unless an analysis satisfactory to the building official shows that shrinkage of the wood framing will not have adverse effects on the structure or any plumbing, electrical or mechanical systems, or other equipment installed therein due to excessive shrinkage or differential movements caused by shrinkage. The analysis shall also show that the roof drainage system and the foregoing systems or equipment will not be adversely affected or, as an alternate, such systems shall be designed to accommodate the differential shrinkage or movements.

Comments

Often architects and builders will introduce different-sized members of the same material as components of a building system. Materials that are known to shrink noticeably should be avoided in these situations, as they can cause uneven settlement. This condition may cause a variety of building defects, including uneven and/or squeaking floors, stress cracks, and other defects in interior floor and wall finishes. For the same reasons, care should be taken when selecting structural members comprised of different materials or different grades of the same material.

Composite building materials—including wood and steel open-web trusses; laminated veneer lumber; parallel strand lumber beams, headers, columns, and posts; and laminated strand lumber—are manufactured to approximately equal moisture content, and they generally do not shrink, warp, or change shape after installation. This quality should be taken into consideration when composite members are used in conjunction with conventional framing systems.

Effects of Moisture Content

Industry Standards

Timber Construction Manual
(John Wiley & Sons, Inc.)

Between zero moisture content and the fiber-saturation point, wood shrinks as it loses moisture and swells as it absorbs moisture. Above the fiber saturation point there is no dimensional change with variation in moisture content.
The amount of shrinkage and swelling differs in the tangential, radial, and longitudinal dimensions of the piece. Engineering design should consider shrinkage and swelling in the detailing and use of lumber.

Comments

Wood expands or shrinks in relation to its moisture content. Wood with 19% or more moisture content is commonly used in new construction. As the wood dries to equilibrium (around 8%), the wood shrinks.

Wood shrinkage can have a dramatic effect on the height of a building. It is reported that a four-story building shrank four inches because of the change in moisture content of the framing lumber. The shrinkage was detected because the building had an internal stucco cement-lined shaft that raised at the roof line as the building shrank. Even though most single-family homes have three or less stories, the effect of lumber shrinkage must be addressed. At one extreme is a production multi-story home that is built fast with green lumber, and at the other extreme is a slowly built single-level home constructed with kiln-dried lumber.

Temperature changes can also cause wood to expand and contract, but the effect is usually not significant. In fact, other common building materials expand three to ten times the amount for the same change in temperature. Consideration should be given to the other materials used in conjunction with wood and the differential in thermal expansion and contraction.

Shrinkage occurs when the moisture content (MC) is reduced to a value below the fiber saturation point (for purposes of dimensional change, commonly assumed to be 30% MC) and is proportional to the amount of moisture lost below this point. Swelling occurs when the moisture content is increased until the fiber saturation point is reached; then the increase ceases. For each 1% decrease in moisture content below the fiber saturation point, wood shrinks about 1/30th of the total possible shrinkage, and, for each 1% increase in moisture content, the piece swells about 1/30th of the total possible swelling. The total swelling is equal numerically to the total shrinkage. Shrinking and swelling are expressed as percentages based on the green dimensions of the wood. Wood shrinks most in a direction tangent to the annual growth rings, and somewhat less in the radial direction, or across these rings. (See **Figure 5.2**.) In general, shrinkage is greater in heavier pieces than in lighter pieces of the same species, and greater in hardwoods than in softwoods.

As a piece of green or wet wood dries, the outer parts are reduced to a moisture content below the fiber saturation point much sooner than are the inner parts. Thus the whole piece may show some shrinkage before the average moisture content reaches the fiber saturation point.

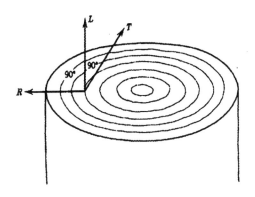

THE THREE PRINCIPAL AXES OF WOOD.
L. Longitudinal (parallel to grain); *R*, radial (perpendicular to grain, radial to annual rings); *T*, tangential (perpendicular to grain, tangential to annual rings).

Courtesy of John Wiley & Son, Inc., *Timber Construction Manual*

Figure 5.2

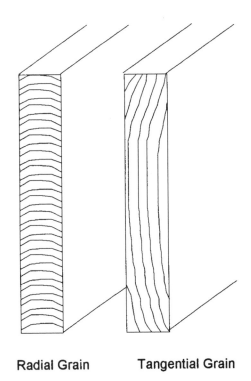

Radial Grain   **Tangential Grain**

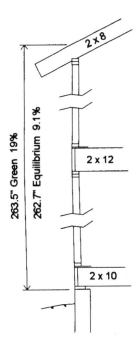

Drawings by Keith Everhart

Figure 5.3

Comments

Each species of wood has its own value of shrinkage. For example, as Douglas fir, Interior West, passes from fiber saturation of 30% to oven dry (0%), it shrinks 4.8% across radial growth rings and 7.5% tangential to growth rings.

The moisture content of materials such as wood, soil, masonry units, or roofing materials is expressed as a percentage of the total dry weight. At 70° and 50% humidity, the equilibrium moisture content of wood is 9.1%.

The information about wood shrinkage and moisture content can be usefully applied to a typical two-story house built on a raised foundation. At the foundation there is a 2x plate with a 2x10 rim joist, then ply and a 2x bottom plate, a stud and double top plate with a 2x12 rim joist with ply above and a 2x plate and stud with a double 2x top plate on which 2x8 rafter tails rest.

The foundation plate (1-1/2"), first floor joist (9-1/2"), bottom plate (1-1/2") and two top plates (3") and second floor joist (11-1/2") with a bottom plate (1-1/2") and two top plates (3") and rafter (8") add to a total wood thickness of 39-1/2". These portions of the wall height are either tangential or radial grain and will shrink or swell with moisture change.

Averaging the tangential and radial percentages, we find that we can expect the noted framing to shrink 6.2% from fiber saturation to oven dry. If the wood in our example is at saturation and reduced to oven dry, it will shrink 6.2%, or 2-7/16" (39-1/2" x .062). However, the moisture content in our example only moves from 19% green to 9.1% equilibrium. This is a reduction of 9.9%, which is about 1/3 of the total 30% possible. If 30% reduction will give us 2-7/16" shrinkage, 9.9% will result in shrinkage of .80", or just over 3/4". The reduction in height occurs after ply shear wall, sheet siding, or plaster is already attached. There is a possibility that the exterior siding or shear wall will show signs of compression stress as the weight of the house comes to bear on it. Ripples or bulges in the siding or cracking and bulges in the plaster finish can occur. This effect is often observed where narrow sections of walls are carrying heavy loads. It is often thought to be a structural defect, but is usually caused by framing shrinkage.

The effects of wood shrinkage on building construction may be noticed in other parts of the structure as well. Plumbing pipes, particularly ABS plastic plumbing

drainpipes, have been known to fail because of framing shrinkage. This situation is most frequently manifested in fittings that split at floor level. Similarly, nail pops are the direct result of lumber shrinkage. The best procedure for reducing nail pops is using the smallest legal nail allowed, which gives the nail a chance to move with the lumber.

Protecting Wood from Moisture and Decay

UBC — 1997

Section 3302. Preparation of the Building Site.

All stumps and roots shall be removed from the soil to a depth of at least 12 inches (305 mm) below the surface of the ground in the area to be occupied by the building.

All wood forms that have been used in placing concrete, if within the ground or between foundation sills and the ground, shall be removed before a building is occupied or used for any purpose. Before completion, loose or casual wood shall be removed from direct contact with the ground under the building.

Comments

In this section we have combined information concerning wood products embedded in the earth, placed close to or in contact with the earth, or in contact with concrete slabs placed on earth. The use of pressure-treated lumber is common in all areas of the country. While some of these code sections may apply, this section is not intended to cover wood foundations. For wood foundations, see UBC Chapter 18, Division II, Section 1810 through Section 1814.8.

Dryrot, which is really wet rot, and advanced fungal growth are common factors in defect claims. Water should not be allowed to come into prolonged contact with structural wood components. However, when it occurs, the best defense is use of the proper wood products.

Any discussion of wood in contact with the earth should begin with a reminder that all construction wood debris and concrete forms must be removed from the site. This wood material is an attraction to termites and encourages infestation in the building lumber.

2306.2. Wood Support Embedded in Ground. Wood embedded in the ground or in direct contact with the earth and used for the support of permanent structures shall be treated wood unless continuously below the groundwater line or continuously submerged in fresh water. Round or rectangular posts, poles and sawn timber columns supporting permanent structures that are embedded in concrete or masonry in direct contact with earth or embedded in concrete or masonry exposed to the weather shall be treated wood. The wood shall be treated for ground contact.

2306.3 Under-Floor Clearance. When wood joists or the bottom of wood structural floors without joists are located closer than 18 inches (457 mm) or wood girders are located closer than 12 inches (305 mm) to exposed ground in crawl spaces or unexcavated areas located within the periphery of the building foundation, the floor assembly, including posts, girders, joists and subfloor, shall be approved wood of natural resistance to decay as listed in Section 2306.4 or treated wood.

When the above under-floor clearances are required, the under-floor area shall be accessible. Accessible under-floor areas shall be provided with a minimum 18-inch-by-24-inch (457 mm by 610 mm) opening unobstructed by pipes, ducts and similar construction. All under-floor access openings shall be effectively screened or covered. Pipes, ducts and other construction shall not interfere with the accessibility to or within under-floor areas.

2306.4 Plates, Sills and Sleepers. All foundation plates or sills and sleepers on a concrete or masonry slab, which is in direct contact with earth, and sills that rest on concrete or masonry foundations, shall be treated wood or Foundation redwood, all marked or branded by an approved agency. Foundation cedar or No. 2 Foundation redwood marked or branded by an approved agency may be used for sills in territories subject to moderate hazard, where termite approved by the building official. In territories where hazard of termite damage is slight, any species of wood permitted by this code may be used for sills when specifically approved by the building official.

2306.5. Columns and Posts. Columns and posts located on concrete or masonry floors or decks exposed to the weather or to water splash or in basements and that support permanent structures shall be supported by concrete piers or metal pedestals projecting above floors unless approved wood of natural resistance to decay or treated wood is used. The pedestals shall project at least 6 inches (152 mm) above exposed earth and at least 1 inch (25 mm) above such floors.

Individual concrete or masonry piers shall project at least 8 inches (203 mm) above exposed ground unless the columns or posts that they support are of approved wood of natural resistance to decay or treated wood is used.

2306.6. Girders Entering Masonry or Concrete Walls. Ends of wood girders entering masonry or concrete walls shall be provided with a 1/2-inch (12.7 mm) air space on tops, sides and ends unless approved wood of natural resistance to decay or treated wood is used.

2306.8. Wood and Earth Separation. Protection of wood against deterioration as set forth in the previous sections for specified applications is required. In addition, wood used in construction of permanent structures and located nearer than 6 inches (152 mm) to earth shall be treated wood or wood of natural resistance to decay, as defined in Section 2302.1. Where located on concrete slabs placed on earth, wood shall be treated wood or wood of natural resistance to decay. Where not subject to water splash or to exterior moisture and located on concrete having a minimum thickness of 3 inches (76 mm) with an impervious membrane installed between concrete and earth, the wood may be untreated and of any species.

Where planter boxes are installed adjacent to wood frame walls, a 2-inch-wide (51 mm) air space shall be provided between the planter and the wall. Flashings shall be installed when the air space is less than 6 inches (152 mm) in width. Where flashing is used, provisions shall be made to permit circulation of air in the air space. The wood frame wall shall be provided with an exterior wall covering conforming to the provisions of Section 2310.

Pressure-Treated Wood Application

RETENTION (IBS/FT³)	PRODUCTION APPLICATION
0.25	Above Ground
0.40	Ground Contact
0.60	Permanent Wood Foundation
2.50	Salt Water

Source: American Wood Preservers Institute, www.awpi.org

Figure 5.4

Comments

The UBC *Section 2304.1. Quality and Identification* requires all pressure-treated wood to be identified by the quality mark of an inspection agency that has been accredited by an accreditation body complying with the requirements of the American Lumber Standard Committee Treated Wood Program, or its equivalent. *Figure 5.5* denotes the typical quality mark for waterborne preservatives for pressure-treated lumber. Waterborne preservatives are the only type of preservative commonly used to treat wood for residential and commercial construction. This information may help in selection of the proper products for an intended application.

LEGEND:

Typical Quality Mark for Pressure-treated Lumber

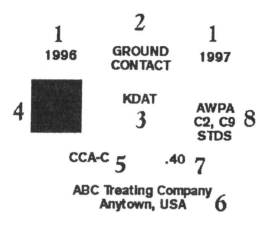

1. Year of Treatment
2. Proper Exposure Conditions
3. Dry or kiln-dried after treatment (if applicable)
4. Trademark of inspection agency approved by the American Lumber Standards Committee (ALSC)

5. Preservative used
6. Treating Company and Location
7. Retention Level
8. Applicable American Wood-Preservers' Association (AWPA) standards

Source: American Wood Preservers Institute, www.awpi.org

Figure 5.5

Section 2302. Definitions.

2302.1 Definitions. The following terms used in this chapter shall have the meanings indicated in this section:

Wood of Natural Resistance to Decay or Termites is the heartwood of the species set forth below. Corner sapwood is permitted on 5 percent of the pieces provided 90 percent or more of the width of each side on which it occurs is heartwood. Recognized species are:

Decay resistant: Redwood, Cedars, Black Locust

Termite resistant: Redwood, Eastern Red Cedar

Comments

1. Damage from rot (fungi decay) may be prevented or controlled by providing roof overhangs and gutters that will keep water off the building. Insect damage may be prevented by using properly seasoned wood that is well ventilated, in conjunction with properly installed vapor barriers. In some areas of the country, codes specify use of pressure-treated or other specially treated materials.

2. Good drainage is very important for any structure. Care should be taken to eliminate puddling and ponding adjacent to the foundation. Check the ground slope requirements in your building code.

3. Shrub beds and planting areas next to a structure should be checked from time to time to ensure that they are draining properly and that mulch and organic material are not building up against wood members and/or siding materials.

Ventilation

UBC — 1997

Section 1505 — Attics: Access, Draft Stops and Ventilation

1505.1 Access. An attic access opening shall be provided to attics of buildings with combustible ceiling or roof construction.

Exception: Attics with a maximum vertical height of less than 30 inches (762 mm).

The opening shall not be less than 22 inches (559 mm) by 30 inches (762 mm) and shall be located in a corridor, hallway or other readily accessible location. Thirty-inch-minimum (762 mm) unobstructed headroom in the attic space shall be provided at or above the access opening.

1505.2 Draft Stops. Attics, mansards, overhangs and other concealed roof spaces formed of combustible construction shall be draft stopped as specified in Section 708.3.

1505.3 Ventilation. Where determined necessary by the building official due to atmospheric or climatic conditions, enclosed attics and enclosed rafter spaces formed where ceilings are applied directly to the underside of roof rafters shall have cross ventilation for each separate space by ventilating openings protected against the entrance of rain and snow. Where eave or cornice vents are installed, insulation shall not block the free flow of air. A minimum of 1 inch (25 mm) of air space shall be provided between the insulation and the roof sheathing. The net free ventilating area shall not be less than 1/150 of the area of the space ventilated.

Exceptions:

1. The opening area may be 1/300 of the area of the space ventilated provided 50 percent of the required opening area is provided by ventilators located in the upper portion of the space to be ventilated at least 3 feet (914 mm) above eave or cornice vents with the balance of the required ventilation provided by eave or cornice vents.

2. The opening area may be 1/300 of the area of the space ventilated provided a vapor barrier not exceeding 1 perm [5.7 10^{-11} kg/(Pa - s - m^2)] is installed on the warm side of the attic insulation.

Comments

Although code requires 1/300 of the area of the space, it is good practice to exceed this figure when building in extreme cold climates. Heavy frost accumulation has been found in attics with the code minimum ventilation.

Openings for ventilation shall be covered with corrosion-resistant metal mesh with mesh openings of 1/4 inch (6.4 mm) in dimension.

Smoke and heat venting shall be in accordance with Section 906.

Section 1203 — Light and Ventilation in Group R Occupancies

1203.1 General. For the purpose of determining the light or ventilation for Group R Occupancies required by this section, any room may be considered as a portion of an adjoining room when one half of the area of the common wall is open and unobstructed and provides an opening of not less than one tenth of the floor area of the interior room or 25 square feet (2.3 m^2), whichever is greater.

Exterior openings for natural light or ventilation required by this section shall open directly onto a public way or a yard or court as set forth in Section 1203.4.

Exceptions:

1. Required exterior openings may open into a roofed porch where the porch:

    1.1 Abuts a public way, yard or court;

    1.2 Has a ceiling height of not less than 7 feet (2134 mm); and

    1.3 Has a longer side at least 65 percent open and unobstructed.

2. Skylights.

1203.3 Ventilation. Guest rooms and habitable rooms within a dwelling unit or congregate residence shall be provided with natural ventilation by means of openable exterior openings with an area of not less than 1/20 of the floor area of such rooms with a minimum of 5 square feet (0.46 m^2).

In lieu of required exterior openings for natural ventilation, a mechanical ventilating system may be provided. Such system shall be capable of providing two air changes per hour in guest rooms, dormitories, habitable rooms and in public corridors with a minimum of 15 cubic feet per minute (7 L/s) of outside air per occupant during such time as the building is occupied.

Bathrooms, water closet compartments, laundry rooms and similar rooms shall be provided with natural ventilation by means of openable exterior openings with an area not less than 1/20 of the floor area of such rooms with a minimum of 1-1/2 square feet (0.14 m^2).

Exception: Laundry rooms in Group R, Division 3 Occupancies.

In lieu of required exterior openings for natural ventilation in bathrooms containing a bathtub, shower or combination thereof; laundry rooms; and similar rooms, a mechanical ventilation system connected directly to the outside capable of providing five air changes per hour shall be provided. Such systems shall be connected directly to the outside, and the point of discharge shall be at least 3 feet (914 mm) from any opening that allows air entry into occupied portions of the building. Bathrooms that contain only a water closet, lavatory or combination thereof and similar rooms may be ventilated with an approved mechanical recirculating fan or similar device designed to remove odors from the air.

Under-Floor Ventilation

2306.7 Under-Floor Ventilation. Under-floor areas shall be ventilated by an approved mechanical means or by openings into the under-floor area walls. Such openings shall have a net area of not less than 1 square foot for each 150 square feet (0.067 m^2 for each 10 m^2) of under-floor area. Openings shall be located as close to corners as practical and shall provide cross ventilation. The required area of such openings shall be approximately equally distributed along the length of at least two opposite sides. They shall be covered with corrosion-resistant wire mesh with mesh openings of 1/4 inch (6.4 mm) in dimension. Where moisture due to climate and groundwater conditions is not considered excessive, the building official may allow operable louvers and may allow the required net area of vent openings to be reduced to 10 percent of the above, provided the under-floor ground surface area is covered with an approved vapor retarder.

Comments

It is important to stay abreast of code changes on ventilation, as well as other requirements.

Nails, Fasteners & Bolts

Nails

Comments

Nails are the most numerous and common ingredient in the construction of a new home. Using the wrong nail, having the wrong spacing between nails, and improperly installing nails has been the cause of considerable property damage, and the subject of many construction defect lawsuits. For example, in high-wind areas, buildings have lost their roofs and/or siding; and in areas prone to earthquakes, buildings have collapsed—partially due to the improper use of the nails and other fasteners.

Note that the 1997 UBC includes a change from the 1994 UBC, which allowed an exception to the use of special nails or fasteners when the treated wood was not below grade or exposed to weather. The 1997 UBC stipulates that pressure-preservative treated and fire-retardant treated wood require hot-dipped galvanized or one of the other designated fasteners. Treated sill plates require hot-dipped galvanized, stainless steel, silicon bronze, or copper fasteners.

Pneumatic nailers and staplers may be used to connect a variety of materials to both concrete and steel, in addition to wood. Manufacturers should be consulted for correct selection of fasteners as well as for appropriate pressure settings. If the power nailer is not set correctly, fasteners may penetrate too deeply, or not deeply enough, jeopardizing their holding performance.

For more information on nail selection (how nail diameter, length, shape, and surface affect holding power), contact the National Frame Builders Association (Telephone: 913-843-2444 for appropriate

publications). For staples and nails for pneumatic fasteners, refer to the Industrial Stapling and Nailing Technical Association and HUD-FHA Bulletin No. UM–25d.

UBC — 1997

2304.3 Timber connectors and fasteners. Safe loads and design practices for types of connectors and fasteners not mentioned or fully covered in Division III, Part III, may be determined in a manner approved by the building official.

The number and size of nails connecting wood members shall not be less than that set forth in Tables 23-II-B-1 and 23-II-B-2. (See the 1997 Uniform Building Code.)

Other connections shall be fastened to provide equivalent strength. End and edge distances and nail penetrations shall be in accordance with the applicable provisions of Division III, Part III.

Fasteners for pressure-preservative treated and fire-retardant treated wood shall be of hot-dipped zinc coated galvanized, stainless steel, silicon bronze or copper. Fasteners for wood foundations shall be as required in Chapter 18, Division II. Fasteners required to be corrosion resistant shall be either zinc-coated fasteners, aluminum alloy wire fasteners or stainless steel fasteners.

Connections depending on joist hangers or framing anchors, ties, and other mechanical fastenings not otherwise covered may be used where approved.

Fasteners

Comments

Nails are available in different sizes and with various holding capacities. Common nails, with a broad head and thick shank, are used for rough framing. Ring shank nails, with ridges to increase their holding capacity, are used for subflooring (underlayment). Roofing nails, with broad heads, hold shingles, building paper, and vapor barrier materials in place. Galvanized steel nails are suitable for exterior work, such as siding that will be exposed. Their zinc coating prevents marks and stains on the wood materials they contact.

For detailed technical data on seismic, hurricane or high-wind areas, consult the UBC, Volume 2, Chapter 16, Divisions III and IV.

UBC — 1997
Section 2318 — Timber Connectors and Fasteners

2318.1 General. Timber connectors and fasteners may be used to transmit forces between wood members and between wood and metal members. Allowable design values, Z and W, shall be determined in accordance with Division III, Part I or this section. Modifications to allowable design values, and installation of timber connectors and fasteners shall be in accordance with the provisions set forth in Division III, Part I.

2318.2 Bolts. Allowable lateral design values, in pounds for bolts in shear in seasoned lumber of Douglas fir- larch and Southern pine shall be as set forth in Tables 23-III-B-1 and 23-III-B-2.

2318.3 Nails and Spikes

2318.3.1 Allowable lateral loads. Allowable lateral design values, Z, for common wire and box nails driven perpendicular to the grain of the wood, when used to fasten wood members together, shall be as set forth in Tables 23-III-C-1 and 23-III-C-2.

A wire nail driven parallel to the grain of the wood shall not be subjected to more than two thirds of the lateral load allowed when driven perpendicular to the grain. Toenails shall not be subjected to more than five sixths of the lateral load allowed for nails driven perpendicular to the grain.

2318.3.2 Allowable withdrawal loads. Allowable withdrawal design values, W, for wire nails driven perpendicular to the grain of the wood shall be as set forth in Table 23-III-D.

Nails driven parallel to the grain of the wood shall not be allowed for resisting withdrawal forces.

2318.3.3 Spacing and penetration. Common wire nails shall have penetration into the piece receiving the point as set forth in Tables 23-III-C-1 and 23-III-C-2. Nails or spikes for which the gages or lengths are not set forth in Tables 23-III-C-1 and 23-III-C-2 shall have a required penetration of not less than 11 diameters, and allowable loads may be interpolated. Allowable loads shall not be increased when the penetration of nails into the member holding the point is larger than required by this section.

Comments

The following section of the UBC code, while technical, gives us the information that nails driven into end-grain have only 2/3 the shear value of nails driven into the side or edge of the wood. Also, toenails achieve 5/6 the value of side or edge nails.

Note also that the code states that "nails driven parallel to the grain of the wood shall not be allowed for resisting withdrawal forces."

Ed. Note: The following notes from UBC Table 23–II–I–1 explain that when nailing is closer than 6" to the edge of ply panels (which relates to 3" on center into the framing member) using 10d or larger nails, the wood member must be 3X.

1. All panel edges backed with 2-inch (51 mm) nominal or wider framing. Panels installed either horizontally or vertically. Space nails at 6 inches (152 mm) on center along intermediate framing members for 3/8-inch (9.5 mm) and 7/16-inch (11 mm) panels installed on studs spaced 24 inches (610 mm) on center and 12 inches (305 mm) on center for other conditions and panel thicknesses. These values are for short-time loads due to wind or earthquake and must be reduced 25 percent for normal loading.

   Allowable shear values for nails in framing members of other species set forth in Division III, Part III, shall be calculated for all other grades by multiplying the shear capacities for nails in Structural I by the following factors: 0.82 for species with specific gravity greater than or equal to 0.42 but less than 0.49, and 0.65 for species with a specific gravity less than 0.42.

2. Where panels are applied on both faces of a wall and nail spacing is less than 6 inches (152 mm) on center on either side, panel joints shall be offset to fall on different framing members or framing shall be 3-inch (76 mm) nominal or thicker and nails on each side shall be staggered.

3. In Seismic Zones 3 and 4, where allowable shear values exceed 350 pounds per foot (5.11 N/mm), foundation sill plates and all framing members receiving edge nailing from abutting panels shall not be less than a single 3-inch (76 mm) nominal member. Nails shall be staggered.

4. The values for 3/8-inch (9.5 mm) and 7/16-inch (11 mm) panels applied direct to framing may be increased to values shown for 15/32-inch (12 mm) panels, provided studs are spaced a maximum of 16 inches (406 mm) on center or panels are applied with long dimension across studs.

5. Galvanized nails shall be hot-dipped or tumbled.

1806.6 Foundation Plates or Sills. Wood plates or sills shall be bolted to the foundation or foundation wall. Steel bolts with a minimum nominal diameter of 1/2 inch (12.7 mm) shall be used in Seismic Zones 0 through 3. Steel bolts with a minimum nominal diameter of 5/8 inch (16 mm) shall be used in Seismic Zone 4. Bolts shall be embedded at least 7 inches (178 mm) into the concrete or masonry and shall be spaced not more than 6 feet (1829 mm) apart. There shall be a minimum of two bolts per piece with one bolt located not more than 12 inches (305 mm) or less than seven bolt diameters from each end of the piece. A properly sized nut and washer shall be tightened on each bolt to the plate. Foundation plates and sills shall be the kind of wood specified in Section 2306.4.

Comments

Green Vinyl Sinkers

For the last two decades on the West Coast, green vinyl sinkers have been used almost exclusively for residential construction. The 16d green vinyl sinker used for framing for the most part meets the requirement of the code, which allows either 16d box or 16d common nails to be interchanged. The sinker nail is mid-point between box and common on shank diameter and has the same head diameter as a common nail. The sinker is 3-1/4" long, which is 1/4" shorter than either the box or common.

This shorter length does not violate the specifications if used for 2X material, which is 1-1/2" thick. The 16d green vinyl sinker is out of spec on 3X lumber.

Another area in which the green vinyl sinker fails to comply with code is in nailing structural panels, subfloor or wall sheathing, to framing. In some cases, this can be corrected by using a larger sinker as described below. Code specifically requires common nails or in some cases deformed shank (screw or ring) nails for structural panels. Smooth shank green vinyl sinkers cannot be substituted for deformed shank nails.

The 8d sinker is 3/8" longer, but otherwise identical to the 6d common nail. The 8d sinker can be substituted for the 6d common to attach 1/2" or thinner structural panels, subfloor, or wall sheathing to framing.

The 16d sinker has the same diameter shaft as the 10d common, but has a larger diameter head and is 1/4" longer. The 16d sinker can be substituted for the 10d common for nailing 1-1/8" – 1-1/4" structural panels, subfloor, subfloor-underlayment, or wall sheathing to framing.

Anchor Bolts

Industry Standards

House Framing
(Creative Homeowner Press®)

You must install most anchor bolts in the foundation when the concrete is still wet. It's best to position your anchor bolts before pouring concrete, tie them in place with wire, then pour your walls or slab around them.

No matter what kind of anchor you use in your foundation, the technique for fastening the sill to the foundation is essentially the same. Always use bolts of at least 1/2-inch diameter and, ideally, embed the end of the anchor at least 7 inches into reinforced concrete (15 inches in unreinforced

Seismic Anchors

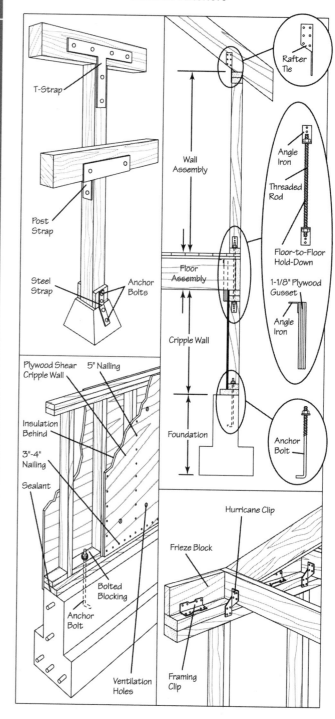

Building codes in seismic- or hurricane-prone areas may require T-straps, post caps, and anchor bolts wherever beams and posts meet or contact the foundation (top left). They may also require plywood shear panels on cripple walls and hurricane ties, floor-to-floor angle-iron-and-all-thread hold downs, and extra long anchor bolts at the foundation (top right and bottom left). Framing clips and hurricane ties can reinforce the connection between rafters, top plate, and rim joists or frieze blocks (bottom right).

Courtesy of Creative Homeowner Press®, *House Framing*

Figure 5.6

concrete). Space the bolts no more than 6 feet apart and within 12 inches of the ends of the sill plates. No matter how short a sill section is, it needs at least two anchor bolts. Always use washers beneath nuts when cinching the sills down to keep the nuts from sinking into the sill plates.

Comments

Hangers, Ties and Anchors

Metal hangers, ties, and anchors are required in some geographic areas to protect structures from hurricane strength winds. Local codes, in areas where hurricane damage is most common have specific guidelines for these items. Hangers and ties are generally required for the following connections:

- *bottom to sill plates*
- *ceiling or floor joists to headers or rim joists*
- *rafters to top plates (of walls)*

(Refer to the "Roof Framing" section later in this chapter for more on hurricane anchors.)

Seismic fastener requirements are described in local codes for earthquake-prone areas such as California. Some typical bracing and fastener requirements are shown in Figure 5.6.

Joist hangers are intended for use with specific sizes of framing members. If the hanger is too big for the member, it will not perform properly.

Load Resistance Values

Comments

Manufacturers of construction hardware generally set standards or load resistance values based on the American Forest and Paper Association's National Design Specification (NDS®).

Load resistance values may change from time to time; it is important to be aware of current values.

Manufacturers' catalogs and product information may be used as a general reference for the selection of standard or typical connectors. To achieve allowable loads, all specified fasteners must be used and proper installation procedures observed. This includes verifying that support members' dimensions are sufficient to receive the specified fasteners. If products are modified without the written permission of the manufacturer, the manufacturer will not be liable for building failure.

In most cases, products are sized for standard surfaced lumber or manufactured wood products.

Custom or special hardware is available for composite wood members. Nails are generally 8d, 10d, 16d, 20d common wire and bolts that conform to ASTM A 307–89 standards or better. All structural-rated products should meet ASTM–D1761, the testing standard recognized by all model agencies.

Construction hardware manufacturers offer custom design services and have the capability to produce connectors to meet all common and many unusual framing needs. (Due to regional builder preferences, code listings, or other factors, products may be offered in both Western Region and Eastern Region versions.)

Wood Joists & Plywood Decks

Industry Standards

Means Graphic Construction Standards
(R.S. Means Co., Inc.)

Wood joists may be used with all types of bearing wall or support systems. They may also be used in conjunction with various deck materials to provide economical floor and roof systems with moderate spans and loadings. The spacing of the wood joists may be varied to suit deck span or loading requirements.

Joists

UBC — 1997

2320.8.1 General. Spans for joists shall be in accordance with Tables 23-IV-J-1 and 23-IV-J-2.

2320.8.2 Bearing. Except where supported on a 1-inch by 4-inch (25 mm by 102 mm) ribbon strip and nailed to the adjoining stud, the ends of each joist shall not have less than 11/2 inches (38 mm) of bearing on wood or metal, or less than 3 inches (76 mm) on masonry.

Timber Connectors

Post Base

Comments

Joists are part of the floor framing system, along with the girder, sill plates, sill sealer, and subfloor sheathing. Joists provide the support for the floor. They are usually spaced at 12", 16" and 24" on center, between the girder and the sill on the foundation wall. A band or box joist (also called a "rim" or "perimeter" joist) is attached at the ends of the joists at the perimeter of the subfloor system.

Floor Systems

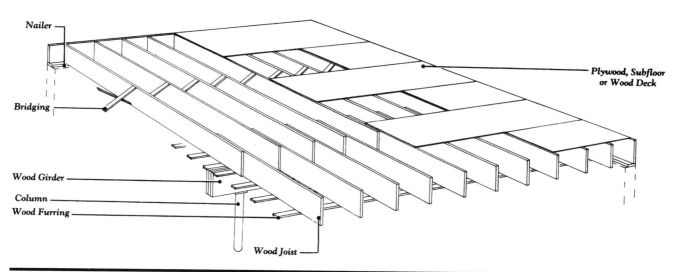

Nailer

Plywood, Subfloor or Wood Deck

Bridging

Wood Girder

Column

Wood Furring

Wood Joist

R.S. Means Co., Inc., *Means Graphic Construction Standards*

Figure 5.7

Headers & Trimmers

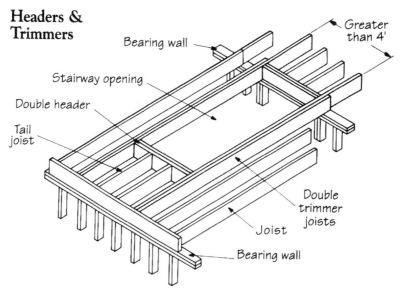

Bearing wall

Greater than 4'

Stairway opening

Double header

Tail joist

Double trimmer joists

Joist

Bearing wall

Interrupted joists must be headed off to transfer their loads to adjacent joists. If the header spans more than 4 feet, it must be doubled and the loads transferred to double trimmer joists.

Courtesy of Western Wood Products Association, *Field Guide to Common Framing Errors*

Figure 5.8

2320.8.3 Framing details. Joists shall be supported laterally at the ends and at each support by solid blocking except where the ends of joists are nailed to a header, band or rim joist or to an adjoining stud or by other approved means. Solid blocking shall not be less than 2 inches (51 mm) in thickness and the full depth of joist.

Notches on the ends of joists shall not exceed one fourth the joist depth. Holes bored in joists shall not be within 2 inches (51 mm) of the top or bottom of the joist, and the diameter of any such hole shall not exceed one third the depth of the joist. Notches in the top or bottom of joists shall not exceed one sixth the depth and shall not be located in the middle third of the span.

Joist framing from opposite sides of a beam, girder or partition shall be lapped at least 3 inches or the opposing joists shall be tied together in an approved manner.

Joists framing into the side of a wood girder shall be supported by framing anchors or on ledger strips not less than 2 inches by 2 inches (51 mm by 51 mm).

2320.8.4 Framing around openings. Trimmer and header joists shall be doubled, or of lumber of equivalent cross section, when the span of the header exceeds 4 feet (1219 mm). The ends of header joists more than 6 feet (1829 mm) long shall be supported by framing anchors or joist hangers unless bearing on a beam, partition or wall. Tail joists over 12 feet (3658 mm) long shall be supported at header by framing anchors or on ledger strips not less than 2 inches by 2 inches (51 mm by 51 mm).

2320.8.5 Supporting bearing partitions. Bearing partitions perpendicular to joists shall not be offset from supporting girders, walls or partitions more than the joist depth.

Joists under and parallel to bearing partitions shall be doubled.

Comments

Most codes require that joists adjacent to floor openings be doubled. Joists must also be doubled under partitions that run parallel to the joists. Joist hangers should be used to support joists whose ends do not bear on anything.

Joists must be stabilized by blocking (blocks installed square between joists) or bridging ("x-" shaped components made of 5/4 x 3s, angled at 45°). Bridging is installed along the length of the joist at 6' intervals. Prefabricated metal bridging can also be used.

Tapered Joists
Industry Standards
Field Guide to Common Framing Errors
(Western Wood Products Association)

It is sometimes necessary (or at least convenient) to taper the ends of ceiling joists or beams to keep them under the plane of the roof, as in **Figure 5.10**. But by reducing the depth of the joist or beam, you reduce its load carrying capacity.

If you must taper-cut the ends of ceiling joists, make sure the length of the taper cut does not exceed three times the depth of the member, and that the end of the joist or beam is at least one-half the member's original depth.

With taper-cut beams, you should also check the shear rating. If you can't meet this criteria, you'll probably have to lower the beam into a pocket so that enough cross-section can be left, after taper-cutting, to carry the applied load.

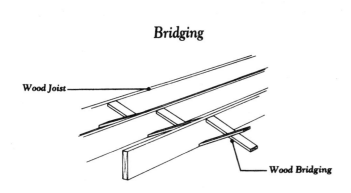

Bridging

Wood Joist

Wood Bridging

R.S. Means Co., Inc., *Means Graphic Construction Standards*

Figure 5.9

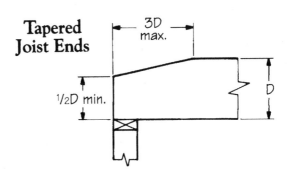

Tapered Joist Ends

3D max.

1/2D min.

D

Overtapering joists to fit beneath roofs create inadequate joist depth at the plate. A proper cut leaves at least half the depth of the joist.

Courtesy of Western Wood Products Association, *Field Guide to Common Framing Errors*

Figure 5.10

Comments

For information on tolerances in wood flooring and wood joists, see Sections 3–7 through 3–9 in Residential Construction Performance Guidelines, published by the National Association of Home Builders (Telephone: 800-368-5242).

Bored Holes & Notching

UBC 1997

2320.11.7 Pipes in walls. Stud partitions containing plumbing, heating, or other pipes shall be so framed and the joists underneath so spaced as to give proper clearance for the piping. Where a partition containing such piping runs parallel to the floor joists, the joists underneath such partitions shall be doubled and spaced to permit the passage of such pipes and shall be bridged. Where plumbing, heating or other pipes are placed in or partly in a partition, necessitating the cutting of the soles or plates, a metal tie not less than 0.058 inch (1.47 mm) (16 galvanized gage) and 1-1/2 inches (38 mm) wide shall be fastened to each plate across and to each side of the opening with not less than six 16d nails.

2320.11.9 Cutting and notching. In exterior walls and bearing partitions, any wood stud may be cut or notched to a depth not exceeding 25 percent of its width. Cutting or notching of studs to a depth not greater than 40 percent of the width of the stud is permitted in nonbearing partitions supporting no loads other than the weight of the partition.

2320.11.10 Bored holes. A hole not greater in diameter than 40 percent of the stud width may be bored in any wood stud. Bored holes not greater than 60 percent of the width of the stud are permitted in nonbearing partitions or in any wall where each bored stud is doubled, provided not more than two such successive doubled studs are so bored.

In no case shall the edge of the bored hole be nearer than 5/8 inch (16 mm) to the edge of the stud. Bored holes shall not be located at the same section of stud as a cut or notch.

Guide for Cutting, Notching, and Boring Joists

Joist Size	Maximum Hole	Maximum Notch Depth	Maximum End Notch
2x4	None	None	None
2x6	$1^1/2$	$^7/8$	$1^3/8$
2x8	$2^3/8$	$1^1/4$	$1^7/8$
2x10	3	$1^1/2$	$2^3/8$
2x12	$3^3/4$	$1^7/8$	$2^7/8$

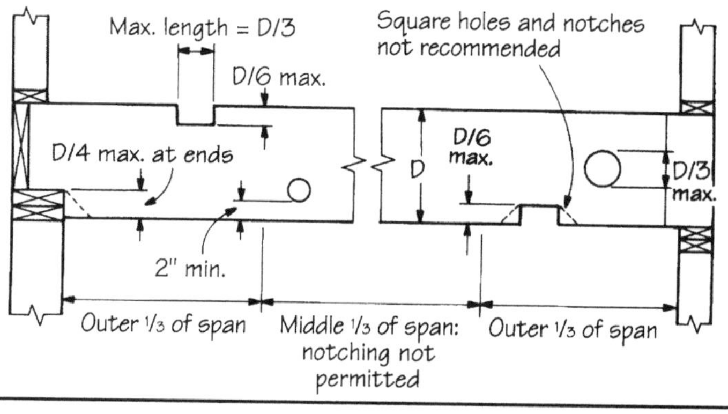

In joists, never cut holes closer than 2 inches to joist edges, nor make them larger than 1/3 the depth of the joist. Also, don't make notches in the middle third of a span where the bending forces are greatest. They should also not be deeper than 1/6 the depth of the joist, or 1/4 the depth if the notch is at the end of the joist. Limit the length of notches to 1/3 of the joist's depth. Use actual, not nominal, dimensions.

Courtesy of Western Wood Products Association, *Field Guide to Common Framing Errors*

Figure 5.11

Accommodating Wiring, Plumbing & Ductwork

Industry Standards

House Framing
(Creative Homeowner Press®)

A piece of lumber's strength depends on its entire dimension, without any notches or holes made in it. The more holes and notches you put in the lumber, the weaker it becomes. During house construction, it's often necessary to drill or notch lumber to make room for running wires, heating ducts, and pipes through the walls. It's easy to do this the wrong way, by hacking at the wood wherever it's convenient. By following a few simple rules, however, you can safely notch and drill wood. When calculating the sizes of notches and holes, use actual, not nominal, dimensions.

- Try not to cut a hole in a joist closer than 2 inches to the edge. Doing so weakens the joist considerably and increases the risk of nicking wires, pipes, or ducts with fasteners screwed or nailed through the decking.

- Never cut a hole bigger than one-third the depth of the joist. This weakens the joist too much, because you're removing one-third of its strength at that particular point. If you're using 2x10 joists, make the maximum hole size 3 inches; for 2x12s, make it 3-3/4 inches.

- Never make a notch in the middle third of a joist's length. This is where the loads really test the joist, at its mid-span, so avoid anything that would compromise its strength in this crucial section.

- Notches in joists should be no deeper than one-sixth the joist's depth (one-quarter the depth near the end of the joist) and no longer than one-third the joist's depth. Cover notches with steel plates.

The rules listed above apply mostly to running wires or pipes. If you get into running ducts, zero-clearance chimney pipes, or items larger than one-third the depth of the joists, you'll likely either build a special chase or passageway for running these services or suspend them using metal straps.

Additionally, be aware that electricians and plumbers commonly over-drill and over-notch joists for running their wires and pipes.

- Drywall screws can easily puncture or penetrate copper pipe or wire, so you must set plumbing and wiring back from the side of the stud that will be receiving screws. Mark for holes so that when the tubing or wire is in place it will be no closer than 1-1/2 inches from the stud edge.

- Maintain a consistent elevation from one stud bay to the next, especially for pipes, which are inflexible.

- Drill for wires with a 5/8-inch spade bit and for tubing with a 5/8- to 1-inch spade bit, depending on the size of the tubing. Drill for larger plumbing members like drains only in nonstructural partition walls.

- Where it is impossible to set the wire or tubing back from the wall at least 1-1/2 inches, install a metal shield (1/16 inch in thickness) on the edge of the stud's inside face to prevent screws from entering.

Comments

For engineered or manufactured building components such as wooden I-joists, composite wood and steel open-web trusses; laminated veneer lumber; parallel strand lumber beams, headers, columns and posts, refer to the manufacturers' installation standards.

Load conditions and hole sizes should be obtained from manufacturers' hole charts. Do not cut or notch flanges without approved engineered or manufacturers' drawings. If an improper cut or notch is made, the integrity of the member is compromised and the manufacturer may not be liable for related construction defects or failure.

Holes & Notches in Framing Members

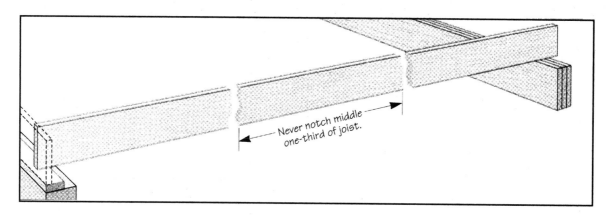

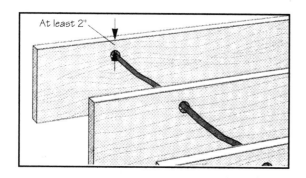

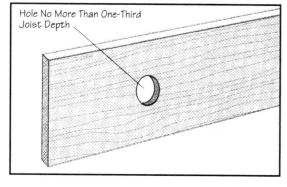

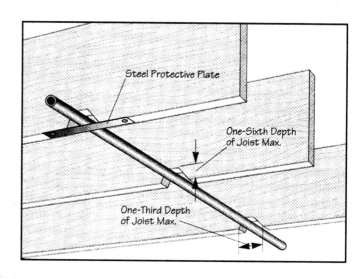

Courtesy of Creative Homeowner Press®, *House Framing*

Figure 5.12

Walls

Wall Partition/Framing Assembly

Industry Standards
Plan Reading & Material Takeoff
(R.S. Means Co., Inc.)

The wall and partition framing consists of the exterior walls and sheathing, the interior load-bearing walls, and the interior nonload-bearing partitions. *Load-bearing* walls carry live and dead loads from a part of the structure above, such as a floor, roof, or ceiling. A major component of the load-bearing wall is the *header*. Headers span the openings in load-bearing walls above windows and doors. They are structural members that transmit the load from above the opening to the framing on either side of the opening. Typical header construction consists of 2" x 6", 8", 10", or 12" (nominal) framing lumber nailed

together with 1/2" plywood spacers to equal the thickness of the wall. **Figure 5.13** illustrates a typical wood header.

The vertical members that support the header are called *trimmers* or *jack studs*. The jack studs are nailed to full studs at each side of the header, sometimes referred to as *king studs*.

All partitions and walls have horizontal members that hold the *studs*, or vertical members at the desired spacing. These horizontal members are called *plates*. The plate at the top of the wall is referred to as the *top plate*, and the one at the bottom is called the *sill plate* or *sole plate*. Most load-bearing wall construction requires that the top plate be doubled. The horizontal member that runs parallel to the header at the window sill height is called the *sill*. The short studs that fill in under the window sill or above the header are called *cripples*. **Figure 5.14** illustrates typical load-bearing wall framing.

To complete the exterior wall system, plywood or similarly rated sheathing is installed over the framed wall. This helps give the wall rigidity and bracing against the wind. Just as in floor framing, wall sheathing is nailed with the 8' length perpendicular to the studs.

Wood Header

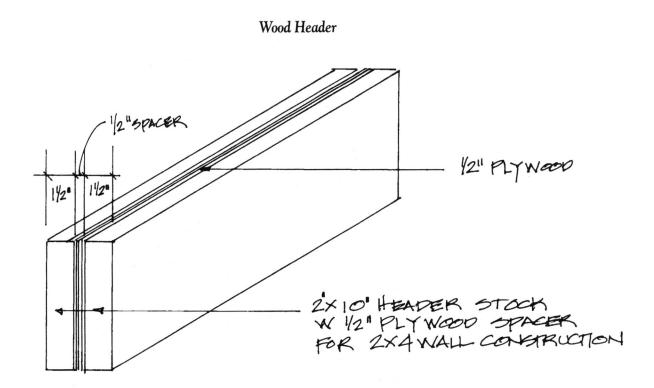

R.S. Means Co., Inc., *Plan Reading & Material Takeoff*

Figure 5.13

Load-Bearing Wall Framing

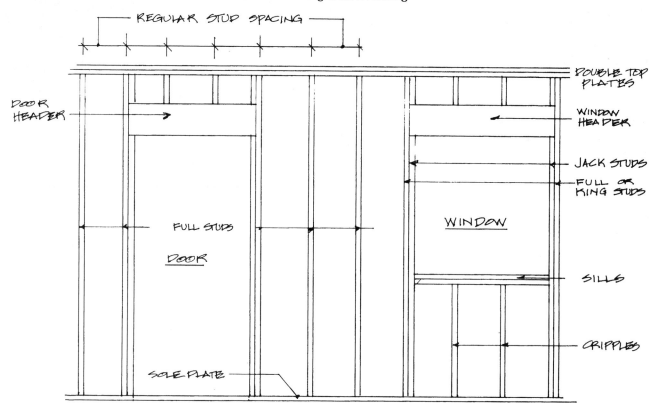

R.S. Means Co., Inc., *Plan Reading & Material Takeoff*

Figure 5.14

UBC — 1997
Section 2302 — Definitions

Diaphragm is a horizontal or nearly horizontal system acting to transmit lateral forces to the vertical-resisting elements. When the term "diaphragm" is used, it includes horizontal bracing systems.

Section 2320 — Conventional Light-Frame Construction Design Provisions

2320.5.6 Interior braced wall support. In one-story buildings, interior braced wall lines shall be supported on continuous foundations at intervals not exceeding 50 feet (15 240 mm). In buildings more than one story in height, all interior braced wall panels shall be supported on continuous foundations.

Exception: Two-story buildings may have interior braced wall lines supported on continuous foundations at intervals not exceeding 50 feet (15 240 mm) provided:

1. Cripple wall height does not exceed 4 feet (1219 mm).

2. First-floor braced wall panels are supported on doubled floor joists, continuous blocking or floor beams.

3. Distance between bracing lines does not exceed twice the building width parallel to the braced wall line.

2310.6 Hardboard. When hardboard siding is used for covering the outside of exterior walls, it shall conform to Table 23-II-C.

Lap siding shall be installed horizontally and applied to sheathed or unsheathed walls. Corner bracing shall be installed in conformance with Division IV. A weather-resistive barrier shall be installed under the lap siding as required by Section 1402.1.

2320.11.3 Bracing. Braced wall lines shall consist of braced wall panels, which meet the requirements for location, type and amount of bracing specified in Table 23-IV-C-1 and are in line or offset from each other by not more than 4 feet (1219 mm). Braced wall panels shall start at not more than 8 feet (2438 mm) from each end of a braced wall line. All braced wall panels shall be clearly indicated on the plans. Construction of braced wall panels shall be by one of the following methods:

1. Nominal 1-inch by 4-inch (25 mm by 102 mm) continuous diagonal braces let into top and bottom plates and intervening studs, placed at an angle not more than 60 degrees or less than 45 degrees from the horizontal, and attached to the framing in conformance with Table 23-II-B-1.

2. Wood boards of 5/8-inch (16 mm) net minimum thickness applied diagonally on studs spaced not over 24 inches (610 mm) on center.

3. Wood structural panel sheathing with a thickness not less than 5/16 inch (7.9 mm) for 16-inch (406 mm) stud spacing and not less than 3/8 inch (9.5 mm) for 24-inch (610 mm) stud spacing in accordance with Tables 23-II-A-1 and 23-IV-D-1.

4. Fiberboard sheathing 4-foot by 8-foot (1219 mm by 2438 mm) panels not less than 1/2 inch (13 mm) thick applied vertically on studs spaced not over 16 inches (406 mm) on center when installed in accordance with Section 2315.6 and Table 23-II-J.

5. Gypsum board sheathing 1/2 inch (13 mm) thick by 4 feet (1219 mm) wide, wallboard or veneer base] on studs spaced not over 24 inches (610 mm) on center and nailed at 7 inches (178 mm) on center with nails as required by Table 25-I.

6. Particleboard wall sheathing panels where installed in accordance with Table 23-IV-D-2.

7. Portland cement plaster on studs spaced 16 inches (406 mm) on center installed in accordance with Table 25-I.

8. Hardboard panel siding when installed in accordance with Section 2310.6 and Table 23-II-C.

Method 1 is not permitted in Seismic Zones 2B, 3 and 4. For cripple wall bracing, see Section 2320.11.5. For Methods 2, 3, 4, 6, 7 and 8, each braced panel must be at least 48 inches (1219 mm) in length, covering three stud spaces where studs are spaced 16 inches (406 mm) apart and covering two stud spaces where studs are spaced 24 inches (610 mm) apart.

For Method 5, each braced wall panel must be at least 96 inches (2438 mm) in length when applied to one face of a braced wall panel and 48 inches (1219 mm) when applied to both faces.

All vertical joints of panel sheathing shall occur over studs.

Horizontal joints shall occur over blocking equal in size to the studding except where waived by the installation requirements for the specific sheathing materials.

Braced wall panel sole plates shall be nailed to the floor framing and top plates shall be connected to the framing above in accordance with Table 23-II-B-1. Sills shall be bolted to the foundation or slab in accordance with Section 1806.6. Where joists are perpendicular to braced wall lines above, blocking shall be provided under and in line with the braced wall panels.

2320.11.5 Cripple walls. Foundation cripple walls shall be framed of studs not less in size than the studding above with a minimum length of 14 inches (356 mm), or shall be framed of solid blocking. When exceeding 4 feet (1219 mm) in height, such walls shall be framed of studs having the size required for an additional story.

Cripple walls having a stud height exceeding 14 inches (356 mm) shall be braced in accordance with Table 23-IV-C-2. Solid blocking or wood structural panel sheathing may be used to brace cripple walls having a stud height of 14 inches (356 mm) or less. In Seismic Zone 4, Method 7 is not permitted for bracing any cripple wall studs.

Spacing of boundary nailing for required wall bracing shall not exceed 6 inches (152 mm) on center along the foundation plate and the top plate of the cripple wall. Nail size, nail spacing for field nailing and more restrictive boundary nailing requirements shall be as required elsewhere in the code for the specific bracing material used.

Bearing Walls
Industry Standards
Field Guide to Common Framing Errors
(Western Wood Products Association)

Misaligned bearing walls, in other instances, loads carried by bearing walls or posts must be transferred through floor systems. If the bearing wall or post above doesn't line up closely enough with a bearing wall, post, or beam below, the floor joists in between can be overstressed, causing severe deflection. This can eventually split the joists, as well as cause finish cracking problems.

Bearing walls supported by floor joists must be within the depth of the joist from their bearing support below (just as with cantilevers), as in **Figure 5.15.**

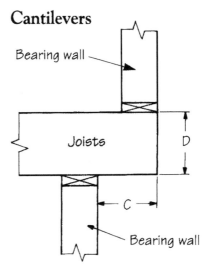

Cantilevers

When a cantilever supports a bearing wall, the distance it extends beyond its support (C) should not exceed the depth of the joist (D).

Courtesy of Western Wood Products Association, *Field Guide to Common Framing Errors*

Figure 5.15

This code requirement applies only to solid-sawn wood joists. Engineered products such as wood I-beams are required to have the loads line up directly over each other, and special blocking is required. Special engineering of either dimensional or engineered lumber may allow placing loads at other locations, but you shouldn't try it without consulting an engineer first.

Bearing Walls on Cantilevers

Industry Standards

Field Guide to Common Framing Errors
(Western Wood Products Association)

How far can a conventionally framed cantilever extend and still support a bearing wall?

Most of the confusion about how far a cantilever can extend beyond its support stems from an old rule of thumb used by builders and code officials alike: the rule of "one-to-three." This states that a joist should extend back inside the building at least three times the length of the cantilevered section — if the cantilevered section hangs 2 feet out, the joists should extend at least 6 feet in.

This rule works fine for nonbearing situations. But it does not apply to a cantilever that supports a bearing wall. In this situation, the maximum distance that joists can be cantilevered without engineering them is a distance equal to the depth of the joists, as in **Figure 5.15**. So if you are using 2x10 floor joists, the maximum cantilever for those joists supporting a bearing wall is 9-1/4 inches. Beyond this distance, shear becomes a serious factor, as does the bending moment at the support. This combination could eventually cause splitting of the cantilevered joists. The only way to work around this problem is to have it engineered.

> ## Comments
>
> *Composite joists may be cantilevered up to a maximum of 2'–0" when supporting roof load, but may require reinforcement. Manufacturers' loading tables should be consulted to determine the required reinforcement.*
>
> *Composite joists may be cantilevered up to one-third of the adjacent span if not supporting concentrated loads on the cantilever. Cantilevers exceeding 4' may require special construction. Manufacturers should be contacted for assistance.*

Aligning Bearing Walls

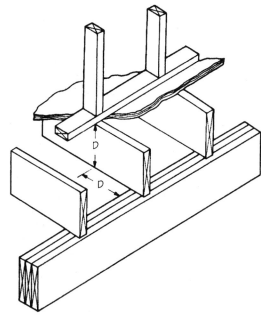

If a bearing wall doesn't line up with the support below, it should lie no farther than the depth of the joists (D). If the joists are engineered lumber, the walls and support must align exactly.

Courtesy of Western Wood Products Association, *Field Guide to Common Framing Errors*

Figure 5.16

Bracing Framing

UBC — 1997

2306.4 Plates, Sills and Sleepers. All foundation plates or sills and sleepers on a concrete or masonry slab, which is in direct contact with earth, and sills that rest on concrete or masonry foundations, shall be treated wood or Foundation redwood, all marked or branded by an approved agency. Foundation cedar or No. 2 Foundation redwood marked or branded by an approved agency may be used for sills in territories subject to moderate hazard, where termite damage is not frequent and when specifically approved by the building official. In territories where hazard of termite damage is slight, any species of wood permitted by this code may be used for sills when specifically approved by the building official.

1806.6 Foundation Plates or Sills. Wood plates or sills shall be bolted to the foundation or foundation wall. Steel bolts with a minimum nominal diameter of 1/2 inch (12.7 mm) shall be used in Seismic Zones 0 through 3. Steel bolts with a minimum nominal diameter of 5/8 inch (16 mm) shall be used in Seismic Zone 4. Bolts shall be embedded at least

7 inches (178 mm) into the concrete or masonry and shall be spaced not more than 6 feet (1829 mm) apart. There shall be a minimum of two bolts per piece with one bolt located not more than 12 inches (305 mm) or less than seven bolt diameters from each end of the piece. A properly sized nut and washer shall be tightened on each bolt to the plate. Foundation plates and sills shall be the kind of wood specified in Section 2306.4

2320.6 Foundation Plates or Sills. Foundations and footings shall be as specified in Chapter 18. Foundation plates or sills resting on concrete or masonry foundations shall be bolted as required by Section 1806.6.

Ed. Note: Section 1806.6 provides detailed requirements on sizes, types and placement of bolts and reinforcement for various seismic zones.

2320.11.2 Framing details. Studs shall be placed with their wide dimension perpendicular to the wall. Not less than three studs shall be installed at each corner of an exterior wall.

Exception: At corners, a third stud may be omitted through the use of wood spacers or backup cleats of 3/8-inch-thick (9.5 mm) wood structural panel, 3/8-inch (9.5 mm) Type M "Exterior Glue" particleboard, 1-inch-thick (25 mm) lumber or other approved devices that will serve as an adequate backing for the attachment of facing materials. Where fire-resistance ratings or shear values are involved, wood spacers, backup cleats or other devices shall not be used unless specifically approved for such use.

Bearing and exterior wall studs shall be capped with double top plates installed to provide overlapping at corners and at intersections with other partitions. End joints in double top plates shall be offset at least 48 inches (2438 mm).

Exception: A single top plate may be used, provided the plate is adequately tied at joints, corners and intersecting walls by at least the equivalent of 3-inch by 6-inch (76 mm by 152 mm) by 0.036-inch-thick (0.9 mm) galvanized steel that is nailed to each wall or segment of wall by six 8d nails or equivalent, provided the rafters, joists or trusses are centered over the studs with a tolerance of no more than 1 inch (25 mm).

When bearing studs are spaced at 24-inch (610 mm) intervals and top plates are less than two 2-inch by 6-inch (51 mm by 152 mm) or two 3-inch by 4-inch (76 mm by 102 mm) members and when the floor joists, floor trusses or roof trusses which they support are spaced at more than 16-inch (406 mm) intervals, such joists or trusses shall bear within 5 inches (127 mm) of the studs beneath or a third plate shall be installed.

Interior nonbearing partitions may be capped with a single top plate installed to provide overlapping at corners and at intersections with other walls and partitions. The plate shall be continuously tied at joints by solid blocking at least 16 inches (406 mm) in length and equal in size to the plate or by 1/8-inch by 11/2-inch (3.2 mm by 38 mm) metal ties with spliced sections fastened with two 16d nails on each side of the joint.

Studs shall have full bearing on a plate or sill not less than 2 inches (51 mm) in thickness having a width not less than that of the wall studs.

2320.11.6 Headers. Headers and lintels shall conform to the requirements set forth in this paragraph and together with their supporting systems shall be designed to support the loads specified in this code. All openings 4 feet (1219 mm) wide or less in bearing walls shall be provided with headers consisting of either two pieces of 2-inch (51 mm) framing lumber placed on edge and securely fastened together or 4-inch (102 mm) lumber of equivalent cross section. All openings more than 4 feet (1219 mm) wide shall be provided with headers or lintels. Each end of a lintel or header shall have a length of bearing of not less than 1-1/2 inches (38 mm) for the full width of the lintel.

Comments

See "Nails, Fasteners & Bolts" for information on hurricane and seismic requirements.

For further information about variances in wall structure, see sections 4–1 and 4–2 in Residential Construction Performance Guidelines, *published by the National Association of Home Builders (call 800-368-5242 for publications information).*

Columns

Industry Standards

Field Guide to Common Framing Errors
(Western Wood Products Association)

Bringing Columns to Foundation Properly

If you use a column to support a beam or other member, make sure it bears on something that can in turn support it. A common mistake is to rest one on the floor, without extra blocking or support beneath. Doing this can crush the underlying joists. Columns shouldn't rest on unsupported floor joists; they should run continuously to the foundation, or (if you must have a clear space beneath) to an engineered beam or header to transfer the load out to other columns or bearing members.

Columns shouldn't rest on rim (perimeter) joists either, for similar reasons. If you need to rest a column at the rim, add full-depth vertical blocking inside the rim joist the full depth and width of the column base, so that the load is transferred through the blocking to the foundation.

Wood Columns, Girders, Beams, and Wood Decks

Industry Standards

Means Graphic Construction Standards
(R.S. Means Co., Inc.)

Wood columns, girders, and beams may be used with wood deck, or joists and plywood deck, to provide a floor or roof-framing system. The system is sometimes called "post and beam construction." This system is primarily used in situations where the floor or roof loading is relatively moderate, and where clear spans are not excessive.

Wood Girder Supported by Square Tube Column

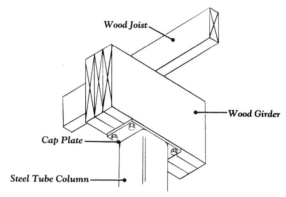

Wood Girder Supported by Pipe Column

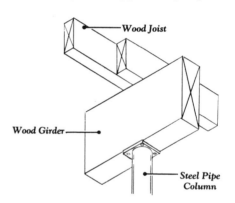

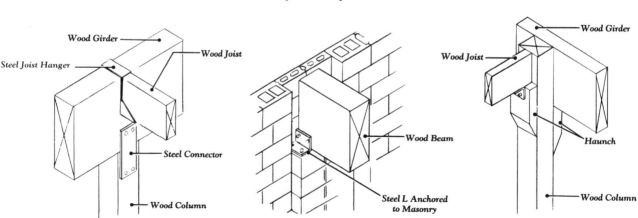

Wood Column Girder and Joist · Wood Girder Supported by Masonry Wall · Wood Column with Laminated Haunches

R.S. Means Co., Inc., *Means Graphic Construction Standards*

Figure 5.17

Laminated Girders & Beams With Wood Deck

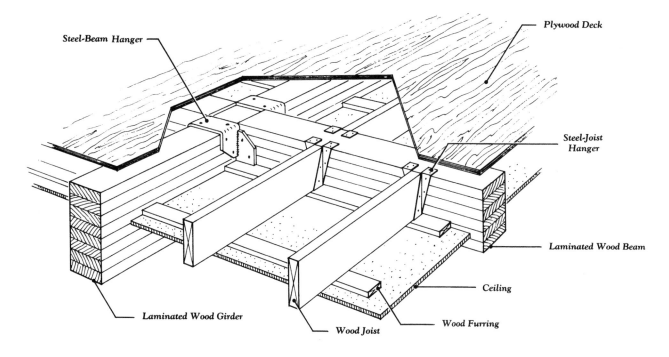

Laminated Wood Floor Beams

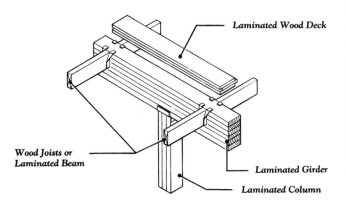

Laminated Wood Deck

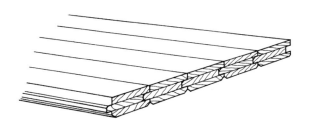

R.S. Means Co., Inc., *Means Graphic Construction Standards*

Figure 5.18

Laminated Columns, Girders, Beams, and Wood Decks

Industry Standards

Means Graphic Construction Standards
(R.S. Means Co., Inc.)

Laminated wood members and decking (or plywood) may be used to frame floors and roofs with varied spans and loadings. Both the framing members and decking may be left unfinished or supplied factory-stained. The connectors are usually fabricator-designed and supplied.

Roof Framing

Industry Standards

Plan Reading & Material Takeoff
(R.S. Means Co., Inc.)

The rafters are supported at the base by the top plate at the top of the exterior wall. In the same way that floor joists are spaced along the pressure-treated sills, rafters are spaced along the top plate. Common spacing is 12", 16", or 24" on center. The part of the rafter that extends beyond the face of the exterior wall is called the *rafter tail*, or *tail*. It provides the nailing for the fascia and soffit (discussed later in this chapter), and constitutes the roof's overhang. The highest point of the rafter terminates at a perpendicular member in the horizontal plane called the *ridge*, or *ridge board*. To complete the triangular shape of the roof frame, horizontal members called *ceiling joists* provide the follor of the attic space or ceiling of the floor below. Ceiling joists extend from the top plates of bearing walls and span the space, much like floor joists that span from sill to girder or sill. Ceiling joists for gable-end roofs run parallel to rafters. *Strapping* (called furring when applied to walls) is typically comprised of 1" x 3" (nominal) boards nailed to the ceiling side of the ceiling joists. Strapping runs at right angles to the ceiling joists in the same horizontal plane. Strapping is used to maintain the spacing of ceiling joists between bearing points and to provide furring for the ceiling finish. Strapping is commonly spaced at 12" or 16" on center.

To increase the rigidity of the roof frame, horizontal members called *collar ties* are installed from rafter to rafter on opposite sides of the ridge. Collar ties are typically located in the top third of the imaginary triangle created by the roof frame.

The *roof sheathing* extends from the rafter tail to the ridge board along the top surface of the rafter and provides a substrate for the application of the roofing. **Figure 5.19** shows a typical roof frame as viewed in a building cross-section.

UBC — 1997
2320.12 Roof and Ceiling Framing
2320.12.1 General. The framing details required in this section apply to roofs having a minimum slope of 3 units vertical in 12 units horizontal (25% slope) or greater. When the roof slope is less than 3 units vertical in 12 units horizontal (25% slope), members supporting rafters and ceiling joists such as ridge board, hips and valleys shall be designed as beams.

Comments
For seismic, hurricane or high wind areas, reference the UBC Volume 2, Chapter 16, Divisions III and IV.

2320.12.2 Spans. Allowable spans for ceiling joists shall be in accordance with Tables 23-IV-J-3 and 23-IV-J-4. Allowable spans for rafters shall be in accordance with Tables 23-IV-R-1 through 23-IV-R-12, where applicable.

2320.12.3 Framing. Rafters shall be framed directly opposite each other at the ridge. There shall be a ridge board at least 1-inch (25 mm) nominal thickness at all ridges and not less in depth than the cut end of the rafter. At all valleys and hips there shall be a single valley or hip rafter not less than 2-inch (51 mm) nominal thickness and not less in depth than the cut end of the rafter.

Section at Roof Frame

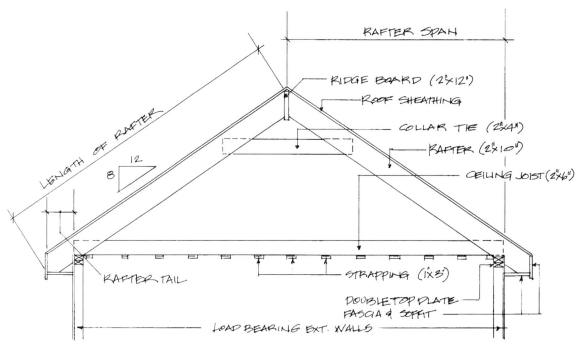

Figure 5.19

2320.12.5 Framing around openings. Trimmer and header rafters shall be doubled, or of lumber of equivalent cross section, when the span of the header exceeds 4 feet (1219 mm). The ends of header rafters more than 6 feet (1829 mm) long shall be supported by framing anchors or rafter hangers unless bearing on a beam, partition or wall.

2320.12.6 Rafter ties. Rafters shall be nailed to adjacent ceiling joists to form a continuous tie between exterior walls when such joists are parallel to the rafters. Where not parallel, rafters shall be tied to 1-inch by 4-inch (25 mm by 102 mm) (nominal) minimum size crossties. Rafter ties shall be spaced not more than 4 feet (1219 mm) on center.

2320.12.7 Purlins. Purlins to support roof loads may be installed to reduce the span of rafters within allowable limits and shall be supported by struts to bearing walls. The maximum span of 2-inch by 4-inch (51 mm by 102 mm) purlins shall be 4 feet (1219 mm). The maximum span of the 2-inch by 6-inch (51 mm by 152 mm) purlin shall be 6 feet (1829 mm) but in no case shall the purlin be smaller than the supported rafter. Struts shall not be smaller than 2-inch by 4-inch (51 mm by 102 mm) members. The unbraced length of struts shall not exceed 8 feet (2438 mm) and the minimum slope of the struts shall not be less than 45 degrees from the horizontal.

2320.12.8 Blocking. Roof rafters and ceiling joists shall be supported laterally to prevent rotation and lateral displacement when required by Division III, Part I, Section 4.4.1.2. Roof trusses shall be supported laterally at points of bearing by solid blocking to prevent rotation and lateral displacement.

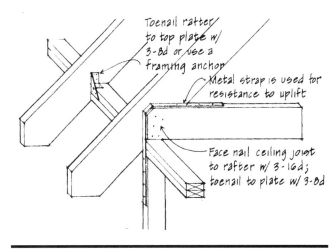

Courtesy of Western Wood Products Association, *Field Guide to Common Framing Errors*

Figure 5.20

Wood Rafters
Industry Standards
Means Graphic Construction Standards
(R.S. Means Co., Inc.)

Wood roof rafters are fabricated in the field from dimensional lumber, for high or low pitched roofs, hipped roofs, mansard roofs, and flat roofs. They are typically used in conjunction with plywood decking to provide a roof structure compatible with many types of bearing wall systems. The spacing and slope of wood rafter systems may be varied to suit the loading span and aesthetic requirements of the installation.

Gable End Roof

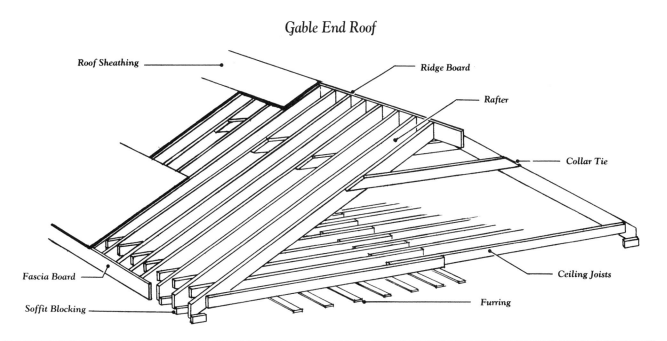

R.S. Means Co., Inc. *Means Graphic Construction Standards*

Figure 5.21

Shed Roof

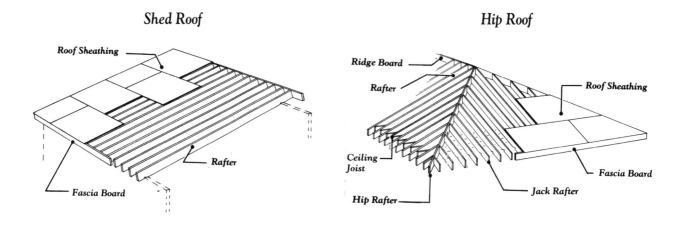

Hip Roof

Gambrel Roof

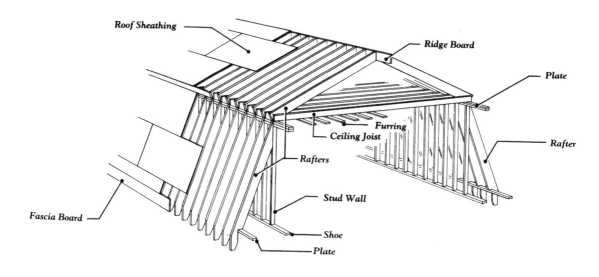

Mansard Roof

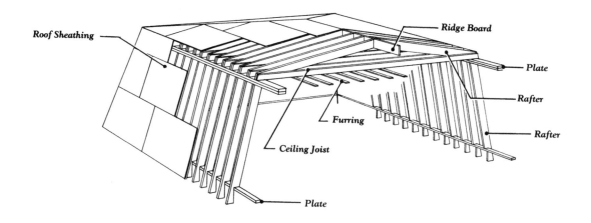

R.S. Means Co., Inc. *Means Graphic Construction Standards*

Figure 5.21 continued

Comments

Based on regional differences in load (wind, snow) placed on the roof structure, code may require different structural members.

Roof Support Structures

The roof frame furnishes the base to which the roofing material is attached. The frame must be made strong and rigid to withstand imposed, live and dead loads. Rafters are structural-in nature and are arranged at equal intervals, along walls and extending up from the top of the wall to the ridge.

All lumber should be inspected for compliance with the specification. Grade stamps should be checked to ensure proper type and structural properties. Members that are damaged or have gross defects should never be used.

Lumber should be stored on blocking off the ground, and in properly drained areas.

Framing members should not be cut or notched without leaving sufficient strength to carry the load. (See "Bored Holes & Notching" earlier in this chapter.)

Rafter Bearing

Industry Standards
Field Guide to Common Framing Errors
(Western Wood Products Association)

Another area that inspires excessive cutting is the level cut of the seat of a rafter. Many times, especially on low slope rafters, this level cut becomes a long taper cut on the tension (lower) side of the rafter, as in **Figure 5.22**. If the bearing point on the rafter is at the heel (interior side) of the cut, there is no problem. But usually these long cuts put the bearing point near the toe. This reduces the effective size of the rafter, producing stresses that can create splits at the bearing point, and eventually a sagging rafter.

To prevent this, cut your rafters so that the heel rests on the plate. This will mean using a slightly longer rafter. It will also give you a few extra inches between the top of the exterior wall and the roof sheathing. This translates into more room for attic insulation to extend over your outside wall, reducing those cold spots that can cause condensation or ice dam problems at the eaves.

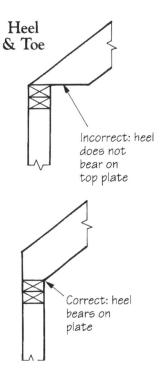

Heel & Toe

Setting a rafter's toe on the top plate (top) risks splitting the rafter and causing the roof to sag. The inside edge of the level cut, or heel, should rest on the plate (bottom).

Courtesy of Western Wood Products Association, *Field Guide to Common Framing Errors*
Figure 5.22

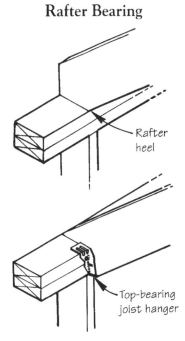

Rafter Bearing

It's best to have the rafter heel on the plate (top). Where this isn't possible, you can sometimes support it with a joist hanger (above). The joist hanger also keeps the rafter from rotating, a job that normally requires ceiling joists or solid blocking.

Courtesy of Western Wood Products Association, *Field Guide to Common Framing Errors*
Figure 5.23

Rafter-to-Wall Connection

Industry Standards

Field Guide to Common Framing Errors
(Western Wood Products Association)

Connecting Rafter to Wall

Conventional construction leaves too little connection between rafters and walls. Nails connect rafter to plate and plate to stud, but do nothing to connect the rafters to the wall itself. Such structures are subject to damage from the high, near-hurricane force winds that sooner or later blow across virtually every roof.

As a result, the building codes are beginning to get more restrictive about how rafters and trusses are tied to the rest of the building. For example, the 1991 Uniform Building Code has added Appendix Chapter 25 which applies to high wind areas. Under its requirements, rafters or trusses must be tied not just to the top plate, but to the studs below at 4 foot intervals. This means using some kind of metal connector to provide a positive tie to the studs.

The answer is the hurricane anchor (see **Figure 5.24**). You don't need to face a hurricane to need it — winds of roof-damaging gale force blow in most parts of the country. If you build in an area subject to high winds (or seismic conditions), you should consider using these or other holddowns.

Comments

For seismic, hurricane or high wind areas, reference the U.B.C. Volume 2, Chapter 16, Divisions III and IV. (See also "Seismic Bracing" later in this chapter.)

Wood Roof Trusses

Industry Standards

Means Graphic Construction Standards
(R.S. Means Co., Inc.)

Wood roof trusses are factory fabricated of dimension lumber for high- or low-pitched roofs, hipped roofs, mansard roofs, and flat roofs. They are available from manufacturers in many different configurations. Members are connected with wood or metal gussetts and are glued and/or power nailed in a jig to ensure uniformity.

The clear span characteristics of trusses provides flexibility for interior planning and partition layout. A considerable cost savings results from the fact that ceilings or decking can be applied directly to the truss chords. Truss spacing is dictated by maximum allowable span of the sheathing material. Normal span wood trusses can be erected by hand due to their light weight, but are also efficiently erected utilizing a boom truck or crane and a small erection crew.

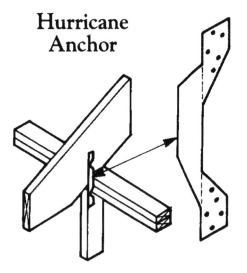

Hurricane Anchor

Nailing rafters to plates, and plates to studs, is not always enough to resist high winds. Hurricane anchors at 4-foot intervals will securely tie rafters to studs.

Courtesy of Western Wood Products Association, *Field Guide to Common Framing Errors*

Figure 5.24

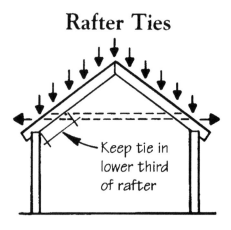

Rafter Ties

Keep tie in lower third of rafter

As rafters settle, their outward thrust pushes out on exterior walls. Rafter ties should be placed in the lower third of the rafter span so they have enough leverage to resist this thrust.

Courtesy of Western Wood Products Association, *Common Roof-Framing Errors*

Figure 5.25

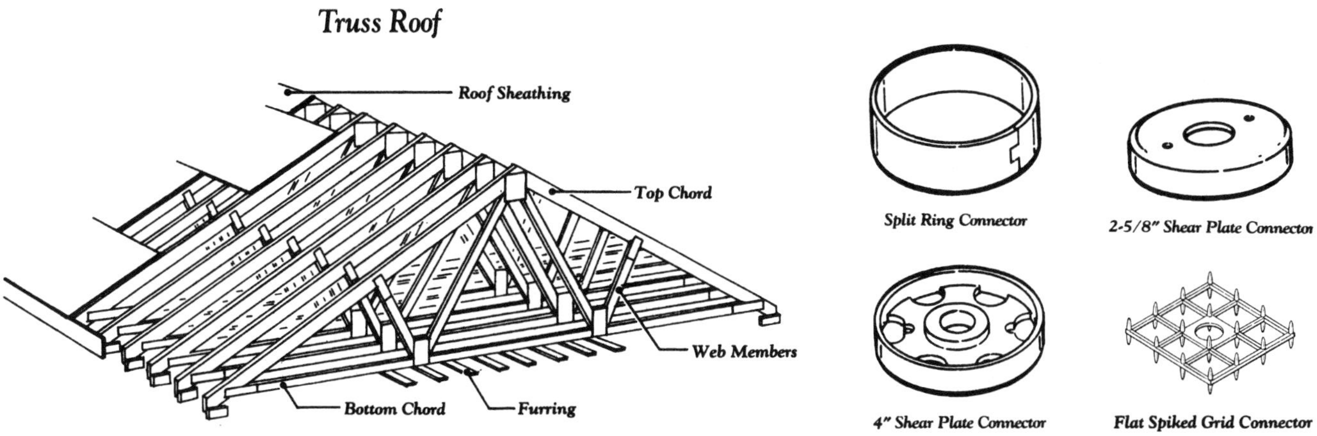

Truss Roof

R.S. Means Co., Inc., *Means Graphic Construction Standards*

Figure 5.26

Fire Blocks & Draft Stops

Industry Standards

House Framing
(Creative Homeowner Press®)

Most building codes require fire blocking — two-by stud material that runs horizontally from stud to stud — every 10 feet measured vertically in stud bays, the spaces between the studs. Fire blocking interrupts the upward flow of flames and heat. If there were no blocking and a fire started in the basement walls, it could easily and quickly reach the roof and consume the house in flames by following the unobstructed chimney-like path of the stud bays.

If you're framing typical 8-foot walls, the first-floor top plate will serve as fire blocking for the first 10 feet and the second-floor top plate for the next 10 feet. If you're building walls that extend 10 feet or more vertically without blocking of some sort, however, you must install fire blocking.

UBC — 1997

708.1 General. In combustible construction, fireblocking and draftstopping shall be installed to cut off all concealed draft openings (both vertical and horizontal) and shall form an effective barrier between floors, between a top story and a roof or attic space, and shall subdivide attic spaces, concealed roof spaces and floor-ceiling assemblies. The integrity of all fire blocks and draft stops shall be maintained.

708.2 Fire Blocks

708.2.1 Where required. Fireblocking shall be provided in the following locations:

1. In concealed spaces of stud walls and partitions, including furred spaces, at the ceiling and floor levels and at 10-foot (3048 mm) intervals both vertical and horizontal. See also Section 803, Item 1.

Exception: Fire blocks may be omitted at floor and ceiling levels when approved smoke-actuated fire dampers are installed at these levels.

2. At all interconnections between concealed vertical and horizontal spaces such as occur at soffits, drop ceilings and cove ceilings.

3. In concealed spaces between stair stringers at the top and bottom of the run and between studs along and in line with the run of stairs if the walls under the stairs are unfinished.

4. In openings around vents, pipes, ducts, chimneys, fireplaces and similar openings that afford a passage for fire at ceiling and floor levels, with noncombustible materials.

5. At openings between attic spaces and chimney chases for factory-built chimneys.

Comments

Installed fire blocks and draft stops should be checked after all wall penetrations have been made (for piping, electrical, and ductwork) and prior to installation of insulation materials. Subtrades may remove fire blocks and draft stops, not realizing that these elements are essential to code compliance.

708.2.2 Fire block construction. Except as provided in Item 4 above, fireblocking shall consist of 2 inches (51 mm) nominal lumber or two thicknesses of 1-inch (25 mm) nominal lumber with broken lap joints or one thickness of 23/32-inch (18.3 mm) wood structural panel with joints backed by 23/32-inch (18.3 mm) wood structural panel or one thickness of 3/4-inch (19.1 mm) Type 2-M particleboard with joints backed by 3/4-inch (19.1 mm) Type 2-M particleboard.

Fire blocks may also be of gypsum board, cement fiber board, batts or blankets of mineral or glass fiber, or other approved materials installed in such a manner as to be securely retained in place.

Loose-fill insulation material shall not be used as a fire block unless specifically tested in the form and manner intended for use to demonstrate its ability to remain in place and to retard the spread of fire and hot gases.

Walls having parallel or staggered studs for sound-transmission control shall have fire blocks of batts or blankets of mineral or glass fiber or other approved flexible materials.

708.3 Draft Stops

708.3.1 Where required. Draftstopping shall be provided in the locations set forth in this section.

708.3.1.1 Floor-ceiling assemblies.

708.3.1.1.1 Single-family dwellings. When there is usable space above and below the concealed space of a floor-ceiling assembly in a single-family dwelling, draft stops shall be installed so that the area of the concealed space does not exceed 1,000 square feet (93 m2). Draftstopping shall divide the concealed space into approximately equal areas.

708.3.1.1.2 Two or more dwelling units and hotels. Draft stops shall be installed in floor-ceiling assemblies of buildings having more than one dwelling unit and in hotels. Such draft stops shall be in line with walls separating individual dwelling units and guest rooms from each other and in line with walls separating individual dwelling units and guest rooms from each other and from other areas.

Attics

708.3.1.2.1 Two or more dwelling units and hotels. Draft stops shall be installed in the attics, mansards, overhangs, false fronts set out from walls and similar concealed spaces of buildings containing more than one dwelling unit and in hotels. Such draft stops shall be above and in line with the walls separating individual dwelling units and guest rooms from each other and from other uses.

Exception:

Draft stops may be omitted along one of the corridor walls, provided draft stops at walls separating individual dwelling units and guest rooms from each other and from other uses, extend to the remaining corridor draft stop.

Where approved sprinklers are installed, draftstopping may be as specified in the exception to Section 708.3.1.2.2.

708.3.1.3 Draft stop construction. Draftstopping materials shall not be less than 1/2-inch (12.7 mm) gypsum board, 3/8-inch (9.5 mm) wood structural panel, 3/8-inch (9.5 mm) Type 2-M particleboard or other approved materials adequately supported.

Openings in the partitions shall be protected by self-closing doors with automatic latches constructed as required for the partitions.

Ventilation of concealed roof spaces shall be maintained in accordance with Section 1505.

Structural Sheathing

UBC — 1997
Section 2312 — Sheathing

2312.1 Structural Floor Sheathing. Structural floor sheathing shall be designed in accordance with the general provisions of this code and the special provisions in this section.

Sheathing used as subflooring shall be designed to support all loads specified in this code and shall be capable of supporting concentrated loads of not less than 300 pounds (1334 N) without failure. The concentrated load shall be applied by a loaded disc, 3 inches (76 mm) or smaller in diameter.

Flooring, including the finish floor, underlayment and subfloor, where used, shall meet the following requirements:

1. Deflection under uniform design load limited to 1/360 of the span between supporting joists or beams.

2. Deflection of flooring relative to joists under a 1-inch-diameter (25 mm) concentrated load of 200 pounds (890 N) limited to 0.125 inch (3.2 mm) or less when loaded midway between supporting joists or beams not over 24 inches (610 mm) on center and 1/360 of the span for spans over 24 inches (610 mm).

Floor sheathing conforming to the provisions of Table 23-II-D-1, 23-II-D-2, 23-II-E-1, 23-II-F-1 or 23-II-F-2 shall be deemed to meet the requirements of this section.

Moisture changes in plywood make it expand or contract. It is very important to install the panels with a 1/8" gap at the edges and the ends.

1/8" space required at panel edges and ends unless otherwise directed by panel manufacturer.

Drawing by Keith Everhart
Figure 5.27

Comments

Sheathing Nailed to Composite Joist Flanges and Engineered Wood

Refer to manufacturers' tables for maximum spacing of nails related to specific flange size. If more than one row of nails is used, rows should be offset and nails staggered. If staples or pneumatic nails are substituted for common nails, consult manufacturer recommendations for gauge and wire size.

Roof Sheathing

Industry Standards

House Framing
(Creative Homeowner Press®)

Sheathing stabilizes the roof and provides a nailing surface for the roofing material. Roof sheathing can be 3/8 inch (only for 16-inch on-center rafters) or 1/2 inch thick (for 16- or 24-inch-on-center rafters). Plywood is the choice sheathing material, but your building code may allow less expensive nonveneer sheathing materials like oriented-strand board (OSB). Whether you use plywood or OSB, be sure that panels are APA-rated exposure 1 where you'll enclose the soffit. For open soffits, use panels marked exterior or exposure 1 of the appropriate grade to permit painting or staining. Be sure to stagger the sheathing-panel joints so the seams don't line up.

Prolonged exposure to the weather can damage the framing, so waterproof the structure as soon as possible.

Use H panel clips on panels installed on 24-inch-on-center rafters. Locate clips mid-point between the rafters. Make the panel edges flush with rafter ends and the edge of fascia rafters. Leave a 1/8-inch space between panels for expansion.

Fasten each panel using 8d common, spiral-threaded, or ring-shank nails. Space nails 6 inches apart along panel ends and 12 inches at intermediate supports. If you use a powered staple gun, use 1-1/2-inch staples for 1/2-inch plywood. Drive the staples 4 inches apart along the edges and 8 inches in the interior of the sheathing. Start the second course with a half (4x4-foot) panel. Stagger the panels by at least one rafter as you go up the roof.

UBC — 1997

2312.2 Structural Roof Sheathing. Structural roof sheathing shall be designed in accordance with sheathing shall be designed to support all loads specified in this code and shall be capable of supporting concentrated loads of not less than 300 pounds (1334 N) without failure. The concentrated load shall be applied by a loaded the general provisions of this code and the special provisions in this section. Structural roof disc, 3 inches (76 mm) or smaller in diameter. Structural roof sheathing shall meet the following requirement:

Deflection under uniform design live and dead load limited to 1/180 of the span between supporting rafters or beams and 1/240 under live load only.

Roof sheathing conforming to the provisions of Tables 23-II-D-1 and 23-II-D-2 or 23-II-E-1 and 23-II-E-2 shall be deemed to meet the requirements of this section.

Wood structural panel roof sheathing shall be bonded by intermediate or exterior glue. Wood structural panel roof sheathing exposed on the underside shall be bonded with exterior glue.

Seismic Bracing
Industry Standards
House Framing
(Creative Homeowner Press®)

Whether you are using structural reinforcement to protect against wind or earthquake, the object is to keep the various framing components somehow tied together, including connections between the sill and foundation, between the first- and second-floors, between the second floor's top plate and the rafters, and between the rafters and the ridgeboard.

There are a variety of specialized hurricane and earthquake connectors available for framing. Extended anchor bolts between the foundation and the sill are essential in areas subject to seismic forces. Between the first floor and the foundation, a hold-down anchor in the form of a metal strap is a good idea. This strap will wrap around the bottom plate, span across and attach to the sill plate, and anchor it into the foundation. If you're attaching posts to your foundation, foundation hold-downs in the form of heavy-duty L-brackets may be required.

Between the first floor's top plate and the second floor, a strap-type hold-down may also be required to tie these sections of the house together. Roof connectors or hurricane ties may be required for tying the rafters to the second floor's top plate where the frieze blocks, top plates, and rafters meet. Strap-type connectors are sometimes used to tie rafters to the ridgeboard. Between floors, some codes call for a floor-to-floor hold-down consisting of a steel rod and angle brackets, and even a 1-1/8-inch plywood gusset between floor joists. As a matter of course, codes require the use of plywood sheathing to strengthen walls. Some carpenters install plywood on both the inside and outside of first floor walls, especially if they're cripple walls, which are particularly susceptible to collapse during earthquakes.

Framing Clip

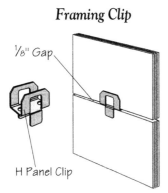

¹⁄₈" Gap

H Panel Clip

Courtesy of Creative Homeowner Press®, *House Framing*
Figure 5.28

Seismic Bracing

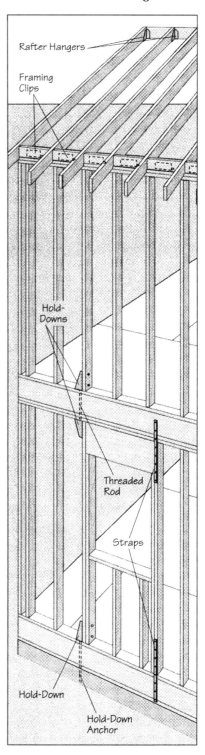

Rafter Hangers

Framing Clips

Hold-Downs

Threaded Rod

Straps

Hold-Down

Hold-Down Anchor

Seismic connectors include hangers between the ridge and rafters, framing clips between rafter blocking and top plates, hurricane hold-downs and straps between floors, straps that hold walls to rim joists, and foundation hold-downs between the first floor and the foundation.

Courtesy of Creative Homeowner Press®, *House Framing*
Figure 5.29

Comments

The UBC *Chapter 23, Division II, Part II — Requirements Applicable to Engineered Design of Wind and Earthquake Load-Resisting Systems* has provisions for interior structural wall sheathing. If the building under construction is subject to these events, check with the local building official to determine if this portion of the code is enforced. Frequently, a registered engineer is required to prepare or approve plans for buildings in these areas.

Note that both floor and roof sheathing has a maximum deflection requirement. The code also states that the use of sheathing within the span rating as stamped on the panel is deemed to meet the deflection requirement.

Plywood for use on floors or roofs will typically have two numbers separated by a slash, such as 32/16. The first number is the maximum spacing of supports for use on roofs and the second number is the maximum spacing of supports for use on floors. Plywood for use on floors is required to be tongue and groove if edge blocking is not used.

Comments

Plywood is available in two basic types: exterior, which has a 100% waterproof glueline, and interior, which has a moisture-resistant glueline. Exposure 1 panels (produced with exterior glue) can be used where the materials must resist moisture while construction is delayed or where there is some exposure of the installed material. For long-term exposure to moisture and weather conditions, only exterior-type plywood should be used.

The APA—The Engineered Wood Association has rated plywood performance as follows:

Exterior—For use in areas subject to continuous weather/moisture exposure (comparable to PS 1 as "Exterior").

Exposure 1—For use in protected situations requiring resistance to moisture for limited periods of time (e.g., construction delays); comparable to PS 1 as "Exposure 1" or "Interior" with exterior glue.

Exposure 2—For use in protected situations where there may be limited exposure to moisture, water leakage, or high humidity; (comparable to PS 1 "Interior"-type with intermediate glue).

Exterior Wall Coverings

UBC — 1997

2310.1 General. Exterior wood stud walls shall be covered on the outside with the materials and in the manner specified in this section or elsewhere in this code. Studs or sheathing shall be covered on the outside face with a weather-resistive barrier when required by Section 1402.1. Exterior wall coverings of the minimum thickness specified in this section are based on a maximum stud spacing of 16 inches (406 mm) unless otherwise specified.

2310.3 Plywood. When plywood is used for covering the exterior of outside walls, it shall be of the exterior type not less than 3/8 inch (9.5 mm) thick. Plywood panel siding shall be installed in accordance with Table 23-II-A-1.

Unless applied over 1-inch (25 mm) wood sheathing or 15/32-inch (12 mm) wood structural panel sheathing or 1/2-inch (13 mm) particleboard sheathing, joints shall occur over framing members and shall be protected with a continuous wood batten, approved caulking, flashing, vertical or horizontal shiplaps; or joints shall be lapped horizontally or otherwise made waterproof.

Section 2315 — Wood Shear Walls and Diaphragms

2315.1 General. Diaphragm sheathing nails or other approved sheathing connectors shall be driven flush but shall not fracture the surface of the sheathing.

Subfloor

UBC — 1997

2320.9.1 Lumber subfloor. Sheathing used as a structural subfloor shall conform to the limitations set forth in Tables 23-II-D-1 and 23-II-D-2.

Joints in subflooring shall occur over supports unless end-matched lumber is used, in which case each piece shall bear on at least two joists.

Subflooring may be omitted when joist spacing does not exceed 16 inches (406 mm) and 1-inch (25 mm) nominal tongue-and-groove wood strip flooring is applied perpendicular to the joists.

2320.9.2 Wood structural panels. Where used as structural subflooring, wood structural panels shall be as set forth in Tables 23-II-E-1 and 23-II-E-2. Wood structural panel combination subfloor underlayment shall have maximum spans as set forth in Table 23-II-F-1.

When wood structural panel floors are glued to joists with an adhesive in accordance with the adhesive manufacturer's directions, fasteners may be spaced a maximum of 12 inches (305 mm) on center at all supports.

Stair Framing

stairs with a concrete-framed building; steel stairs with a steel-framed building; and wood stairs with a wood-framed building.

Industry Standards
Means Graphic Construction Standards
(R.S. Means Co., Inc.)

Stairs may be prefabricated or built in place from aluminum, concrete, cast iron, steel, or wood. In many instances stairs are designed to conform to the structural framing system: concrete

Comments

See "Egress" later in this chapter for code information on stair construction. See the section titled "Wood Stairs and Railings" in Chapter 6, "Finish Carpentry & Cabinetry," for more information on stair installations, including UBC requirements.

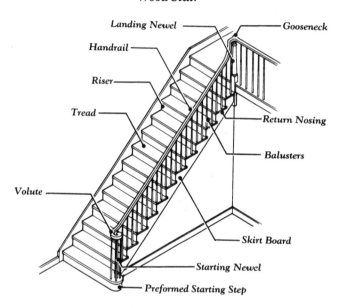

Wood Stair

Landing Newel — Gooseneck
Handrail
Riser
Tread — Return Nosing
— Balusters
Volute
— Skirt Board
— Starting Newel
Preformed Starting Step

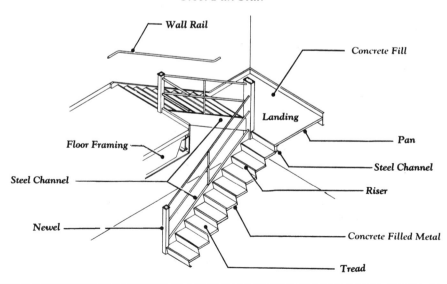

Steel Pan Stair

— Wall Rail
Concrete Fill
Landing
Floor Framing — Pan
Steel Channel — Steel Channel
Newel — Riser
— Concrete Filled Metal
— Tread

R.S. Means Co., Inc., *Means Graphic Construction Standards*
Figure 5.30

Industry Standards
Basics for Builders: Framing & Rough Carpentry
(R.S. Means Co., Inc.)

The three main dimensions in stair building are those for risers, treads, and headroom. Check for minimum clearance of 6'8" to finish straight up from line to bottom of headroom. The riser height and the tread width are usually given on the plans. You can generally use the tread width given on the plans. The riser height, however, is often not accurate enough to use.

Standard Riser and Tread Dimensions

If the riser and tread dimensions are not given on the plan, you need to calculate them. To do this, you should consider the following points:

- Make sure all risers and treads are equal, so the stairs will not cause people to fall.
- The lower the riser, the longer the tread needs to be to feel comfortable.
- Common dimensions for riser and tread are 7" rise and 10-1/2" tread.
- Use the following three rules to check to see if your stair dimensions are in the comfortable range.

    Rule 1: Two risers and one tread added should equal 24" to 25".

    Rule 2: One riser and one tread added should equal 17" to 18".

    Rule 3: Multiply one riser by one tread, and the result should equal 71" to 75".

Egress (Stairs, Ramps & Guardrails)

Comments

There are many elements to consider in providing safe access and egress to residences. In this section, we will begin with the minimum window opening for sleeping rooms, and progress to doors and stairways.

We have not included comprehensive information here on accessibility for the physically and sensorially disabled. The code and regulations vary from state to state and even from jurisdiction to jurisdiction. See UBC Chapter 11, "Accessibility," CABO/ANSI A117.1, "Accessible and Usable Buildings and Facilities," and the Americans with Disabilities Act for more information. Your local building official will provide local regulations and code requirements for your project.

This section of the code is integrated with the commercial requirements. We have extracted only the residential portions, so that the intent of the code would remain clear.

UBC — 1997
Stairways

1003.3.3.1 General. Every stairway having two or more risers serving any building or portion thereof shall comply with the requirements of Section 1003.3.3. For the purposes of Section 1003.3.3, the term "stairway" shall include stairs, landings, handrails and guardrails as applicable. Where aisles in assembly rooms have steps, they shall comply with the requirements in Section 1004.3.2.

Exception: Stairs or ladders used only to attend equipment or window wells are exempt from the requirements of this section.

For the purpose of this chapter, the term "step" shall mean those portions of the means of egress achieving a change in elevation by means of a single riser. Individual steps shall comply with the detailed requirements of this chapter that specify applicability to steps.

1003.3.3.2 Width. The width of stairways shall be determined as specified in Section 1003.2.3.

Stairways serving an occupant load less than 50 shall not be less than 36 inches (914 mm) in width.

1003.3.3.3 Rise and run. The rise of steps and stairs shall not be less than 4 inches (102 mm) nor more than 7 inches (178 mm). The greatest riser height within any flight of stairs shall not exceed the smallest by more than 3/8 inch (9.5 mm). Except as permitted in Sections 1003.3.3.8.1, 1003.3.3.8.2 and 1003.3.3.8.3, the run shall not be less than 11 inches (279 mm) as measured horizontally between the vertical planes of the furthermost projection of adjacent treads or nosings. Stair treads shall be of uniform size and shape, except the largest tread run within any flight of stairs shall not exceed the smallest by more than 3/8 inch (9.5 mm).

Exceptions:

1. Private steps and stairways serving an occupant load of less than 10 and stairways to unoccupied roofs may be constructed with an 8-inch-maximum (203 mm) rise and a 9-inch- minimum (229 mm) run.

2. Where the bottom or top riser adjoins a sloping public way, walk or driveway having an established grade (other than natural earth) and serving as a landing, the bottom or top riser may be reduced along the slope to less than 4 inches (102 mm) in height with the variation in height of the bottom or top riser not to exceed 1 unit vertical in 12 units horizontal (8.3% slope) of stairway width.

1003.3.3.4 Headroom. Every stairway shall have a headroom clearance of not less than 6 feet 8 inches (2032 mm). Such clearances shall be measured vertically from a plane parallel and tangent to the stairway tread nosings to the soffit or other construction above at all points.

1003.3.3.5 Landings. There shall be a floor or a landing at the top and bottom of each stairway or stair run. Every landing shall have a dimension measured in the direction of travel not less than the width of the stairway. Such dimension need not exceed 44 inches (1118 mm) where the stair has a straight run. At least one intermediate landing shall be provided for each 12 feet (3658 mm) of vertical stairway rise measured between the horizontal planes of adjacent landings. Landings shall be level except that exterior landings may have a slope not to exceed l/4 unit vertical in 12 units horizontal (2% slope). For landings with adjoining doors, see Section 1003.3.1.7.

Exceptions:

In Group R, Division 3, and Group U Occupancies and within individual units of Group R, Division 1 Occupancies, such length need not exceed 36 inches (914 mm) where the stair has a straight run.

Stairs serving an unoccupied roof are exempt from these requirements.

Comments

Adequate blocking must be installed during the framing to accommodate spacing of brackets and other stair-related hardware that may fall on center with framing members.

Guardrails

509.1 Where Required. Unenclosed floor and roof openings, open and glazed sides of stairways, aisles, landings and ramps, balconies or porches, which are more than 30 inches (762 mm) above grade or floor below, and roofs used for other than service of the building shall be protected by a guardrail.

509.2 Height. The top of guardrails shall not be less than 42 inches (1067 mm) in height.

Exception:

1. The top of guardrails for Group R, Division 3 and Group U, Division 1 Occupancies and interior guardrails within individual dwelling units, Group R, Division 3 congregate residences and guest rooms of Group R, Division 1 Occupancies may be 36 inches (914 mm) in height.

2. The top of guardrails for stairways, exclusive of their landings, may have a height as specified in Section 1003.3.3.6 for handrails.

509.3 Openings. Open guardrails shall have intermediate rails or an ornamental pattern such that a sphere 4 inches (102 mm) in diameter cannot pass through.

Comments

In addition to meeting the above code requirements for guardrails, it is important to anchor guardrails so that they provide adequate resistance to any potential load that may come in contact with them.

Exceptions:

1. The open space between the intermediate rails or ornamental pattern of guardrails in areas of commercial and industrial-type occupancies which are not accessible to the public may be such that a sphere 12 inches (305 mm) in diameter cannot pass through.

2. The triangular openings formed by the riser, tread and bottom element of a guardrail at the open side of a stairway may be of such size that a sphere 6 inches (152 mm) in diameter cannot pass through.

Circular Stairways

1003.3.3.8.1 Circular stairways. Circular stairways conforming to the requirements of this section may be used as a means of egress component in any occupancy. The minimum width of run shall not be less than 10 inches (254 mm) and the smaller stairway radius shall not be less than twice the width of the stairway.

1003.3.3.8.2 Winding stairways. In Group R, Division 3 Occupancies and in private stairways in Group R, Division 1 Occupancies, winding stairways may be used if the required width of run is provided at a point not more than 12 inches (305 mm) from the side of the stairway where the treads are narrower, but in no case shall the width of run be less than 6 inches (152 mm) at any point.

1003.3.3.8.3 Spiral stairways. In Group R, Division 3 Occupancies and in private stairways within individual units of Group R, Division 1 Occupancies, spiral stairways may be installed. A spiral stairway is a stairway having a closed circular form in its plan view with uniform section shaped treads attached to and radiating about a minimum diameter supporting column. Such stairways may be used as a required means of egress component where the area served is limited to 400 square feet (37.16 m^2).

The tread shall provide a clear walking area measuring at least 26 inches (660 mm) from the outer edge of the supporting column to the inner edge of the handrail. The effective tread is delineated by the nosing radius line, the exterior arc (inner edge of railing) and the overlap radius line (nosing radius line of tread above).

Effective tread dimensions are taken along a line perpendicular to the center line of the tread. A run of at least 7-1/2 inches (191 mm) shall be provided at a point 12 inches (305 mm) from where the tread is the narrowest. The rise shall be sufficient to provide a headroom clearance of not less than

6 feet 6 inches (1981 mm); however, such rise shall not exceed 9-1/2 inches (241 mm).

1003.3.3.9 Interior stairway construction. Interior stairways shall be constructed based on type of construction requirements as specified in Sections 602.4, 603.4, 604.4, 605.4 and 606.4.

Except where enclosed usable space under stairs is prohibited by Section 1005.3.3.6, the walls and soffits of such enclosed space shall be protected on the enclosed side as required for one-hour, fire-resistive construction.

Stairways exiting directly to the exterior of a building four or more stories in height shall be provided with a means for emergency entry for fire department access. (See the Fire Code.)

Access

UBC — 1997

1004.2.3.1 General. Exits shall be provided from each building level. Additionally, access to such exits shall be provided from all occupied areas within building levels. The maximum number of exits required from any story, basement or individual space shall be maintained until arrival at grade or the public way.

1004.2.3.2 From individual floors. For the purposes of Section 1004.2, floors, stories, occupied roofs, mezzanines, and similar designations of building levels other than basements shall be considered synonymous.

Every occupant on the first story shall have access to not less than one exit and not less than two exits when required by Table 10-A. Every occupant in basements and on stories other than the first story shall have access to not less than two exits.

Exceptions:

1. Second stories having an occupant load less than 10 may be provided with access to only one exit.

2. Two or more dwelling units on the second story or in a basement may have access to only one exit where the total occupant load served by that exit does not exceed 10.

3. Except as provided in Table 10-A, access to only one exit need be provided from the second floor or a basement within an individual dwelling unit or a Group R, Division 3 congregate residence.

4. Where the third floor within an individual dwelling unit or a Group R, Division 3 congregate residence does not exceed 500 square feet (46.45 m2), access to only one exit need be provided from that floor.

5. Occupied roofs on Group R, Division 3 Occupancies may have access to only one exit where such occupied areas are less than 500 square feet (46.45 m2) and are located no higher than immediately above the second story.

1004.2.3.3 From individual spaces. All occupied portions of the building shall have access to not less than one exit or exit-access doorway.

1006.3.5 Exit courts.

1006.3.5.1 General. Exit courts serving as a portion of the exit discharge in the means of egress system shall comply with the requirements of Section 1006.3.5. An exit court is a court or yard that provides access to a public way for one or more required exits.

1006.3.5.2 Width. The width of exit courts shall be determined as specified in Section 1003.2.3, but such width shall be not less than 44 inches (1118 mm), except as specified herein. Exit courts serving Group R, Division 3 and Group U Occupancies shall not be less than 36 inches (914 mm) in width.

The required width of exit courts shall be unobstructed to a height of 7 feet (2134 mm).

Exception: Doors, when fully opened, and handrails shall not reduce the required width by more than 7 inches (178 mm). Doors in any position shall not reduce the required width by more than one half. Other nonstructural projections such as trim and similar decorative features may project into the required width 1-1/2 inches (38 mm) from each side.

Where an exit court exceeds the minimum required width and the width of such exit court is then reduced along the path of exit travel, the reduction in width shall be gradual. The transition in width shall be affected by a guardrail not less than 36 inches (914 mm) in height and shall not create an angle of more than 30 degrees with respect to the axis of the exit court along the path of exit travel. In no case shall the width of the exit court be less than the required minimum.

Garages

UBC — 1997

Section 312 — Requirements for Group U Occupancies

312.1 Group U Occupancies Defined. Group U Occupancies shall include buildings or structures, or portions thereof, and shall be:

Division 1. Private garages, carports, sheds and agricultural buildings.

312.2 Construction, Height and Allowable Area.

Comments

In this section, we have organized the information as follows:

First, the code definition of a residential garage and carport. Then, the required separation from a residence, fire blocking, and draft stops.

Note that a home with an attached garage is considered mixed-occupancy, as it is Group U Division 1 (Garage) and Group R Division 3 (Dwelling).

312.2.1 General. Buildings or parts of buildings classed as Group U, Division 1 Occupancies because of the use or character of the occupancy shall not exceed 1,000 square feet (92.9 m²) in area or one story in height except as provided in Section 312.2.2.

Any building or portion thereof that exceeds the limitations specified in this chapter shall be classed in the occupancy group other than Group U, Division 1 that it most nearly resembles.

312.2.2 Special area provisions. The total area of a private garage used only as a parking garage for private or pleasure-type motor vehicles where no repair work is done or fuel dispensed may be 3,000 square feet (279 m²), provided the provisions set forth in Item 1 or 2 are satisfied. More than one 3,000-square-foot (279 m²) Group U, Division 1 Occupancy may be within the same building, provided each 3,000-square-foot (279 m²) area is separated by area separation walls complying with Section 504.6.

For a mixed-occupancy building, the exterior wall and opening protection for the Group U, Division 1 portion of the building shall be as required for the major occupancy of the building. For such mixed-occupancy building, the allowable floor area of the building shall be as permitted for the major occupancy contained therein.

For a building containing only a Group U, Division 1 Occupancy, the exterior wall and opening protection shall be as required for a building classified as a Group R, Division 1 Occupancy.

312.4 Special Hazards. Chimneys and heating apparatus shall conform to the requirements of Chapter 31 and the Mechanical Code.

Under no circumstances shall a private garage have any opening into a room used for sleeping purposes.

Mixed Use

Ed. Note: The following excerpt from the Uniform Building Code *includes only those items that are relevant to residential or light commercial construction.*

UBC — 1997

302.1 General. When a building is used for more than one occupancy purpose, each part of the building comprising a distinct "occupancy," as described in Section 301, shall be separated from any other occupancy as specified in Section 302.4.

Exceptions:

3. An occupancy separation need not be provided between a Group R, Division 3 Occupancy and a carport having no enclosed uses above, provided the carport is entirely open on two or more sides.

302.2 Forms of Occupancy Separations. Occupancy separations shall be vertical or horizontal or both or, when necessary, of such other form as may be required to afford a complete separation between the various occupancy divisions in the building.

Where the occupancy separation is horizontal, structural members supporting the separation shall be protected by equivalent fire-resistive construction.

302.3 Types of Occupancy Separations. Occupancy separations shall be classed as "four-hour fire-resistive," "three-hour fire-resistive," "two-hour fire-resistive" and "one-hour fire-resistive."

4. A one-hour fire-resistive occupancy separations shall not be of less than one-hour fire-resistive construction. All openings in such separation shall be protected by a fire assembly having a one-hour fire-protection rating.

302.4 Fire Ratings for Occupancy Separations. Occupancy separations shall be provided between the various groups and divisions of occupancies as set forth in Table 3–B. For required separation of specific uses in Group I, Division 1 hospitals and nursing homes, see Table 3–C. See also Section 504.6.1.

Exceptions:

3. In the one-hour occupancy separation between Group R, Division 3 and Group U Occupancies, the separation may be limited to the installation of materials approved for one-hour fire-resistive construction on the garage side and a self-closing, tightfitting solid-wood door 1-3/8 inches (35 mm) in thickness, or a self-closing, tightfitting door having a fire-protection rating of not less than 20 minutes when tested in accordance with Part II of UBC Standard 7–2, which is a part of this code, is permitted in lieu of a one-hour fire assembly. Fire dampers need not be installed in air ducts passing through the wall, floor or ceiling separating a Group R, Division 3 Occupancy from a Group U Occupancy, provided such ducts within the Group U Occupancy are constructed of steel having a thickness not less than 0.019 inch (0.48 mm) (No. 26 galvanized sheet gage) and have no openings into the Group U Occupancy.

Comments

A carport open on two or more sides does not need an occupancy separation. However, Section 302.4, Exception 3 (above), clearly defines the required separation between home and attached garage. Section 302.2 stipulates that when a home extends above a garage, a one-hour fire assembly is required on the ceilings of the garage.

Note that a garage may not have any opening into a room used for sleeping.

310.7 Efficiency Dwelling Units. An efficiency dwelling unit shall conform to the requirements of the code except as herein provided:

1. The unit shall have a living room of not less than 220 square feet (20.4 m²) of superficial floor area. An additional 100 square feet (9.3 m²) of superficial floor area shall be provided for each occupant of such unit in excess of two.

2. The unit shall be provided with a separate closet.

3. The unit shall be provided with a kitchen sink, cooking appliance and refrigeration facilities, each having a clear working space of not less than 30 inches (762 mm) in front. Light and ventilation conforming to this code shall be provided.

4. The unit shall be provided with a separate bathroom containing a water closet, lavatory and bathtub or shower.

Hurricane and Earthquake Resistance

Comments

See "Nails, Fasteners & Bolts" and "Seismic Bracing" earlier in this chapter for more information on framing in seismic and hurricane-prone areas.

Industry Recommendations
Building Strong Walls with Plywood and OSB
(APA — The Engineered Wood Association)

When a high wind or earthquake strikes a house, the brunt of the forces hit the walls and roof. That's why the construction of the walls and roof is particularly important to a building's overall strength. In walls, wind and seismic forces can be resisted by shear walls that are composed of wood structural sheathing fastened to wood framing and properly connected to the foundation below and roof above. Similarly, the installation of wood structural panels over roof or floor supports creates a diaphragm — a flat structural unit that acts like a deep, thin beam — that resists forces. The overall strength of a building is a function of all the walls, roof, floor, and foundation, and how those key components are tied together.

Industry Recommendations
Introduction to Lateral Design
(APA — The Engineered Wood Association)

Lateral loads are those that act in a direction parallel to the ground. The two major contributors to lateral load are high winds, such as those from a hurricane, and seismic (earthquake) forces.

The structure must be designed to withstand lateral loads in two directions at right angles to each other. As a result, three separate load designs must be calculated for every building: one vertical load design and two lateral load designs (one for each direction). Then, the load capacity of all major building elements and *every* connection between each element must be calculated to make sure each has the capacity to resist all three loads and transfer lateral and vertical forces between them.

Correct lateral design, however, is essential. A building that has not been specifically designed and built to resist lateral loads will likely collapse when subjected to these forces.

The elements of a wood-framed building that enable it to withstand lateral forces are *shear walls* and *diaphragms*. These elements must be designed to resist the lateral loads applied, and connections between elements must be strong enough to transfer the loads between elements.

Shear Walls and Diaphragms

Wind and seismic forces are resisted by *shear walls* that are composed of wood structural sheathing fastened to wood framing, properly connected to the foundation below and the roof above. Similarly, the installation of wood structural panels over a roof or floor supports creates a *diaphragm*, a flat structural unit that acts like a deep, thin beam that resists lateral forces.

Shear walls and diaphragms are building elements necessary for proper lateral design. Aside from the fact that a shear wall is vertical and the diaphragm is horizontal (or nearly horizontal), they are essentially the same kind of structural element. A diaphragm is designed as a simply supported beam while the shear wall is designed like a vertical, cantilevered diaphragm.

A diaphragm acts in a manner similar to a deep I-beam or girder, where the panels act as a "web" resisting shear, while the diaphragm edge members perform the function of flanges, resisting bending stresses. These edge members are commonly called *chords* in diaphragm design, and may be joists, ledgers, trusses, etc.

Engineered versus Prescriptive Requirements

Current model building codes allow the designer to use either of two methods to design light frame wood structures. Both are appropriate for detached one and two family dwellings as well as many other wood structures. These two methods are by the use of *engineering design* or *prescriptive* requirements.

Chapter 16 of the current editions of all three major model building codes is the chapter that provides the information required to *engineer* a structure, the design-based requirements. This chapter provides all of the vertical and horizontal design loads (gravity, snow, wind, seismic impact, construction, live and dead loads, etc.) that must be considered when doing an engineering design of *any type* of structure covered by the building codes.

This data must be interpreted by a designer or engineer whose responsibility it is to provide all of the details necessary to resist the applied loads.

The wood chapter of each of the three model building codes (Chapter 23 in all three) contains *prescriptive requirements* for the design of wood structures. Prescriptive requirements provide a "cookbook" method for the design of wood structures within certain limitations. They tell the designer what size and grade lumber to use for the different applications, what anchor bolt spacing to use, what size joists to use for various floor spans, the fastening schedule for all applications, etc. Because prescriptive requirements ignore specific factors such as the actual geometry of the structure, actual loads seen by the structure and their location, this design method is limited

for use in locations with low wind and minimal risk of seismic activity.

Bracing versus Shear Walls

The design method chosen, engineered or prescriptive, will determine whether shear walls or wall bracing are used to provide lateral bracing and resistance in the structure.

In the process of designing a "box-type" structure, as the great majority of all residences are, the engineer/designer will find that he or she must provide a number of vertical wall elements designed to resist the horizontal forces acting on the building (earthquake, wind or both). The elements used in a box-type structure to resist lateral loads are *shear walls*. These shear walls also act as interior and exterior walls, load bearing and non-load bearing walls required to meet the architectural goals of the building as well as the requirements of other design loads.

While shear walls may look similar to other walls, they often contain a number of important differences, including:

- Additional base shear anchor bolts in the bottom plate (the size and number may be different from the prescriptive requirements of the code).

- Holddown anchors at each end of the shear wall.

- Tighter-than-conventional nailing of the sheathing/siding.

- Thicker-than-conventional sheathing/siding.

- Different framing grades, species and sizes.

- Limitations on the placement of the shear wall segments (e.g., shear walls on upper floors must be placed directly over shear walls below).

- Special fastening requirements at the top of the shear wall elements to insure load transfer from the roof/floor diaphragm into the shear wall.

When the building is designed using *prescriptive requirements*, lateral forces are resisted by *wall bracing* instead of by shear walls. This wall bracing must be placed at prescribed locations throughout the structure: e.g., "located at each corner and at every 25 ft (7620 mm) of each exterior wall" (taken from Table 2308.2.2A of the 1994 SBC). While these bracing panels serve the same function as the engineered shear wall — provide resistance to the lateral forces acting on the structure — they have few elements in common with the shear walls described above. Their lack of detailing severely limits the strength and stiffness of the wall bracing when compared with an engineered shear wall. For this reason, wall bracing is relegated to low-load situations.

What Is Wall Bracing?

The codes give various options. Most commonly used: one "unit" of wall bracing could be 4 lineal feet of studs sheathed with wood structural panels, 8 lineal feet of studs sheathed with gypsum board, 8 lineal feet of wall containing a let-in brace at 45 degrees (limited to single story or second story of a two story building), etc.

Comments

See the "Roof Framing," "Fasteners" and "Structural Sheathing" sections of this chapter for more information on hurricane and seismic framing requirements. For detailed technical data on seismic, hurricane, and high-wind areas, consult the UBC, Volume 2, Chapter 16, Divisions III and IV.

Allowable Tolerances

Industry Standards
Handbook of Construction Tolerances
(The McGraw-Hill Companies)
Wall Framing
6-6. Rough Lumber Framing

Description

Rough lumber framing includes posts, beams, joists, rafters, studs, and other wood framing for residential or commercial construction. It also includes glued laminated timber and heavy timber construction.

Allowable Tolerances

There is not a single, fixed standard for rough lumber framing tolerances. Various documents and industry practices refer to a variety of measurements. In most cases, positional tolerances of framing members of dimensional lumber [less than 5 in. (127 mm) in nominal dimension] are not critical for the application of finish materials. A tolerance of +/- 1/4 in. (6 mm) is frequently used and is acceptable. For heavy timber construction a tolerance of +/- 1/2 in. (13 mm) is often used. However, plumbness tolerance is important because out-of-plumb walls and partitions can be noticeable and can affect the successful application of many finish materials. The *Quality Standards for the Professional Remodeler* and the Insurance/Warranty Documents require that walls be plumb to within 1/4 in. (6 mm) in any 32-in. (813-mm) vertical measurement. However, a smaller tolerance of 1/4 in. in 10 ft (6 mm in 3050 mm) is often recommended for gypsum wallboard and plaster applications. For gypsum wallboard application, the maximum misalignment of adjacent framing members must not exceed 1/8 in. (3.2 mm).

A tolerance of 1/4 in. in 10 ft provides a reasonable tolerance for carpenters while allowing gypsum wallboard to be installed without excessive shimming when tighter tolerances of the wallboard surface are required. For example, if a 1/8 in. in 8 ft (3.2 mm in 2440 mm) plumbness is required for a thin-set mortar application of ceramic tile, the gypsum board can be

shimmed from a 1/4-in. tolerance to the 1/8-in. tolerance. However, most wallboard contractors prefer not to shim, so the specifier may want to require that the smaller tolerance be built into the framing specifications.

Floor Framing
6-7. Wood Floor Framing and Subflooring

Description

This section includes wood fools framed with standard wood joists and covered with sub-flooring of plywood, particleboard, or other sheet material as a base for underlayment and other finish flooring.

Allowable Tolerances

As with rough framing, there is no single accepted tolerance for flatness of wood subfloors. In most cases, the required level depends on the type of finish surface used and other considerations, such as whether factory built cabinets will be placed on an uneven floor, requiring shimming. In general, a level tolerance of +/-1/4 in. in 10 ft (6 mm in 3050 mm) for new construction is a reasonable expectation and is less than the maximum allowable deflection (L/240 for dead and live load) stated by the Uniform Building Code. It also allows for slight misalignments of supporting members. However, the *Quality Standards for the Professional Remodeler* and Insurance/Warranty Documents state a more generous maximum out-of-level tolerance of 1/4 in. in 32 in. (O mm in 813 mm) measured parallel to the joists. For total variation in a floor surface of a room, the Quality Standards for the Professional Remodeler state a tolerance of +/-1/2 in. in 20 ft (13 mm in 6100 mm) while the recommended specification of the Spectext master specifications is 1/2 in. in 30 ft (13 mm in 9144 mm).

If the floor framing is also supporting a gypsum wallboard ceiling below, the Gypsum Association requires that deflection not exceed L/240 of the span at full design load, where L is the span. In addition, the fastening surface of adjacent joists should not vary by more than 1/8 in. (3mm).

As with other rough framing, if a smaller tolerance than those mentioned above is required for finish materials, such as ceramic tile or wood flooring, it should be specified.

Comments

For further information on wood floor framing tolerances, see Sections 3–1 through 3–4 in Residential Construction Performance Guidelines, *published by the National Association of Home Builders (Telephone: 1-800-368-5242).*

Panelized Roof

The panelized roof is primarily used on commercial warehouse buildings. It is an engineered lightweight wood assembly to create wide spans with minimum cost. There are is no standard design criteria that can be used without engineering because of the nature of the individual design and locale.

This application commonly uses glue lam beams to form a grid. These grids are then broken into smaller grids with purlins, usually 4x dimensional beams. The fill between the purlins is usually comprised of 2x subpurlins dropped into hangers

and covered with plywood sheathing. These panels can be assembled on the ground and dropped by crane into the supporting hangars in module.

Areas that support mechanical equipment must have additional stiffening and load transfer.

These roofs are usually very lightweight and will deflect some from live load. Drainage is critical as excessive water buildup may cause a catastrophic failure of the roofing members. Consideration should be made on roofing materials and roof design to allow for flexing especially at curbs and parapets.

Framing Tolerances

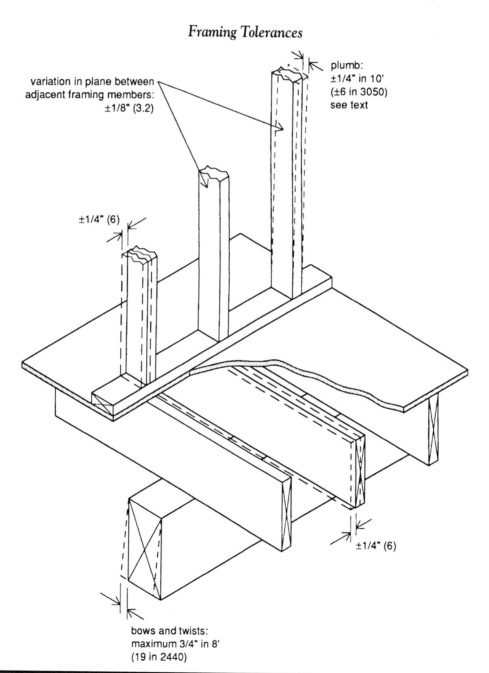

variation in plane between adjacent framing members: ±1/8" (3.2)

plumb: ±1/4" in 10' (±6 in 3050) see text

±1/4" (6)

±1/4" (6)

bows and twists: maximum 3/4" in 8' (19 in 2440)

Courtesy of The McGraw-Hill Companies, *Handbook of Construction Tolerances*

Figure 5.31

CHAPTER

6

FINISH CARPENTRY & CABINETRY

Table of Contents

(continued on next page)

Text in blue print indicates excerpts from model building code(s). "Comments" (in solid blue boxes) were written by the editors, based on their own experience.

For building product information, use this book's special Internet gateway to thousands of manufacturers: www.rsmeans.com/prodsupp/rlstand.html

CHAPTER 6

FINISH CARPENTRY & CABINETRY

Common Defect Allegations

Generally, there is a statute of limitations on patent defects of between two and five years, depending on the nature of the failure. Patent defects are observable, as opposed to latent defects, which are concealed. Since patent defects are generally conspicuous, they tend to be handled as part of the punch list after initial occupancy. Claims are often associated with water or flood and are related to particleboard expansion. Particleboard is, in fact, an acceptable material in all grades of cabinetry, contrary to some opinion.

Other claims may involve gaps at mitered or non-mitered trim and moulding joints, visible nails or nail holes (usually considered a defect in painting and finishing), and visible hammer marks on interior trim.

Cabinet installation defects include gaps between cabinet and wall, or failure of doors or drawers to operate properly. Countertop issues include scratched surfaces, delamination, and installation out of level.

Introduction

Finish carpentry and wood cabinetry are categorized under Finishes and Furnishings and are not usually associated with the structural integrity of a building. Consequently, building codes have very little to address in these areas. Standards for these aspects of construction are, therefore, set primarily by professional associations and published textbooks.

This chapter provides standards for finish carpentry and cabinetry, mostly from those developed by the Architectural Woodwork Institute, the Woodwork Institute of California, and the National Kitchen & Bath Association. The Kitchen Cabinet Manufacturers Association also provides a standard for cabinet manufacture. The addresses of all these organizations are given below as a source of further information.

Architectural Woodwork Institute
1952 Isaac Newton Square West
Reston, VA 20190
Telephone: 703-733-0600
www.awinet.org

AWI's mission is to improve industry standards, provide technical help for design professionals, and research new and better materials and methods for engineering, fabricating, finishing, and installing fine architectural woodwork. AWI has published *Architectural Woodwork Quality Standards Illustrated*, 7th Edition, which includes specifications and specifically defines quality grades for architectural woodwork. The AWI Quality Standards have been used for over 35 years by owners' representatives for the specification of architectural woodwork.

The *Architectural Woodwork Institute* has established and defined three grades of quality for wood finishes and woodwork: Economy, Custom, and Premium. When AWI standards are referenced in the specifications, but no grade is specified, AWI Custom Grade Standards are considered the Prevailing Grade. Economy is defined as "areas out of public view, such as mechanical rooms"; Custom as "high quality, appropriate for most jobs"; and Premium as "special jobs with exceptional requirements."

AWI members include manufacturers who own a mill and woodworking equipment, supplier/vendors, and affiliates.

Woodwork Institute of California (WIC)
P.O. Box 980247
West Sacramento, CA 95798-0247
Telephone: 916-372-9943
www.wicnet.org

WIC also defines quality grades (materials and installation requirements) for architectural woodwork, with particular emphasis on cabinetry and millwork. WIC's grades are included in this chapter.

National Kitchen & Bath Association (NKBA)
687 Willow Grove Street
Hackettstown, NJ 07840
Telephone: 908-852-0033
www.nkba.org
The National Kitchen & Bath Association (NKBA) has a certification program "to test minimum competencies on all topics that are pertinent" to a kitchen and bath designer's or distributor's job. The exams are based primarily on the NKBA's installation manuals, technical manuals, and universal planning books. NKBA's *Kitchen & Bathroom Installation Manuals* detail methods of kitchen and bathroom installation. Call 800-843-6522 for order information.

Kitchen Cabinet Manufacturers Association (KCMA)
1899 Preston White Drive
Reston, VA 20191
Telephone: 703-264-1690
www.kcma.org

Ed. Note: Comments and recommendations within this chapter are not intended as a definitive resource for construction activities. For building projects, contractors must rely on the project documents and applicable code requirements pertaining to their own particular locations.

Finish Carpentry

Comments

*Finish carpentry involves the installation of finish woods (and trim made of plastic or molded polyurethane materials) to provide a finished appearance to installed doors, windows, stairs, and other features of a structure's interior. Elements include **casing** (the trim around window perimeters and the sides and head of doors), **baseboard** (the trim around the base perimeter of rooms) and (for stairs) **railings**, **newel posts**, **balusters**, **skirt boards** and **cheek boards**. Interior trim installations also include **cornice moulding**, **chair rails**, **columns**, **mantels**, **grilles**, **louvers**, **paneling**, and **shelving**.*

Contractors should find information on the location, size, type and proposed arrangement of interior finish carpentry items on the project drawings — particularly the interior elevations and wall sections. Details are often provided to clarify a section of work.

Ed. Note: "Cabinetry, Millwork, & Countertops," the second section of this chapter, contains an excerpt from the Woodwork Institute of California. To maintain its continuity, we have left this WIC text intact, rather than breaking out references such as "Trim" and "Shelving" and combining them with information presented under those headings in the first section. We recommend referring to both "Finish Carpentry" and "Cabinetry, Millwork & Countertops" for the most complete perspective on architectural woodwork items.

Storage of Materials & Timing of Installation

Ed. Note: See also "Cabinetry, Millwork & Countertops" later in this chapter, which provides the Woodwork Institute of California's guidelines for delivery and storage of casework and countertops.

Comments

In regions with high humidity, wood trim, paneling and doors should be allowed 24 hours to acclimate the material to the ambient humidity before installation.

No interior finish work should begin before the structure has been closed in and protected by a waterproof roof. Windows and doors should be in place (or openings at least temporarily closed) in order to control humidity and temperature.

Wood materials intended for use as trim should not be stored in an excessively moist environment. If job conditions are damp, materials should be delivered close to the time they will be installed. Prefinished materials require extra care in storage and handling.

Following is the order in which finish carpentry items are typically performed.

- *Install trim window openings, mouldings (except base), stair rails and stairs.*
- *Install cabinets, interior doors and trim, and wood flooring. (Wood flooring may be installed before or after the cabinets.)*
- *Install hardware. (If painting will follow, hardware may be fit, then removed for painting, then permanently installed.)*

Standing and Running Trim

Comments

Interior trim (finish) is generally broken into two categories:

- ***Standing trim*** — *such as window and door casings — which can be created using single lengths of wood.*
- ***Running trim*** — *trim of continuing length — such as baseboard, cornices, chair rail, and shoe moulding.*

The applications of trim are not structural in nature, but proper installation may contribute to the integrity of the building element they serve to enhance. A door or window casing, when correctly applied, becomes an integral part of the assembly and can extend the utility of the unit.

AWI's publication Architectural Woodwork Quality Standards Illustrated provides standards for sawing and planing, and also recommends methods of cutting that will not only make cost-effective use of materials, but also reduce stress on the finished component, thereby reducing the chance of twisting, warping and bowing. AWI's standards also describe their recommended methods for creating radius mouldings.

Figures 6.1–6.4 are tables showing AWI's standards for material and workmanship for moulding installation, custom cabinetry tightness and flushness of plant-assembled joints, and field-assembled joints.

Standing & Running Trim: Standards for Material & Workmanship

Materials

Hardwood members exceeding dimensions defined in Section 100 may be glued for width and thickness.

If total length exceeds the available length of the species as defined in Section 100, members can have plant-prepared joints for field assembly. Unless otherwise specified or detailed, the following standards shall apply:

	Premium		Custom		Economy	
	Transparent	Opaque	Transparent	Opaque	Transparent	Opaque
Lumber Grade	I	II	II	II	II	II
Cut of Lumber	Plain sawn	Plain sawn or MDF*	Plain sawn	Plain sawn or MDF*	Plain sawn	Plain sawn or MDF*

Workmanship

	Premium	Custom	Economy
Finger-jointed lengths	Not permitted	Not permitted	Permitted
Exposed End (Return)	Plant Made	Not Req'd	Not Req'd
Win Non Exposed Ends*	Backed Out	Backed Out	Flat Back
Plant Assembly of Trim Members (Must be Specified)	Lemon Spline, Scarf or Dowel	Clamp Nails	Not Required
Factory Manufactured Radius Mouldings	Factory shaped and glued to longest practical lengths, for installation with smooth transitions.		Not Required
Minimum Lengths	Lengths of trim pieces are governed by material availability. Consult Section 100 for data.		

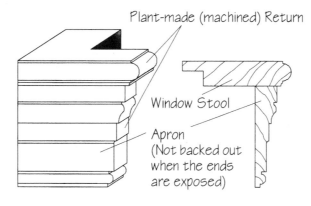

Plant-made (machined) Return

Window Stool

Apron
(Not backed out when the ends are exposed)

Machined Return

*Medium Density Fiberboard

Courtesy of Architectural Woodwork Institute, *Architectural Woodwork Quality Standards Illustrated [Tables 300-S-2 and 300-S-3]*

Figure 6.1

Table of Section Installation Standards

Section Standards - Apply to Specific Sections of Work	Premium	Custom	Economy
For All Sections - Up to any height			
Filling nail and /or screw holes unfinished work	No	No	No
Electrical/telephone/mechanical/plumbing	No	No	No
Grounds and /or blocking inside partitions or ceiling	No	No	No
Caulking to fill for wall and/or ceiling imperfections	No	No	No
Site finishing of unfinished work	No	No	No
Exposed or capped fasteners on exposed HPDL surfaces	No, except exposed access panels		Yes
Plumb and level within 1/8" in 96" tolerance, normal site	Yes	Yes	No
Allow wood products to acclimatize to area 72 hours	Yes	Yes	Yes
Standing and Running Trim (Section 300) - Up to 118" [3 m] above finished floor etc.			
Exposed end returns profiled or mitered	Yes	Yes	No
Back prime unfinished trim before installation (if specified at bid)	Yes	Yes	Yes
Joints staggered on multi-member trims	Yes	Yes	No
Trim installed in maximum available lengths	Yes	Yes	No
Running joints to be diagonal or "scarf" joints	Yes*	Recommended	No
unless a properly executed doweled, biscuit, or spline butt joint is less conspicuous, more sound or required due to site conditions.			
Miters over 4" long splined or doweled with glue	Yes	Recommended	No
Blind nailing and concealed fastening	When practical	No	No
Exposed wood base scribed (if specified at bid)	Yes	Yes	Yes
Cope inside corners, moulded trim	Yes	No	No
Miter inside corners, moulded trim	No	Yes	Yes
Custom Cabinetry (Section 400) - Up to 118" [3 m] above finished floor, etc.			
Base and/or toe kick scribed to uneven floor	Yes	No	No
Cabinets installed end-to-end with countersunk fasteners	Yes	No	No
Harware installed neatly with no tear out of surrounding	Yes	Yes	No
Exposed surfaces scribed to wall with scribe strip	Yes	No	No
Exposed surfaces trimmed to wall with overlay trim	Yes	Yes	No
Cabinets mounted plumb and square w/ adequate screws	Yes	Yes	Yes
Doors and drawers meet gap tolerances, work smoothly	Yes	Yes	Yes
Wall & Base cabinets fastened thru back and/or cleat	Yes	Yes	Yes
Semi-Exp. countersunk fasteners filled/color matched	Yes	Yes	No
Open cabinets installed by concealed methods	Yes	No	No
Countertops and splashes scribed to wall and anchored	Yes	No	No
Loose joints in tops secured with mechanical fasteners	Yes	Yes	No
Paneling (Section 500) - Up to 118" [3 m] above finished floor, etc.			
Paneling shall be factory finished	Recommended to specifier		No
Back of all panels shall be sealed, minimum 2 coats	Yes	Recommended	No
Grounds set plumb and true	Yes	Yes	Yes
Flush Panels hung on aluminum clips or wood grounds	Yes	Yes	No
Ceiling reveal, maximum	3/4"	1"	No limit
Expansion joints/reveals = ±1/16" per 4'-0" elevation	Yes	Yes	Yes
Stile and Rail Panel hung w/ screws	Hidden	Hidden	Site option
Loose joints between sections doweled/splined, no glue	Yes	Yes	No

Courtesy of Architectural Woodwork Institute, *Architectural Woodwork Quality Standards Illustrated, [Table 1700-S-3]*

Figure 6.2

Tightness and Flushness of Plant Assembled Joints

Plant Assembled Joint Table	Premium		Custom		Economy	
	Interior	**Exterior**	**Interior**	**Exterior**	**Interior**	**Exterior**
Maximum Gap: Test A	.015" wide by 20% of joint length	.025" wide by 30% of joint length	.025" wide by 20% of joint length	.050" wide by 30% of joint length	.050" wide by 20% of joint length	.075" wide by 30% of joint length
Maximum Gap: Test B* *typographical correction made-7th ed. 2nd printing	.015" x 3", and no gap may occur within 72" of a similar gap	.025" x 6", and no gap may occur within 30" of a similar gap	.025" x 6", and no gap may occur within 60" of a similar gap	.050" x 8", and no gap may occur within 26" of a similar gap	.050" x 8", and no gap may occur within 48" of a similar gap	.075" x 10", and no gap may occur within 24" of a similar gap
Maximum Gap: Test C	.015"	.025"	.025"	.050"	.050"	.075"
Flushness Variation	.001"	.015"	.005"	.025"	.025"	.050"

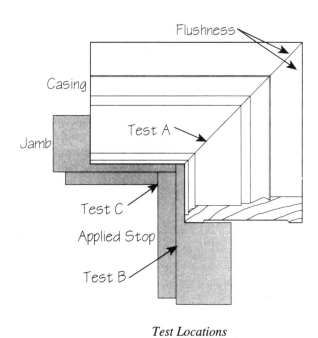

Test Locations

Courtesy of Architectural Woodwork Institute, *Architectural Woodwork Quality Standards Illustrated [Table 300-S-5]*

Figure 6.3

Field Joints: Table of General Installation Standards

Grade and Description	Smoothness minimum	Sanding cross scratch (by finish type)		Flushness Variation	Gap Width	Gap Length
General Standards - Apply to all Sections of Work						
		Transparent	Opaque	Max. allowed	Max. allowed	Max. allowed
Field Joints Wood-to-Wood - Up to 118" [3 m] above finished floor, balcony, deck or walkway customarily exposed to view and open to the building occupants and/or general public						
Premium Grade						
Flat Surface	150 grit	None	.025" [.65 mm]	.012" [.3 mm]	.012" [.3 mm]	30% joint
Shaped Surface	120 grit	.025" [.65 mm]	.050" [1.2 mm]	.025" [.65 mm]	.025" [.65 mm]	30% joint
Custom Grade						
Flat Surface	120 grit	None	.025" [.65 mm]	.025" [.65 mm]	.025" [.65 mm]	30% joint
Shaped Surface	20 KCPI	*	*	.050" [1.2 mm]	.050" [1.2 mm]	30% joint
Economy Grade						
Flat Surface	15 KCPI	*	*	.050" [1.2 mm]	.050" [1.2 mm]	30% joint
Shaped Surface	15 KCPI	*	*	.075" [1.9 mm]	.075" [1.9 mm]	30% joint
Field Joints Wood-to-Non-Wood - Up to 118" [3 m] above finished floor, balcony, deck or walkway customarily exposed to view and open to the building occupants and/or general public						
Premium Grade						
Flat Surface	*	*	*	.025" [.65 mm]	.025" [.65 mm]	30% joint
Shaped Surface	*	*	*	.050" [1.2 mm]	.050" [1.2 mm]	30% joint
Custom Grade						
Flat Surface	*	*	*	.050" [1.2 mm]	.050" [1.2 mm]	30% joint
Shaped Surface	*	*	*	.075" [1.9 mm]	.075" [1.9 mm]	30% joint
Economy Grade						
Flat Surface	*	*	*	.075" [1.9 mm]	.075" [1.9 mm]	30% joint
Shaped Surface	*	*	*	.100" [2.5 mm]	.100" [2.5 mm]	30% joint
Field Joints Non-Wood-to-Non-Wood - Up to 118" [3 m] above finished floor, balcony, deck or walkway customarily exposed to view and open to the building occupants and/or general public						
Premium Grade						
Flat Surface	*	*	*	.050" [1.2 mm]	.050" [1.2 mm]	30% joint
Shaped Surface	*	*	*	.075" [1.9 mm]	.075" [1.9 mm]	30% joint
Custom Grade						
Flat Surface	*	*	*	.075" [1.9 mm]	.075" [1.9 mm]	30% joint
Shaped Surface	*	*	*	.100" [2.5 mm]	.100" [2.5 mm]	30% joint
Economy Grade						
Flat Surface	*	*	*	.100" [2.5 mm]	.100" [2.5 mm]	30% joint
Shaped Surface	*	*	*	.125" [3.2 mm]	.125" [3.2 mm]	30% joint
Field Joints All Elements - Above 118" [3 m] above finished floor, balcony, deck or walkway customarily exposed to view and open to the building occupants and/or general public						
Premium Grade						
Flat Surface	20 KCPI	*	*	.050" [1.2 mm]	.050" [1.2 mm]	30% joint
Shaped Surface	20 KCPI	*	*	.075" [1.9 mm]	.075" [1.9 mm]	30% joint
Custom Grade						
Flat Surface	20 KCPI	*	*	.075" [1.9 mm]	.075" [1.9 mm]	30% joint
Shaped Surface	20 KCPI	*	*	.100" [2.5 mm]	.100" [2.5 mm]	30% joint
Economy Grade						
Flat Surface	15 KCPI	*	*	.100" [2.5 mm]	.100" [2.5 mm]	30% joint
Shaped Surface	15 KCPI	*	*	.125" [3.2 mm]	.125" [3.2 mm]	30% joint

* - Indicates there is no minimum, maximum, or the test does not apply to this element.

Courtesy of Architectural Woodwork Institute, *Architectural Woodwork Quality Standards Illustrated [Table 1700-S-2]*

Figure 6.4

Field Joints: Table of General Installation Standards (cont.)

Cup	Twist	Bow	Warp	Scribe to adjacent surface	Visible finish nails	Visible trim screws	Glue or Adhsv. Required	Wood Plug	Filler, wood insert	Filler, putty	Filler, wax	Well Matched	Compat ible
							General Standards - Apply to all Sections of Work						
Field Joints Wood-to-Wood - Up to 118" [3 m] above finished floor, balcony, deck or walkway customarily exposed to view and open to the building occupants and/or general public													
Premium Grade													
None	None	None	None	Yes	No	No	Yes	Yes	Yes	No	Yes	Yes	*
*	*	*	*	Yes	No	No	Yes	Yes	Yes	No	Yes	Yes	*
Custom Grade													
None	None	None	None	Yes	No	No	Yes	Yes	Yes	No	Yes	*	Yes
*	*	*	*	No	Yes	Yes	No	No	Yes	Yes	Yes	*	Yes
Economy Grade													
*	*	*	*	No	Yes	Yes	No	No	Yes	Yes	Yes	*	*
*	*	*	*	No	Yes	Yes	No	No	Yes	Yes	Yes	*	*
Field Joints Wood-to-Non-Wood - Up to 118" [3 m] above finished floor, balcony, deck or walkway customarily exposed to view and open to the building occupants and/or general public													
Premium Grade													
None	None	None	None	Yes	No	No	Yes	*	*	*	*	*	*
*	*	*	*	Yes	No	No	Yes	*	*	*	*	*	*
Custom Grade													
None	None	None	None	Yes	No	No	Yes	*	*	*	*	*	*
*	*	*	*	No	Yes	Yes	No	*	*	*	*	*	*
Economy Grade													
*	*	*	*	No	Yes	Yes	No	*	*	*	*	*	*
*	*	*	*	No	Yes	Yes	No	*	*	*	*	*	*
Field Joints Non-Wood-to-Non-Wood - Up to 118" [3 m] above finished floor, balcony, deck or walkway customarily exposed to view and open to the building occupants and/or general public													
Premium Grade													
None	None	None	None	No	No	Yes	Yes	*	*	*	*	*	*
*	*	*	*	No	No	Yes	Yes	*	*	*	*	*	*
Custom Grade													
None	None	None	None	No	No	Yes	Yes	*	*	*	*	*	*
*	*	*	*	No	No	Yes	Yes	*	*	*	*	*	*
Economy Grade													
*	*	*	*	No	No	Yes	Yes	*	*	*	*	*	*
*	*	*	*	No	No	Yes	Yes	*	*	*	*	*	*
Field Joints All Elements - Above 118" [3 m] above finished floor, balcony, deck or walkway customarily exposed to view and open to the building occupants and/or general public													
Premium Grade													
None	None	None	None	No	No	Yes	Yes	*	*	*	*	*	*
*	*	*	*	No	No	Yes	Yes	*	*	*	*	*	*
Custom Grade													
None	None	None	None	No	No	Yes	Yes	*	*	*	*	*	*
*	*	*	*	No	No	Yes	Yes	*	*	*	*	*	*
Economy Grade													
*	*	*	*	No	No	Yes	Yes	*	*	*	*	*	*
*	*	*	*	No	No	Yes	Yes	*	*	*	*	*	*

* - Indicates there is no requirement or the test does not apply to this element.

Courtesy of Architectural Woodwork Institute, *Architectural Woodwork Quality Standards Illustrated.* [Table 1700-S-2]

Figure 6.4 continued

Paneling

Comments

Paneling, generally produced in 4' x 8' sheets, is available in a wide range of wood materials and quality. Manufacturers' recommendations should be strictly adhered to, both in installation and in the proper storage and handling of the panels. Following are some general guidelines:

- *Vertical panels should be installed in a plumb manner, and horizontal panels should be level.*

- *Panels may be fastened in a variety of ways including nailed, glued, mechanically fastened, or a combination of these methods.*

- *Paneling accessories include jointing devices, corner mouldings, and ceiling and base mouldings which may be used to finish the applications. Or, panels may be "scribed," thereby eliminating the need for any type of finish moulding.*

- *For commercial applications, the installer must follow the installation instructions which are generally included within the specification. A specification usually requires the contractor to submit manufacturers' literature regarding the quality, color, characteristics, and other information specific to the panel materials selected.*

- *Unless otherwise specified, panel joints should be tight and free of rough edges and defects.*

- *Unless otherwise specified, fasteners and adhesives should not be noticeable.*

- *Panels should be flat, without buckling or deformity of surfaces.*

Wood Stairs and Railings

Comments

Building stairs is generally considered a specialty within the carpentry field. Stair components are often fabricated in a mill, and assembled by the carpenter on-site. Stairs must conform to rigid construction standards and adhere to codes. Standard riser heights and tread widths have been established around ranges that may vary depending on tolerances developed by building code officials. Designers and builders should consult with local regulating authorities for their most current standards. Interpretation of current code requirements is particularly important when designing and constructing special stairs, such as winders and curved stairways. Requirements for landing size and locations, and door swings are also key factors.

Because finished stair tread, riser, and other dimensional requirements must be established before stairs are framed, excerpts from the building code requirements are included in Chapter 5, "Wood Framing." However, here are some rules of thumb:

- *Stairs should be at least 36" wide, for a building occupant load of 49 or fewer, and at least 44" for more than 50 occupants.*

- *Riser height (distance between finished treads) should be no more than 7" for an occupant load greater than 10, and up to 8-1/4" (check local code) for fewer than 10 occupants. All risers should be a consistent height.*

- *Tread length (or "run") should also be consistent, a minimum of 11" (9-1/2" for an occupant load less than 10).*

- *Handrails should be installed between 30"–38" above the tread. If a stairway is wider than 44", there should be a handrail on both sides. A space of 1-1/2" should be provided between wall and handrail.*

- *Balustrades on landings or balconies should be 36" above the finish landing, and 44" for commercial projects. A guardrail may also be necessary.*

ADA-Compliant Stairs

Industry Standards

Means ADA Compliance Pricing Guide
(R.S. Means Co., Inc.)

Ed. Note: "ADAAG" stands for Americans with Disabilities Act—Act Guidelines. For further information, or to obtain copies of this material, call the ADA Technical Assistance Center at 800-949-4232.

ADAAG Reference Numbers:

4.1.3(4), Accessible Buildings, New Construction

4.9 Stairs

4.26 Handrails, Grab Bars, and Tub and Showers Seats

Where Applicable
All stairs connecting levels that are not accessible by elevators, ramps, or lifts.

Design Requirements
- Minimum tread width of 11".

- Slip-resistant surface.

- No protruding nosings greater than 1-1/2".

- No open risers.

- Rails on both sides, 34"-38" above nosings, 1-1/4"–1-1/2" diameter, round or oval, continuous inside rail, 1-1/2" from wall.

- If rails are not continuous, 12" extensions at the top parallel to the floor, and 12" plus width of one tread extensions at the bottom, sloped for the width of one tread and parallel to the floor for the remaining distance.

Ornamental Woodwork

Comments

This finish carpentry item includes decorative and functional components such as mantels, grilles, columns, corbels, and balusters.

Industry Standards

Architectural Woodwork Quality Standards Illustrated
(Architectural Woodwork Institute)

700–G–5: Installation Recommendation
This section does not cover field installation of woodwork; however, the methods and skill involved in the installation of woodwork in large measure determine the final appearance of the project. The design, detailing, and fabrication should be directed toward achieving installation with a minimum of exposed face fastening. The use of interlocking wood cleats or metal hanging clips combined with accurate furring and shimming will accomplish this. Such hanging of woodwork has the additional advantage of permitting movement that results from humidity changes or building movement. Depending upon local practice, in many areas woodworkers will perform the wall preparation and installation of the woodwork.

700–G–6: Finishing Recommendation
This section does not cover finishing. However, site conditions for finishing are rarely conducive to good results. Poor lighting, dust-laden air, and techniques available are limiting factors. Depending upon local practice, in many areas woodworkers will factory finish, yielding better results than can be achieved from field finishing.

Moulded Urethane

Comments

Moulded urethane products are designed for weather-resistant exterior applications, and are suitable for most interior applications. The Standard Building Code, the Uniform Building Code, BOCA and sections of the National Fire Protection Code address moulded urethane products. Section 3007 of the UBC restricts plastic veneer attached to the exterior walls of a building to heights equal to or less than 50' above grade. Local fire officials must be consulted to determine approval for the type of material and allowable height at which it may be applied. Most codes address plastic interior trim and require specific information on smoke generation and flame test data. For interior use it is suggested that applicable codes be consulted for compliance with flame-spread values.

Guidelines for Installation

- *Urethane millwork with the exception of balustrade systems and porch posts should be used for decorative purpose only, not for structural support.*

- *For best results noncorrosive fasteners should be used with the manufacturer's recommended adhesives.*

- *Materials should not be stored in extreme heat and humidity. The material should be acclimated to the site prior to installation.*

- *Cut surfaces should be primed and painted within a few days of installation.*

- *Urethane millwork should never be placed in an area subject to solar temperature buildups, such as behind a storm door.*

- *Joinery for urethane millwork should be to the same standard as for wood millwork — finishes should be better than or equal to wood.*

Shelving

Comments

The designer of a project has no control over the weight of contents that may eventually be placed on shelving by the building user. The probability exists that shelves will be overloaded beyond their design strength. While the shelves may not break, they may deflect, or sag, severely enough to jeopardize the shelf support system, and become aesthetically unacceptable to the user.

The following information was developed for use primarily by manufacturers of custom casework. While it includes technical data such as the formula to compute deflection, it also provides information a contractor needs to answer these questions: How much weight will the proposed shelves hold? What material, thickness, span and width will result in functional shelving that retains an acceptable appearance?

Industry Standards

Architectural Woodwork Quality Standards Illustrated
(Architectural Woodwork Institute)

Shelf Deflection Information

The Department of Wood Science in the Division of Forestry at West Virginia University conducted a study for the Architectural Woodwork Institute regarding the deflection of wood shelving materials under various amounts of stress. The following table represents their findings with the various products tested.

The table shows total uniformly distributed load requirements necessary to cause deflection of 1/4" in shelves and 8" and 12" wide with spans (i.e. unfixed, supported at each end) of 30, 36, 42, and 48 inches. Load required to deflect shelves more or less than 1/4" may be estimated by direct proportion. For example, the uniformly distributed load required to cause a deflection of 1/8" is one-half that of the value in the table. For width different than 8" or 12" (the values used in the table), load required to cause a 1/4" deflection may also be determined by direct proportion. A 6" wide shelf, for example, will deflect twice as much as a 12" wide shelf under the same load.

Shelf Deflection of 1/4" by Estimated Total Distributed Load in Pounds

Material	Thickness	Span	30"		36"		42"		48"	
		Width	8"	12"	8"	12"	8"	12"	8"	12"
Yellow-Poplar Red Gum Sweet Gum	lumber 3/4" 1-1/16"		322 lbs. 912	483 lbs. 1368	189 lbs. 538	284 lbs. 807	117 lbs. 332	175 lbs. 498	78 lbs. 221	117 lbs. 332
Hard Maple Pecan Red Oak	lumber 3/4" 1-1/16"		356 1011	534 1516	209 592	313 888	133 373	206 560	88 249	232 374
Birch Hickory	lumber 3/4" 1-1/16"		400 1134	600 1701	232 660	348 990	146 414	219 621	977 277	146 415
Medium Density Particleboard (raw or covered with "melamine")	3/4" 1"		78 185	117 277	46 109	69 164	29 69	43 102	19 45	28 66
Medium Density Fiberboard (raw or covered with "melamine")	3/4" 1"		100 237	150 356	58 137	87 206	36 85	54 128	25 59	38 90
Birch faced plywood, veneer core	3/4"		145	218	86	129	54	81	36	54
Birch faced plywood, medium density particleboard core	3/4"		125	188	72	109	46	68	31	46
Medium density particleboard covered two sides and one edge with nominal 0.028" high pressure decorative laminate	3/4" (core)		174	261	100	139	64	96	42	63
Medium density particleboard covered two sides and one edge with nominal 0.050" high pressure decorative laminate	3/4" (core)		234	350	137	205	86	129	58	87
Medium density particleboard with 1/8" solid lumber edge	3/4"		89	139	53	79	33	50	22	33
Medium density particleboard with 3/4" solid lumber edge	3/4"		100	150	60	90	42	63	25	38
Medium density particleboard with 3/4" x 1-1/2" solid lumber dropped edge	3/4"		384	435	216	241	132	152	92	107

NOTE: All medium density particle board is Type 1-M-2.
The information and ratings stated here pertain to material currently offered and represent results of tests believed to be reliable. However, due to variation in handling and methods not known or under our control, the Architectural Woodwork Institute cannot make any warranties or guarantees as to end result.

Courtesy of Architectural Woodwork Institute, *Architectural Woodwork Quality Standards Illustrated*

Figure 6.5

The following equation shows how deflection is related to shelf dimensions, width, thickness, span, load per inch of span and E-value, a material property which measures stiffness or resistance to deflection. The higher the E-value the less the deflection. When a shelf is made with several materials, each with its own E-value, a composite E-value must be determined.

To compute deflection:

$$D = \frac{0.1563wl^4}{Ebh^3}$$

In which the values are:
 D = deflection (in inches)
 w = load per lineal inch of span
 l = span (length)
 E = modulus of elasticity
 b = base (width)
 h = depth (thickness)

Ed. Note: See "Finishing of Millwork," item III D ("Library Shelving") later in this chapter for information on finishing shelves.

Cabinetry, Millwork & Countertops

Millwork

Industry Standards

Means Graphic Construction Standards
(R.S. Means Co., Inc.)

Millwork refers to finish material made of wood, plastic, and sometimes molded gypsum or polyurethane. Millwork can be custom designed and fabricated, or factory fabricated or milled.

The millwork contractor will commonly furnish the following wood items: doors, windows, factory- and custom-fabricated cabinetry and casework, columns, mantels, grilles, louvers, mouldings, paneling, railings, shelving, siding and stairs.

Plastic materials include laminates, cabinets, mouldings, doors and windows.

Factory-molded gypsum and polyurethane, medallions, mantels, stair brackets, door and window features and mouldings may also be supplied under the millwork contract.

Comments

Solid surface items, such as countertops, may be included in millwork packages.

Delivery & Storage

Industry Standards

WIC Manual of Millwork
(Woodwork Institute of California)

Ed. Note: The following excerpts from the Woodwork Institute of California (WIC) include only those informational items that apply directly to finish carpentry and cabinetry.

Recommended Care and Storage of Architectural Woodwork

II. Delivery and Storage

  A. The delivery of all items of architectural millwork shall be as required by a progress schedule furnished by the general contractor, and subject to conditions as follows:

    1. Delivery of architectural millwork shall be made only when the area of operation is enclosed, all plaster and concrete work dry, and the area broom clean.

    2. A clean storage area, well ventilated and protected from direct sunlight, excessive heat, rain or moisture, in which the relative humidity is between 45% and 65% at 60° to 90° F, and EMC (Equilibrium Moisture Content) conditions between 8% and 12%, shall be provided and maintained at the building site by the general contractor. The air conditioning or heating system shall be on and functioning, and the architectural millwork shall be acclimated to these conditions for 72 hours prior to installation.

    3. Millwork should not be subjected to abnormal heat, extreme dryness, humid conditions, sudden changes in temperature, or direct sunlight.

    4. If the above paragraphs are not adhered to, severe damage could result to the millwork. The fabricator of the work shall not be held responsible for any damage that might develop by not adhering to the above paragraphs.

  E. Cabinets should be handled carefully and set or stored on a level floor. Care should be taken to protect the exposed finished portions from bumping, scratching, etc. Never use cabinets or counters for "work benches" or convenient places to store other materials.

  F. Plastic tops should be stacked flat if possible, at least 4" off the floor, with a protective covering under the bottom unit, and covered on top to protect surfaces from scratching. Strips of wood or other suitable materials should be placed between tops. If tops are fully-formed or have splashes attached, extreme care must be taken to prevent breaking. Never stand or stack plastic tops on end against a wall where they can be broken or damaged by falling.

Wood Casework

Comments

Successful cabinetry begins with a complete set of shop drawings. These drawings should include the following: Cabinet Grade, Door Schedule & Details, Hardware, Elevations and Profiles, Finishes, Drawer Assembly Details, Floor & Wall Connections, Countertop & Splash, Overhang, Laminate Selections, Adhesive Selection, Backpriming Treatments, Method of Joining, and Sealant Specifications.

The drawings should be issued first as a preliminary and reissued after approvals, so that corrections can be incorporated in the working set.

Cabinetry can generally be separated into three categories: Commercial, Industrial/Laboratory, and Residential. Classifying cabinets into one of the categories is one way to establish a grade standard for the product. As with many other trades, cabinet contractors or millshops often specialize in either commercial/industrial fabrication or residential cabinetry.

Commercial and industrial cabinets require full design and specifications due to special requirements, finishes, or aesthetics of a project. Architects or designers are usually retained to provide specifications.

In recent years, the industry has moved toward "European" frameless construction and prefabricated modular cabinets built in a factory assembly line. Factory-built modular cabinets offer more standardized construction and incorporate the latest technology for cabinet finishes at a more economical price.

Some cabinet contractors build the cabinet boxes in their shops and purchase prefinished doors and drawer fronts from a supplier. This is because many states now prohibit the use of oil-based paint products and lacquers unless there are elaborate ventilating and hazardous waste systems installed at the shop. Now terms such as "conversion varnish" and "thermafoil" have replaced sprayed polyurethane and lacquer.

The cabinet industry is one of the fastest growing and evolving trades. A large contributor to this growth has been the dramatic increase of residential kitchen remodeling over the last 10 years. We can expect that new standards will continue to be established and published in the near future.

Good planning will keep damage to millwork and cabinetry to a minimum. After fabrication, there should be only one more handling – the delivery to the jobsite and the installation.

I. Wood Casework — Scope

A. Casework shall be fabricated complete in the mill to field dimensions. At manufacturer's option one of the following will be supplied unless specified otherwise:

   a. Type I — multiple self-supporting units fastened together to form a larger unit.

   b. Type II — a single length section as required, or in such sections as access openings will permit.

II. Casework Grades

A. Economy Grade establishes a standard to meet the requirements of lower cost residential and commercial construction where economy is the principal factor, and for use in storage and utility areas.

B. Custom Grade includes all the requisites of high quality casework and is suitable for all normal uses in high grade construction, such as higher quality construction for residential, school, medical facilities, and commercial buildings.

C. Premium Grade as the name implies, is a superior quality of materials and craftsmanship, with a corresponding increase in cost. It is intended, primarily, for the best of natural hardwood construction; but any species of wood may be specified.

D. Laboratory Grade is intended for usage in chemistry or "hard acid" areas where exposed or semi-exposed portions of the cabinet require additional protection. This grade shall meet all the requirements of Premium Grade. Grades contain additional requirements. (Specifications shall indicate any special finishing requirements for exposed and semi-exposed surfaces.)

Special Note: All grades shall meet requirements for Economy Grade. Custom, Premium, and Laboratory Grades contain additional requirements.

Seismic Zones 3 & 4

Seismic Forces Requirements: The WIC has had tests performed for several types of cabinet construction that meet the seismic forces requirements for Title 24. The types of construction are: Doweled, Confirmat Screws, Modeez®, Fully Plowed-in Back, and Backs Screwed on in rabbeted ends, tops, and bottoms. The exact method of cabinet construction for each of these tests would be available from organizations the Woodwork Institute of California.

III. Casework Specification Requirements

For clarity of bid and fabrication, the job drawings and specifications should clearly indicate or specify the following:

A. Grade Desired. If the grade is not specified, it shall be Custom Grade.

C. Construction Style and Type Desired.

   1. Construction Style. At manufacturers' option, one of the following will be supplied, unless otherwise specified.

      a. Style A — Frameless

      b. Style B — Face Frame

Plan View: Casework Construction Style & Type

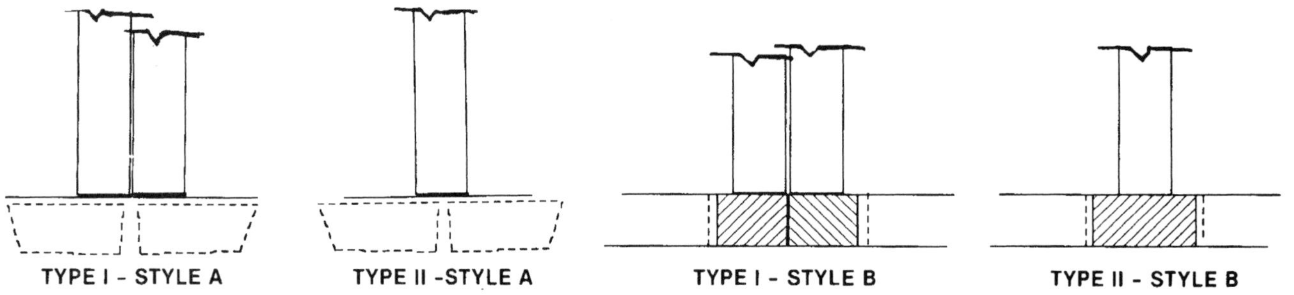

| TYPE I – STYLE A | TYPE II – STYLE A | TYPE I – STYLE B | TYPE II – STYLE B |

Courtesy of Woodwork Institute of California, *WIC Manual of Millwork*

Figure 6.6

2. Construction Type. At manufacturers' option, one of the following will be supplied, unless otherwise specified.

   a. Type I Construction. Multiple self-supporting units fastened together to form a larger unit.

   Note: For Type I Construction, Custom and Premium Grades, joints are permitted where ends are flush with cabinet tops. In each unit, the exposed edges of the ends shall be banded with the same material as the exposed surfaces. If other construction is desired, it shall be so specified.

D. WIC Cabinet Design Series

1. Individual cabinets may be listed by a **Standard Design Number System.**

2. Cabinets shall be Type I frameless construction only and are limited to flush overlay or reveal overlay styles, unless otherwise specified.

3. Finished ends shall be either applied panels or integral members on the end cabinet. Gaps at wall-to-wall installations shall be closed by filler panels not to exceed 1-1 /2" in width.

4. Cabinets may be specified to be any desired dimensions. Industry standards indicate outside dimensions, unless otherwise specified.

E. Exposed Material. Indicate the following:

1. Intended finish, opaque or transparent.

2. Species and veneer cut. If veneer cut is not specified, Rotary Cut or Plain Sliced will be furnished at the option of the manufacturer.

3. Flame-Spread Class, if required.

F. Toe space will be considered concealed, unless otherwise specified.

G. Special Treatment of Semi-Exposed Surfaces

1. Interior surfaces of open cabinets or behind glass doors for WIC Economy and Custom Grades are considered semi-exposed. If it is desired that these open surfaces match the exposed, it shall be specified.

2. If it is desired that a particular portion of any semi-exposed surface be a material other than minimum requirements of this section, it shall be specified.

H. Door and Drawer Front Style Desired

1. Flush overlay.

2. Reveal overlay (specify reveal dimension).

3. Lipped.

4. Flush.

J. If security or dust panels, tote trays, and levelers are desired, they shall be so specified.

K. Backs

1. If backs are desired for Economy Grade.

2. The thickness if other than 1-1/4" minimum for Custom and Premium Grade.

L. Shelves

1. If thicker shelves or center shelf supports are desired due to heavy loads, it shall be specified.

2. Thickness and type of glass for shelves shall be specified.

M. Cabinet Hardware Desired, Type, Manufacturer, and Finish

If not specified, selection shall be at the option of the manufacturer from Supplement 1, except in the case of pre-engineered drawer box systems whose use must be pre-approved in the specifications.

O. Cabinet installation by manufacturer, if desired, shall be specified.

P. Run and Match of Wood Grain

If it is desired that wood grain pattern is to run and match vertically, it shall be so specified, otherwise the drawer fronts may run horizontally at the option of manufacturer. For Premium Grade, vertical match is required.

Q. If provisions for the WIC Grade specified are in conflict with or modified by the drawings and specifications, the drawings and specifications shall govern.

R. Factory Finishing

1. If desired, it shall be specified.

2. Any special finish desired for Laboratory Grade exposed and semi-exposed portions.

Ed. Note: See "Finishing of Millwork" later in this chapter for more information on factory finishing.

S. For job site finishing, it is recommended that the following be included in the painting specifications:

"Before finishing the exposed surface of all millwork, the finishing contractor shall remove handling marks or effects of exposure to moisture with a thorough final sanding over all surfaces of the exposed portions, using at least 150 grit or finer sandpaper, and shall thoroughly clean all surfaces before applying sealer and finish."

IV. Casework Definitions
A. Exposed Portions

1. All surfaces visible when doors and drawers are closed, including knee spaces.

2. Underside of bottoms of cabinets over 4' – 0" above finished floor, including bottoms behind light valances.

3. Cabinet tops under 6' – 0" above finished floor or if 6' – 0" and over and visible from an upper building level or floor.

4. Visible front edges of web frames, ends, divisions, tops, shelves, and hanging stiles.

5. Sloping tops of cabinets that are visible.

6. Visible surfaces in open cabinets or behind glass for Premium Grade.

7. Interior faces of hinged doors for Premium Grade.

8. Visible portions of bottoms, tops, and ends in front of sliding doors in Custom and Premium Grades only.

B. Semi-Exposed Portions

1. Shelves.

2. Divisions.

3. Interior face of ends, backs, and bottoms.

4. Drawer sides, sub-fronts, backs, and bottoms. Also included are the interior surfaces of cabinet top members when the top member is 36" or more above the finished floor.

5. The underside of bottoms of wall cabinets between 2' – 0" and 4' – 0" above the finished floor.

6. Interior faces of hinged doors, except Premium Grade.

7. Visible surfaces in open cabinets or behind glass for Economy and Custom Grades and all rooms designated as storage, janitor, closet, or utility.

8. Visible portion of bottoms, tops, and ends in front of sliding doors in Economy Grade only.

C. Concealed Portions

1. Toe space unless otherwise specified.

2. Sleepers.

3. Web frames, stretchers, and solid sub-tops.

4. Security panels.

5. Underside of bottoms of cabinets less than 2' – 6" above the finished floor.

6. Flat tops of cabinets 6' – 0" or more above the finished floor, except if visible from an upper building level.

7. The three non-visible edges of adjustable shelves.

8. The underside of countertops, knee spaces, and drawer aprons.

9. The faces of cabinet ends of adjoining units that butt together.

VI. Workmanship

A. The assembled cabinet shall present **First Class Workmanship.**

B. Assembly. Cabinets shall be assembled complete in the mill with doors, drawers, and hardware installed, unless otherwise specified.

C. Rigidity. Where essential to produce a rigid assembly, mechanical fasteners or glue shall be used.

D. Casework Protection. Casework shall be protected with skids, bracing, and corner guards or other protection as may be required to assure protection from rough handling.

E. Casework shall be free of adhesive overspray, fabrication marks, and shop accumulated dirt.

VIII. Material Requirements — Grade Rules
A. Exposed Portions

1. All wood grains shall be furnished as rotary cut or plain sliced at fabricator's option unless otherwise

specified. Plywood grain and color do not match with grain and color of solid stock.

2. For transparent finish, if the species is not specified, the use of hardwood or softwood (plywood or solid stock) of one species for the entire job is permitted, at the option of the manufacturer.

    a. For Custom Grade, solid stock and/or plywood shall be compatible in color and grain.

    b. For Premium Grade, solid stock shall be well matched for color and grain; plywood shall be compatible in color with solid stock; and adjacent plywood panels shall be well matched for color and grain.

    c. See Glossary for definition of compatible in color and well-matched for color and grain.

3. For Economy Grade, opaque finish, softwood plywood, particleboard, medium density fiberboard, medium density overlay, hardwood plywood, and solid stock are permitted.

4. For Custom Grade, opaque finish, particleboard, medium density fiberboard, medium density overlay, hardwood plywood, and solid stock are permitted.

5. For Premium Grade, opaque finish, softwood plywood is **not** permitted; medium density fiberboard, hardwood plywood are permitted. Hardwood plywood and solid stock shall be close grained only (i.e., birch and maple).

B. Semi-Exposed Portions

1. May be of species and grain other than exposed portions. When any surface is required to be the same species and grain as the exposed portion or if all materials are required to be one species and grain, it shall be so specified. For Premium Grade, all semi-exposed portions behind glass or in open cases shall be the same species, color, grain and grade as the exposed material.

2. For transparent finish, particleboard or medium density fiberboard is not permitted for open cabinets or behind glass doors.

3. May be of material other than exposed portions. Acceptable materials include any overlay material identified in Section 15, paragraph VIII, B, 1, a through g, or any mill option hardwood plywood. Color or species will be consistent throughout semi-exposed surfaces on entire job.

Casework Specification Requirements: Definitions

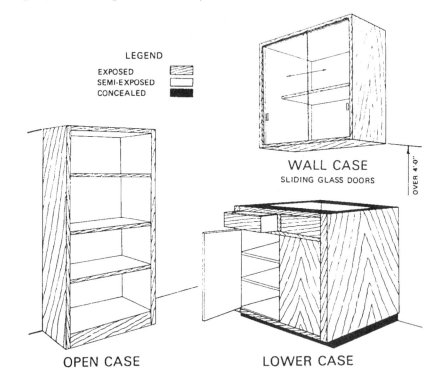

NOTE: Inside surfaces of open shelf cabinets and surfaces behind glass are considered exposed for **Premium Grade.** Tops of tall cabinets and upper cabinets 6' and over that are visible from upper levels are considered exposed.

LEGEND

EXPOSED
SEMI-EXPOSED
CONCEALED

WALL CASE
SLIDING GLASS DOORS

OPEN CASE

LOWER CASE

Courtesy of Woodwork Institute of California, *WIC Manual of Millwork*

Figure 6.7

C. Concealed Portions, Cores, and Substrates

4. Concealed portions shall be any species of sound, dry, solid stock, plywood, particleboard, medium density fiberboard, or a combination thereof.

D. Visible Edges, Exposed and Semi-Exposed, except door and drawer fronts. (See Paragraphs VIII. E. and VIII. F., respectively.)

1. Exposed or semi-exposed shall be treated as follows:

   a. For Economy Grade only, all voids filled and sanded.

   b. Banded with veneer or veneer tape. Finger joints are not permitted for Premium Grade.

   c. Banded with solid wood.

2. Only the front edge of adjustable shelves shall be considered visible.

3. Medium density fiberboard does not require edge filling.

4. Custom and Premium Grades shall be edge banded.

5. Premium Grade shall have concealed edge bands, except at shelves and bottoms.

6. For Custom and Premium Grades, the visible top edge of the end of cabinets 6' – 0" or more from the floor does not require an edge band, but shall have all voids filled and sanded.

7. For Economy and Custom Grades Type II construction, the visible bottom edge of the end of upper cabinets does not require an edge band but shall have all voids filled and sanded. For Premium Grade, this edge shall be concealed, banded or shoulder mitered, and when specified to receive a transparent finish, edge bands shall be the same species, color and WIC Grade as the exposed material.

8. For all grades Type I construction, the visible bottom edge of the end of upper cabinets shall be edge banded.

E. Drawers

1. Drawer fronts.

   a. For Economy Grade, drawer fronts shall be a minimum of 3/4" in thickness; all edges of plywood and particleboard are to be filled and sanded.

   b. For Economy and Custom Grade opaque finishes, medium density fiberboard does not require an edge band. Edge banding is required for Premium Grade.

   c. For transparent finish, banding shall be on all four edges.

   d. For transparent finish, edges visible after doors and drawers are closed are required to be the same species, color, grain, and grade as the exposed portions.

   e. For Custom and Premium Grades, banding shall be on all four edges. For Custom Grade, solid stock may be used and shall not require banding.

2. Sides, backs, and sub-fronts.

   a. For Economy Grade shall be a minimum of 7/16" in thickness of any approved semi-exposed material except hardboard. Vinyl wrapped drawers are permitted. The same material shall be used for all parts of the drawer box.

   b. Hardwood or softwood plywood shall be filled and sanded on the top edges.

   c. For Custom Grade shall be a minimum of 12 mm and a maximum of 5/8" in thickness, and shall be one species of material and thickness for all parts for the entire job.

   d. Hardwood plywood shall be 7- or 9-ply with no core voids in the inner plies, or 5-ply edge banded.

Comments

Where available, lumber core ply panels are recommended, as they are very stable.

   e. Particleboard or medium density fiberboard shall have an overlay surface and be edge banded.

   f. For Premium Grade if solid stock, it shall be a minimum of 0.37 specific gravity hardwood. Hardwood shall be the same species of wood for the entire drawer box and job. If approved overlay material, the same material shall be used for the entire drawer box and job.

3. Drawer bottoms.

   a. For Economy Grade, drawer bottoms shall be a minimum of 1/8" in thickness, except if width exceeds 18", it shall be 1/4" in thickness and shall be any of the approved semi-exposed materials.

   b. For Custom Grade, drawer bottoms shall be a minimum of 1/4" in thickness, except if width exceeds 30", it shall be a minimum of 3/8" in thickness or reinforced with 1/2" x 2-1/2" strip at center. Exposed particleboard or medium density fiberboard is not permitted.

   c. For Premium Grade, drawer bottoms of Grade AD softwood plywood and hardboard is not permitted.

4. For Premium Grade only if solid stock, shall be a minimum of 0.37 specific gravity hardwood. Hardwood shall be the same species of wood for the entire drawer box and job. If overlay material, the same material shall be used for the entire drawer box and job.

F. **Cabinet Doors** (Maximum width shall be 24". Maximum height 80". Larger sizes are not recommended.)

1. Hinged.

   a. Shall conform to the same thickness and banding requirements as drawer fronts (see Paragraph E, 1).

   b. Interior faces for Economy and Custom Grades may be Economy Grade of the same species as exposed portion.

   c. For Premium Grade, interior faces shall be the same species, color, grain, cut, and grade as the exposed portion of the cabinet. The faces of adjacent cabinet doors that are visible when closed shall be well matched for color and grain.

2. Sliding doors. (Bottom of upper cabinet may require reinforcement to prevent sagging.)

   a. Shall be a minimum of 1/4" in thickness, except when over 2'–0" high they shall be a minimum of 3/4" in thickness.

   b. Interior faces may be the same as exposed portion, or any balancing species.

   c. Top and bottom edges are not required to be banded or filled.

   d. Both vertical edges of sliding doors are considered visible.

3. Frameless glass doors shall be a minimum of 1/4" thick clear safety glass with all exposed edges ground. For Premium Grade, all exposed edges shall be polished.

4. Stile and rail cabinet doors.

   a. Solid lumber stile and rails shall be a minimum of 3/4" in thickness and 2-1/4" in width. Stiles and rails consisting of MDF or particleboard cores shall be a minimum of 3/4" in thickness and 3-1/2" in width.

   b. Glass shall be a minimum of clear double strength, secured with removable stops of the same species of wood.

   c. Panels shall be flat, unless otherwise specified.

   d. For opaque finish, door components may be manufactured from solid stock of medium density fiberboard, at the mill's option.

I. **Face Frames**

Shall be solid stock, a minimum of 3/4" in thickness.

J. **Ends and Divisions**

1. Shall be a minimum of 3/4" in thickness, except for face frame construction, where Economy Grade permits a minimum of 1/2" in thickness and Custom and Premium Grades permit a minimum of 5/8" in thickness.

2. Paneled construction, stiles and rails shall be a minimum of 3/4" in thickness and panels a minimum of 1/4" in thickness. For Custom and Premium Grades for transparent finish, hardboard is not permitted.

K. **Shelves**

1. For Economy Grade, shelves shall be solid stock or particleboard a minimum of 3/4" in thickness or may be veneer core plywood, a minimum of 5/8" in thickness.

2. For Custom and Premium Grades, fixed shelves with spans in excess of 4'-0" are not recommended; if desired, a center support shall be specified. Shelves shall be solid stock, plywood or particleboard a minimum of 3/4" in thickness. Fixed shelves 3'-6" in length with particleboard core between vertical members of the cabinet body shall be a minimum of 1" in thickness. If not specified, the material shall be the option of the manufacturer subject to the 40 lb. load capacity, unless it is to be used in a school or hospital, which will require the 50 lb. load test.

3. If thicker shelves or center shelf supports are required due to heavy loads, they shall be so specified.

4. For Custom and Premium Grades, when hardboard is used for shelves, vertical or horizontal dividers, it must be smooth on two sides and tempered.

5. The grain of the face veneer of plywood shall run the length of the shelf.

L. **Tops and Bottoms**

1. For Economy Grade, tops and bottoms of cabinets shall conform to requirements of Paragraph J,1.

2. For Custom and Premium Grades, tops and bottoms are required and shall be a minimum of 3/4" in thickness.

3. Bottoms of upper cabinets (see Paragraph K,2 and 3).

4. Wood tops, if an integral part of a cabinet, shall be a minimum of 3/4" in thickness.

N. **Backs**

1. For Economy Grade when backs are used, backs shall be hardboard or plywood, a minimum of 1/8" in thickness.

2. For Custom and Premium Grades, backs shall be hardboard, plywood, particleboard or medium density fiberboard, a minimum of 1/4" in thickness.

3. Exposed backs shall be a minimum of 1/2" in thickness.

4. If 1/2" or thicker back is used, anchor strips are **not** required.

O. Breadboards and Pullout Boards

1. Breadboards

   a. Shall be solid stock, a minimum of 3/4" in thickness, except for Economy Grade exterior grade plywood is permitted.

   b. When solid stock is glued for width, Type II adhesive shall be used.

2. Pullout Boards

   a. Shall be veneer core plywood, a minimum of 3/4" in thickness.

IX. Construction Requirements — Grade Rules

A. Joinery

1. All cabinet members shall be securely fastened together using one or more acceptable joinery methods (see paragraph A,5, a through e).

2. All joints shall be securely glued (see Glossary for definition).

3. Casework shall be assembled square and true, with a tolerance not to exceed 1/32" difference in measurement at top versus bottom, and 1/16" in diagonal measurement.

4. To assemble cabinet bodies and components, the use of finish nails is allowed. They shall be a maximum of 4" on center (except face frames — 8" on center), with a minimum of 2 fasteners per joint for cabinet body and drawer construction. Staples, screws and T nails are not permitted for exposed surfaces.

5. For Custom and Premium Grades, at the option of the manufacturer, construction joinery shall be as follows:

   a. Dadoes or lock joints, plows or rabbets.

   b. Doweled Joints. The dowels shall be a minimum of 8 mm x 30 mm with a minimum of 2 dowels per joint. The first dowel shall be spaced a maximum of 37 mm from each edge or end, and the second dowel shall be a maximum of 32 mm on center from the first dowel. Subsequent dowels shall be spaced a maximum of 128 mm on center. All dowel construction shall be glued and clamped.

   c. Confirmat-Type Screws. Maximum of 37 mm from each end with subsequent screws being spaced 128 mm on center. Glue is **not** required with this system.

   d. Lamello-Type Jointing Plates. The plate shall be a maximum of 2 inches from each edge or end to the center of the plate. Subsequent plates shall be spaced a maximum of 6 inches on center. All joints shall be glued and clamped.

   e. Mod-eez Type Fastening Systems. The fasteners shall be a maximum of 16" on center and 4" from any edge or end. They shall be fastened with #10 full-thread sheet metal screws for cabinet body construction. Glue is not required with this system.

Typical Joints

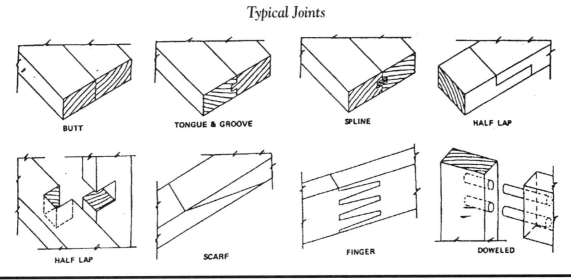

6. For Premium Grade, no exposed fastening is permitted except for access panels.

B. Edges of Exposed Portions

Blind or stop dadoes are not required for Economy Grade or for open shelving in rooms designated as janitor, closet, or utility.

2. For Custom Grade, when specified to receive a transparent finish, blind or stop dadoes are required. When lock joints are used, they shall not run through the edge band.

3. For Premium Grade, blind or stop dadoes are required.

C. Ends and Divisions

1. Cabinet ends are required.

2. Open ends or skeleton frames against walls are not permitted in any grade in any WIC Grade.

3. Exposed ends shall be rabbeted or plowed to receive backs if used.

4. For Custom and Premium Grades, drawer compartments shall be separated from shelf or open compartments by a solid vertical division unless design or usage prevents. A solid division shall occur behind all vertical face frame members or hanging stiles.

D. Face Frames

1. For cabinet doors flush with face frame, the use of a bottom member of the face frame is optional with the fabricator, unless otherwise specified.

2. Face frames shall be mortised and tenoned, doweled with wood or metal screw dowels, or Lamello type plates, and securely glued.

3. The grain shall run horizontally and vertically respectively.

4. For Economy and Custom Grades, frames shall be glued to cabinet bodies and may be face nailed.

5. For Premium Grade, all exposed corners shall be shoulder mitered, lock mitered, spline mitered, or mitered with a Lamello-type plate. Exposed nailing of face frames to cabinet bodies is not permitted.

E. Shelves

1. For Economy Grade, fixed shelves shall be nailed 4" or less on center to ends and divisions. Shelves in excess of 4'–0" shall be supported on cleats at the back or nailed through the back if a back is used.

2. Adjustable shelves shall be supported on metal shelf standards and metal shelf rests, or, in evenly spaced, cleanly bored holes a maximum of 2" o.c. with metal shelf rests. Holes shall be bored from front and back edge of shelves a minimum of 1" to a maximum of 2-3/4". For shelves over 24" deep, there shall be three (3) supports at each end for Title 24 — schools and hospitals. Cabinets over 30" deep shall have three (3) supports at each end of shelf.

3. For Custom and Premium Grades, if metal shelf standards are used, they shall be properly attached, recessed, and shall run continuous from top to bottom of plow. The particleboard edges shall not be visible.

Typical Joints

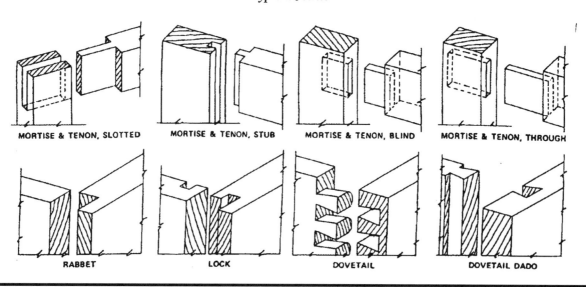

MORTISE & TENON, SLOTTED · MORTISE & TENON, STUB · MORTISE & TENON, BLIND · MORTISE & TENON, THROUGH

RABBET · LOCK · DOVETAIL · DOVETAIL DADO

Courtesy of Woodwork Institute of California, *WIC Manual of Millwork*

Figure 6.9

4. The minimum length of adjustable shelves shall be 1/8" less than the inside dimension of the cabinet.

5. For cabinets over 72" high from the floor and that is not immediately abutting a structural wall or another cabinet, a fixed shelf is required at mid-height.

F. **Tops, Bottoms, Intermediate Horizontal Members, Web Frames, Sub-Tops, and Stretchers**

1. Design permitting, bottoms and tops are required.

2. All members shall be assembled with any of the approved methods under "Joinery Requirements."

3. At concealed ends, tops and bottoms may extend past the concealed end.

4. At exposed ends, horizontal members, except countertops, shall not extend beyond the exposed end.

5. Stretchers shall be provided at both front and back under countertops.

6. For sink compartments, stretchers may run front to back.

7. For Custom and Premium Grades, web frames shall be provided under drawers that operate on wood center guides. When banks of drawers operate on wood corner guides, side runner guides, metal side or bottom mount slides, front stretcher is only required when total drawer opening height exceeds 2'-6".

8. Wood countertops.

   a. For Economy Grade, may be surface nailed.

   b. For Custom and Premium Grades, all countertops shall be attached with concealed clips, screws, or other equivalent fastening.

9. Exposed tops.

   a. For Economy and Custom Grades, tops which are flush with exposed ends do not require mitered joints. Exposed ends of the top shall be banded with the same material as other exposed surfaces.

   b. For Type I Construction (multiple self-supporting units fastened together to form a larger unit), Custom and Premium Grades, joints are permitted where ends are flush with tops. In each unit, the exposed edges of the ends shall be banded with the same material as the exposed surfaces.

   c. For Type II Construction (a single length section as required, or in such sections as access openings will permit), Premium Grade tops (other than countertops) which are flush with exposed ends shall be shoulder mitered, lock mitered, spline mitered or mitered with a Lamello-type plate, or dowel mitered.

10. Sub-tops for tile shall be supplied with base cabinets.

11. Bottoms of upper cabinets.

   a. For Economy Grade Type I and Type II construction, joints are permitted where ends are flush with bottoms in each unit. If ends extend below the bottom, the interior exposed surface of the end may be the same material as the semi-exposed surface.

Typical Joints

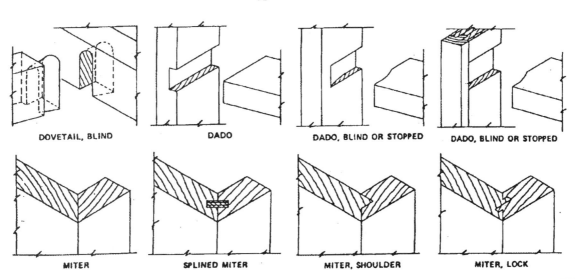

DOVETAIL, BLIND   DADO   DADO, BLIND OR STOPPED   DADO, BLIND OR STOPPED

MITER   SPLINED MITER   MITER, SHOULDER   MITER, LOCK

Courtesy of Woodwork Institute of California, *WIC Manual of Millwork*

Figure **6.10**

b. For Custom and Premium Grades Type I and Type II construction, joints are permitted where ends are flush with bottoms in each unit. The exposed edges of the ends shall be banded with the same material as the exposed surfaces. If ends extend below the bottom, the interior exposed surface of the end shall be the same material as the exposed surface.

12. Security and dust panels (if specified) shall be supplied above locked doors and drawers.

G. Backs

1. For Economy Grade, backs are required only when specified or where the cabinet will be set in an unfinished recess, or where the back would be exposed to view.

2. For Custom and Premium Grades, backs are required.

3. Shall be rabbeted or dadoed into exposed ends unless a plant-on end is used.

4. Shall be securely nailed, stapled, doweled or dadoed to the case body, divisions, or fixed shelves. Gluing is not required.

H. Breadboards and Pullout Boards

1. Shall operate smoothly in channels or other rigid guides.

2. Breadboards shall be provided with tongue and groove bands at each end, securely glued with Type II adhesive.

3. Pullout Board shall be banded on three edges.

I. Drawers

1. All joints shall be securely glued.

2. Provision shall be made to prevent drawers from tipping when extended.

3. Hardwood guides of corner, center, side or side runner type, and all metal slides shall be as indicated in hardware supplement.

4. Drawers, trays, and sliding bins shall be properly fitted to the cabinet and operate smoothly without excessive play. Drawer boxes, trays and sliding bins must fill the cabinet opening, front to back, less than a maximum of 2", from top to bottom to the greatest extent possible, while remaining fully functional.

5. File drawers shall be provided with a follower mechanism or be of a size to allow use of pendaflex folders on a systems stand. All file drawers shall have full-extension slides. Direction of file is at the discretion of the designer. Legal-sized drawers with hanging file suspension bars must provide for both legal and letter-sized hanging files.

6. For Premium Grade, spring loaded tip-down stops shall be provided on all drawers (design permitting) unless a stop is built into a metal drawer slide.

7. For Style B face frame construction.

a. For Economy Grade, the fronts or sub-fronts may be rabbeted to receive the sides. Backs may be butt jointed and nailed to the sides.

b. For Custom and Premium Grades, drawer sides shall be multiple dovetailed (dovetail joints with exposed substrates are acceptable in all WIC Grades. Exposed particleboard and medium density fiberboard substrates must be painted to match the drawer box color), dovetail dadoed, doweled, lock jointed and nailed, fastened with Confirmat type screws, or rabbets with #8 screws, a minimum of 2 screws for each side, a maximum of 2" on center, to the fronts or sub-fronts and backs. Sides may be dadoed to receive backs. Nails shall be a maximum of 2" on center.

c. For Premium Grade construction, top edges of side shall be stop shaped.

8. For flush overlay type construction.

a. Drawer sides shall be blind dovetail dadoed, unless a sub-front is used.

b. For Premium Grade, top edges of sides shall be stop shaped.

9. Sub-fronts.

a. For Economy Grade, drawer sides may be nailed to sub-fronts and backs.

b. For Custom and Premium Grades, drawer sides shall be multiple dovetailed or dovetail dado, doweled, lock jointed and nailed, fastened with Confirmat type screws, or rabbets with #8 screws, a minimum of 2 screws for each side, and a maximum of 2" on center to the fronts or sub-fronts and backs. Sides may be dadoed to receive backs. Nails shall be at a maximum of 2" on center.

c. The finished front shall be securely attached to a sub-front with #8 x 1" pan head sheet metal screws a maximum of 1-1/2" from inside corners of the finished front and a maximum of 12" on center.

d. When a lock joint is used in the construction of a drawer box, attach the sub-front to the sides of the drawer, 1/8 of an inch of exposed particleboard and solid stock is permitted on the drawer sides.

10. Drawer bottoms.

a. Shall be plowed into sides, fronts, or sub-fronts.

b. Bottoms shall be securely attached to the backs either by plow or by nailing at a maximum of 4" on center if the bottom runs through, and shall be securely glued or glue blocked to form a rigid unit.

c. The use of surface applied bottoms need not to be plowed or glued into sides, sub-fronts and backs is permitted in conjunction with approved metal bottom mounted side slides.

d. Bottoms are not required to be plowed into drawer fronts or sub-fronts with the use of integral metal drawer side/slide systems if a minimum of 1/2" thickness bottom is used.

e. Wood trays, bins, and similar items shall be similarly constructed.

11. Drawer stops.

a. For Custom and Premium Grades, to prevent drawer fronts from hitting the cabinet body, stops shall be provided at the back of both sides of all drawers unless a stop is built into a metal drawer slide and provision made to stop the drawer in both the in and out position without impact on the drawer front.

12. Unless otherwise specified, the following drawer box and drawer slide dynamic weight capacity standard will apply. Pencil drawers — 50 lbs., general purpose drawers — 75 lbs., file drawers — 100 lbs., lateral file drawers longer than 24" in length — 125 lbs., special weight requirements must be specified.

J. Doors

1. Sliding doors.

a. For Economy Grade, sliding doors 3'-0" in height or less shall be equipped with adequate top and/or bottom guides or runs. Sliding doors in excess of 3'-0" in height shall be installed on hardware of a type optional with the manufacturer.

b. For Custom and Premium Grades, doors over 2'-10" in height shall be installed on either overhead metal track with nylon roller hangers, or metal bottom track with sheaves and top guide.

c. For Custom and Premium Grades, doors 2'-10" and under in height shall be installed on appropriate fiber or metal track, with top guide.

d. For Custom and Premium Grades, for face frame type construction a continuous vertical filler strip shall be provided in the opening behind the face frame and in front of the rear sliding door.

e. For Custom and Premium Grades, frameless sliding glass doors shall be installed on carriers with metal track and top guide. To prevent sagging, the bottoms of upper cabinets shall be increased

in thickness or provided with a hardwood track member of sufficient thickness or a strongback screwed and glued to the underside.

2. Hinged doors.

a. For all WIC Grades, doors shall stop against the body of the cabinet. Doors and door faces must overlap cabinet sides, top stretchers and bottoms, with the exception of handicapped units.

b. For concealed European style hinges, doors less than 40" in height shall have a minimum of two hinges. Doors 40" to 60" in height shall have a minimum of three hinges. Doors more than 60" and up to 80" high shall have a minimum of four hinges. Doors over 80" in height shall have an additional hinge for every 18" of additional height.

c. For wraparound style hinges, doors under 48" in height shall have a minimum of two hinges. Doors 48" to 84" high shall have a minimum of three hinges, and over 84" shall have a minimum of four hinges. Wraparound hinges shall be let into the edge of the door.

d. Cabinet door hinges shall be installed by the cabinet fabricator unless otherwise specified. Installed doors shall operate properly without binding and shall be in proper alignment.

e. For Custom and Premium Grades flush construction, a stop shall be provided at the top of hinged door openings. Hinges shall be either self closing or doors shall be provided with a catch.

f. For Custom and Premium Grades, Style A construction, a stop-stretcher shall be provided at the top of pairs of hinged door openings.

g. For Custom and Premium Grades, where drawers occur above pairs of doors, a stop-stretcher shall be required above the pairs of hinged door openings.

h. For Premium Grade face frame flush construction, a stop shall be provided at both sides of the door opening.

i. For Custom and Premium Grades, locking full height pairs of cabinet doors must be equipped with either two sliding bolts — one at top and one at bottom — or a single elbow catch at cabinets with fixed middle shelves.

K. Bases and Sleepers

1. Shall be fabricated of solid stock, plywood or particleboard, a minimum of 3/4" in thickness and as either a separate unit or integral with the cabinet body at the manufacturers option unless otherwise specified. Sleepers shall be provided at a maximum of 3'-0" on center.

L. Clothes Poles

1. Shall be wood a minimum of 1-1/4" in diameter or 1-1/16" minimum diameter metal as approved in the hardware supplement at fabricator's option, unless otherwise specified.

2. Shall be supported a maximum of 4'-0" on center. Poles shall be supported at each end by rosettes or hook strips with bored holes. Nailing is not acceptable.

M. Wardrobes

1. Horizontal members at the top rail of sliding doors in wardrobes 5'-0" in width or over shall be rigidly supported with a vertical 1-3/8" round pole or two strips a minimum of 3/4" x 1-1/4", forming a "T" member and securely positioned behind the door lap.

N. Anchor Strips

1. For Economy Grade, anchor strips are not required.

2. For Custom and Premium Grades, anchor strips of solid stock, plywood, particleboard, or medium density fiberboard shall be a minimum of 1/2" in thickness and a minimum of 2-1/2" in width, and shall be provided at the wall side of the cabinet back on both top and bottom of wall hung cabinets and at top only of base cabinets. Anchor strips of semi-exposed material may be provided on the inside of the cabinet providing the back is flush with the top, bottom, and ends of the cabinet body and is attached to the cabinet body as well as the back. Base cabinets with integral base shall have anchor strips at top and bottom.

3. Cabinets over 5'-0" in height shall have an intermediate anchor strip.

4. Where 1/2" or thicker cabinet backs are used, anchor strips are not required.

5. Anchor strips shall be securely attached.

O. Sanding

1. For Economy Grade, all flat exposed and semi-exposed portions shall be machine sanded with all exposed edges and mouldings smoothly machined and clean.

2. For Custom and Premium Grades, the bottom edges of drawer fronts and aprons at knee spaces shall be smoothly sanded.

3. For Custom Grade, all exposed portions shall be smoothly sanded and all semi-exposed portions shall be machine sanded and free from tool marks and other blemishes.

4. For Premium Grade, all exposed portions shall be hand sanded and free from tool marks and other blemishes, scraped or otherwise completely smoothed, ready for finishing. All semi-exposed portions shall be smoothly sanded and free from tool marks or other blemishes.

P. Scribing

1. For Economy Grade, scribing is not required.

2. For Custom Grade, provision shall be made for scribing or scribe moulds furnished where cabinets contact finished walls or ceiling at the option of the manufacturer unless otherwise specified. End joints of scribe moulds shall be beveled and corners mitered.

3. For Custom and Premium Grades, the use of wood filler strips not to exceed 1-1/2" in width, scribe strips, and cellulose sponge a minimum of 1/2" is permitted. Color compatible caulking is permitted not to exceed 1/16".

4. For Premium Grade, provisions shall be made for scribing unless otherwise specified.

5. For Custom and Premium Grades, closure panels and scribe moulds shall be provided at top and bottom of upper cabinets and at the top of tall cabinets requiring angle turns so that open spaces are not visible.

Q. Movable Cabinets

1. When metal glides are specified in lieu of casters, they shall be adjustable.

2. For casters see hardware supplement.

3. All lock joint corners of bottoms and top webs of movable cabinets shall be reinforced with a continuous 1" metal angle strip or a continuous wood reinforcing cleat securely screwed into the inside of both sides of the corner.

4. Movable cabinets with doors and without fixed stabilizing vertical or horizontal partitions shall be built with a diaphragm type double bottom.

Table of Recommended Door and Drawer Tolerances

GRADE	MAXIMUM CLEARANCE ALLOWED			WARP[1] OR TWIST[1] TOLERANCE PER LINEAL FOOT	
	FLUSH OVERLAY TYPE		FLUSH TYPE		
	SINGLE UNIT	ADJACENT UNIT			
Premium	0.1250" 4 mm	0.2500" 8 mm	0.0938" 3/32"	0.0313" 1/32"	
Custom	0.1250" 4 mm	0.2500" 8 mm	0.1250" 1/8"	0.0469" 3/64"	
Economy	0.1563" 5/32"	0.3125" 5/16"	0.1563" 5/32"	0.0625" 1/16"	

[1] Not to exceed 1/4" in any size door.

Reveal overlay shall be as specified.

Courtesy of Woodwork Institute of California, WIC *Manual of Millwork*

Figure 6.11

R. Door and Drawer Tolerances

1. The recommended clearances allowed between any edge of doors or drawers, or between doors hung in pairs, or between flush face frames and doors and drawers, or any edge of doors and drawers and the surrounding border; and the warp and twist tolerances for doors less than 1-3/8" in thickness are indicated in the table above for all grades.

2. The test for warp and twist is made by placing a string, wire, or straight edge on the concave face of the door diagonally, horizontally, or vertically and measuring the maximum distance between the face of the door and the straight edge, wire, or string.

3. For reveal overlay construction, the maximum clearance allowed shall be as specified or indicated.

4. Doors and drawers shall align vertically and horizontally.

Plastic Laminate

Industry Standards
WIC Manual of Millwork
(Woodwork Institute of California)

Ed. Note: See also "Kitchen & Bathroom Countertops" at the end of this chapter for more information on plastic laminates.

Laminated Plastic Countertops, Splashes and Wall Paneling

I. Scope of Classification. All decorative high-pressure laminated plastic for facings, tops, splashes, wainscot, shelves, wall caps and window sills with plastic or metal trim applicable to these items.

A. Inclusions:

1. Decorative high-pressure laminated plastic, bonded to proper core.

2. WIC approved backing sheet.

3. Cutouts for sinks or other accessories.

4. Metal, wood, or self-edge trim.

5. Jobsite installation, if specified.

B. Excluded:

1. Stripping, furring, blocking, or grounds.

2. Furnishing or installation of sinks and sink rims.

II. Specification Requirements

A. The drawings and specifications should clearly indicate or specify the following:

1. WIC Grades.

   a. If the Grade is not specified, countertops of the same grade as specified for casework shall be furnished.

4. Type of edge covering; i.e., self-edged, rolled, no-drip bullnose, no-drip tilt edge, metal, wood, etc.

   a. If the above is not specified, self-edged will be furnished.

5. Type of back splash; i.e., square butt joint or integral cove.

   a. If the above is not specified, integral cove backsplash will be furnished.

6. Whether top of backsplash is to be waterfall or square with self-edge.

   a. If the above is not specified, top of splash will be square with self-edge.

7. Height of backsplash.

   a. If height is not indicated, splashes shall be a minimum of 4" in height above deck surface, unless job conditions do not permit.

   b. Unless specified otherwise, backsplashes are required at all countertops with sinks.

8. If solid colors, wood grains, or special finishes are desired.

   a. If the above is not specified, colors will be selected from non-premium priced standard patterns.

   b. If the brand, color and/or design numbers are not shown, the selection shall be based on sheet sizes available consistent with dimensions indicated on the drawings.

9. If Colorcore® or Solicor® are desired, they shall be specified. Colors selected by the architect/designer.

10. If other than textured-surfaced laminated plastic is desired for wall paneling, it must be specified, unless it is a part of a top.

11. Height of wainscot.

   a. If height is not indicated, the top of the wainscot shall be 4'-0" above the floor.

12. It is recommended that metal trim rims at sinks should overlap both countertop and sink by a minimum of 3/16". A self-rimming sink should overlap the countertop by a minimum of 3/16".

13. Cut-outs within countertops and paneling that are to be finished by the fabricator shall be so specified.

III. Grades

A. Economy: This grade establishes a standard to meet the requirements of lower cost residential and commercial construction wherein economy is the principal factor.

B. Custom: This grade includes all the requisites of a high-quality product and is suitable for all normal uses in high-grade construction, such as higher quality residential, school and commercial buildings.

C. Premium: This grade is a superior quality of workmanship and materials, with a corresponding increase in cost.

IV. Shop Drawings and Submittals

A. Shop drawings shall be submitted to the contractor, architect/designer, or owner for approval prior to fabrication.

C. Drawings shall show each typical plastic top or plastic wall panel with sufficient details to clearly indicate all unusual features in construction and shall conform to the requirements set forth in the WIC policy and procedures for Millwork Shop Drawings.

V. Workmanship

A. The assembled plastic top or plastic wall paneling shall present First Class Workmanship for Grade Specified.

VII. Material Standards

A. Surface material shall be high-pressure laminated plastic conforming to NEMA LD-3 latest edition.

   1. Tops, splashes, and shelves shall be faced with general purpose type laminated decorative sheets a minimum of .050" in thickness or .042" post forming grade if required.

   3. Formica Colorcore® or Wilsonart Solicor® conforming to manufacturer's standards.

B. Backing sheets shall be any one of the following for the entire job and WIC Grade indicated.

Premium Grade

   1. A minimum of .020" thickness conforming to NEMA LD latest edition or Gator Ply® .028" thickness, is permitted for all grades and is required as the only backing sheet for Premium Grade.

Economy and Custom Grades

   1. Man-made wood-fiber veneers that are impregnated with acrylic melamine fortified high load resin system, a minimum of .020". (Gator Ply®, produced by International Paper Co.) is permitted for Economy and Custom Grades only.

   2. Synthetic polymer treated backing sheet .017–.019 nominal thickness designed for use with decorative high pressure laminate known as Dynopregh-ply, thickness of .020 and .026 produced by Dyno Overlays, Inc., formerly Reichold Chemical Co., is permitted for Economy and Custom Grades only.

3. Dark brown colored .015 nominal thickness phenolic resin impregnated craft paper (Simpson Backing sheet #.015 produced by Simpson Timber Co.) is permitted for Economy and Custom Grades only.

4. Thermoset resin treated wood-fibered brown color 3-ply construction, a minimum thickness of .020, known as Resobak #184C produced by Pioneer Plastic Corporation is permitted for Economy and Custom Grades only.

Economy Grade Only

1. Hot melt coat brown colored .002" minimum thickness factory applied to particleboard core coat of blended wax petroleum, copolymer resins and anti-oxidants and swip controlling agents (HMC, produced by Willamette Industries) is required for Economy Grade only.

2. Low pressure polyester or melamine laminate (ALA 851) (to PB 1M-2) for Economy Grade only.

C. Core material for tops, splashes, and shelves shall be a minimum of 3/4".

1. Unsupported spans should be reinforced to prevent deflection in excess of 1/4" with a 50 lb. load.

D. Cove Stick.

1. For a 3/4" radius, a moulded cove stick shall be used with no voids permitted between the plastic laminate and the cove stick. The cove stick shall be the same thickness as the core material, and no voids are permitted at either joint.

2. For a 1/4" radius, a square stick is permitted with all voids filled with glue between laminate and cove stick, providing it is the same thickness as the core material.

E. Adhesives.

1. Contact adhesive laminations must pass the WIC Heat Resistance Test and must comply with Type II adhesive moisture resistance testing (see **Figure 6.13**).

VIII. Grade Rules—Tops, Splashes, and Shelves

A. Economy Grade.

1. Core material shall be particleboard.

2. The laminated plastic shall be securely glued to the core with Type II adhesive applied as recommended by the adhesive manufacturer.

Ed. Note: See **Figure 6.12**, *"Technical Bulletin: Selection Guide to Adhesives."*

3. The underside of tops and the backside of splashes shall be covered with HMC backing sheet or any other approved backing sheet.

4. Exposed edges of core material shall be neatly and entirely covered by trim as shown or specified. Where tops are subject to excessive moisture, edges shall be sealed before the metal trim or sink rim is installed.

5. Holes for sinks will be cut, but the furnishing or installation of metal sink rims is not included.

6. All joints shall be neatly and carefully made. Care shall be taken to make all joints water tight. Waterproof sealant shall be used at all square butt joint splashes and shall be color matched. All connecting surfaces shall be flush within the manufacturing tolerance of the process used. Tops which require field joints shall be joined with bolt-up type fasteners, if practicable.

7. All exposed edges shall be eased.

8. Appropriate scribe allowance shall be provided.

9. Wood grained patterns for an L-shaped top shall have a diagonal joint approximately 45 degrees. A butt joint is not permitted.

10. Exposed fastening will not be allowed, except for access panels.

11. Maximum unsupported countertop spans shall not exceed 48", unless otherwise specified.

12. Sink cut-outs will not fall within 18" of discretionary field joints.

B. Custom Grade.

All requirements of Economy Grade are included herein, with additional requirements as follows:

1. Core material (1) shall be particleboard, rotary cut Lauan, or other hardwood plywood with "Sound" (2) Grade face veneer; and the crossband under the face veneer shall be Industrial (3) Grade or better.

2. The laminated plastic shall be securely glued to the core with Type II adhesive applied as recommended by the adhesive manufacturer. In addition to meeting the requirements of Type II, the adhesive shall meet WIC Heat Resistant Test Requirements.

3. The underside of tops and the backside of splashes shall be covered with an approved backing sheet.

4. Plastic tops requiring more than one sheet of laminate shall have the plastic prematched to minimize color variation within the scope of the manufacturer's guarantee, and shall be fabricated from the longest sheet lengths available.

WOODWORK INSTITUTE OF CALIFORNIA
TECHNICAL BULLETIN

SELECTION GUIDE TO ADHESIVES

ADHESIVE:	PERFORMANCE TEST:
Type I — Fully Waterproof (Exterior)	2 Cycle Boil/Shear Test
Type II — Water Resistant (Interior)	3 Cycle Soak Test
Type III — Water Resistant (Interior)	2 Cycle Soak Test

GENERIC NAME	USED FOR BONDING	TYPE ANSI/HPMA 1983 NWWDA I.S.1986	CHARACTERISTICS
1. Aliphatic (Carpenter's Glue)	Wood and wood products	Type II	Non-toxic; non-flammable; and non-staining; **NOT** waterproof; water resistant
2. Casein	Wood and wood products	Type II	Highly water resistant, **NOT** waterproof
3. Contact Cement	Plastic laminates and veneers to wood	Type II	Highly water resistant; not waterproof (see WIC approved list)
4. Epoxy	Wide range; wood; wood to metals	Type I	Two-part glue — Formulas vary; Completely waterproof
5. Hot-melt Glue	Wide range; bonds wood to vinyl, metal and wood	Not tested for moisture resistance	Liquefies when heated; bonds in a liquid state; solidifies as it cools. Used extensively for edge banders and other automatic equipment.
6. Polyvinyl Acetate PVA	Wood and wood products	Slight moisture resistance	Good for cabinet work and interior woodwork. Not recommended for joints with sustained loads.
7. Polyvinyl Acetate PVA (Polyvinyl Acetate Catalyzed)	Wood and Wood Products	Type I	Used for assembly gluing where exterior waterproof bonds are required.
8. Polyvinyl Chloride PVC	Wide variety of materials	Not tested for moisture resistance	Crystal clear, fast drying.
9. Resorcinol Resin	Wood, wood products and laminates	Type I	Fully waterproof; purple glue line; two parts; liquid resin and powdered catalyst. Pot life — 3 hours.
10. Urea Resin	Wood and wood products	Type II	Plastic resin glue; mixed with water; excellent for cabinet work; must be clamped. Drying time — 3 to 7 hours at 70 degrees Fahrenheit.
11. Liquid Nail or "Lock-Tite"	Metal to wood, particleboard, or plywood; also plastic surfaces	Type II	Plastic epoxy base; liquid state; dries fast; very difficult to remove. Can be used to permanently set adjustment screws in European type hinges.

Courtesy of Woodwork Institute of California, *Technical Bulletin: Selection Guide to Adhesives*

Figure 6.12

5. Where self-edge trim is used, the top laminate may extend over the edge laminate, or the edge laminate may be face applied.

   a. Where self-edge front trim is used, the built-up member shall be particleboard, solid stock, plywood, or particleboard with backing sheet or liner. The bottom edge shall be free of dents, torn grain, glue, etc., and shall be smoothly sanded if a backing sheet is not used.

6. When backsplashes are required, square butt joint end splashes of a corresponding height shall be furnished at wall or closed end.

7. Exposed shelves (shelves not in cabinets) shall be covered on both sides with the same material. Shelves less than 4'-0" above the floor may have a backing sheet in lieu of exposed material securely glued to the underside of the core with identical adhesive and under identical circumstances as the face sheet.

   b. All visible edges shall be edge-banded with the same material as the face of the shelf, unless otherwise specified.

8. Exposed fastening will not be allowed, except for access panels.

9. Unless specified otherwise, an integral cove backsplash shall be provided.

C. Premium Grade. All requirements of Custom Grade are included herein, with additional requirements as follows:

1. The undersides of tops and the backside of splashes shall be covered with .020 thickness backing sheet conforming to NEMA LD 3.

2. Where self-edging trim is used, the top laminate shall extend over the edge laminate on the front edges of the top only.

3. Application of Colorcore® or Solicor® as set forth in manufacturer's literature. Strictly conform to manufacturer's recommendation for adhesives. A high pressure laminate backing sheet is required.

4. Exposed fastening will not be allowed except for access panels.

5. Raw core at joint between countertop deck and backsplash shall be sealed before assembly.

Finishing of Millwork
Industry Standards
WIC Manual of Millwork
(Woodwork Institute of California)

WIC has made no effort to determine whether any of these finishing systems complies with Air Quality Management District regulations in California or any other state. A firm that performs factory finishing should contact the local EPA or Air Quality Management District to determine what types of finish material are approved.

I. Scope of Classification

All Architectural Millwork that is to be factory finished prior to delivery and installation, shall be specified properly to attain the desired aesthetic effect, such as color, gloss, and thickness of finish. Also, serviceability, toughness, adhesion, good wearing characteristics, and moisture resistance.

(For obvious reasons it is very difficult to determine "how many coats" of each step in the system are needed. The desirable end result should be to provide a finish that adds beauty to the wood, and gives desirable color, tone, smoothness, and depth.)

A. Inclusions:

1. All architectural millwork specified to be prefinished, including wood doors with special finish systems.

2. All preparatory work.

3. Labor to apply materials.

4. Shop facility including spray room and equipment.

5. All materials as specified.

6. All related supplies needed.

B. Exclusions:

1. Any items not specified in architectural millwork contract.

2. All exterior or interior painting or priming of walls or surfaces not specified.

II. Specification Requirements

A. Drawings and specifications should clearly specify:

2. Indicate if factory or jobsite finishing is desired.

3. Architectural millwork including interior trim; miscellaneous interior millwork; interior wood jambs; interior wood stairwork; wood casework, counters, and fixtures; wood doors; wall paneling; wainscot; and other specialty wood items.

4. The type of finish required. Generic classifications are:

System #1 — Lacquers, Water reducible acrylic
System #2 — Varnish
System #3 — Polyurethane
System #4 — Epoxy
System #5 — Penetrating Oils
System #6 — Synthetic Enamels
System #7 — Fire-Retardant Coatings

6. If a Laboratory-Type finish is desired. Systems 1, 2, 3, or 4 must be specified as Catalyzed Lacquer, Catalyzed Conversion Varnish, Catalyzed Polyurethane, Catalyzed Vinyl Lacquer, or Epoxy for acid resistance.

7. If to be stained for transparent finish or opaque finish.

8. If back priming is to be done by manufacturer.

9. Whether Fire-Retardant Coatings are required.

III. Standards

A. General Information.

1. Finishing of Architectural Woodwork can be applied at the jobsite, provided there is no violation of local, state, or EPA codes or regulations.

2. If the Architect/Specifier requires a high-quality finish, then the factory controlled finishing environment offers a superior finished product.

3. The basic purpose of finishing woodwork is to protect it from potential damage caused by moisture in the atmosphere, from day-to-day usage, and to maintain good appearance for the life of the project.

   a. Each finish system should be selected to give the best performance results. Costs of each system vary considerably and should be weighed carefully to accomplish the results desired.

4. Before making the final selection of a finish system, there are some other considerations, namely:

5. Some species of wood contain a chemical (oak, particularly) which reacts unfavorably with certain finishes. Where possible, a test sample should be made to check for unfavorable reactions. Application of a sealer before finishing will usually prevent this difficulty.

6. Oil stain shall be wiped — small areas at a time. Non-grain raising dye stains can be sprayed.

7. Open grain wood and veneers shall be stained first, before applying sealer. If filler is specified, it shall be tinted to required color before finish is applied, unless an oil finish is used. Where a dark stained finish is to be used, the wood surface shall be wash coat sealed. For finishing purposes, some hardwoods may be classified as follows:

Hardwoods with Open Grain	
Ash	Oak, Red
Butternut	Oak, White
Chestnut	Walnut
African Mahogany	Honduras Mahogany
Philippine Mahogany (Lauan)	

Hardwoods with Close Grain	
Alder, Red	Cherry
Beech	Gum
Birch, Red*	Maple*
Birch, White*	

* Birch or Maple have pores large enough to take wood filler effectively when desired, but small enough as a rule to be finished without filler. Dark stains are not recommended; but if they are desired, it is recommended that Birch or Maple be filled and/or wash coat sealed before the stain is applied. It is very difficult to obtain a uniform dark color on Birch or Maple.

8. Panel products require special finishing consideration. A "balanced" panel product is specially constructed for stability. To remain free from warp, the panel should be finished with balanced coats of finishing material.

9. The Architect/Specifier after selecting the desired Finish System, should select the final color or sheen. If special colors or matching are required, the Architect/Specifier shall provide the woodworker/finisher with preferred color samples. This should be accomplished during the pricing stage, otherwise a price will be agreed upon for additional expense of a special finish match. In the event that grain and color of veneers vary widely the finisher may find it necessary to do substantial toning and color blending to arrive at the desired final color or sheen. It is mandatory that adequate finish samples be submitted. (See IV, "Submittals")

10. Generally speaking the grade of finishing selected should be the same as the grade of woodwork fabrication. Exceptions to the above statement can occur when a fabrication grade is chosen to meet budget needs and perhaps a higher or lower grade of finishing will suffice. In any event, the specifications should clearly call for any such change in finishing grade.

11. The finishing of architectural woodwork is always critical to the final results. The Architect/Specifier is always free to modify suggested standards in any way he sees fit.

12. Standard door manufacturers will usually only produce their own standard finishes. If the specifier lists one or more acceptable door manufacturers in his or her specifications, this indicates that the door manufacturers standard finishes are acceptable. If special door finishes are required they must be so specified to be applied by the woodworker.

13. Glossary of Special Terms:

    Non-Grain Raising Stains contain no pigmented solids and are usually spray applied.

    Wiping Stains do contain color particles and many color variations are available. Can be applied by spray, brushing, or hand wiped.

    Bleaching lightens the base color of the wood to give a more uniform appearance.

    Fillers are used to close or fill the pores to give a smooth appearance. Apply by brush, roller, or spray. Wipe or squeeze off against the grain.

    Glazing is a specialty step to achieve color uniformity where the natural wood color may be too strong in contrast.

    Toning is the use of semi-transparent colors to block out or reduce the color of the wood.

    Sealers lock in the stain or fillers and provide a knit or base for the final top coat or coats. It contributes to the "build" and resists moisture penetration.

    Washcoats are thinned coats of sealer to act as a barrier against over penetration of stains which cause blotchiness.

    Hand Rubbing is performed to smooth, flatten or give a more uniform finished effect. Represents additional costs.

    High-Polished Finish involves several operations of wet sanding, buffing and final high gloss polishing. This also represents additional costs.

    Distressing of Aging gives the appearance of being older. Can be done by hand, mechanical, or chemical methods.

14. **Color and light:** Lighting can drastically affect the color of the finish system applied to the wood surface. The color we see is the result of the surrounding light reflected off the wood surface.

When a color is observed under more than one light source, such as fluorescent lighting, incandescent lighting, or natural sunlight, or when colors match under one of the light sources just mentioned but look different if all sources of light are in play, there undoubtedly will be a sharp contrast or difference in appearance. This phenomenon is known as "metamerism." Care must be taken to emphasize this to the Architect/Specifier to avoid conflict.

B. Casework: All items of casework shall include exposed, semi-exposed, and concealed areas as previously defined.

  1. Both sides of cabinet doors and all edges shall receive the same number of coats to prevent warping and twisting.

C. Running and Standing Trim and Wood Door Frames: Normally include finishing of exposed faces and edges only. If back priming is desired, specifications should clearly state if it is to be done by the architectural millwork manufacturer.

D. Library Shelving; Store and Bank Fixtures; Wall Paneling and Decorative Items: These items shall be finished as specified with the materials and system selected to match approved color samples submitted. Before finishing, remove all handling marks or effects of exposure to moisture with a complete, thorough, and final block over all surfaces using at least 150 grit sandpaper, followed by 220 grit finishing paper, then carefully cleaned with dry brush or tack cloth before applying sealer or other coats. Deep scratches must be steamed out before sanding. Sharp edges shall be eased by sanding.

E. Wood Doors: Before finishing all hardware must be removed or properly masked. The entire surface of wood doors including faces, top and bottom edges, as well as hinge and lock edges, shall receive two coats of oil-base mixed paint, varnish, or lacquer immediately after fitting, cutting for closures, weatherstrips, and/or thresholds. Exterior wood doors shall be finished before exposure to weather. Adequate drying time must be allowed between coats. An equal number of finish coats shall be applied to each side, and the same system and material shall be used on each side. Pairs of doors and openings with sidelights and transoms shall be finished and toned together to achieve maximum uniformity of color.

IV. Submittals

A. Samples: Submit samples of sufficient size to clearly show grain and color variations with finish type specified. At least 16" x 24" for plywood; 6" x 10" long for solid stock. Each sample should bear a label identifying the job name, the Architect/Designer, the general contractor, and the Finish System number. The sample materials submitted shall be representative of that to be used for the project.

V. Delivery, Storage, and Handling

A. Provide adequate storage facilities.

Ed. Note: See the WIC excerpt, "Delivery & Storage," earlier in this chapter.

VI. Environmental Requirements

A. Measure moisture content of wall surfaces such as drywall, plaster, etc, using an electronic moisture meter. **Do not** apply finish unless moisture content of surfaces is below 12%.

B. Minimum application temperature for varnish and lacquer finishes is 65° F.

C. Provide adequate continuous ventilation and sufficient heating facilities to maintain temperatures above 65° F for 24 hours before, during, and 48 hours after application of finishes.

D. All waste materials must be properly disposed of to conform to all local, state, and federal requirements.

VII. Materials

A. Paint, varnish, stain, enamel, sealers, filters, and necessary thinners to apply finish system specified.

B. Provide all other materials not specifically indicated but necessary to achieve the finishes specified.

C. Coatings to have good flowing properties and capable of drying or curing free of streaks or sags.

VIII. Preparation

A. Examine carefully all surfaces to be finished before commencement of work. Report in writing to Architect/Designer/Engineer any condition that may affect proper application.

B. Remove handling marks or effects of exposure to moisture with a complete, thorough, and final sanding of all surfaces. The sanded surface shall be smooth and free from raised grain, cross-sanding, burnishing, machining, and manufacturing marks. Clean surfaces with dry brush or tack cloth before applying sealer, stain, or primer. Deep scratches must be steamed out before sanding. Ease sharp edges with light sanding. The finish sanding quality of unfinished woodwork will determine the quality of the final finished product. It is required that all sanding inconsistencies and defects be removed before the finish is applied.

C. As required for the finish system specified, open grain woods and veneers, if desired to have a paste wood filler prior to sealing, it shall be so specified. Tint the filler to approximate stain or grain color if transparent finishes are specified.

D. Opaque finishes require hard closed grain surfaces such as medium density fiberboard (MDF) or a closed grain hardwood such as Birch.

E. For transparent finish to prevent sharp color contrast from member to member, panel to panel, flitch to flitch, solid stock to adjacent veneers, toning or sap staining to obtain compatible and uniform color is required.

F. For transparent finish, if the species is not specified, the use of either hardwood or softwood (plywood or solid stock) of one species for the entire job is permitted, at the option of the manufacturer.

1. For Custom Grade, solid stock and/or plywood shall be compatible in color and grain.

2. For Premium Grade, solid stock shall be well matched for color and grain; plywood shall be compatible in color with solid stock; and adjacent plywood panels shall be well matched for color and grain.

IX. Protection

A. For factory finishing of cabinets, doors, trim, and specialty items, provide adequate protection to adjacent surfaces and items from overspray and damage. Repair damage as a result of inadequate or unsuitable protection.

B. Furnish sufficient drop cloths, shields, and protective equipment to prevent spray or droppings from fouling surfaces not being finished and, in particular, surfaces within storage and preparation area.

C. Place cotton waste, cloths, and material which may constitute a fire hazard in closed metal containers and remove daily from site. Be careful to avoid spraying near electric motors, compressors, or other spark inducing contact. Steel wool can be extremely dangerous on or near electrical outlets.

X. Application

A. Apply each coat at proper consistency, as recommended by the paint manufacturer.

B. Sand lightly between coats with an appropriate grit finishing paper to provide a smooth, scratch-free finish.

C. Do not sand or apply finishes to surfaces that are not dry.

D. Allow each coat to thoroughly dry before applying next coat.

E. In book matching plywood, every other leaf of veneer is turned over as the leaves are taken in sequence from the flitch, similar to turning or unfolding the pages of a book. Since one leaf will be loose side up and the next tight side up, book matching produces a color shading. In book matching, obtain a match for color and grain at the joints. The tight and loose faces alternating in adjacent leaves may refract light differently, and cause a noticeable color variation in some species. *Proper finishing techniques will minimize this variation.*

Adjacent panels, like pairs of doors, should be finished together to achieve maximum uniformity of color. If possible, entire elevations should be finished together.

F. First class workmanship shall be required for WIC Grade specified.

Where woodwork is to be factory-primed only, one coat of primer is to be applied to appropriate surfaces. Sanding of factory-primed only surfaces is not mandatory.

XI. Cleaning

A. Promptly remove all finish materials spilled, splashed, or spattered.

XII. Finishing Schedule

G. Field Touch-Up: Field touch-up after installation is important to the overall appearance expected. All scratches, dents, marks, screw and nail holes, raw or rough edges resulting from job installation, shall be properly sanded, puttied, stained, filled and coated to match the original finish. A final dusting of all exterior and interior surfaces, including drawers, shall be carefully done including the removal of fingerprints or other marks. Advised when items are ready for back priming, if specified. A quantity of touch-up materials shall be provided, after completed, to allow the owner to do minor touch-up. Materials must be properly labeled.

H. Back Priming

1. If back priming is not a part of the architectural millwork manufacturer's contract, the general contractor will be advised when items are ready for back priming, if specified.

2. Material requirements for back priming are based on the type of finish to be applied to exposed portions of installed millwork.

   a. Lacquer or Vinyl Finish — One Coat Lacquer or Vinyl Sanding Sealer.

   b. Varnish Finish — One Coat Semi-gloss Varnish.

   c. Opaque Finish — One Coat Primer or Undercoater.

   d. Plastic Laminate Faced Millwork — One Coat Primer, Sealer, or suitable Backing Sheet.

I. Wood Finish Systems: Several generic types of finishes are available to finish wood products. These systems vary in composition from alkyd clears to phenolic varnishes, polyurethane, epoxy, vinyls, epoxy-polyesters, acrylic, polymeric oils, and lacquers. A finish system should be chosen that will perform properly for the end use required.

Kitchen Cabinets

Comments

Before kitchen cabinets can be installed, the job must be thoroughly planned, and the space prepared. Pre-planning includes sharing plan information with all involved subcontractors, and careful review of all their work to avoid potential conflicts. This is also the time to make sure that any structural issues have been identified and planned for, to ensure that the electrical service is adequate for equipment and proposed new outlets, and that proposed plumbing rough-ins are correctly located.

Prior to cabinet installation, all electrical, mechanical and plumbing work should be roughed-in and preparation work for the walls, ceiling and floor should be completed. Any finished surfaces should be protected with cardboard or tarps. Cabinets that have been removed from their boxes should be protected with padded coverings.

Since cabinets must be installed plumb and level, level floor and ceiling lines must be established, based on high (floor) and low (ceiling) points. Unevenness in walls should be identified and remedied.

*Both Imperial and metric dimensions are used by cabinet manufacturers, and many provide both units of measure for ease in integrating systems. **Figure 6.14** shows the standard height and depth dimensions for base and wall cabinets, counter heights, and wall cabinet mounting heights. Note: On occasion, an owner may request or agree to a minor adjustment in these heights to accommodate factors such as wheelchair access or low ceilings.*

Cabinet Performance Standards

Industry Standards

Kitchen & Bathroom Installation Manual, Volume 1
(National Kitchen & Bath Association)

The most recognized and specified standard for kitchen cabinets is ANSI/KCMA A.161.1.1990. This is a performance standard that measures the ability of cabinets to withstand various strict tests that replicate typical household usage and measures desirable construction and performance characteristics. The Kitchen Cabinet Manufacturers Association administers a nationally recognized testing and certification program. Companies that successfully pass this annual battery of tests, performed on randomly selected products, are able to display the blue and white seal. A directory of certified manufacturers and their approved lines is available from KCMA.

Ed. Note: See the Introduction to this chapter for NKBA and KCMA contact information.

Types of Cabinets

Framed Cabinets

In framed cabinet construction, thin component parts make up the sides, back, top, and bottom of the cabinet. These parts are then joined together and attached to a frame that is the primary support for the cabinet. Framed cabinets do not have the minimal clearance tolerances found in the frameless method of cabinet construction.

Comments

Three types of doors are used with framed cabinets: partial overlay (most frequently used), full overlay, and inset. Partial overlay doors can be adjusted fairly easily, so tolerances are not as crucial. Full overlay doors can also be adjusted vertically or horizontally, but the installer must be careful not to allow any obstructions between doors, drawers, or hardware.

Frameless Cabinets

With this method of construction, 5/8" to 3/4" (1.59 cm to 1.91 cm) core material sides are connected, with either a mechanical fastening system or a dowel method of construction. Because of their thickness, these case parts form a box that does not need a front frame for stability or squareness. Whether the doors are full overlay or inset, the very tight tolerance for the reveal between doors or between doors and the cabinet box is critical. This reveal is usually 1/8" (3 mm) or less. The slightest misalignment is obvious with such tight tolerances, which is why the doors usually have (and need) 6-way adjustable hinges.

With full overlay doors, *scribing fillers* are required wherever a cabinet is being installed adjacent to a wall. This is necessary to allow for sufficient clearance for the door to hinge open. Scribing fillers are scribed or cut to follow the exact contour of the wall. Similar fillers may be required to allow for proper functioning of cabinets directly adjacent to appliances, when cabinets meet at right angles, or if the cabinet unit has roll-out drawers requiring the cabinet door to swing a little more than 90°. These fillers do not generally need to be scribed.

European Cabinets

European or *Euro-style* cabinets are frameless, and all the shelf supports and connecting hardware are inserted into pre-drilled holes a standard 32 mm (1-1/4") on center. European wall cabinets are hung on hanging rails that are generally furnished with the cabinet units. The wall cabinet units themselves are not permanently attached to the wall. The hanging rail is a length of steel approximately 1-1/4" wide. It has an offset channel that is designed to accept the adjustable hooks on the back of each wall cabinet unit. The rail length corresponds to the width of the wall cabinet being installed. The hanging rail is drilled and screwed to wall studs. Most manufacturers recommend that 1/4" holes be pre-drilled in the rails for mounting. Use #14, 2-1/2" pan head screws to attach the rails to the wall studs. European cabinet hinges are fully adjustable, allowing the typical full overlay doors to be easily adjusted.

Some cabinets are designed to have the hanging rail behind the wall cabinet units, while others use a rail that is run above the wall cabinets. When the rail is exposed, crown moulding or trim should be planned above the cabinets to conceal the hanging rail. If the hanging rail runs behind the wall cabinets, the backs of the cabinets should be notched so that the cabinets will sit tight against the back wall. However, do not notch the exposed end panel of a wall cabinet at the end of a run of cabinets. Instead, stop the rail at the inside of this end panel.

European base cabinets are not as deep as their North American counterparts, so standard-depth countertops will overhang these base cabinets too far. Some North American installers place blocking behind the cabinets to push them forward to the standard 24" (60.96 cm) depth. You will need special end panels on exposed cabinet ends to cover the gap between the wall and the base cabinets. Make sure you use washers or some other means of keeping the screws from pulling through the back of the cabinet if you choose to screw the base cabinets to the wall.

Typical Imperial and Metric Cabinet Dimensions

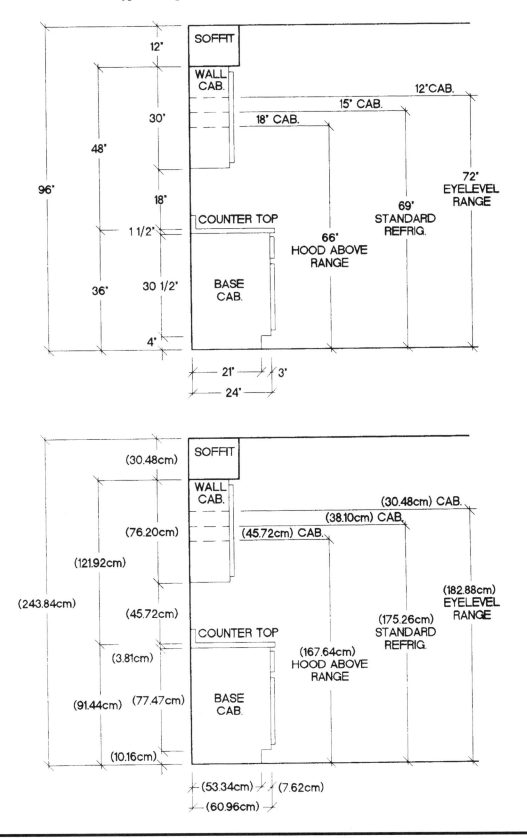

Figure 6.13

Cabinet Fasteners

All manufacturers agree that screws are the fastener of choice in almost all installation applications.

The fasteners most commonly used are #8 and #10 screws, with the recommended head types varying by cabinet manufacturer. Wall cabinets are generally attached to wood studs with #8 or #10 wood screws or drywall screws of sufficient length to pass through the cabinet and wall finish and penetrate the wall stud by at least 3/4" (1.905 cm). A minimum of four (4) screws are mounted through the top and bottom horizontal mounting rails of each wall cabinet. Cabinets over 42" wide should have six (6) screws. This is somewhat dependent on the stud layout. If you were not able to locate a wall stud, or if a stud does not exist at the point where the cabinet is being mounted, install what you can and then use the next cabinet to add support. Toggle bolts can be used in some cases in lieu of attaching to a stud, but in no case should a wall cabinet be installed without being secured to at least one wall stud.

Solid masonry walls offer an additional challenge, since there are no studs to screw into and no hollow walls to bolt through. Most manufacturers recommend the use of electrician rawls or some type of lag bolt system for mounting to masonry walls, with the quantity required being the same as for regular screw installations.

Alternatively, lag bolt a hanging rail to the masonry wall first, and then mount the cabinets to the rail. The hanging rail is usually a 1x4 (2.54 cm x 10.16 cm). Some installers will notch out the wall finish so that the rail can set directly against the masonry and thus reduce the gap between the back of the cabinets and the wall.

To attach adjacent wall cabinet units, #8 x 2-1/4" or 2-1/2" (5.715 cm or 6.35 cm) wood screws or drywall screws should be fastened through the vertical stile of one cabinet into the vertical stile of the adjacent cabinet. The length is dependent on the thickness of the stiles, which varies from manufacturer to manufacturer. Two (2) screws per pair of wall cabinets being connected are generally sufficient for cabinets up to 36" (91.44 cm). Cabinets taller than this should have three (3) screws.

Fasteners for base cabinets are similar to those used for wall cabinets. However, because base cabinets are resting on the floor surface, fasteners are used basically to secure the unit in place once it has been leveled. If the base cabinet backs up to only one wall surface, two screws placed through the center of the mounting rail into wall studs are generally sufficient to stabilize the unit. Adjacent units are screwed together through the vertical stiles or through the adjoining cabinet side panel, depending on whether they are framed or frameless cabinets.

Brads or other suitable types of nails are recommended only for use with wood trim, panels, and other types of mouldings. Nails are not considered sufficient fasteners for either base or wall cabinets.

Professional Tips for Cabinet Installation

- When a wall cabinet is planned that is continuous from countertop to soffit or ceiling (a 48"- to 60"-high unit) (122 – 152 cm), consider special clearance. Reduce overall cabinet slightly. A countertop platform should be planned beneath the wall cabinet, finished either to match the cabinet with moulding, or the counter material, so doors will not rest on the countertop. Scribing room is built in. A 3/4" to 1-1/2" (2-4 cm) platform is recommended.

- When installing wall cabinets to the ceiling, make sure there are not recessed lights designed with the lamp below the edge of the diffuser (which is flush with the ceiling), nor any surface-mounted light closer than the dimension of the cabinet door when open. Ideally, the cabinet should be down from the ceiling an inch or so and trimmed out with moulding to let doors open and close.

- If placing a drawer unit against a wall with a window or door opening, use a 1" to 1-1/2" (2.5–4 cm) filler between cabinet and wall so drawer will miss casing. Do the same with a drawer unit in a corner so drawers at right angles will miss each other.

- (For roll-out shelves) make sure the door opens past 90° to allow the shelves to roll out.

- Corbel brackets support extended counters. Generally, an overhang more than 12" (30 cm) needs a support bracket every 36" (91 cm).

- Outside corner moulding is used to seal a joint between two panels at right angles. Scribe moulding is used to finish along an uneven ceiling. Batten moulding is used to cover joints between adjacent cabinets.

- Countertop edge mouldings and backsplash mouldings are used to finish the top with solid surface, ceramic tiles and laminates. These surfaces should be finished all the way around if used with tile. With solid surface, mouldings may be installed unfinished so they can be sanded flush with the top, then finished. Or finished mouldings can be installed slightly offset from the solid surface edgings.

Comments

Cabinets should not be forced into position. Use of shims and scribes should be the rule. Forcing will only rack the cabinet out of square and make operation of drawers and doors sticky.

Kitchen & Bathroom Countertops

Industry Standards

Kitchen & Bathroom Installation Manual, Volume 1
(National Kitchen & Bath Association)

Kitchen and bathroom countertop surfaces must stand up to heavy use, and be very resilient. Typical surface materials for countertops include decorative laminates, cast polymers, solid surface composites, ceramic tile, marble, granite, wood, and stainless steel. These materials may be used alone or in combination.

Decorative Laminates

Decorative laminate surfacing materials are generally adhered to a substrate of 3/4" (1.91 cm) plywood or particle board. A 3/4" (1.91 cm) thick wood frame is attached to the bottom of the substrate material to give the countertop rigidity. The countertop is attached to the base cabinets by screwing into this wood frame. The wood frame is generally applied at the perimeter of the countertop and at all seams in the substrate material.

Solid-Surfacing

Solid surface materials are man-made composites, made of polymers and acrylics in combination with other materials that produce tough, rigid, high performance countertop surfaces.

Installation tips for solid-surface countertops:

- A quality installation is largely dependent on the skill and experience of the fabricator. Most manufacturers of solid surface materials train and certify fabricators.

- When properly fabricated, the seam between two pieces of the solid-surfacing materials is almost imperceptible.

- All manufacturers recommend that unsupported overhangs should not exceed 12" (30.48 cm) with 3/4" sheets or 6" (15.24 cm) with 1/2" sheets.

- All manufacturers recommend that the material "float" on the substrate. Most recommend perimeter frames and a web support system 18" on center rather than a full substrate.

- Because solid surface materials expand when heated, all manufacturers recommend at least 1/8" clearance on wall-to-wall installations.

- While only one manufacturer specifically requires the use of biscuit splines, some installers find that it is wise to use biscuits for most installations to allow for accurate alignment of the two sections being joined. Generally three biscuits are used for each joint: one set in about 3" from each outside edge and one in the middle.

Comments

Most manufacturers of solid surface countertops do not recommend their use for exterior applications. Exposure to temperature variations and sunlight can cause changes in color, and expansion and contraction of the material.

Cast Polymers

Cultured marble, cultured onyx, cultured granite and *solid-colored polymer-based materials* are all used for cast mineral-filled polymer fixtures. Although generally referred to as "cultured marble," a better term to use when describing all of these materials is *cast polymer*. Cast polymers are created by pouring a mixture of ground marble and polyester resin into a treated mold where curing takes place at room temperature or in a curing oven.

The best way to ensure that you will receive a quality countertop is to use suppliers who are certified under the joint Cultured Marble Institute (CMI) — National Association of Home Builders Research Center (NAHB RC) Certification Program.

Comments

Cast polymers are also known as "cultured marble," "cultured onyx," and "cultured granite."

Ceramic Tile

Ed. Note: See also Chapter 10, "Drywall & Ceramic Tile," for more information on ceramic tile.

Make certain that the type of ceramic tile specified for the installation project is manufactured with all the specially designed edge and trim pieces required to put together a countertop. Trim pieces are generally manufactured with a 3/4" (1.91 cm) radius for conventional mortar installations and a 1/4" (.64 cm) radius for organic adhesive installations.

Ceramic tile countertops are installed directly on a deck or substrate by one of three installation methods: *mastic* (organic adhesive), *conventional mortar bed* (mud), or *thin set* over a backerboard.

While plywood decking is the most common substrate material for countertops, some installers prefer traditional lumber decking. Traditional decking is often used to provide flexibility under the tile. Generally, grade-one or grade-two kiln dried Douglas fir, 1"x 4" (2.54 cm x 10.16 cm) or 1" x 6" (2.54 cm x 15.24 cm) spaced 1/4" (.64 cm) apart, is used. It may be installed perpendicular to the backsplash (from the front of the counter to the back) or running parallel with the cabinet space.

The decking should be delivered to the project site several days before the installation to allow the wood to reach the relative humidity of the room. The decking should overhang the cabinets and be flush with the face of the drawers and doors.

Fixture cutouts are made during the tile decking installation. Whenever possible, any cutout should be a minimum of 2" (5.08 cm) away from a wallboard or plastered backsplash.

Elimination of stress is critical when countertop overhangs are planned. The tile must have a solid base. If any movement occurs when pressure is placed on the top, the tile and/or grout will crack. The underside of the decking should be finished to match the cabinets or correspond with other products used in the project.

Granite

Granite countertops are prefabricated and delivered to the job site ready for installation. Accurate field dimensions are a must, since modification of a granite countertop in the field is nearly impossible.

For most granite countertops, the optimum thickness is 1-1/4" (3.18 cm). The difference in cost over the more fragile 3/4" (1.91 cm) slabs is minimal and the added thickness gives more strength for extensions and cutouts, while reducing the risk of breakage during transport and installation. For example, a 1-1/4" (3.18 cm) granite slab can support 12" (30.48 cm) of overhang. Keep in mind the weight of these countertops as you plan your installation.

Granite slabs for countertops can measure up to 4'-6" (137.16 cm) wide and up to 9' (274.32 cm) long. This allows flexibility in countertop design. Should more than one piece be necessary, the slabs can be matched for color and grain consistency and then cut to butt squarely against each other. You want to plan seams at the most inconspicuous locations possible, such as around cutouts or back corners. However, avoid seams in the vicinity of the sink cutout due to the possibility of moisture infiltration.

Marble

Marble is extremely brittle, and must be handled like glass during installation. Marble is soft and porous. This means it will stain easily if it is not sealed with at least two coats of penetrating sealer. And it must be frequently resealed.

Wood

Countertops made from laminated wood products are commonly referred to as butcher block. In addition to full countertops, insert blocks are often installed in other types of kitchen countertops as cutting boards. The intended use of block should determine the finish selection. Unfinished wood is most desirable if the entire counter surface is wood and local fabrication of seams or miters is required. (Seams do not adhere properly with prefinished tops, and the wood must be refinished if any sanding is done.) For prefinished wood, the factory finish will include a penetrating sealer and non-toxic lacquer finish. This type of finish is appropriate for countertop sections, such as island tops or sandwich centers. Wood treated with varethane sealer is not appropriate for use as a chopping surface or in contact with food. The finish is, however, very good on countertops that will be exposed to moisture or liquids.

Clean-Up

Comments

When all kitchen components have been installed, all debris and temporary protective materials should be removed. All surfaces should be left "maid-clean." Scratches or nicks that may have occurred can usually be patched using a touch-up kit available from the manufacturer. In anticipation of these minor repairs, the kit can be ordered along with the cabinets.

CHAPTER

7

INSULATION & VAPOR RETARDERS

Table of Contents

(continued on next page)

185

Text in blue print indicates excerpts from model building code(s). "Comments"
(in solid blue boxes) were written by the editors, based on their own experience.

For building product information, use this book's special
Internet gateway to thousands of manufacturers:
www.rsmeans.com/prodsupp/rlstand.html

CHAPTER 7

INSULATION & VAPOR RETARDERS

Common Defect Allegations

- *Insufficient filling of wall space with blown-in insulation: This situation usually results from obstructions inside the wall or because the installer does not keep the nozzle moving during installation. An opening that fills too quickly usually indicates an obstruction. The trained installer knows the average time and pressure required to fill a wall space. This type of claim is usually discovered at a later date when a wall is opened for repairs or remodeling.*

- *Blowout of interior walls on blown insulation: The pressure generated by the machine can cause interior nail pops and even entire walls to blow out. This type of complaint is usually directed toward the installer, but the situation can also be caused by incorrect nail size or insufficient nailing of the drywall during original construction.*

- *Failure to allow on air gap between the roof sheathing and the insulation space when installing insulation in ceiling joist spaces on vaulted ceiling: The gap is intended to allow condensation that forms against the sheathing to evaporate before saturating the insulation. Condensation forms when there are extreme differentials in temperature between the inside and outside air. Insulation that becomes wet will compress and lose its R-Value. Additionally wet insulation will hold water against a wood structure and promote mold, fungus, and the subsequent dryrot.*

- *Blocked vents at the frieze blocks: This prevents the necessary air circulation required in that void. This condition can cause miscellaneous water intrusion to stay in the building, leading to some of the above-described problems. Also we find that ceiling/wall cracking is prevalent when the vents are blocked due to expansion from excessive heat buildup.*

- *Insulation covering vented recessed light fixtures such as heat lamps in violation of the 3" rule for clearance: Be sure to check with the electrician on which rough-ins may require special clearances, or read the label on the unit.*
- *Electrical and plumbing holes not properly filled: In cold climates the insulator is usually tasked with the job of filling the holes (electrical and plumbing) in the top and bottom plates with expanding foam. This is an important task and should be watched and checked.*
- *Foam roofing failures on commercial buildings where the roof slope has been achieved with sprayed foam under the roof membrane: When water enters this system, there is no way that we have found to save the system. The remedy is to remove the entire system and reinstall. Building owners should be given instructions on maintaining this system when they purchase the building, and an aggressive maintenance program must be applied to keep out water intrusion.*

Introduction

Many defect claims, especially in cold climates, are related to moisture entrapment in insulation and unvented areas. While this chapter provides an overview of general requirements for the United States, it is important to understand the specific and proper procedures and requirements for installation of insulation and vapor barriers for your particular location.

The purpose of insulation is to reduce the transmission of heat, cold, or sound. Insulation materials are rated for thermal resistance, expressed as R-value. Insulation requirements for a particular project are typically specified on the plan cross section, wall sections, and details through the exterior building envelope. (See **Figure 7.1.**)

This chapter addresses common insulation applications in residential and light commercial construction. The chapter is broken down into types and uses of various insulation materials, followed by requirements for building components that are commonly insulated.

While the UBC lists some insulation requirements (see "Insulation Materials" later in this chapter), it does not address the requirements for wall, floor, roof, and window ratings for thermal protection.

The other major regional building codes have somewhat different and sometimes more extensive requirements. Local building codes should always be consulted. Some types of housing may have to meet additional Federal government requirements, such as H.U.D. (Housing and Urban Development).

Insulation Details

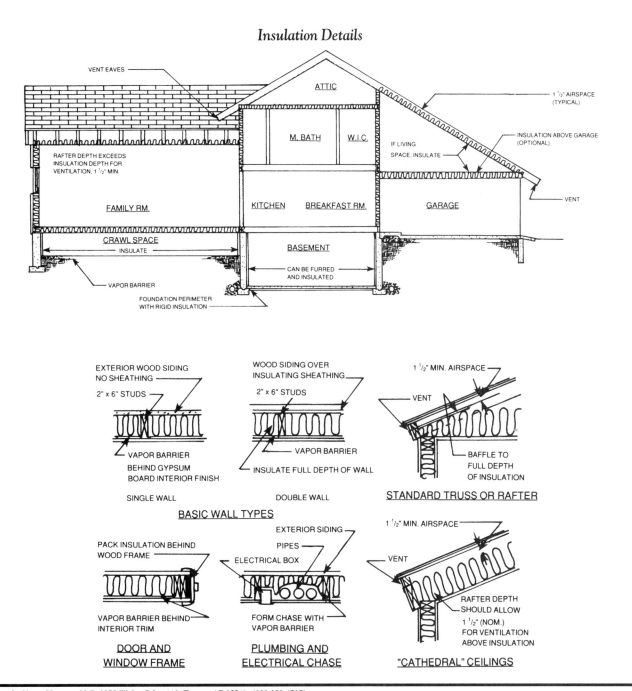

Figure 7.1

The U.S. government created the *Model Energy Code* when there was an energy shortage. It includes minimum requirements for the use of energy in new building construction or additions to existing structures and is now maintained by the International Code Council (ICC). In this chapter, we refer to the *Model Energy Code* only in a general way because the code relates to energy calculations from an engineering approach. A builder applying for a permit conveys the proposed type and R-value of the insulation to be used. It is important to note that the contractor needs to determine the thickness and type of insulation required to meet the specified R-value. In some cases, such as cathedral ceilings, special high-density (and higher-cost) batt insulation may be required due to space limitations.

The Consumer Update Bulletin #1, published by the Cellulose Insulation Manufacturers Association (CIMA), indicates that although R-value is an essential component in selecting the best insulation for a project, it is only one factor in the actual performance of insulated building assemblies. Other key factors include:

- air infiltration from leaks through gaps in the system.
- permeability of system elements.
- convective flows within insulation systems.
- thermal bridging across the building envelope.
- thermal mass of building occupants.

Note: Pipe and duct insulation are covered more fully in Chapter 15, "HVAC."

The following professional associations may be helpful in locating more information about insulation:

Association of the Wall and Ceiling Industries—International
(AWCI—International)
307 East Annandale Road, Suite 200
Falls Church, VA 22042-4233
Telephone: 703-534-8300
www.awci.org

Cellulose Insulation Manufacturers Association (CIMA)
136 South Keowee Street
Dayton, OH 45402
Telephone: 937-222-2462
www.cellulose.org

Central States Insulation & Abatement Contractors Association (CSIAC) and **Eastern States Insulation Contractors Association (ESICA)**
136 South Keowee Street
Dayton, OH 45402
Telephone: 937-222-1024

Insulation Contractors Association of America (ICAA)
1321 Duke Street, #303
Alexandria, VA 22314
Telephone: 703-739-0356
www.insulate.org
The ICAA offers a buyer's guide and homeowner's referral.

Midwest Insulation Contractors Association (MICA)
2017 South 139th Circle
Omaha, NE 68144
Telephone: 402-342-3463 or 800-747-6422
www.micainsulation.org

National Insulation Association (NIA)
99 Canal Center Plaza, Suite 222
Alexandria, VA 22314
Telephone: 703-683-6422
www.insulation.org
The NIA represents the mechanical and specialty insulation industry. It provides information on insulation uses and an introduction to insulation contracting.

North American Insulation Manufacturers Association (NAIMA)
44 Canal Center Plaza, Suite 310
Alexandria, VA 22314
Telephone: 703-684-0084
www.naima.org
NAIMA provides information on standards for installing cellulose insulation, including definitions and guidance on ASTM and government standards.

Polyisocyanurate Insulation Manufacturers Association (PIMA)
1001 Pennsylvania Avenue, N.W.
5th Floor
Washington, DC 20004
Telephone: 202-624-2709
www.pima.org

Southwestern Insulation Contractors Association (SWICA)
3033 Chimney Rock, Suite 101
Houston, TX 77056
Telephone: 713-977-0909

Thermal Insulation Association of Canada (TIAC)
371A Richmond Rd., Unit 8
Ottawa, Ontario K2A 0E7
Telephone: 613-724-4834

Western Insulation Association (WIA)
669 South 200 East
Salt Lake City, UT 84111
Telephone: 801-364-0050

Ed. Note: Comments and recommendations within this chapter are not intended as a definitive resource for construction activities. For building projects, contractors must rely on the project documents and any applicable local building code requirements.

General Types & Forms of Insulation

Industry Standards

National Insulation Association

(NIA Internet Web Site: www.insulation.org)

Insulations will be discussed according to their generic types and forms. The type indicates composition (i.e., glass, plastic) and internal structure (i.e., cellular, fibrous). The form implies overall shape or application (i.e., board, blanket, pipe covering).

General Types of Insulation

Fibrous Insulation — Composed of small diameter fibers, which finely divide the air space. The fibers may be perpendicular or horizontal to the surface being insulated, and they may or may not be bonded together. Silica, rock wool, slag wool and alumina silica fibers are used. The most widely used insulations of this type are glass fiber and mineral wool.

Cellular Insulation — Composed of small individual cells separated from each other. The cellular material may be glass or foamed plastic, such as polystyrene (closed cell), polyurethane and elastomeric.

Granular Insulation — Composed of small nodules which contain voids or hollow spaces. It is not considered a true cellular material, since gas can be transferred between the individual spaces. This type may be produced as a loose or pourable material, or combined with a binder and fibers to make a rigid insulation. Examples of these insulations are calcium silicate, expanded vermiculite, perlite, cellulose, diatomaceous earth, and expanded polystyrene.

General Forms of Insulation

Insulations are produced in a variety of forms suitable for specific functions and applications. The combined form and type of insulation determine its proper method of installation. The forms most widely used are:

1. **Rigid boards, blocks, sheets, and pre-formed shapes such as pipe covering, curved segments, lagging, etc.** Cellular, granular, and fibrous insulations are produced in these forms.

2. **Flexible sheets and pre-formed shapes.** Cellular and fibrous insulations are produced in these forms.

3. **Flexible blankets.** Fibrous insulations are produced in flexible blankets.

4. **Cements (insulating and finishing).** Produced from fibrous and granular insulations and cement, they may be of the hydraulic setting or air drying type.

5. **Foams.** Poured or froth foam is used to fill irregular areas and voids. Spray is used for flat surfaces.

Uses of Insulation

Insulation materials have been developed for specific uses and are produced in many forms. Some of these are as follows:

- **Loose fill** — Used for pouring or blowing in attic or wall spaces of buildings.

- **Batts** — A loose, fluffy insulation material with little structural strength which must be placed in an enclosure or laid flat.

- **Blanket** — A flexible material used to wrap different shapes and forms. (Example: duct wrap)

- **Semi-Rigid Boards** — Sheets and pre-formed shapes with little "give." (Example: fiberglass boards and pipe insulation)

- **Flexible** — Plastic sheets and tubing insulation used in various applications such as refrigerant pipe on residential air conditioning systems. (Example: Armaflex)

- **Rigid Boards** — Block, sheets, and pre-formed shapes with little "give" used on straight sections of flat surfaces. May be fabricated for curved and irregular surfaces. (Example: Calcium silicate pipe and block insulation)

- **Tapes** — Used to wrap small diameter apparatus where other forms are not practical.

- **Cements** — Used for molding various shapes and surfaces.

- **Foam-in-Place Plastic Materials** — A liquid mixed at time of application which sets or hardens to insulate surfaces or cavities.

- **Spray-On-Fiber, Granular, or Cement Materials** — Used for building and equipment insulation in a wide temperature application range. (Example: spray-on fireproofing)

- **Reflective Insulation** — Layers of reflective stainless steel foil. It is used extensively in nuclear power plants. Another type is reflective glass or film for plate glass windows that reflect the heat from the sun.

Loose-Fill Insulation

Comments

Loose-fill insulation can be applied by hand-pouring, machine-blowing, or spraying. Loose-fill is specified by R-value rather than inches of thickness because manufacturers can vary slightly in the R-value to thickness of insulation ratio. Information on coverage and the inches of thickness necessary to attain a specific R-value is provided by each manufacturer on the package. Cellulose R-values should always be stated at settled density. Insulation blown in the direction of the joist, rather than across them, ensures complete filling of the joist spaces.

Loose-Fill Insulation Defect Claims

Loose fill insulation of existing walls usually involves two different types of defect claims.

1. Insufficient filling of wall space—This situation usually results from obstructions inside the wall or because the installer does not keep the nozzle moving during installation. An opening that fills too quickly usually indicates an obstruction. The trained installer knows the average time and pressure required to fill a wall space. This type of claim is usually discovered at a later date when a wall is opened for repairs or remodeling.

2. Blowout or distortion of interior walls— The pressure generated by the machine can cause interior nail pops and even entire walls to blow out. This type of complaint is usually directed toward the installer, but the situation can also be caused by incorrect nail size or insufficient nailing of the drywall during original construction.

UBC — 1997

707.3 Insulation. Cellulose loose-fill insulation shall comply with CPSC 16 CFR, Parts 1209 and 1404. All other insulation materials, including facings, such as vapor barriers or breather papers installed within floor-ceiling assemblies, roof-ceiling assemblies, walls, crawl spaces or attics, shall have a flame-spread rating not to exceed 25 and a smoke density not to exceed 450 when tested in accordance with UBC Standard 8–1.

Exceptions:

1. Foam plastic insulation shall comply with Section 2602.

2. When such materials are installed in concealed spaces of Types III, IV and V construction, the flame-spread and smoke-developed limitations do not apply to facings, provided that the facing is installed in substantial contact with the unexposed surface of the ceiling, floor or wall finish.

Comments

Cellulosic Fiber

Cellulosic fiber insulation is applied by blowing, pouring, and sometimes by combining with adhesives for spraying.

Cellulosic fiber insulation is primarily used for insulating walls and attic spaces. Rated materials can also be used in commercial applications.

Care must be taken to keep cellulosic insulations at least 3" away from light fixtures or any other heat-generating item. (See Chapter 16, "Lighting Outlets," and "Lighting Fixtures" for electrical code requirements.) Blown or pourable cellulosic insulations should not be installed in locations where temperatures will exceed 180°F.

Be sure to follow the cellulosic fiber installation methods exactly as stated on the manufacturing label. Chemicals that are mixed in cellulosic insulations have been known to cause chemical corrosion of electrical wiring and plumbing when blown-in products were improperly installed as a spray-on application.

Rigid Insulation: Types & Applications

Comments

Rigid insulation is fabricated in boards or sheets and is predominantly used in exterior walls, foundations, and roofs. The materials commonly used for rigid insulations include **polystyrene** (often called "beadboard"), **perlite, polyurethane, polyisocyanurate, phenolic, cellular glass block, organic fiber** or **glass fiber.**

Polystyrene insulations are similar to other plastic foam insulations, but they generally have lower R-values. Prolonged exposure to sunlight will cause polystyrene to deteriorate.

In industrial and commercial buildings, polystyrene is commonly used for foundations, floors, walls, and roofs. In residential construction, it is used for perimeter slabs, foundations, exterior sheathing, and siding backerboards.

Perlite does not burn, but has a tendency to absorb water, so it should be kept dry.

Polyisocyanurate foam, like other urethanes, will burn and must be protected from flame and damage. In industrial and commercial buildings, polyisocyanurate is commonly used in foundations, floors, walls, and roofs. In residential construction, it is principally used for sheathing, exterior foundations, and slab-on-grade.

Phenolic insulation is used for roofs and walls. It has a higher R-value than other foam plastic insulations, but it is fragile and must be handled carefully.

Cellular glass is used on roof and exterior decks, and as perimeter insulation for foundations and slabs. Cellular glass must be handled carefully and protected from freezing and thawing.

Organic fiber rigid insulation and rigid glass fiber insulation are primarily used for roofing systems in which the boards are tapered to provide positive drainage.

Mineral Fiber Insulation

Mineral fiber insulation is resistant to fire, moisture, and vermin.

Semi-rigid boards, 1"–3" thick, are primarily used as curtain walls between exterior wall furring and in locations requiring a semi-rigid product.

Batts and blankets are primarily used for insulating walls and partitions, below floors, in crawl spaces, above ceilings, in attic spaces, and as a sound barrier. Batts or blankets can be manufactured with facings that can act either as a vapor barrier or as breather paper. Only one face on the batt or blanket is a vapor barrier. Any other facing is a breather paper, which is installed for easier handling or to provide flanges for stapling. Unfaced batts or blankets are designed to be friction fit and are held in place by pressure.

According to the UBC (601.5.7), combustible insulating boards can be used under finished flooring.

Flexible Piping Insulation

Comments

Hot water piping can be insulated with preformed lengths of insulation, which is made from fiberglass or closed cell foam. To ensure a snug fit, the insulation (which is usually in 4' lengths) is manufactured to fit a specific pipe type and size. A slit along the length of the insulation allows it to be slipped onto the pipe after the waterline is in place. Tape wrapped around the insulation secures it to the pipe.

See Chapter 15, "HVAC," and Chapter 14, "Plumbing," for more information on pipe insulation.

UBC — 1997

707.2 Insulation and Covering on Pipe and Tubing
Insulation and covering on pipe and tubing shall have a flame-spread rating not to exceed 25 and a smoke density not to exceed 450 when tested in accordance with UBC Standard 8–1.

Exception: Foam plastic insulation shall comply with Section 2602.

Classifying Installation Work

Industry Standards

National Insulation Association
(NIA Internet Web Site: www.insulation.org)

Conventional building insulation is usually installed by laborers or carpenters and is not considered a skilled trade. Foam-in-place and spray-on materials are installed by those specializing in the specific materials and applications. Low temperature space insulation (cold storage rooms) is usually installed by carpenters, as it is part of the structure and requires room finishes similar to regular building construction.

Industrial contractors specialize in the installation of pipes, ducts, and equipment. They employ skilled insulation trade mechanics. Some industrial contractors also participate in specialized fields of insulation, especially in low temperature space insulation and foam-in-place applications.

Two broad classifications of insulation work are industrial and commercial. Industrial consists of pipe, duct, and equipment insulation applied in manufacturing plants, power plants, ships, refineries, chemical plants, and other industrial facilities.

Commercial work is performed in buildings other than industrial plants. For example, an office building would have plumbing which would consist of cold water, hot water, and drain pipes. It may also have a heating and air conditioning system on pipes and ducts. Pipe and duct would be insulated to hold heat in hot pipes and/or ducts, to prevent condensation (sweating) on cold pipes or ducts, and to keep them cold. These uses conserve energy.

In industrial work, pipe and equipment are insulated for many important reasons. These include:

- Energy conservation.
- Employee protection from hot pipe burns.
- Maintenance of consistent manufacturing processing temperatures.
- Prevention of fire hazards.
- Noise reduction (to meet legal or company requirements).
- Prevention of moisture condensation damage (sweating) from low-temperature lines or equipment.
- Increase in equipment working life as a result of reduced internal corrosion.
- Environmental protection due to reduced fuel consumption and the emission of air pollutants such as sulfur oxides.
- Reduced requirements for air-conditioning and heat generating systems.

Building Codes & Material Standards

Comments

Building codes are in one of two forms—a specification or a performance code. The specification code provides the technical description of the material, and the performance code describes how the product or system should perform. One must also be aware of any additional code or energy requirements as established by the local building authority that has actual jurisdiction over the structure.

Insulation materials generally meet standards determined by the American Society for Testing and Materials (ASTM) *and those set by the* General Services Administration (GSA), *which are known as Federal Specifications. Also, all material standards, tests, and codes are revised at various intervals, and it is important that architects and contractors are aware of the latest revisions. In addition to manufacturers' recommended standards, the following resources may be helpful in providing information on insulation requirements:*

- *Model Energy Code*
- *HUD MPS (Minimum Property Standards)*
- *Farmers Home Administration (FMHA)*
- *State energy codes*
- *NAHB Research Center Certification and Labeling Program*

Insulation Materials & R-Value

Comments

*Energy standards list insulation products according to their ability to resist heat flow at a given thickness. This measurement is commonly known as the R-value or U-factor. However, the following terms may sometimes be used: **thermal resistance** or **thermal conductivity (k-value)**.*

R-value listings are preferred, because they can be added directly to calculate the overall thermal resistance of an assembly. The overall R-value is the reciprocal of the assembly's U-factor, which is used to calculate the heat loss through the assembly.

R-values of the same product may vary slightly with each manufacturer. In most cases, specific minimum R-values are dictated by code. Manufacturers then fabricate and package their finished products to meet the code.

Manufacturers of loose fill and sprayed-on-foam list a specific thickness that must be installed for their product to meet the specified R-value.

R-values are not directly related to the thickness of the insulation product. Density determines an insulation's R-value. The more fibers per square inch of insulating material, the greater its density, and the higher its R-value.

Figure 7.2 *shows the formulas for calculating heat transfer, using a masonry wall example to illustrate the changing R- and U-values when different insulating materials are applied.* ***Figure 7.3*** *is a chart listing the R-values of common building materials.*

Builder Compliance with Federal Consumer Law

Insulation Contractors Association of America
(ICAA Internet Web Site: www.insulate.org)

Federal Consumer Law on Insulation

There is a federal consumer law that requires specific information on insulation be included in a homebuilder's sales contract with home buyers.

If you are a homebuilder, federal consumer law (FTC Home Insulation Rule 460) requires that the R-value of any insulation installed in the homes you sell cannot be below the R-value shown in your sales contract. You must put the following information in every sales contract: the *type*, *thickness*, and *R-value* of the insulation that will be installed in each part of the house.

Builders are subject to a $10,000 fine each time the Rule is broken. FTC regulates the home insulation industry under its Rule 460, which covers builders who sell new homes.

To ensure that insulation's savings and comfort are achieved, adequate R-values must be installed. Where attic R-values are deficient, builders have been found to be culpable.

R-value deficiency occurs when:

1. Some types of loose-fill insulations are easily "fluffed" (more air, less material), so that it appears as if a lot more insulation has been installed;

2. A particular type of loose-fill insulation *settles to a level below* the minimum installed thickness indicated on the product bag label;

3. Loose-fill insulation is *installed to a level below* the minimum installed thickness indicated on the product bag label.

ICAA has endorsed *guaranteed R-value* products as the best way to ensure that R-value is present. These products are guaranteed by the manufacturer to provide specific R-values at designated thickness levels. For a list of these products and manufacturers or for more information on FTC Rule 460, contact ICAA at 703–739–0356.

"U" and "R" Factors

Example Using 14″ Masonry Cavity Wall with 1″ Plaster for the Exterior Closure

Total Heat Transfer is found using the equation
$Q = AU (T_2 - T_1)$ where:

Q = Heat flow, BTU per hour
A = Area, square feet
U = Overall heat transfer coefficient
$(T_2 - T_1)$ = Difference in temperature of the air on each side of the construction component in degrees Fahrenheit

Coefficients of Transmission ("U") are expressed in BTU per (hour) (square foot) (Fahrenheit degree difference in temperature between the air on two sides) and are based on 15 mph outside wind velocity.

The lower the U-value the higher the insulating value.

$U = 1/R$ where "R" is the summation of the resistances of air films, materials and air spaces that make up the assembly.

Example Using 14″ Masonry Cavity Wall with 1″ Plaster for the Exterior Closure

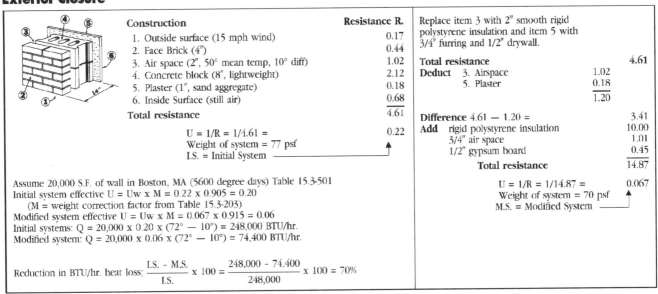

Construction	Resistance R.
1. Outside surface (15 mph wind)	0.17
2. Face Brick (4″)	0.44
3. Air space (2″, 50° mean temp, 10° diff)	1.02
4. Concrete block (8″, lightweight)	2.12
5. Plaster (1″, sand aggregate)	0.18
6. Inside Surface (still air)	0.68
Total resistance	4.61

$U = 1/R = 1/4.61 = 0.22$
Weight of system = 77 psf
I.S. = Initial System

Replace item 3 with 2″ smooth rigid polystyrene insulation and item 5 with 3/4″ furring and 1/2″ drywall.

Total resistance		4.61
Deduct 3. Airspace	1.02	
5. Plaster	0.18	
	1.20	

Difference 4.61 − 1.20 =	3.41
Add rigid polystyrene insulation	10.00
3/4″ air space	1.01
1/2″ gypsum board	0.45
Total resistance	14.87

$U = 1/R = 1/14.87 = 0.067$
Weight of system = 70 psf
M.S. = Modified System

Assume 20,000 S.F. of wall in Boston, MA (5600 degree days) Table 15.3-501
Initial system effective U = Uw x M = 0.22 x 0.905 = 0.20
   (M = weight correction factor from Table 15.3-203)
Modified system effective U = Uw x M = 0.067 x 0.915 = 0.06
Initial systems: Q = 20,000 x 0.20 x (72° − 10°) = 248,000 BTU/hr.
Modified system: Q = 20,000 x 0.06 x (72° − 10°) = 74,400 BTU/hr.

Reduction in BTU/hr. heat loss: $\frac{\text{I.S.} - \text{M.S.}}{\text{I.S.}} \times 100 = \frac{248,000 - 74,400}{248,000} \times 100 = 70\%$

R.S. Means Co., Inc., *Assemblies Cost Data*

Figure 7.2

General Recommendations

UBC — 1997

Section 707 — Insulation

707.1 General. Thermal and acoustical insulation located on or within floor-ceiling and roof-ceiling assemblies, crawl spaces, walls, partitions and insulation on pipes and tubing shall comply with this section. Duct insulation and insulation in plenums shall conform to the requirements of the Mechanical Code.

Exception: Roof insulation shall comply with Section 1510.

Comments

For tolerances on insulation installation, see Section 4-4 in Residential Construction Performance Guidelines, published by the National Association of Home Builders (Telephone: 1-800-368-5242).

"U" and "R" Factors

Thermal Coefficients of Exterior Closures

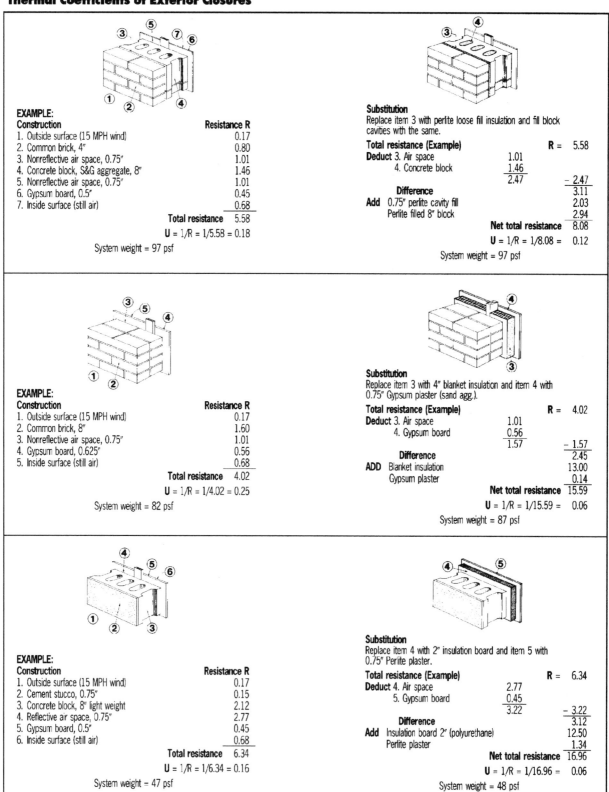

EXAMPLE:

Construction	Resistance R
1. Outside surface (15 MPH wind)	0.17
2. Common brick, 4″	0.80
3. Nonreflective air space, 0.75″	1.01
4. Concrete block, S&G aggregate, 8″	1.46
5. Nonreflective air space, 0.75″	1.01
6. Gypsum board, 0.5″	0.45
7. Inside surface (still air)	0.68
Total resistance	5.58

U = 1/R = 1/5.58 = 0.18

System weight = 97 psf

Substitution
Replace item 3 with perlite loose fill insulation and fill block cavities with the same.

Total resistance (Example)		**R =** 5.58
Deduct 3. Air space	1.01	
4. Concrete block	1.46	
	2.47	− 2.47
Difference		3.11
Add 0.75″ perlite cavity fill		2.03
Perlite filled 8″ block		2.94
Net total resistance		8.08

U = 1/R = 1/8.08 = 0.12

System weight = 97 psf

EXAMPLE:

Construction	Resistance R
1. Outside surface (15 MPH wind)	0.17
2. Common brick, 8″	1.60
3. Nonreflective air space, 0.75″	1.01
4. Gypsum board, 0.625″	0.56
5. Inside surface (still air)	0.68
Total resistance	4.02

U = 1/R = 1/4.02 = 0.25

System weight = 82 psf

Substitution
Replace item 3 with 4″ blanket insulation and item 4 with 0.75″ Gypsum plaster (sand agg.).

Total resistance (Example)		**R =** 4.02
Deduct 3. Air space	1.01	
4. Gypsum board	0.56	
	1.57	− 1.57
Difference		2.45
ADD Blanket insulation		13.00
Gypsum plaster		0.14
Net total resistance		15.59

U = 1/R = 1/15.59 = 0.06

System weight = 87 psf

EXAMPLE:

Construction	Resistance R
1. Outside surface (15 MPH wind)	0.17
2. Cement stucco, 0.75″	0.15
3. Concrete block, 8″ light weight	2.12
4. Reflective air space, 0.75″	2.77
5. Gypsum board, 0.5″	0.45
6. Inside surface (still air)	0.68
Total resistance	6.34

U = 1/R = 1/6.34 = 0.16

System weight = 47 psf

Substitution
Replace item 4 with 2″ insulation board and item 5 with 0.75″ Perlite plaster.

Total resistance (Example)		**R =** 6.34
Deduct 4. Air space	2.77	
5. Gypsum board	0.45	
	3.22	− 3.22
Difference		3.12
Add Insulation board 2″ (polyurethane)		12.50
Perlite plaster		1.34
Net total resistance		16.96

U = 1/R = 1/16.96 = 0.06

System weight = 48 psf

R.S. Means Co., Inc., *Assemblies Cost Data*

Figure 7.2 continued

Thermal Properties of Materials

Resistances ("R") of Building and Insulating Materials

Material	Wt./Lbs. per C.F.	R per Inch	R Listed Size
Air Spaces and Surfaces			
Enclosed non-reflective spaces, E=0.82			
50°F mean temp., 30°/10°F diff.			
.5"			.90/.91
.75"			.94/1.01
1.50"			.90/1.02
3.50"			.91/1.01
Inside vert. surface (still air)			0.68
Outside vert. surface (15 mph wind)			0.17
Building Boards			
Asbestos cement, 0.25" thick	120		0.06
Gypsum or plaster, 0.5" thick	50		0.45
Hardboard regular	50	1.37	
Tempered	63	1.00	
Laminated paper	30	2.00	
Particle board	37	1.85	
	50	1.06	
	63	0.85	
Plywood (Douglas Fir), 0.5" thick	34		0.62
Shingle backer, .375" thick	18		0.94
Sound deadening board, 0.5" thick	15		1.35
Tile and lay-in panels, plain or			
acoustical, 0.5" thick	18		1.25
Vegetable fiber, 0.5" thick	18		1.32
	25		1.14
Wood, hardwoods	48	0.91	
Softwoods	32	1.25	
Flooring Carpet with fibrous pad			2.08
With rubber pad			1.23
Cork tile, 1/8" thick			0.28
Terrazzo			0.08
Tile, resilient			0.05
Wood, hardwood, 0.75" thick			0.68
Subfloor, 0.75" thick			0.94
Glass			
Insulation, 0.50" air space			2.04
Single glass			0.91
Insulation Blanket or Batt, mineral, glass			
or rock fiber, approximate thickness			
3.0" to 3.5" thick			11
3.5" to 4.0" thick			13
6.0" to 6.5" thick			19
6.5" to 7.0" thick			22
8.5" to 9.0" thick			30
Boards			
Cellular glass	8.5	2.63	
Fiberboard, wet felted			
Acoustical tile	21	2.70	
Roof insulation	17	2.94	
Fiberboard, wet molded			
Acoustical tile	23	2.38	
Mineral fiber with resin binder	15	3.45	
Polystyrene, extruded,			
cut cell surface	1.8	4.00	
smooth skin surface	2.2	5.00	
	3.5	5.26	
Bead boards	1.0	3.57	
Polyurethane	1.5	6.25	
Wood or cane fiberboard, 0.5" thick			1.25

Material	Wt./Lbs. per C.F.	R per Inch	R Listed Size
Insulation Loose Fill			
Cellulose	2.3	3.13	
	3.2	3.70	
Mineral fiber, 3.75" to 5" thick	2-5		11
6.5" to 8.75" thick			19
7.5" to 10" thick			22
10.25" to 13.75" thick			30
Perlite	5-8	2.70	
Vermiculite	4-6	2.27	
Wood fiber	2-3.5	3.33	
Masonry Brick, Common	120	0.20	
Face	130	0.11	
Cement mortar	116	0.20	
Clay tile, hollow			
1 cell wide, 3" width			0.80
4" width			1.11
2 cells wide, 6" width			1.52
8" width			1.85
10" width			2.22
3 cells wide, 12" width			2.50
Concrete, gypsum fiber	51	0.60	
Lightweight	120	0.19	
	80	0.40	
	40	0.86	
Perlite	40	1.08	
Sand and gravel or stone	140	0.08	
Concrete block, lightweight			
3 cell units, 4"-15 lbs. ea.			1.68
6"-23 lbs. ea.			1.83
8"-28 lbs. ea.			2.12
12"-40 lbs. ea.			2.62
Sand and gravel aggregates,			
4"-20 lbs. ea.			1.17
6"-33 lbs. ea.			1.29
8"-38 lbs. ea.			1.46
12"-56 lbs. ea.			1.81
Plastering Cement Plaster,			
Sand aggregate	116	0.20	
Gypsum plaster, Perlite aggregate	45	0.67	
Sand aggregate	105	0.18	
Vermiculite aggregate	45	0.59	
Roofing			
Asphalt, felt, 15 lb.			0.06
Rolled roofing	70		0.15
Shingles	70		0.44
Built-up roofing .375" thick	70		0.33
Cement shingles	120		0.21
Vapor-permeable felt			0.06
Vapor seal, 2 layers of			
mopped 15 lb. felt			0.12
Wood, shingles 16"-7.5" exposure			0.87
Siding			
Aluminum or steel (hollow backed)			
oversheathing			0.61
With .375" insulating backer board			1.82
Foil backed			2.96
Wood siding, beveled, ½" x 8"			0.81

(r) = rate of heat through a homogeneous material one-inch thick measured by the temperature difference in degrees (F) between the two exposed faces required to cause one British thermal unit (Btu) to flow through one square foot per hour.

R.S. Means Co., Inc., *Assemblies Cost Data*

Figure 7.3

Summary of Model Building Code Requirements
(BOCA, ICBO, SBCCI)

1. **Flame Spread Rating**

   • Optimum rating is 0-25, called Class I by BOCA and ICBO or Class A by SBCCI and NFPA.

   • Unfaced building insulation, special Flame-Resistant Foil (FSK 25) and InsulSafe III are classified Class I or Class A.

2. **Noncombustibility**—Unfaced building insulation and InsulSafe III are noncombustible per criteria of ASTM E 136.

3. **Fire Resistance Ratings**—Depend on type of building construction and location of assembly.

4. **Sound Transmission Loss Rating (STC)**—

   • BOCA & SBCCI–STC 45 where a rating is required.

   • ICBO–STC 45 (field test) or STC 50 (lab test) where rating is required.

Note: HUB/FHA (MPS)–STC 45, except STC 50 for assemblies separating living units from public spaces or high noise areas.

Comments

Some insulation is manufactured from materials that are flammable or produce toxic fumes when burned or subjected to extreme heat. Most building codes require these materials to be protected by fire-resistant finishes, such as gypsum wallboard.

Insulation materials containing polyurethane, polyisocyanurate and polystyrene should not be exposed to sunlight because they will be subject to ultraviolet deterioration. Molded polystyrene and expanded perlite boards must be protected from water, as they will absorb moisture.

Ventilation

Comments

Ventilation can be accomplished through a natural (static) or a power ventilation system. Static systems (simple vent openings) are most common in attics. Ridge, eave, and/or gable vents can be used. Insulation must not be allowed to cover vent openings. Two or more vent openings allow air to flow through.

There should be 1 square foot of vent area for each 150 square feet of ceiling area if there is no vapor retarder in the ceiling. If there is a ceiling vapor retarder, allow 1 square foot for each 300 square feet of ceiling area. Optimally, vents located in the upper portion of the attic should accommodate 50 percent of the required ventilating area. The other 50 percent should be addressed by eave vents.

In cathedral ceilings, insulation is installed in rafter spaces, and the ceiling finish layer is fastened to the rafters. A vented air space between insulation and roof sheathing is desirable.

***Figure 7.4** shows various types of gable vents.*

Ed. Note: *Refer to Chapters 5, 14 and 15 for more information on code requirements for ventilation. See also "Foundations, Basements, & Crawl Spaces" at the end of this chapter.*

Gable Vents

Rectangular
Gable-End Vent

Pitched Triangular
Gable-End Vent

Half-Round
Gable-End Vent

R.S. Means Co., Inc., *Exterior Home Improvement Costs*

Figure 7.4

Roof Insulation

UBC — 1997

Section 1510 — Roof Insulation

Roof insulation shall be of a rigid type suitable as a base for application of a roof covering. Foam plastic roof insulation shall conform to the requirements of Section 2602. The use of insulation in fire-resistive construction shall comply with Section 7101.1.

The roof insulation, deck material and roof covering shall meet the fire-retardancy requirements of Section 1504 and Table 15–A.

Insulation for built-up roofs shall be applied in accordance with Table 15–E. Insulation for modified bitumen, thermoplastic and thermoset membrane roofs shall be applied in accordance with the roofing manufacturer's recommendations. For other roofing materials such as shingles or tile, the insulation shall be covered with a suitable nailing base secured to the structure.

Comments

The roof will have a significant impact on a building's heat transmission. Heat transmission through a roof can be reduced by:

1. *Use of shiny or light-colored roofing materials for heat reflection.*
2. *Use of optimum insulation quantities.*
3. *Increased ventilation in attic spaces.*
4. *Design of roof pitches and overhangs to increase the lag time of heat flow.*
5. *Use of building materials that reduce heat transmission.*

Many building jurisdictions require roofs with a Class A rating and will no longer allow installation of a wood shake roof. Composition residential roofs simulate the color of wood shakes. Popular colors for these roofs tend to be dark brown or gray, and the differences in roof colors affect heat transmission. The darker colors absorb more heat than lighter-colored roofs, creating hotter attic spaces. Proper attic ventilation—passive or active— will decrease the temperature of the attic space and, therefore, decrease the degree of heat transmission through the ceiling.

Flat roof systems should use a type of rigid board insulation that provides a base for the roofing as well as thermal resistance.

Industry Standards

Roofing: Design Criteria, Options, Selection
(R.S. Means Co., Inc.)

Roof insulation can serve a dual purpose: to reduce heat transfer, and to act as a stable, uniform substrate for the roof membrane. In most cases, roof insulation is installed *between the structural deck and the roof membrane*. **Figure 7.5** is an illustration of a conventional roof insulation system. One exception, the Inverted Roof Membrane Assembly (IRMA), is used in severely cold climates. In this arrangement, the insulation rests above the waterproofing membrane. This system, also known as Protected Membrane Roofing (PMR), is also shown in **Figure 7.5.**

There are many types and thicknesses of material available for roof insulation. **Figure 7.6** is a chart comparing the characteristics of various roof insulation materials. The most common are described in the following paragraphs.

Note: Composite board is a combination of two of the following boards, with a facing of a different material. The two boards are laminated in the factory to produce a product with the advantages of both materials.

Polyisocyanurate Foam Board

Polyisocyanurate board is a dimensionally stable, closed-cell foam which normally has a glass fiber facing bonded to it in order to receive hot moppings or adhesive. It has a high thermal efficiency (R = 7.2 in.) and relatively low cost.

There have been some problems with polyisocyanurate board. The most publicized is thermal drift of the "R" value as the insulation ages. There have also been incidences of facer separation. It is best to use materials from the same supplier whenever practical, and to ensure that the board manufacturer also cross-references, or approves, the bitumen and adhesive(s) used.

Polyurethane Foam Board

Polyurethane and urethane foam boards have been in common use for a longer period than polyisocyanurate, and were the efficiency "leaders" before the advent of phenolic and polyisocyanurate. Urethane has had the same "thermal drift" problems as polyisocyanurate, but overall, it is still an efficient insulation board.

Polystyrene Foam Board

Expanded polystyrene: Expanded polystyrene (EPS) is a polymer (plastic) impregnated with a foaming agent, which—when exposed to heat—creates a uniform structure resistant to moisture penetration. Polystyrene has an "R" value of 3.85–4.76 per inch and a compressive strength of 21–27 psi (pounds per square inch) at 1.5 pounds per cubic foot of density. As a comparison, the compressive strength of mineral board (perlite) is 35 psi.

Conventional Roof Insulation System

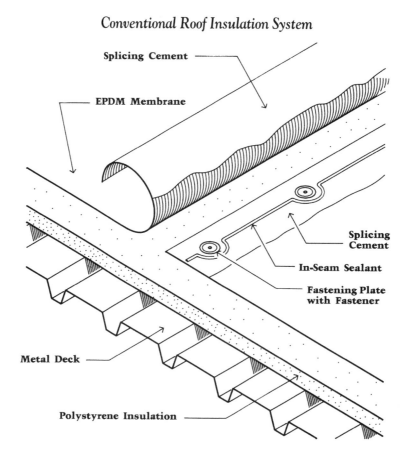

Protected Membrane Roofing

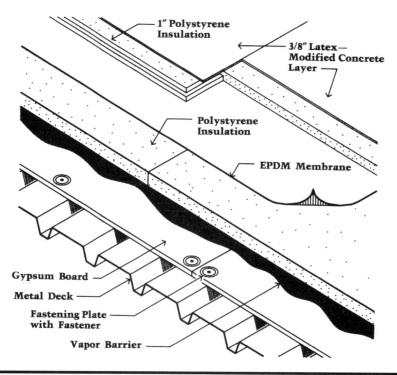

R.S. Means Co., Inc., *Roofing: Design Criteria, Options, Selection*

Figure 7.5

Characteristics of Various Roof Insulation Materials

Characteristics	Polyisocyanurate Foam	Polyurethane Foam	Extruded Polystyrene	Molded Polystyrene	Cellular Glass	Mineral Fiber	Phenolic Foam	Wood Fiber	Glass Fiber
				TYPE OF INSULATING BOARD					
Impact resistant	G	G	G	F	G	E	G	E	F
Moisture resistant	E	G	E	G	E	G	E		
Fire Resistant	E				E	E	E		E
Compatible with bitumens	E	G	F	F	E	E	E	E	G
Durable	E	E	E	E	E	G	F	E	E
Stable "k" value			E	E	E	E		E	E
Dimensionally stable	E	E	E	E	E	E	E	E	G
High thermal resistance	E	E	E	G	F	F	E	F	G
Available tapered slabs	Y	Y	Y	Y	Y	Y	Y	Y	Y
"R" value per in. thickness*	7.20	6.25	4.76	3.85-4.35	2.86	2.78	8.30	1.75-2.00	4.00
Thicknesses available	1"-3"	1"-4"	1"-3½"	½"-24"	1½"-4"	¾"-3"	1"-4"	1"-3"	¾"-2½"
Density (lb./ft.³)	2.0	1.5	1.8-3.5	1.0-2.0	8.5	16-17	1.5	22-27	49
Remarks	Prone to "thermal drift"	Prone to "thermal drift" Note "A": Should be overlaid with a thin layer of wood fiber, glass fiber or perlite board, with staggered joints.	Somewhat sensitive to hot bitumen & adhesive vapors Note "A": Should be overlaid with a thin layer of wood fiber, glass fiber or perlite board, with staggered joints.	Somewhat sensitive to hot bitumen & adhesive vapors Note "A": Should be overlaid with a thin layer of wood fiber, glass fiber or perlite board, with staggered joints.			Prone to "Thermal drift" relatively new & untested.	Expands with moisture —holds moisture.	Prone to damage from moisture infiltration.

E = EXCELLENT
G = GOOD
F = FAIR

R.S. Means Co., Inc., *Roofing: Design Criteria, Options, Selection*

Figure 7.6

Most expanded polystyrene is used under loose-laid, ballasted single-ply systems. The type of expanded polystyrene often used in these cases is a material with a density of one pound per cubic foot, with an average "R" value of 4.2 per inch. This type of polystyrene is similar to that used in the manufacture of inexpensive picnic coolers.

Using mechanized gravel buggies for ballast installation tends to damage this lighter density EPS. The lighter material is also more likely to "shuffle" or crack under the membrane. The industry favors using a board with a minimum density of 1.5 pounds of the extruded material, which is far more durable.

Extruded polystyrene: Extruded polystyrene is a closed-cell foam with a low capacity for water absorption (.06% by volume), which makes it ideal for use in the insulated roof membrane assembly (IRMA). Its "R" value is approximately 4.8 per inch.

Installation: Most building codes require the installation of a 1/2 inch fire-rated gypsum board underlayment when polystyrene is used over a steel deck. The NRCA also recommends that, when using polystyrene board, a thin (minimum 1/4 inch) layer of perlite of fiberboard "recover board" be overlaid, with joints staggered from the insulation board joints below. Polystyrene board must also be protected from ultraviolet light.

Cellular Glass Board

Cellular glass board is no longer used as often as it once was for roof insulation. Its lower "R" value per inch and relatively high density (thus, weight) has rendered it less popular than the newer materials. It is, however, a moisture-resistant, stable, and durable material.

Mineral Board

Mineral board is composed of expanded perlite, cellulose binders, and waterproofing agents. Low water absorption, stability, superior fire-resistance, and the best compressive resistance of all the insulations currently used, make this material extremely popular. The biggest drawback of mineral board is its relatively low "R" value (2.78 per inch). It becomes impractical and expensive to use 4 inches of this material to achieve an "R" value of 10 when the same value can be attained using only 1-1/2 inches of foam insulation.

When mineral board is used as the base layer of a two-layer insulation system, it must be mechanically attached to the deck. A vapor retarder should then be installed or mopped over the mineral board, followed by a high performance insulation. This system ensures secure attachment to the deck and positive control of vapor, which would otherwise tend to be driven into the insulation during the winter months. By installing two separate layers of insulation with staggered joints, thermal bridging of the fasteners is eliminated, as is bridging at joints. Placing the vapor retarder above the fasteners and maintaining a temperature at the fasteners above the dew point reduces corrosion of the fasteners and the deck.

Phenolic Foam Board

Phenolic foam is popular with specifiers because of its "R" value of 8.3 per inch and its competitive pricing. It is a fire-resistant, dimensionally stable, foamed plastic. It is friable (subject to crumbling), and will fracture if abused. There have been instances where phenolic foam "dished" (raised at the corners) under single-ply membranes. If soaked, phenolic foam will absorb moisture and lose much of its thermal efficiency. Although not fully tested, it is reasonable to assume that phenolic foam is affected by thermal drift, as are the other foams that use fluorocarbon blowing agents. (Thermal drift is the reduction in "R" value that occurs when the fluorocarbon used as the foaming agent in manufacture vacates the material over time, and is replaced with atmospheric air, which has a lower "R" value.)

Wood Fiber Board

Wood fiber is used as a combination decking and insulation board for many roof systems. It is stronger and more durable than the other board insulation products, and makes a far better attachment substrate. However, these attributes are offset by its relatively low thermal resistance. Many specifiers use a composite board or a combination of wood fiber board and one of the high efficiency foams to create a solid, efficient system upon which to overlay a roof membrane.

Glass Fiber Board

Glass fiber insulation board is comprised of glass fibers, bound by a resinous binder and rolled into rigid board. A top surface (*facing*) of asphalt-adhered kraft paper or foil is applied as protection. This type of insulation is very efficient (R = 4 per inch) and has been tested by both Factory Mutual and Underwriters' Laboratory. This board is relatively soft and prone to moisture, which attacks the binder and causes the material to collapse.

Comments

While the preceding materials for roof insulation can be used for both commercial and residential buildings, the foam and fiberboard density requirements may differ depending on the application.

Associated Roofing Insulation Materials

Industry Standards
Roofing: Design Criteria, Options, Selection
(R.S. Means Co., Inc.)

Recover Boards
When installing single-ply membranes over hard-surfaced insulation board, fasteners or gravel can work their way up through the membrane, causing leaks that are very difficult to locate. Some specifications call for the use of *recover boards*, made of pressed fibers, over the insulation board. Recover boards are susceptible to moisture contamination and, therefore, should not be used over wet decks.

Vapor Retarders

Comments
Household activities such as cooking and bathing, as well as the presence of occupants, can generate 2 to 3 gallons of water vapor per day. If moisture vapor travelling into attics and exterior walls is not slowed by a vapor retarder or vapor barrier, condensation can result when the vapor contacts cold surfaces. Prolonged condensation can lead to wood rot, mildew, and mold. Furthermore, damp insulation has reduced thermal performance.

Vapor retarders are materials used to limit water vapor transmission. Vapor retarders are typically kraft or foil facings on building insulation. Polyethylene (4- or 6-mil) can also be used with unfaced insulation to provide a continuous, airtight vapor retarder.

Vapor retarders should generally be installed on the side of the insulation that is warmer in winter (usually toward the interior, but on the exterior in some warm, humid areas; check local practice and/or building codes).

In cold climate construction, 4- or 6-mil polyethylene must be installed on the interior side of the insulation. All seams and penetrations must be sealed with a non-hardening adhesive (butyl caulk or acoustical caulk).

Vapor retarders are not required in some dry, high-temperature climates, such as parts of Arizona and California. Vapor retarders are not required if there is sufficient ventilation.

Industry Standards
Roofing: Design Criteria, Options, Selection
(R.S. Means Co., Inc.)

Vapor retarders used to be referred to as "vapor barriers," until the industry conceded that no true "barrier" may be devised against moisture intrusion using readily available sheet materials or mopped membranes. Every vapor retarder allows *some* moisture to permeate. Moisture permeability through a vapor retarder is measured in *perms*.

A vapor retarder is strongly recommended when the average outside January temperature is below 40 degrees and the indoor relative humidity in winter is 45 percent or above. The NRCA recommends that when a vapor retarder is specified, moisture relief venting must be installed as a means of allowing any trapped moisture to escape from the system. There is, however, strong evidence that roof vents do not significantly contribute to moisture removal in insulation that is already wet. The primary source of moisture in roof insulation is breaks in the membrane. Therefore, it stands to reason that adding many roof vents in the system will only increase the chances for a leak.

Vapor retarders *should not be used* unless dew point vapor flow calculations clearly indicate that these devices are necessary, or unless the previously stated January temperature and humidity ranges prevail in that location. For most areas of the U.S., the "downward drying" that occurs in the building space during warm seasons of the year will far exceed the "upward wetting" which occurs in the colder periods. There is one clear exception to this rule: in wet-process applications, such as laundries, canneries, and swimming pools, the "upward-wetting" potential virtually demands a vapor retarder to restrict contamination of the insulation.

It is very important that vapor retarders, when used, be as homogeneous as possible, with as few seams or breaks as practical.

Ceilings

Comments

Flexible insulation with vapor barriers should be installed in ceilings so that the vapor barrier is facing the living space. (See "Vapor Retarders" on previous page.) Loose fill, batt, or blanket insulation without a vapor barrier should have a separate polyethylene film placed below the insulation facing the living space. Batt or blanket insulation at the ceilings is usually installed at the same time as the wall insulation, from underneath the ceiling joists.

For maximum effectiveness, the vapor barrier facing on the insulation should overlap the faces of the framing members. The insulation should extend across the entire top plate to prevent heat loss at the joint. If necessary, the junction between the insulation and the plate should be stuffed with loose insulation.

Loose fill insulation is installed over the top of the finished ceiling by pouring or blowing it in to fill the joist space. Since loose fill is installed later in the construction process, the ceiling insulation is usually inspected as part of the final overall inspection.

When eave vents are used, the insulation should not block the air movement between the vent and the space above the insulation. Eave baffles should be installed to prevent loose fill insulation from covering the vents.

As mentioned earlier, cellulose insulation should be kept from contact with potential heat sources, such as light fixtures. A minimum 3" clearance should be provided around each fixture. (Note: Some recessed light fixtures are now rated to allow direct contact with insulation. However, many local building jurisdictions still require the installation of a gypsum wallboard or plywood box around recessed light fixtures, prior to installation of insulation, to prevent contact.)

Cathedral Ceilings

If cathedral ceilings are insulated, they require both a vapor barrier and ventilation. Faced fiberglass insulation can be installed between ceiling rafters, or unfaced insulation can be used in combination with a 4- or 6-mil polyethylene vapor barrier stapled to ceiling rafters. (In areas such as Florida and the Gulf Coast, an interior vapor barrier may not be required.)

Insulation should be friction-fit (no inset stapling). Any stapling should be to the front-side of the rafters.

Ventilation space of 1" should be provided between the roof sheathing and the insulation. Baffles and eave vents can be installed along the ceiling space to create air flow.

Finish materials, such as gypsum wallboard, should be installed when the insulation is in place. Faced insulation should never be left exposed. Kraft and foil-faced materials are flammable, and should be covered by approved wall, ceiling, or floor materials.

Framed Walls

Comments

Insulation requirements for framed walls are usually similar to ceiling applications. The maximum R-value of material that can be installed in a framed wall is dictated by the thickness of the framing material. The stud cavity of a standard 2x4 framed wall permits 3-1/2" of blanket insulation, with an R-value ranging from about 11 to 17, depending upon the insulation material and its density.

The insulation values recommended in many climate zones require a wall R-value of 19 or higher and are often difficult to accomplish using a single layer of insulation. Sometimes the other portions of the wall, such as interior and exterior finishes and sheathing, may contribute enough insulating value to provide sufficient total wall R-value. The only other means of increasing the R-value of the wall is to increase the thickness of the insulation. This can be accomplished by using 6" stud walls, which provides 5-1/2" of stud cavity, or by adding additional layers of insulation to the interior or exterior surface of the wall.

The most common material used for framed wall insulation is fiberglass batts or blankets. Exterior walls are insulated with batts or blankets faced with kraft paper or foil as a vapor barrier.

Fiberglass batts or blankets are manufactured to fit between the standard stud spacing of 16" or 24" on center. The batts or blankets should fit snugly at all sides and at the top and bottom plates. The batts or blankets with a vapor barrier are held in place by "face" (on the edge of the room side of the stud) or "inset" (on the inside cavity space of the stud) stapling.

When adding batts or blankets to an existing condition, install a layer of batts or blankets between the joist spaces, then, install a second, unfaced layer at a right *angle across the joists. This installation method provides a higher insulating value because the wood joists are covered with insulation. (Note: This method cannot be effectively used with engineered trusses.)*

Loose fill insulation can be applied to framed walls in new construction if the manufacturer has designed a system that will keep the insulation in place. One method is to install a vapor barrier material to the interior side of the wall to enclose the stud cavity. The loose fill insulation is blown in through a hole in the vapor barrier near the top of the stud cavity.

Some manufacturers have a system of spraying the insulation into the stud cavities and then scraping off the excess material even with the interior edge face of the studs. This process involves a wetting agent that is mixed with the insulation at the spray nozzle, thus activating a binding action to keep the loose fill insulation in place. Loose fill insulation can also be used to insulate existing sidewalls. Openings are drilled—usually from the exterior—at various intervals, and the insulation is pumped into the stud cavity. The exterior openings are then plugged and finished.

It is important to determine whether there are obstructions in the walls, such as fire blocking. Blowing loose fill insulation through a single opening at the top of an 8' wall would leave much of the stud cavity without insulation. Most walls require two, if not three, openings per stud cavity. Openings should be located vertically at 4' to 5' intervals, depending upon any predetermined obstacles.

Generally, the lower holes are filled first to ensure that insulation has reached the lowest portion of the wall in the correct density. The blowing machine is equipped with a pop-off valve that will bleed off pressure as the wall cavity is filled, preventing the interior wall from blowing out. Pressures for drywall applications are considerably less than lath and plaster walls.

Crawl Spaces and Floors

Industry Standards

Construction Principles, Materials, and Methods
(John Wiley & Sons, Inc.)

Ventilation Requirements

In crawl space construction, adequate cross-ventilation should be provided under the floor. The total area of vent openings should equal 1.5% of the first floor area.

A groundcover of 4- to 6-mil polyethylene film is essential as a moisture retarder. Inadequate moisture control can harm any floor installation by contributing to warping or discoloration of the flooring.

Comments

Crawl spaces can be insulated by placing the insulation between the floor joists. Fiberglass batts are the common material used for this purpose. The vapor barrier should be facing towards the living space, just as it would for walls and ceilings.

Installing insulation in existing conditions can be very difficult when the crawl space is tight—sometimes only 18" to 24" high. Often plumbing, as well as electrical and HVAC ducts, complicate the installation. In this case, the insulation can be installed from above, prior to the installation of the subfloor.

In new construction, mesh can be installed from the top of the joists before the subfloor is laid by rolling out the mesh and creating pockets at each joist space. The mesh is then stapled to the top edge of the joists. The batts or blankets are laid into the mesh pocket, and the subfloor is installed over the top of the insulation.

In existing construction, mesh can be stapled to the bottom face of the joists after the insulation has been installed.

Another option is wire lacing, which can be created by interweaving malleable wire and securing it to the bottom face of the joists by stapling or nailing.

Standard wall insulation has the stapling flange on the vapor barrier side. For new construction, we do not recommend relying on only staples applied from the top side of the wall insulation. The weight of the insulation may eventually cause the flange to tear from the staples, and the insulation will fall to the ground. Some method of support from the bottom of the insulation is needed.

Foundations, Basements & Crawl Spaces

Comments

In basements and heated crawl spaces, the foundation walls must be insulated and ventilated. Providing a minimum of two crawl space vents provides a positive flow of air in and out of the crawl space.

The common insulation materials used for basements include polystyrene, polyurethane, polyisocyanurate, phenolic and cellular glass block. The advantages and disadvantages of each are described in the material sections at the beginning of this chapter.

Crawl spaces that are unheated and/or have a dirt floor should be covered with a polyethylene vapor barrier.

Exterior Walls

Comments

Exterior wall insulation is often installed when the exterior finish is remodeled. Rigid board insulation in foundation and basement applications is installed between the existing wall and new siding material.

Soundproofing

Industry Standards

House Framing
(Creative Homeowner Press®)

You can attempt soundproofing 2x4 partition walls, the non-load-bearing walls that divide the interior of a structure. Although you can't expect to make any walls in the house truly soundproof, you can effectively attenuate, or cut down, the transmission of sound through some walls. Walls separating bedroom and bathroom are prime candidates for soundproofing. There are a number of approaches, ranging from the simple to the complex, depending on how much sound you want to block.

A simple approach to controlling sound involves filling the interior partition wall with batts of R–11 unfaced fiberglass insulation or rigid foam rated at around R–11. The mass of the insulation helps cut down sound transmission. If you want to make the wall even more soundproof, double the drywall on each side of the wall.

Probably the best soundproofing technique involves using 2x6s for the top and bottom plates and framing the wall with staggered 2x4 studs. Set the studs at 12 inches on center, so that every other stud is at 24 inches on center on the same plane. Though this wall arrangement alone is effective, it's best to weave unfaced fiberglass insulation between the studs and use double layers of drywall on each side of the wall. (See **Figure 7.7** for an illustration of soundproofing procedures.)

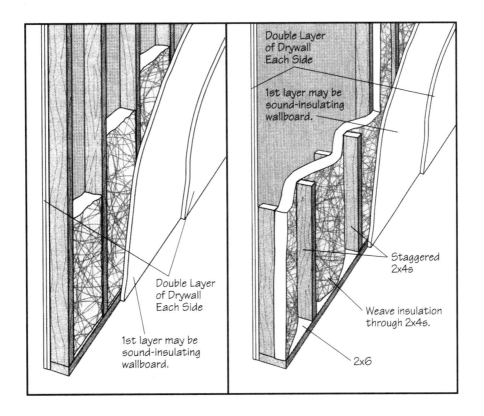

Figure 7.7

CHAPTER 8

ROOFING, SIDING & MOISTURE PROTECTION

Table of Contents

(continued on next page)

Text in blue print indicates excerpts from model building code(s). "Comments" (in solid blue boxes) were written by the editors, based on their own experience.

For building product information, use this book's special Internet gateway to thousands of manufacturers: www.rsmeans.com/prodsupp/rlstand.html

ROOFING, SIDING & MOISTURE PROTECTION

Common Defect Allegations

Roofing

Roofing is a frequent defect allegation. Few roofs fully comply with building code and roofing manufacturers' recommendations. Claims often include one or more of the following:

- *Overexposure of roofing shingle or tile to weather. Production roofers usually make the field equal from eave to ridge without cutting, stretching the courses a little, if necessary, to make it even. Occasionally, the tiles or shingles are stretched to a point where the underlayment is exposed at the joints due to insufficient lap.*

- *Penetrations through flashing, or flashing that does not extend high enough.*

- *Water intrusion at plumbing and other utility penetrations.*

- *Improperly configured valleys. Open valleys are required to be larger at the bottom than at the top so that they will not have a tendency to trap debris.*

- *Shingles at the eaves failing to project (as they should) beyond the edge of the roof framing. Many concrete shingles shave a drip lip to reduce the water curl as it is discharged from the roof. The more metal transition and drip flashing that can be incorporated in the installation, the better, including gutters. These are not mandatory; however, in defect investigation, wood damage is often seen from poor eave performance and is shown as the standard of care that the builder used in their construction.*

- *Insufficient penetration of fasteners. In cement fiber shingle construction, many installations have not used a staple that fully penetrates the sheathing, or a minimum of 3/4". The result is that high winds will lift off large sections of the shingles.*

- *Failure to install an upslope cricket in skylights over 30" in width. The skylight curb must be high enough to support this cricket with a minimum of 5-1/2" curb height. The cricket rule also applies to chimneys over 30".*

- *Failure to use pressure-treated wood for sleepers and nailers under roofing shingles. The sleepers and nailers should be in 4' lengths with spacing to allow water to drain off of the underlayment.*

Siding

- *Two of the most common siding defects are: (1) the wood material is not backprimed prior to installation, and (2) the siding does not terminate far enough above the surrounding grade. The absence of an air gap between the wood framing/siding assembly and paving or soil is the defect that causes the greatest damage. This is because it does not really show up until wood fails, which takes about five years. Mold odor will occur in the living space, but the source is not easily detectable. The mold and fungal attack creates an unhealthy air quality inside the building. When the damage is discovered, it usually is a very expensive changeout.*

- *Failure of the shiplap siding due to improper maintenance. Shiplap siding has a distinct maintenance requirement. It is important that the builder deliver notice to the building owner that the siding and trim will require caulking and paint as frequently as every two years to maintain the structure.*

- *Failure to follow the manufacturers' recommended installation instructions for wood siding products in shingle and clapboard may result in unnecessary splitting and cracking, and uneven shrinkage. The result may be water penetration and exposure of fasteners that should not be visible.*

- *EIFS systems have received some bad press in the last few years. An EIFS building that is properly flashed and has watertight doors and windows is a durable and efficient building. The only drawback to this type of construction is the acoustic transmission. Acoustic problems are easily solved with additional layers of gypboard and sealants.*

Introduction

A tremendous number of construction claims involve defective roofing. Not only is the roof itself susceptible to defects and weather damage, but the building's interior finishes and contents can experience costly damage if the roof fails. Preventing roof leaks may be the single most important item in a strategy to prevent lawsuits and defect claims. Because this is such an important issue, we have included excerpts from publications that go beyond technical discussion to reflect opinions on failures and leaks. Material definitions and product ingredients/components are also covered to help clarify the discussion of proper application.

Flashing, the thin, impervious material used in construction to prevent water penetration or to direct the flow of water, has numerous applications — at roof hips and valleys, for roof penetrations, at joints between a roof and a vertical wall, and in masonry walls to direct the flow of water and moisture. The requirements also vary with the various types of roofing materials. For these reasons, information on flashing will be found throughout the chapter rather than in one specific section. Valley requirements are also covered within the text on the different types of roofing.

The **National Roofing Contractors Association (NRCA)** has generously allowed us to reprint some construction details. While these definitions and designs may not reflect the minimum standards for every type of installation, they certainly do represent the correct way to build. We hope that this section, above all others, is used as a reference on every construction project you encounter.

Roofing designers, specifiers, consultants, inspectors, and installers should have the following resources at their disposal.

- The latest edition of the applicable Building Code(s)
- The Factory Mutual Research Corporation Approval Guide
- The UL Building Materials Directory
- The UL Fire Resistance Directory
- The ASTM Board of Standards, Vol. 04.04, *Roofing, Waterproofing, and Bituminous Materials*
- The NRCA Roofing & Waterproofing Manual

All of the following professional associations may be helpful in locating further information about roofing and moisture control.

American Society for Testing & Materials (ASTM)
100 Barr Harbor Drive
West Conshohocken, PA 19428-2959
Telephone: 610-832-9500
www.astm.org

Asphalt Roofing Manufacturers Association (ARMA)
4041 Powder Mill Road, Suite 404
Calverton, MD 20705
Telephone: 302-348-2002
www.asphaltroofing.org

Factory Mutual Research Corporation
1151 Boston — Providence Turnpike
P.O. Box 9102
Norwood, MA 02062
Telephone: 781-762-4300
www.factorymutual.com

Metal Building Manufacturers Association (MBMA)
1300 Sumner Avenue
Cleveland, OH 44115-2851
Telephone: 216-241-7333
www.mbma.com

National Roofing Contractors Association (NRCA)
10255 W. Higgins Road, Suite 600
Rosemont, IL 60018-5607
Telephone: 800-323-9545
www.roofonline.org

National Tile Roofing Manufacturers Association (NTRMA)
P.O. Box 40337
Eugene, OR 97404
Telephone: 541-689-0366
www.ntrma.com

Roof Coatings Manufacturers Association (RCMA)
4041 Powder Mill Road, Suite 404
Calverton, MD 20705-3106
Telephone: 301-348-2003

Rubber Manufacturers Association (RMA)
1400 K Street, N.W.
Washington, DC 20005
To Order: 800-325-5095
Telephone: 202-682-4800
www.rma.org

SPRI
Single-Ply Roofing Institute
200 Reservoir Street, Suite 309A
Needham, MA 02494
Telephone: 781-444-0242
www.spri.org

Underwriters' Laboratories, Inc. (UL)
333 Pfingsten Road
Northbrook, IL 60062
Telephone: 847-272-8800
www.ul.com

Siding is another area where defect claims frequently occur. Improper attachment of siding can lead to aesthetic problems and damage — to the structure, the interior finishes, and the building's contents.

The latter part of this chapter covers common exterior closure systems, from wood shingles and clapboards to brick, metal, stucco, and exterior insulation finish systems (EIFS).

The following associations provide information on siding and other exterior closure installations.

Brick Industry Association (BIA)
11490 Commerce Park Drive
Reston, VA 20191
Telephone: 703-620-0010
www.bia.org

The Cedar Shake & Shingle Bureau
P.O. Box 1178
Sumass, WA 98295
Telephone: 604-462-8961
www.cedarbureau.org

EIFS Industry Members Association (EIMA)
3000 Corporate Center Drive, Suite 270
Morrow, GA 30260
Telephone: 800-294-3462
www.eifsfacts.com

Plastering Information Bureau
21243 Ventura Blvd., Suite 115
Woodland Hills, CA 91364
Telephone: 818-340-6767

The Western Red Cedar Lumber Association
1200 – 555 Burrard Street
Vancouver, BC V7X 1S7
Telephone: 604-684-0266
www.wrcla.org

The moisture protection section at the end of this chapter is concerned primarily with waterproofing and dampproofing of walls, floors and substrates, and foundation drains. It also includes site grading and placement of backfill. For moisture protection for concrete foundation walls, see Chapter 2, "Concrete."

Ed. Note: Comments and recommendations within this chapter are not intended as a definitive resource for construction activities. For building projects, contractors must rely on the project documents and local building codes.

Typical Roofing Problems and Correction

Industry Standards
Building Materials, Technology, Structural Performance & Environmental Impact
(The McGraw-Hill Companies)

The following questions are asked frequently:

1. Why is water coming down the wall in a room on the top floor of a building? Flashing against the parapet wall on the roof has probably pulled loose and the opening allowed rain to run down the wall to the floor below. The flashing at parapet walls is probably the most common source of roof leaks, and regular maintenance could prevent this complaint. Metal flashings should not exceed 3 to 4 meters (10 to 12 feet) in length because thermal expansion can cause them to buckle and pull away from the parapet walls. To repair, anchor the flashing securely to the wall and caulk the edge, touching the wall with a flexible caulking material. If the metal needs to be replaced, a flexible plastic flashing will be less apt to be a problem.

2. Why does the attic ceiling have patches of mold covering it, but no sign of water leaks? Evidently the temperature of the ceiling has been chilled below the dew point by the freezing temperature on the rooftop. The moisture condensed on the ceiling from the hot, humid air in the attic. The wet areas of the ceiling caused mold to form and thrive on the ceiling. Correction for this problem is to provide more or better insulation for the roof so that the extreme cold on the roof does not chill the ceiling below the dew point.

3. What is the cause of most roof leaks? Leakage at the parapet wall and the junctures of roofing materials with vent pipes and rooftop equipment are frequent causes of roof leaks. Regular maintenance could prevent this complaint. Drains should prevent water from standing in this area. Thermal expansion and contraction cause the metal flashing to pull away from the parapet wall, allowing rain to run down the wall to the floor below. The solution is to press the flashing into the wall — sometimes a groove is provided — and recaulk.

4. What should be done about a large blister (bubble) on a built-up roof! These are spectacular, but usually do not mean that there is a membrane failure and water leakage. They are inflated by the expansion of water vapor. Once the top layer of felt is raised, it stiffens and remains inflated. The bubble can be pierced, gently deflated, and the hole where it was pierced can be sealed with a covering of asphalt emulsion. However, if there is little danger of the bubble being torn open, it can be left undisturbed since it is not a source of leakage.

5. What should be done if water is pending around the drain on the edge of the roof, especially during heavy showers? Evidently a scupper (a drain going into the wall) was overlooked. Scuppers in a parapet wall behind and above the level of the surface drain are usually supplied as an emergency overflow in case the surface drain is clogged. The drain should be unclogged and a scupper constructed in the wall.

6. The ceiling is leaking near the center of the building, where the electrical and drainage facilities service the building. The pipe connected to the roof drain is clogged with roof gravel and the extra weight of the gravel has pulled apart a pipe connection. Gravel is put on top of a built-up roof as a protective sun screen and to help hold down the membrane in order to keep it from blowing away during heavy winds. A low curb near the edge of the roof can keep the gravel from being carried off the roof by heavy rains, ice, and snow. Roof drains should be covered with a coarse grating to keep gravel from filling the drain pipes. Gravel is becoming scarce and is being replaced by a highly reflective aluminum paint to reflect the sun's rays and avoid excessive heating.

7. What should be done about puddles of water standing on an asphalt built-up roofing membrane after a rain? To ensure drainage, roof membranes should have a gentle slope toward the drains. Too often, perhaps due to poor design or construction or to repeated roof coverings with one layer on top of the other, the layers of felt are lower in some regions and provide a depression for water to collect.

Although these are usually tolerated, they can be filled with a few patching layers of roofing felt carefully cemented down with an asphalt emulsion or cut-back asphalt.

8. Water is leaking down the vent pipes that emerge from the roof. Lead sheet flashing has pulled away from the pipe or is not tightly wrapped around the pipe. Lead is malleable and can be readily shaped to the pipe.

9. There are ceiling water stains, but no leaks have been found around the edge of the roof or the drains. There is some danger of a leak developing wherever the roof changes slope. The flashing may be too small and difficult to caulk because of insufficient overlapping of materials.

10. Shingles (wood or asphalt) are ripped from the roof in a strong windstorm. The shingles may have been installed with too much of the shingle showing (insufficient overlap). Also, the shingles may have been stapled in place mechanically with a varying depth of penetration into the roof. A better practice in regions of frequent strong winds is to hand nail the shingles and individually tab or cement them into place. In hurricane-force winds roof coverings are likely to be ripped loose. In this case even the hurricane straps holding the roof structure to the wall beams might loosen and let portions of the deck blow away.

Comments

Residential Construction Performance Guidelines, *published by the National Association of Home Builders (Telephone: 1-800-368-5242), provides tolerances for the following: roof installation and leaks (Sections 5–5 through 5–17), roof rolling (Sections 5–18 through 5–20), chimney (Sections 5–21 and 5–22), chimney flashing (Section 5–23), and gutters and downspouts (Sections 5–24 through 5–26).*

Roofing Definitions

UBC — 1997

Section 1502 — Definitions

Built-Up Roofing is two or more layers of felt cemented together and surfaced with a cap sheet, mineral aggregate, smooth coating or similar surfacing material.

Built-Up Roofing Ply is a layer of felt in built-up roofing.

Cap Sheet is roof covering made of organic or inorganic fibers, saturated and coated on both sides with a bituminous compound, surfaced with mineral granules, mica, talc, ilmenite, inorganic fibers or similar materials.

Cementing is solidly mopped application of asphalt, cold liquid asphalt compound, coal tar pitch or other approved cementing material.

Combination Sheet is a glass fiber felt integrally attached to kraft paper.

Roof Drainage

UBC — 1997

1506.1 General. Roofs shall be sloped a minimum of 1 unit vertical in 48 units horizontal (2% slope) for drainage unless designed for water accumulation in accordance with Section 1611 and approved by the building official.

1506.2 Roof Drains. Unless roofs are sloped to drain over roof edges, roof drains shall be installed at each low point of the roof.

Roof drains shall be sized and discharged in accordance with the Plumbing Code.

1506.3 Overflow Drains and Scuppers. Where roof drains are required, overflow drains having the same size as the roof drains shall be installed with the inlet flow line located 2 inches (51 mm) above the low point of the roof, or overflow scuppers having three times the size of the roof drains and having a minimum opening height of 4 inches (102 mm) may be installed in the adjacent parapet walls with the inlet flow line located 2 inches (51 mm) above the low point of the adjacent roof.

Overflow drains shall discharge to an approved location and shall not be connected to roof drain lines.

1506.4 Concealed Piping. Roof drains and overflow drains, where concealed within the construction of the building, shall be installed in accordance with the Plumbing Code.

1506.5 Over Public Property. Roof drainage water from a building shall not be permitted to flow over public property.

Exception: Group R, Division 3 and Group U Occupancies.

Ed. Note: See "Built-Up Roofing" later in this chapter for a roof drain illustration.

Gutters & Downspouts

Industry Standards

Means Graphic Construction Standards
(R.S. Means Co., Inc.)

Gutter and downspout systems are used to collect and distribute water from roof edges. Metal gutters of aluminum, copper, lead-coated copper, galvanized steel, and stainless steel are available in stock lengths with accessories such as mounting brackets, connectors, corners, end caps, downspout connectors, and leaf guards. They may be box, round, or ogee in configuration and are often prepainted. Plastic or vinyl gutters in stock lengths and various cross-sectional shapes are manufactured with matching accessories. These types of gutters have the advantage that they deteriorate less from the effects of weather. Treated wood gutters are premilled in quarter round or ogee patterns. They may be job fabricated in box or V configurations. Downspouts, round or rectangular in cross section, are available with accessories to match the gutter systems. Pipe of black steel or cast iron may be used to provide a more durable downspout.

Flat Roof with Gutter

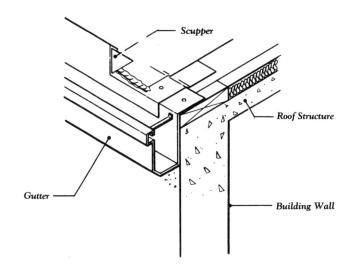

Metal or Vinyl Gutter

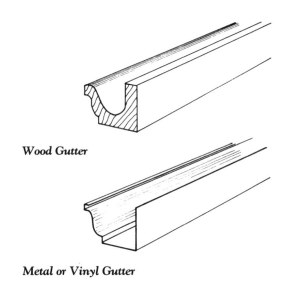

Wood Gutter

Metal or Vinyl Gutter

Flat Roof with Leader Box

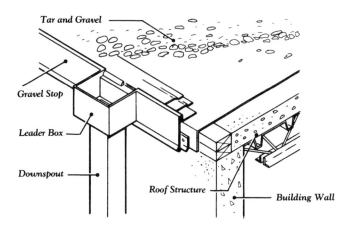

R.S. Means Co., Inc., *Means Graphic Construction Standards*

Figure 8.1

Industry Standards
Roofing: Design Criteria, Options, Selection
(R.S. Means Co., Inc.)

Gutters Versus Scuppers

Because of problems with maintenance, deterioration, and cleaning, it is best to avoid the use of gutters when possible on larger commercial structures, where they may be required to move the water a great distance, thereby increasing the chance of blockage by debris or ice. The best way to remove water from this type of roof is with interior ("field") drains. These drains should be installed along with tapered insulation, to ensure a positive slope and thus minimize ponding. Short lengths of gutter, *scuppers* or *heads*, and downspouts are another solution. With this approach, water is directed away from the raised portion of the fascia by the use of *crickets* between the scuppers (see **Figure 8.2, "Downspout Scupper"**). The most economical downspout is the 26-gauge corrugated rectangular type, readily available in most areas at sheet metal supply wholesalers. These downspouts are usually available in three sizes:

Area in Square Inches	Actual Size	Nominal Size
7.73	2-3/8" x 3-1/4"	2" x 3"
11.70	2-3/4" x 4-1/4"	3" x 4"
18.75	3-3/4" x 5"	4" x 5"

Scuppers should be spaced no more than 50 feet on center; they should be closer if there are large areas to drain. The area to be drained by each downspout should be calculated. Then, using rainfall data derived from charts in the *SMACNA Architectural Manual*, *AIA Graphic Standards*, or a similar resource, the size of the downspouts can be determined, and the distance between the downspouts adjusted as necessary to produce practical spacing. If the downspouts are over 40 feet in length, relief valves or heads should be installed to admit air and prevent formation of a vacuum.

Ed. Note: See "Bituminous Roofing Products" later in this chapter for an illustration of a gutter system for that type of roof.

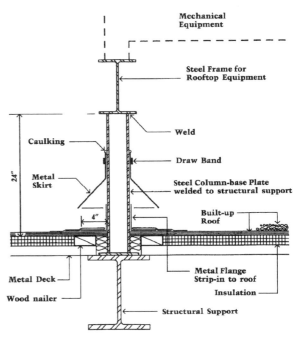

Mechanical Equipment Support

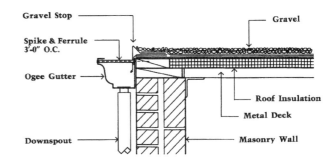

Gutter & Downspout

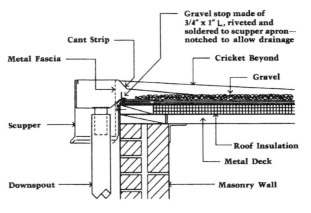

Downspout Scupper

R.S. Means Co., Inc., *Roofing: Design Criteria, Options, Selection*

Figure 8.2

Roofing Fire Safety & Wind Resistance

Industry Standards

Roofing Handbook
(The McGraw-Hill Companies)

Fire safety is an important consideration, especially since the roof is particularly vulnerable to fire from overhead or airborne sources.

The fire resistance of roofing materials is tested by the Underwriters' Laboratories, Inc. (UL), an independent, not-for-profit public safety testing laboratory. UL established the standard for the testing of roofing materials with the assistance of nationally recognized fire authorities.

Manufacturers voluntarily submit materials for testing. The materials then are classified and labeled according to the classes below. The American Society for Testing and Materials (ASTM) is a voluntary organization concerned with the development of consensus standards, testing procedures, and specifications.

Class A The highest fire-resistance rating for roofing as per ASTM E-108. This class rating indicates that the roofing material is able to withstand severe exposure to fire that originates from sources outside the building.

Class B This fire-resistance rating indicates that the roofing material is able to withstand moderate exposure to fire that originates from sources outside the building.

Class C This fire-resistance rating indicates that the roofing material is able to withstand light exposure to fire that originates from sources outside the building.

UL also tests shingle performance against high winds. To qualify for the UL wind-resistant label, shingles must withstand continuous test winds of at least 60 miles per hour for two hours without a shingle tab lifting.

Labelling of Roof Materials

UBC — 1997

1507.1 Materials. The quality and design of roofing materials and their fastenings shall conform to the applicable standards listed in Chapter 35, Part II.

1507.2 Identification. All material shall be delivered in packages bearing the manufacturer's label or identifying mark. Each package of asphalt shingles, mineral surfaced roll roofing, fire-retardant-treated shingles and shakes, modified bitumen,

thermoplastic, and thermoset membranes, and built-up roofing ply materials shall bear the label of an approved agency having a service for the inspection of material and finished products during manufacture.

Each bundle of wood shakes or shingles shall comply with UBC Standard 15-3 or 15-4, respectively. Each bundle of wood shakes or shingles and slate shingles shall bear the label or identification mark of an approved inspection bureau or agency showing the grade.

Asphalt shall be delivered in cartons indicating the name of the manufacturer, the flash point and the type of product. Bulk shipments shall be accompanied with the same information issued in the form of a certification or on the bill of lading by the manufacturer. Coal tar pitch shall bear the manufacturer's name and type. Additional information, such as equiviscous temperature (EVT), may be furnished.

1507.3 Asbestos-cement Roofing. Corrugated asbestos-cement roofing shall be applied in an approved manner.

1507.5 Asphalt Shingles. Asphalt shingles shall be fastened according to the manufacturer's instructions and Table 15-B-1.

1507.6 Built-up Roofs. Built-up roofing shall be applied in accordance with the manufacturer's instructions and Tables 15-E through 15-G.

Roof Structure

Comments

For tolerances on roof ridge beam deflection, see section 5.1 in Residential Construction Performance Guidelines, *published by the National Association of Home Builders (Telephone: 800-368-5242).*

Industry Standards

Roofing: Design Criteria, Options, Selection
(R.S. Means Co., Inc.)

Structural Roof Deck

The structural roof deck is the foundation upon which the roofing system is built. The following basic principles should be kept in mind:

- In new design, provide a deck and its supporting structure with the strength and stability to accommodate loading for a variety of roofing systems, attachment of components, and temporary loading during construction. Re-roofing will inevitably be required in the future.

- Provide slope for positive drainage, using a minimum of 1/4 " per foot.

- Check special loading conditions, such as concentrated equipment loads, snow slides or banks at base of walls of high roof sections, and ponding behind potential ice dam locations.

- Check roof load bearing capacity for any roof that will have more dead load added by re-roofing. Steel and wood structures are more likely to be overloaded by the added weight, but do not overlook potential problems in reinforced or pre-stressed concrete. Long span "flat roof" members with perimeter drainage can be especially troublesome if they have lost their initial camber.

The structural roof deck is an integral part of the light-commercial building structure. It supports not only the roofing system, consisting of insulation, membrane, and surfacing, but also live loads, such as wind and various forms of precipitation. In addition, economy of design often dictates that the deck perform beyond the simple function of carrying the roofing and gravity loading. The deck also acts as lateral bracing for compressive sections of slender framing, such as joists or purlins. Additionally, the structural deck may be used as a diaphragm to receive, distribute, and deliver lateral forces to walls or other buttressing elements of the building.

All roof decks must be compatible not only with their accompanying system components, but also with the service environment. To successfully support a roofing system, the deck must have the necessary strength, stiffness, dimensional stability, and durability to provide a good foundation for that system. If the building designer is not an expert on roofing technology, a professional should be consulted who can match the roofing system to the structure.

Steel Roof Decks

Industry Standards

Means Graphic Construction Standards
(R.S. Means Co., Inc.)

Steel roof decking (used in commercial structures) has the advantages of being a lightweight material that covers a large area and can be installed in a minimum amount of time. Decking is manufactured in depths ranging from 1-1/2" to 7-1/2", thicknesses from 18 gauge to 22 gauge, and various cover widths. Economy dictates that lengths cover a minimum of two supporting members. Roof deck measuring 1-1/2" thick is rolled in three configurations: narrow rib, intermediate rib, and wide rib. The interior finish may be galvanized or factory painted.

Steel deck stored on site should be blocked off the ground with one end higher than the other to provide drainage. They should be covered with ventilated waterproof material for protection from the elements. The deck may be welded to supporting members, including bearing walls, or fastened with screws. Welds are made from the top side of the deck with puddle welds at least 1/2" diameter and fillet welds at least 1" long. Screws should be a minimum size No. 12. Spacing of welds or screws are as follows for all widths of deck: all side laps plus a sufficient number of interior ribs to limit the spacing between adjacent points of attachment to 18". For spans greater than 5', side laps shall be fastened between supports, center-to-center, at a maximum spacing of 3'.

Comments

Roof Deck Classification

Decks are classified in a number of different ways, based on different criteria. Codes or insurance-related agencies classify decks as combustible or noncombustible; built-up roofing manufacturers and their specifiers classify them as nailable or non-nailable. Structural engineers and architects usually classify decks by material, such as concrete, cementitious wood fiber, steel, or wood.

As some roof system components may be incompatible with certain deck types, the designer or roof specifier should be aware of potential problems with certain combinations in advance. This section covers characteristics of each of the various types of decks and potential problems these arrangements may present to the roof system. Such problems can be avoided through optimal system selection and design.

Comments

Steel deck surfaces that will remain exposed when the project is complete should be galvanized or painted on the underside to prevent rust and eventual staining.

Deck sheets should be placed in accordance with an approved erection-layout drawing supplied by the deck manufacturer and in accordance with the deck manufacturer's standards. Roofs having a slope of 1/4" in 12" or more should be erected from the low side up to produce a shingle effect. The ends of the sheet should lap a minimum of 2" and be located over a support.

The deck erector normally cuts openings in the roof deck, which are shown on the erection drawings, and are less than 16 square feet in area, as well as skew cuts. Openings for stacks, conduits, vents, etc. should be cut (and reinforced if necessary) by trades requiring the openings.

Roof Deck System with Insulation

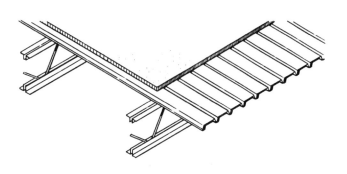

Acoustic Deck System

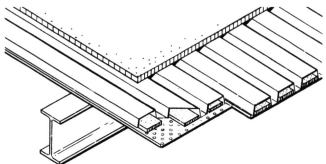

Composite Beam, Deck and Slab

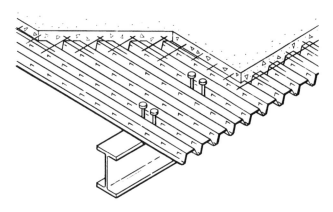

Cellular Deck System

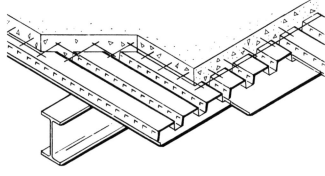

R.S. Means Co., Inc., *Means Graphic Construction Standards*

Figure 8.3

Steel Roof Deck

Acoustic Deck

Cellular Deck

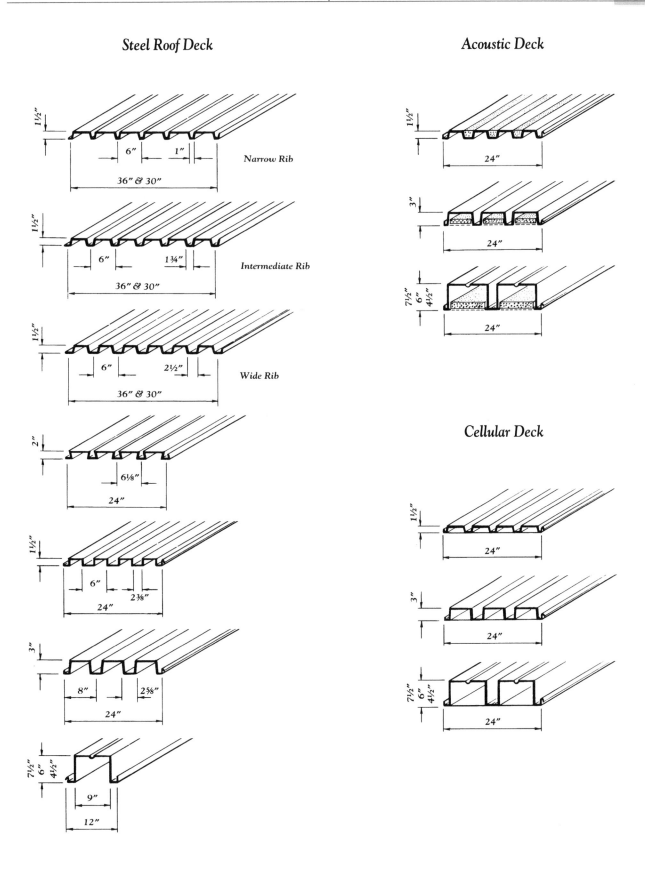

R.S. Means Co., Inc., *Means Graphic Construction Standards*

Figure 8.3 continued

Metal Deck and Steel Joists on Beams

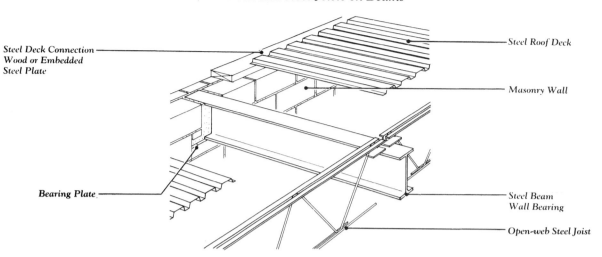

Steel Deck Connection
Wood or Embedded
Steel Plate

Steel Roof Deck

Masonry Wall

Bearing Plate

Steel Beam
Wall Bearing

Open-web Steel Joist

Metal Deck and Steel Joists on Walls

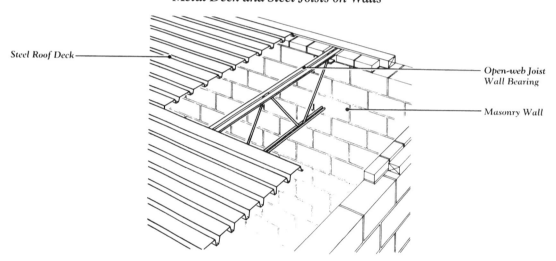

Steel Roof Deck

Open-web Joist
Wall Bearing

Masonry Wall

Formboard Deck, Bulb Ts, and Steel Joists

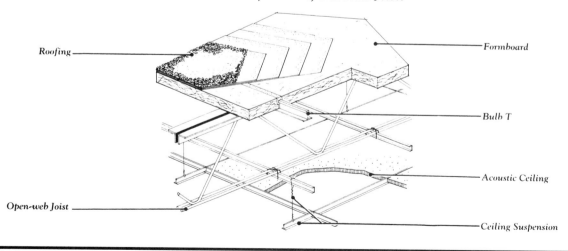

Roofing

Formboard

Bulb T

Acoustic Ceiling

Open-web Joist

Ceiling Suspension

R.S. Means Co., Inc., *Means Graphic Construction Standards*

Figure 8.4

Concrete Roof Decks

Industry Standards

Roofing: Design Criteria, Options, Selection
(R.S. Means Co., Inc.)

Structural Concrete

Structural concrete decks (also used for commercial applications) may be *cast-in-place* or *precast*. Cast-in-place concrete decks are either *conventionally reinforced* or *post-tensioned*. Precast decks are also either conventionally reinforced (commonly designated "reinforced") or pre-stressed, but pre-stressed is by far more commonly used.

Concrete decks are superior to lightweight decks for ballasted roofing systems. For insulated or mechanically attached single-ply systems, however, the cost of attaching insulation to the deck becomes a factor. When not topped with cast-in-place concrete or underlayment, the insulation board may fracture or membranes may split. Adjacent deck sections must be properly attached structurally in order to prevent differential vertical movement. It is also necessary to level the butted ends of sections if they are out of level. If lateral movements are possible in the deck system, the roofing membrane must have adequate flexibility in order to prevent splitting.

Pre-stressed members deflect a greater distance than cast-in-place reinforced structural slabs under comparable loads. They also gain and lose camber from heating and cooling of the upper surface, if not well insulated. Considerable movement can also take place between the ends of members in multiple span arrangements; this movement must be addressed in the selection of the roofing system, its attachment, and flashings. Flashing along terminal (side) edges of long members must often accommodate several inches of vertical movement between the deck and the parapet.

In lightweight insulating concrete decks, venting is not provided beneath the concrete. Thus, efforts should be made to assure proper drying of the overlay prior to roofing. Attention should also be paid to lateral venting of moisture vapor between the concrete and the underside of a built-up roof (BUR) membrane. This may be accomplished with a *venting base sheet*; one-way *roof vents* may also be helpful.

Hot mopping of BUR membranes to lightweight fills is discouraged by roofing authorities. Instead, special fasteners are recommended to attach base sheets to this nailable substrate. Such fasteners usually have a two-piece shank and an oversized head. The shanks mechanically anchor into the media by expanding, deforming, or barbing as they are driven. The plain shanks of standard roofing nails do not offer sufficient resistance to withdrawal. To mechanically attach insulation boards to lightweight fill, special fasteners are

Truss Tees, Formboard, Mesh, and Poured Gypsum Deck

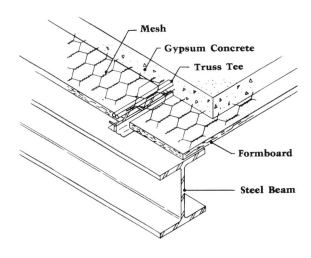

R.S. Means Co., Inc., *Roofing: Design Criteria, Options, Selection*

Figure 8.5

available with large, coarse threads and integral, or two-piece, disc heads. Some also have internal "barbs" that are actuated from the top after setting the screw. These special screws are spaced more widely than nails (up to three times more widely spaced), for attaching a base sheet.

The larger value of uplift resistance required for the insulation fasteners is often beyond the pull-out strength of lightweight insulating concrete. Uplift tests should be run, using the planned fastener in the lightweight concrete on-site, to confirm that the required design values can be achieved. Otherwise, alternative methods of attachment must be used.

Wood Roof Decks

Ed. Note: For more information on wood framing, see Chapter 5.

Industry Standards

Roofing: Design Criteria, Options, Selection
(R.S. Means Co., Inc.)

Ventilation

Wood roof framing, if not pressure-treated against decay, *must be ventilated*. Air, wood, and decay-propagating organisms are ever present; suitable decay-producing temperatures are anywhere between 45° and 110°F. To prevent decay, wood moisture content should be kept below 20 percent, or the wood should be pressure-treated to make it toxic, or unacceptable, to fungi or termites.

Cementitious Wood Fiber Decks

Cementitious wood fiber decks are often used in structures that do not have a suspended ceiling, such as gymnasiums and schools. The planks or panels are plant-produced, using treated wood fibers and a binder of Portland cement or gypsum. They are molded with controlled pressure and temperature to modular widths. When used with bulb tees, the planks have rabbeted edges to lay on bottom flanges of the tees (see **Figure 8.6**). The tees are usually spaced at 2'-9" on center and the planks span transversely between them. When used to span longitudinally between joists or purlins, the planks are generally 8' long and have tongue and groove edges.

Bulb Tees and 3" Thick Deck

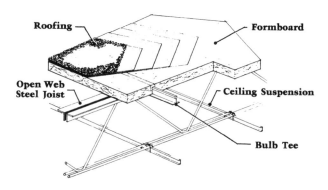

R.S. Means Co., Inc., *Roofing: Design Criteria, Options, Selection*

Figure 8.6

Asphalt Coating

Comments

Kettle temperature must be monitored, because overheating asphalt causes a number of problems. When it is overheated, asphalt will apply too thin; when it is cool, it will become brittle. Overheated asphalt puddles at the bottom of slopes, resulting in future alligatoring, or checking, in the areas where the puddle thickens.

The National Roofing Contractors Association (NCRA) recommends the following mop application:

Type I   ASTM D 312   Level Asphalt   350°F ± 25°F

Type II   ASTM D 312   Flat Asphalt   400°F ± 25°F

Type III ASTM D 312   Steep Asphalt   425°F ± 25°F

Refer to the manufacturer's recommendations for appropriate temperatures for a particular application. See also "Built-Up Roofing, Rule 5," later in this chapter.

Roof Shingles & Tiles: Definitions

Industry Standards

Plan Reading & Material Takeoff

(R.S. Means Co., Inc.)

Shingles and tiles are popular materials for covering sloped roofs. Both are *watershed* materials, which means they are designed to direct water away from the building by means of the slope or pitch of the roof. Shingles and tiles are used on roofs with a pitch of 3" or more per foot. Shingles are installed in layers with staggered joints over roofing felt underlayment. Nails or fasteners are concealed by the course above. Shingle materials include wood, asphalt, fiberglass, metal, and masonry tiles. Asphalt and fiberglass are available in a variety of weights and styles, with three-tab being the most common. **Figure 8.7** illustrates an asphalt shingle roof system and its components.

Wood shingles may be either shingle or shake grade; cedar is the most common species of wood used. Metal shingles are either aluminum or steel and are generally available prefinished. Slate and clay tiles are available in a variety of shapes, sizes, colors, weights, and textures. These are typically heavier materials and therefore require specialized installation techniques, and a stronger structural roof system to support the added loads imposed by the weight of the tile.

In addition to the shingle or tile materials, special metal trim pieces are required to protect the edge of the roof deck and allow water to drip free of the roof edge. *Drip edge* (available in vented and nonvented) is a corrosion-resistant metal, typically aluminum; it may be omitted with wood shingles or slates when the edge of the shingle or slate projects beyond the roof edge. Metal flashings for the valleys of the shingled and tiled roofs may also be specified. Valley flashing can be lead-coated copper, copper, or zinc alloy.

To provide venting for the attic space, ridge vents are sometimes used. They allow the transfer of air from the attic or rafter space to the outside, to prevent the buildup of moisture along the underside of the roof sheathing. Ridge-venting materials are available in a variety of styles and compositions.

Shingles and tile roof systems require special shingles or tiles, called *cap shingles* at the ridge or hip of the roof. A cap shingle may be a regular three-tab shingle modified for use as a cap, as in the case of asphalt or fiberglass shingles, or a special prefabricated cap (as in the case of some clay tile or metal tile designs).

Shingled Roof

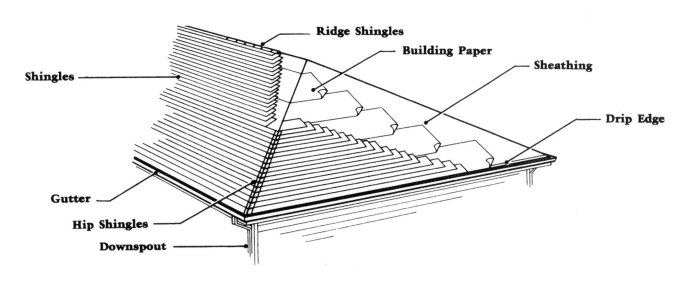

R.S. Means Co., Inc., *Plan Reading & Material Takeoff*

Figure 8.7

Special membrane material installed under the first couple of courses, and at the hips and valleys or the shingle or tile roof, is called an *ice/water barrier*. Most of these products are a bitumen-based self-adhering membrane for use in cold climates where ice and water may dam along the eaves and valleys and cause water to back up under the roof shingles.

Asphalt Shingles

Industry Standards
Roofing Handbook
(The McGraw-Hill Companies)

Specifying Underlayments
When a single-layer underlayment is required, apply one layer of No. 15 asphalt-saturated, nonperforated felt horizontally. Heavier underlayment usually is not necessary, but might be required by local codes or area practice. Lap all felt sheets a minimum of 2 inches over the preceding felt sheet. Endlaps should be a minimum of 4 inches. Nail the felts under the lap only as necessary to hold the felts in place until the asphalt roofing material is applied. Laps can be sealed with plastic asphalt cement as required.

If specifications call for a double-layer underlayment, apply two layers of No. 15 (minimum) asphalt-saturated, nonperforated felt horizontally. Apply a 19-inch-wide starter sheet to the eaves. Cover the starter sheet with a full width sheet. Lap succeeding sheets 19 inches over the preceding sheets with a 17-inch exposure. Endlaps should be a minimum of 6 inches. Backnail the felts under the laps only as necessary to hold tile felts in place until the asphalt roofing material is applied. Laps can be sealed with plastic asphalt cement as required.

In locations where the January mean temperature is 30° F or lower, apply two plies of No. 15 felt or one ply of No. 50 felt. Set in hot asphalt or mastic, or an adhered bitumen membrane underlayment to roof decks with slopes less than 4 inches per foot, regardless of the slope. Work from the eaves to a point 24 inches inside the building's inside wall line to serve as an ice shield.

The limitations imposed by the slope, or pitch, of the roof deck are factors that must be considered when the roof is designed and underlayments specified.

For instance, self-sealing strip shingles, with tabs, can be applied on roof decks that have a slope of 4 inches per 12 inches or more if at least one layer of No. 15 asphalt-saturated, nonperforated felt is applied horizontally to serve as the underlayment.

Self-sealing strip shingles, with tabs, also can be applied to roof decks with a slope of 3 inches per 12 inches or more if at least two layers of No. 15 asphalt-saturated, nonperforated felt is applied horizontally to serve as the underlayment.

Using Staples and Nails

Staples can be used in place of roofing nails on a one-for-one basis. If there is any doubt about the acceptability of staples in a particular application, consult the shingle manufacturer.

Selecting Nails

Use large-headed, sharp-pointed, hot-dipped, galvanized, or the equivalent, steel or aluminum nails with barbed or otherwise deformed shanks to apply asphalt shingles. The best roofing nails are made from 11- or 12-gauge wire, have heads that are 3/8 or 7/16 inch in diameter, and are long enough to penetrate the roofing materials. The nails should extend through plywood decks and at least 3/4 inch into wooden plank decks.

If a fastener does not penetrate the deck properly, remove the fastener and repair the hole in the shingle with asphalt plastic cement or replace the entire shingle. Then place another fastener nearby.

Do not nail into or above factory-applied adhesives. Carefully align each shingle. Whenever possible, make sure that no cutout or end joint is less than 2 inches from a nail in an underlaying course. To prevent buckling, start nailing from the end nearest the shingle just laid and proceed across. To prevent distortion, do not attempt to realign a shingle by shifting the free end after two nails are in place.

Place the fasteners according to the shingle manufacturer's specifications. Align the shingles properly to avoid exposing fasteners in the course below. Drive the nails straight and flush with the shingle surface. Do not sink the nail into or break the shingle's surface.

Applying 3-Tab Strip Shingles

In areas with normal weather conditions, fasten each of these shingles with 4 fasteners. When the shingles are applied with a 5-inch exposure, apply the fasteners on a line 5/8 inch above the top of the cutouts, 1 inch from each end, and centered over each cutout.

For high wind areas, use six fasteners instead of four. The fastener locations should be on a line 5/8 inch above the top of the cutouts, 1 inch from each end and 1 inch to the left and right of center of each cutout.

If a roof surface is broken by a dormer or valley, start applying the shingles from a rake and work toward the break. If the surface is unbroken, start at the rake that is most visible. If both rakes are equally visible, start at the center and work both ways. No matter where the application begins, apply the shingles across and diagonally up the roof. This ensures that each shingle is fastened properly.

Straight-up application or racking can result in less than the recommended number of nails being used because of the manner in which the shingles are applied.

Comments

*Improperly driven nails (see **Figure 8.10**) can be addressed by removing and replacing the incorrect nail, or by adding another, correctly driven nail next to the original one. A small amount of roof cement can be applied over the nailhead or hole in the shingle.*

Asphalt Roofing — 6-inch Pattern

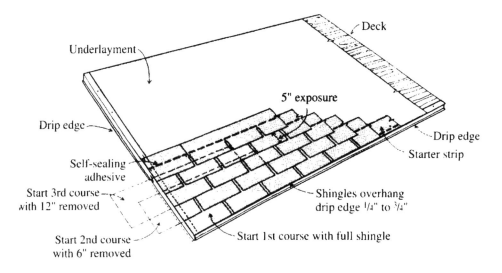

Courtesy of The McGraw-Hill Companies, *Roofing Handbook*

Figure 8.8

Asphalt Shingle Application

Roof Slope	ASPHALT SHINGLES	
	Not Permitted below 2 Units Vertical in 12 Units Horizontal (16.7% Slope)	
	2 Units Vertical in 12 Units Horizontal (16.7% Slope) to Less than 4 Units Vertical in 12 Units Horizontal (33.3% Slope)	4 Units Vertical in 12 Units Horizontal (33.3% Slope) and Over
1. Deck requirement	Asphalt shingles shall be fastened to solidly sheathed roofs. Sheathing shall conform to Sections 2312.2 and 2320.12.9.	
2. Underlayment Temperate climate	Asphalt strip shingles may be installed on slopes as low as 2 units vertical in 12 units horizontal (16.7% slope), provided the shingles are approved self-sealing or are hand sealed and are installed with an underlayment consisting of two layers of nonperforated Type 15 felt applied shingle fashion. Starting with an 18-inch-wide (457 mm) sheet and a 36-inch-wide (914 mm) sheet over it at the eaves, each subsequent sheet shall be lapped 19 inches (483 mm) horizontally.	One layer nonperforated Type 15 felt lapped 2 inches (51 mm) horizontally and 4 inches (102 mm) vertically to shed water.
Severe climate: In areas subject to wind-driven snow or roof ice buildup	Same as for temperate climate, and the two layers shall be solid cemented together with approved cementing material between the plies extending from the eave up the roof to a line 24 inches (610 mm) inside the exterior wall line of the building. As an alternative to the two layers of cemented Type 15 felt, an approved self-adhering, polymer modified, bituminous sheet may be used.	Same as for temperate climate, except that one layer No. 40 coated roofing or coated glass base shall be applied from the eaves to a line 12 inches (305 mm) inside the exterior wall line with all laps cemented together. As an alternative to the layer of No. 40 felt, a self-adhering, polymer modified, bituminous sheet may be used.
3. Attachment Combined systems, type of fasteners	Corrosion-resistant nails, minimum 12-gage $^3/_8$-inch (9.5 mm) head, or approved corrosion-resistant staples, minimum 16-gage $^{15}/_{16}$-inch (23.8 mm) crown width. Fasteners shall comply with the requirements of Chapter 23, Division III, Part III. Fasteners shall be long enough to penetrate into the sheathing $^3/_4$ inch (19 mm) or through the thickness of the sheathing, whichever is less.	
No. of fasteners[1]	4 per 36-inch to 40-inch (914 mm to 1016 mm) strip 2 per 9-inch to 18-inch (229 mm to 457 mm) shingle	
Exposure Field of roof Hips and ridges	Per manufacturer's instructions included with packages of shingles. Hip and ridge weather exposures shall not exceed those permitted for the field of the roof.	
Method	Per manufacturer's instructions included with packages of shingles.	
4. Flashing Valleys Other flashing	Per Section 1508.2 Per Section 1509	

[1]Figures shown are for normal application. For special conditions, such as mansard application and where roofs are in special wind regions, shingles shall be attached per the manufacturer's instructions.

Courtesy of ICBO, UBC — 1997 [Table 15-B-1]

Figure 8.9

Nailing Diagram

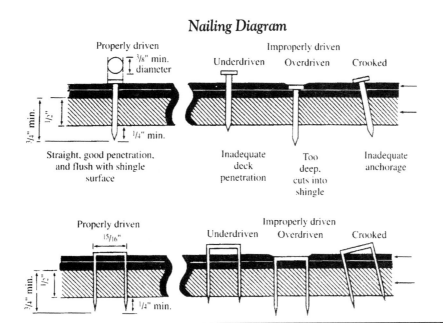

Courtesy of The McGraw-Hill Companies, *Roofing Handbook*

Figure 8.10

Open Valley Using Metal Valley Flashing

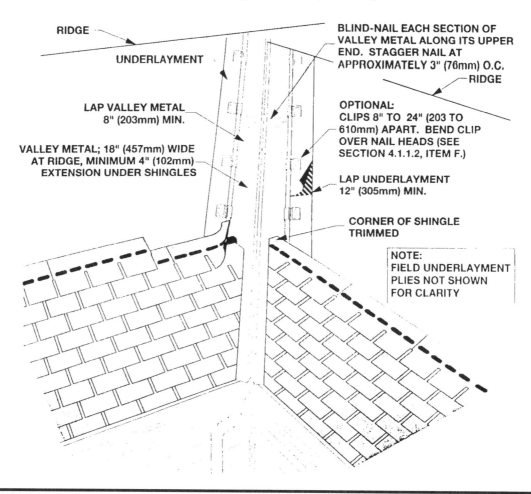

RIDGE

UNDERLAYMENT

LAP VALLEY METAL
8" (203mm) MIN.

VALLEY METAL; 18" (457mm) WIDE
AT RIDGE, MINIMUM 4" (102mm)
EXTENSION UNDER SHINGLES

BLIND-NAIL EACH SECTION OF
VALLEY METAL ALONG ITS UPPER
END. STAGGER NAIL AT
APPROXIMATELY 3" (76mm) O.C.

RIDGE

OPTIONAL:
CLIPS 8" TO 24" (203 TO
610mm) APART. BEND CLIP
OVER NAIL HEADS (SEE
SECTION 4.1.1.2, ITEM F.)

LAP UNDERLAYMENT
12" (305mm) MIN.

CORNER OF SHINGLE
TRIMMED

NOTE:
FIELD UNDERLAYMENT
PLIES NOT SHOWN
FOR CLARITY

Courtesy National Roofing Contractors Association, NRCA *Roofing & Waterproofing Manual*

Figure 8.11

Applying Successive Courses

The first course is the most crucial. Be sure it is laid perfectly straight. Check it regularly during application against a horizontal chalkline. A few vertical chalklines aligned with the ends of the shingles in the first course ensure the proper alignment of the cutouts.

If applying three-tab shingles or roll roofing for the starter strip, bond the tabs of each shingle in the first course to the starter strip by placing a spot of asphalt plastic cement about the size of a quarter on the starter strip beneath each tab. Then press the tabs firmly into the cement. Avoid excessive use of cement as this can cause blistering.

Comments

To adequately anchor asphalt roofing materials, special fasteners and/or details are required in certain deck materials, for example, gypsum concrete plank and tile, fiberboard, or similar nonwood deck materials. It is important to follow the manufacturers' instructions carefully when working with these types of materials, to ensure that responsibility for performance remains with the manufacturer.

Asphalt Shingles: Valleys & Flashing

Open Valleys

Open valleys can be formed by laying strips of at least 26-gauge galvanized metal, or an equivalent noncorrosive, nonstaining material in the valley angle and lapping the roofing material over the metal on either side. This leaves a space between the edges of the roofing material to channel the water down the valley.

UBC — 1997

1508.1 Valleys. Roof valley flashings shall be as noted in this section. Shingle application shall be consistent with applicable Table 15-B-1, 15-B-2, 15-D-1 or 15-D-2.

1508.2 Asphalt Shingles. The roof valley flashing shall not be provided of less than 0.016-inch (0.41 mm) (No. 28 galvanized sheet gage) corrosion-resistant metal, and shall extend at least 8 inches (203 mm) from the center line each way. Sections of flashing shall have an end lap of not less than 4 inches (102 mm). Alternatively, the valley shall consist of woven asphalt shingles applied in accordance with the manufacturer's printed instructions.

In each case, the roof valley flashing shall have a 36-inch-wide (914 mm) underlayment directly under it consisting of one layer of Type 15 felt running the full length of the valley, in addition to the underlayment specified in Table 15-B-1. In severe climates, the metal valley flashing underlayment shall be solid cemented to the roof underlayment for slopes under 7 units vertical in 12 units horizontal (58.3% slope).

Industry Standards

NRCA Roofing & Waterproofing Manual
(National Roofing Contractors Association)

NRCA recommends that valley metal, for use with asphalt shingles, be approximately 24 inches (610 mm) wide. This means that the NRCA recommends that the valley metal be formed with a "W"-shaped splash diverter, or rib,

Woven Valley

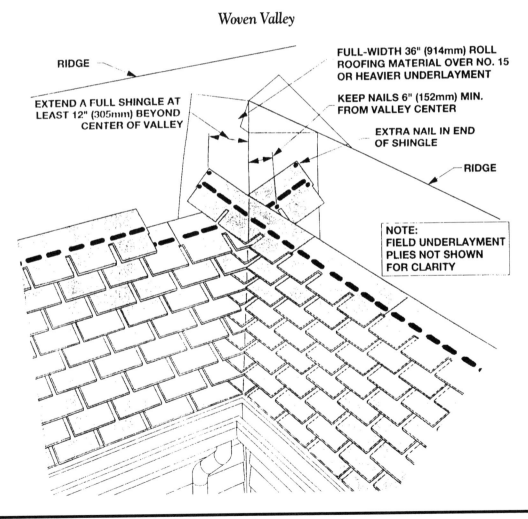

RIDGE

EXTEND A FULL SHINGLE AT LEAST 12" (305mm) BEYOND CENTER OF VALLEY

FULL-WIDTH 36" (914mm) ROLL ROOFING MATERIAL OVER NO. 15 OR HEAVIER UNDERLAYMENT

KEEP NAILS 6" (152mm) MIN. FROM VALLEY CENTER

EXTRA NAIL IN END OF SHINGLE

RIDGE

NOTE:
FIELD UNDERLAYMENT PLIES NOT SHOWN FOR CLARITY

Courtesy National Roofing Contractors Association, *NRCA Roofing & Waterproofing Manual*

Figure 8.12

in the center. A center rib can be especially beneficial in valleys where adjoining roof areas are of unequal slope, as the rib helps to prevent "wash over" of runoff. The center rib should not be less than 1 inch (25 mm) high. For easier installation, and for controlling thermal expansion and contraction, NRCA suggests that metal valleys, used with asphalt shingle roofing, be no longer than 12 feet (4 m).

3.7.2 Woven Valleys

The woven valley method illustrated in **Figure 8.12** is preferred by some roofing professionals, but its use is generally limited to 3-tab strip shingles on roofs where the valley slope is at least 4 inches per foot (33%). However, in areas of the country where heavy accumulations of moss may grow between the shingle cutouts, a woven valley may hamper runoff. Therefore, as with all types of valleys, specifying a woven valley should be carefully considered to be sure it is beneficial for the particular project.

Some dimensional or architectural shingles can be difficult to use to create a rapidly draining woven valley. When dimensional shingles from opposite sides of the valley are woven, they can make for a relatively thick build-up of material, which can make the resultant valley irregularly sloped and slower draining. Individual locking-type shingles cannot be used with woven valley construction because nails are required for each tab, which would mean placing nails at or near the center of the valley.

Comments

While it is legal to construct the valley flashing from rolled roofing (both the Roofing Handbook *and the* NRCA Roofing & Waterproofing Manual *address the acceptable methods), we exclude this method from this text as it does not reflect common practice for new construction.*

Closed-Cut Valley

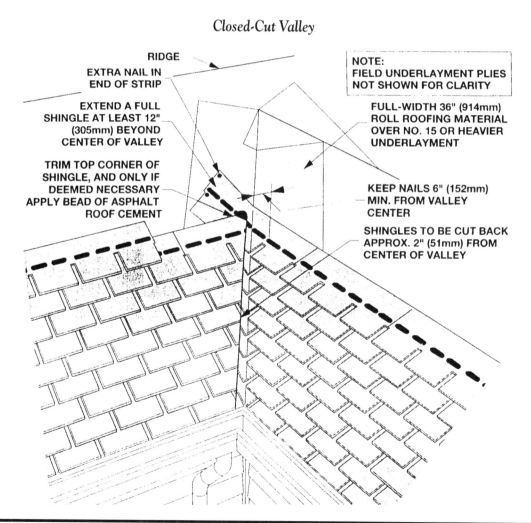

RIDGE

EXTRA NAIL IN END OF STRIP

EXTEND A FULL SHINGLE AT LEAST 12" (305mm) BEYOND CENTER OF VALLEY

TRIM TOP CORNER OF SHINGLE, AND ONLY IF DEEMED NECESSARY APPLY BEAD OF ASPHALT ROOF CEMENT

NOTE: FIELD UNDERLAYMENT PLIES NOT SHOWN FOR CLARITY

FULL-WIDTH 36" (914mm) ROLL ROOFING MATERIAL OVER NO. 15 OR HEAVIER UNDERLAYMENT

KEEP NAILS 6" (152mm) MIN. FROM VALLEY CENTER

SHINGLES TO BE CUT BACK APPROX. 2" (51mm) FROM CENTER OF VALLEY

Courtesy National Roofing Contractors Association, *NRCA Roofing & Waterproofing Manual*

Figure 8.13

Note: It is important, with all types of asphalt shingle valley construction, to keep from placing nails near the center of a valley. Nails should be kept away from the center of the valley to avoid leakage. Generally, nails should be kept back from the center of the valley by a minimum of 6 inches (152mm).

However, on relatively low-sloped roofs with valleys oriented into prevailing wind-driven rain, or in climates where freeze-thaw cycling may be regularly anticipated, holding nails back 6 to 8 inches (150 to 203 mm) or further from the center of the valley is not uncommon.

With 3-tab shingles, the last shingle in a particular course may not extend fully through the valley. If the shingle were nailed, the last nail would be too close to the valley center line. Placing a nail too close to the center of a woven valley can be avoided by simply cutting the shingle that falls short of extending through the valley.

Industry Standards

Roofing Handbook
(The McGraw-Hill Companies)

Closed-Cut Valleys

This design can be used only with strip-type shingles and roll roofing materials. To install flashings at closed-cut valley locations, center a 36-inch-wide strip of No. 15 asphalt-saturated, nonperforated felt in the valley over the existing No. 15 asphalt-saturated felt underlayment. Use only enough nails to hold the sheet smoothly in place.

Lay the first course of shingles along the eaves of one roof area up to and over the valley. Extend it along the adjoining roof area for at least 12 inches. Continue to apply the second and successive courses over the valley in the same manner as the first course. Tightly press the shingles into the valley and nail in place. Locate no nail closer than 6 inches to the valley's centerline. Locate two nails at the end of each terminal sheet.

Apply the first course of shingles along the eaves of the intersecting roof area and extend it over the previously applied shingles. Trim a minimum of 2 inches back from the centerline of the valley. Clip in place the upper corner of each end shingle to prevent water from penetrating under the courses and then embed it in a 3-inch-wide strip of plastic asphalt cement.

Flashing Against Chimneys

To avoid stresses and distortions due to the uneven settling of roofing materials, the chimney is usually built on a separate foundation from the building and normally is subject to some differential settling. Therefore, flashing at the point where the chimney projects through the roof requires a type of construction that allows for movement without damaging the water seal. To satisfy this requirement, use base flashings that are secured to the roof deck and counterflashings that are secured to masonry.

Counterflashing

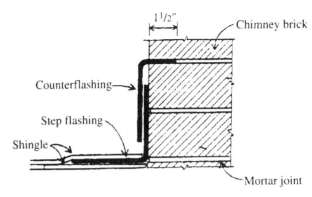

Courtesy of The McGraw-Hill Companies, *Roofing Handbook*

Figure 8.14

Step Flashing & Counterflashing Against Chimney

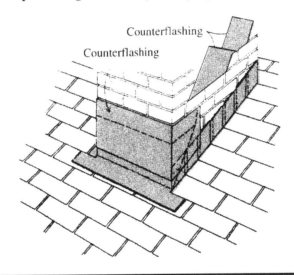

Courtesy of The McGraw-Hill Companies, *Roofing Handbook*

Figure 8.15

Before any flashings are installed, apply shingles over the roofing felt up to the front face of the chimney and construct a cricket or saddle between the back face of the chimney and the roof deck. Design the cricket to prevent the accumulation of snow and ice and to deflect water around the chimney.

Begin the flashing construction by installing at least 26-gauge galvanized metal, or an equivalent noncorrosive, nonstaining material, between the chimney and the roof deck on all sides. Apply the base flashing to the front first. Bend the base flashing so that the lower section extends at least 4 inches over the shingles and the upper section extends at least 12 inches up the face of the chimney. Set both sections of the base flashing in plastic asphalt cement.

Use metal step flashing for the sides of the chimney. Position the pieces in the same manner as flashing for a vertical sidewall. Secure each piece to the masonry with plastic asphalt cement and use nails to secure to the roof deck. Embed the overlapping shingles in plastic asphalt cement.

Place the rear base flashing over the cricket and the back of the chimney. The metal base flashing should cover the cricket and extend onto the roof deck at least 6 inches. It should also extend 6 inches up the brickwork. Bring the asphalt shingles up to or over the cricket and cement in place.

Place counterflashings over all apron, cricket, and step flashings to keep water from the joint. Begin by setting the metal counterflashing into the brickwork. This is done by raking out the mortar joint to a depth of 1-1/2 inches and inserting the bent edge of the flashing into the cleared joint. Once it is in place and has a slight amount of spring tension, the flashing cannot be dislodged easily. Refill the joint with Portland cement mortar. Finally, bend the flashing down to cover the flashing and to lie snugly against the masonry.

Drip Edges

Drip edges provide efficient watershedding at the eaves and rakes and keeps the underlying wood or plywood deck from rotting. Use 28-gauge galvanized metal, at a minimum, or an equivalent noncorrosive, nonstaining material to make drip edges along eaves and rakes and at edges of the deck. Provide an underlayment between the metal edge and the roof deck along the rake and over the metal edge along the eave.

Extend the drip edge back from the edge of the deck not more than 3 inches and secure with appropriate nails spaced 8 to 10 inches apart along the inner edge. In high-wind areas, space nails 4 inches on center.

Asphalt Shingles: Hips & Ridges

For hips and ridges, use individual shingles cut down to 12 x 12 inches from 12 x 36 inch three-tab shingles or to a minimum of 9 x 12 inches on two tab or no cutout asphalt shingles. Taper the lap portion of each cap shingle slightly so that it is narrower than the exposed portion. Some shingle manufacturers supply ready-cut hip and ridge shingles and specify how they should be applied.

To apply the cut ridge shingles, bend each shingle along its centerline so that it extends an equal distance on each side of the hip or ridge. Chalklines can assist in proper alignment. In cold weather, warm the shingle until it is pliable before bending. Apply the shingles with a 5-inch exposure, beginning at the bottom of the hip or from the end of the ridge opposite the direction of the prevailing winds.

Secure each shingle with one fastener on each side, placed 5-1/2 inches back from the exposed end and 1 inch up from the edge. The fastener length for hip and ridge shingles should be 1/4 inch longer than that recommended for shingles.

Asphalt Shingles: Shading & Discoloration

Shading

As a completed asphalt shingle roof is viewed from different angles, certain areas can appear darker or lighter. This difference in appearance is called shading. Shading also depends on the position of the sun and overall intensity of light. For example, slanting sun rays emphasize shading, while direct, overhead rays cause color shading to disappear.

Shading is a visual phenomenon that in no way affects the performance of the shingles. It occurs primarily as a result of normal manufacturing operations that produce slight differences in surface texture that cannot be detected during the production process. These unavoidable variations in texture simply affect the way the surface reflects light.

Algae Discoloration

A type of roof discoloration caused by algae and commonly referred to as fungus growth is a frequent problem throughout the country. It is often mistaken for soot, dirt, moss or tree droppings. The algae that cause this discoloration do not feed on the roofing material and, therefore, do not affect the service life of the roofing.

Fiber Cement Shingles

Industry Standards

NRCA Roofing & Waterproofing Manual
(National Roofing Contractors Association)

Fiber cement products are generally a blend of a Portland cement, synthetic or natural fibers and, in some cases, lightweight aggregate that are manufactured to simulate natural slate, wood shakes or shingles, and tile. Others may be based on a cementitious resin or epoxy compound. With some of these products the coloring is created with mineral oxides or pigments. The resulting products can typically be fastened, and sawn or cut for use on steep-slope roofs. Currently, these products are cement-based, non-asbestos fiber reinforced.

2.2 Manufacturing Processes for Fiber Cement Roofing Products

Generally, the non-asbestos fibers, cement, and other ingredients are mixed together, then poured into a mold or formed for shape, and heated under pressure to form the shingles or roofing units. Some products are predrilled with fastener holes before packaging.

Shingle Measurements

E   *Exposure*
TL   *Toplap*
HL   *Headlap*
SL   *Sidelap*
W   *Width for Strip Shingles*
      or Length for Individual Shingles

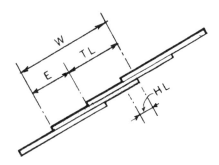

Courtesy of John Wiley & Sons, Inc., *Construction Principles, Materials, and Methods*

Figure 8.16

2.3 Some General Guidelines and Application Information Applicable to Various Fiber Cement Roofing Products

2.3.1 Roof Deck With some products, both solid and spaced sheathing may be used. When solid sheathing is to be used, a minimum of 1-5/32 inch (12mm) plywood sheathing is recommended. However, with some products in certain climates more conservative roof deck and framing spacings are important to consider. Manufacturers' instructions and roof deck recommendations should be consulted.

NRCA recommends a minimum roof deck slope of 4 inches per foot (33%). Some manufacturers will allow application on lower slopes, such as 3 inches per foot (25%), if special precautions and underlayment configurations are followed (refer to Item 2.5.4, Slope Limitations).

2.3.2.1 Underlayment and Interlayments

Underlayments and interlayments are often essential components for use with fiber cement roof systems. With some systems, underlayments or interlayments are critical. NRCA suggests underlayments (and/or interlayments where applicable) be used with all fiber cement roof systems, particularly where wind-driven rain and snow are anticipated.

2.3.2.2 Additional Underlayment Requirements and Ice Dam Protection Membranes

A. When a single layer of underlayment is required, the non-perforated felt should be applied horizontally. NRCA recommends that the asphalt-saturated felt meet or exceed the standards set forth by ASTM D 226 or

ASTM D 4869. In single layer applications, all felts should be lapped a minimum of 2 inches (51mm) over the preceding felt sheet. End laps should be a minimum of 4 inches (102mm). The underlayment should be fastened appropriately for the slope of the roof, as necessary to hold the felts in place until the installation of the primary roof covering materials.

B. When a double-layer underlayment is required, two layers of non-perforated felt should be applied horizontally. First, a 19-inch (483mm) wide starter sheet should be applied along the downslope roof edge (e.g., eave). A full-width sheet should then be applied, completely covering the starter sheet. Succeeding sheets should be lapped 19-inches (483mm) over the preceding sheets, leaving a 17-inch (432mm) exposure. End laps should be a minimum of 6 inches (152mm). It is suggested that the felts be nailed as necessary to hold the felts in place until the primary steep-slope roofing material is applied.

C. Regardless of the type of underlayment required, or the slope of the roof, in locations where the January mean temperature is 30° F (-1° C) or less, NRCA suggests installation of an ice dam protection membrane. An ice dam protection membrane may consist of:

- Two plies of No. 15 asphalt saturated organic felt, one nailed to the deck and the second set in hot, Type III (steep) or Type IV (special steep) asphalt or asphalt lap cement.

- A combination of heavyweight coated base sheet nailed to the deck, and another felt ply or ply sheet set in hot steep asphalt or asphalt lap cement.

- A self-adhering polymer-modified bitumen membrane, ASTM D 1970.

The ice dam protection membrane should be applied starting from the eaves and extending upslope a minimum of 24 inches (610 mm) from the inside of the exterior wall line of the building. Note: On slopes less than 4 inches per foot (250/4), NRCA recommends the ice dam protection membrane be extended a minimum of 36 inches (914 mm) upslope from the inside of the exterior wall line of the building.

Note: Ice dam protection membranes, by themselves, cannot be relied upon to keep leaks or moisture infiltration from occurring. Careful consideration of roof insulation, ventilation, and project specific detailing for the particular climatic conditions is vital. Also, self-adhering modified bitumen underlayment must not be left exposed for long periods of time. Self-adhering modified bitumen underlayments should be covered with the primary roofing material as soon as practical to prevent premature degradation of the modified bitumen material.

Fasteners

2.3.3.1 Nails, Screws, and Staples. Non-corroding copper, stainless steel, or galvanized fasteners are often required. Consult with the specific fiber cement product manufacturer for recommended fasteners.

2.3.3.1.2 Length. Fasteners should be long enough to penetrate through all layers of roofing materials and achieve secure anchorage into the roof deck. Fasteners should extend through the underside of plywood sheathing or other acceptable wood panel decks, and penetrate at least 3/4 inch (19 mm) into wood plank decks.

2.3.3.2 Wind Clips. Wind clips (sometimes referred to as storm anchors) may be used with some products to secure the butt or downslope edge of the individual roofing unit. Generally, wind clips are made of stainless steel or copper wire, sometimes fashioned with an elongated shaft and disc base. Wind clips are recommended where wind uplift pressures may exceed the product's uplift resistance when through-fastened in the typical manner, or where required by code.

2.3.5 Hips and Ridges

Hips and ridges may be covered with a premanufactured hip and ridge unit supplied by the manufacturer, or a metal saddle ridge covering; with some products, a site-fabricated ridge covering may be made from field material.

In some cases, hip and ridge units are used in conjunction with an overlayment material covering the hip or ridge. With some fiber cement products, a site-fabricated unit made from field material that is cut to the proper size may be recommended by the manufacturer. Consult the fiber cement product manufacturer's recommendations for hip and ridge coverings.

2.4 Valleys and Other Flashings

2.4.1 Description. Because steep-slope roofs are frequently interrupted by the intersection of adjoining roof sections, adjacent walls, or penetrations such as chimneys and plumbing soil-pipe stacks, all of which create opportunities for leakage, special provisions for weather protection must be made at these locations. The components used to control water entry at these locations are commonly called flashings. Careful attention to flashing details is essential to successful long-term roof performance, regardless of the type of roof construction. Consult the fiber cement product manufacturer for recommendations regarding valley construction and various flashing details, and consider upgrading detail designs as necessary for the particular project, giving special attention to local climatic expectations.

2.5 Precautions

NRCA is concerned about potential problems that may be associated with some fiber cement products as they are exposed to severe, repetitive freeze-thaw and/or wet-dry cycling. NRCA suggests close examination of the manufacturer's test

data before specifying a particular material, to ensure that the material will withstand the climatic conditions it will be expected to endure.

Ed. Note: For building code requirements on valleys with asbestos-cement shingles, see the end of the "Slate Shingles" section later in this chapter.

Wood Shingles & Shakes

Comments

Although wood shakes and wood shingles are available in pressure-treated wood, enabling them to meet UL 790 fire-rated standards for Class A roofs, many areas of the country have outlawed their use because of fire proliferation. Pressure treatment increases the cost of the product, and there is a possibility that, over time, some of the fire-retardant chemicals may leach out of the wood, reducing the effectiveness of the fire-resistant feature.

One other negative to the use of wood shingles on roofs is that skip sheathing (normally recommended to discourage fungal growth on wood shingles) makes a very poor shear diaphragm structurally.

Following are installation standards for those areas where wood shakes and wood shingles are still allowed.

The UBC addresses wood roof shingles and shakes in 1507 in a brief statement that references UBC Standard 15-3 and 15-4. Those standards address quality grades, inspection and labelling.

UBC — 1997

1508.5 Wood Shingles and Wood Shakes. The roof valley flashing shall not be provided of less than 0.016-inch (0.41 mm) (No. 28 galvanized sheet gage) corrosion-resistant metal, which shall extend at least 8 inches (203 mm) from the centerline each way for wood shingles and 11 inches (279 mm) from the centerline each way for wood shakes. Sections of flashing shall have an overlap of not less than 4 inches (102 mm). The metal valley flashing shall have a 36-inch-wide (914 mm) underlayment directly under it consisting of one layer of Type 15 felt running the full length of the valley, in addition to underlayment specified in Table 15-B-2. In severe climates, the metal valley flashing underlayment shall be solid cemented to the roofing underlayment for roof slopes under 7 units vertical in 12 units horizontal (58.3% slope).

Exception: Where local practice indicates satisfactory performance, the building official may permit valley flashing without underlayment.

Industry Standards
NRCA Roofing & Waterproofing Manual
(National Roofing Contractors Association)

2.1.1 Perimeter Flashing and Downslope Underlayment

Depending upon climate severity, anticipated amounts of rainfall and freeze-thaw cycling, the use of perimeter drip-edge flashing may be considered for use with wood shakes. However, a metal drip-edge flashing may not be necessary with many types of steep-slope roof coverings that are rigid, and are capable of being extended beyond the edge of the roof without deformation to achieve a positive drip-edge. When perimeter flashings are specified, NRCA recommends the use of metal flashing with a formed drip-edge to allow water to drip off the edge of the roof without affecting the underlying construction. Where climate dictates the need for the use of perimeter flashing with wood roofing, NRCA recommends that a minimum of 26-gauge galvanized prepainted metal, or a non-corrosive flashing material of an expected longevity comparable to that of the shake roof, be specified for use along perimeter roof edges.

2.1.2 Starter Course for Shakes

In order for the shake roof to be two or three (whichever is specified) layers thick at all locations, including the downslope portion of the roof, a starter course is necessary. Generally, if the length of the shakes and the exposure specified will provide for a two layer thick wood roof, then the starter course may contain only one layer. If the length of the shakes and the exposure specified will provide for a three-layer-thick wood roof, then the starter course should contain two layers. The starter course is applied directly over the underlayment or ice-dam protection membrane along the downslope portion of the roof. In addition to providing longevity to the finished roof, the primary purpose of the starter course is to shed water that may migrate through the gaps or joints between the shakes in the overlying first course.

The following procedures may be used to apply the starter course:

A. After the downslope underlayment or ice dam protection membrane has been installed, the starter course of wood roofing may be applied. Generally, the starter course may consist of 15- to 24-inch (380 to 610 mm) wood shakes or shingles as the exposure specified for the project allows.

B. The shakes in the starter course should be laid so that the butt ends extend a minimum of 1-1/2 inches (38 mm) beyond the finished fascia board or outer sheathing board edge (if there is no fascia). When gutters or eaves troughs are used, the overhang may be reduced to approximately 1 inch (25 mm). Shakes should be laid to extend approximately 1-1/2 inches (38 mm) beyond the rake edge.

C. Space the individual starter units approximately 1/4 to 1/2 inch (6 to 13 mm) apart, and fasten each unit with two fasteners. Place the nails approximately 3/4 to 1 inch (19 to 25 mm) from the sides.

D. If the starter course consists of two layers, offset the joints between neighboring shakes in the adjacent courses a minimum of 1-1/2 inches (38 mm).

2.1.3 First Course of Shakes

A. After the starter course has been installed along the downslope portion of the roof, the first course of shakes is applied. The first course is installed directly over the starter course. The joints between shakes in neighboring courses should be offset by a minimum of 1-1/2 inches (38 mm). In some roof layouts, shakes less than 4 inches (102 mm) wide should not be used.

B. The butt ends of the shakes in the first course should extend to approximately the same point as the butt ends of the starter course units, so that the downslope end of the first course is flush with the downslope end of the starter course.

C. Space the shakes in the first course approximately 1/4 to 1/2 inch (6 to 13mm) apart, and fasten each shake with two fasteners (the type and size specified). Note: Non-corroding staples are considered acceptable by NRCA for attachment of wood shakes, as the varied grain structure of the wood and the manner in which it affects staple shank deformation generally provide for good withdrawal resistance. Place the fasteners approximately 3/4 to 1 inch (19 to 25 mm) from the sides, and 1-1/2 to 2 inches (38 to 51 mm) above the butt line that will be created by the next overlying course.

2.1.4 Interlayment

A. After the first course of shakes has been applied, an 18-inch (457mm) strip of No. 30 asphalt-saturated (non-perforated "shake felt") roofing felt meeting ASTM D 226 or ASTM D 4869 should be installed as an interlayment. This felt interlayment helps to serve as a shield to protect from wind-driven rain and snow entry, and sheds water. A No. 30 asphalt saturated roofing felt is the minimum felt recommended for use as interlayment.

B. The felt interlayment is laid over the top portion of the shakes in the first course, and should extend up slope so that it rests on top of the sheathing. The bottom edge of the interlayment felt should be set at a distance that is equal to twice the exposure dimension specified for the shakes. For example, if 24-inch (610 mm) shakes are specified to be applied at a 10-inch (254 mm) exposure, that would require the felt interlayment be set 20 inches (508 mm) above the shake butts in the first course. This would provide for coverage of the top 4 inches (102 mm) of the shakes.

C. The top edge of the felt interlayment must rest on the sheathing. Stagger fasten the interlayment along the upper portion to hold it in place until the next course of shakes is installed. Interlayment fasteners should be covered by the next consecutive course of interlayment.

2.1.5 Second and Succeeding Courses of Shakes

A. After the first course of shakes and the first layer of felt interlayment have been applied, the second and succeeding courses of shakes and their interlayment are applied.

B. Set the second course of shakes at the specified exposure.

C. Space the individual shakes approximately 1/4 to 1/2 inch (6 to 13 mm) apart, and offset the shakes from the joints in the underlying course by a minimum of 1-1/2 inches (38 mm).

D. Fasten each shake with two fasteners. Place the fasteners approximately 3/4 to 1 inch (19 to 25 mm) from the sides, and approximately 1-1/2 to 2 inches (38 to 51 mm) above the butt line that will be created by the next overlapping course of shakes.

E. The fasteners should be driven flush to the surface of the shake.

F. After fastening each course of shakes in place, the felt interlayment is applied prior to setting the next succeeding course of shakes.

2.3 Wood Shakes for Hip and Ridge Locations

To weatherproof the roof at hips and ridges, wood shakes may be used as hip and ridge coverings. Mills assemble bundles of premade hip and ridge units, or contractors may make their own. However, both types of hip and ridge units must have alternate overlaps, and the units must be blind nailed during application. Typically, the exposure for hip and ridge units is the same as is specified for the field of the roof, although the exposure can be shortened to create hip and ridge lines for visual accent.

After both roof areas have been roofed with shakes up to the adjoining hip or ridge intersection, and the shakes in each intersecting course have been cut to the apex of the hip or ridge, then the hip or ridge coverings may be applied. The following procedures may be used to apply shakes at hip and ridge locations.

A. Felt plies of interlayment can be wrapped and nailed over the hip or ridge centerline. Wrapping the hips and ridges with the field felts provides an additional layer of protection from wind-driven rain and snow. Note: At ventilating ridges, felt is not wrapped over the ridge, as it would be closed off to ventilation.

B. For additional weather protection of the hip or ridge, a strip of asphalt-saturated felt may be fastened over the exposed juncture along the hip or ridge. This layer of felt should overlap the shakes on either side of the centerline by a minimum of 4 inches (102 mm). Note: At ventilating ridges, this extra strip of felt is not used.

C. Beginning at the downslope end of a hip or at the leeward end of a ridge, the shake hip or ridge units are applied in shingle fashion with each unit lapping over the previous unit. Note: Beginning the ridge shake application at the leeward end of the ridge orients each ridge shake's overlap away from the prevailing wind and weather. Applying ridge shakes with their laps facing away from the prevailing wind helps to keep wind-driven rain and snow from entering the roof and can help to minimize problems with wind blow-off.

D. Typically, hip and ridge shakes are made to provide a relatively uniform overlap of the hip or ridge centerline, covering the adjacent trimmed field shake by approximately 4 to 6 inches (102 to 152 mm). However, it is a good idea to chalk a straight line on one side of the hip or ridge, so that hip or ridge shakes can be set to the line for proper alignment.

E. Select and lay the hip or ridge units so the overlap along the top of each unit is alternated. One unit's overlap faces the roof area on one side of the hip or ridge; then the next sequential hip or ridge unit that is laid must face the opposite roof area.

F. Fasten each hip or ridge covering unit with two fasteners. Because hip and ridge fasteners must penetrate through more layers of roofing in order to securely attach the hip and ridge coverings to the underlying roof deck, the fasteners for hip and ridge units are recommended to be longer than those fasteners specified for the shakes covering the field of the roof. Place the fasteners approximately 3/4 to 1 inch (19 to 25 mm) up from the sides, and approximately 1-1/2 to 2 inches above the butt line that will be created by the next overlapping hip or ridge unit. The fasteners should be driven flush to the surface of the wood.

G. When reaching the upslope end of the hip or windward end of the ridge, the last unit is placed and fastened. These fasteners in the last hip or ridge unit will be exposed to the weather.

H. Sometimes hip and ridge boards are specified, in lieu of shakes, to cover hips or ridges, to enhance the aesthetic appeal of the wood roofing. Occasionally, the ridge boards are clad with sheet metal ridge covers.

Industry Standards

Roofing: Design Criteria, Options, Selections
(R.S. Means Co., Inc.)

A minimum of 4" in 12" slope is required to properly drain a wood roof. Two nails per shingle are required, as are baffles. Nails should always be galvanized or copper, placed one inch from each side and just high enough to be covered by the next course of shakes (see **Figure 8.17**). Nails should be driven flush to the surface and not into the fiber of the wood. The nails should penetrate the wood substrate by at least 1/2".

Sequence: The roof should be pre-loaded with bundles of wood shakes or shingles the day before application is to begin. Thirty-pound felt should then be applied to the entire deck. The installation should begin at the eave with an overlay of 1-1/2". Caulk lines should always be struck to ensure uniformity and alignment. The 18" strips of 30 pound felt (the baffles) should be placed to overlap the shakes by four inches. Cut shakes or shingles should be saved to use along the valleys. Proper planning should provide orderly coursing. Pre-manufactured hip and ridge units can be obtained from the supplier to ensure uniformity. It is recommended that a 3/8" to 1/2" space be left between shakes to prevent buckling. Side lap should be 1-1/2" for each succeeding course, as shown in **Figure 8.17**.

Wood Shake Application

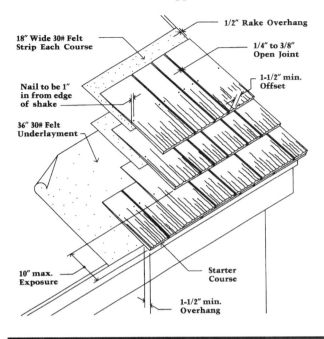

R.S. Means Co., Inc., *Roofing: Design Criteria, Options, Selection*

Figure 8.17

Wood Shingle & Shake Wall or Chimney Flashing

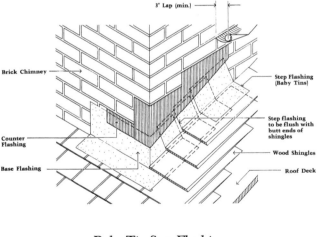

Baby Tin Step Flashing

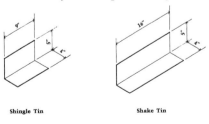

R.S. Means Co., Inc., *Roofing: Design Criteria, Options, Selection*

Figure 8.18

Slate Shingles

Industry Standards

Roofing: Design Criteria, Options, Selection
(R.S. Means Co., Inc.)

The most common thickness used for roofing slate is 3/16". **Figure 8.19** shows the available sizes of standard slate, the minimum number of slates required per square, the exposures, and the quantity (by weight) of nails required per square of roof surface. Copper nails are the only suitable nails for use with slate. Nail length may be determined by adding one inch to twice the thickness of the slate. Nails should be large head, diamond-pointed, #10 gauge shank.

Some basic guidelines for slate roof installation are as follows. (See **Figure 8.20** for an illustration of a slate roof system.)

- No through joints should occur from the roof surface to the felt.

- The overlapping slate should be joined as near the center of the underlying slate as possible, and not less than three inches from any underlying joint. A standard three-inch *headlap* should be used. (Headlap is that portion of the slate which overlaps the lowest slate course beneath it.) The exposure (weathering surface) should be determined by subtracting three inches from the length of the slate and dividing by two.

Ridge Construction: Several methods may be used to construct the ridge on a slate roof, but the most common, shown in **Figure 8.20**, is called the *saddle ridge*. Using this method, the slates are brought together at the ridge so that the opposing slates will butt flush (see **Figure 8.20**). Wood lath is then nailed to the ridge so that the top row of slate will be properly aligned. To ensure that no moisture can be driven

Schedule for Standard Slate

Size of Slate (In.)	Slates Per Square	Exposure with 3" Lap	Nails Per Square		Size of Slate (In.)	Slates Per Square	Exposure with 3" Lap	Nails Per Square	
			(lbs.)	(ozs.)				(lbs.)	(ozs.)
26x14	89	11^1/$_2$″	1	0	16x14	160	6^1/$_2$″	1	13
					16x12	184	6^1/$_2$″	2	2
24x16	86	10^1/$_2$″	1	0	16x11	201	6^1/$_2$″	2	5
24x14	98	10^1/$_2$″	1	2	16x10	222	6^1/$_2$″	2	8
24x13	106	10^1/$_2$″	1	3	16x9	246	6^1/$_2$″	2	13
24x11	125	10^1/$_2$″	1	7	16x8	277	6^1/$_2$″	3	2
24x12	114	10^1/$_2$″	1	5					
					14x12	218	5^1/$_2$″	2	8
22x14	108	9^1/$_2$″	1	4	14x11	238	5^1/$_2$″	2	11
22x13	117	9^1/$_2$″	1	5	14x10	261	5^1/$_2$″	3	3
22x12	126	9^1/$_2$″	1	7	14x9	291	5^1/$_2$″	3	5
22x11	138	9^1/$_2$″	1	9	14x8	327	5^1/$_2$″	3	12
22x10	152	9^1/$_2$″	1	12	14x7	374	5^1/$_2$″	4	4
20x14	121	8^1/$_2$″	1	6	12x10	320	4^1/$_2$″	3	10
20x13	132	8^1/$_2$″	1	8	12x9	355	4^1/$_2$″	4	1
20x12	141	8^1/$_2$″	1	10	12x8	400	4^1/$_2$″	4	9
20x11	154	8^1/$_2$″	1	12	12x7	457	4^1/$_2$″	5	3
20x10	170	8^1/$_2$″	1	15	12x6	533	4^1/$_2$″	6	1
20x9	189	8^1/$_2$″	2	3					
					11x8	450	4″	5	2
18x14	137	7^1/$_2$″	1	9	11x7	515	4″	5	14
18x13	148	7^1/$_2$″	1	11					
18x12	160	7^1/$_2$″	1	13	10x8	515	3^1/$_2$″	5	14
18x11	175	7^1/$_2$″	2	0	10x7	588	3^1/$_2$″	7	4
18x10	192	7^1/$_2$″	2	3	10x6	686	3^1/$_2$″	7	13
18x9	213	7^1/$_2$″	2	7					

R.S. Means Co., Inc., *Roofing: Design Criteria, Options, Selection*

Figure 8.19

into the ridge, a strip of 60 mil. EPDM roof membrane is then placed over and along the ridge. The final *combing slate* is then placed over the top row of slate, with a three-inch overlap. The ridge course should be run with the "grain" horizontal. The ridge slates are secured to the deck with two nails, which are then covered with plastic cement. All nails, except the last one on each side of the ridge, are concealed with a cover of cement.

Hip Construction: There are also several methods that can be used to form the hips. Again, the most common is the *saddle hip*, shown in **Figure 8.21**. Here, as in the ridge, a wooden lath strip should be run along both sides of the hip. The ridge slate (of the same size as the exposure in the roof slates) should be attached with four nails per slate, with a strip of EPDM membrane underneath, as shown, to prevent moisture infiltration. All nail heads should be covered with plastic cement.

Valleys: Most valleys in slate roofs are "open," as shown in **Figure 8.22.** However, slate may also have closed valleys (see **Figure 8.22**). The valley is first lined with sheet metal (preferably 16 oz. cold-rolled copper sheet) so that water will be channeled between the slate on both sides. The width of this channel should uniformly increase, at the rate of one inch per eight feet, down the valley toward the eave in order to carry the additional volume of water.

Saddle Hip

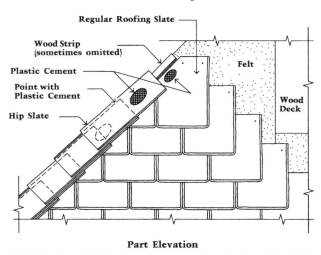

Part Elevation

R.S. Means Co., Inc., *Roofing: Design Criteria, Options, Selection*

Figure 8.21

Slate Roof System (Saddle Ridge)

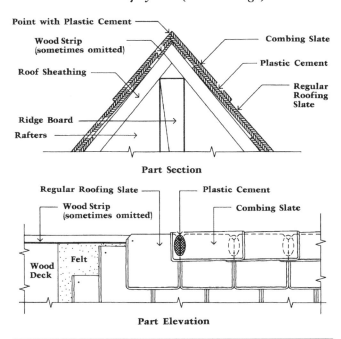

Part Section

Part Elevation

R.S. Means Co., Inc., *Roofing: Design Criteria, Options, Selection*

Figure 8.20

Open Valley

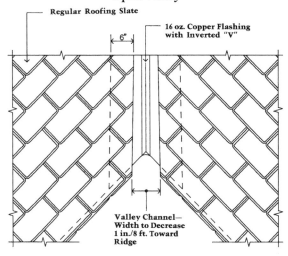

Closed Valley

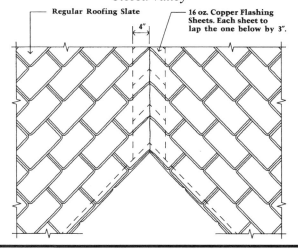

R.S. Means Co., Inc., *Roofing: Design Criteria, Options, Selection*

Figure 8.22

The slate application should begin two inches from the inverted "V" at the top and should taper away at the rate of one-half inch for every eight feet down to the eave. The function of the inverted "V" in the valley is to "break up" the flow from each side and thereby prevent water from being driven up under the slate on the opposite side. The valley flashing should extend at least six inches under the slate and should be crimped back to intercept any moisture. The metal valley should be secured with cleats at eight inches on center, along both sides of the valley.

UBC — 1997

1508.4 Asbestos-Cement Shingles, Slate Shingles, and Clay and Concrete Tile. The roof valley flashing shall not be provided of less than 0.016-inch (0.41 mm) (No. 28 galvanized sheet gage) corrosion-resistant metal, which shall extend at least 11 inches (279 mm) from the centerline each way and shall have a splash diverter rib not less than 1 inch (25 mm) high at the flow line formed as part of the flashing. Sections of flashing shall have an end lap of not less than 4 inches (102 mm). For roof slopes of 3 units vertical in 12 units horizontal (25% slope) and over, the metal valley flashing shall have a 36-inch-wide (914 mm) underlayment directly under it consisting of one layer of Type 15 felt running the full length of the valley, in addition to the underlayment specified in Tables 15-D-1 and 15-D-2. In severe climates, the metal valley flashing underlayment shall be solid cemented to the roofing underlayment for slopes under 7 units vertical in 12 units horizontal (58.3% slope).

Tile Roofing: Definitions & Considerations

Industry Standards

NRCA Roofing & Waterproofing Manual
(National Roofing Contractors Association)

1.3.1 Plain

Plain tiles are also referred to as flat slab or shingle tiles, as they are non-interlocking pieces. Plain tile is meant to be laid in a double thickness similar to asphalt shingles, and some wood shakes and slate.

With plain tile applications, an actual headlap is achieved, and the customary headlap dimensions are 2 or 3 inches (51 or 76 mm). Generally, plain tile thicknesses range from 1/4 inch to 3/4 inch (6 mm to 19 mm). Butts are usually square, but there are some with rounded and other cut-butt patterns. Some plain tiles have a roughened end that has a handmade appearance. A wide variety of surface treatments are applied during manufacture, including smooth, scored, grooved, sanded, ash coated, or others that create textures to achieve traditional appearances. In different parts of the world, plain tiles are also referred to as flat tiles, slab tiles, or shingle tiles.

1.3.2 Pan and Cover

Pan and cover tiles (also referred to as barrel tile or mission tile in some regions) are typically made in rounded pieces, half-circular pieces, or pairs. Pan and cover tiles are installed with one laid concave, the other laid convex. In some traditional styles, the pan is flatter, with side ribs or lips. Typically, depending on how the tile is specified to be installed, there is only one layer of tile throughout the field of the roof. Pan and cover tiles can be either straight or tapered. They are available with surface textures ranging from smooth and uniform to scored and rough surfaces.

Pans and covers are laid in a variety of ways. Pans can be laid tight to one another at the sides, or spaced apart (providing a minimum side lap by the covers). Straight barrel pans are sometimes used with tapered covers for added laying flexibility and aesthetics. Some covers have clipped-top corners that fit against clipped-bottom corners of the pans, which provides for a tight and relatively precise fit. Some pan and cover styles incorporate an interlocking feature to help keep out wind-driven rain and snow. Common styles are called Mission, Barrel, Straight Barrel Mission, and Tapered Barrel Mission.

1.3.3 Interlocking

Interlocking tile is laid in a single thickness with only a course-to-course overlap. The sides are channeled or ribbed so that neighboring tiles are lapped in an interlocking arrangement. The heads and butts may also interlock. Where there is no head-to-butt interlock, a simple overlap is used. With some styles the exposed surfaces are flat, and either smooth or textured. Many interlocking tiles are profiled, and the contours help direct runoff away from the interlocking side of the tile. Some contoured tiles are available that have the appearance of pan and cover tiles. Some molded-in contours add strength to the tile. Reinforcing ribs on the underside are used to add strength and reduce weight. The thickness at the butt, and, sometimes, the overall height of the flat styles range from 1/2 inch (13 mm) to 2 inches (51 mm).

1.3.4 S-Tile

S-tile refers to the profile of the tile. Sometimes S-tile is also referred to as one-piece pan and cover. S-tiles are laid in a single thickness with a course-to-course overlap. Thickness varies, but typical tile thickness is approximately 1/2 inch (13mm). Surfaces are available in smooth or a variety of textures. In some styles, the convex portion is slightly larger than the concave part. The concave portions may be rounded or flattened in contour. Common styles are referred to as S-tile.

Comments

Weight of roofing is an important part of the design and construction of any structure. An S-Tile roof can have a weight of 950 lbs per square (100 sq. ft.). A pan and cover can have 1100 lbs per square, while an asphalt roof is 250 lbs per square. A square of roofing equals 100 square feet. Review the NRCA Roofing & Waterproofing Manual and the Roofing Handbook for further detail and comparison of options.

Tile Roofing: Installation Procedures

Industry Standards

Roofing: Design Criteria, Options, Selection
(R.S. Means Co., Inc.)

Decks: If plywood deck is used, the sheets should be separated by at least 1/16". It should be exterior grade plywood of a thickness adequate to satisfy nailing requirements. If wood planking is used, it should be a minimum of 1 x 6 nominal lumber, spanning no more than 24 inches between rafters.

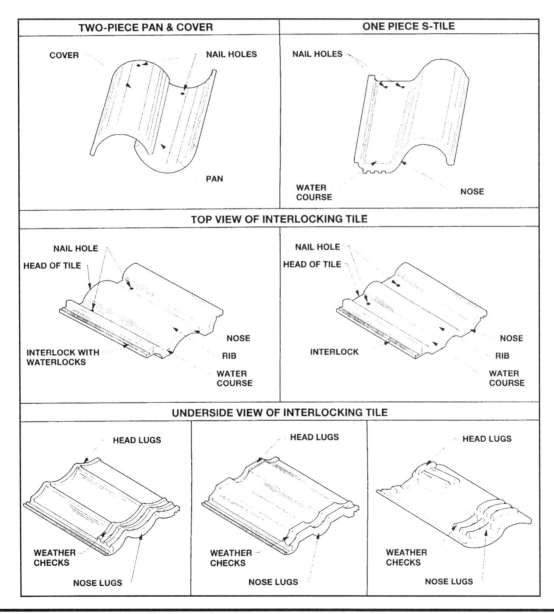

Courtesy of National Roofing Contractors Association, NRCA *Roofing & Waterproofing Manual*

Figure 8.23

When the underlayment has been installed, vertical laths should then be nailed directly above all rafters, through the felt. Horizontal battens (stringers) are nailed across the lath, and spaced according to tile dimensions.

Stringers (Nailing strips): Hip and ridge stringers (see **Figure 8.24**) vary in height depending on the type of tile and the roof slope. It is best to lay out a few tiles at the ridge and determine the proper height for the ridge stringer.

Clay Tile Application

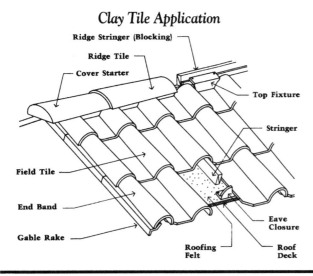

R.S. Means Co., Inc., *Roofing: Design Criteria, Options, Selection*

Figure 8.24

Required Slopes for Tile Roof

The slope of a tile roof should be no less than four-in-twelve. For low-sloped roofs (three inches to the foot), all configurations of clay tile may be installed *if* two layers of #43 base sheet are used; the first ply nailed and the second mopped in steep asphalt. Flat shingle tile without an interlocking feature should not be installed on roof decks having a slope of less than 5" per foot. A minimum of one layer of #30 roofing felt should be applied as an underlayment. Since the underlayment is the waterproofing course, it is best to use a #43 base sheet for this purpose. While a high density clay tile roof will last several hundred years, most underlayment will not.

Ice Shields

For installations where the January mean temperature is below 30 degrees Fahrenheit, an ice shield consisting of #43 felt mopped in steep asphalt should be installed. The ice shield should extend from the eave to the inside of the wall line.

Valleys

Special attention must be paid to the manner in which open valleys are installed in tile roofs. The requirements include an extra ply of dry-in felt installed before the metal valleys are fitted. The metal valleys should be "V" crimped in the middle

in order to lessen the force of the water running down the slope and prevent it from driving up under the tiles on the opposite side.

At the valleys, tiles must be cut along a line to form an even edge, using a power saw and carborundum blade. Metal valleys and flashing should always be fabricated out of copper, stainless steel, or other noncorrosive metal.

Industry Standards
NRCA Roofing and Waterproofing Manual
(National Roofing Contractors Association)

With tile roofs, there are two basic types of valleys:

2.9.3.1 Open Valleys

Open valleys are lined with sheet metal valley material. Note: The tiles are held back from the center of the valley so the valley flashing is exposed or open. Open valleys permit clear, unobstructed drainage, and are advantageous in locations where fallout from surrounding foliage (e.g., leaves, needles, and debris) settles on the roof and tends to accumulate in the valley. Open valleys constructed with durable heavy-gauge metal can be very long lasting.

Tiles from the adjoining roof areas are mitered to form a closed valley.

Generally, closed or mitered tile valleys are lined with sheet metal material. However, when metal flashing is used to line a closed tile valley, the metal is typically not exposed and lies under the courses of tile. With mitered tile valleys, the tiles are brought together over the metal liner at the valley centerline and mitered along the length of the valley to form a closed valley.

Note: With tile roofing, closed valleys are considered decorative because water can migrate through the layers of tile and it is the underlying metal valley that carries the runoff. Closed valleys are not recommended where surrounding foliage exists because fallout (e.g., leaves, needles, or debris) onto the roof can impede rapid runoff.

The two types of valleys described above are constructed only after the necessary layer(s) of underlayment, and any valley lining membrane material specified, have been applied to the roof deck.

Typically valley underlayment construction consists of a full width 36-inch sheet of No. 40 minimum asphalt-saturated felt, or an ice dam protection membrane. This valley underlayment is centered in the valley. Typically, valley underlayment sheets are secured with only enough roofing nails to hold them in place until the balance of valley materials are applied. The courses of underlayment from the fields of the two adjoining roof areas are extended so that each course overlaps the valley underlayment by at least 12 inches (305 mm). The valley is then lined with the balance of the valley flashing and tile roofing.

2.9.3.1.1 Open Valleys Using Valley Metal

Open valleys are usually constructed with sheet metal valley material. The metal valley is constructed by laying lengths (typically 8 or 10 feet) of 24-gauge pre-painted galvanized steel or an equivalent non-corrosive metal through the valley. The tile (and with some area practices, the underlayment) is lapped onto the flange on either side of the valley metal, leaving a clear space between the roofing material to channel runoff water down the valley. The width of the valley, or the amount of space between the intersecting tile should increase uniformly, so the valley widens as it continues downslope. The difference in the width of the upper end of the valley and the lower end of the valley is referred to as the valley taper. In most climates, the amount of this valley taper is recommended to be 1/8 inch (3 mm) for every lineal foot (305 mm) of valley length. For example, in a valley 16 feet (5 m) long, the distance between tiles should be approximately 2 inches (51 mm) greater at the bottom of the valley than at the top.
Note: Tapering valleys with tile roofing is not a common practice in all areas of the United States.

Tapering the valley has the following advantages:

- Allows tile to be laid closer to the valley at the upper end.

- Allows for increase in volume of runoff water to be received at the downslope end.

- Allows any ice that may form within the valley to free itself when melting, and slide down and exit the valley rather than lodging somewhere along the length of the valley.

2.9.3.2 Closed Valleys

Closed valley methods are preferred by some roofing professionals, but closed valley use with tile is generally limited to roofs where the valley slope is at least 8 inches per foot (67%). However, in areas of the country where heavy accumulations of foliage fallout are anticipated, or if moss can be expected to grow between the tile roofing joints, a closed valley can hamper runoff. Therefore, specifying a closed valley should be carefully considered to be sure it is beneficial for the particular project.

Comments

Closed valleys should have a minimum gap of 2" at the bottom and 1/2" at the top to allow debris to self-clean during heavy rains.

UBC — 1997

1508.4 Asbestos-Cement Shingles, Slate Shingles, and Clay and Concrete Tile. The roof valley flashing shall not be provided of less than 0.016-inch (0.41 mm) (No. 28 galvanized sheet gage) corrosion-resistant metal, which shall extend at least 11 inches (279 mm) from the centerline each way and shall have a splash diverter rib not less than 1 inch (25 mm) high at the flow line formed as part of the flashing. Sections of flashing shall have an end lap of not less than 4 inches (102 mm). For roof slopes of 3 units vertical in

Roof to Masonry Wall with Gutter Flashing

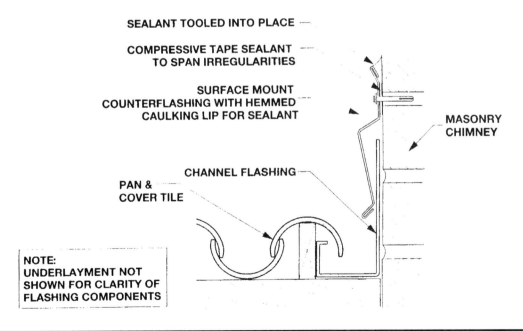

Courtesy of National Roofing Contractors Association, *NRCA Roofing & Waterproof Manual*

Figure 8.25

12 units horizontal (25% slope) and over, the metal valley flashing shall have a 36-inch-wide (914 mm) underlayment directly under it consisting of one layer of Type 15 felt running the full length of the valley, in addition to the underlayment specified in Tables 15-D-1 and 15-D-2. In severe climates, the metal valley flashing underlayment shall be solid cemented to the roofing underlayment for slopes under 7 units vertical in 12 units horizontal (58.3% slope).

Section 1509 — Other Flashing

At the juncture of the roof and vertical surfaces, flashing and counterflashing shall be provided per the roofing manufacturer's instructions and, when of metal, shall not be less than 0.019-inch (No. 26 galvanized sheet gage) corrosion-resistant metal.

UBC Table 15-D-2

Underlayment. (In climate areas subject to wind-driven snow, roof ice or special wind regions, as shown in UBC, Chapter 16, Figure 16-1.)

Ed. Note: UBC Figure 16.1 shows minimum basic wind speeds.

Solid sheathing one layer of Type 30 felt lapped 2 inches (51 mm) horizontally and 6 inches (152 mm) vertically, except that extending from the eaves up the roof to line 24 inches (610 mm) inside the exterior wall line of the building, two layers of the underlayment shall be applied shingle fashion and solid cemented together with approved cementing material.

Other Climates. For spaced sheathing, approved reinforced membrane. For solid sheathing, one layer heavy-duty felt or Type 30 felt lapped 2 inches (51 mm) horizontally and 6 inches (152 mm) vertically.

Ed. Note: See "Roof Penetrations & Flashing" later in this chapter for more on flashing.

Tile Roofing: Water Migration

Industry Standards
NRCA Roofing & Waterproofing Manual
(National Roofing Contractors Association)
1.4.1 Water Migration Potential

In steep roofing, water migration refers to the movement of water beyond the primary roof covering material. For example, water may migrate between the side-lap joints of tile and enter the roof system — this is one reason that underlayment materials can be so vital to the success of many types of tile roofs. Wind-driven rain and snow may migrate into some types of tile roofs. Also, the physical phenomenon of capillary action and surface tension, combined with wind, is a factor in the water migration characteristics of some types of tile.

Roof to Wall Flashing

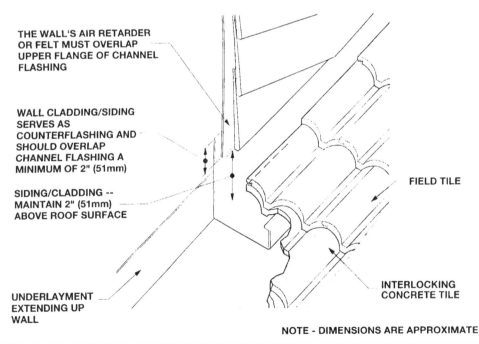

THE WALL'S AIR RETARDER OR FELT MUST OVERLAP UPPER FLANGE OF CHANNEL FLASHING

WALL CLADDING/SIDING SERVES AS COUNTERFLASHING AND SHOULD OVERLAP CHANNEL FLASHING A MINIMUM OF 2" (51mm)

SIDING/CLADDING -- MAINTAIN 2" (51mm) ABOVE ROOF SURFACE

UNDERLAYMENT EXTENDING UP WALL

FIELD TILE

INTERLOCKING CONCRETE TILE

NOTE - DIMENSIONS ARE APPROXIMATE

Courtesy of National Roofing Contractors Association, NRCA *Roofing & Waterproof Manual*

Figure 8.26

Different types of tile have different water migration potentials depending upon the tile's interlock (and waterlock) features, the headlap (if any) and the course-to-course overlap, the surface texture and finish, and the joint tolerances.

1.4.1.1 Water Migration Potential of Plain Tile

Plain tile functions as most other multiple layered watershedding roof coverings, in that there is an actual headlap. Wind, ice damming, and capillary action may cause water to migrate beyond the exposed portion of the overlying tile at the butt and the vertical or side joints. However, with plain tile, the width of the underlying tile, the location of its fastener holes, the slope of the roof, and the anti-capillary characteristics of the tile-to-tile surfaces, especially the headlap, all function to keep the roof weathertight. However, in extreme climates during harsh conditions (e.g., during hard wind-driven rains), water may migrate beyond the joints of plain tile. For the above reasons, underlayments are necessary with plain tile.

1.4.1.2 Water Migration Potential of Interlocking Tile

Interlocking types of tile function as a single layer, watershedding, primary roof covering, as there is just a course-to-course overlap, with individual interlocking tile shedding water downslope from one course to the next. Wind and capillary action can cause water to migrate beyond the exposed part of the tile at the edges. A wide variety of interlocking and waterlock configurations are used to limit water migration. Typical waterlocks include ribs and channels, although some have lips, angled diverters, and weeps to provide additional protection against water migration into the tile roof system. Different types of waterlock configurations function with different degrees of effectiveness. The width of the tile and the location of fastener holes, the slope of the roof, and the anti-capillary characteristics of the tile-to-tile surfaces are all important factors.

Therefore, on projects using interlocking tile, underlayments are necessary.

1.4.1.3 Water Migration Potential of Pan and Cover; and S-Tile

Two-piece pan and cover tile is applied so that the sides of the covers overlap the sides of the pan tile. The convex-shaped portions, or covers, shed water into the pans. The concave-shaped portion, or pans, channel the water downslope. The amount of overlap and the resistance to water migration vary with different styles, and with methods of laying pan and cover tile. Overlaps of both the pans and covers are typically 3 inches (76 mm). The dimensions of the laps, the location of fastener holes, and the slope of the roof are factors that affect the amount of water that may migrate beyond the tile edges. Therefore, on projects using pan and cover tile, underlayments are necessary.

One-piece S-tile functions as a single layer interlocking tile system where only a course-to-course overlap is achieved. With S-tile, both the sides and the head and butt overlap. The height of the pan side and point of overlap by the cover, play a large role in limiting the water that may migrate beyond the tiles edges. Overlaps are typically 3 inches (76 mm). With some styles, an interlock feature is added at the overlaps to restrict wind driven rain and capillary action. The dimensions of the lap, the type of interlock and waterlock configurations, the location of fastener holes, the slope of the roof, and surface conditions are all factors that affect the amount of water that may migrate beyond the tile. Therefore, on projects using S-tile, underlayments are necessary.

1.4.2 Wind and Seismic Considerations

Wind and seismic performance characteristics of tile roofs are being scrutinized more than in years past. The relatively regular occurrence of high wind events and seismic (earthquake) activities have caused designers to consider securing tile more conservatively than in the past. Different parts of the roof, such as the field, rakes, ridges, and downslope perimeters are subject to different wind-uplift pressures, and possibly different seismic loading forces.

Other factors affecting tile performance in wind and some seismic events include building height, eave overhang, tile size and weight, tile style and shape, the roof slope, and the securement method.

1.4.2.1 Information on Wind

The Standard Building Code provides information on evaluation of the wind loading and resistance of loose laid and mechanically attached tile.

1.4.2.2 Seismic Information

In areas prone to moderate or strong seismic activity (e.g., Uniform Building Code seismic zones 3 and 4), it is recommended that designers consider seismic effects on tile roof coverings.

1.4.3.1 Water Absorption

The porosity of roof tile is an indication of its ability to endure freeze-thaw cycling. The lower the porosity the less water the material may hold, thus the less likely the tile is to be damaged (by crack, spall, etc.) when frozen. Porosity of some materials may indicate the possibility of increased decomposition of water soluble particles in the tile. Porosity is typically expressed as a percent of the weight of water that is absorbed by the tile. Dense well-baked clay tile may have porosity values under 2% when fully vitrified. The porosity values of some clay tiles range up to 10%. Concrete tiles have porosity values in the range of 3 – 20%. Sealers are sometimes used to reduce porosity. The service life of the sealers and some surfacings should be considered during the roof design phase, as should the possible need to reseal the tile's surface in the future.

Strength of the tile along the joints, where it is joined or lapped, is important because this is a likely location for cracking or breaking under loading.

Strength is typically measured as a breaking load. Generally, the breaking loads of roof tile range from 250 to 1,000 pounds (44 to 175 kN/m). Typical breaking loads are approximately 650 pounds (114 kN/m) for clay tile and approximately 400 pounds (70 kN/m) for concrete tile.

1.6.4 Types of Fasteners, and Fastening and Attachment Devices

Many different types and combinations of securement methods are used for the various types of roof tile. Early methods included setting the tile in a bed of mud or mortar; or loose-laying the tile, using gravity and friction to keep tile in place on lower slopes. Tapered tiles were used to help prevent slippage. Head lugs were used where open sheathing or battens were common, and at a time when metal fasteners were handmade and nearly as expensive as the tile. Wire-tie methods were used by the Romans for their tile roofs installed over concrete roof decks.

Recent developments in fastener and attachment technology have impacted the once simple methods of tile securement. The types of fasteners and various attachment methods must now be examined, along with the type of tile and roof deck, when securement is being considered during roof design.

1.6.4.1 Nails

Nailing is the most common method of fastening tile. The trend is toward more stringent nailing schedules along perimeters, especially in high wind and seismic areas. Designers should consult local code requirements. There are

a wide variety of non-corrosive metal nail types, with differing mechanical and physical properties, depending upon the metal, nail shape, size, shank type, head type, and point type.

1.6.4.2 Screws

Screws are also used to fasten tile. There are a wide variety of non-corrosive metal screws, with differing mechanical and physical properties, depending upon the metal, screw shape, size, shank style, tread type, head type, and point type.

1.6.4.3 Wire

Hanging tile with wire is often used as a method of attachment on non-nailable or insulated decks, or in some areas where fastening through metal flashing needs to be avoided. Attaching entire tile roofs with wire is relatively common with concrete roof decks and other types of non-nailable substrates. For non-nailable roof decks, there is quite a variety of wire and strapping systems available. Wire-tying tile is also specified where penetrating the underlayment is undesirable, such as on low-slope applications. In strong earthquake zones, wire-tying tile (in some configurations) can allow for more movement of the tile than some rigid attachment methods, and can be an effective securement method. Nails, screws, and expanding fasteners are commonly used in conjunction with wire-tie systems to affix the wire to certain substrates.

1.6.4.4 Clips

Nose or butt clips and side clips are sometimes used in conjunction with other attachment methods in high wind and seismic areas. Some tile clips are commonly referred to as wind clips or storm anchors. Clips can hold the tile in place and help reduce stress at the primary attachment point. Some types of clips may also hold the tile in place if the tile's primary nailing fails.

Rake Nailer

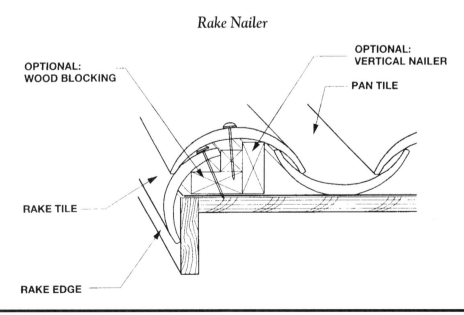

Courtesy of National Roofing Contractors Association, *NRCA Roofing & Waterproof Manual*

Figure 8.27

1.6.4.5 Lug-Hung Tile

When battens are used, many types of tile have lugs formed on the underside, near the head of the tile, on which the tile may be hung over the batten. In some areas, on roofs with shallow slopes, when tiles are loose laid they are simply hung over the battens. However, in most areas of the country, lug hanging of tile is usually used in combination with other securement methods, and some building codes require attachment of perimeter tile.

1.6.4.6 Bedding Tile

Laying tile in a full or partial bed of mortar is common in some areas of the United States (e.g., parts of the South) where freeze/thaw conditions are not encountered. Vertical-grade asphalt-based roof cements or cement mortars are commonly used to bed tile at hips and ridges. Tile laid along eaves, rakes and valleys, and some other flashing locations are sometimes bed in mortar. A variety of other roof cements, such as vertical-grade polymer-modified asphalt roof cement and slater's cement, are also used for bedding tile. Bedding is often used in combination with other securement methods.

2.7 Rakes

To weatherproof a tile roof along the rake edges, different details may be used depending upon the type and profile of the tile, the climate, and regional or area practices. Many of the clay tile rake details use specialty rake tile to complete the exterior edges of the roof. With plain tile, there is usually no rake tile or perimeter metal flashing used. A plain tile roof's rake edge may be detailed similar to the rake edge of a slate roof, where the perimeter tiles are simply extended beyond the rake edge to provide a watershedding drip edge for runoff, and to help provide some weather protection for the underlying building components.

2.7.1 Rake Tile Attachment

Note: Where tiles are specified to be used along rake edges, the rake tiles should be fastened with two fasteners for prudent securement. However some types of tile are manufactured with only one fastener hole — which means that only one fastener can be used to attach the tile along the rake edge of the roof.

2.8 Clay Tiles for Hip and Ridge Locations

To weatherproof the roof at hips and ridges, special hip and ridge tiles are used as hip and ridge coverings. Often, with pan and cover tiles, the covers are used for hip and ridge coverings. Typically, the exposure for hip and ridge tiles is the same as the field of the roof, although with some types of tile the exposure can be shortened to create different hip and ridge lines for visual accent and increased weather resistance.

After the field tile has been applied to both roof areas up to the adjoining hip or ridge intersection, and the tiles in each intersecting course have been cut to the apex of the hip or ridge, the hip or ridge coverings may be applied. The following procedures may be used to apply tiles at hip and ridge locations.

Ridge & Hip

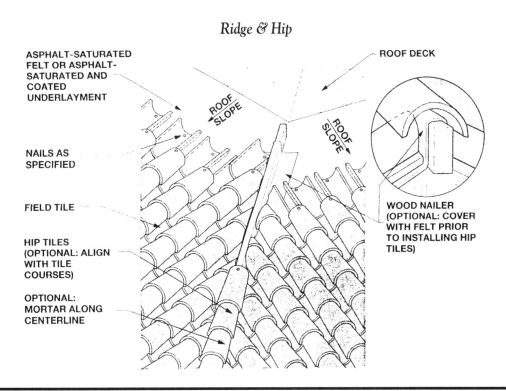

Courtesy of National Roofing Contractors Association, NRCA *Roofing & Waterproof Manual*

Figure **8.28**

A. The plies of underlayment can be wrapped and nailed over the hip or ridge centerline. Wrapping the hips and ridges with the field underlayment provides an additional layer of protection from wind-driven rain and snow. Note: At ventilating ridges, felt should not be wrapped over the ridge as it would close off ventilation.

B. For additional weather protection with some types of tile roofs, the hip or ridge may be overlaid with a strip of heavyweight asphalt-saturated felt, or modified bitumen membrane material, secured over the exposed juncture along the hip or ridge. Note: At ventilating ridges, this extra strip of felt is not used.

C. Beginning at tile downslope end of a hip or at the leeward end of a ridge, the hip or ridge tiles are applied in shingle fashion with each unit lapping over the previous unit. Note: Beginning the ridge tile application at the leeward end of the ridge orients each ridge tile overlap away from the prevailing wind and weather. Applying ridge tile with their laps facing away from the prevailing wind helps to keep wind-driven rain and snow from entering the roof.

D. Typically, hip and ridge tiles are installed to provide a relatively uniform overlap of the hip or ridge center line, covering the adjacent cut field tile by approximately 3 to 6 inches (76 to 152mm), depending upon the type of tile. However, it is a good idea to chalk a straight line on one side of the hip or ridge, so that hip or ridge tiles can be set to the line.

Metal Roofs

Industry Standards

Roofing: Design Criteria, Options, Selection
(R.S. Means Co., Inc.)

Custom-fabricated

Custom metal roofs are the most visually appealing and versatile types of systems for use on custom designs or in achieving intricate details, such as barrel roofs and convex mansards. Commonly used materials are standing seam and batten seam terneplate, copper, or galvanized steel.

Terneplate: A terneplate roof should not be installed over structures with a slope of less than three inches to the foot. The deck should be stable and of a material capable of receiving and holding nails. Plywood is the preferred deck material and should be a minimum of 5/8" thick. Tongue-and-groove wood sheathing decks are also commonly used. The deck should be covered with a #30 asphalt felt. The felt should be covered with a red resin paper slip sheet to avoid bonding of the felt to the metal.

Pre-formed

Between the relatively inexpensive pre-engineered metal building systems and the custom-designed, site-formed metal system is the largest sector of the metal roofing market — pre-formed, pre-painted metal roofing.

There are two predominant methods of joining pre-formed metal roof panels: *snap-on seam clips*, and *automated seaming* using electric field-seaming machines. The seaming operation locks concealed, sliding clip fasteners into place, forms the seam. Joint sealant can be applied as a part of the operation.

Formed Metal Roofing

Formed metal roofing (copper, lead, and zinc alloy) is used on sloped roofs over a base of plywood or concrete. This material comes in flat sheets, which are joined with flat, batten or standing seams, followed by soldering or an application of adhesive.

Comments

Manufacturers recommend a minimum pitch when using preformed metal roofing on sloped roofs. Self-tapping screws with attached neoprene washers (to prevent leakage) are used to attach metal roofing to the supporting members. Lapped ends may be sealed with preformed sealant (available from the manufacturer) to match the deck configuration.

Where self-tapping screws are used to attach the metal roofing, be sure the entire roof is swept first to prevent the expelled metal chips and burrs from rusting and ruining the finish.

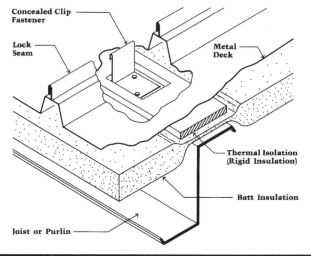

Standing Seam & Batten Seam: Custom-Fabricated

R.S. Means Co., Inc., *Roofing: Design Criteria, Options, Selection*
Figure 8.29

Metal Shingles

UBC — 1997

1508.3 Metal Shingles. The roof valley flashing shall not be provided of less than 0.016-inch (0.41 mm) (No. 28 galvanized sheet gage) corrosion-resistant metal, which shall extend at least 8 inches (203 mm) from the centerline each way and shall have a splash diverter rib not less than 3/4 inch (19 mm) high at the flow line formed as part of the flashing. Sections of flashing shall have an end lap of not less than 4 inches (102 mm). The metal valley flashing shall have a 36-inch-wide (914 mm) underlayment directly under it consisting of one layer of Type 15 felt running the full length of the valley, in addition to underlayment required for metal shingles. In severe climates, the metal valley flashing underlayment shall be solid cemented to the roofing underlayment for roof slopes under 7 units vertical in 12 units horizontal (58.3% slope).

Comments

Metal shingles are used for roofing or mansards on residential and commercial projects. They are available in decorative diamond shapes, in a standing seam, and in panels that simulate the look of wood-grained shingles. Metal shingles are very durable and virtually maintenance-free. A product with a quality finish should not fade, chalk, crack, peel, warp or rot. Any surface residue can be cleaned with normal methods, and minor scratches touched up with matching paint from the manufacturer. Accessories are available from the manufacturers.

Metal shingles should be installed by roofers who are trained in the particular techniques required. Manufacturers provide installation manuals and seminars. (Contact their Technical Service Advisors for information.) The recommended slope is typically 3 in 12. Decorative, diamond-shaped metal shingles may be arranged in a design using different colors. The shingles have a turned-down front edge and turned up back edge for double-sealing protection. The fastening system is concealed. Standing seam metal shingles are installed vertically up the roof slope, interlocking for weathertightness. Panel seams are staggered for an attractive appearance. Simulated wood-grain panels, also interlocking, are installed horizontally from eave to ridge, with panel seams staggered.

Single-Ply Roofing

Comments

Single-ply roofing (SPR) systems originated as an alternative to built-up roofing (BUR). Manufacturer research, warranty programs, and incentives for quality installation have contributed to the success of SPR in the U.S. While the membrane for built-up roofing is constructed on the roof by the contractor from felts and asphalt, single-ply roofing is built from flexible sheets of compounded synthetic materials manufactured in a controlled environment.

SPRI, the Single-ply Roofing Institute, maintains that "primary among the physical and performance properties these materials provide are strength, flexibility, durability, versatility in their attachment methods, and broad applicability."

Industry Standards

Roofing: Design Criteria, Options, Selection
(R.S. Means Co., Inc.)

Single-ply roofing is used in light commercial applications. Rolls of SPR membrane should be placed on the roof (over structural supports) as soon as the deck structure is in place. The SPR membrane should not be laid out on the ground. The rolls should not be concentrated in one area of the roof, but distributed immediately and evenly to avoid overloading the structure. Roof insulation should be placed on pallets not more than two tiers high, and covered with secured tarpaulins.

The roof area should be laid out in advance to utilize the largest sheets possible. This approach to layout should be carried out in advance by all bidders, who should include in their submittals to the architect a roof sheet layout, showing seams and penetrations.

Before the membrane is unrolled, the roof surface should be checked to ensure that there are no sharp objects, such as gravel or bits of metal, that might pierce the membrane. After the sheets are unrolled and positioned, seam splicing begins. There is little margin for error in splicing seams, since SPR offers no second or third ply of membrane to back up the first in the event of a leak. A manufacturer's representative should be on site during this phase, at least initially, to assure the quality of the splices. To make a field seam in an EPDM roof, the top sheet should be folded back 12 inches, showing at least the same amount of membrane of the adjoining sheet. This 24-inch wide area should be wiped clean of talc and debris, using solvent or cleaner furnished by the manufacturer. Inadequately cleaned splices are a common cause of seam failure.

The splice cement should be labeled by the manufacturer of the membrane and thoroughly mixed using a drill-activated stirring device. Most manufacturers' specifications call for a three-to-four inch minimum splice. However, most professional roofing contractors generally require about six inches. The extra cost of the materials is negligible, and the added splice area strengthens this critical juncture. One manufacturer specifies in-the-splice sealant for all of its mechanically attached systems. Most manufacturers specify that adhesive be brush-applied, but most roofing contractors prefer a four-inch long-handled roller. The object is to achieve a thin, even film of adhesive on both mating surfaces; too much adhesive distorts the membrane. When the adhesive becomes tacky, but is not yet dry, the installer should carefully fold the top sheet over, and brush toward the seam with a roller or the palm of the hand, avoiding wrinkles or "fishmouths."

If fishmouths do occur, they should not be "pressed down," but cut out. A patch should then be applied over the area of the cut-out, in accordance with the manufacturer's directions. The splice should then be rolled toward the seam with a heavy metal hand roller.

After the joint is cleaned, a bead of lap sealer should be applied along the exposed edge. It is important that this be done at the end of each day's work to prevent moisture from contaminating the seam adhesive overnight.

Attachment Methods

There are four methods of attaching the SPR membrane to the substrate or deck: using gravel slag ballast, mechanically fastening, partially adhering using "spots" or "lines" of adhesive, and fully adhering. As illustrated in **Figure 8.30**, many of the SPR products may utilize any of the attachment methods.

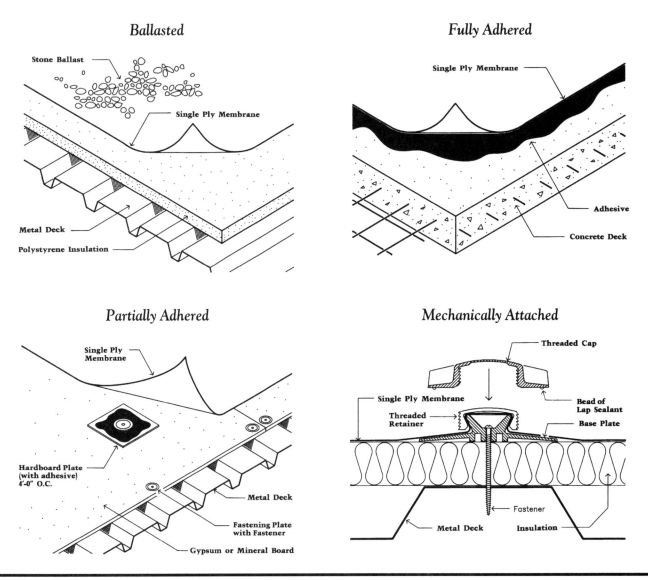

Ballasted

Fully Adhered

Partially Adhered

Mechanically Attached

R.S. Means Co., Inc., *Roofing: Design Criteria, Options, Selection*

Figure 8.30

Bituminous Roofing Products

Industry Standards

Construction Principles, Materials, and Methods
(John Wiley & Sons, Inc.)

Four basic materials are used in the manufacture of bituminous roofing products. These are (1) a reinforcing base that is either organic dry felt or glass fiber mat; (2) bitumen (asphalt or coal tar); (3) mineral stabilizers; and (4) either fine or coarse surfacings.

In general, the manufacture of organic felt bituminous roofing products includes processing cellulose fibers into dry felt, saturating and coating the felt with asphalt or coal tar, and then, depending on the type of finished product, surfacing the coated felt with selected mineral aggregates. When glass fiber mat is used as a reinforcing base instead of organic felt, the saturating process is bypassed. The mat goes directly from a dry looper into a coater.

7.5.1.1 Dry Organic Felt

Dry organic felt, used as a base for making reinforcing felts for built-up roofing and waterproofing, underlayment, smooth and mineral-surfaced roll roofing, and asphalt shingles, is made from combinations of cellulose fibers, such as those derived from rags, paper, and wood, on a machine similar to the type used for making paper. The fibers are prepared by various pulping methods, then blended and proportioned to produce felt with the necessary weight, tensile strength, absorptive capacity, and flexibility required to make a suitable roofing product. The felt must be able to absorb from one and a half to two times its weight in asphalt saturants and be strong and flexible enough to withstand strains placed on it during the manufacturing process.

7.5.1.2 Glass Fiber Mat

Dry glass fiber mats are used as a base for reinforcing felts for built-up roofing and waterproofing, coated smooth rolls and mineral-surfaced roll roofing, and asphalt shingles. To make glass fiber mats, sand, soda ash, and limestone are first combined to make chopped strand glass fibers. These fibers then are mixed with a binding agent and cured to produce a mat with the thickness, tensile strength, tear strength, weight, and flexibility required to produce roofing and waterproofing products.

7.5.1.3 Bitumens

The bitumens used in bituminous roofing products are asphalt and coal tar. They are used to saturate and coat dry organic felts and coat glass fiber mats in the manufacture of roofing felt and to weld or fuse roofing or waterproofing felts together to form a built-up roof or waterproofing membrane. Both asphalt and coal tar bitumens are thermoplastic, which means they become more fluid when heated and return to their former solid state when they are cooled.

A bitumen's equiviscous temperature (EVT) is the optimum temperature at which it should be used. Each asphalt and coal tar bitumen has its own EVT. The lowest type number has the lowest EVT.

Asphalt

Asphalt used to make roofing and waterproofing products, known as asphalt flux, is a petroleum product obtained from the fractional distillation of crude oil. Asphalt flux is processed to produce roofing grades of asphalt, called saturants, or when combined with mineral stabilizers, coating asphalts. Both forms combine with dry felt to make asphalt roofing or waterproofing membranes.

The preservative and waterproofing characteristics of asphalt reside largely in certain oily constituents. In the making of roofing products, the body of the highly absorbent felt sheet first is impregnated (saturated) to the greatest possible extent with saturants that are oil-rich asphalts. The saturant then is sealed in with an application of a harder, more viscous coating asphalt, which in turn can be further protected by a covering of opaque mineral granules. A primary difference between saturants and coating asphalts is the temperature at which they soften. The softening point of saturants varies from 100° to 160° F; that of coatings is as high as 260° F. Saturant asphalt is not used with glass fiber mat. The coating mixture is used to completely surround the glass fibers and to provide a layer of coating on both sides of the mat. Asphalt flux is also the base material used to make asphalt plastic cement, quick-setting roof adhesives, asphalt primers, other roof coatings, and adhesives.

Coal Tar

Coal tar used to make roofing products is a distillation of bituminous coal. It is considered basically superior to asphalt for use in low-slope roofing. It is most effective at a slope of 1/4 in./ft. and can be used on slopes up to 1/2 in./ft., but no higher.

7.5.1.4 Mineral Stabilizers

Finely ground minerals called stabilizers, such as silica, slate dust, talc, micaceous materials, dolomite, and trap rock, when combined with coating bitumens control hardness, elasticity, adhesion, and weathering. Coated bitumens that contain stabilizers resist weather better, are more shatterproof and shockproof in cold weather, and significantly increase the life of roofing products.

Built-Up Roofing

Types & Installation Guidelines

Industry Standards

Roofing Handbook
(The McGraw-Hill Companies)

There are three basic types of BUR systems.

Surfacing Smooth Systems

Smooth-surfaced inorganic BURs offer several advantages. For example, they are lightweight, generally less than 1/3 the approximate 400 to 700 pounds per square of gravel-surfaced roofs. They are easy to inspect and repair. The absence of gravel facilitates fast visual inspection of the smooth surface. If damaged, patching takes little time and there is no need to scrape away gravel. Because of these advantages, maintenance of smooth-surfaced roofs is simpler than other BUR roofs.

When reroofing is desired, or necessary, the job can often be done without removing the old smooth-surfaced membrane. If removal is necessary, there is less material to remove. In addition to all these, surfaced roofs often cost less than 3 gravel-surfaced roofs with the same design life.

Surfacing Gravel Systems

Gravel-surfaced, inorganic BUR systems are similar in construction to smooth-surfaced roofs, except in the final surfacing. Instead of the light mopping of asphalt or a light application of one of the other roof coatings used on smooth-surfaced roofs, a flood coat of approximately 60 pounds per square of hot bitumen is applied and followed by the appropriate aggregate.

Gravel-surfaced systems are typically more durable than smooth-surfaced BUR systems. The aggregate covering helps the asphalt flood coat resist the aging effects of the elements. The gravel also helps stabilize the flood-coat bitumen and permits heavier pours than typically are used in systems that do not employ gravel. This results in additional waterproofing material in the assembly.

Other, more obvious advantages are the improved fire resistance offered by the aggregate and added protection from penetrating forces, such as hail. Gravel-surfaced roofs generally are limited to slopes of 3 inches or less to minimize gravel loss and membrane slippage.

Comments

In high-wind areas, loose aggregates may become projectiles. Be sure all aggregates are fully embedded in bitumen.

There are differing opinions about how many layers of roofing can be applied over an existing roof before a tearoff is required. Section 1516 "Reroofing Overlays Allowed," in the 1997 UBC states that, in general, "not more than one overlay shall be applied over an existing built-up roof." See the section on reroofing later in this chapter for more details.

Surfacing Mineral Systems

Mineral-surfaced cap sheets form the last visible ply in this type of BUR membrane. The inorganic mat is coated with weather-grade asphalt, into which is embedded opaque, noncombustible, ceramic-coated granules. The resulting sheet yields a roof that enhances the appearance of the building it protects.

Mineral-surfaced cap sheets provide BURs with several unique properties. Tile ceramic-coated granules on these products offer a uniform, factory-applied surfacing that helps the underlying bitumen resist weathering and aging. Unlike coatings, these granules are not typically a maintenance item. Many smooth-surfaced, coated roofs require periodic recoating. The cap sheet system also has improved fire resistance and reflective properties.

Industry Standards

Roofing: Design Criteria, Options, Selection
(R.S. Means Co., Inc.)

The following guidelines offer a good starting point for proper installation of built-up roofing.

Rule 1: Slope the Roof

Never design a flat or "dead level" roof! The design of near-level or dead-level roofs will eventually result in ponding and deterioration of flashing and roofing materials.

Rule 2: Inspection

Provide *continuous* inspection during the placement of roofing by a knowledgeable inspector. Carefully follow manufacturers' published specifications.

Rule 3: Restore Temporary Roofs

Always restore temporary roofing before applying the permanent built-up system. The practice of installing the first plies and one "mopping," then allowing other trades to use it as a staging area, and finally mopping in the additional plies and ballast, has become common as time becomes a crucial factor on construction projects. If a temporary roof is required, it should be properly restored before the permanent roof is installed.

All accessories, curbs, and penetrations through the roof should also be in place before the roof is installed.

Rule 4: Keep Materials Dry

Protect roofing and insulation materials from moisture *before,* as well as *during,* construction. The system is susceptible to moisture before, during, and after the roof installation. Prior to installation, roofing materials (especially insulation) must be protected from moisture infiltration. Simply covering these materials may not be sufficient. Some insulations have been found to absorb moisture while stored in a warehouse, to the extent that they are too "wet" to install. It is important to store material off the floor or ground on pallets, and cover it with tarpaulins. The lightweight plastic wrapping that the materials are shipped in is usually not a sufficient covering because it tends to tear easily.

Lightweight concrete decks must be properly vented. Most specifications call for the roofing contractor to "approve" the deck design before plans for proceeding with roof installation. The roof installer should perform a deck dryness test.

Rule 5: Avoid the Void

Prevent voids between plies in a BUR. The most prominent cause of failure in BURs, according to an NRCA survey, was interply blistering.

To prevent voids, an even bitumen application is essential; this can be obtained when the application temperature of the bitumen is in the equiviscous temperature range (EVT). The EVT is usually printed on the asphalt container. The roofing contractor must heat the bitumen in the kettle to a temperature above the EVT, but below the flash point, in order to allow for the chilling of the asphalt as it is transported and applied. The bitumen should "roll" (spread out) along the laps on application, and plies should be installed "shingle fashion," as shown in **Figure 8.31**.

Typical Built-Up Roof

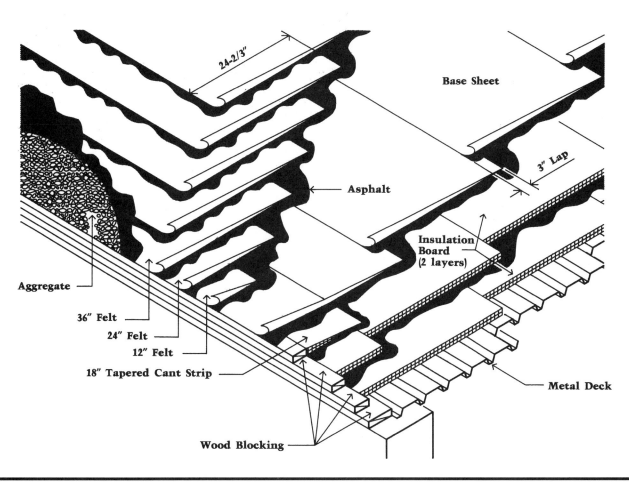

R.S. Means Co., Inc., *Roofing: Design Criteria, Options, Selection*

Figure 8.31

Roof Drain—Built-Up Roofing

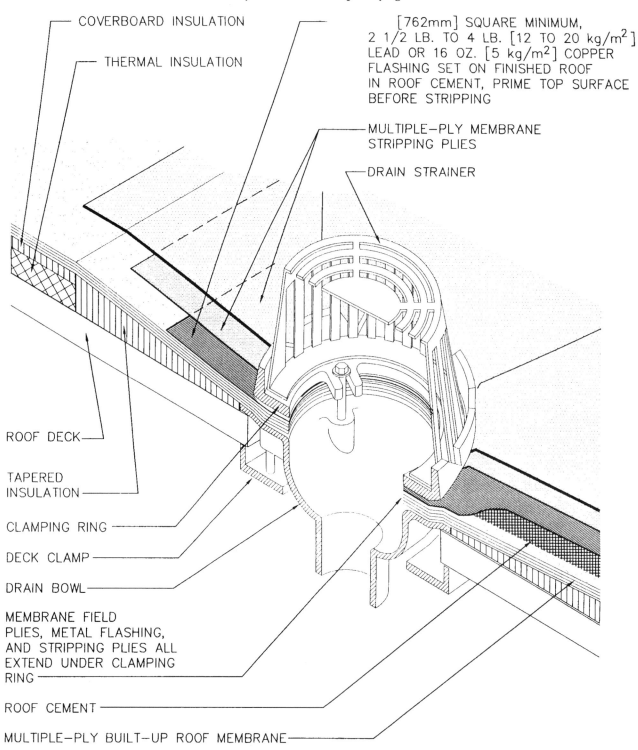

COVERBOARD INSULATION

THERMAL INSULATION

[762mm] SQUARE MINIMUM, 2 1/2 LB. TO 4 LB. [12 TO 20 kg/m^2] LEAD OR 16 OZ. [5 kg/m^2] COPPER FLASHING SET ON FINISHED ROOF IN ROOF CEMENT, PRIME TOP SURFACE BEFORE STRIPPING

MULTIPLE–PLY MEMBRANE STRIPPING PLIES

DRAIN STRAINER

ROOF DECK

TAPERED INSULATION

CLAMPING RING

DECK CLAMP

DRAIN BOWL

MEMBRANE FIELD PLIES, METAL FLASHING, AND STRIPPING PLIES ALL EXTEND UNDER CLAMPING RING

ROOF CEMENT

MULTIPLE–PLY BUILT–UP ROOF MEMBRANE

NOTES:

1. THE USE OF A METAL DECK SUMP PAN IS NOT RECOMMENDED. HOWEVER, DRAIN RECEIVER/BEARING PLATES ARE APPLICABLE WITH SOME PROJECTS.
2. DO NOT APPLY COAL TAR OR DEAD LEVEL ASPHALT INTO DRAIN SUMP.

Courtesy of National Roofing Contractors Association, *NRCA Roofing & Waterproofing Manual*

Figure 8.32

Skylights & Roof Accessories

Ed. Note: Skylights are considered roof accessories, along with roof hatches, pipes and conduits, and roof curbs for HVAC units. All of these items, though they may be installed by other trades, must be flashed into the roof.

Comments

Roof plans, sections and elevations should contain information about roof accessories. These drawings should also show requirements and locations of gutters and downspouts. HVAC curbs, piping, and conduits should be indicated on the mechanical and electrical drawings.

UBC — 1997

Section 2409 — Sloped Glazing and Skylights

2409.1 Scope. This section applies to the installation of glass or other transparent, translucent or opaque glazing material installed at a slope of 15 degrees or more from the vertical plane, including glazing materials in skylights, roofs and sloped walls.

2409.2 Allowable Glazing Materials. Sloped glazing shall be any of the following materials, subject to the limitations in this section:

1. Laminated glass with a minimum 0.015-inch (0.38 mm) polyvinyl butyl interlayer for glass panes 16 square feet (1.5 m²) or less in area and with the highest point of the glass no more than 12 feet (3658 mm) above a walking surface; for larger or higher panes, the minimum interlayer thickness shall be 0.030 inch (0.76 mm).

2. Fully tempered glass.

3. Heat-strengthened glass.

4. Wired glass.

5. Approved rigid plastics meeting the requirements of Section 2603.7.

For multiple-layer glazing systems, each light or layer shall consist of any of the glazing materials specified above.

Annealed glass may be used as specified within Exceptions 2 and 3 of Section 2409.3.

2409.3 Screening. Heat-strengthened glass and fully-tempered glass, when used in single-layer glazing systems, shall have screens installed below glazing. The screens shall be capable of supporting the weight of the glass and shall be substantially supported below and installed within 4 inches (102 mm) of the glass.

They shall be constructed of a noncombustible material not thinner than 0.08 inch (2.03 mm) with a mesh not larger than 1 inch by 1 inch (25 mm by 25 mm). In a corrosive atmosphere, structurally equivalent noncorrosive screening materials shall be used. Heat-strengthened glass, fully-tempered glass and wired glass, when used in multiple-layer glazing systems as the bottom glass layer over the walking surface, shall be equipped with screening that complies with the requirements for monolithic glazing systems.

Exception:

1. Fully tempered glass may be installed without required protective screens when located between intervening floors at a slope of 30 degrees or less from the vertical plane if the highest point of the glass is 10 feet (3048 mm) or less above the walking surface.

2. Allowable glazing material, including annealed glass, may be installed without required screens if the walking surface or any other accessible area below the glazing material is permanently protected from falling glass for a minimum horizontal distance equal to twice the height.

3. Allowable glazing material, including annealed glass, may be installed without screens in the sloped glazing systems of commercial or detached greenhouses used exclusively for growing plants and not intended for use by the public, provided the height of the greenhouse at the ridge does not exceed 20 feet (6096 mm) above grade.

4. Screens need not be provided within individual dwelling units when fully tempered glass is used as single glazing or in both panes of an insulating glass unit when all the following conditions are met:

   4.1 The area of each pane (single glass) or unit (insulating glass) shall not exceed 16 square feet (1.49 m²).

   4.2 The highest point of the glass shall not be more than 12 feet (3658 mm) above any walking surface or other accessible area.

   4.3 The nominal thickness of each pane shall not exceed 3/16 inch (4.76 mm).

2409.4 Framing. In Types I and II construction, skylight frames shall be constructed of noncombustible materials.

Exception: In foundries or buildings where acid fumes deleterious to metal are incidental to the use of the buildings, approved pressure-treated woods or other approved noncorrosive materials may be used for sash and frames. Skylights set at an angle of less than 45 degrees from the horizontal plane shall be mounted at least 4 inches (102 mm) above the plane of the roof on a curb constructed of materials as required for the frame. Skylights may be installed in the plane of the roof when the roof slope is 45 degrees or greater from horizontal.

2603.7 Skylights.

2603.7.1 General. Skylight assemblies may be glazed with approved plastic materials in accordance with the following provisions:

1. The plastics shall be mounted at least 4 inches (102 mm) above the plane of the roof by a curb constructed consistent with the requirements for the type of construction classification.

   Exception: Curbs may be omitted on roofs of Group R, Division 3 Occupancies with a minimum slope of 3 units vertical in 12 units horizontal (25% slope) when self-flashing skylights are used.

2. Flat or corrugated plastic skylights shall slope at least 4 units vertical in 12 units horizontal (33.3% slope). Dome-shaped skylights shall rise above the mounting flange a minimum distance equal to 10 percent of the maximum span of the dome, but not less than 5 inches (127 mm).

   Exception: Skylights that pass the Class B Burning Brand Test specified in UBC Standard 15-2.

3. The edges of the plastic lights or domes shall be protected by metal or other noncombustible materials or shall be tested to show that equivalent fire protection is provided.

   Exception: The metal or noncombustible edge is not required where nonrated roof coverings are permitted.

4. Each skylight unit may have a maximum area within the curb of 100 square feet (9.3 m^2) for CC2 material and 200 square feet (18.6 m^2) for CC1 material.

Skylights

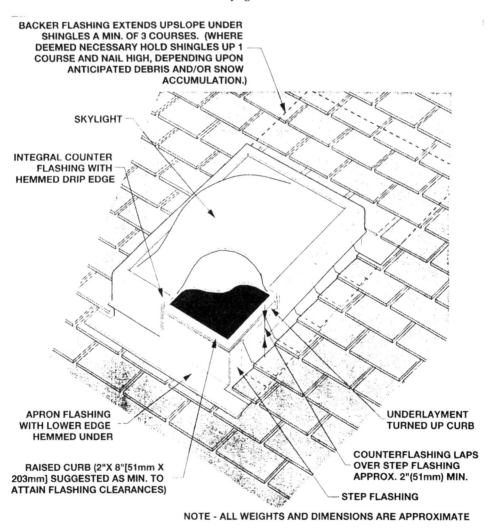

Courtesy of National Roofing Contractors Association, *NRCA Roofing & Waterproofing Manual*

Figure 8.33

Exceptions: The maximum area within the curb need not be limited if the building on which the skylights are located is not more than one story in height, the building has an exterior separation from other buildings of at least 30 feet (9144 mm), and the room or space sheltered by the roof is not classified in a Group I, Division 1.1, 1.2 or 3 Occupancy or as a required means of egress. Except for Groups A, Divisions 1 and 2; I, Divisions 1.1, 1.2 and 2; and H, Divisions 1 and 2 Occupancies, the maximum area within the curb need not be limited where skylights are:

    2.1 Serving as a fire venting system complying with this code, or

    2.2 Used in a building completely equipped with an approved automatic sprinkler system complying with UBC Standard 9-1 or 9-3.

5. The aggregate area of skylights installed in the roof shall not exceed 33-1/3 percent of the floor area of the room or space sheltered by the roof when CC1 materials are used and 25 percent when CC2 materials are used.

6. Skylight units shall be separated from each other by a distance of not less than 4 feet (1219 mm), measured in a horizontal plane.

Exceptions:

1. Except for Groups A, Divisions 1 and 2; I, Divisions 1.1, 1.2 and 2; and H, Divisions 1 and 2 Occupancies, the separation is not required where the skylights are:

    1.1. Serving as a fire venting system complying with this code, or 1.2 Used in a building completely equipped with an approved automatic sprinkler system complying with UBC Standard 9-1 or 9-3.

    1.2. Multiple skylights located above the same room or space with a combined area not exceeding the limits set forth in Section 2603.7.1, Item 4.

7. Skylights shall not be installed within that portion of a roof located within a distance to property line or public way where openings in exterior walls are prohibited or required to be protected, whichever is most restrictive.

2603.7.2 Plastics over stair shafts. Approved plastic materials that will not automatically vent but are able to be vented may be used over stairways and shafts, provided the installation conforms to the requirements of Section 2603.7.1.

Comments

For further information about skylight leaks, see Section 5–27 in Residential Construction Performance Guidelines, *published by the National Association of Home Builders (Telephone: 1-800-368-5242).*

Industry Standards
Roofing: Design Criteria, Options, Selection
(R.S. Means Co., Inc.)

Skylights

Figure 8.34 is an illustration of the components and configuration of a skylight roof curb. It is imperative that curbs be built and located while the deck is being installed. If decks are not cut and curbs not installed until *after* the roof membrane is in place, there is a much greater chance of roofing failure at the point of curb installation.

Other Roof Curbs

Like skylights, other penetrations requiring curbs should also be coordinated early in the roof installation process. Items such as smoke vents and hatches should be detailed on construction documents. Without this information, field fabrication and setting of the curbs may result in damage to the roof membrane.

Skylight Roof Curb

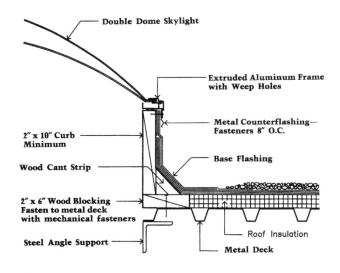

R.S. Means Co., Inc., *Roofing: Design Criteria, Options, Selection*

Figure 8.34

Roof Penetration Flashing — Pipes

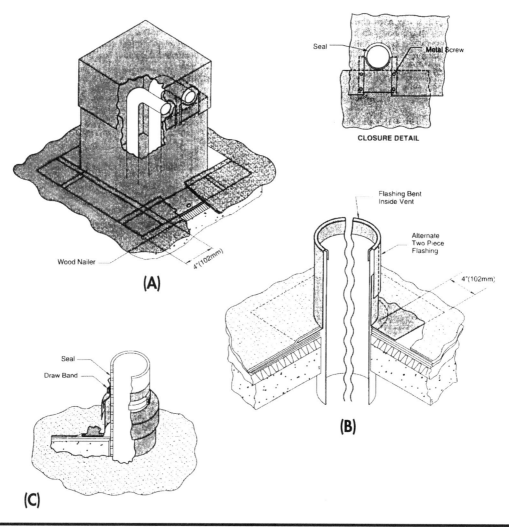

Reprinted from the SMACNA *Architectural Sheet Metal Manual, Fifth Edition,* Copyrighted 1993, with permission.

Figure 8.35

Roof Penetrations & Flashing

Comments

Flashing is a thin, impervious sheet of material that is used in building construction to prevent water penetration or to direct the flow of water. Flashing is used especially at roof hips and valleys, roof penetrations, joints between a roof and a vertical wall, and in masonry walls. Refer to the information on different types of flashing and flashing materials throughout the chapter.

Pipe

Industry Standards

SMACNA Architectural Sheet Metal Manual
(Sheet Metal and Air Conditioning Contractors' National Association)

Figure 8.35, drawing A illustrates a method of flashing a roof opening where curb is not used. This method is recommended only if pipes are turned horizontally within 24 inches (610 mm) of the roof and the opening is not greater than 18 in. x 18 in. (460 mm x 460 mm).

The flashing is made in pieces with base portion being flanged 4 in. (102 mm) onto the roof. The flange is fastened through the roofing felts and is then stripped in by the roofer. Top section is notched to fit over the pipes and metal screwed to the base section. The closure is attached as shown in Closure

Detail. Recommended minimum gage for flashing in **Figure 8.35, drawing A** is 16 oz. (.55 mm) copper, 26 ga (.477 mm) stainless steel, or 24 ga (.607 mm) galvanized steel.

Figure 8.35, drawing B illustrates two methods of flashing a vent pipe. The flange extends 4 inches (102 mm) on roof and is stripped in by roofer. The top of flashing is turned down inside the vent pipe. The flashing may be one piece or a two piece style. When a vent pipe extends above the roof so far that it is impractical to completely cover it with flashing (**Figure 8.35, drawing B**), it is recommended that it be flashed as shown in **Figure 8.35, drawing C** [minimum 2 in. (51 mm)].

Roof Vent Flashing

Upper and side shingles overlap flange and are set in asphalt plastic cement

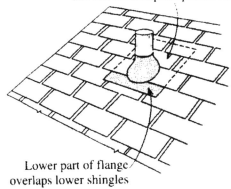

Lower part of flange overlaps lower shingles

Courtesy of The McGraw-Hill Companies, *Roofing Handbook*

Figure 8.36

Comments

For tolerances regarding roof vents and louvres, see Section 5.4 in Residential Construction Performance Guidelines, published by the National Association of Home Builders (Telephone: 1-800-368-5242).

Cants, Curbs, Nailers, and Flashings

Ed. Note: Refer to the individual roof types (Asphalt, Fiber Cement, Wood and Tile) earlier in this chapter for more on flashing installations.

Industry Standards
Means Graphic Construction Standards
(R.S. Means Co., Inc.)

Flashings are required to ensure that discontinuities in the roofing system are protected from water penetration. Typical flashing locations include the roof perimeter, around penetrations such as vents, hatches, skylights, and equipment curbs, along roof expansion joints, and sometimes at changes in slope.

Typical flashing materials include aluminum, copper, lead-coated copper, lead, polyvinyl chloride, butyl rubber, copper-clad stainless steel, stainless steel, zinc and copper alloy, and galvanized metal. Flashing materials should be compatible with roofing system and all adjacent materials.

Comments

Flashing can be formed on site, or preformed in the shop. Metal flashing should be a minimum of 26 gauge and corrosion-resistant.
Flashing is used not only on the roof, but over windows and doors, around skylights, and for some masonry installations.

Expansion joints are required to compensate for the change in dimensions or volume of building materials due to thermal variations, moisture, or other environmental conditions. In the roof structure, a joint or gap is placed at appropriate intervals to allow for expansion and contraction of the building parts. Expansion joints typically consist of job-built or prefabricated blocking material designed to raise the joint covering above the roofing material. The joint may be filled with a compressible material, such as felt, rubber, or neoprene to keep it clean and dry. A prefabricated protective covering of rubber, neoprene, or metal inhibits moisture penetration while allowing for movement. This covering, together with the necessary flashings, completes the joint system.

Gravel stop is used at the edges of flat or nearly flat roofs to contain the gravel on the roof, as a counter flashing, and as a decorative edge strip. It is usually used in conjunction with treated-lumber blocking and a cant strip to protect the flashing at the roof edge. The exposed face height varies from 4" to 12" or more and the flashing return is usually fabricated to suit the roof edge conditions.

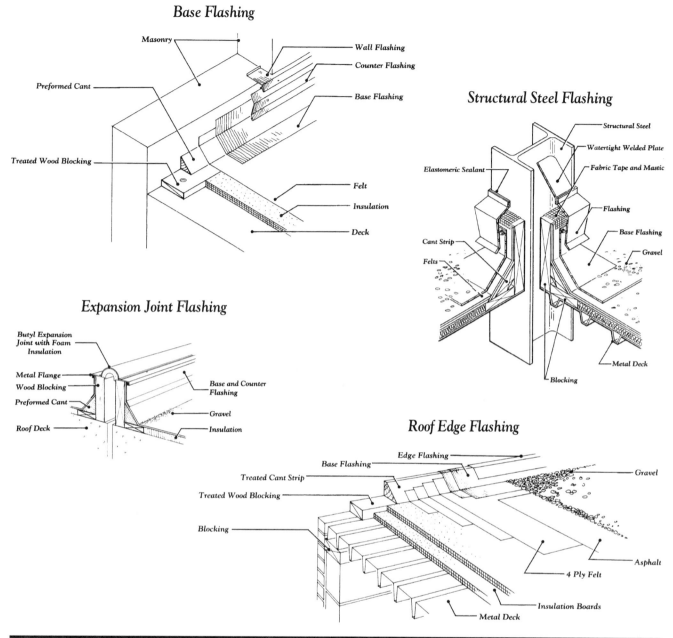

Base Flashing

Structural Steel Flashing

Expansion Joint Flashing

Roof Edge Flashing

R.S. Means Co., Inc., *Means Graphic Construction Standards*

Figure 8.37

Gravel stop may be fabricated from aluminum, copper, lead-coated copper, polyvinyl chloride, galvanized steel, or stainless steel. The finish may be natural or painted. A duranodic finish is commonly used with aluminum gravel stops.

Industry Standards
NRCA Roofing & Waterproofing Manual
(National Roofing Contractors Association)

15.1 Cants
The bending radius of bituminous roofing materials is generally limited to 45 degrees. To allow for this limited bending radius, cant strips must be provided at any 90-degree angle change, such as those created by roof-to-wall, roof-to-curb, or other roof-to-vertical surface intersections. Generally, the installation of cant strips to accommodate roof-to-wall or other horizontal-to-vertical plane change is consistent with good roofing practice.

15.2 Unit Curbs
Mechanical units using curbs that have built-in metal base flashing flanges can be difficult to seal for the long term and, therefore, are not recommended for use with bituminous roof membranes.

Some single-ply roof membranes may utilize prefabricated curbs with metal "self-flashing" flanges to be embedded in the roof membrane. However, the use of raised curbs that provide for proper application of the roof membrane, vertical extension, and proper termination of membrane base flashings, and installation of sheet metal counterflashing, promote good roofing and flashing practices with any membrane roof system.

15.3 Nailers

It is recommended that well-secured, decay-resistant (e.g., preservative pressure-treated) wood blocking/nailers be carefully designed and provided at all roof perimeters and penetrations for fastening membrane flashings and sheet metal components. Wood nailers should be provided on all prefabricated curbs and hatches for attachment of membrane base flashings.

15.4 Flashings

There are two types of flashings: membrane flashings and sheet metal flashings.

15.4.1 Membrane Base Flashing

Membrane base flashing is generally composed of strips of compatible membrane materials used to close-in or flash roof-to-vertical surface intersections or transitions. NRCA recommends the height of the membrane base flashing be not lower than (a nominal) 8 inches (203 mm), and generally not higher than (a nominal) 14 inches (356 mm) above the finished roof surface. Walls requiring flashings higher than 14 inches (356 mm) should receive special moisture-proofing, membrane wall flashing/waterproofing plies, or cladding.

A wood nailer strip or suitable fixture allowing mechanical fastening of the membrane base flashing, along its upper edge, must be provided. Membrane base flashings should be fastened to prevent displacement and/or slippage.

Depending upon the roof system, fastening may be accomplished with cap-head nails, securely fastened termination bars, or other appropriate mechanical fastening devices approved by the membrane manufacturer. Generally, membrane base flashing fasteners should be spaced 6 to 12 inches (152 to 305 mm) apart, depending upon the type of membrane and base flashing configuration being installed.

Sprayed polyurethane foam is said to be a self-flashing roofing system; however, NRCA recommends metal counterflashings be designed and installed to overlap and shield the foam and coating along points of termination. The polyurethane foam is sprayed to form a smooth transition between the horizontal roof structure and the vertical projection. The foam should be sprayed to a point at least 4 inches (102 mm) above the roof surface, and the protective coating should be carried 4 inches (102 mm) above the foam. Metal components should then be installed to the foam and coating points of termination.

For wall-supported roof decks scheduled to receive bituminous membrane systems, the vertical masonry or concrete surfaces scheduled for membrane base flashing should be primed with a compatible bituminous primer. Well-secured, decay-resistant (e.g., preservative pressure-treated) wood blocking/nailers should be designed and provided at all roof perimeters and penetrations for fastening membrane flashings and sheet metal components. Wood nailers should be provided on all prefabricated curbs and hatches for membrane base flashing attachment.

For non-wall-supported roof decks, raised wood blocking or curbing is recommended to isolate differential wall and roof assembly movement. The wood curbing that facilitates flashing application should be placed against the wall and secured only to the deck.

Membrane flashings on expansion joint curbs (allowing expansion and contraction) should be constructed, according to the NRCA Construction Details. The designer is cautioned to consider that building components are subjected to thermal movements at different rates and directions from the roof membrane. If the roof is to be tied into these components, special consideration should be given to the design of that juncture.

15.4.2 Metal Flashing (Counterflashing and Cap Flashing)

On mechanical units, and other raised curb equipment, sheet metal counterflashing should be installed to cover the top edge and overlap the upper portion of membrane base flashings. On units that will be frequently serviced, the counterflashings may extend down over membrane flashings covering the cant and terminate near the roof surface so that membrane base flashings are protected.

Surface-mount counterflashing for concrete walls

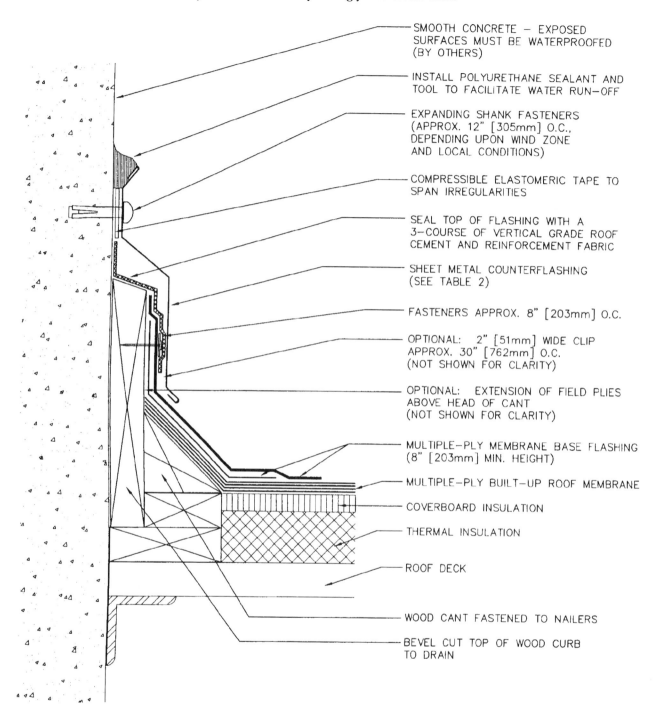

SMOOTH CONCRETE — EXPOSED SURFACES MUST BE WATERPROOFED (BY OTHERS)

INSTALL POLYURETHANE SEALANT AND TOOL TO FACILITATE WATER RUN—OFF

EXPANDING SHANK FASTENERS (APPROX. 12" [305mm] O.C., DEPENDING UPON WIND ZONE AND LOCAL CONDITIONS)

COMPRESSIBLE ELASTOMERIC TAPE TO SPAN IRREGULARITIES

SEAL TOP OF FLASHING WITH A 3—COURSE OF VERTICAL GRADE ROOF CEMENT AND REINFORCEMENT FABRIC

SHEET METAL COUNTERFLASHING (SEE TABLE 2)

FASTENERS APPROX. 8" [203mm] O.C.

OPTIONAL: 2" [51mm] WIDE CLIP APPROX. 30" [762mm] O.C. (NOT SHOWN FOR CLARITY)

OPTIONAL: EXTENSION OF FIELD PLIES ABOVE HEAD OF CANT (NOT SHOWN FOR CLARITY)

MULTIPLE—PLY MEMBRANE BASE FLASHING (8" [203mm] MIN. HEIGHT)

MULTIPLE—PLY BUILT—UP ROOF MEMBRANE

COVERBOARD INSULATION

THERMAL INSULATION

ROOF DECK

WOOD CANT FASTENED TO NAILERS

BEVEL CUT TOP OF WOOD CURB TO DRAIN

NOTES:

1. THIS DETAIL SHOULD BE USED ONLY WHERE THE DECK IS SUPPORTED BY THE WALL.
2. ATTACH NAILER TO DECK WITH SUITABLE FASTENERS.
3. OPTION: IF WOOD NAILERS ARE NOT USED, A FIBER CANT STRIP SET IN BITUMEN OR ADHESIVE MAY BE USED.
4. COUNTERFLASHING DETAIL MAY BE A TWO—PIECE REGLET AND COUNTERFLASHING (SEE TABLE 2.2, "C" FOR ALTERNATE SHEET METAL COUNTERFLASHING.)

Courtesy of National Roofing Contractors Association, NRCA *Roofing & Waterproofing Manual*

Figure 8.38

Flashing at Roof Parapet

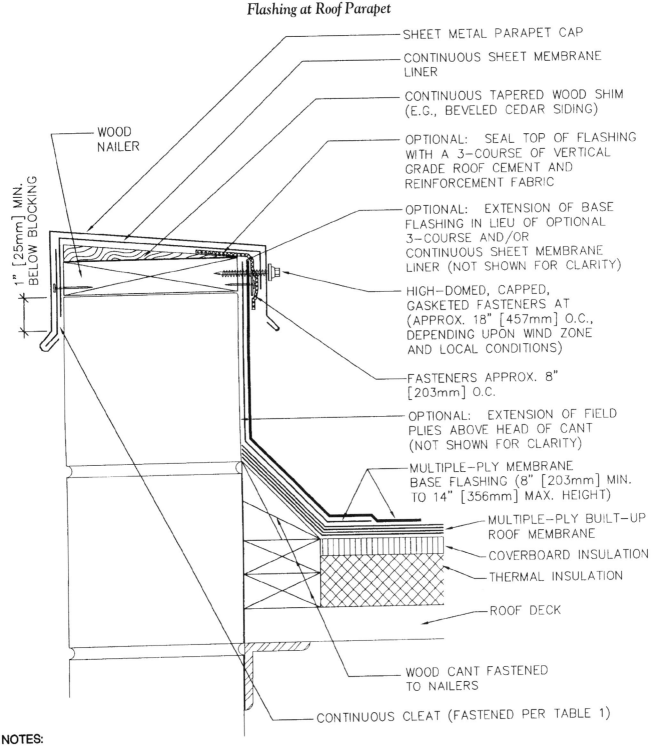

SHEET METAL PARAPET CAP

CONTINUOUS SHEET MEMBRANE LINER

CONTINUOUS TAPERED WOOD SHIM (E.G., BEVELED CEDAR SIDING)

OPTIONAL: SEAL TOP OF FLASHING WITH A 3-COURSE OF VERTICAL GRADE ROOF CEMENT AND REINFORCEMENT FABRIC

OPTIONAL: EXTENSION OF BASE FLASHING IN LIEU OF OPTIONAL 3-COURSE AND/OR CONTINUOUS SHEET MEMBRANE LINER (NOT SHOWN FOR CLARITY)

HIGH-DOMED, CAPPED, GASKETED FASTENERS AT (APPROX. 18" [457mm] O.C., DEPENDING UPON WIND ZONE AND LOCAL CONDITIONS)

FASTENERS APPROX. 8" [203mm] O.C.

OPTIONAL: EXTENSION OF FIELD PLIES ABOVE HEAD OF CANT (NOT SHOWN FOR CLARITY)

MULTIPLE-PLY MEMBRANE BASE FLASHING (8" [203mm] MIN. TO 14" [356mm] MAX. HEIGHT)

MULTIPLE-PLY BUILT-UP ROOF MEMBRANE

COVERBOARD INSULATION

THERMAL INSULATION

ROOF DECK

WOOD CANT FASTENED TO NAILERS

CONTINUOUS CLEAT (FASTENED PER TABLE 1)

WOOD NAILER

1" [25mm] MIN. BELOW BLOCKING

NOTES:

1. THIS DETAIL SHOULD BE USED ONLY WHEN THE ROOF DECK IS SUPPORTED BY THE WALL. DETAIL BUR-4 SHOULD BE USED FOR NON-WALL SUPPORTED DECK.
2. ATTACH NAILER TO DECK WITH SUITABLE FASTENERS.
3. OPTION: IF WOOD NAILERS ARE NOT USED, A FIBER CANT STRIP SET IN BITUMEN OR ADHESIVE MAY BE USED.
4. REFER TO BUR/MB TABLE 1 FOR METAL THICKNESS AND CLEAT REQUIREMENT.
5. SEE TABLE 3 FOR ALTERNATE SHEET METAL PARAPET CAP SECUREMENT AND LOCKS AND SEAMS FOR JOINTS IN SHEET METAL.

Courtesy of National Roofing Contractors Association, *NRCA Roofing & Waterproofing Manual*

Figure 8.39

Embedded Edge Metal Flashing — Thermoset Roofing

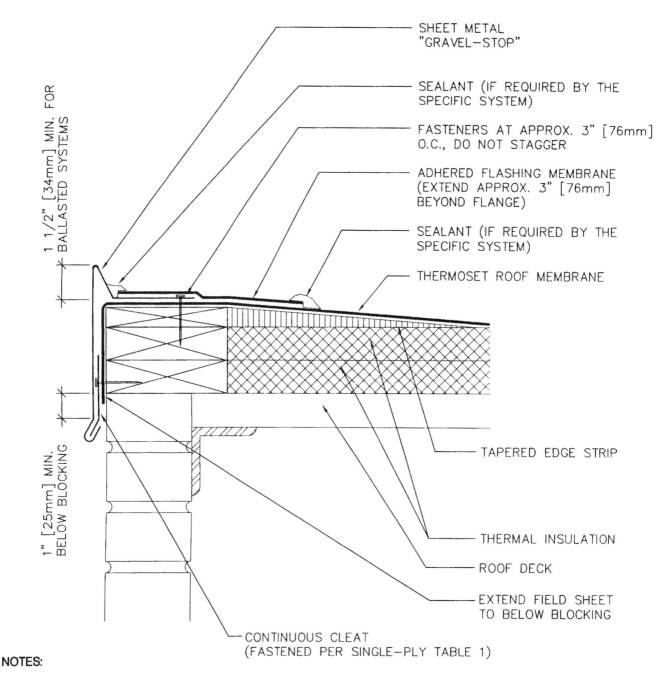

SHEET METAL "GRAVEL-STOP"

SEALANT (IF REQUIRED BY THE SPECIFIC SYSTEM)

FASTENERS AT APPROX. 3" [76mm] O.C., DO NOT STAGGER

ADHERED FLASHING MEMBRANE (EXTEND APPROX. 3" [76mm] BEYOND FLANGE)

SEALANT (IF REQUIRED BY THE SPECIFIC SYSTEM)

THERMOSET ROOF MEMBRANE

TAPERED EDGE STRIP

THERMAL INSULATION

ROOF DECK

EXTEND FIELD SHEET TO BELOW BLOCKING

CONTINUOUS CLEAT (FASTENED PER SINGLE-PLY TABLE 1)

1 1/2" [34mm] MIN. FOR BALLASTED SYSTEMS

1" [25mm] MIN. BELOW BLOCKING

NOTES:

1. NRCA SUGGESTS AVOIDING (WHERE POSSIBLE) FLASHING DETAILS THAT REQUIRE RIGID METAL FLANGES TO BE EMBEDDED OR SANDWICHED INTO THE ROOF MEMBRANE.
2. THIS DETAIL SHOULD BE USED ONLY WHERE THE DECK IS SUPPORTED BY THE OUTSIDE WALL.
3. ATTACH NAILER TO WALL WITH SUITABLE FASTENERS.
4. WOOD BLOCKING MAY BE SLOTTED FOR VENTING OF WET-FILL DECKS OR OTHER CONSTRUCTIONS WHERE APPLICABLE.
5. FREQUENT NAILING OF SHEET METAL FLANGE IS NECESSARY TO MINIMIZE THERMAL MOVEMENT.
6. REFER TO SINGLE-PLY TABLE 1 FOR METAL THICKNESS AND CLEAT REQUIREMENT.
7. TOP LAYER OF INSULATION CAN BE EITHER THERMAL INSULATION OR COVERBOARD INSULATION.

Courtesy of National Roofing Contractors Association, NRCA Roofing & Waterproofing Manual

Figure 8.40

Gutter & Flashing—Modified Bitumen Roofing

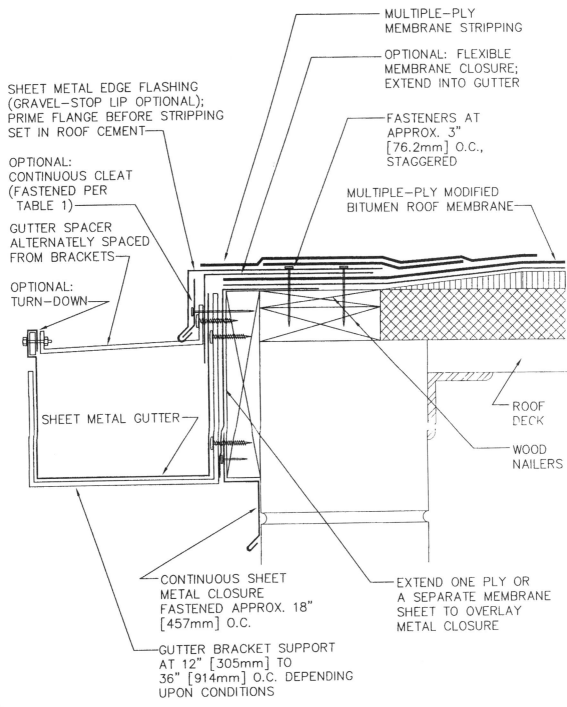

MULTIPLE-PLY
MEMBRANE STRIPPING

OPTIONAL: FLEXIBLE
MEMBRANE CLOSURE;
EXTEND INTO GUTTER

FASTENERS AT
APPROX. 3"
[76.2mm] O.C.,
STAGGERED

MULTIPLE-PLY MODIFIED
BITUMEN ROOF MEMBRANE

SHEET METAL EDGE FLASHING
(GRAVEL-STOP LIP OPTIONAL);
PRIME FLANGE BEFORE STRIPPING
SET IN ROOF CEMENT

OPTIONAL:
CONTINUOUS CLEAT
(FASTENED PER
TABLE 1)

GUTTER SPACER
ALTERNATELY SPACED
FROM BRACKETS

OPTIONAL:
TURN-DOWN

SHEET METAL GUTTER

ROOF
DECK

WOOD
NAILERS

CONTINUOUS SHEET
METAL CLOSURE
FASTENED APPROX. 18"
[457mm] O.C.

GUTTER BRACKET SUPPORT
AT 12" [305mm] TO
36" [914mm] O.C. DEPENDING
UPON CONDITIONS

EXTEND ONE PLY OR
A SEPARATE MEMBRANE
SHEET TO OVERLAY
METAL CLOSURE

NOTES:

1. IN CLIMATES WHERE THE WINTER TEMPERATURE REMAINS BELOW FREEZING FOR EXTENDED PERIODS OF TIME, NRCA SUGGESTS USING BUR-1 AND INTERIOR DRAINS OR THROUGH-CURB SCUPPERS TO DRAIN THE ROOF.
2. GUTTER BRACKETS ARE RECOMMENDED TO BE AT LEAST ONE GAUGE HEAVIER THAN GUTTER STOCK.
3. ATTACH WOOD NAILER TO WALL/DECK WITH SUITABLE FASTENERS.
4. DESIGN GUTTER EXPANSION JOINTS PLACED AT APPROPRIATE INTERVALS COMMENSURATE WITH TYPE OF METAL

Courtesy of National Roofing Contractors Association, *NRCA Roofing & Waterproofing Manual*

Figure 8.41

On certain prefabricated metal roof hatches, skylight assemblies, and other roof-mounted curbed units, or on equipment that has a relatively short, built-in metal counterflashing flange, it may be necessary to attach an additional sheet metal counterflashing "skirt." In certain climates and geographic regions a sheet metal skirt is useful to extend the premanufactured counterflashing, so as to ensure adequate overlap of the membrane base flashing, thus restricting wind driven rain and snow from entering the roof assembly.

Since metals generally have a high coefficient of expansion, metal flashing must be isolated from the roof membrane wherever possible to prevent metal movement from fatiguing and/or splitting the membrane. NRCA suggests avoiding (where possible), flashing details that require metal flanges to be embedded or sandwiched into the roof membrane.

For all walls that receive membrane base flashing, metal counterflashing should be installed in or on the wall above the base flashing. NRCA suggests the design of this counterflashing detail consist of separate reglet and counterflashing pieces, allowing installation of the sheet metal counterflashing after the membrane base flashing is complete. Projects where single-piece counterflashing has been installed will be difficult to base flash properly during future reroofing, and when membrane flashing maintenance is necessary, without deforming the metal. Sheet metal is not recommended to be used as an embedded base flashing material with bituminous and certain other membrane roof designs where differential movement may attribute to fatiguing, cracking, or splitting of the aging, weathering membrane.

When precast walls are used, the designer should carefully consider the flashing provisions required to properly interface the roof to the precast wall units. Cast-in raggles (often mistakenly called reglets), frequently used for this purpose, are difficult to align. When they are not aligned, they hinder the proper installation of sheet metal reglets and counterflashing components. For this reason the use of cast-in raggles is not recommended. In all such flashing situations, consideration should be given to camber, creep, and the independent thermal movement of the walls, roof membrane, and flashings.

For non-wall-supported roof decks, the membrane base flashing should be fastened to a vertical wood upright whose horizontal base is attached to the deck only. After the membrane base flashing has been attached to the wood upright, the metal counterflashing can extend down over the top of the base flashing. This method allows independent movement of the wall and metal flashings without damage to the roof membrane and membrane base flashing.

Metal cap flashing or coping is often used to cover the top of a wall in lieu of masonry copings. In some cases (e.g., with intermediate-height parapet walls) metal counterflashing is attached to the inside face of metal cap flashing.

When used, metal gravel stops should be raised above the waterline or surface of the roof by using tapered wood blocking and edge strips. The metal flanges of metal gravel stops should be set on top of the completed roof membrane, and be fastened at approximately 3 inches (76 mm) on center to the perimeter wood nailer. The metal flange should then be stripped-in with membrane flashing plies or stripping plies.

Plumbing soil pipe stacks and all other pipe projections through the membrane require metal flashing collars or membrane pipe flashing "boots." Metal flashing flanges should be stripped-in with membrane flashing plies or strips.

Slope & Pitch

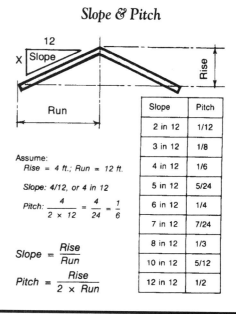

Courtesy of John Wiley & Sons, Inc., *Construction Principles, Materials, and Methods*

Figure 8.42

Chimney Flashing

Tile Roof Flashing

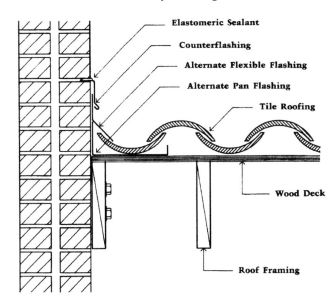

Ed. Note: For more information, see "Tile Roofing" earlier in this chapter.

R.S. Means Co., Inc., *Roofing: Design Criteria, Options, Selection*

Figure 8.43

Reroofing

UBC — 1997

Section 1515 — Inspection and Written Approval

1515.1 Written Approval Required. New roofing shall not be applied without first obtaining written approval from the building official.

The building official may allow existing roof coverings to remain when inspection or other evidence reveals all of the following:

1. The roof structure is sufficient to sustain the weight of the additional dead load of the new roofing.
2. The roof deck is structurally sound.
3. Roof drains and drainage are sufficient to prevent extensive accumulation of water.
4. The existing roofing is securely attached to the deck.
5. Existing insulation is not water soaked.
6. Fire-retardant requirements are maintained.

1515.2 Required Inspections.

1515.2.1 Preroofing inspection. Inspection prior to the installation of new roofing must be obtained from the building official to verify the existing roofing meets all the conditions in Section 1515.1. The building official may accept an inspection report of above-listed conditions prepared by a special inspector.

1515.2.2 Final inspection. A final inspection and approval shall be obtained from the building official when the reroofing is complete.

Section 1516 — Reroofing Overlays Allowed

1516.1 General. No roof shall have in any combination more than that allowed in Table A-15-A. Roofing conforming to Section 1503 overlaid on existing roofing shall comply with the provisions of this section and manufacturer's installation requirements as an overlay when approved by the building official.

1516.2 Overlay on existing built-up roofs. The building official may allow reroofing over existing built-up roofing when the conditions specified in Section 1515.1 have been met. When an existing built-up roof has been removed and prior to application of new roofing on a nailable deck that has residual bitumen, rosin-sized or other dry sheet shall be installed. Prior to the application of any reroofing, the existing surface shall be prepared as follows:

1. **Gravel-surfaced roofing.** Not more than one overlay shall be approved over an existing built-up roof. The existing built-up roof shall be cleaned of all loose gravel and debris. All blisters, buckles and other irregularities shall be cut and made smooth and secure. On nonnailable decks, minimum 3/8-inch (9.5 mm) insulation board shall be securely cemented to the existing roofing with hot bitumen after the existing surface has been adequately primed.

On nailable decks, a rosin-sized or other dry sheet shall be installed and a base sheet shall be mechanically fastened in place.

2. **Smooth or cap-sheet surface.** Not more than one overlay shall be applied over an existing built-up roof. All blisters, buckles and other irregularities of existing built-up roof shall be cut and made smooth and secure. On nonnailable decks, a base sheet shall be spot cemented to the existing roof. On nailable decks, a base sheet shall be mechanically fastened in place and where residual materials on the existing surface may cause the new base sheet to adhere to the old roof, a rosin-sized or other dry sheet shall be installed under the new base sheet.

3. **Intersecting walls.** All concrete and masonry walls shall be completely cleaned and primed to receive new flashing. All other walls shall have the surface finish material removed to a minimum height of 6 inches (152 mm) above the new roof deck surface to receive new roofing and flashing. All rotted wood shall be replaced with new material. Surface finish material shall be replaced or reinstalled.

4. **Parapets.** Parapets of area separation walls shall have noncombustible faces, including counterflashing and coping materials.

   Exception: Combustible roofing may extend 7 inches (178 mm) above the roof surface.

5. **Cant strips.** Where space permits, cant strips shall be installed at all angles. All angles shall be flashed with at least two more layers than in the new roof with an exposed finish layer of inorganic felt or mineral surfaced cap sheet.

6. **Asphalt and wood shingle application.** Not more than one overlay of asphalt shingles shall be applied over one existing built-up roof on structures with a slope of 2 units vertical in 12 units horizontal (16.7% slope) or greater. Not more than one overlay of wood shingles shall be applied over one existing built-up roof on structures with a slope of 3 units vertical in 12 units horizontal (25% slope) or greater. The existing built-up roof shall have all surfaces cleaned of gravel and debris, all blisters and irregularities cut and made smooth and secure, and an underlayment of not less than Type 30 nonperforated felt shall be installed prior to reroofing.

7. **Spray-applied polyurethane foam application.** Spray-applied polyurethane foam may be applied directly to existing built-up roofing systems when the completed assembly is a Class A, B, or C fire-retardant roofing assembly and complies with Section 2602.5.3. When applied on a fire-resistive roof-ceiling assembly, the completed assembly shall also comply with Section 710.1.

   Base sheets or dry sheets are not required over existing surfaces when applying spray polyurethane foam roofing systems.

Miscellaneous materials such as adhesives, elastomeric caulking compounds, metal, vents and drains shall be a composite part of the roof system.

1516.3 Overlay on existing wood roofs or asphalt shingle roofs. The building official may allow reroofing over existing wood shingle roofing or asphalt shingle roofing. Only fire-retardant roofing assemblies or noncombustible roof covering may be applied over existing wood shake roofs, in accordance with the listing or manufacturer's installation requirements, when approved by the building official.

When the application of new roofing over existing wood shingle or wood shake roofs creates a combustible concealed space, the entire existing surface shall be covered with gypsum board, mineral fiber, glass fiber or other approved materials securely fastened in place. Hip and ridge cover on existing shake or shingle roofing shall be removed prior to reroofing application. Roofing overlays may be installed in accordance with the following:

1. **Asphalt shingles.** Not more than two overlays of asphalt shingles shall be applied over an existing asphalt or wood shingle roof. Asphalt shingles applied over wood shingles shall not have less than Type 30 nonperforated felt underlayment installed prior to reroofing.

2. **Wood shakes.** Not more than one overlay of wood shakes shall be applied over an existing asphalt shingle or wood shingle roofing on structures with a slope of 4 units vertical in 12 units horizontal (33% slope) or greater. One layer of 18-inch (457 mm), Type 30 nonperforated felt shall be shingled between each course in such a manner that no felt is exposed to the weather below the shake butts.

3. **Wood shingles.** Not more than one overlay of wood shingles shall be applied over existing wood or asphalt shingles. Wood shingles applied over asphalt shingles shall not have less than Type 30 nonperforated felt underlayment installed prior to reroofing.

Section 1517 — Tile

Tile may be applied to roofs with a slope of 4 units vertical in 12 units horizontal (33% slope) or greater over existing roof coverings in accordance with Table A-15-A. (See **Figure 8.44**.) Such installations shall be substantiated by a report prepared by an engineer or architect licensed by the state to practice as such, indicating that the existing or modified framing system is adequate to support the additional tile roof covering.

Tile shall be applied in accordance with the original manufacturer's specifications or when the original manufacturer's specifications are no longer available, in accordance with Section 1507.7.

Tile may be repaired to match the prior installation except that clay and terra-cotta hips and ridge tile shall be reinstalled with portland cement mortar.

Allowable Reroofs Over Existing Roofing (Inspection and Written Approval Required Prior to Application)

EXISTING ROOFING	NEW OVERLAY ROOFING							
	Built Up	Wood Shake	Wood Shingle	Asphalt Shingle	Tile Roof	Metal Roof	Modified Bitumen	Spray Polyurethane Foam
Built Up	Yes	NP	Yes (3:12)	Yes (2:12)	Yes (2.5:12)	Yes	Yes	Yes
Wood Shake[1]	NP	NP	NP	NP	Yes[2]	Yes[2]	NP	NP
Wood Shingle[1]	NP	Yes[3] (4:12)	Yes[4]	Yes[4]	Yes[2]	Yes[2]	NP	NP
Asphalt Shingle[1]	NP	Yes[3] (4:12)	Yes[4] (3:12)	Yes	Yes (2.5:12)	Yes	Yes	NP
Asphalt over Wood	NP	NP	NP	Yes	Yes[2]	Yes[2]	Yes	NP
Asphalt over Asphalt	NP	NP	NP	Yes	Yes	Yes	Yes	NP
Tile Roof	NP	NP	NP	NP	NP	NP	NP	NP
Metal Roof	NP	NP	NP	NP	NP	Yes	NP	NP
Modified Bitumen	Yes	NP	Yes (3:12)	Yes	Yes (2.5:12)	Yes	Yes	NP

NP = Not Permitted.
Note: (Minimum Roof Slope)
[1]See Section 1515.2 for specific requirements.
[2]Board and batten leveling system must be firestopped in accordance with Section 1516.3.
[3]One layer 18-inch (457 mm) Type 30 nonperforated felt interlaced between shake courses required.
[4]Type 30 nonperforated felt underlayment required for reroofing.

Courtesy of ICBO, UBC — 1997, [Table A–15–A]

Figure 8.44

Section 1518 — Metal Roof Covering

Metal roof covering may be applied over existing roofing in accordance with Table A-15-A. Reroofing with metal roof covering shall be in accordance with the original manufacturer's specifications or when the original manufacturer's specifications are no longer available as required by Section 1507.8.

Section 1519 — Other Roofing

Reroofing with systems not covered elsewhere in Chapter 15 or this appendix, such as, but not limited to, those that are fluid applied or applied as nonasphaltic sheets, shall be done with materials and procedures approved by the building official.

Section 1520 — Flashing and Edging

Missing, rusted or damaged flashing and counterflashing, vent caps, and metal edging shall be installed or replaced with new materials. When existing built-up roofs remain, vent flashing, metal edging, drain outlets, metal counterflashing and collars shall be removed and cleaned. All metal allowed to be reinstalled shall be primed prior to reroofing installation. Collars and flanges shall be flashed per the roofing manufacturer's instructions.

Siding

Industry Standards
Plan Reading & Material Takeoff
(R.S. Means Co., Inc.)

Air Infiltration Barriers

Air infiltration barriers provide resistance to drafts caused by wind and water penetration. Air barriers are installed at the exterior of the sidewall sheathing under the exterior siding. There are a variety of products available, such as asphalt felt paper and synthetic wraps (such as TYVEK® Housewrap). The efficiency of the building insulation is influenced by humidity (moisture in the air) and the exterior temperature. The best possible scenario is to have a drywall cavity free from moisture; however, the building needs to "breathe."

The contractor should refer to the architectural wall sections for the location, and the exterior elevations for the limits of air infiltration barriers. Specifications should be reviewed for the particular product(s) required.

Comments

Air infiltration barriers should be in place and properly lapped before exterior windows, doors and trim are installed. This is critical to ensure that the vertical joints created between the exterior window casing (or trim) and the sheathing are sealed. Otherwise, moisture may be driven into the sheathing. The air infiltration barrier should be lapped in the direction that water naturally flows.

Consult manufacturers' recommendations regarding allowable time between application of the air infiltration barrier and the application of siding. The integrity of air infiltration barrier materials can be compromised by prolonged exposure to sunlight.

Leaks or excess condensation may occur on the inside of the building in cases where the contractor failed to use an air infiltration barrier, or did not install this material behind the window casings. See Chapter 9, "Windows & Doors," for more information on flashing.

Caulking and Sealants

Sealants and caulking compounds are used to provide a water, vapor, and air barrier between joints or gaps of adjacent but dissimilar materials. A classic example is the joint between a steel door frame and a masonry wall opening. Caulking and sealants are manufactured for a full range of applications, such as interior or exterior use, ability to expand and contract, service temperature range, paintability, and compatibility with the material to be sealed.

Joint sealants are normally applied over a backup material that controls the depth of the joint. They serve as bond breaks to allow free movement of the joint and prevent water penetration. The backup material, called *backer rod*, is available in a variety of compositions, such as butyl, neoprene, polyethylene, or rubber.

The contractor should refer to the architectural drawings, specifically elevations, wall sections, and details that show window and exterior door installations. Refer to the specifications for the appropriate location and type of caulking and sealants needed and their respective application.

Wood Siding

Industry Standards
Plan Reading & Material Takeoff
(R.S. Means Co., Inc.)

Wood siding is usually milled of wood species that can withstand extreme variations of weather. Redwood and cedar are two moisture-resistant woods used for board and sheet siding, as well as for shingles. Fir and pine are also used for board and sheet siding, but they must be finished with stain or paint after installation. Man-made material can also qualify for exterior applications. For example, hardboard and medium-density-overlay products can be used, but they also must be painted or stained. Plywood sheet siding is manufactured with waterproof glue to provide weather protection.

Watertight installation of siding is essential. Cedar and redwood clapboard siding are beveled in widths from 4" to 10". Proper installation dictates that upper boards should overlap the lower boards by a minimum of 1" and be nailed through plywood-sheathing backup to wall studs. Horizontal boards are butted and caulked into vertical corner boards at exterior and interior corners.

Vertical tongue-and-groove board siding is blind-nailed together through the sheathing to horizontal blocking spaced at 24" on center. It is manufactured in widths from 4" to 12" on center. Channel and shiplap board siding are also lapped, but are face-nailed to the blocking. Vertical boards are installed with a 1/2" joint between the boards and are held in place with a nailed batten strip. All vertical board siding should extend to the corners and be overlapped with corner boards. Vertical siding is usually interrupted at floors with a horizontal wood beltline and flashing strip, or flashing strip alone.

Plywood sheet siding can be installed directly to the stud wall, without sheathing, and nailed along all panel edges and intermediate stud supports. Vertical edges can be lapped, battened, or simply butted and caulked. Horizontal joints are usually flashed.

Clapboard siding comes in the better grades of cedar and redwood, i.e., B, A, and clear grade. Rough sawn and channel cedar are available in no. 3 grade and better.

Comments

Humidity can cause some buckling in installed clapboard siding. Refer to Residential Construction Performance Guidelines, published by the National Association of Home Builders, for an interpretation of allowable tolerances for bowing and buckling, end gaps, and straightness of siding.

Wood Shingles: Installation

Industry Standards

Cedar Shake & Shingle Bureau
(Cedar Bureau Internet Web Site: www.cedarbureau.org)

Ed. Note: The **Cedar Shake & Shingle Bureau** *recommends a procedure (summarized in the following paragraphs) for applying siding to a new exterior wall.*

- **Preparation:** Be sure that the walls are smooth, without protuberances. Nail ends or points should be removed or pounded flush.

- **Building paper:** An approved paper should be applied over the sheathing. Apply it horizontally with a staple gun, starting at the base of the wall, with a 2" horizontal overlap with each succeeding course, and a 6" overlap vertically when starting a new roll. Wrap the paper 4" each way around both inside and outside corners.

- **Corner Boards:** Install corner boards at this time. (See **Figure 8.50.**)

- **Flashing:** Install flashing and caulking over doors, windows, and other points of potential water entry.

- **Laying Out:** (Determining the number of courses and laying them out on all other walls.) Whenever possible, butt lines should align with tops or bottoms of windows or other openings, and for appearance the exposure of the final course at the top should match those below. (See **Figure 8.47.**)

Wood Shingle Siding

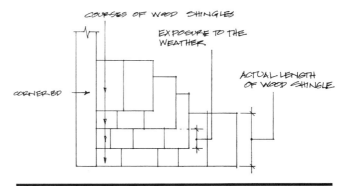

R.S. Means Co., Inc., *Plan Reading & Material Takeoff*

Figure 8.46

Clapboard Siding

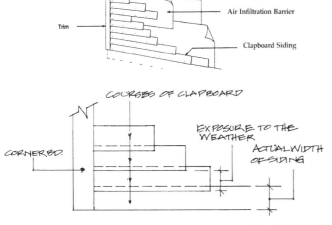

R.S. Means Co., Inc., *Plan Reading & Material Takeoff*

Figure 8.45

Storypole

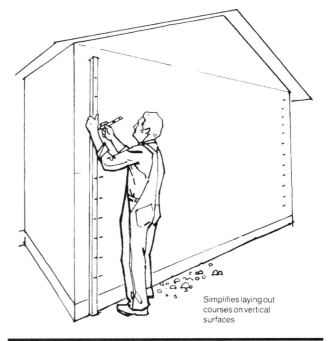

Simplifies laying out courses on vertical surfaces

Source: Cedar Shake & Shingle Bureau, www.cedarbureau.org

Figure 8.47

Single Coursing: Double the starting course at the base of the wall. Apply with 1/8" to 1/4" vertical space between shingles allowing for expansion. Primed shingles can be butted close together. A natural shingle, if applied with tight joints, should be primed or stained soon after application to prevent buckling due to expansion caused by moisture absorption. (See **Figure 8.48.**)

Double Coursing: The maximum weather exposures recommended for #1 grade shingles are 12" for 16" shingles, 14" for 18" shingles, and 16" for 24" shingles. With shakes, the #1 grade 18" lengths can be laid at weather exposures up to 14" and 24", shakes up to 18".

Corners: It is standard practice to lace outside corners. On wide exposures this method requires small nails near the shingle butts to tighten and hold the lapped corners. Use only nails that are corrosion resistant. Corner boards also can be used to advantage by nailing 1" x 4" cedar board to a 1" x 3" cedar board, then attaching the preassembled corner to the building. It is good practice to use flashing behind shingles or shakes at the inside corners. (See **Figure 8.50.**)

Staggered Coursing Apply the shingle irregularly at variable distances below (but not above) the horizontal line. Maximum distances are 1" for 16" and 18" shingles, and 1-1/2" for 24" shingles.

Ribbon Coursing A double shadow line effect can be obtained by raising the outer course shingles approximately 1" above the undercoursing. Use #1 grade for undercoursing when applying ribbon coursing.

Non-Wood Sheathing

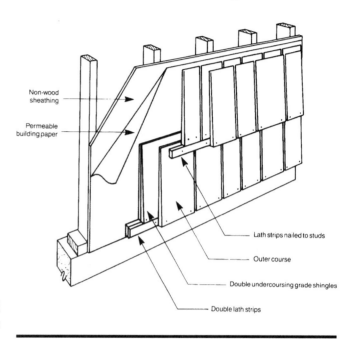

Source: Cedar Shake & Shingle Bureau, www.cedarbureau.org

Figure 8.49

Spacing Details

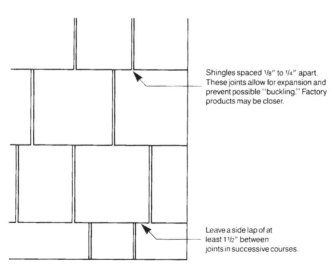

Shingles spaced 1/8" to 1/4" apart. These joints allow for expansion and prevent possible "buckling." Factory products may be closer.

Leave a side lap of at least 1 1/2" between joints in successive courses.

Source: Cedar Shake & Shingle Bureau, www.cedarbureau.org

Figure 8.48

Corner Details

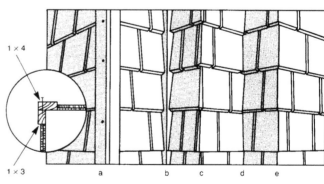

a) Shingles butted against corner boards
b) Shingles butted against square wood strip on inside corner, flashing behind
c) Laced outside corner
d) Laced inside corner with flashing behind
e) Mitered corner

Source: Cedar Shake & Shingle Bureau, www.cedarbureau.org

Figure 8.50

Bevel Siding: Installation

Industry Standards

Western Red Cedar Lumber Association
(WRCLA Internet Web Site: www.wrcla.org)

Spacing for the siding should be laid out beforehand. The number of board spaces between the soffit and bottom of the lowest piece of siding at the foundation should be such that the minimum overlap is not less than 1". (See table below.)

Recommended Overlap for Bevel Siding	
Normal Width (in.)	Overlap (In.)
4	1
6	1
8	1–1–1/8
10	1–1–1/2
12	1–2 max*

*Use for unseasoned 10 in. bevel siding.

Notes: Do not exceed 2 in. overlap. Use the larger overlaps for unseasoned sidings to allow for shrinkage and expansion. Take care not to overdrive fasteners when using larger overlaps.

Start with the bottom course using a furring strip to support the lower edge. Each succeeding course overlaps the upper edge of the previous one by a minimum of 1". Rabbeted patterns are self-spacing, but leave 1/8 in. expansion clearance. Where possible, the bottom of the board that is placed across the top of the windows should coincide with the window cap.

Bevel siding should be face nailed to studs with 1-1/2" penetration into solid wood using one nail per bearing spaced at a maximum of 24" on center. Place nail just above the 1" overlap. Take care not to nail through the overlap of two pieces.

Butt joints between boards should be staggered and made on studs. Fit snugly to other pieces and to trim and flashing. Ends should be caulked.

Bevel Siding Dimensions (Seasoned)		
Thickness (in.)	Nominal Width (in.)	Finished Width (in.)
1/2	4, 6, 8	3-1/2, 5-1/2, 7-1/2
5/8	6, 8	5-1/2, 7-1/2
3/4	6, 8, 10	5-1/2, 7-1/2, 9-1/2
7/8	10, 12	9-1/2, 11-1/2
5/4	8, 10, 12	7-1/2, 9-1/2, 11-1/2

Siding: Brick Veneer

Industry Standards

Means Graphic Construction Standards
(R.S. Means Co., Inc.)

Brick is among the most popular of wall materials because it is durable, economical to maintain, readily available in most areas, and varied in size and color. Also, brick can be installed rapidly with local labor and with a limited number of specialized tools and equipment. Brick can be used alone in single wythe walls or as the facing material in composite or cavity walls. Although the insulating value of a single wythe brick wall is a low 1.6R rating, it has the relatively high fire rating of one hour.

Because brick walls are not waterproof, provisions must be made to limit the amount of water penetration through the exterior face. Flashing should be installed at the junction of walls and floors, as well as over and under openings. In cavity walls, the outside face of the backup wall or the insulation between the wythes should be waterproofed. Weepholes should be located above the flashing at brick shelves, relieving angles, and lintels to provide a means of escape for moisture that has penetrated the wall.

Brick Veneer with Wood Frame Construction

Industry Standards

Technical Note 28 — Anchored Brick Veneer, Wood Frame Construction
(Brick Industry Association Internet Web Site: www.bia.org)

Ed. Note: The following excerpts from the Brick Industry Association's Technical Note 28 apply to new construction of buildings no more than three stories high. The excerpts describe the brick veneer/wood stud system, selection of materials, construction details, and workmanship techniques. For the complete Technical Note 28, contact the Brick Industry Association directly (see the Introduction to this chapter for the association's address, telephone number, and Web site).

According to the BIA, the minimum requirements given have proven successful for this type of wall construction.

Anchored brick veneer construction consists of a nominal 3" (75 mm) or 4" (100 mm) thick exterior brick wythe anchored to a backing system with metal ties in such a way that a clear air space is provided between the veneer and the backing system. The backing system may be wood frame, steel frame, concrete or masonry. By definition, a veneer wall is a wall having a facing of masonry units, or other weather-resisting, noncombustible materials, securely attached to the backing, but not so bonded as to intentionally exert common action under load. The brick veneer is designed to carry loads due to its own weight, no other loads are to be resisted by the veneer.

The minimum requirements given in this *Technical Notes* are based on successful past performance of brick veneer anchored to wood frame systems. The proper design, detailing and construction of anchored brick veneer walls ensure that these walls function as complete systems. It is important to understand that the failure of any part of the system, whether in design or construction, can result in improper performance of the entire system. Satisfactory performance of brick veneer wood frame systems is achieved with: (1) an adequate foundation, (2) a sufficiently strong, rigid, well-braced backing system, (3) proper attachment of the veneer to the backing system, (4) proper detailing, (5) the use of proper materials, and (6) good workmanship in construction.

Brick Veneer/Metal Stud Backup Wall System

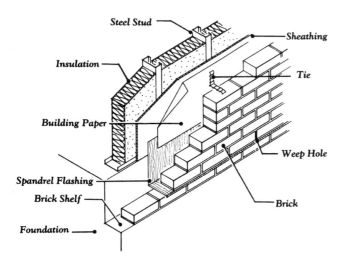

Brick Veneer/Wood Stud Backup System

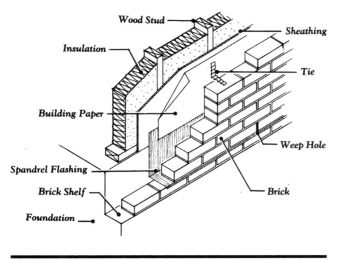

R.S. Means Co., Inc., *Means Graphic Construction Standards*
Figure 8.51

DESIGN & DETAILS: Foundations for Brick Veneer

Brick veneer with wood frame backing must transfer the weight of the veneer to the foundation. The foundation or foundation wall supporting the brick veneer should be at least equal to the total thickness of the brick veneer wall assembly. Many building codes permit a nominal 8" (200 mm) foundation wall under single-family dwellings constructed of brick veneer, provided the top of the foundation wall is corbeled. The total projection of the corbel should not exceed 2" (50 mm) with individual courses projecting beyond the course below, not more than one-third the thickness of the unit nor one-half the height of the unit. The top course of the corbel should not be higher than the bottom of the floor joist and shall be a full header course.

Foundations must extend beneath the frost line as required by the local building code. Design of the foundation should consider differential settlement and the effect of concentrated loads such as those from columns or fireplaces. Appropriate drainage must be provided in order to maintain soil bearing capacity and prevent washout.

Brick walls which enclose crawl spaces must have openings to provide adequate ventilation. Openings should be located to achieve cross ventilation.

DESIGN & DETAILS: Ties

There should be one tie for every 2-2/3 sq. ft. (0.25 m²) of wall area with a maximum spacing of 24 in. (600 mm) o.c. in either direction. The nail attaching a corrugated tie must be located within 5/8 in. (16 mm) of the bend in the tie. The best location of the nail is at the bend in the corrugated tie, and the bend should be 90°.

Wire ties must be embedded at least 5/8 in. (16 mm) into the bed joint from the air space and must have at least 5/8 in. (16 mm) cover of mortar to the exposed face. Corrugated ties must penetrate to at least half the veneer thickness and have at least 5/8 in. (16 mm) cover. Ties should be placed so that the portion within the bed joint is completely surrounded by the mortar.

DESIGN & DETAILS: Flashing and Weepholes

Flashing and weepholes should be located above and as near to grade as possible at the bottom of the wall, above all openings, and beneath sills. Weepholes must be located in the head joints immediately above all flashing. Clear, open weepholes should be spaced no more than 24 in. (600 mm) o.c. Weepholes formed with wick materials or with tubes should be spaced at a maximum of 16 in. (400 mm) o.c. If the veneer continues below the flashing at the base of the wall, the space between the veneer and the backing should be grouted to the height of the flashing. Flashing should be securely fastened to the backing system and extend through the face of the brick veneer. The flashing should be turned up at least 8 in. (200 mm). Flashing should be carefully installed to prevent punctures or tears. Where several pieces of flashing are required to flash a section of the veneer, the ends of the flashing should be lapped a minimum of 6 in. (150 mm) and the joints properly sealed. Where the flashing is not continuous, such as over and under openings in the wall, the ends of the flashing should be turned up into the head joint at least 2 in. (50 mm) to form a dam.

DESIGN & DETAILS: Lintels, Sills and Jambs

Brick veneer backed by wood frame must always be supported by lintels over openings unless the masonry is self-supporting. Lintel design information may be found in *Technical Notes* 17H and 31B. Loose steel, stone or precast lintels should bear at least 4 in. (100 mm) at each jamb. All lintels should have space at the end of the lintel to allow for expansion. The clear span for 1/4 in. (6.3 mm) thick steel angles varies between 5 ft. (1.5 m) and a maximum of 8 ft. (2.4 m), depending on the size of the angle selected. Steel lintels with spans greater than 8 ft. (2.4 m) may require lateral bracing for stability. The maximum clear span may be restricted by the fire protection requirements of some building codes. Concrete, cast stone and stone lintels must be appropriately sized to carry the weight of the veneer.

Reinforced brick lintels are also a viable option. Some of the advantages of reinforced brick lintels are: more efficient use of materials; built-in fireproofing; elimination of differential movement which may occur with steel lintels and brick veneer; and no required painting or other maintenance.

DESIGN & DETAILS: Eave Details

Residential eave detail is suggested for the area at the top of the veneer. The air space between the top of the brick veneer and wood framing is necessary to accommodate movement. Larger overhangs and gutters are helpful to keep water from contacting the wall below.

DESIGN & DETAILS: Movement Provisions

Design provisions for movement which include bond breaks, expansion joints, and joint reinforcement are not usually required in residential and low-rise brick veneer construction. However, they may be required in specific situations and the designer should analyze the project to determine such need.

Bond Breaks. Significant differential foundation settlement and horizontal movement may cause cracking in walls rigidly attached to the foundation. Bond breaks will help to relieve the stresses caused by these movements between the wall and the supporting foundation. Flashing at the base of the wall between the veneer and the foundation will provide sufficient break in the bond.

Expansion Joints. Expansion joints to allow for horizontal movement may be required in brick veneer when there are long walls, walls with returns, or large openings. The placement of expansion joints and the materials used should be in accordance with the information given in *Technical Notes* 18 Series.

DESIGN & DETAILS: Horizontal Joint Reinforcement

Masonry materials subject to shrinkage stresses, such as concrete masonry, require horizontal joint reinforcement for control of cracking from such movement. Brick is *not* subject to shrinkage, therefore horizontal joint reinforcement is never required in brick masonry for this purpose. It may be beneficial to use limited amounts of horizontal joint reinforcement in brick veneer for added strength at the corners of openings and at locations where running bond in the masonry is not maintained.

Horizontal joint reinforcement should be used to add integrity to veneer constructed in locations with intermediate and higher seismic activity or when the units are laid in stack bond. It may be either single- or double-wire joint reinforcement. In seismically active areas, the wire should engage the veneer ties. When using horizontal joint reinforcement, it *must* be discontinuous at *all* movement joints.

DESIGN & DETAILS: Sealant Joints

Exterior joints at the perimeter of exterior door and window frames to be filled with sealant should be formed by the adjacent materials or be a reservoir type joint. The joint should be no less than 1/4 in. (6.3 mm) nor more than 1/2 in. (12.7 mm) wide and 1/4 in. (6.33 mm) deep. If wider joints are required, the sealant depth should be one-half of the joint width. A compressible backer rod or sealant bond break tape must be used. Fillet joints are not recommended, but if used, should be at least 1/2 in. (12.7 mm) across the diagonal. Sealant joints should be solidly filled with an elastic sealant forced into place with a pressure gun. All joints should be properly prepared before placing sealants. Appropriate primers should be applied as necessary. Expansion joints must be clear of all material for the thickness of the veneer wythe and closed with a backer rod and sealant.

MATERIALS: Flashing and Weepholes

There are many types of flashing available which are suitable for use in brick veneer walls. Sheet metals, plastics, laminates or combinations of these have been used successfully. Plastic flashing should be at least 30 mil thick. Asphalt impregnated felt (building paper) or air-infiltration barrier is *not* acceptable for use as flashing. These materials serve other purposes in the wall assembly. Building paper is applied as a moisture barrier to the sheathing. Air-infiltration barriers function as their name implies and may also serve as a moisture barrier.

Selection of flashing is often determined by cost; however, it is recommended that only superior materials be used, as replacement in the event of failure is exceedingly expensive.

Weepholes can be made in several ways. Some of the most common ways are leaving head joints open, using removable oiled ropes or rods, using plastic or metal tubes, or using rope wicks. There are also plastic or metal vents which are installed in lieu of mortar in a head joint. Clear openings without obstructions produce the best weepholes. For further discussion on flashing and weepholes see *Technical Notes* 7A.

MATERIALS: Horizontal Joint Reinforcement

Horizontal joint reinforcement should be fabricated from wire conforming to ASTM A 82. It should have a corrosion-resistant coating which conforms to ASTM A 153, Class B-2.

MATERIALS: Lintel Materials

Lintels may be reinforced brick masonry, reinforced concrete, stone or steel angles. Reinforcement for reinforced brick masonry lintels should be steel bars manufactured in accordance with ASTM A 615, A 616 or A 617, Grades 40, 50, 60 and should be at least No. 3 bar size. Joint reinforcement can also be used in reinforced brick masonry lintels.

Steel for lintels should conform to ASTM A 36 Standard Specification for Structural Steel. Steel angle lintels should be at least 1/4 in. (6.3 mm) thick with a horizontal leg of at least 3 1/2 in. (89 mm) for use with nominal 4 in. (100 mm) thick brick veneer, and 3 in. (75 mm) for use with nominal 3 in. (75 mm) thick brick veneer. Steel lintels should be painted before installation.

MATERIALS: Sealants

There are numerous types of sealants available that are suitable for use with brick veneer. The material selected should be flexible and durable. Superior sealants may have a higher initial cost, but their high flexibility and increased durability result in savings of maintenance costs due to the reduced frequency of reapplication. Good grades of polysulfide, butyl or silicone rubber sealants are recommended. Oil-based caulking compounds are *not* recommended since most lack the desired flexibility and durability, see *Technical Notes* 7A. Regardless of the type of sealant chose, proper primers and backer rods must be selected. Follow the recommendations of the sealant manufacturer.

CONSTRUCTION: Protection of Materials

Masonry. Prior to and during construction, all materials should be stored off of the ground to prevent contamination by mud, dust or other materials likely to cause stains or defects. The masonry materials should also be covered for protection against the elements.

To limit water absorption, it is recommended that all brick masonry be protected by covering at the end of each workday and for shutdown periods. The cover should be a strong, weather-resistant membrane securely attached to and overhanging the brickwork by at least 24 in. (600 mm). Partially completed masonry exposed to rain may become so saturated with water that it may require months after the completion of the building to dry out. This saturation may cause prolonged efflorescence. See *Technical Notes*, 23 Series, for more information.

Flashing. Flashing materials should be stored in places where they will not be punctured or damaged. Plastic and asphalt coated flashing materials should not be stored in areas exposed to sunlight. Ultraviolet rays from the sun break down these materials, causing them to become brittle with time. Plastic flashing exposed to the weather at the site for months before installation should not be used. During installation, flashing must be pliable so that no cracks occur at corners or bends.

CONSTRUCTION: Workmanship

Good workmanship is as essential in constructing brick veneer as it is in all types of brick masonry construction. All joints intended to receive mortar, including head joints with hollow brick, should be completely filled. Joints or spaces not intended to receive mortar should be kept clean and free of droppings. Courses of brick laid on foundations or lintels must have at least two-thirds of the brick thickness on the support.

The joints should be tooled with a jointer as soon as the mortar has become thumbprint hard. The types of joints recommended for exterior use with brick veneer are concave, "V" and grapevine. These joints firmly compact the mortar against the edges of the adjoining brick. Other joints are not recommended because they do not provide the necessary resistance to moisture penetration. See *Technical Notes*, 7B Revised, for further information.

It is essential when constructing brick veneer, to keep the 1 in. (25.4 mm) minimum air space between the veneer and the backing clean and free of all mortar droppings, so that the wall assembly will perform as a drainage wall. If mortar blocks the air space, it may provide a bridge for water to travel to the interior. In addition, all flashing, weepholes, ties and other accessories must be properly installed.

Brick Veneer: Moisture Control

Industry Standards
Technical Note 28 — Anchored Brick Veneer, Wood Frame Construction
(Brick Industry Association Internet Web Site: www.bia.org)

Brick veneer wall assemblies are classified as drainage type walls. Walls of this type provide good resistance to rain penetration. It is essential to maintain the clear air space between the brick veneer and the backing to ensure proper drainage. Flashing and weepholes work with the air space to provide moisture penetration resistance. Refer to *Technical Notes*, 7 Series, for more information. Brick veneer with wood frame backing has historically been built with a 1 in. (25 mm) minimum air space. The protection provided by roof overhangs and the relatively low wall heights aid in reducing water penetration.

Industry Standards
Technical Note 13 — Ceramic Glazed Brick Facing for Exterior Walls
(Brick Industry Association Internet Web Site: www.bia.org)

"Excessive moisture continuously gets into the walls and *must be eliminated before it causes trouble*. It usually enters as rain water (1) through the pores in building materials, (2) into incompletely bonded mortar joints, (3) around copings, sills, and belt courses, (4) as condensation of vapor from the interior of the structure (this action is more insidious and far-reaching than most people realize), (5) through capillary contact with the ground.

"Without water in the wall there would be little or no problem of masonry disintegration and disruption. The only ways to get rid of the excess moisture are (1) through continuous cavities within walls (hollow wall construction) with adequate weep holes at various locations in the wall, (2) by evaporation through the exterior of the masonry."

When exterior walls are faced with ceramic glazed brick or when an impervious coating is applied to the exterior face of walls, water cannot enter the walls through the pores of the brick nor can it escape by this means from the face of the wall. For this reason, it becomes especially important to reduce the water entering the wall to an absolute minimum and to provide positive means to escape for water that permeates the wall, either as rain or as condensed vapor. The amount of the water that may be expected to enter a wall as a result of rain varies with the exposure which may be defined roughly in terms of the resultant wind pressure and precipitation as follows:

Severe: Annual precipitation 30 in. or over; wind pressure 30 lb. per sq. ft. or over.

Moderate: Annual precipitation 30 in. or over; wind pressure 20 to 25 lb. per sq. ft..

Slight: Annual precipitation less than 30 in.; wind pressure 20 to 25 lb. per sq. ft. or annual precipitation less than 20 in.

The following recommendations covering wall design and construction are applicable to severe and moderate exposures as defined above.

Recommendations: Design
1. Cavity wall construction recommended.
2. For walls enclosing heated areas, provide vapor barrier on warm side of cavity.
3. For walls exposed on both sides; such as free-standing walls, wing walls and parapet walls; ventilate cavity.
4. Provide adequate flashing.
5. Provide adequate expansion joints (3/4" per 100 ft of wall) and an expansion joint on each side of each corner, located not more than 10' nor less than 4' from the corner.
6. Provide flexible anchorage to columns and beam.

Recommendations: Specifications
1. Specify highly plastic mortar; 1 cement: 1 type S lime: 6 sand or 1 cement: 1/2 S lime: 4 1/2 sand are recommended.
2. Specify full head and bed joints and that cavity be kept clean and weepholes open.
3. The Specifications of the Facing Tile Institute for Select Quality Ceramic Glaze Structural.
4. Facing Tile, dated November 1959, provide: "Where ceramic glaze units are required for exterior use, the manufacturers should be consulted for material suitable for this purpose."

Specifiers of ceramic glazed brick for exterior use are urged to comply with this recommendation and, in so doing, to indicate to the manufacturers the geographic location of the project, the type of construction, that is, enclosure walls, parapets, etc., and the wall design, including flashing details and mortar specified.

Brick Veneer: Methods of Thin Brick Installation
Industry Standards
Technical Note 28C — Thin Brick Veneer
(Brick Industry Association Internet Web Site: www.bia.org)

Adhered Veneer
Adhered veneer relies on a bonding agent between the thin brick units and the backup substrate. Adhered veneer construction may be classified as either thin bed set or thick bed set.

Thin Set. The thin bed set procedure typically utilizes an epoxy or organic adhesive, and is normally used on interior surfaces only. For areas subject to dampness, only clear and dry masonry surfaces or concrete surfaces should be used for backup. For dry locations, the backing material (substrate) may be wood, wallboard, masonry, etc.

Thick Set. The thick bed set procedure is used on interior and exterior surfaces. The backing material may be masonry, concrete, steel, or wood stud framing. The wire lath may be eliminated if the masonry wall is heavily scarified (sand-blasted). (Williams, Griffith, Jr., "New Bricklike Tile Veneer," *Building Standards*, July-August, 1982). For applications over steel studs, procedures are similar to those used for concrete or masonry backup; however, wallboard and building felt must be installed over the studs before lath and mortar bed are placed.

Comments

For further information on brick veneer tolerance, refer to sections 4-38, 4-40, and 5-22 in Residential Construction Performance Guidelines, *published by the National Association of Home Builders (Telephone: 800-368-5242).*

Stucco & EIFS Systems

Industry Standards

Means Graphic Construction Standards
(R.S. Means Co., Inc.)

Stucco is a facing material applied like plaster to the exterior of buildings to provide a decorative and weather-resistant surface. Stucco is usually a mixture of sand, cement, lime, and water, but it may be composed of patented mixes with manufactured additives.

Stucco mixes differ from plaster mixes because portland cement and lime are the basic ingredients in lieu of gypsum. Portland cement plasters are more difficult to trowel and finish, but are durable, relatively unaffected by water, and withstand repeated cycles of wetting, drying, freezing, and thawing.

The two common methods of applying stucco are the open-frame method and the direct-application system. In the open-frame method, the stucco is applied to galvanized metal lath attached directly to wood or steel studs. Three coats of stucco are normally required: (1) a scratch or first coat, (2) a brown or leveling coat, and (3) a finish coat.

The frame should be sufficiently braced to prevent movement. The flashings and drips should be carefully placed to prevent water penetration. Waterproof building paper applied over the studs or self-furring lath with integral waterproof paper are used for moisture protection. The system may also be waterproofed by backplastering or applying a coat of stucco on the interior side of the wall.

Directly applied stucco may be placed over sheathed wood or steel stud systems, or applied on concrete or masonry walls. One coat of stucco, with a bonding agent, or two coats of stucco may be used if the backing material possesses the surface characteristics required for adequate bonding. If the surface is not suitable for direct stucco application, the surface should first be covered with building paper and then furred with self-furring metal lath.

Exterior stucco is usually highly textured and coarse in appearance, to conceal staining and shrinkage cracks. Finish stucco coats may be tinted, painted, or treated with colorless coating materials to help prevent water penetration.

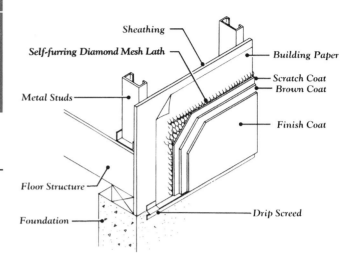

Stucco

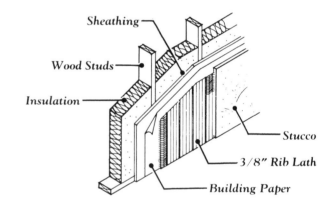

Stucco on Rib Lath

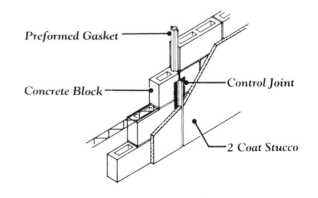

Stucco on Masonry

R.S. Means Co., Inc., *Means Graphic Construction Standards*

Figure 8.52

Exterior Lath

UBC — 1997

Section 1402 — Weather Protection

1402.1 Weather-resistive Barriers. All weather-exposed surfaces shall have a weather-resistive barrier to protect the interior wall covering. Such barrier shall be equal to that provided for in UBC Standard 14-1 for kraft waterproof building paper or asphalt-saturated rag felt. Building paper and felt shall be free from holes and breaks other than those created by fasteners and construction system due to attaching of the building paper, and shall be applied over studs or sheathing of all exterior walls. Such felt or paper shall be applied horizontally, with the upper layer lapped over the lower layer not less than 2 inches (51 mm). Where vertical joints occur, felt or paper shall be lapped not less than 6 inches (152 mm).

A weather-resistive barrier may be omitted in the following cases:

When exterior covering is of approved weatherproof panels.

In back-plastered construction.

When there is no human occupancy.

Over water-repellent panel sheathing.

Under approved paperbacked metal or wire fabric lath.

Behind lath and portland cement plaster applied to the underside of roof and eave projections.

1402.2 Flashing and Counterflashing. Exterior openings exposed to the weather shall be flashed in such a manner as to make them weatherproof.

All parapets shall be provided with coping of approved materials. All flashing, counterflashing and coping, when of metal, shall have a minimum thickness of 0.019-inch (0.48 mm) (No. 26 galvanized sheet metal gage) corrosion-resistant metal.

Section 2506 — Exterior Lath

2506.1 General. Exterior surfaces are weather-exposed surfaces as defined in Section 224. For eave overhangs required to be fire resistive, see Section 705.

2506.2 Corrosion Resistance. All lath and lath attachments shall be of corrosion-resistant material. See Section 2501.4.

2506.3 Backing. Backing or a lath shall provide sufficient rigidity to permit plaster application.

Where lath on vertical surfaces extends between rafters or other similar projecting members, solid backing shall be installed to provide support for lath and attachments.

Gypsum lath or gypsum board shall not be used, except that on horizontal supports of ceilings or roof soffits it may be used as backing for metal lath or wire fabric lath and cement plaster.

Backing is not required under metal lath or paperbacked wire fabric lath.

2506.4 Weather-resistive Barriers. Weather-resistive barriers shall be installed as required in Section 1402.1 and, when applied over wood base sheathing, shall include two layers of Grade D paper.

2506.5 Application of Metal Plaster Bases. The application of metal lath or wire fabric lath shall be as specified in Section 2505.3 and they shall be furred out from vertical supports or backing not less than 1/4 inch (6.4 mm) except as set forth in Table 25-B, Footnote 2.

Where no external corner reinforcement is used, lath shall be furred out and carried around corners at least one support on frame construction.

A minimum 0.019-inch (0.48 mm) (No. 26 galvanized sheet gage) corrosion-resistant weep screed with a minimum vertical attachment flange of 31/2 inches (89 mm) shall be provided at or below the foundation plate line on all exterior stud walls. The screed shall be placed a minimum of 4 inches (102 mm) above the earth or 2 inches (51 mm) above paved areas and shall be of a type that will allow trapped water to drain to the exterior of the building. The weather-resistive barrier shall lap the attachment flange, and the exterior lath shall cover and terminate on the attachment flange of the screed.

Comments

Horizontal Surfaces

Stucco can be used at the tops of walls and/or on patio and balcony railings. Good performance is dependent on plaster thickness and integrity, finishing, a proper weather barrier under the top, and adequate water control.

Moisture Barrier

To reduce the incidence of cracking, two layers of building paper are commonly used over the plywood sheathing. Moisture might enter the first layer, but the second layer tends to keep moisture from reaching the plywood, thereby minimizing expansion and contraction.

To maintain the integrity of the weather barrier, fasteners should not be installed on horizontal surfaces. Lath from the adjacent vertical surface should continue onto the horizontal surface. A weep screed is recommended where the vertical plaster ends on patio or balcony railings.

Plaster should be the same thickness over the cap as it is on the walls (generally 7/8"). Corner reinforcement, when used, must be embedded in a minimum of 1/8" of plaster to form a solid plaster corner. If nose wire is exposed, it can lead to corrosion and staining.

Application of acrylic polymer finish over the cap (the same color and texture as stucco) is recommended. This material is applied starting about 6" below the cap. It is applied across the horizontal surface, and should continue 6" down the other side.

Weep Screeds

Weep openings at the base of stucco walls are required by codes to eliminate water that may inadvertently reach the back plane of the stucco. (Water could enter as a result of missing or improperly installed flashing, or where dissimilar elements meet, such as stucco abutting wood).

Weep screeds must provide for free passage of water between the stucco termination and the "ground" (the part of the weep screed that extends outward from the vertical plane).

The weep screed ground (usually 3/4" or 7/8") provides a thickness gauge for plaster, and as well as a place where the plaster can be leveled out.

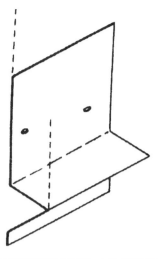

Courtesy of BNI Publications, Inc., *Plaster and Drywall Systems Manual*

Figure 8.53

Cement Plaster Cracking

Industry Standards

Cracking in Portland Cement Plaster
(Plastering Information Bureau)

Portland cement plaster, often referred to as stucco, as a 2- or 3-coat system is usually a 7/8" to 1" thick inflexible membrane which most commonly provides the exterior skin for structures in Southern California and in some other parts of the country.

Structural penetrations such as windows, doors, plumbing, electric accessory outlets, light boxes, wall refrigeration units, vents, etc. pierce the thin plaster membrane. Such penetrations function as focus points or lines for stresses inherent in the supportive skeleton of the building.

Cracking in plaster occurs when the forces or stresses acting on it exceed the tensile strength of the plaster itself. Since portland cement plaster gains strength gradually, it is most susceptible to cracking during its early, weaker stage.

There are two and only two factors which produce all cracking in portland cement plaster. One is that normal change in volume of portland cement plaster intrinsic to the hydration and curing of the cement binder and/or the loss of the mix water in excess of the moisture required for hydration. This process causes internal stresses. The other factor is stress transferred to the plaster membrane from external sources. It is classed as an external stress. Examples of transferred stresses are sonic resonance, seismic vibration, deflections of supporting members, thermal sock, wind loads, settlement and/or subsidence.

Portland cement plaster, like concrete, must be mixed with sufficient water to render it plastic and workable. Part of the water chemically combines with the cement for hydration. A significant amount of water is lost either by evaporation or by absorption. Accompanying the setting of portland cement plaster there is a natural shrinkage or loss of mass of its bulk. If the loss of moisture is not uniform throughout the thickness of the plaster, shrinkage will create internal stresses within the plaster membrane. Normally, contraction occurs towards the center of the portland cement area or panel. This is one of several possible factors which may affect shrinkage cracking.

Assuming that there are no deficiencies in either mix proportioning of the ingredients of the portland cement plaster or in the ensuing curing, the plaster will gain its largest percentage of ultimate strength during the first 7 days following its placement. This is the same period during which most shrinkage of the plaster takes place. The two natural, but counteractive, processes develop during a period of time when portland cement plaster should be expected to achieve its greatest gain in strength while at the same time, the greatest distortional stress from loss of volume occurs.

The second major factor in cracking, transferred stresses to the plaster membrane, is found in almost every structure built. The buildup of stresses is most pronounced in wood-framed construction. When framing, lumber loses the free moisture it contains, it is subject to volume change dimensionally through shrinkage, twisting, warping, bowing, bending, etc. Even kiln-dried lumber contains a considerable amount of water. Even when lumber is free of knots and is relatively straight-grained, it is subject to distortion to some degree.

In wood framing the natural deformation of supports and structural members may exert tremendous pressure perpendicularly to or in alignment with the plane of the plaster. Problems may be compounded if leaks occur and water is introduced into framing members after construction. Wet lumber swells and generates tremendous expansive forces.

In metal framing, a significant degree of transferred stressing often is generated in thermally-induced expansion and contraction of wall framing metal elements and of steel structural elements. The problem is worsened where the wall systems are welded in a unitized fashion without relief mechanisms.

Control joints in the lath-plaster areas should limit panel sizes.

Construction expansion joints should separate structural components into reasonable areas.

Other examples of transferred stresses are thermal shock, temperature-induced expansion and contraction, sonic vibrations, seismic temblors, concrete creep and sag, foundation settlement, structural subsidence, wind loads, live loading of floors, mechanical vibrations or other stress-producing impingements on the plaster membranes. Such transferred stresses are usually well within the range

of accommodation by the building structure and pose little threat to serviceability, structural performance, weather resistivity or safety. These stresses are normally minimal in measurement or hardly measurable at all. However, they can sometimes reach a magnitude which exceeds the resistive strength of the nominal 7/8" thickness of metal reinforced portland cement plaster. While minimal in detection, such stresses may react on the hard, brittle plaster skin to such a degree as to find relief in fractures in the cement membrane.

Transferred stresses are of two types. One is a static force and the other a live or dynamic force. In the former the crack-induction potential is relieved once the stress has expended its energy in the fracture.

The other is the live crack which responds cyclically to recurrent stresses which may be reimposed on the plaster membrane in either a fixed or an uncertain periodicity. Where stress loads recur, live cracks may re-open, even if fractures have been repaired.

Some hairline cracking is almost always found in portland cement plaster and should be expected as normal. Movements in the supporting building structure most commonly cause cracks at the header and sill corners of windows and doors, over concentrations of large dimension wood framing members, and at focus points of stress buildup.

The use of control joints or other properly designed and installed stress relief mechanisms may reduce or prevent the focusing and concentration of both internal and external stresses. The building's designer and/or engineer should determine lines and points at which stresses may be expected and make relief provisions. Plaster panels should be limited in size to a maximum of 100 square feet and one dimension of the panel should not exceed 2-1/2 times the other dimension.

Control joints which allow for some expansion and contraction movement are preferable to those which are rigid.

When unrelieved portland cement plaster panels exceed the recommended spacing of relief mechanisms, cracking is almost certain to occur in the plaster. While the use of relief joints is not an absolute guarantee of crack prevention, it minimizes stress fracturing. Where control joints are omitted in the design of a structure, the designer and/or owner, by default, must shoulder the major responsibility for cracking.

Portland cement plaster over solid wood shear panels, such as plywood sheathing, is subject to tremendous stress action. Even minutia amounts of water may cause swelling and buckling of the plywood. This is particularly true when plywood sheets are placed without a minimum 1/8" spacing between joints. Industry practice and building requirements dictate a double layer of Grade D weather barrier paper or its equivalent in asphalt-saturated felt, be placed over wood sheathing when in direct contact with the back face of the plaster membrane.

If the plywood is wet at the time of installation of the lath, cracking of the plaster is almost assured.

An application of a moisture barrier coating over plywood prior to lathing may reduce cracking problems. Over wood shear panelling, control joints or other stress relief mechanisms are most urgently recommended.

Special relief provisions should be made at the juncture of dissimilar bases such as along the line of abutment of masonry and open framing construction. Relief should be designed at lines where wall membranes pass over concrete floors.

In some areas there is a strong opinion that the addition of short glass or polypropylene fibers added to portland cement plaster during the last stage of mixing provide considerable resistance to plaster fracture. Test results tend to confirm the theory that the plaster's ability to resist cracking is enhanced by the embedment of such reinforcing fibers in the plaster base coats.

Cracking is more apparent in certain stucco textures. Where the surface has been steel trowelled to a dense, smooth finish, cracking is almost always present. Sand float and to a lesser degree light machine dash textures highlight cracks more than skip-trowel or other coarse texture patterns which tend to absorb or conceal the cracks.

A plastering expert can usually tell from the location, dimension, state of spalling and pattern of the cracks whether the source of the stresses creating the fractures originate in the plaster membrane or were transferred to it.

Hairline surface cracking usually presents no leaking problems or other sub-standard performance of the plaster skin. It is usually a mere cosmetic or aesthetic consideration.

Most cracking ceases when the wooden skeleton of the building is in a condition of equilibrium, with the lumber set in its final configuration, as the building is occupied, loaded, stabilized and interior temperature brought to a fixed level. Because of the nature of the material, some hairline cracking in portland cement plaster is very normal and should be expected. Such cracks may easily be filled the first time the exterior is redecorated.

Penetration Flashing

Industry Standards

Plaster and Drywall Systems Manual
(BNI Publications, Inc.)

Penetration Flashing Material

Material for flashing shall be barrier-coated reinforced flashing material and shall provide for 4-hour minimum protection from water penetration when tested in accordance with ASTM D-779. Flashing material shall carry continuous identification. Sealant shall be Butyl to comply with Fed. Spec. TT-S-1657.

Application

To flash penetrations, a strip of approved flashing material at least nine inches wide must be applied in weatherboard fashion around all openings. Apply the first strip horizontally immediately underneath the sill.

The penetrating fixture then is installed by pressing the nailing flange positively into a continuous bead of sealant which extends around the bottom and vertical perimeter of the inserted fixture.

Note: The continuous head of sealant that is applied to the underneath side of the nailing flange of windows, doors, and vents is not to be construed as a substitute for flashing.

Apply the top horizontal section of flashing last, overlapping and sealed against the full height of the outer face of the top nailing flange with a continuous bead of sealant. Cut the top piece of flashing sufficiently long so that it will extend to the outer edge of both vertical strips of side flashing.

Installation of Exterior Plaster Weather-resistant Paper Underlayment to Complete Acceptable Penetration Flashing

Commence at the bottom of the wall, and overlapping the weep screed flange, lay the approved weather-resistant paper up the wall, overlapping 2" min. in weatherboard fashion. Be sure that the first layer is placed under the sill strip flashing.

Ed. Note: While the requirements for flashing and counterflashing are briefly addressed in Section 1402.2 of the 1997 UBC, this area — along with roofing — is the focus of frequent complaints in construction litigation. The problems resulting from improper flashing (dryrot and fungal growth) are easily visible. They not only weaken the structure, but spoil its appearance. Flashing and counterflashing claims are preventable by following the manufacturers' instructions, the project specifications, and any local building code requirements.

See Chapter 9, "Windows & Doors," for more information on flashing penetrations.

UBC — 1997

Section 2508 — Exterior Plaster

2508.1 General. Plastering with cement plaster shall not be less than three coats when applied over metal lath or wire fabric lath and shall not be less than two coats when applied over masonry, concrete, or gypsum backing as specified in Section 2506.3. If plaster surface is completely covered by veneer or other facing material, or is completely concealed by another wall, plaster application need be only two coats, provided the total thickness is as set forth in Table 25-F.

On wood-frame or metal stud construction with an on-grade concrete floor slab system, exterior plaster shall be applied in such a manner as to cover, but not extend below, lath and paper. See Section 2506.5 for the application of paper and lath, and flashing or weep screeds.

Only approved plasticity agents and approved amounts thereof may be added to portland cement. When plastic cement is used, no additional lime or plasticizers shall be added. Hydrated lime or the equivalent amount of lime putty used as a plasticizer may be added to cement plaster or cement and lime plaster in an amount not to exceed that set forth in Table 25-F.

Gypsum plaster shall not be used on exterior surfaces. See Section 224.

2508.2 Base Coat Proportions. The proportion of aggregate to cementitious materials shall be as set forth in Table 25-F.

2508.3 Base Coat Application. The first coat shall be applied with sufficient material and pressure to fill solidly all openings in the lath. The surface shall be scored horizontally sufficiently rough to provide adequate bond to receive the second coat.

The second coat shall be brought out to proper thickness, rodded and floated sufficiently rough to provide adequate bond for the finish coat. The second coat shall have no variation greater than 1/4 inch (6.4 mm) in any direction under a 5-foot (1524 mm) straight edge.

2508.4 Environmental Conditions. Portland cement-based plaster shall not be applied to frozen base or those bases containing frost. Plaster mixes shall not contain frozen ingredients. Plaster coats shall be protected from freezing for a period of not less than 24 hours after set has occurred.

2508.5 Curing and Interval. First and second coats of plaster shall be applied and moist cured as set forth in Table 25-F.

When applied over gypsum backing as specified in Section 2506.3 or directly to unit masonry surfaces, the second coat may be applied as soon as the first coat has attained sufficient hardness.

2508.6 Alternate Method of Application. As an alternate method of application, the second coat may be applied as soon as the first coat has attained sufficient rigidity to receive the second coat.

When using this method of application, calcium aluminate cement up to 15 percent of the weight of the portland cement may be added to the mix.

Curing of the first coat may be omitted and the second coat shall be cured as set forth in Table 25-F.

2508.7 Finish Coats. Finish coats shall be proportioned and mixed in an approved manner and in accordance with Table 25-F.

Cement plaster finish coats shall be applied over base coats that have been in place for the time periods set forth in Table 25-F. The third or finish coat shall be applied with sufficient material and pressure to bond to and to cover the brown coat and shall be of sufficient thickness to conceal the brown coat.

2508.8 Preparation of Masonry and Concrete. Surfaces shall be clean, free from efflorescence, sufficiently damp and rough to ensure proper bond. If surface is insufficiently rough, approved bonding agents or a portland cement dash bond coat mixed in proportions of one and one half parts volume of sand to one part volume of portland cement or plastic cement shall be applied.

Dash bond coat shall be left undisturbed and shall be moist cured not less than 24 hours. When dash bond is applied, first coat of base coat plaster may be omitted. See Table 25-D for thickness.

Section 2510 — Pneumatically Placed Plaster (Gunite)

Pneumatically placed portland cement plaster shall be a mixture of portland cement and sand, mixed dry, conveyed by air through a pipe or flexible tube, hydrated at the nozzle at the end of the conveyor, and deposited by air pressure in its final position.

Rebound material may be screened and reused as sand in an amount not greater than 25 percent of the total sand in any batch.

Pneumatically placed portland cement plaster shall consist of a mixture of one part cement to not more than five parts sand. Plasticity agents may be used as specified in Section 2508.1. Except when applied to concrete or masonry, such plaster shall be applied in not less than two coats to a minimum total thickness of 7/8 inch (22.2 mm). The first coat shall be rodded as specified in Section 2508.3 for the second coat. The curing period and time interval shall be as set forth in Table 25-F.

Exterior Insulation and Finish System (EIFS)

Industry Standards
Plan Reading & Material Takeoff
(R.S. Means Co., Inc.)

Exterior insulation and finish system (EIFS), sometimes referred to as *synthetic stucco,* is an exterior siding material that has the durability and thermal insulation value of stucco. It is composed of expanded polystyrene insulation board and cementitious base coat applied in varying thicknesses, with a synthetic woven mesh that acts as a reinforcement. The top or finish coat is an acrylic stucco, available in a variety of textures and colors. The insulation is adhered or mechanically fastened to the sidewall substrate of plywood, masonry, or gypsum sheathing. The base coat is troweled on, similar to a conventional stucco system, and the mesh reinforcing is embedded in the base coat. The finish coat is applied after the base coat has had sufficient time to dry.

The contractor should refer to the architectural drawings for sections and details of the system, with attention to the details at the abutting surfaces of dissimilar materials, door frames, windows, and wood surfaces. Control and expansion joints are required as per the manufacturer's recommendations to control expansion and contraction associated with the product. The specifications should indicate the individual product specified as well as the manufacturer's standard application and installation procedures.

Comments

EIFS systems, often referred to by the trade names "Dryvit" (Dryvit Systems, Inc.) and "Sto" (Sto Corporation) should be installed by a contractor approved and certified by the system manufacturer. Some projects may require that samples of finish coating (for color and texture) be submitted to and approved by the architect.

Following are some guidelines for the preparation and use of EIFS: Materials should be stored under cover in their original containers with manufacturer's seals and labels intact, with each production lot identified by batch number. Storage should be in a cool, dry location, at a temperature no less than 40°F. Installation should also be in conditions not less than 40°F. Adjacent areas need to be protected, and completed sections of the work must also be protected from moisture not only during the application, but until the coatings are dry.

Before EIFS installation can begin, it is important to make sure that the substrate is properly prepared. All areas should be even and free of surface irregularities. A substrate approved by the EIFS manufacturer should be in place. If exterior gypsum sheathing is to be used, it must meet the required standard, be clean, dry, and properly fastened with no deterioration or defects. The insulation board is installed in a running bond pattern with the long dimension applied horizontally. Board joints must be tightly butted. At least three fasteners per board should be used to tack the board to the substrate or framing. Boards should be interlocked at corners. (Rasp boards if necessary to ensure they are flush.) The installed insulated wall surface should be sound, flat and level in all directions. Fiber mesh reinforcing should be applied mechanically over the insulation board with fasteners spaced 12" on center vertically and 24" on center horizontally. Control joints should be installed as indicated by the manufacturer. When the basecoat is applied over the reinforcing mesh, no mesh should

be visible on the finished surface. The surface should be flat and even. The finish coat is then applied per manufacturer's instructions.

EIFS has not been around long enough to see performance over the life of the building (40 years). However, properly installed, EIFS has so far had excellent results. Detractors have claimed that the system has a low performance rating; but in reviewing numerous studies, we have not seen a single failure of the EIFS product itself. Problems typically stem from improper flashing and termination techniques.

EIFS Backwrapping, Flashing, Expansion Joints & Penetrations

An EIFS should not extend below grade. It should be a minimum of 8" above grade, held in place either by backwrapping with reinforcing mesh and base coat, or by returning the reinforcing mesh and base coat onto the foundation.

All terminations should be backwrapped, which means continuing the reinforced base coat from the face of the insulation board across the edge and onto the back side, which it should overlap by at least 2-1/2".

When the system terminates at a dissimilar material such as wood or block, it should be held back 3/4" to allow for an expansion joint and caulking. In wood frame construction, expansion joints are installed at each floor line as well as at areas where the substrate changes or significant structural movement is anticipated.

Where EIFS terminates at penetrations (light fixtures, hose bibs, dryer vents, wall receptacles, etc.) it requires backwrapping with reinforcing mesh and base coat. The insulation board must be held back from the opening a minimum of 3/8"-1/2" for proper sealant application.

Flashing is installed between the plywood and the ledger board, with one piece turned onto the sleeper or nailer to prevent water from entering behind the deck or ledger boards. The EIFS should overlap the flashing where it is backwrapped and held up from the deck at least 2".

If a gap can be detected between the sill and jamb of a window, it should be caulked with the window manufacturer's recommended sealant. The heads of multiple openings (such as ganged windows) should have a continuous piece of drip flashing to prevent water entry.

Terminations at expansion joints, windows, and other openings must be caulked with sealants that are approved for use with the materials to which it must adhere. Use closed-cell backer rods and sealant primer.

Where the roof intersects a vertical wall, it is necessary
to use a kickout or diverter flashing as the first piece of
flashing. Diverter joints must be soldered. Step flashing
should extend upward a minimum of 6". The step
flashing and the diverter are intended to shed the water
off the roof and away from the vertical wall below.

Glass Blocks

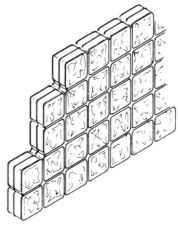

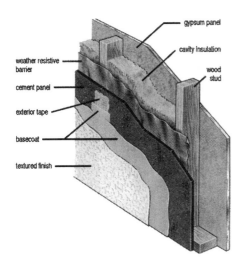

Courtesy of United States Gypsum Company

Figure 8.54

Glass Block

Industry Standards

Means Graphic Construction Standards
(R.S. Means Co., Inc.)

Glass block can be placed on a raised base, plate, or sill,
provided that the surfaces to be mortared are primed with
asphalt emulsion. Wall recesses and channel tract that receive
the glass block should be lined with expansion strips prior
to oakum filler and caulking. Horizontal joint reinforcing is
specified for flexural as well as shrinkage control and is laid
in the joints along with the mortar. End blocks are anchored
to the adjacent construction with metal anchors, if no other
provisions for attachment exist. If intermediate support is
required, vertical I-shaped stiffeners can either be installed
in the plane of the wall or adjacent to it, but the stiffeners
should be tied to the wall with wire anchors. The top of the
wall is supported between angles or in a channel track similar
to the jambs.

Glass Block Head Section

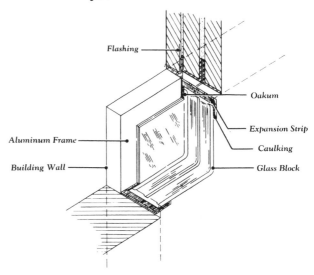

Glass Block Sill Section

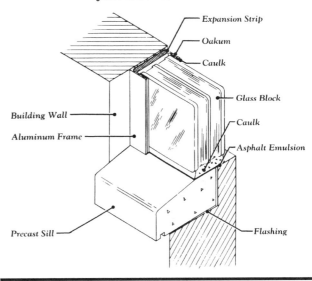

R.S. Means Co., Inc., *Means Graphic Construction Standards*

Figure 8.55

Metal Siding

Industry Standards

Means Graphic Construction Standards
(R.S. Means Co., Inc.)

Formed metal panels are used for mansard roofing and building fascia, as well as for siding. The panels are made from sheet metal, aluminum, or steel and can span distances from 3' to 12'. The ability to transfer wind loads across these spans depends on the gauge of the sheet metal and the profile that is formed with the sheet during rolling. Where structural strength is not required, the corrugation can be regarded as merely an architectural feature.

Sheet metal can be finished with a variety of coatings for corrosion protection. Steel panels may be galvanized, aluminized, or stainless. Both aluminum and steel panels can have a baked enamel or porcelain finish.

Canopy fascia and mansard panels can be fastened or clipped to extruded or channel-shaped metal girts. They are placed horizontally at the required span distance and are supported on channel truss frames. Panels may also be fastened to solid backing (sheathing mounted on stud framing) directly or with metal clips. Where a backup wall exists, metal panels may simply be mounted on channel or stud furring. The top of the panels are supplied with matching coping or gravel stops, and the panel bottom with nose or sill trim. Conversion trim pieces are available for slope transitions. Inside and outside corners are finished with post or cap assemblies. Smooth or ventilated ceiling panels are used for soffits.

For a more custom installation, panel ribs and flat sheets can be supplied as separate components to be installed to a stud and sheathing backup system within the constraints of the field conditions. The exposed open ends of ribs can be closed with "plugs," should coping not be desirable. Ribs may also be field crimped at slope transitions. A very dramatic vertical rib effect can be obtained by mounting a standard 4" wide panel on horizontal carriers that will support the ribs in a variety of angles to the plane of the exterior wall, giving a "louvered" appearance.

A total siding system involves the metal panels fastened to a structural girt support, as mentioned above, with the addition of insulation and backup (liner) panels. In some metal siding systems, the liner panel and insulation are installed to the girt first. The face panel then interlocks with grooves in the liner panel. The thickness of the face and liner panels range from 24 to 20 gauge, and the span can reach 8'.

When the face and liner panels are stiffened by inserting a subgirt between them, the allowable span will increase to 15" for 22 gauge and to 30' for 18 gauge (and a deeper profile). The structural girt may be eliminated altogether if the liner panel is given a deeper profile or a structural stud is integrated

into the liner design. This insulated panel and liner system can be factory assembled to save installation time in the field. The liner panel may be perforated to provide sound absorption. A multi-leaf gypsum wallboard layer can also be enclosed in a double-subgirt system with the face and liner panel to provide a fire-rated wall panel. Some factory assembled panels have a foamed-in-place insulation that is bonded to the face and liner sheet to provide composite structural action.

Vinyl Siding

UBC — 1997

1404.1 General. Vinyl siding conforming to the requirements of this section and complying with UBC Standard 14-2 may be installed on exterior walls of buildings of Type V construction located in areas where the wind speed specified in Figure 16-1 does not exceed 80 miles per hour (129 km/h) and the building height is less than 40 feet (12 192 mm) in Exposure C. If construction is located in areas where wind speed exceeds 80 miles per hour (129 km/h) or building heights are in excess of 40 feet (12 192 mm), data indicating compliance with Chapter 16 must be submitted. Vinyl siding shall be secured to the building to provide weather protection for the exterior walls of the building.

1404.2 Application. The siding shall be applied over sheathing or materials listed in Section 2310. Siding shall be applied to conform with the weather-resistive barrier requirements in Section 1402.1. Siding and accessories shall be installed in accordance with approved manufacturer's instructions.

Nails used to fasten the siding and accessories shall have a minimum 3/8-inch (9.5 mm) head diameter and 0.120-inch (3.05 mm) shank diameter. The nails shall be corrosion resistant and shall be long enough to penetrate the studs or nailing strip at least 3/4 inch (19mm). Where siding is installed horizontally, the fastener spacing shall not exceed 16 inches (406 mm) horizontally and 12 inches (305 mm) vertically. Where the siding is installed vertically, the fastener spacing shall not exceed 12 inches (305 mm) horizontally and 12 inches (305 mm) vertically.

Ed. Note: Refer to Residential Construction Performance Guidelines, *published by the National Association of Home Builders (Telephone: 800-368-5242), for further information on tolerances for vinyl siding installation.*

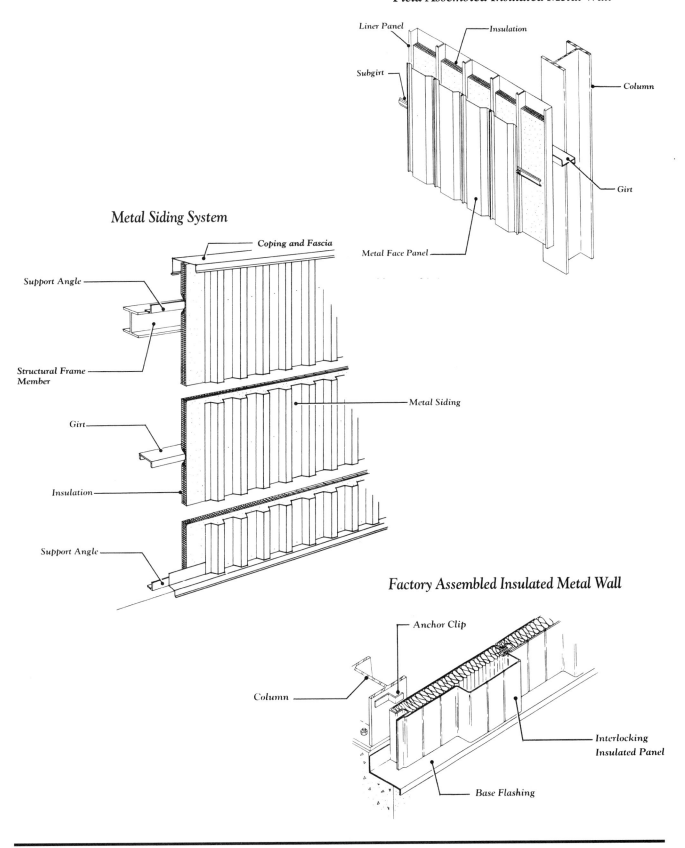

Field Assembled Insulated Metal Wall

Liner Panel

Insulation

Subgirt

Column

Metal Face Panel

Girt

Metal Siding System

Coping and Fascia

Support Angle

Structural Frame Member

Girt

Insulation

Support Angle

Metal Siding

Factory Assembled Insulated Metal Wall

Anchor Clip

Column

Interlocking Insulated Panel

Base Flashing

Waterproofing & Dampproofing

Industry Standards

NRCA Roofing & Waterproofing Manual
(National Roofing Contractors Association)

2.1.1 Waterproofing

Waterproofing is defined as the treatment of a surface or structure to prevent the passage of water under hydrostatic pressure. Water exerts a pressure of 62.4 pounds of force per foot (1000 kg per meter) of depth. Therefore, water lying against a barrier exerts a steadily increasing pressure as the depth increases. The waterproofing treatment must keep the water from penetrating into the building interior.

Waterproofing is used:

- To protect floors and walls below grade of buildings, tunnels, and similar structures from ground water.

- To protect spaces beneath roofs and plaza decks.

- To isolate wet spaces such as kitchens, showers, and mechanical equipment rooms from other areas of buildings.

- On bridge decks to protect against deterioration from de-icing salts and to help minimize the negative effects of thermal expansion of the structural elements and topping materials.

- To keep water from leaking from pools, planters, lagoons, irrigation trenches and dams, or into basements and other underground structures.

An understanding of the different loads and stresses placed upon the waterproofing material is important to the proper design of structures and facilities. Some of these forces are similar to those to which roofing membranes are exposed, but others are quite different. The following are some of the performance attributes required of waterproofing materials:

- Perform for an extended period of time, preferably for the life of the structure. It is usually quite costly, if not impossible, to excavate around the foundation walls or to remove a reinforced concrete floor slab to repair or replace the waterproofing material.

  Consequently, unlike a roof membrane, a waterproofing membrane must perform completely trouble- and maintenance-free for an indefinite period of time.

- Perform successfully in a constantly wet environment. While there may be relatively dry periods depending on where the material is employed and the level of ground water, waterproofing is usually in continuous contact with ground water, or is retaining water, such as in a planter or pool.

- Resist environmental contaminants, such as acids or alkalis, and other contaminants. Soil chemistry varies from location to location, and sometimes from foot to foot of excavated depth. The material must be compatible with both the soil and the substrate to which it is applied. Some waterproofing materials are intolerant of certain soil salts, and others are affected by oils that could be spilled onto floors in mechanical equipment rooms. These contaminants are much different from those to which roof membranes are exposed.

- Withstand construction activity. The material must remain in place and intact until excavations can be backfilled or the protective wearing course can be applied. During backfill placement, rocks, construction debris, and other sharp objects may be dumped against the waterproofing material. However, the greatest threat to waterproofing often comes from other construction trades. Even though horizontal surfaces are usually covered with a protection course, other trades often use the waterproofed surface as a staging area or for access to adjacent work areas. Although this can also be a problem for roof membranes, it is more critical for waterproofing because once in use the waterproofing membrane is not readily accessible for repair.

- Accommodate anticipated structural movement in the substrate to which it has been applied. Below-grade concrete and masonry structures may experience settlement and/or shrinkage as the substrate materials cure. Horizontal plaza decks experience thermal movement and load deflection. These characteristics make it necessary for the waterproofing material to be able to bridge small cracks, and expand and contract to some degree without rupture or failure.

Waterproofing materials are generally concealed and often placed into more shielded environments than roof membranes. Therefore, materials used for waterproofing may not perform if used for roofing applications. The following are some conditions favorable to waterproofing membranes:

- Subjected to limited thermal stress. Below-grade waterproofing materials are usually kept at near constant temperatures because of their contact with earth backfill on the exterior and proximity to relatively constant interior temperatures. Further, the materials are usually directly adhered to thermally and dimensionally stable structural decks or wall surfaces.

- Not usually exposed to direct ultraviolet radiation because they are most often buried in the ground, covered with a plaza deck surface, or used inside the building. Sunlight and other environmental exposures cannot affect them once the building is completed.

- Most have the advantage of being adhered directly to structural substrates. Structural decks and walls are typically dimensionally stable. When the materials are fully adhered to the substrates, water penetrating the waterproofing cannot freely move laterally. Therefore, leaks tend to appear very close to the point of moisture penetration.

- Protected from physical abuse. After installation, waterproofing materials are usually covered with a protection course and backfill or with a permanent protection slab. People should not walk directly on the waterproofing membrane.

2.1.2 Dampproofing

Dampproofing is defined as the treatment of a surface or structure to resist the passage of water in the absence of hydrostatic pressure. Dampproofing methods will not work when hydrostatic pressures are present, and are generally employed above grade, or below grade in the absence of ground water. For this reason, many of the design factors that are critical to the performance of a waterproofing system are not as critical to the successful performance of dampproofing.

Dampproofing is employed to prevent moisture from wicking through the structure and damaging interior finishes. Some dampproofing materials are transparent and can be exposed above grade.

2.1.3 Hydrostatic Pressure Relief Systems

A hydrostatic pressure relief system is a system of perimeter and/or under-slab drains used to regulate the hydrostatic pressure in the earth surrounding a below-grade structure.

Clearly, the most effective way to waterproof walls and floors placed against earth is to remove the water from the earth prior to it reaching the wall or floor. Each of the waterproofing materials described in this manual will resist hydrostatic pressure to varying degrees. However, the waterproof integrity of any building can be greatly improved if the hydrostatic pressure against the waterproofing material can be reduced or eliminated entirely.

In below-grade structures, the determination of whether a hydrostatic pressure relief system can be used depends upon the quantity of water that must be handled and how it is to be handled or resisted. When gravity can be used to direct water from around the building foundation into a storm sewer, greater amounts of water can be handled than when pumping must be used to lower the water table. Operating the pumps can be costly if there is a great amount of water to handle, and there is always the threat of problems should the pumps fail.

If it is determined that a hydrostatic relief system cannot be economically employed, then the foundation floor slab must be designed with sufficient concrete mass and reinforcement to resist the uplift pressures of the anticipated water table, and the construction has to be carefully waterproofed, which can be an expensive construction process. If a hydrostatic pressure relief system can be employed, then the slab-on-grade can be designed with only surface load considerations, thereby greatly reducing construction costs. Furthermore, waterproofing of the floor slab may not be necessary.

The decision to use a hydrostatic pressure relief system depends upon a careful analysis of soil borings and water table level readings, and should be made with the input of an experienced soils or geotechnical engineer. A site with coarse, permeable soil that freely permits water percolation, combined with a water table level that is above the top of the foundation floor slab, is probably an unlikely candidate for a hydrostatic pressure relief system, particularly if the water table must be lowered by pumping. Conversely, a site with a dense clay soil resistant to water percolation could be an excellent candidate for a hydrostatic pressure relief system, even if the water table level is considerably higher than the foundation floor slab.

Hydrostatic pressure can be relieved from perimeter walls below grade by using a coarse aggregate backfill or a prefabricated drainage product known as a "geocomposite." These systems channel ground water traveling toward the building down to a perimeter drainage system located below the bottom of the foundation floor slab. The drain system may be installed either at the exterior or interior perimeter of the foundation walls or both, depending upon the specific type of hydrostatic pressure relief system being used. When aggregate is used to relieve hydrostatic pressure against wall surfaces, a separate protection course must be placed against the waterproofing membrane to protect the membrane from damage during aggregate placement.

Loose aggregate should not be placed directly against the waterproofing membrane. Alternatively, geocomposites relieve hydrostatic pressure and some also serve as protection for the waterproofing membrane during backfill operations.

Consideration should also be given to relieving water pressure from the surface of horizontal suspended structural slabs, such as a plaza deck slab. When water that permeates its way through upper layers down to the membrane surface can drain freely to deck drains, the horizontal waterproofing membrane will perform better. This drainage can be achieved by placing a suitable insulation board specially designed with drainage channels or grooves on its underside, or a protection course and a layer of aggregate, or a geocomposite directly above the waterproofing membrane surface.

2.1.4 Substrate Preparation

Most waterproofing materials are bonded or applied to surfaces that are installed by other trades. It is essential to the performance of the waterproofing material that these substrates be structurally sound and free from excessive cracks, holes or projections. Certain curing compounds and finishes may affect or interfere with the performance of the waterproofing material. The use of oils, waxes, and other surface contaminates should be avoided or the contaminates must be removed prior to waterproofing. The waterproofing contractor should visually inspect the substrate surfaces before the application of waterproofing materials, and report any deficiencies so that they may be corrected by the responsible trade.

Following are recommended surface preparation procedures acceptable for most waterproofing materials. Other procedures may be recommended or required by the waterproofing material manufacturer.

2.1.4.1 Masonry Substrates

Holes, joints, and voids in masonry substrates should be pointed flush with the surface. The masonry surface should be smooth and free from projections. Penetrations through the masonry surface should be grouted tightly. Irregular existing masonry surfaces that will be waterproofed with a membrane should receive an approximate 1/2 inch (13mm) thick parging, consisting of one part cement to three parts sand, finished to a smooth steel trowel surface. Block filler may be used in lieu of parging where conditions warrant.

2.1.4.2 Concrete Substrates

NRCA recommends that horizontal concrete decks cure a minimum of 28 days, or as specified by the material manufacturer, to allow moisture to dissipate from the top surface (forming systems typically prevent dissipation of moisture from the underside of horizontal decks) prior to applying waterproofing materials.

Form release agents and concrete curing compounds must be compatible with the waterproofing materials being used, or must be removed from the concrete surface by the responsible trade. Honeycombs, tie-wire holes, and other voids in the concrete substrate must be cut out and re-pointed with a non-shrinking concrete patching compound. Concrete fins or other projections should be removed to provide a smooth surface. Horizontal concrete slabs should be free from gouges, voids, depressions, ridges, and concrete droppings, and should preferably be sloped to drains.

ASTM D 5295, *Standard Guide for Preparation of Concrete Surfaces for Adhered (Bonded) Membrane Waterproofing System*, provides additional recommendations regarding the preparation of concrete deck surfaces prior to the installation of waterproofing.

2.1.4.3 Plywood Substrates

The grade of plywood utilized is critical to the performance of the waterproofing. NRCA suggests the use of marine grade plywood as a substrate for waterproofing applications.

The surface of plywood substrates must be smooth, and holes, open joints, or gaps between panels should be plugged or covered. Knot holes are not acceptable for waterproofing purposes. Plywood panel edges should bear on joists or blocking to reduce deflection from traffic. The thickness and deflection characteristics of plywood substrates are important design considerations. Plywood decks should be sloped for drainage.

Fasteners used for attaching plywood must be corrosion-resistant-type, either resin coated, ribbed, screw or ring shanked nails; or screws countersunk to prevent their backing out and puncturing the waterproofing membrane.

Comments

French drain systems that use a perforated pipe in an envelope of crushed rock must incorporate a method of filtering out the fines and clays from filling the gravel and sealing the system. The standard method is to lay a filter wrap material in the trench on base soil before placement of gravel or pipe. The filter wrap should be of sufficient width to eventually overlap itself after the pipe and gravel placement is complete. The gravel is then placed on the wrap and drainage gradients are established for the pipe. The perforated pipe is then placed on the rock and more rock is placed over the pipe. The filter wrap is then completely wrapped and overlapped around the entire french drain installation. The whole french drain should be approximately 12 to 24 inches in diameter, depending on the application.

Backfilling behind block walls with crushed rock in lieu of soil is not an acceptable procedure. While this method omits the need for compaction and appears to be a good water filter, it eventually allows surface grade to erode into the rock, allowing surface water to directly impact the backfill. The french drain system is for percolated water only.

Waterproofing & Dampproofing Foundations

UBC — 1997

Section 1820 — Scope

Walls, or portions thereof, retaining earth and enclosing interior spaces and floors below grade shall be waterproofed or dampproofed according to this appendix chapter.

Exception: Walls enclosing crawl spaces.

Section 1821 — Groundwater Table Investigation

A subsurface soils investigation shall be made in accordance with Section 1804.3, Item 3, to determine the possibility of the groundwater table rising above the proposed elevation of the floor or floors below grade. The building official may require that this determination be made by an engineer or architect licensed by the state to practice as such.

Exceptions:

1. When foundation waterproofing is provided.

2. When dampproofing is provided and the building official finds that there is satisfactory data from adjacent areas to demonstrate that groundwater has not been a problem.

Section 1822 — Dampproofing Required

Where the groundwater investigation required by Section 1821 indicates that a hydrostatic pressure caused by the water table will not occur, floors and walls shall be dampproofed and a subsoil drainage system shall be installed in accordance with this appendix chapter.

Exception: Wood foundation systems shall be constructed in accordance with Chapter 18, Division II.

Section 1823 — Floor Dampproofing

1823.1 General. Dampproofing materials shall be installed between the floor and base materials required by Section 1825.2.

Exception: Where a separate floor is provided above a concrete slab, the dampproofing may be installed on top of the slab.

1823.2 Dampproofing Materials. Dampproofing installed beneath the slab shall consist of not less than 6-mil (0.152 mm) polyethylene, or other approved methods or materials. When permitted to be installed on top of the slab, dampproofing shall consist of not less than 4-mil (0.1 mm) polyethylene.

Section 1824 — Wall Dampproofing

1824.1 General. Dampproofing materials shall be installed on the exterior surface of walls, and shall extend from a point 6 inches (152 mm) above grade, down to the top of the spread portion of the footing.

1824.2 Surface Preparation. Prior to application of dampproofing materials on concrete walls, fins or sharp projections that may pierce the membrane shall be removed and all holes and recesses resulting from the removal of form ties shall be sealed with a dry-pack mortar, bituminous material, or other approved methods or materials.

1824.3 Dampproofing Materials. Wall dampproofing shall consist of a bituminous material, acrylic modified cement base coating, any of the materials permitted for waterproofing in Section 1828.4, or other approved methods or materials. When such materials are not approved for direct application to unit masonry, the wall shall be parged on the exterior surface below grade with not less than 3/8 inch (9.5 mm) of portland cement mortar.

Section 1825 — Other Dampproofing Requirements

1825.1 Subsoil Drainage System. When dampproofing is required, a base material shall be installed under the floor and a drain shall be installed around the foundation perimeter in accordance with this subsection.

Exception: When the finished ground level is below the floor level for more than 25 percent of the perimeter of the building, the base material required by Section 1825.2 need not be provided and the foundation drain required by Section 1825.3 need be provided only around that portion of the building where the ground level is above the floor level.

1825.2 Base Material. Floors shall be placed over base material not less than 4 inches (102 mm) in thickness consisting of gravel or crushed stone containing not more than 10 percent material that passes a No. 4 sieve (4.75 mm).

1825.3 Foundation Drain. The drain shall consist of gravel, crushed stone or drain tile. Gravel or crushed stone drains shall contain not more than 10 percent material that passes a No. 4 sieve (4.75 mm). The drain shall extend a minimum of 12 inches (305 mm) beyond the outside edge of the footing. The depth shall be such that the bottom of the drain is not higher than the bottom of the base material under the floor, and the top of the drain is not less than 6 inches (152 mm) above the spread portion of the footing. The top of the drain shall be covered with an approved filter membrane material.

When drain tile or perforated pipe is used, the invert of the pipe or tile shall be not higher than the floor elevation. The top of joints or the top of perforations shall be protected with an approved filter membrane material. The pipe or tile shall be placed on not less than 2 inches (51 mm) of gravel or crushed stone complying with this section and covered with not less than 6 inches (152 mm) of the same material.

1825.4 Drainage Disposal. The floor base and foundation perimeter drain shall discharge by gravity or mechanical means into an approved drainage system.

Exception: Where a site is located in well-drained gravel or sand-gravel mixture soils, a dedicated drainage system need not be provided.

Section 1826 — Waterproofing Required

Where the groundwater investigation required by Section 1821 indicates that a hydrostatic pressure caused by the water table does exist, walls and floors shall be waterproofed in accordance with this appendix chapter.

Exceptions:

1. When the groundwater table can be lowered and maintained at an elevation not less than 6 inches (152 mm) below the bottom of the lowest floor, dampproofing provisions in accordance with Section 1822 may be used in lieu of waterproofing.

   The design of the system to lower the groundwater table shall be based on accepted principles of engineering which shall consider, but not necessarily be limited to, the permeability of the soil, the rate at which water enters the drainage system, the rated capacity of pumps, the head against which pumps are to pump, and the rated capacity of the disposal area of the system.

2. Wood foundation systems constructed in accordance with Chapter 18, Division II, are to be provided with additional moisture-control measures as specified in Section 1812.

Section 1827 — Floor Waterproofing

1827.1 General Floors required to be waterproofed shall be of concrete designed to withstand anticipated hydrostatic pressure.

Comments

Hydrostatic pressure can result in "uplift." An alternative approach is placing a double layer of concrete with a waterproof membrane in between.

1827.2 Waterproofing Materials. Waterproofing of floors shall be accomplished by placing under the slab a membrane of rubberized asphalt, polymer-modified asphalt, butyl rubber, neoprene, or not less than 6-mil (0.15 mm) polyvinyl chloride or polyethylene, or other approved materials capable of bridging nonstructural cracks. Joints in the membrane shall be lapped not less than 6 inches (152 mm) and sealed in an approved manner.

Section 1828 — Wall Waterproofing

1828.1 General. Walls required to be waterproofed shall be of concrete or masonry designed to withstand the anticipated hydrostatic pressure and other lateral loads.

1828.2 Wall Preparation. Prior to the application of waterproofing materials on concrete or masonry walls, the wall surfaces shall be prepared in accordance with Section 1824.2.

1828.3 Where Required. Waterproofing shall be applied from a point 12 inches (305 mm) above the maximum elevation of the groundwater table down to the top of the spread portion of the footing. The remains of the wall located below grade shall be dampproofed with materials in accordance with Section 1824.3.

1828.4 Waterproofing Materials. Waterproofing shall consist of rubberized asphalt, polymer-modified asphalt, butyl rubber, or other approved materials capable of bridging nonstructural cracks. Joints in the membrane shall be lapped and sealed in an approved manner.

1828.5 Joints. Joints in walls and floors, and between the wall and floor, and penetrations of the wall and floor shall be made watertight using approved methods and materials.

Section 1829 - Other Dampproofing and Waterproofing Requirements

1829.1 Placement of Backfill. The excavation outside the foundation shall be backfilled with soil which is free of organic material, construction debris and large rocks. The backfill shall be placed in lifts and compacted in a manner which does not damage the waterproofing or dampproofing material or structurally damage the wall.

Comments

A physical barrier can be placed between the backfill and the waterproof membrane to prevent sharp objects from piercing the membrane. Suitable materials for such a barrier include: asphalt-impregnated fiberboard, styrofoam, and treated plywood.

1829.2 Site Grading. The ground immediately adjacent to the foundation shall be sloped away from the building at not less than 1 unit vertical in 12 units horizontal (8.3% slope) for a minimum distance of 6 feet (1829 mm) measured perpendicular to the face of the wall or an approved alternate method of diverting water away from the foundation shall be used. Consideration shall be given to possible additional settlement of the backfill when establishing final ground level adjacent to the foundation.

1829.3 Erosion Protection. Where water impacts the ground from the edge of the roof, downspout, scupper, valley, or other rainwater collection or diversion device, provisions shall be used to prevent soil erosion and direct the water away from the foundation.

CHAPTER 9 WINDOWS & DOORS

Table of Contents

(continued on next page)

297

Text in blue print indicates excerpts from model building code(s). "Comments" (in solid blue boxes) were written by the editors, based on their own experience.

For building product information, use this book's special Internet gateway to thousands of manufacturers: www.rsmeans.com/prodsupp/rlstand.html

CHAPTER
9 WINDOWS & DOORS

Common Defect Allegations

Windows

- *When extensive or destructive inspections are required, construction analysts find that most windows and doors show evidence of some water intrusion. To avoid these kinds of claims, many builders have begun using a flexible, rubberized, self-adhesive flashing to create a positive watertight installation.*

- *Aluminum window frame assemblies are usually screwed together. The corners are metal to metal, with a dab of sealant, and many of these connections leak. It is good practice to apply extra high-grade flexible sealant in those corners. Another problem occurs when the frames are installed upside down, with the weepholes at the top of the window. Sometimes the windows are installed correctly, but plaster has filled the weepholes, which traps the water in the track.*

- *Wood windows very often deteriorate quickly. Problems often result from insufficient maintenance. Another factor is the use of paint with less durability in many areas where air quality regulations limit paint choices. In some conditions, windows will require repainting every two years. Failures can also result from the paint being cut back from the glass by the cleanup workers with a razor-type scraper that breaks the water seal.*

UBC — 1997

- 1402.2 Flashing and Counterflashing. Exterior openings exposed to the weather shall be flashed in such a manner as to make them weatherproof.

The above excerpt is the extent of the 1997 UBC requirements for window and door flashing. Yet, (along with roofing and HVAC/plumbing problems), improper flashing is one of the most frequent complaints in construction defect litigation. It creates significant

299

visual defects due to the consequential dryrot and fungal growth. Flashing problems are among the most easily preventable defects.

There are two sources of water intrusion from windows: the mechanical connection of the frame to the wall, and the interior of the window assembled by the manufacturer. We address only the frame wall connection.

The basic problem is that there is no minimum method that can be enforced by the building official during the wrap of the building with regard to the integration of flashing materials, especially over radius windows or on windows that have a plant-on or reveal adjacent to the window frame itself.

The acceptable minimum standard flashing around residential windows is a sisal-type, reinforced paper flashing. This is considered to be a baffle system that is not caulked to the building paper, but is simply overlapped, assuming that gravity will take the water and shed it over the next layer before it travels horizontally and enters the interior of the wall cavity. This treatment gives the window the four-hour rating required to meet ASTM D-779.

Doors
- Wood doors, like windows, often suffer from lack of maintenance. Very often, exterior doors are not painted top and bottom, which allows water to be absorbed into the wood assembly. Sometimes the door top and bottom are painted correctly, but a security system company drills a round magnet into the top of the door without sealing it.

- A very common problem is water intrusion under thresholds. The threshold must be caulked to the exterior building layer with a high grade flexible caulking. This includes shaping an end dam where the threshold ends at the wall.

- Exterior wood doors, especially french doors, are often scheduled to be stain grade with a clear finish. The finish will not stand up to extended exposure to weather, particularly on west- and south-facing walls. If it is a must to employ this finish, then clear instructions must be delivered to the owner that it will require annual refinishing.

(See also "Common Window & Door Problems" following the introduction to this chapter.)

Introduction

This chapter begins by listing common window and door problems (with corrective measures). It goes on to provide specific standards for window and then door installations, including basic installation requirements, finishing, flashing, trim application, testing, quality certifications, and tolerances. Chapter 5, "Wood Framing," contains information on code requirements for egress.

Successful window and door installations begin with appropriate selection of the type of window or door for the particular application. Not only climate, but specific performance requirements should be considered. A perfect installation of a quality window or door could still fail if inappropriate materials are chosen for the site conditions and/or building use.

Windows and doors are built in a controlled environment, and defects in manufacture of the basic unit are generally attributed to the manufacturer, not the installer. Check the specifics of the product warranty. Typical warranty exclusions are cracked or broken glass; damage caused by improper installation, use, or maintenance; damage caused by improper finish-painting; and labor charges for repairs or replacements.

Flashing is such a common complaint in construction defect litigation that we address the topic in the first section following "General Information" at the beginning of this chapter. We explore the options available according to the latest technologies recommended by restoration specialists and include comments on the plant-on cure.

Please note that there are several excerpts from different authoritative sources on door installation. Because each of these source organizations may have a somewhat different focus, their coverage of this subject may occur in a different order and may give more, or less, attention to certain aspects of the door installation process. We recommend checking all of these source references for the most complete understanding of what is required and/or desirable.

The following organizations may be helpful in providing additional information on window and door installation requirements.

National Fenestration Rating Council (NFRC)
1300 Spring Street, Suite 120
Silver Spring, MD 20910
Telephone: 301-589-6372
www.nfrc.org
The National Fenestration Rating Council (NFRC) has developed a window energy rating system based on whole product performance. This system is designed to accurately account for the energy-related effects of all the products' component parts.

Insulated Steel Door Institute (ISDI)
30200 Detroit Road
Cleveland, OH 44145
Telephone: 440-899-0010
www.isdi.org

National Wood Window & Door Association (NWWDA)
1400 E. Touhy Avenue, Suite 470
Des Plaines, IL 60018
Telephone: 847-299-5200
www.nwwda.org

Steel Door Institute (SDI)
30200 Detroit Road
Cleveland, OH 44145
Telephone: 440-899-0010
www.sdi.org

California Association of Window Manufacturers (CAWM)
Although CAWM was dissolved in the spring of 1998, many of the association's publications are distributed as a courtesy by the **American Architectural Manufacturers Association (AAMA).** For information or to inquire about CAWM publications, call the AAMA at 888-323-5664.

Ed. Note: Comments and recommendations within this chapter are not intended as a definitive resource for construction activities. For building projects, contractors must rely on a copy of the project documents and local building codes.

Common Window & Door Problems & Corrective Measures

Door Problems

Comments

- Temperature and/or humidity changes or improper finishing of one of a door's six sides can cause the door to warp and stick or to appear uneven. The National Wood Window & Door Association (NWWDA) allows 1/4" warpage, measured from corner to diagonal corner. If the warp exceeds this amount, or the sides have not been finished correctly, the door may have to be refit.

- There are gaps around the exterior edges of the door, the threshold, and the door jamb. The door can be repaired or adjusted to acceptable parameters.
Note: See the NAHB's Residential Construction Performance Guidelines for suggested specific tolerances.

- Unpainted wood is exposed at the edge of a door panel. This condition may occur when wood door panels shrink and expand in accordance with humidity and temperature changes. This is considered to be a normal condition, rather than a defect. The door may require refinishing.

- A door panel splits, showing light through the crack. Depending on the severity of the split, the panel may be repaired and refinished as necessary, or the door may have to be replaced.

- Sliding glass or screen doors do not slide smoothly. A true malfunction resulting from improper installation can be corrected by carefully adjusting the track. While the doors should function properly when the job is completed, the project owner must maintain the doors to ensure continued smooth operation. This involves keeping the track clean, free of debris, and protected from damage.

Window Problems

Comments

- The thermal seal in a double- or triple-paned window yields, resulting in clouding of glass. One possible cause may be intense heat on one side of the window, or heat build-up between the panes. Another reason for thermal break problems is deterioration of the original window, especially caulking and sealant, over time. Improvements in these materials have reduced the incidence of these problems. Check the manufacturer's warranty for specific coverage. Many window manufacturers include air seal failures in their warranties and will replace either glass or glass in sash, depending on the type of window.

- The window glass breaks as a result of stress forces. Stress may be placed on the window frame if it was not installed plumb and level, if it is touching a structural member, or if uneven settlement occurs. All are situations that should be avoided in the installation. To correct the problem, remove the trim to discover the source of the stress, eliminate the source of stress, and then replace the window. Depending on the number of lights of glass and the severity of the damage, the contractor will generally opt for the most economical solution. In the case of a thermal glazed window, generally only the sash is replaced. These components are easily obtained from the distributor. In the case of small, single-glazed or multiple-pane custom windows, it may be less expensive to reglaze a single lite.

Note: **The window frame and sash act as a unit and serve to support the functionality of the window itself; they should never be considered part of the structural system, nor are they a source of any structural support.**

- The window binds as a result of insulation packed too tightly around it, between the window frame and the rough opening frame. This situation also causes problems in the installation of the interior trim. To correct the problem, remove the trim and reinstall the insulation properly; then re-trim the window.

- The flashing is improperly installed, resulting in leaks around the window. **A general rule: Flashing should be installed to allow moisture and water to flow away from and over joints.** Follow manufacturer's specific instructions.

Note: **See the "Flashing" section early in this chapter.**

- *There are scratches on the window glass. Manufacturers' warranties generally exclude "minor" scratches or other imperfections as long as this condition is not visible from a distance of several feet, and does not obscure "normal visibility" or compromise the window's structural integrity.*

- *The window leaks at the point of glazing. This is a defect in a new window, and is usually covered by the manufacturer's warranty. Window glazing, unless of vinyl or similar material, should be painted according to the manufacturer's specification. The paint should seal to the glass. Sometimes on a construction job, the paint is scraped off of a window pane too aggressively, breaking the seal between the glazing, sash, glass, and finish.*

- *Moisture buildup has occurred in the wall due to clogged or plugged weepholes. Some window manufacturers depend on the use of weepholes to relieve the accumulation of moisture in areas inside the wall frame. The idea is that any moisture that penetrates this space is drained to the exterior of the building. If weepholes become clogged, problems may ensue. Occasionally, owners and contractors intentionally plug weepholes in a misguided attempt to prevent leakage of air and moisture, not realizing that they are creating a moisture problem. The problem is solved by unplugging the weepholes and educating owners and others about the way these components function.*

General Information

Industry Standards

Construction Principles, Materials, and Methods
(John Wiley & Sons, Inc.)

The finest window or door design and the highest quality of manufacture will not compensate for poor installation. Weathertight installation, although simple, can be ensured only if a window or sliding glass door is installed by an experienced worker following the guidelines and instructions supplied by the manufacturer. A rough opening should be prepared to receive the unit in such a manner that it can be installed, and will finish out square, plumb, level, straight, and true. The design of most windows and doors provides for minor adjustments at the job site, but no unit will operate or weather properly if it is twisted and misaligned during installation.

A properly selected and manufactured window or sliding glass door will be weather resistant as a unit; but if the building is insulated, the space between the rough opening and the windows or sliding glass doors should be filled with insulation. In addition, the spaces between the unit and adjacent materials must be closed with a sealant, trim members, or both, to prevent the passage of air, dust, and water around the frame.

Windows and sliding glass doors should be supported (nailed, screwed, or otherwise fastened) around the entire frame and anchored securely to the supporting construction in a firm and rigid position. They should also be flashed at their heads and sills to provide a path back to the exterior for water that finds its way into the wall.

Anchoring materials and flashing should be of aluminum or material compatible with aluminum, such as stainless steel, cadmium-coated steel, or galvanized steel. Dissimilar materials, such as copper or bronze, should be insulated from direct contact with aluminum by waterproof, nonconductive materials, such as neoprene, waxed papers, or coated felts. Dissimilar metals located where water passing over them may contact a window or door should be painted to prevent staining of the aluminum.

Concealed aluminum in contact with concrete, masonry, or absorbent material, such as wood, paper, or insulation, should be permanently protected by coating either the aluminum or the adjacent material with a bituminous or aluminum paint or by coating the aluminum with a zinc chromate primer, to minimize the chance of chemical corrosion of the aluminum by acids, alkalies, and salts leached out of the adjacent materials. Creosote and tar coating, which might damage the aluminum, should not be used.

Because aluminum windows and sliding glass doors are prefinished building components, they should be handled and treated with care to prevent damage.

Window & Door Components Defined

Industry Standards

Nail-On Windows
(DTA, Inc.)

Windows once installed are part of the exterior wall assembly and should resist leakage as much as the principal wall construction. The main components of the window assembly can be identified as the supporting frame, the wall sheathing, the flashing, the window, and the surrounding exterior cladding. Each of these interrelated components can be analyzed as complete assemblies themselves.

Wall Frame
The frame provides the structural support around the window/door opening. The frame often supports the wall, too.

The frame type can be further categorized by the material used to construct the wall, e.g. wood-frame; masonry (includes brick and concrete block); light-gage steel (steel studs), steel (as in high-rise construction); poured concrete and other material or structural systems.

The window or door opening in the wall frame must be properly constructed for size and support. The manufacturers of aluminum windows and doors have standard frame-to-rough opening sizes. Many also provide custom sizes. They recommend sizes for the framed opening to be slightly larger in order to fit the window. The framed opening is typically called the "rough opening." Often the rough opening is 1/2 inch larger all around than the overall window dimensions. This dimension may change from manufacturer to manufacturer.

This part of the wall framing must be built square, with each corner at 90 degrees. The top and bottom of the opening must be parallel and level. The sides or jambs must be plumb, both in the plane of the wall as well as perpendicular to the wall plane. The top of the window is spanned by framing called a header. The header must be structurally adequate to support the weight of building materials and any occupants on floors above, the same as with a "bearing" wall. The building code and structural engineering practice determines the size of the header for window and sliding glass door openings.

Problems in framing which can effect the performance of the window or flashing include:

- Undersized header which sags or deflects to distort the window flashings or tears flashing from fasteners.
- Wood shrinkage or warping can cause wood framing to get out of alignment from being square, plumb or level.
- Severe framing distortion can affect window operation, leak resistance and distress flashings and sealants.

Mechanical damage to the framing, installed window, flashing or exterior cladding can unexpectedly occur any time during construction where portions of buildings can be subject to physical abuse. Protection from environmental abuse may also be lacking during construction where building elements which are partially completed may be exposed to rain, wind or prolonged sunlight effects.

Wall Sheathing

Wall sheathing is usually a rigid paneling applied on the outside of the wall frame. It may be omitted in some construction, where the wall system would be termed "open framing."

Wall sheathing is provided for the purposes of structural strength improvement to the wall frame, fire resistive protection and insulation or energy conservation value. The wall sheathing provides a stable and uniform plane to support the easily damaged building papers and flashings. Wall sheathing also provides support for the exterior wall cladding.

Window/Sliding Glass Door

Window and sliding glass doors are manufactured products completely assembled in the factory or partially assembled in the field.

The components manufactured in the factory can vary in quality due to the stoutness of the aluminum extrusion, the type of joint connection used for corners, the sealants or gaskets used and the quality of the glazing components.

Product integrity is affected by the packing and shipping means used between the factory and the site or between the factory and a distributor. Transportation can cause stress to assembled windows and doors. Distributors, contractors, or installers receiving a product may not always recognize transportation damage which could influence later performance.

On-site storage precautions and the location on the construction site provides another period of risk for damage to the window/door units before installation.

Rough handling can damage glazing units during the process of installation, especially if a single mechanic is trying to maneuver a heavy glazed unit. This is a likely period where the nail-on flange corner can get distorted from being used as a pivot while being hauled around a construction site.

Exterior Wall Cladding

The wall covering providing weather protection is the exterior cladding of a building. The wall finish materials in common use today for residential construction with wood frame buildings include stucco (cement plaster), plywood siding, wood lap siding, hardboard siding, as well as different stucco systems (e.g. EIFS — Exterior Insulation Finish Systems).

Each of these different materials needs to be either integrated with the penetrations through the wall cladding with a concealed weather barrier or exclude moisture with an effective surface barrier. The exterior cladding installation has to be integrated with and compliment the window/door flashings, as well as any vapor barrier system on the wall.

Ed. Note: See the CAWM references (5.2) under "Window Installation & Flashing" and "Door Installation & Flashing" for more information on protection from dissimilar materials.

Storm Exposure

The performance of windows and sliding glass doors depends in large part on weather exposure. Manufacturers fabricate products for different weather performances. There are categories for performance established by AAMA. The AAMA publication 10 1–9: *Voluntary Specifications for Aluminum and Poly (Vinyl Chloride) (PVC) Prime Window and Glass Doors* provides a method for selecting a performance rating for water resistance based on the location in wind zones around the country and height of the window door above ground level. There are many areas of the country which experience wind speeds up to 70 and 80 mph in conjunction with rain. This should be considered in window selection.

The weather exposure of building openings is often an important contributing cause for leaks. Wind driven rain from the predominant local storm direction can result in openings facing the weather to demonstrate leakage. Precautions in the building design, product selection and methods of installation of window and door openings facing the storm exposure should be considered.

Comments

Select thermal requirements for windows based on climate. Also note that Government agencies, such as HUD (Department of Housing and Urban Development) and institutions responsible for other publicly-funded projects require certain thermal ratings for windows.

Flashing

Comments

Most wood windows come with factory-installed flashing, metal flange, or the flashing components. The jambs should have a membrane between the brick mold or stucco mold, and the window jambs and should overlap the building wrap a minimum of 6". The top of the wood window should have a Z-Metal drip head flashing that extends beyond the jamb a minimum of 2" on either side.

Industry Standards
Nail-On Windows
(DTA, Inc.)
Flashing Materials

Flashing is a separate sheet of waterproof or water-resistant material used to cover or lap the edges of a window or door frame installed in a rough opening of the wall frame.

Flashing materials range from sheet metal, building paper, building felt, specialty flashing papers with asphalt cores, and recently developed self-adhering membrane flashings.

Most window leaks (which we have investigated) are attributable to a lack of flashing, poor flashing, or deteriorated flashing. The window product is often not the source of leaks

observed around windows. Flashing is necessary to integrate the weather-resistant qualities of the window product with the weather-resistant functions of the exterior cladding system.

Flashings are typically concealed by the finished construction and are not intended as the primary source of water resistance around windows. However, flashings often become the only source of protection when the primary weather barrier fails. The primary weather barrier should be the exterior cladding system selected for the wall covering. The exterior surface of the wall cladding will keep out most of the water which falls against it.

In time, flashings will fail if the exterior cladding system does not properly exclude most of the water from the weatherexposed cracks, crevices, joints and penetrations in the building.

Conditions Affecting Successful Flashing Assemblies
1. A solid, framed opening in which to be installed
2. Protection from physical abuse
   a. During construction
   b. During its useful life
3. Protection from environmental abuse
   a. During construction
   b. During its useful life
4. Correct sequencing of the materials
5. Correct method of attachment
6. Compatible flashing and wall cladding materials
7. Durable materials. Materials that will provide the assembly with the "expected life of that particular assembly."

Window Installation & Flashing

Comments

While the following text from CAWM addresses aluminum windows, the basic installation requirements are the same for wood, vinyl, vinyl-clad, and metal windows.

*The installation method shown in **Figure 9.1** would include a requirement to caulk the side and top flashings to the nailing flange with a butyl caulking. The building paper is then interwoven under the bottom sisalkraft flashing and over the upper flashing. The bottom tails of the sisalkraft are not caulked until the wrap is installed.*

Industry Standards

Standard Practices for Installation of Windows (CAWM 400-95)
(California Association of Window Manufacturers)

5. Procedure

5.1 Framing Requirements — The rough framed opening to receive the window shall be sufficiently larger in width and height than the actual frame dimensions of the window. To assure adequate clearance, the framer shall consult the manufacturer's literature for the recommended rough opening dimensions. The framing shall be plumb, square and level.

5.2 Protection from Dissimilar Materials

5.2.1 Aluminum products shall be isolated from dissimilar or corrosive materials with a nonconductive coating or sealant material.

5.2.2 All fasteners shall be corrosive resistant, in accordance with ASTM B 633, B 766, or B 456.

Flashing Requirements

Proper flashing and/or sealing is necessary as a secondary barrier to prevent water from entering the wall between the window frame and the adjacent wall materials. Flashing and/or an appropriate method of sealing shall be designed as a part of an overall weather-resistive barrier system. It is **not** the responsibility of the window manufacturer to design or recommend a flashing system appropriate to each job condition.

Note 1 — The responsibility for protecting any flashing material from damage caused by weather, other trades, or vandalism, and properly integrating the flashing system into the weather-resistive barrier for the entire building, will be the responsibility of the general contractor or his designated agent.

5.3.1 Penetration Flashing Material— Flashing material shall be barrier coated reinforced and shall provide four (4) hour minimum protection from water penetration when tested in accordance with ASTM D–779. Flashing material shall carry continuous identification.

Comments

The California Association of Window Manufacturers (CAWM) has established two acceptable methods for installing windows with an integral mounting flange. Method A puts the vertical flashing material over the flange on the vertical window jamb, while Method B places the flashing material under the flange of the vertical window jamb. It is imperative that the caulking be installed as described so that the building wrap can be properly lapped. (See **Figure 9.1***.)*

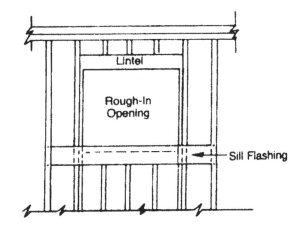

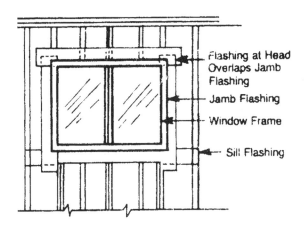

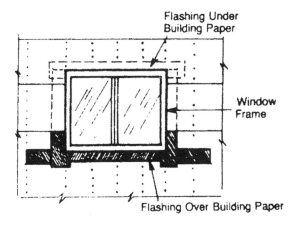

Courtesy of BNI Publications, Inc., *Plaster and Drywall Systems Manual*

Figure 9.1

5.4 Application

5.4.1 One of the two following methods shall be selected as the application to be followed. Once a method is selected, all procedures of that method must be performed in the described sequence. Substitution of a procedure from one method to the other is not permitted.

Method A

5.4.1.1.1 A strip of approved flashing material should be at least nine inches wide. Flashing shall be applied in a weatherboard fashion around the full perimeter of the opening.

5.4.1.1.2 Apply the first strip horizontally immediately below the sill, cut it sufficiently long to extend past each side of the window, so that it projects beyond the vertical flashing to be applied later.

5.4.1.1.3 Fasten the top edge of the sill flashing to the framing, but do not fasten the lower edge, so the weather resistant building paper applied later may be slipped up and underneath the flashing in weatherboard fashion.

5.4.1.1.4 Apply a continuous seal to the back side (interior) of the sill mounting flange. The window shall then be installed in accordance with Section 5.5 installation procedures.

5.4.1.1.5 Next, apply a continuous seal to the exposed mounting flange at the top (head) and sides (C jambs) of the installed window. For mechanically joined frames, apply seal at corners the full length of the seam where mounting flanges meet.

5.4.1.1.6 Starting at each jamb, embed the jamb flashing into the seal and fasten in place. Run this flashing beyond the sill flashing and above where the head flashing will intersect.

5.4.1.1.7 Finally, embed the flashing into the sealant on the mounting flange at the window head. Cut this flashing sufficiently long so that it will extend beyond each jamb flashing.

Comments

Figure 9.2 shows recommended flashing for window installation in wood siding. This description parallels the recommendations of the Plaster and Drywall Systems Manual and the California Association of Window Manufacturers (CAWM) on plaster walls, including setting the window frame in mastic against the sisalkraft. Manufacturers may specify different methods for various exterior skins.

Method B

5.4.1.2.1 A strip of approved flashing material should be at least nine inches wide. Flashing shall be applied in a weatherboard fashion around the full perimeter of the opening.

5.4.1.2.2 Apply the first strip horizontally immediately below the sill, cut it sufficiently long to extend past each side of the window, so that it projects beyond the vertical flashing to be applied later.

5.4.1.2.3 Fasten the top edge of the sill flashing to the framing, but do not fasten the lower edge, so the weather resistant building paper applied later may be slipped up and underneath the flashing in weatherboard fashion.

5.4.1.2.4 Next, fasten strips of flashing at each vertical edge (jamb) of the opening. Run this flashing beyond the sill flashing and above where the head flashing will intersect.

5.4.1.2.5 Apply a continuous seal to the backside (interior) of the mounting flange near the outer edge or a continuous seal to the perimeter of the opening at a point to assure contact with the backside (interior) of the mounting flange.

Note 2 — Caution must be taken to avoid disrupting the continuous seal.

5.4.1.2.6 The window shall then be installed in accordance with Section 5.5 installation procedures.

5.4.1.2.7 For mechanically joined frames, apply seal at corners the full length of the seam where mounting flanges meet.

5.4.1.2.8 Next, apply a continuous seal at the top (head) mounting flange and embed the bottom of the head flashing over the sealant and the mounting flange. Cut this flashing sufficiently long so that it will extend beyond each jamb flashing. Fasten in place.

Installation Requirements

5.5.1 Depending on the size and weight of the window, shim blocks may be required under the sill to maintain straight and level condition and to prevent rotation. Consult manufacturer's recommendations.

5.5.2 Shim and adjust the window as necessary to achieve a plumb, square and level condition, as well as an even reveal around the frame opening, securing it the full perimeter with the equivalent of 6d fasteners on a maximum 16-inch center. Hinged and pivoted windows may require additional fasteners located near the hinge or pivot points. For certain windows it may be appropriate to fasten the head in a manner to allow for possible deflection.

Comments

Shims should be placed at equal distance opposite one another, top and bottom, and side to side.

Window Flashing

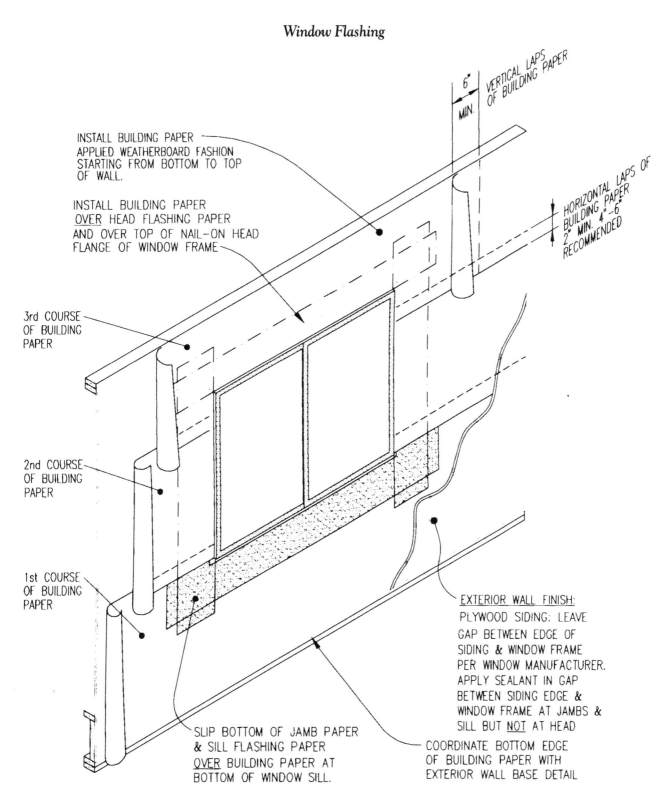

INSTALL BUILDING PAPER
APPLIED WEATHERBOARD FASHION
STARTING FROM BOTTOM TO TOP
OF WALL.

INSTALL BUILDING PAPER
OVER HEAD FLASHING PAPER
AND OVER TOP OF NAIL−ON HEAD
FLANGE OF WINDOW FRAME

6" MIN. VERTICAL LAPS OF BUILDING PAPER

HORIZONTAL LAPS OF BUILDING PAPER 2" MIN. 4"−6" RECOMMENDED

3rd COURSE
OF BUILDING
PAPER

2nd COURSE
OF BUILDING
PAPER

1st COURSE
OF BUILDING
PAPER

EXTERIOR WALL FINISH:
PLYWOOD SIDING: LEAVE
GAP BETWEEN EDGE OF
SIDING & WINDOW FRAME
PER WINDOW MANUFACTURER.
APPLY SEALANT IN GAP
BETWEEN SIDING EDGE &
WINDOW FRAME AT JAMBS &
SILL BUT NOT AT HEAD

SLIP BOTTOM OF JAMB PAPER
& SILL FLASHING PAPER
OVER BUILDING PAPER AT
BOTTOM OF WINDOW SILL.

COORDINATE BOTTOM EDGE
OF BUILDING PAPER WITH
EXTERIOR WALL BASE DETAIL

NOTE: ATTEMPT TO KEEP FASTENER FOR TRIM & SIDING AWAY FROM WINDOW. FIN AS MUCH AS
POSSIBLE, ESPECIALLY NEAR CORNERS. THE NAILS WHICH PENETRATE THE FIN CAN DISTORT
THE FRAME'S CORNER JOINT SEAL.

Courtesy of DTA, Inc., *Nail-On Windows*

Figure 9.2

Aluminum Window with Wood Plant-On

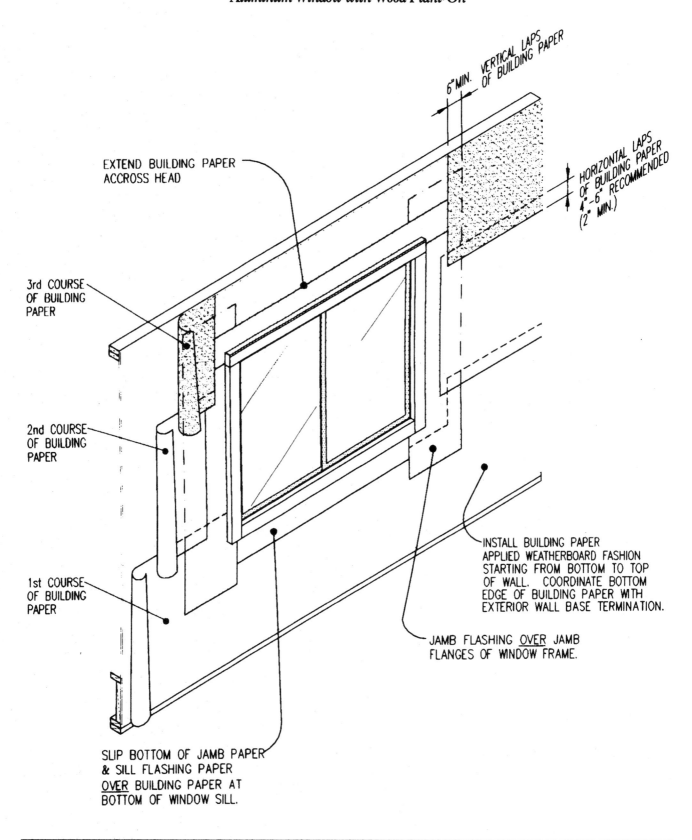

6"MIN. VERTICAL LAPS OF BUILDING PAPER

HORIZONTAL LAPS OF BUILDING PAPER 4"-6" RECOMMENDED (2" MIN.)

EXTEND BUILDING PAPER ACCROSS HEAD

3rd COURSE OF BUILDING PAPER

2nd COURSE OF BUILDING PAPER

1st COURSE OF BUILDING PAPER

INSTALL BUILDING PAPER APPLIED WEATHERBOARD FASHION STARTING FROM BOTTOM TO TOP OF WALL. COORDINATE BOTTOM EDGE OF BUILDING PAPER WITH EXTERIOR WALL BASE TERMINATION.

JAMB FLASHING <u>OVER</u> JAMB FLANGES OF WINDOW FRAME.

SLIP BOTTOM OF JAMB PAPER & SILL FLASHING PAPER <u>OVER</u> BUILDING PAPER AT BOTTOM OF WINDOW SILL.

Courtesy of DTA, Inc., *Nail-On Windows*

Figure 9.3

310

5.5.3 In each direction from all corners there must be a fastener within 10 inches, but no closer than 3 inches, to prevent frame distortion or fracture of joint seals.

5.5.4 In all cases consult manufacturer's instructions for any special procedures or applications.

Comments

While these listed installation requirements apply to most windows, every manufacturer has its own specific instructions, which may include unique details essential to successful product performance.

Note 3 — If any damage to window frame joint seals is observed during installation, it must be repaired by the installer.

5.5.5 Where weather-resistant building paper, insulating board, or other materials *by other trades* may constitute the primary weather barrier behind the exterior wall finish (i.e., stucco, masonry, siding, etc.), Owner/General Contractor is responsible to ensure that the weather barrier is continuous by effectively sealing the material to the window frame.

Plant-On Trim

Comments

The following drawing recommends placement of the plant-on trim over the standard wrap. Use treated lumber for the plant-on, because exposure to moisture will cause the wood to swell. The plant-on should be made of foam or lightweight plaster that will not increase dimensionally from water absorption.

Also note the sheet metal flashing over the top of the wood plant-on header.

Radius windows with integral flange should use small pieces of paper-reinforced flashing that have been folded and set in sealant to "step flash" the radius to a keystone center piece at the top.

While the sisalkraft can perform well when it is properly installed, a self-sticking bitumen flashing is far superior to the reinforced paper products.

Plant-On Detail

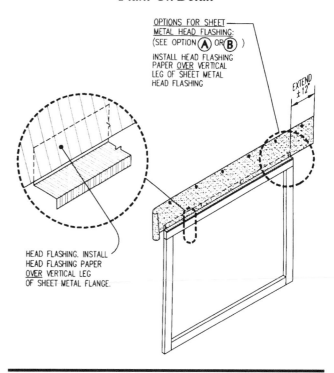

OPTIONS FOR SHEET METAL HEAD FLASHING: (SEE OPTION (A) OR (B))
INSTALL HEAD FLASHING PAPER OVER VERTICAL LEG OF SHEET METAL HEAD FLASHING

EXTEND ± 12"

HEAD FLASHING. INSTALL HEAD FLASHING PAPER OVER VERTICAL LEG OF SHEET METAL FLANGE.

Courtesy of DTA, Inc., *Nail-On Windows*

Figure 9.4

Finish & Sealant Protection

Industry Standards

Standard Practices for Installation of Windows (CAWM 400-95)
(California Association of Window Manufacturers)

5.7.1 Caution shall be used to avoid damage to windows during and after installation. Prior to installation, store windows in a near vertical position in a clean area, free of circulating dirt or debris and protected from exposure to weather elements.

5.7.2 Field-applied protective coatings can damage window sealants and gaskets and are not recommended. Contact the window manufacturer before applying any such coatings.

5.7.3 Masking tapes shall not be used on window surfaces as they may cause damage when they are removed.

5.7.4 Stucco or concrete left to cure on frames and glass will damage these surfaces. Remove and clean all such materials from surfaces before any curing action takes place.

5.7.5 Glass and frame surfaces exposed to leaching water from new concrete or stucco must be rinsed immediately with clear water to prevent permanent damage.

Doors: General Information

Grading
Industry Standards
WIC Manual of Millwork
(Woodwork Institute of California)

The following are the grades established for architectural millwork products:

Economy
This grade establishes a standard to meet the requirements of lower cost residential and commercial construction wherein economy is the principal factor, and use in storage room and utility areas.

Custom
This grade includes all the requisites of high quality millwork and is suitable for all normal uses in high grade construction, such as higher quality residential, school, and commercial building.

Premium
This grade, as the name implies, is a superior quality of materials and craftsmanship, with a corresponding increase in cost. It is intended primarily for the best of hardwood construction, but any species of wood may be specified.

Types of Doors
Industry Standards
Fundamentals of the Construction Process
(R.S. Means Co., Inc.)

Wood Doors
Wood doors are available in two basic designs: flush and panel. Flush wood doors have two smooth faces and are manufactured as hollow core, particleboard core, or solid core. Flush facings are single sheets of lauan mahogany, birch, other hardwood veneers, or synthetic veneers created from a medium density overlay and high-pressure plastic laminate. These veneers require only a clear finish. The core materials used for flush doors depend, to a certain extent, on the quality of the interior finishes and the soundproofing provided by the denser cores. The design is the most common, having a universal appeal to commercial as well as residential owners.

Paneled-wood doors are manufactured from pine or fir. This type of door typically has a solid wood stile (vertical-edge member) and rail (cross-membrane), and one-, two-, five-, six-, or eight-panel design. Simulated six-panel doors with hollow cores and molded hardboard facings are also available. These doors are painted.

Hollow Metal Doors
The most common hollow metal (steel) doors are flush design, but residential doors are available in several decorative patterns that are embossed into or applied onto the face sheets. Metal doors can be galvanized and primed, or factory-finished with enamel in a variety of colors.

There are several grades of hardware: light duty or residential, standard duty, and heavy duty. For hinges, this is expressed in terms of usage: low, average, and high frequencies.

Most general contractors order doors, frames, and hardware from various suppliers or manufacturers and then install them with their own carpenters. The door frame schedule and supplier must be closely coordinated with the hardware schedule and supplier. For example, templates are transmitted to hollow metal suppliers immediately following approval of the door schedule. In this case, time can be a critical factor; custom hollow metal frames, doors, and hardware are long lead items.

Ed. Note: See also "Metal Doors" later in this chapter.

Door Installation

Industry Standards

Specifiers Guide to Wood Windows and Doors
(National Wood Window & Door Association)

The utility or structural strength of the doors must not be impaired in fitting to the opening, in applying hardware, in preparing for lights, louvers, plant-ons or other detailing.

Use two hinges for solid core doors up to 60' in height, three hinges for doors up to 90' in height and an additional hinge for every additional 30" of door height or portion thereof. Interior hollowcore doors weighing less than 50 pounds and not over 7'6" in height may be hung on two hinges. Use heavy weight hinges on doors over 175 pounds. Consult manufacturer with regard to weight and site of hinges required.

Clearances between door edges and door frame should be a minimum of 1/16" on the hinge edge. For latch edge and top rail the clearance should be 1/8" (+0, –1/16".)

All hardware locations, preparations for hardware and methods of hardware attachment must be appropriate for the specific door construction. Templates for specific hardware preparation are available from hardware manufacturers or their distributors.

Comments

Hollow Core Door

If hardware is specified that is not commonly used with hollow core doors, it is possible to have inserts or stiffeners inserted during the manufacturing process that will compensate for any unusual loads or stresses that may be imposed by the hardware application.

When light or louver cutouts are made for exterior doors, they must be protected in order to prevent water from entering the door core. Metal flashing at the bottom of the cutout is one satisfactory method.

Pilot holes must be drilled for all screws that act as hardware attachments. Threaded-to-the-head screws are preferable for fastening hardware to nonrated doors and are required on fire rated doors.

In fitting for height, do not trim top or bottom edge by more than 3/4" unless accommodated by additional blocking. Do not trim top edge of fire doors.

Doors and door frames should be installed plumb, square and level. When installed in exterior applications, doors must be properly sealed and adequately protected from the elements. Flashing should be applied at the head, jambs and sill.

Cleaning and Touchup

Inspect all wood doors prior to hanging them on the job. Repair noticeable marks or defects that may have occurred from improper storage and handling.

Field touchup shall include the filling of exposed nail or screw holes, re-finishing of raw surfaces resulting form job fitting, repair of job inflicted scratches and mars, and final cleaning of finished surfaces. Field repairs and touchups are the responsibility of the installing contractor.

When cleaning door surfaces, use a non-abrasive commercial cleaner designed for cleaning wood door or paneling surfaces, that do not leave a film residue that would buildup or effect the surface gloss of the door finish.

Adjustment and Maintenance

Inspect all wood doors prior to hanging them on the job. Repair noticeable marks or defects that may have occurred from improper storage and handling.

Review with the owner/owner's representative how to periodically inspect all doors for wear, damage and natural deterioration.

Review with the owner/owner's representative how to periodically inspect and adjust all hardware to insure that it continues to function as it was originally intended.

Wood & Plastic Laminate Doors

Industry Standards

WIC Manual of Millwork
(Woodwork Institute of California)

Install with a maximum clearance of 1/8" on the hinge side, 1/8" on the lock side, 1/8" between the meeting edge of doors in pairs, and 1/8" between the top of the door and the frame header. The installer is not responsible for clearances in excess of these dimensions if the door supplier has erred on the prefit widths or locations for mortise hardware. Clearance at the bottom of the door will be as specified by Architect/Designer on nonrated doors and conform to NFPA 80 on fire-rated doors. Prefit and premachined doors are to be installed in accordance with manufacturers' data. Notify the contractor or owner if there is a problem before proceeding.

If not premachined, use a minimum of one hinge for each 30 inches of door height on all exterior doors and all solid core doors.

When using three or more hinges, they are to be equally spaced. Interior hollow core doors weighing less than fifty pounds and not over 7'-6" in height may be hung on two hinges.

All screws must be applied into each piece of hardware.

Doors may not extend beyond 1/16" from the face of the jamb, nor more than 1/8" behind the jamb face.

Wood doors that are part of a matched paneled area must be installed by the paneling installer.

The utility or structural strength of the doors must not be impaired in fitting to the opening, in applying hardware, in preparing for lights, louvers, or plant-ons or other detailing.

All hardware locations, preparation for hardware, and methods of hardware attachment must be appropriate for the specific door construction. Templates for specific hardware preparation are available from hardware manufacturers, NWWDA, or DHI.

When light or louver cutouts are made for exterior doors, they must be protected in order to prevent water from entering the door core. Metal flashing at the bottom of the cutout is one satisfactory method.

Wood doors seldom need to be replaced due to warp. Temporary distortions will usually disappear when humidity is equalized.

Extreme care must be used to prevent chipping veneer when cutting length.

The best manufactured door still requires skilled workmanship and proper care at the jobsite.

Installation of Doors & Jambs

The installation standard of doors and jambs shall be equal to the Premium or Custom Quality Standard of the manufactured doors and jambs being used.

Doors

In the fitting for width, trim equally from both sides. In order to preserve the label on fire-rated doors, trim per manufacturers' requirements.

If fitting for height, do not trim top or bottom rails more than 3/4". Fire-rated doors shall be trimmed only from the bottom rails and shall be trimmed no more than 3/4".

Threaded-to-the-head wood screws are preferable for fastening all hardware on non-rated doors and required on all rated doors. Pilot holes must be drilled for all screws.

Do not remove labels from fire-rated doors.

Door Jambs

Jambs must be set plumb.

Jambs legs must be set square with header and parallel to each other within 1/16" on Premium, 1/8" on Custom, 3/16" on Economy.

Jambs must be securely seated directly onto floor.

Jambs must be securely anchored with concealed fasteners for Premium Grade.

Cleaning

Upon completion of the installation, the installer shall clean all items installed; pencil or ink marks shall be removed, and broom clean the area of operations, depositing his debris in containers provided by the general contractor.

Wood Doors

Industry Standards

Specifiers Guide to Wood Windows and Doors
(National Wood Window & Door Association)

Ed. Note: NWWDA I.S.I-A is a general industry standard that provides quality levels for the construction of architectural wood flush doors.

Exterior Use

In exterior use, temperature and humidity are not controlled on both sides of the door. Care must be taken when specifying Architectural wood flush doors in exterior openings. Consult individual manufacturers for specific recommendations and warranty limitations.

Wood Door Finishing
Job Site Finishing

Because of the many uncontrollable variables that exist at a site, such as temperature and moisture variation, dust and other factors, door manufacturers' warranties do not cover the appearance of finishes applied at the job site.

Finishing

Wood is hygroscopic and dimensionally influenced by changes in moisture content caused by changes within its surrounding environment. To assure uniform moisture exposure and dimensional control all surfaces must be finished equally.

Doors may not be ready for finishing when initially received. Before finishing, remove all handling marks, raised grain, scuffs, burnishes and other undesirable blemishes by block sanding all surfaces in a horizontal position with a 120, 150 or 180 grit sandpaper. To avoid cross grain scratches, sand with the grain.

Certain species of wood, particularly oak, contain chemicals which react unfavorably with foreign materials in the finishing system. Eliminate the use of steel wool on bare wood, rusty containers or any other contaminate in the finishing system.

A thinned coat of sanding sealer should be applied prior to staining to promote a uniform appearance and avoid sharp contrasts in color or a blotchy appearance.

All exposed wood surfaces must be sealed including top and bottom rails. Cutouts for hardware in exterior doors must be sealed prior to installation of hardware and exposure to weather. Dark-colored finishes should be avoided on all surfaces if the door is exposed to direct sunlight, in order to reduce the chance of warping or veneer checking. Oil-based sealers or prime coats provide the best base coat for finishing. If a water-based primer is used it should be an exterior grade product. Note: Water-based coatings on unfinished wood may cause veneer splits, highlight joints and raise wood grain and therefore should be avoided. If a water-based primer is desired, please contact the finish supplier regarding the correct application and use of these products.

Be sure the door surface being finished is satisfactory in both smoothness and color after each coat. Allow adequate drying time between coats. Desired results are best achieved by following the finish manufactures' recommendations. Do not finish door until a sample of the finish has been approved.

Finishes on exterior doors may deteriorate due to exposure to the environment. In order to protect the door it is recommended that the condition of the exterior finish be inspected at least once a year and re-finished as needed.

Note: Certain wood fire doors have fire retardant salts impregnated into various wood components that makes the components more hygroscopic than normal wood. When exposed to high moisture conditions, these salts will concentrate on exposed surfaces and interfere with the finish. Before finishing, reduce moisture content in the treated wood below 11% and remove the salt crystals with a damp cloth followed by drying and light sanding. For further information on fire doors see NWWDA publications regarding Installing, Handling & Finishing Fire Doors.

Comments

For wood entry systems, the final finish should be applied to the door as soon as it has been fit and hung (but not during periods of significant moisture). Surfaces should be clean and dry, and any dust, grease, and marks from handling removed. Any damage from handling must be repaired, and the entire door sanded lightly.

Best results are obtained if the door is lying flat when finished. All sides, including edges, should be finished. Dark-colored stain or paint is generally not

recommended for surfaces that receive direct sunlight. Dark colors contribute to heat buildup, resulting in moisture loss, shrinkage, and checking.

Exterior finishes or stains should contain ultraviolet (UV) inhibitors. When painting glazed doors, apply the top coats such that they form a "bridge" between the wood and the glass. The lapping of paint onto glass by 1/16" provides protection from moisture penetration.

Basic Wood Door Installation Guidelines

The following guidelines are in keeping with the general recommendations of wood door manufacturers. (Be sure to consult the specific instructions accompanying a particular door.)

- *Allow 1/8" clearance between frame and door.*
- *For doors 7' maximum height, and 3' maximum width, use 3 hinges in a straight line to prevent distortion.*
- *For doors over 7' high, or over 3' wide, use 4 hinges.*

For more on hinge requirements, see "Door Installation," NWWDA guidelines in the previous section.

Panels on stile and rail wood doors are designed to move (or "float") during climate changes. Before the door is finished, the installer should make sure the panels are properly aligned with the rails and stiles. Panels can be adjusted with a soft wood block and rubber mallet. Manufacturers do not generally consider the need for this realignment as a defect.

Wood Entry Doors

Scope

2.1 This standard provides minimum performance requirements for exterior wood door primary entry systems. Provisions are included in Section 4 for testing and identifying systems which fully comply with this standard.

3. General Requirements

3.1.1 Doors (panels). All wood doors used in exterior wood door systems shall meet the appropriate requirements of the latest revision of NWWDA I.S.1 "Industry Standard for Wood Flush Doors" or NWWDA 1.S.6 "Industry Standard for Wood Stile and Rail Doors."

3.1.2 Tolerances. A tolerance of plus or minus 1/8 inch (3.2 mm) from the specifications of the door system tested will be permitted.

3.1.3 Weather-stripping. All exterior wood door systems shall be weather-stripped. The materials and locations of the weather-stripping shall enable the unit to meet the performance requirements of Section 4 and have the durability reasonably adequate for normal and continuous usage.

Appearance of Individual Pieces of Veneer

 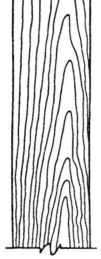 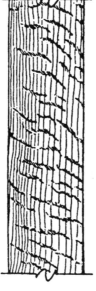 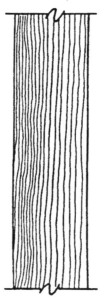 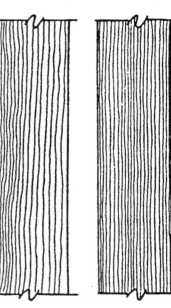

| Rotary Cut | Flat Cut:
Plain Sliced | Quarter Cut:
Red & White Oak | Quarter Cut:
Other Species | Rift-Cut:
Red & White Oak | Comb Grain:
Red & White Oak |

Veneer Cuts

The way in which a log is cut, in relation to the annual growth rings, determines the appearance of veneer. The beauty of veneer is in the natural variations of texture, grain, figure, color, and the way it is assembled on a door face.

Faces will have the natural variations in grain inherent in the species and cut. Natural variations of veneer grain and pattern will vary from these illustrations.

Rotary

This cut follows the log's annual growth rings, providing a general bold random appearance.

Flat Cut (Plain Sliced)

Slicing is done parallel to a line through the center of the log. Cathedral and straight grained patterns result. The individual pieces of veneer are kept in the order they are sliced, permitting a natural grain progression when assembled as veneer faces.

Quarter Cut

A series of stripes is produced. These stripes vary in width from species to species. Flake is a characteristic of this cut in red and white oak.

Rift-Cut (only in Red & White Oak)

The cut slices slightly across the medullary rays, accentuating the vertical grain and minimizing the "flake." Rift grain is restricted to red and white oak.

Comb Grain (only in Red & White Oak)

Limited availability. This is a rift-cut veneer distinguished by the tightness and straightness of the grain along the entire length of the veneer. Slight angle in the grain is allowed. Comb grain is restricted to red and white oak. See section G-11 for maximum grain slope. There are occasional cross bars and flake is minimal.

Courtesy of National Wood, Window & Door Association, *Specifiers Guide to Wood Windows & Doors*

Figure 9.5

Wood Patio Doors

2.1 Scope. This standard provides minimum performance requirements for both the operating and stationary wood, prefinished wood and clad wood sliding patio doors. For purposes of this standard, a sliding patio door covers both wood, prefinished wood and clad wood sliding patio doors. Provisions are included in Section 5.6 for labeling or otherwise identifying each sliding patio door which fully complies with this standard for operating force, air infiltration, water penetration, structural performance and forced entry resistance. Provisions are also included in Section 6.2 for labeling and rating each sliding patio door for thermal performance.

3.0 General Requirements

3.1 All sliding patio doors, which are certified or otherwise indicated or represented as conforming to this standard, shall meet or exceed all the applicable requirements of this standard.

1³/₄ FRONT ENTRANCE DOORS (EXTERIOR)

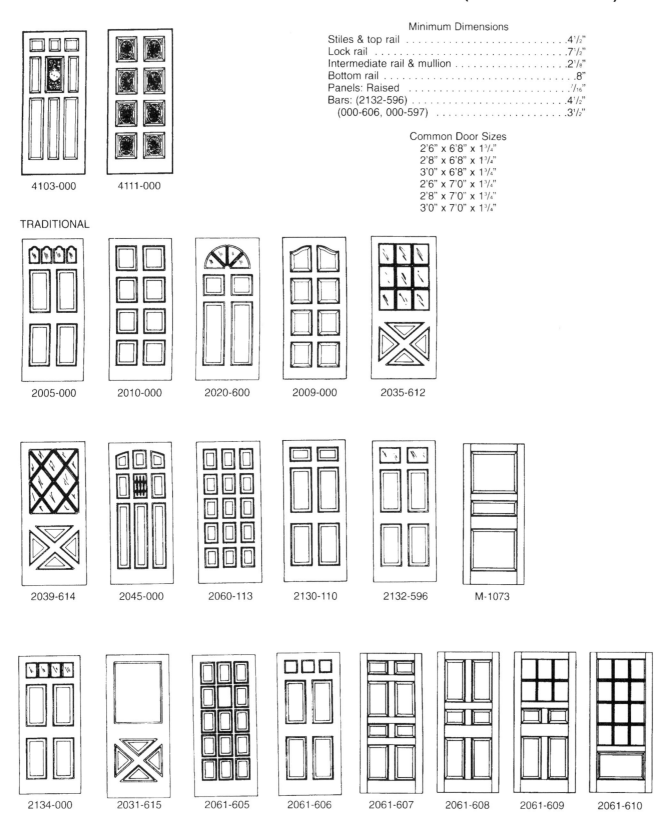

Minimum Dimensions

Stiles & top rail	4¹/₂"
Lock rail	7¹/₂"
Intermediate rail & mullion	2¹/₈"
Bottom rail	8"
Panels: Raised	⁷/₁₆"
Bars: (2132-596)	4¹/₂"
(000-606, 000-597)	3¹/₂"

Common Door Sizes

2'6" x 6'8" x 1³/₄"
2'8" x 6'8" x 1³/₄"
3'0" x 6'8" x 1³/₄"
2'6" x 7'0" x 1³/₄"
2'8" x 7'0" x 1³/₄"
3'0" x 7'0" x 1³/₄"

4103-000   4111-000

TRADITIONAL

2005-000   2010-000   2020-600   2009-000   2035-612

2039-614   2045-000   2060-113   2130-110   2132-596   M-1073

2134-000   2031-615   2061-605   2061-606   2061-607   2061-608   2061-609   2061-610

Courtesy of National Wood Window & Door Association, *Specifiers Guide to Wood Windows and Doors*

Figure 9.6

3.2 Wood. The wood parts of the sliding patio door shall be wood or wood composites that have a moisture content no greater than twelve percent (12%) at the time of fabrication.

3.2.1 All exposed wood surfaces shall be sound. Defects and discolorations are permitted provided the surface is suitable for an opaque finish.

3.3 Tolerances. A tolerance of plus or minus 1/32 inch (1 mm) from the specifications of the sliding patio doors tested will be permitted for all sliding patio door parts.

3.4 Adhesives. The adhesives used in the manufacture of finger jointed and/or edge bonded parts shall meet or exceed the wet use adhesive requirements as defined in the latest revision of ASTM D 5572 "Specification for Adhesives Used for Fingerjoints in Nonstructural Lumber Products".

3.5 Preservative Treatment. All wood parts of sliding patio doors, except inside stops and inside trim, shall be water-repellent preservative treated, after machining, in accordance with the latest revision of NWWDA Industry Standard I.S.4 "Water Repellent Preservative Non-Pressure Treatment for Millwork."

3.6 Weather-strip. All sliding patio doors shall be weather-stripped. Weather-stripping shall be made, at the option of the manufacturer, with any suitable material that has the performance qualities and durability reasonably adequate for normal and continuous operation. The weather-strip shall be installed in a manner which shall effectively enable the unit to meet the air and water infiltration requirements for the performance level specified.

3.7.3 Exposed Exterior Hardware. All hardware exposed to the exterior side of the sliding patio door after assembly and installation shall be, when tested, in accordance with the latest revision of ASTM B 1 17 Standard Method of Salt Spray Apparatus.

3.8 Glazing Material. Glazing materials used in wood sliding patio doors must conform to the requirements of the Consumer Product Safety Commission Safety Standard for Architectural Glazing Materials (16 CFR 1201). Insulated glazing, consisting of two or more pieces of safety glazing material separated by a sealed air space, may be used.

3.8.1 Glazing Sealants. The method of glazing and the materials used shall permit the unit to meet the performance requirements of Section 5. Where glazing sealants are used, they shall be quality elastic type compounds which are designed for bedding safety glazing materials or which are specifically recommended for such use by the sealant manufacturer.

3.8.2 Insulating Glass. Sealed insulating glass shall meet or exceed the requirements of the latest revision of ASTM E 774 "Specifications for Sealed Insulating Glass Units". Each insulating glass unit shall be permanently labeled with a name or code identifying the insulating glass manufacturer.

3.9 Screen Panels. Insect screen panels shall be provided when specified or in accordance with each manufacturer's usual practice. Screen panels shall operate smoothly and shall remain in contact with the track during normal operation. Screen panels shall be equipped with a latch that does not lock automatically, i.e. when the screen panel is closed; the locking device shall not lock without a specific action by the operator. When aluminum framed insect screens are specified, they shall meet or exceed the requirements of the latest revision of ANSI/SMA 2006 "Specifications for Aluminum Sliding Screen Doors".

Wood Swinging Patio Doors

2.1 Scope. This standard provides minimum material and performance requirements for both the operating and stationary portions of all types of wood swinging patio doors. For purposes of this standard wood, prefinished wood and clad wood swinging patio doors are covered. Provisions are included in Section 5 for testing and identifying swinging patio doors which fully comply with this standard for air, water and structural performance certification. Provisions are also included in Section 6.2 for labeling and rating each swinging patio door for thermal performance.

3.2.2 Adhesives. The adhesive used in the manufacture of finger jointed and edge bonded parts shall meet or exceed the "wet use" adhesive requirements of the latest revision of ASTM D 3110 "Adhesives Used in Non-Structural Glued Lumber Products." The adhesive used in the manufacture of fingerjointed parts shall meet or exceed the requirements of the latest revision of ASTM D 5572 "Adhesives Used for Finger Joints in Nonstructural Lumber Products".

3.2.3 Tolerances. Unless otherwise specified at the time the swinging patio door units are ordered, the following tolerances will apply to the overall dimensions of all doors.

3.2.3.1 Height and Width Tolerances. A plus (+)1/8 inch, minus (–) 1/8 inch tolerance (+3 mm, –3 mm) is allowed in overall width and height for swinging patio door units 9 feet or less in width. For units greater than 9 feet wide, a 1/4 inch (6 mm) tolerance in width, +1/8 inch (+3 mm) tolerance in height is allowed.

3.2.3.2 Thickness Tolerances. The following thickness tolerances shall apply to these swinging patio door components.

a) **Doors (panels)** — A plus (+) 1/32 inch, minus (–) 3/32 inch tolerance (+1 mm, – 2 mm) is allowed from the nominal thickness of a door of a unit described in this standard.

b) **Frames/Mouldings** — A plus (+) 1/32 inch tolerance is allowed for the interior wood moulding of the units described in this standard.

3.2.4 Warp. The amount of bow, cup or twist in a door shall not exceed 1/4 inch (6 mm) when measured by placing a straight edge, taut wire or string, on the suspected concave face of the door at any angle (i.e. horizontal, vertical, diagonal). The measurement of bow, cup or twist shall be made at the point of maximum distance between the bottom of the straight edge, taut wire or string, and the face of the door after accounting for glazing recesses.

3.2.5 Grading. All swinging patio door units shall conform to the following specifications.

3.2.5.1 Doors (panels). The doors of the units described in this standard shall meet or exceed the grading requirements in accordance with the latest revision of NWWDA I.S.6 "Industry Standard for Stile and Rail Doors".

3.2.5.2 Frames/Moulding. The interior moulding of the units described in this standard shall meet or exceed the grading requirements in accordance with the latest revision of WM 1-89 "Industry Standard for Interior Wood Door Jambs".

3.2.6.1 Dimensions. The doors (panels) of the units described in this standard shall be constructed to the dimension requirements in accordance with the latest revision of NWWDA 1.S.6 "Industry Standard for Stile and Rail Doors" with the following exceptions:

a) Stile and intermediate rail width must be no less than 2-1/8" (54 mm).

b) Top and bottom rail width must be no less than 3-1/2" (89 mm).

c) Stile and rail thickness must be no less than 1-3/8" (35 mm).

3.3 Glazing Materials

3.3.1 Glazing Material. Glazing materials used in wood swinging patio doors must conform to the requirements of the Consumer Product Safety Commission "Safety Standard for Architectural Glazing Materials (16 CFR 1201)." Insulated glazing, consisting of two or more pieces of safety glazing material separated by a sealed air space, may be used.

3.3.2 Glazing Sealants. The method of glazing and the materials used shall permit the unit to meet the performance requirements of Section 5. Where glazing sealants are used, they shall be quality elastic type compounds which are designed for bedding safety glazing materials or which are specifically recommended for such use by the sealant manufacturer.

3.3.3 Insulating Glass. Sealed insulating glass shall meet or exceed the requirements of the latest revision of ASTM E 774 "Specifications for Sealed Insulating Glass Units." Each insulating glass unit shall be permanently labeled with a name or code identifying the insulating glass manufacturer.

Ed. Note: See "Window Installation & Flashing" earlier in this chapter for information on flashing wood windows and doors.

3.4 Hardware. When hardware is provided, the type and location of hardware installed on a wood swinging patio door shall permit the unit to meet the following requirements, and the performance requirements of Section 5.

3.5 Weather-strip. All operating units shall be weatherstripped. Weather-strip shall be made, at the option of the manufacturer, with any suitable material that has the performance qualities and durability reasonably adequate for normal and continuous operation. The weather-strip shall be installed in the swinging patio door unit so as to effectively enable the unit to meet the air and water infiltration requirements specified in Section 5.

Stile & Rail (Panel) Doors
Industry Standards
Specifiers Guide to Wood Windows and Doors
(National Wood Window and Door Association)

2.1 Scope. This standard covers the principal sizes, types, grades and designs of commercially available wood stile and rail doors. Included are requirements for dimensions, materials and construction. Methods of marking and labeling to indicate compliance with the standard and a glossary of trade terms are also included.

2.2 Classification. The doors covered by this standard are identified by size, species, grade and design. The illustrations in this standard are based on minimum sizes and dimensional requirements for each door design. The sizes and locations of panels, glazing and intermediate members, may vary from manufacturer to manufacturer.

3.1.3.1 Height and Width Tolerances. A plus (+)1/16 in., minus (–)1/8 in. tolerance (+1.6mm, –3.2mm) is allowed in overall width and/or height for all doors except bifold doors. Bifold doors are considered prefit at the time of manufacture and must conform to the tolerances listed in Section 3.3.7.

3.13.2 Thickness Tolerance. A plus (+) 0", minus (–)3/32" tolerance (+ 0 mm, –2.4 mm) is allowed from the nominal thickness of a door or thickness of a raised panel.

3.1.4 Warp. The amount of bow, cup or twist in a door shall be measured by placing a straight edge, taut wire or string on the suspected concave face of the door at any angle (i.e., horizontal, vertical or diagonal). The measurement of bow, cup or twist shall be made at the point of maximum distance between the bottom of the straight edge, taut wire or string and the face of the door, after accounting for panel or glazing recesses. The warp for any nominal 1-3/4" thick by 3'6" wide by 7' high (4.4 cm x 1.07 m x 2.13 m) or smaller door, shall not exceed 1/4" (6.4 mm).

3.2.1 Wood. Unless otherwise stated in this standard, all doors are to be made from wood or wood composites that have been kiln dried to a moisture content no greater than 1246 at the

1³⁄₈ INTERIOR PANEL DOORSᵃ

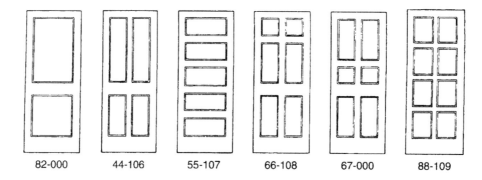

| 82-000 | 44-106 | 55-107 | 66-108 | 67-000 | 88-109 |

Minimum Dimensions

Stiles

1'0" thru 1'6"	.2¹⁄₈"
1'8" thru 2'6"	.3¹⁄₈"
2'8" thru 3'0"	.4¹⁄₈"
over 3'0"	.4¹⁄₂"

Rails

Top Rails	.4¹⁄₂"
Lock Rail (44-106 & 66-108)	.7¹⁄₂"
Intermediate Rail	.3⁷⁄₈"
(Except 55-107)	.3¹⁄₄"
Mullions	.3⁷⁄₈"
Bottom Rail	.8"

Panels

Raised	.⁷⁄₁₆"
Flat	.¹⁄₄"

Common Door Sizesᵇ

1'6" x 6'6" x 1³⁄₈"	2'6" x 6'6" x 1³⁄₈"
1'6" x 6'8"	2'6" x 6'8"
1'8" x 6'8"	2'6" x 7'0"
2'0" x 6'6"	2'8" x 6'6"
2'0" x 6'8"	2'8" x 6'8"
2'0" x 7'0"	2'8" x 7'0"
2'4" x 6'6"	3'0" x 6'8"
3'4" x 6'8"	3'0" x 7'0"
2'4" x 7'0"	

a) Also for exterior use.
b) Doors 1'8" wide and narrower are made one panel wide.

1. Drawings are not to scale. Drawings show only relative position of components.

NOTE: To convert inches to millimeters, multiply by 25.4.

Courtesy of National Wood Window & Door Association, *Specifiers Guide to Wood Windows and Doors*

Figure 9.7

time of fabrication. Any non-wood substrates may be used provided they meet the same performance criteria for solid wood components.

3.2.3 Adhesives. All adhesives used to assemble interior doors shall meet or exceed the requirements for "dry-use" adhesives as described in ASTM D-3110 "Adhesives Used in Non-Structural Glued Lumber Products." Other adhesives used to assemble exterior doors shall meet or exceed the requirements for "wet-use" adhesives as described in the latest revision of ASTM D3110, unless the door manufacturer warrants that doors for exterior installation are fabricated with "dry-use" adhesives.

3.2.4 Glazing Material. All glazing materials used in doors must conform to the requirements for the Consumer Product Safety Commission, "Safety Standard for Architectural Glazing Materials (16CFR 1201)." Insulated glazing, consisting of two or more pieces of safety glazing material separated by a sealed air space, may be used.

3.2.5 Glazing Sealants. Glazing sealants shall be quality, elastic type compounds which are designed for bedding glazing materials or which are specifically recommended for such use by the sealant manufacturer.

3.2.6 Insect Screening. Metal screening shall conform to the requirements of the latest revision of Federal Specification RR-W-365, "Wire Fabric (Insect Screening)." Nonmetal screening shall conform to the requirements of the latest revision of Federal specification L-S-125a, "Screening, Insect, Non-metallic." All tacks, staples, brads or other fasteners used to attach the screen cloth or screen molding shall be of a material which is compatible with the screening being used.

3.3.4 Screening. Metal screening on screen doors or screen sections of a combination door may be rolled into a groove on the stiles and rails, or may be stapled to the stiles and rails. Screen molding on doors may be either raised or flush and shall be fastened with nails, brads or staples. A double row of fasteners shall be used on screen molding 1-3/4" (44.4mm) wide and wider and shall be spaced not more than an average of 10" apart nor more than 3" from each end of the molding. Non-metal screen cloth shall be applied in a groove with a spline sufficiently pliable to engage the filaments of the screen cloth and hold it securely in the groove.

3.3.5 Glazing. All glazed exterior doors, except combination doors, shall have the safety glazing material bedded in sealants and secured in place with mitered wood glazing beads, or shall have the safety glazing material held using sealants or a glazing gasket within a channel or groove machined into the stiles and rails framing the glazed opening. For combination doors, the safety glazed insert shall be framed with wood, plastic or metal, in a manner suitable to the design of the door.

3.3.7 Prefitting. When ordered prefit, all doors shall be sized to the dimensions specified on the order. A tolerance of plus (+) or minus (–) 1/32" (+ or – 0.8 mm) will be allowed from the dimensions specified. The widths of stiles and rails may be reduced by the amount of prefitting.

Comments

As mentioned earlier, in the "Wood Doors" section, panels on stile and rail doors are designed to move, or "float" in response to climate changes. Adjustments required to align them with the stiles and rails are not generally considered by the manufacturer to reflect any defects.

Fire Doors

Industry Standards
WIC Manual of Millwork
(Woodwork Institute of California)
General
Install fire doors as required by NFPA Pamphlet 80. All 45-, 60-, and 90-minute rated doors may be hung with either half surface or full mortise hinges. Core reinforcements can be specified to permit hardware to be surface mounted with screws. Labels shall not be removed from fire-rated doors, 20-, 45-, 60-, and 90-minute rated doors. Preparation of fire door assemblies for locks, latches, hinges, remotely operated or monitored hardware, concealed closures, glass lights, vision panels, louvers, astragals and laminated overlays shall be performed in conformance with the manufactures inspection service procedure and under Label Service.

Exception: Preparation for surface applied hardware, function holes for mortise locks, holes for labeled viewers, a maximum 3/4 inch (19 mm) wood and composite door undercutting, and protection plates may be performed at the jobsite. Surface applied hardware is applied to the face of a door without removing material from the door other than round holes drilled through the face of the door to receive cylinders, spindles, similar operational elements and through bolts. The holes shall not exceed a diameter of 1 inch (25.4 mm) with the exception of cylinders.

Flush Veneer Fire-Rated Doors
Wood veneered fire-rated doors are available in 90-minute label, 60-minute label, 45-minute label, and 20-minute label.

Comments
Fire Rating of Doors
The fire rating of doors applies only when doors have not been altered (for example, by adding louvers, lights, or using nonstandard hardware).

Fire Doors: Storage, Handling, Finishing & Installation
Following are some general recommendations for storage, handling, finishing and installation of fire doors.

Storage
* *Store flat and level in a clean, dry, ventilated area out of sunlight.*
* *Do not expose doors to extreme heat and/or humidity (relative not less than 30% or more than 60%).*
* *Store in enclosed building with operational HVAC systems.*

- *Seal as early as possible (edge sealing is particularly important).*
- *Lift or carry, but do not drag doors.*
- *Handle with clean hands or clean gloves. Do not walk on or place other materials on top of stacked doors.*

Finishing

- *Block sand doors just before staining, sealing, and finishing. Perform sanding with doors in a horizontal position using no less than 150 grit sandpaper, to remove all handling marks and raised grain.*
- *If possible, test surface for compatibility with finish.*
- *Top, bottom, opening, and hardware recess edges should be sealed after fitting with at least two (2) coats of oil-based paint, varnish or lacquer.*
- *Avoid water-based stains, paints or latex primers if possible as they can raise the grain, may cause veneer splits, and highlight veneer joints.*
- *Avoid dark colors on exterior doors that will be exposed to direct sunlight.*
- *Do not use steel wool to prepare oak-veneered or fire-rated doors.*
- *Apply a wash coat (thin sealer) before using a dark stain to avoid a splotchy appearance and/or sharp color contrast.*
- *The appearance of field-applied finishes is not covered by manufacturers' warranties.*

Installation

- *Acclimate doors to finished building heat and humidity before fitting and hanging.*
- *Be sure that applying hardware, plant-ons, or louvers will not adversely affect the door strength.*
- *Trim for width equally from both sides; allow 1/8" clearance at the top and each side.*
- *Do not trim top edges on labeled doors. On nonrated doors, do not trim top and bottom edge more than 3/4" unless using additional blocking.*
- *Threaded-to-the-head wood screws are required on all rated doors. Pilot holes must be drilled for all screws to avoid splitting. Use two (2) hinges for doors up to 60" in height, three (3) hinges for doors up to 90" in height, and an additional hinge for every additional 30" of door height or portion thereof.*

Solid & Hollow Core Veneered Flush Doors

Industry Standards

WIC Manual of Millwork
(Woodwork Institute of California)

1. Standards as established by National Wood Window and Door Association, Industry Standards I.S. 1-A Series, latest edition, for wood flush doors, are adopted as the minimum construction requirements for all WIC Grades of hollow and solid core, mineral core, acoustical, and lead lined flush veneered doors, except as hereinafter modified.

2. Economy, Custom or Premium Grade Architectural doors used for exterior exposure shall have all lite and louver cutouts sealed at the factory with one coat of exterior sealer. The bottom edge of cutouts and top rails of doors shall have flashing, if specified, installed at the factory. The ends of the flashing shall be imbedded in caulking compound.

3. Doors intended for an exterior exposure shall be Type I Adhesive doors. Doors intended for an interior exposure may be Type 1 Adhesive or Type II Bond with choice of adhesive optional with door manufacturer.

4. Typical construction in the industry for wood faced doors is five ply (core, crossband, and face veneer) or seven ply. Typical consideration in the industry for plastic faced doors is three ply (core and plastic). If type is not specified, it shall be optional with the manufacturer.

5. For Custom and Premium Grades, stiles or edge bands shall be securely glued under pressure to the solid block core or particleboard core. Framed Block Non-Glued core is not permitted in these grades.

Cutouts for Lights and Louvers

1. In non-rated doors, combined area of cutouts for lights or louvers shall not exceed 40% of the door area or one-half of the door height. Cutouts shall be a minimum of 5" from door edges, adjacent cutouts, or hardware mortises.

2. In rated doors, combined area of cutouts for lights or louvers shall be governed by the individual manufacturer's fire approval and/or NFPA 80. Cutouts shall be a minimum of 6" from door edges, adjacent cutouts, or hardware mortises.

Prefinished Modular Doors

Comments

Prefinished modular doors and frames are often used in light commercial buildings. Available in a variety of textures, grains, and finishes, they are constructed of interlocking steel frame units with snap-on metal casings. These ready-to-use units offer the advantage of quick installation without the need for finishing. Follow manufacturer's instructions for installation.

Metal Doors

Hollow Metal Doors & Frames

Industry Standards
Plan Reading & Material Takeoff
(R.S. Means Co., Inc.)

Comments

If metal doors are combined with storm doors, painted dark colors, and exposed to direct sunlight, the temperature on the exterior face of the metal door can lead to distortion of the light inserts.

Hollow Metal Frames
Hollow metal frames are formed of 18-, 16-, and 14-gauge steel, and are made to accommodate 1-3/8" and 1-3/4" wood or metal doors. Hollow metal frames are available in a variety of standard wall thicknesses, sometimes called *throat*, typically 4-3/4", 5-3/4", 6-3/4", and 8-3/4". They are available prefinished, galvanized, primed, or unfinished. Hollow metal frames can be installed in wood frame walls, masonry walls, metal stud and drywall walls, and walls that combine wood, steel, and masonry. They are available in two standard levels of fabrication: *knockdown*, where the frame is disassembled into the two jambs and the head piece and assembled on site, and *welded assembly*, where the frame is welded (at the factory) at the corners to produce a rigid, square, and true frame for site installation. Frames can be installed with the frame wrapped around the wall thickness, as in the case of interior partitions, or with the frame butted up to the jamb and the head, as in the case of metal frames installed with a masonry or concrete rough opening. **Figure 9.8** illustrates some typical hollow metal door frames.

Hollow Metal Doors
Hollow metal doors are constructed of 16-, 18-, and 20-gauge face sheets, with interior metal framing for a 1-3/8" or 1-3/4" finished thickness. Hollow metal doors are available in a variety of styles, including flush, small vision panels, full or half glass, and louvered.

In accordance with most building codes, certain locations throughout the building will be required to be fire-rated. Fire rating refers to the door and frame's capacity (label) to slow the transmission of fire. Typical labels are *C Label* for a 3/4-hour rating, *B Label* for a 1-1/2 to 2-hour rating, and *A Label* for a 3-hour rating. Other restrictions and qualifications also govern label doors and frames. Carefully review the plans and specifications.

Hollow Metal Door Frames

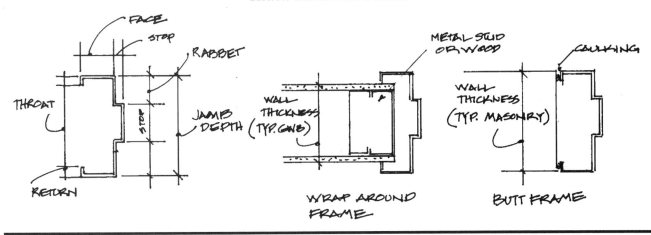

R.S. Means Co., Inc., *Plan Reading & Material Takeoff*

Figure 9.8

Steel Insulating Doors

Steel insulating door units for residential entrances are comprised of thin steel sheets over a wood-and-foam insulating core. They are typically provided prehung in a wood frame with an integral aluminum threshold, bored for locksets and/or deadbolts. Steel door units are available with designs either embossed in the face sheets or surface-applied, in many styles and sizes. Entry units with fiberglass face sheets and similar core construction are also available. Sizes range from 2'-8" to 3'-0" in width and 6'-6" or 6'-8" in height. Steel doors are provided primed for field-applied paint, and fiberglass units are unfinished, ready for field-applied stains or paints.

Comments

The ISDI (Insulated Steel Door Institute) has established criteria for air-infiltration limits, as follows: Air infiltration cannot exceed .2 cfm per foot of crack length at a static pressure of 1.567 lbs./s.f. (approximately equal to a 25 mph wind). The ISDI has also established an index for door insulation systems to rate energy loss. The ISDI acceptable level is 5.0. The lower the number, the better the insulation value, and the greater the energy savings.

Sliding Glass Doors

Comments

The following excerpt from CAWM is similar to the material in an earlier section, "Window Installation & Flashing," but it addresses doors specifically. For more information on exterior cladding and weather protection, see "Window & Door Components Defined," at the beginning of this chapter, under "General Information." While the following recommendations refer to aluminum doors, the same basic principles apply to other types of doors as well.

Industry Standards

Standard Practices for Installation of Sliding Glass Doors (CAWM 410-97)
(California Association of Window Manufacturers)

Protection from Dissimilar Materials

5.2.1 Isolate aluminum products from dissimilar or corrosive materials.

5.2.2 Protect aluminum sills from direct contact with corrosive materials, e.g. concrete, steel and stucco.

5.2.3 All fasteners shall be corrosion resistant, in accordance with ASTM B 633 or B 766.

5.3 Flashing Requirements — Proper flashing and/or sealing is necessary as a secondary barrier to prevent water from entering the wall between the door frame and the adjacent wall materials. Flashing and/or an appropriate method of sealing shall be designed as a part of an overall weather-resistive barrier system. It is not the responsibility of the door manufacturer to design or recommend a flashing system appropriate to each job condition.

Note 1 — The responsibility for supporting and protecting any flashing material from sources of damage, e.g. weather, other trades, or vandalism, and properly integrating the flashing system into the weather-resistive barrier for the entire building, will be the responsibility of the owner/general contractor or his designated agent.

5.3.1 Penetration Flashing Material — Flashing material shall meet Federal Specification UU-B-790a Type I, and shall be Grade C, B or A. Flashing material shall carry continuous identification.

5.4 Application

5.4.1 One of the two following methods shall be selected as the application to be followed. Once a method is selected, all procedures of that method must be performed in the described sequence. Substitution of a procedure from one method to the other is not permitted.

Method A

5.4.1.1.1 A strip of approved flashing material should be at least nine inches wide. Flashing shall be applied in a weatherboard fashion around the top and side perimeters of the opening, as well as below the sill, when applicable.

5.4.1.1.2 Apply continuous sealant beads across the full sill length of the framed opening at a point that makes contact with the door sill or sill pan system. An equivalent of two (2) 3/8" diameter beads should be used. Deposit a sufficient amount of sealant at the framed opening corners so the bottom door frame corners are embedded in sealant when door is installed.

Note 2 — All surfaces contacting sealant must be clean, dry, and free of all contaminants prior to application of sealant. Sealant used must adhere and be chemically compatible with all substrates.

5.4.1.1.3 Apply a continuous seal to the backside (interior) of the sill mounting flange, if provided, near the outer edge or a continuous seal to the perimeter of the opening at a point to assure contact with the backside (interior) of the mounting flange. The door shall then be installed in accordance with Section 5.5 installation.

5.4.1.1.4 Next, apply a continuous seal to the exposed mounting flange at the top (head) and sides (jambs) of the installed door frame. For mechanically joined frames, apply seal at corners the full length of the seam where mounting flanges meet.

5.4.1.1.5 Starting at each jamb, embed the jamb flashing into the seal and fasten in place. Run this flashing beyond the bottom of the rough opening and above where the head flashing will intersect.

5.4.1.1.6 Finally, embed the head flashing into the sealant on the mounting flange at the door head. Cut this flashing sufficiently long so that it will extend beyond each jamb flashing. Fasten in place.

5.4.1.1.7 Next, go to Section 5.5 Installation.

Method B

5.4.1.2.1 A strip of approved flashing material should be at least nine inches wide. Flashing shall be applied in a weatherboard fashion around the top and side perimeters of the opening, as well as below the sill, when applicable.

5.4.1.2.2 Apply continuous sealant across the full sill length of the framed opening at a point that makes contact with the door sill or sill pan system. The equivalent of two 3/8" diameter beads should be used. Deposit a sufficient amount of sealant at the framed opening corners so the bottom door frame corners are embedded in sealant when door is installed.

Note 3 — All surfaces contacting sealant must be clean, dry, and free of all contaminants prior to application of sealant. Sealant used must adhere and be chemically compatible with all substrates.

5.4.1.2.3 Next, fasten strips of flashing at each vertical edge (jamb) of the opening. Run this flashing beyond the bottom of the rough opening and above where the head flashing will intersect.

5.4.1.2.4 Apply a continuous seal to the backside (interior) of the mounting flange near the outer edge or a continuous seal to the entire perimeter of the opening at a point to assure contact with the backside (interior) of the mounting flange.

Note 4— Caution must be taken to avoid disrupting the continuous seal.

5.4.1.2.5 The door shall then be installed in accordance with Section 5.5 installation procedures.

5.4.1.2.6 For mechanically joined frames, apply seal at corners the full length of the seam where mounting flanges meet.

5.4.1.2.7 Next, apply a continuous seal at the top (head) mounting flange and embed the bottom of the head flashing over the sealant and the mounting flange. Cut this flashing sufficiently long so that it will extend beyond each jamb flashing. Fasten in place.

Threshold (Sill) Seal Application

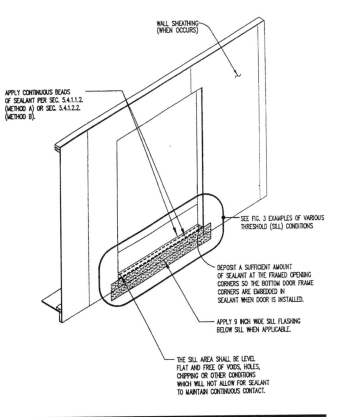

Courtesy of CAWM, *Standard Practices for Installation of Sliding Glass Doors (CAWM 410-97)*

Figure 9.9

5.5 Installation

5.5.1 Depending on rough opening conditions, the mounting flange, if provided on the door sill, may have to be removed. These conditions may include slab on grade that continues to the exterior; metal, plastic or flexible membrane sill pan systems; recessed installations; buildings with exterior decking. Follow door manufacturer's instructions on mounting flange removal.

5.5.2 Depending on the size and weight of the door and the opening conditions, shim blocks may be required under the sill to maintain straight and level condition and to prevent rotation. Consult manufacturer's recommendations.

5.5.3 If shims are needed at the sill, use enough to support the weight of the fixed and operable panels without causing distortion in the sill.

5.5.3.1 If a sill pan system is used, shim between the opening and the pan, not between the pan and the door sill.

5.5.3.2 Use sealant above and below the shims.

Note 5— All surfaces contacting sealant must be clean, dry and free of all contaminants prior to application of sealant.

5.5.4 If necessary, pre-drill and fill holes with sealant and seal over fasteners that penetrate door threshold.

5.5.5 Shim and adjust the door as necessary to achieve a plumb, square and level condition, as well as an even reveal around the frame opening, securing it the full perimeter with the equivalent of 6d fasteners at a maximum 16-inch center.

5.5.5.1 Some door manufacturers may require fasteners at the interior or through the frame members. Consult manufacturer's installation instructions.

Note 6— Consult door manufacturer's installation instructions regarding attachment of head flange to rough opening.

5.5.6 In each direction from all corners there must be a fastener within 10 inches, but no closer than 3 inches, to prevent frame distortion or fracture of joint.

5.5.7 In all cases consult manufacturer's instructions for any special procedures or applications.

Note 7— If any damage to door frame joint seals is observed during installation, it must be repaired by the installer.

5.5.8 Where weather-resistant building paper, insulating board, or other materials by other trades may constitute the primary weather barrier behind the exterior wall finish (i.e. stucco, masonry, siding, etc.), Owner/General Contractor is responsible to ensure that the weather barrier is continuous by effectively sealing the material to the door frame.

5.6 Sealant Requirements

5.6.1 Sealing/caulking required between the door frame and the flashing can be accomplished with caulking conforming to AAMA 800 and/or ASTM C-920 and/or TT-S-00230 C (Type II) Class A, or use sealant recommended and approved by the sealant manufacturer. All sealant and caulking products used must adhere and be chemically compatible with all substrates.

5.6.2 Some exterior wall finishes require additional sealing between the perimeter of the door frame and adjacent finish wall material. Owner/General Contractor is responsible for identifying the need for any additional sealant which will be applied by others. Such sealant shall be elastomeric material, compatible with door framing and adjacent wall materials. All sealant and caulking products used must adhere and be chemically compatible with all substrates.

5.7 Finish, Door and Sealant Protection

5.7.1 Caution shall be taken to avoid damage to doors during and after installation. Prior to installation, store doors in a near vertical position in a clean area, free of circulating dirt or debris and protected from exposure to weather elements.

Concrete or Wood Sub-Floor

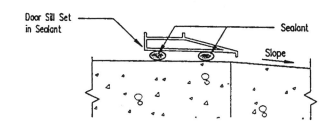

Pan Flashing

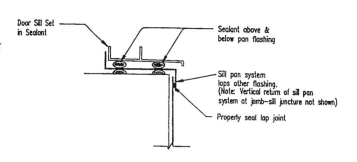

Recessed Sill

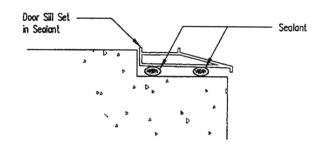

Exterior Decking

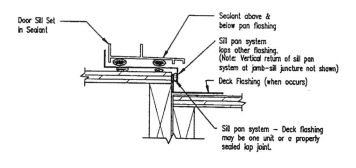

Courtesy of CAWM, *Standard Practices for Installation of Sliding Glass Doors (CAWM 410-97)*

Figure 9.10

ENTRANCE DOORS

Air Infiltration: ASTM E283; not to exceed .50 CFM per linear foot of perimeter crack when tested at 1.57PSF.

Dual Moment: Corner racking test; measures joint separation.

DOOR TYPE	AIR	DUAL MOMENT
250 Narrow Stile 400 Medium Stile 550 Wide Stile	< .50 CFM	Yes
800 Durafront 850 Durafront	< .50 CFM	Yes

STOREFRONTS

Air Infiltration: ASTM E283; not to exceed .06 CFM per square foot of area when tested at 6.24 PSF.

Water Infiltration: ASTM E331; no water penetration allowed.

Structural: ASTM E330; permanent deflection should not exceed .2% of span at 1.5 times the specified design windload (positive and negative).

CRF: AAMA 1503.1 for Condensation Resistance Factor.

U Value: AAMA 1503.1; measures the thermal transmittance for the specific unit in BTU/HR/FT²/°F.

PRODUCT	AIR	WATER	STRUCTURAL	CRF*	U VALUE*
CENTER GLAZED Series 400 & 400-S 450 & 450-S	< .06 CFM	8 PSF	30 PSF		
451 & 451-S	< .06 CFM	10 PSF	30 PSF		
IT 451	< .06 CFM	10 PSF	35 PSF	61	.60
OFFSET GLAZED Series OS 450 OS 451	< .06 CFM	7 PSF	30 PSF		
OS 600 OS 601	< .06 CFM	9 PSF	30 PSF		
THERMO-STACK Series TS 400 II	< .06 CFM	8 PSF	30 PSF	66	.63
FLUSH FRONT Series FF450 FF451 FF600 FF601	< .06 CFM	8 PSF	30 PSF		
FT451 FT601	< .06 CFM	8 PSF	30 PSF	63	.63
BG SYSTEMS Series BG450 BG525 BG520 BG600	< .06 CFM	12 PSF	30 PSF		
BT525 BT600	< .06 CFM	12 PSF	30 PSF	64	.62
THERMO-SET	< .06 CFM	10 PSF	30 PSF	69	.57

Courtesy of United States Aluminum — Commercial Products Group, *Architectural Aluminum Entrances, Storefronts, and Window Walls*

Figure 9.11

CENTER GLAZED SYSTEMS

SERIES 400, 400-S, 450, 450-S, 451 AND 451-S

Fabrication and installation labor costs have always been a decisive factor in selecting framing systems for storefront projects. United States Aluminum offers cost efficient versatile Center Glazed Systems with clean lines and superb performance. Series 400, 450 and 451 offer simple panel type installation. Series 400-S, 450-S and 451-S feature stacking type installation. All series may be inside or outside glazed. A top load E.P.D.M. gasket is used to position and weatherseal the glass in the aluminum pocket. Center Glazed Systems are compatible with most United States Aluminum entrance doors.

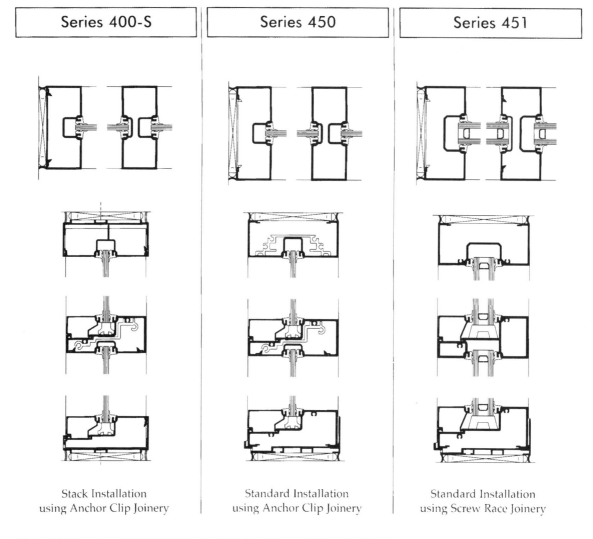

Series 400-S	Series 450	Series 451

Stack Installation using Anchor Clip Joinery | Standard Installation using Anchor Clip Joinery | Standard Installation using Screw Race Joinery

SERIES	WIDTH	DEPTH	GLAZING INFILLS
400 and 400-S	1³/₄″ (44.5)	4″ (101.6)	¹/₄″ (6) or ³/₈″ (9.5)
450 and 450-S	1³/₄″ (44.5)	4¹/₂″ (114.3)	¹/₄″ (6) or ³/₈″ (9.5)
451 and 451-S	2″ (50.8)	4¹/₂″ (114.3)	1″ (25)

Courtesy of United States Aluminum — Commercial Products Group, *Architectural Aluminum Entrances, Storefronts, and Window Walls*

Figure 9.12

5.7.2 Field-applied protective coatings can damage door sealants and gaskets and are not recommended. Contact the door manufacturer before applying any such coatings.

5.7.3 Caution should be used with some masking tapes as they may cause damage when they are removed from door surfaces.

5.7.4 Stucco or concrete left to cure on frames and glass will damage these surfaces. Remove and clean all such materials from surfaces before any curing action takes place.

5.7.5 Glass and frame surfaces exposed to leaching water from new concrete or stucco must be rinsed immediately with clear water to prevent permanent damage.

Aluminum & Glass Storefronts

Comments

Storefront assemblies are rated for Air Filtration, Water Filtration, Structural Deflection, Condensation Resistance Factor, and Thermal Transmittance.

*The door closers in the charts shown in **Figure 9.11** and **Figure 9.12** are recessed in the threshold, with the door swing on a pivot pin or mounted on the header or transom rail.*

See "Doors for Disabled Users" for more on ADA-compliant storefront entry doors.

Doors for Disabled Users

Interior Door in Drywall

Industry Standards

ADA Compliance Pricing Guide
(R.S. Means Co., Inc.)

Americans with Disabilities Act Guidelines (ADAAG) Reference No.: 4.13 Doors
Ed. Note: "ADAAG" stands for Americans with Disabilities Act — Act Guidelines. For further information on the design/ construction requirements or to obtain copies of this material, call the ADA Technical Assistance Center at 800-949-4232, or contact the U.S. Department of Justice at 800-514-0301 or www.usdoj.gov/crt/ada/adahom1.htm.

Where Applicable

Interior doors to accessible areas on accessible routes placed in walls constructed of studs and gypsum wallboard.

Design Requirements

- 32" clear opening width.
- 18" clearance adjacent to the latch on the pull side of the door, 12" on the push side.
- 1/2" maximum beveled threshold.
- 5 lbs. maximum pull or push weight on interior doors (no ADAAG reference for exterior doors).
- Level maneuvering space on both sides of the door, depending on approach. Minimum required dimensions in front of door between 42" to 60", depending on approach and whether door has a closer (see ADAAG Figure 25).
- 60" level surface, inside and outside of door at entrances.
- Accessible hardware (acceptable if operable with a closed fist).
- With door closer, 3 seconds minimum closing time to a point 3" from latch.

Design Suggestions

Because the 32" clear opening is measured from the face of the door in a 90° open position to the stop on the opposite jamb, the door itself has to be wider (usually 36") in order to comply. Doors 2'-10" are the smallest that can be used to comply, but might not meet the requirement. There are several accessible hardware options: a loop (allow at least 3" between inside

R.S. Means Co., Inc. *ADA Compliance Pricing Guide*

Figure 9.13

of loop and face of door), lever handles, push plate, or panic bar. Where opening force is necessarily high or where adequate maneuvering space cannot be provided, installation of an automatic opener may be a solution.

Maneuvering space on each side of the door is determined by how it is approached. A 60" x 60" minimum clear space is best and complies with all approaches cited in ADAAG. Where only a straight-on approach is available, a 60" deep space measured from the face of the door is required on the pull side and a 48" deep space is required on the push side. Where only a side approach is available, the required depth of the clear area in front of the door varies from 42" to 60", and the width is affected by the latch edge clearances and presence or absence of a door opener. Consult ADAAG 4.13 and ADAAG Figure 25 for exact requirements.

Sliding Door

Installation of an accessible sliding door can create an accessible doorway where door swings might otherwise prevent access. Sliding doors can fit within the width of a standard stud wall, and can be a useful and creative method of creating an accessible route between two spaces.

Americans with Disabilities Act Guidelines (ADAAG) Reference No.: 4.13 Doors

Ed. Note: For further information on the ADA's technical requirements, call the ADA Technical Assistance Center at 800-949-4232 or contact the U.S. Department of Justice at 800-514-0301 or www.usdoj.gov/crt/ada/adahom1.htm.

Where Applicable

Doors to accessible areas on accessible routes placed in walls constructed of brick, block, or stone.

Design Requirements

- 32" minimum clear opening width.

- 5 lbs. maximum pull weight on interior doors (no ADAAG reference for exterior doors).

- Thresholds at maximum height of 3/4" for exterior sliding doors, 1/2" maximum for others. All thresholds beveled at a maximum slope of 1:2.

- 48" clearance from face of door for front approach, 42" for side approach.

- Accessible hardware (acceptable if operable with a closed fist).

Design Suggestions

The 32" clear opening requirement is a minimum. Wider sliding doors are only marginally more expensive than narrow doors, and construction costs are the same. Finding compliant hardware for sliding doors is usually more difficult than for swinging doors (sliding doors usually just have a small latch or button), so nonstandard hardware might be needed.

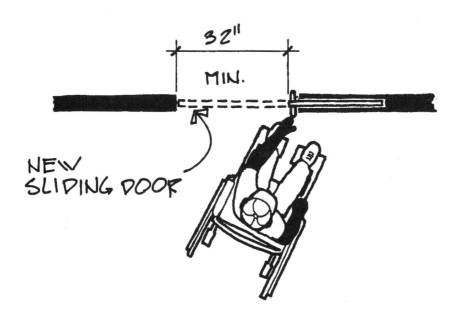

32" MIN.

NEW SLIDING DOOR

R.S. Means Co., Inc. *ADA Compliance Pricing Guide*

Figure 9.14

Exterior Entrance Door in Masonry Wall

Americans with Disabilities Act Guidelines (ADAAG) Reference No.: 4.13 Doors

Where Applicable

Doors to accessible areas on accessible routes placed in walls constructed of brick, block, or stone.

Design Requirements

- 32" clear opening width.
- 18" clearance adjacent to the latch on the pull side of the door, 12" on the push side.
- 1/2" maximum beveled threshold.
- 5 lbs. maximum pull or push weight on interior doors (no ADAAG reference for exterior doors).
- Level maneuvering space on both sides of the door, depending on approach. Minimum required dimensions in front of door between 42" to 60", depending on approach and whether door has a closer (see ADAAG Figure 25).
- 60" level surface, inside and outside of door at entrances. Accessible hardware (acceptable if operable with a closed fist). With door closer, 3 seconds minimum closing time to a point 3" from latch.

Design Suggestions

Ed. Note: See previous section, "Interior Door in Drywall."

Storefront Entrance

Many public facilities have glass storefront facades. Although systems and materials vary widely, many storefronts are made of modules or partitions that can be removed and replaced relatively simply. This allows for the installation of an accessible door in an existing building while maintaining the building design.

Americans with Disabilities Act Guidelines (ADAAG) Reference No.: 4.13 Doors

Ed. Note: For further information on the ADA's technical requirements, call the ADA Technical Assistance Center at 800-949-4232 or contact the U.S. Department of Justice at 800-514-0301 or www.usdoj.gov/crt/ada/adahom1.htm.

Where Applicable

Doors to accessible areas on accessible routes placed in walls constructed of brick, block, or stone.

32" CLEAR OPENING REQUIRED-- MASONRY OPENING DETERMINED BY FIELD CONDITIONS

R.S. Means Co., Inc. *ADA Compliance Pricing Guide*

Figure 9.15

Design Requirements

- 32" clear opening width.
- 18" clearance adjacent to the latch on the pull side of the door, 12" on the push side.
- 1/2" maximum beveled threshold.
- 5 lbs. maximum pull or push weight on interior doors (no ADAAG reference for exterior doors).
- Level maneuvering space on both sides of the door, depending on approach. Minimum required dimensions in front of door between 42" to 60", depending on approach and whether door has a closer (see ADAAG Figure 25).
- 60" level surface, inside and outside of door at entrances. Accessible hardware (acceptable if operable with a closed fist). With door closer, 3 seconds minimum closing time to a point 3" from latch.

Design Suggestions

Because the 32" clear opening is measured from the face of the door in a 90° open position to the stop on the opposite jamb, the door itself has to be wider (usually 36") in order to comply.

Doors 2'-10" are the smallest that can be used to comply, but might not meet the requirement. There are several accessible hardware options: a loop (allow at least 3" between inside of loop and face of door), lever handles, push plate, or panic bar. Where opening force is necessarily high or where adequate maneuvering space cannot be provided, installation of an automatic opener may be a solution.

Maneuvering space on each side of the door is determined by how it is approached. A 60" x 60" minimum clear space is best and complies with all approaches cited in ADAAG. Where only a straight-on approach is available, a 60" deep space measured from the face of the door is required on the pull side and a 48" deep space is required on the push side. Where only a side approach is available, the required depth of the clear area in front of the door varies from 42" to 60", and the width is affected by the latch edge clearances and presence or absence of a door opener. Consult ADAAG 4.13 and ADAAG Figure 25 for exact requirements.

Determining Door Handing

Comments

The term **inswing** *refers to a door that swings into the building, or pulls toward you if you are standing inside the building. If the door opens toward you and the doorknob is on the right-hand side, it is called a* **right-hand door**. *If the knob is on the left, it is a* **left-hand door**.

Door Tolerances
Industry Standards
WIC Manual of Millwork
(Woodwork Institute of California)

A. Size Tolerances (Blank Doors)

Unless otherwise specified, a height and width tolerance of plus or minus 1/16 inch (1.6 mm) will be allowed on the overall door dimensions. Thickness tolerance shall be 1/32", plus or minus.

B. Size Tolerances (Prefit Doors)

1. **Standard Prefitting:** The standard amount of prefitting of a wood flush door to be installed in a wood frame should be 3/16 inch (4.8 mm) in width with a 3-degree bevel on 1 stile only. For wood flush doors to be installed in a steel frame, the standard amount of prefitting shall be 1/4 inch (6.4 mm) in width with a 3-degree bevel on both stiles. A tolerance of plus or minus 1/32 inch (0.8 mm) will be allowed in width only. The lock stile of a prefitted door may be reduced to a minimum 13/16 inch wide (20.6 mm) after prefitting and 3/8 inch wide (9.3 mm) for glued-block core doors. Wood flush doors with standard prefit are book size in height, and rail widths may not be reduced.

2. **Other Prefitting:** Prefitting other than the standard prefit may be specially ordered. However, if such prefitting is ordered, the stile and/or rail widths remaining after prefitting shall not be less than as shown in the following table. A tolerance of plus or minus 1/32 inch (0.8 mm) will be allowed in width only.

C. Squareness Tolerance

All four corners of a door shall be square (right angles) when the dimensions of the door agree with size tolerances as defined

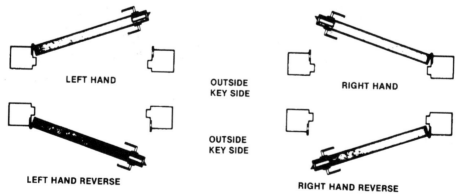

Hand of Door Is Always Determined from the Outside

LEFT HAND

OUTSIDE KEY SIDE

RIGHT HAND

OUTSIDE KEY SIDE

LEFT HAND REVERSE

RIGHT HAND REVERSE

The diagram shown here is for wood doors. The hollow metal door industry is exactly opposite the rule for wood doors. If you do not order doors regularly, it is suggested that you furnish a plan diagram with your confirmed order.

Courtesy of Woodwork Institute of California, *WIC Manual of Millwork*

Figure 9.16

above. Also, the length of the diagonal measurement on the face of the door from the upper right corner to the lower left corner shall be within 1/8 inch (3.2 mm) of the length of the diagonal from the upper left corner to the lower right corner.

D. Warp Tolerance

1.**Measurement of Warp:** Warp is any distortion in the door itself, and does not refer to the relation of the door to the frame or jamb in which it is hung. The amount of bow, cup, and twist shall be measured by placing a straight edge, taut wire or string, on the suspected concave face of the door as any angle (i.e., horizontally, vertically, diagonally). The measurement of bow, cup, or twist shall be made at the point of maximum distance between the bottom of the straight edge, taut wire or string, and the face of the door.

2. **Allowable warp, bow, cup, and twist is determined as follows:**

   a. The warp for any nominal 1-3/4 inches thick (44.4mm) or thicker door shall not be more than 1/4 inch (6.4mm) in any 3 feet 6 inches wide by 7 feet 0 inches high (1067 mm by 2134 mm) section of the door. The measuring section will be reduced to the actual width and/or height of the door, if the actual width and/or height is less than 3 feet 6 inches wide by 7 feet 0 inches high (1067 mm by 2134 mm).

   b. The warp for any nominal 1-3/8 inches thick (34.9 mm) or thinner door that is 3 feet 0 inches wide by 7 feet 0 inches high (914 mm by 2134 mm) or smaller, shall not be more than 1/4 inch (6.4 mm).

3.**Limits on Warp Tolerance:** Allowable warp tolerances are not to be extended to the following doors or situations:

   a. Nominal 1-3/8 inches thick (34.9mm) or thinner doors larger than 3 feet 0 inches wide by 7 feet 0 inches high (914 mm by 2134 mm).

   b. Doors with face veneers of different species.

   c. Doors which are improperly hung or do not swing freely.

   d. Doors with face applied paneling or siding.

   e. Doors that are not sealed with two coats of paint, varnish or sealer on the top and bottom edges and around all cutouts at time of installation.

4.**Photographing stile, rail and core** showing through on hardwood veneered flush doors shall not be considered as a defect unless the faces of the door vary from a true plane in excess of 1/100" in any 3" span.

Ed. Note: See also "Testing for Show-Through and Warpage" in the following section.

Finishing

Prior to finishing, insure that the building atmosphere is dried to a normal, interior relative humidity. Insure that the doors have been allowed to equalize to a stable moisture content.

Windows & Doors: Testing Procedures

Door Tests
Industry Standards
Specifiers Guide to Wood Windows and Doors
(National Wood Window & Door Association)

Ed. Note: Following are pertinent sections of NWWDA I.S.9 Industry Standard for the Performance of Exterior Wood Door Entry Systems. Contractors should refer to the full document for complete details.

4.0 Performance Requirements and Tests

4.1 All exterior wood door systems labeled or otherwise identified as complying with this standard shall conform to the requirements outlined below.

4.2 **Unit Test Size.** The performance tests described in this standard shall be conducted on the largest unit system size for which conformance is desired.

4.3 **Performance Test Criteria.**

4.3.1 Air Infiltration. The unit shall be in a closed and locked position during the test. The unit shall be rested in accordance to ASTM E-283 "Standard Test Method for Rate of Air Leakage Through Exterior Windows, Curtain Walls, and Doors." The rate of air leakage through the test specimen shall not exceed 0.20 cubic feet per minute per foot of crack length when tested under a uniform static air pressure difference of 1.57 pounds per square foot (75PA).

3.3.2 Water Penetration. The unit shall be in a closed and locked position during the test. The unit shall be tested in accordance to ASTM E-547 "Standard Test Method for Water Penetration of Exterior Windows, Curtain Walls, and Doors by Cyclic Static Air Pressure Differential." The unit shall be tested for a minimum of 3 cycles, of no less than 5 minutes each, under a uniform static air pressure difference of 3.86 pounds per square foot. At the conclusion of the test, no water shall have passed beyond the interior face of the unit test specimen and overflowed into the room, or flowed into the wall area.

Note: Joints between the unit test specimen and the adjacent test apparatus shall be caulked, taped or otherwise sealed to prevent extraneous air or water leakage. Since door systems are not normally sold with lock hardware, any air or water leakage through the locking device(s) or between the locking device(s) and the door leaf is to be eliminated or contained and is not to be included in the measured performance of the unit specimen. Sealant may be used to eliminate air or water leakage between the brickmold or extensions and the door jamb; such sealant must be recorded on the test report.

Testing for Show-Through & Warpage

Industry Standards

Specifiers Guide to Wood Windows and Doors
(National Wood Window & Door Association)

T-1: Show-Through

Show-through (telegraphing) of vertical and horizontal edges and cores is considered a defect when the face of the door varies from a true plane in excess of 0.010 inch in any three-inch span.

The selection of high glass laminates or finishes should be avoided, because they tend to accentuate natural telegraphing.

T-2: Warp

Warp is any distortion in the door itself, and is not measured in relation to the frame in which it is hung. Warp is measured by placing a straight edge or a taut string on the concave face and determining the maximum distance from straight edge or string to door face.

Sill Track Test

Industry Standards

Nail-On Windows
(DTA, Inc.)

We recommend that the sill-jamb joints of windows be tested for weather tightness after installation. This is especially critical if the window had any apparent damage from shipping or handling that was not severe enough to have the window replaced.

Method for Testing Allowable Warp Tolerance of Doors

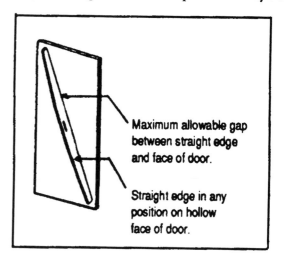

Maximum allowable gap between straight edge and face of door.

Straight edge in any position on hollow face of door.

Courtesy of National Wood, Window & Door Association, *Specifiers Guide to Wood Windows and Doors*

Figure 9.17

To conduct the test, the sill track of the window can be filled with water after plugging and taping the weep holes. Allow the water to sit for 15 minutes to observe if the water level decreases, indicating a leak in the frame joint. This test complies with an industry report outlined in the AAMA publication 502-90, optional Test Method A. Remove weep hole plugs or tape after the test. Refer to **Figure 9.18**.

If the joints leak, then the sill-jamb joints should be cleaned and resealed according to the preparation and scaling procedures recommended by the window manufacturer.

Sill Track Water Test

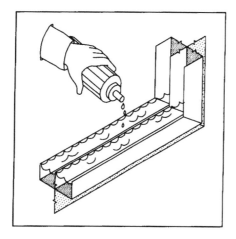

TEST:
1. Plug Weep Holes
2. Fill Sill Track with Water.
3. Observe Water Level 15 Minutes.
4. There should be no leakage or reduction in the water level from sill track.
5. If failure, trace leakage. If pass, remove weep hole plugs.

(Based on AAMA 502-90 Optional Test Method A)

Courtesy of DTA, Inc., *Nail-On Windows*

Figure 9.18

If the flashing procedures are followed and the window sill is watertight, then the window and doors should prove successful for long-term performance.

Water Spray Tests

Section 2.3.1c notes the AAMA water spray tests that can be used to field test installations of windows and sliding glass doors. These field tests can be used to evaluate the flashings and wall claddings around the openings too.

Also effective in locating sources of leaks to windows and doors is a common garden hose used to spray water around the opening. A formalized procedure works from the bottom of the unit towards the top. Observation from inside the building can trace leaks. Removal of interior finishes and the use of a moisture meter can assist in locating leak spots and tracing water paths back to sources of entry. If there is a failure, removal of exterior finishes after water testing can help locate water entry points by following traces of moisture on the layers of building materials around the door or window opening.

Comments

Window warranties usually identify the issues that affect window performance. They also provide tolerances "not considered defects."

Many manufacturers of wood windows utilize varying versions of the Woodwork Institute of California's recommendations for warranty compliance.

These warranty conditions usually include the following:

- *Painting of wood windows must be accomplished on all sides of the windows within 48 hours of delivery to the construction site or immediately upon installation, and must be repainted periodically to avoid damage to the wood parts.*

- *Lap the finish coat 1/16" onto the glass for a proper moisture seal.*

- *Primers usually are not compatible with lacquer and varnishes. Primer paints must be designated to prevent the application of dissimilar products.*

- *Abrasive cleaners or solutions containing solvents should not be used.*

Manufacturers' Quality Certification

Industry Standards

Specifiers Guide to Wood Windows and Doors
(National Wood Window and Door Association)

Quality Certified Wood Windows

NWWDA certifies firms which have demonstrated the ability to manufacture windows according to NWWDA Industry Standard for Wood Window Units I.S. 2. Each NWWDA certified manufacturer's plant is inspected by NWWDA to determine if their production facilities and procedures conform to the Standard. At that time, samples of finger-joints and preservative treating solution are taken and tested.

Window units must meet all of the requirements of the Standard, including air and water infiltration, and uniform and physical loading. I.S.2 also requires that all wood window units be water-repellent preservative treated, and all adhesives used meet the requirements of a Type I "wet use" adhesive in accordance with the appropriate ASTM Standard.

Care

1. Specify that window sash and frames be treated at the factory with a NWWDA approved water-repellent preservative in accordance with Industry Standard I.S.4 Water-Repellent Preservative Non-Pressure Treatment for Millwork.

2. Store in a clean, dry, well ventilated building; not in damp, moist or extremely humid environments.

3. While in storage, cover to keep clean.

4. Windows, frames and sash should be conditioned to the average prevailing moisture (humidity) of the locality before installing.

5. Deliver in clean truck and under cover in wet weather.

6. Handle with clean canvas gloves. Bare hands leave finger marks and soil stains.

7. When moving window units, carry them; do not drag them.

8. Do not drop or jar window units; any jar or shock may break the glass or glazing seal or put the window out of square.

9. In new homes, ventilate rooms thoroughly and install windows after all walls (plaster or cement) are dry.

10. Be sure frame is square before unit is installed in opening. Use a diagonal brace across corners after frame is squared. A horizontal spacer strip at midpoint of height of the frame will maintain equal width between jambs from head to sill. Remove brace and spacer strip after frame is anchored into wall opening.

11. Install and fit windows accurately in accordance with good building practice and/or with manufacturer's instructions.

12. Avoid driving nails into sash balances by marking jamb to indicate position of balance.

13. If nailing through the exterior jamb or wood brick moulding is necessary to ensure the window's structural load capabilities, the anchoring devices (nails, screws, etc.) should be countersunk and the holes puttied flush with the surface prior to coating.

14. Keep channel and weather-strip of window clean so that sash may operate freely.

15. Be sure to install proper close-fitting locks.

16. Keep woodwork clean; do not use caustic or abrasive cleaners.

17. When opening or closing windows, use handle or lift.

18. Install storm sash or insulating glass in colder climates to help prevent condensation on window glass.

19. Make certain to caulk and insulate between the window and the wall rough opening, especially around the nailing fin or brick moulding.

Finishing

1. Temperature and humidity have a major effect on drying and may affect paint film characteristics. Paint should be applied at product, surface, and air temperatures between 50°F (10°C) and 90°F (32°) unless product label specifies differently. Relative humidity should be below 85%.

2. Use only high grade materials and follow manufacturer's instructions carefully to assure a long-lasting beautiful appearance.

3. Surfaces to be painted must be thoroughly dry and free from dust/dirt, oil, grease, wax, chalk and other contaminants. Remove dust/dirt by scrubbing or hosing. Remove oils, waxes and grease with paint thinner. If mildew is present, it must be removed prior to painting. Sand to remove any surface roughness and wipe clean.

4. Be sure that all nail holes, gouges or other surface indentations are filled before coating to ensure the performance of the top coat.

5. As soon as possible, apply a quality prime coat to the exterior of the window if not pre-primed from the factory. Apply two coats of quality trim paint to the exterior of primed units within 30 days of installation. Again, be sure to apply paint in accordance with manufacturer's directions.

6. Each coat of paint should be applied evenly. Make certain the surfaces are dry before applying the next coat.

7. Do not paint weather-strip. Remove unwanted paint from the weather-strip.

8. Be sure to overlap paint or urethane on glass to seal glazing seal joint. Do not break this seal when removing paint from glass surfaces or when cleaning.

9. To the interior of your window units, apply a quality prime coat and two or three coats of trim paint. Or, if you desire a natural finish, apply a coat of sanding sealer and two coats of urethane. Finishing done under the supervision of a reliable painting contractor is the most satisfactory.

10. When cleaning woodwork, avoid the use of caustics or abrasives which dissolve or damage the finish.

11. The exposed exterior surfaces of some wood windows are clad with aluminum or vinyl. Clad windows provide a protective, low-maintenance exterior while still giving the superior thermal performance of wood sash and frames. Clad windows do not require exterior finishing. Consult manufacturer's instructions for care and cleaning instructions.

Glazing

Industry Standards
WIC Manual of Millwork
(Woodwork Institute of California)

I. Thermal Integrity

A. Wood is a natural insulator that needs no artificial "thermal break" to retain heat in winter. ("Thermal breaks" are strips of insulating material — wood, fiberglass, etc. — inserted between layers of aluminum.)

B. Wood as a material resists conductance of cold temperatures 2,000 times better than aluminum. (Thermal conductance is the total measure of heat flow through a material from the inside surface to the outside surface.)

C. A wood window with insulating glass is approximately 30% more thermally efficient than a comparable size and style aluminum window.

D. Wood's minimal conduction of heat and cold keeps inside wood surface of windows warm in winter, cool in summer.

E. Modern, quality wood windows and wood door systems have built-in weather stripping which can reduce air infiltration to less than 0.33 cubic feet per minute.

F. Modern wood windows, and glass-paned wood patio and entry doors, are available with double and triple glazing systems, increasing thermal efficiency.

G. Some wood windows and glass-paned wood doors contain new Low-E glazing. Low-E glazing improves R-value of glass, making these windows and doors more thermally efficient.

II. Key Definitions

A. Low-E — "E" is emissivity; ability of glass to reradiate heat it absorbs. Low-E values represent better heat reradiation. The lower the emissivity ("E") of the glass, the better its insulating quality.

B. U-value — measures thermal transmission; heat flow through material or assembly from inside air to outside air. Low U values represent greater resistance to transmission of interior heat to outside.

C. R-value — measures thermal resistance; how well material stops/resists heat flowing through it. High R-values represent greater ability to stop/resist heat absorption.

III. Types of Low-E Glazing

A. Pyrolitir — applied during manufacture of glass.

B. Sputtered — sprayed on finished glass, used on interior pane of double and triple thermal pane systems. IV.

IV. Benefits of Low-E Glazing

A. In Insulated Glass:
1. Improves U-value (thermal transmission) from 0.49 to 0.32; increases R-value (thermal resistance) from 2.04 to 3.12.

B. In Wood Windows With Insulated Glass:
1. Improves U-value from 0.45 to 0.30; increases R-value from 2.22 to 3.33.

C. In Storm Sashes or Doors (single glazing):
1. Improves U-value from 1.04 to 0.75; increases R-value from 0.96 to 1.33.

V. Durability

A. Wood in quality windows and doors is chemically treated in the factory: to repel decay, warping, insects; protect against heat and humidity.

VI. Options

A. All quality wood windows, wood entry systems, wood patio, stile and rail doors are available as pre-hung units. Prehung units include the door, frames, hardware, and weatherstripping.

Multiple Glazing
Industry Standards
Construction Principles, Materials, and Methods
(John Wiley and Sons, Inc.)

Because of its thinness, a single sheet of glass is a good conductor of heat. One square foot of 1/4-in. clear glass can conduct 6 to 10 times more BTUs per hour than a square foot of a typical frame wall. The rate of heat transfer through the glass is so rapid that added thickness is of almost no value. However, if layers of glass are separated by an air space, the path of conduction is interrupted, and the rate of heat flow is reduced. Heat can then pass through the air space primarily by radiation and convection and only minimally by conduction.

Storm windows can be effective in reducing conduction and infiltration with an air separation between panes of glass of as much as 6 in. However, an air space is most effective in improving thermal performance when it is between 3/16 in. and 5/8 in. wide. Within this range, the heat flow is reduced markedly as the width is increased from 3/16 in. towards 5/8 in. Increasing the air space beyond 5/8 in. does not reduce heat flow to the same extent, because a wider space allows the air in it to circulate more freely and develop convection currents. These currents transport heat from the warmer glass to the colder glass. This increased convection heat loss can more than offset the slight reduction in conductive heat loss through the air. Conversely, a space of less than 3/16 in. is of little value because heat is readily conducted by the air across such a short distance.

Film Coatings

Comments

Sometimes homeowners have mylar film applied to their windows after the installation is complete. Some window manufacturers include disclaimers for window performance under these circumstances. Failures of dual-glazed units due to moisture condensation have been traced to the presence of tinted film on the inside face of the glass. Deflection caused by the tinted film can create heat buildup and expansion within the airspace of the dual unit, which destroys the butyl seal. Water vapor can then be admitted, condensing between the panes. Heat buildup can also cause the decorative grids, or "muntins," within the window to detach from the butyl inside dual-glazed units.

DRYWALL & CERAMIC TILE

Table of Contents

(continued on next page)

Text in blue print indicates excerpts from model building code(s). "Comments" (in solid blue boxes) were written by the editors, based on their own experience.

For building product information, use this book's special Internet gateway to thousands of manufacturers: www.rsmeans.com/prodsupp/rlstand.html

CHAPTER 10

DRYWALL & CERAMIC TILE

Common Defect Allegations

Drywall

Many claims in drywall construction involve issues related to facing, taping and finishing, and fire rating. Since finished drywall telegraphs imperfections through the painted surface, defects that detract from the appearance are often brought to the builder's attention upon occupancy. Even when wallcovering is applied over drywall, proper taping and facing is necessary, as defects may show through.

A common defect allegation is insufficient nailing. Construction defect analysts sometimes place refrigerator magnets on each nailhead to show that the wall was undernailed.

Model building codes allow drywall to be utilized as a shear panel in certain applications. When this occurs, the nailing is critical, and care must be taken to avoid breaking the paper skin while nailing.

Wrinkling or beading sometimes occurs in the horizontal tape joint on walls over eight feet high, as a result of lumber shrinkage. A building can shrink vertically as much as 3/4" per floor, depending on the dryness of the lumber and the lightness of the framer's assembly. Lumber shrinkage causes nail pops, also a common defect allegation. (See Chapter 5, "Wood Framing," for more on wood shrinkage and nail pops.)

Use of green board is a subject of defect claims. Green board has great moisture resistance. Stacks of green board left uncovered in the rain and then measured with a moisture meter have been shown to have resisted moisture even after three weeks. On the other hand, green board used under ceramic tile with missing grout or the wrong mastic (for a shower in regular daily use) can turn into the consistency of pudding after five years.

From time to time, metal corner bead corrodes due to the use of hotmud or quicksetting compound. These products will not only rust the metal trim, but will bleed through light shades of paint, creating yellow blotching.

Ceramic Tile

All installations that are determined to be defective fall under one of two definitions: Observable (Patent Defects), or Concealed (Latent Defects). In the defect litigation business there are statutes of limitation to limit the time period that a builder is responsible for repairs under warranty. Patent Defects are limited to two, three, or five years, according to the type of condition and the interpretation of the owner's responsibility to observe conditions or maintain the installation. Latent Defects are under warranty for ten years.

Ceramic tile allegations reflect the extremes of these rules. Homeowners often add a tile claim of variations in grout joints and water intrusion through the deck, as part of an overall defect claim, seven or eight years after moving into the house. In this case, the observable variations in the grout joints would have expired after two years, while the deck leaking could constitute a valid claim.

The most common defect claim on tile is cracking of tile and/or grout joints, usually in a sawtooth pattern. These problems generally reflect movement in the substrate. Slip-sheet will reduce this condition when wood framing or concrete slabs crack or expand. Occasionally, cracking can result from horizontal stress even over slip-sheet. If tile flooring is grouted tight in a kitchen surrounded by wood cabinets and then experiences a flood or broken pipe, the resulting swelling of the wood cabinet bases will crack the tile floor. This risk can be eliminated by grouting perimeter and key joints with sanded caulking to match the grout.

The most costly of the common defects is exterior deck leaks. The defect, of course, is in the underlayment. The tile was placed over the membrane; however, the membrane did not have water integrity after it was installed, or it was placed in a manner that stressed it sufficiently to tear or break. A regular cause of breaks in membrane is from horizontal expansion breaking the corner where the vertical and horizontal planes meet. Use cant strips whenever possible and use a flexible membrane with slip sheet attached with a rubberized adhesive and no mesh reinforcing to allow stretching. Vertical runs on the membrane must lap under the wall wrap by 2" and at least 2" above the overflow high-level water mark.

Another defect is caused by hand-made shower pans with hot mop roofing as the composite waterproofing. This material continues to be specified on drawings. Destructive testing will almost always uncover a problem using this waterproofing material for this purpose. Installations using vinyl one-piece membrane or vinyl that has been *chemically welded will reduce the frequency of these claims. The pan should be water-checked for 24 hours prior to floating the finishes over the vinyl.*

A common complaint on natural marble floor tiles is where the marble surface begins to deteriorate when certain veins seem to pocket out of the surface. This usually is from excessive moisture vapor being emitted from the concrete floor below, corroding the veins of iron deposits in the marble, thereby causing oxidation or rust expansion.

Introduction

This chapter covers installation issues for gypsum wallboard, followed by a section on skim coat plaster over a gypsum composition base, and ceramic tile. Note that concrete or cement board backing is covered in the ceramic tile section of the chapter.

The chapter begins with a list of common drywall installation problems. Standards for correct drywall installation are detailed in the sections that follow. Tile installation problems are addressed in the section titled, "Avoiding Failures in Ceramic Tile Installation" at the end of this chapter.

For light commercial projects, wall finish information may be provided on the room finish schedule of the architectural drawings. (See Chapter 12 for painting and wallcovering standards.)

The following organizations are sources of additional information:

Association of the Wall & Ceiling Industries (AWCI)
803 West Broad Street, Suite 600
Falls Church, VA 22046
Telephone: 703-634-8300
www.awci.org
AWCI's membership consists of wall and ceiling contractors, product suppliers and manufacturers.

Gypsum Association (GA)
810 First Street NE #510
Washington, DC 20002
Telephone: 202-289-5440
www.gypsum.org
GA has a technical staff for consultation on specific issues relating to the use of gypsum board. The association also publishes technical papers and other publications, and covers many technical issues in the "Frequently Asked Questions" area of its Web site. GA's Evaluation Reports demonstrate code compliance and acceptance of specific gypsum materials and systems.

Ceramic Tile Institute of America, Inc.
12061 Jefferson Blvd.
Culver City, CA 90230
Telephone: 310-574-800

Tile Council of America, Inc. (TCA)
P.O. Box 1787
Clemson, SC 29633
Telephone: 864-646-8453
www.tileusa.com
The TCA publishes the 1998 *Handbook for Ceramic Tile Installation*, which describes in detail the methods and standards for ceramic tile installation.

Ed. Note: Comments and recommendations within this chapter are not intended as a definitive resource for construction activities. For building projects, contractors must rely on the project documents and local building codes.

Gypsum Wallboard: Common Problems

Comments

Also see "Gypsum Base Limitations" and "Effects of Site Conditions" at the end of the Gypsum Wallboard portion of this chapter.

Common Drywall Problems

Paint and finish may show surface irregularities in certain lights. (As with most finishes it is best to judge drywall finish in sunlight or natural light.) The finished product should not show cracked corner bead, excess joint compound, blisters in tape joints or trowel marks. Some causes for imperfections are:

- *Not enough or too much compound used to cover nails, screws, or joints.*
- *Failure to apply enough coats of joint compound or to allow adequate time for the various coats to dry (and shrink) thoroughly before applying the next coat.*
- *The person who applies the tape may be under the impression that other finishes will later cover a particular area. As a result, some nails and joints do not receive the correct amount of attention.*
- *Cracks may develop at corners of openings where small pieces of drywall are used. A taped joint in the board at a corner can also lead to cracking.*

- *Buildup of compound in corners may create shadow line or cause poor fitting of base and other wall moldings.*
- *Too many drywall pieces used instead of full sheets.*
- *End joints stacked on top of each other or four-way joints.*
- *Improper fastening.*
- *Using the drywall to straighten framing members, thereby creating unnecessary pressure points on the board.*
- *Not curing carefully at outlets, switches, or ceiling boxes. (Solid material is always preferable to filling.)*
- *Improper sanding technique.*
  - *—Too little time spent*
  - *—Too aggressive, causing paper to become rough and porous.*
- *Bubbles in tape.*
- *Bubbles in compound.*

Most drywall imperfections can be corrected with a relatively small investment of time and effort, unless whole walls need to be refinished. Persons responsible for the quality control on a job should check finishing and hanging techniques early in the project to ensure that necessary touchup of the drywall will not have to include repainting finished walls. After the painter has applied the first coat of primer, the taper and painter should check for defects before the final coat(s) are applied.

Gypsum Wallboard Installation

Industry Standards
Plan Reading & Material Takeoff
(R.S. Means Co., Inc.)

Drywall sheets are installed on wood or metal framing systems with screws. The seams of abutting drywall sheets and screw holes are taped with a vinyl-based joint treatment compound and reinforcing tape. Joint taping is a multi-step process usually requiring three coats, including the tape coat. The tape is embedded in a coat of joint compound and allowed to dry. Subsequent coats are applied, with sanding between coats to remove the imperfections. The resulting finish conceals the joints, and should be smooth and ready for paint or other finishes.

Comments

Following are some general recommendations for drywall installation.

- *Install the ceiling panels first, then the walls. Begin at a corner.*
- *End-to-end joints should fall at the studs or joists except where back-blocking is used.*
- *On exterior walls, check to make sure adequate insulation has been installed before placing the wallboard. The vapor barrier should be facing into the room, fastened to the sides of the wall studs.*
- *If using adhesive on the bottom of ceiling joists, leave 6" uncovered from the wallboard sides to prevent the adhesive from oozing out at the joints between the boards.*

While fiberglass tape is easier to apply and stronger than paper tape, it has no flexibility and can eventually show through where joints have come apart. Paper tape, on the other hand, contracts and expands along with the gypsum wallboard's paper facing.

Sound-Deadening Measures
The middle and bottom illustrations in Figure 10.1 show two approaches to reduce sound transmission through walls. See Chapter 7, the section titled, "Soundproofing," for more on sound attenuation with insulation and drywall.

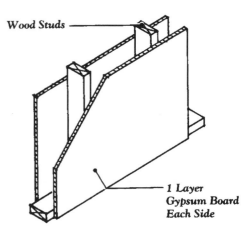

Gypsum Plasterboard

Wood Studs

1 Layer
Gypsum Board
Each Side

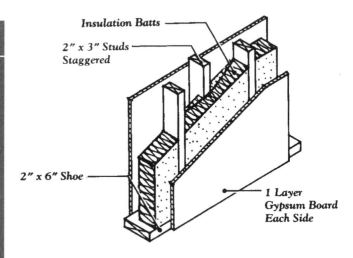

Staggered Stud Wall

Insulation Batts

2" x 3" Studs
Staggered

2" x 6" Shoe

1 Layer
Gypsum Board
Each Side

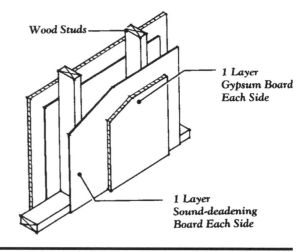

Sound-Deadening Board

Wood Studs

1 Layer
Gypsum Board
Each Side

1 Layer
Sound-deadening
Board Each Side

R.S. Means Co., Inc., *Means Graphic Construction Standards*

Figure 10.1

Single-Layer

UBC — 1997

Section 2511 — Gypsum Wallboard

2511.1 General. Gypsum wallboard shall not be installed on exterior surfaces. See Section 224. For use as backing under stucco, see Section 2506.3. Gypsum wallboard shall not be installed until weather protection for the installation is provided.

Ed. Note: Exterior use of gypsum wallboard is not treated in this chapter. It is addressed as part of stucco & EIFS installations in Chapter 8, "Roofing, Siding & Moisture Protection."

2511.2 Supports. Supports shall be spaced not to exceed the spacing set forth in Table 25-G for single-ply application and Table 25-H for two-ply application [see **Figure 10.2**]. Vertical assemblies shall comply with Section 2503. Horizontal assemblies shall comply with Section 2504.

2511.3 Single-ply Application. All edges and ends of gypsum wallboard shall occur on the framing members, except those edges and ends that are perpendicular to the framing members. All edges and ends of gypsum wallboard shall be in moderate contact, except in concealed spaces where fire-resistive construction or diaphragm action is not required.

The size and spacing of fasteners shall comply with Table 25-G [see **Figure 10.2**], except where modified by fire-resistive construction meeting the requirements of Section 703.2. Fasteners shall not be spaced less than 3/8 inch (9.5 mm) from edges and ends of gypsum wallboard.

Fasteners at the top and bottom plates of vertical assemblies, or the edges and ends of horizontal assemblies perpendicular to supports, and at the wall line may be omitted except on shear-resisting elements or fire-resistive assemblies. Fasteners shall be applied in such a manner as not to fracture the face paper with the fastener head.

Gypsum wallboard may be applied to wood-framing members with an approved adhesive. A continuous bead of the adhesive shall be applied to the face of all framing members, except top and bottom plates, of sufficient size as to spread to an average width of 1 inch (25 mm) and thickness of 1/16 inch (1.6 mm) when the gypsum wallboard is applied.

Where the edges or ends of two pieces of gypsum wallboard occur on the same framing member, two continuous parallel beads of adhesive shall be applied to the framing member. Fasteners shall be used with adhesive application in accordance with Table 25-G.

*Ed. Note: See **Figure 10.6** and **Figure 10.7** for further information about single and double nailing applications.*

Two-Layer

UBC — 1997

2511.4 Two-ply Application. The base of gypsum wallboard shall be applied with fasteners of the type and size as required for the nonadhesive application of single-ply gypsum wallboard. Fastener spacings shall be in accordance with Table 25-H [see **Figure 10.2**], except where modified by fire-resistive construction meeting the requirements of Section 703.2.

The face ply of gypsum wallboard may be applied with gypsum wallboard joint compound or approved adhesive furnishing full coverage between the plies or with fasteners in accordance with Table 25-H [see **Figure 10.2**]. When the face ply is installed with joint compound or adhesive, the joints of the face ply need not occur on supports.

Temporary nails or shoring shall be used to hold face ply in position until the joint compound or adhesive develops adequate bond.

2511.5 Joint Treatment. Gypsum wallboard single-layer fire-rated assemblies shall have joints treated.

Exception: Joint treatment need not be provided when any of the following conditions occur:

1. Where the wallboard is to receive a decorative finish such as wood paneling, battens, acoustical finishes or any similar application that would be equivalent to joint treatment.

2. Joints occur over wood-framing members.

3. Assemblies tested without joint treatment.

TABLE 25-G—SINGLE-PLY GYPSUM WALLBOARD APPLIED PARALLEL (‖) OR PERPENDICULAR (⊥) TO FRAMING MEMBERS

THICKNESS OF GYPSUM WALLBOARD (inch) × 25.4 for mm	PLANE OF FRAMING SURFACE	MAXIMUM SPACING OF FRAMING MEMBER[1] (Center to Center) (inches) × 25.4 for mm	LONG DIMENSION OF GYPSUM WALLBOARD SHEETS IN RELATION TO DIRECTION OF FRAMING MEMBERS ‖	⊥	MAXIMUM SPACING OF FASTENERS[1] (Center to Center) (inches) × 25.4 for mm Nails[3]	Screws[4]	NAILS[2]—TO WOOD × 25.4 for mm
1/2	Horizontal	16	P	P	7	12	No. 13 gage, 1 3/8" long, 19/64" head; 0.098" diameter, 1 1/4" long, annular ringed; 5d, cooler (0.086" dia., 1 5/8" long, 15/64" head) or wallboard (0.086" dia., 1 5/8" long, 9/32" head) nail.
1/2	Horizontal	24	NP	P	7	12	No. 13 gage, 1 3/8" long, 19/64" head; 0.098" diameter, 1 1/4" long, annular ringed; 5d, cooler (0.086" dia., 1 5/8" long, 15/64" head) or wallboard (0.086" dia., 1 5/8" long, 9/32" head) nail.
1/2	Vertical	16	P	P	8	16	No. 13 gage, 1 3/8" long, 19/64" head; 0.098" diameter, 1 1/4" long, annular ringed; 5d, cooler (0.086" dia., 1 5/8" long, 15/64" head) or wallboard (0.086" dia., 1 5/8" long, 9/32" head) nail.
1/2	Vertical	24	P	P	8	12	No. 13 gage, 1 3/8" long, 19/64" head; 0.098" diameter, 1 1/4" long, annular ringed; 5d, cooler (0.086" dia., 1 5/8" long, 15/64" head) or wallboard (0.086" dia., 1 5/8" long, 9/32" head) nail.
5/8	Horizontal	16	P	P	7	12	No. 13 gage, 1 5/8" long, 19/64" head; 0.098" diameter, 1 3/8" long, annular ringed; 6d, cooler (0.092" dia., 1 7/8" long, 1/4" head) or wallboard (0.0915" dia., 1 7/8" long, 19/64" head) nail.
5/8	Horizontal	24	NP	P	7	12	No. 13 gage, 1 5/8" long, 19/64" head; 0.098" diameter, 1 3/8" long, annular ringed; 6d, cooler (0.092" dia., 1 7/8" long, 1/4" head) or wallboard (0.0915" dia., 1 7/8" long, 19/64" head) nail.
5/8	Vertical	16	P	P	8	16	No. 13 gage, 1 5/8" long, 19/64" head; 0.098" diameter, 1 3/8" long, annular ringed; 6d, cooler (0.092" dia., 1 7/8" long, 1/4" head) or wallboard (0.0915" dia., 1 7/8" long, 19/64" head) nail.
5/8	Vertical	24	P	P	8	12	No. 13 gage, 1 5/8" long, 19/64" head; 0.098" diameter, 1 3/8" long, annular ringed; 6d, cooler (0.092" dia., 1 7/8" long, 1/4" head) or wallboard (0.0915" dia., 1 7/8" long, 19/64" head) nail.

Nail or Screw Fastenings with Adhesives (Maximum Center to Center in Inches)

× 25.4 for mm

(Column headings as above)					End	Edges	Field	
1/2 or 5/8	Horizontal	16	P	P	16	16	24	As required for 1/2" and 5/8" gypsum wallboard, see above.
1/2 or 5/8	Horizontal	24	NP	P	16	24	24	As required for 1/2" and 5/8" gypsum wallboard, see above.
1/2 or 5/8	Vertical	24	P	P	16	24	NR	As required for 1/2" and 5/8" gypsum wallboard, see above.

NOTES: Horizontal refers to applications such as ceilings. Vertical refers to applications such as walls.

‖ denotes parallel.

⊥ denotes perpendicular.   P—Permitted.   NP—Not permitted.   NR—Not required.

[1] A combination of fasteners consisting of nails along the perimeter and screws in the field of the gypsum board may be used with the spacing of the fasteners shown in the table.

For fire-resistive construction, see Tables 7-B and 7-C. For shear-resisting elements, see Table 25-I.

[2] Where the metal framing has a clinching design formed to receive the nails by two edges of metal, the nails shall not be less than 5/8 inch (15.9 mm) longer than the wallboard thickness, and shall have ringed shanks. Where the metal framing has a nailing groove formed to receive the nails, the nails shall have barbed shanks or be 5d, No. 13 1/2 gage, 1 5/8 inches (41 mm) long, 15/64-inch (6.0 mm) head for 1/2-inch (12.7 mm) gypsum wallboard; 6d, No. 13 gage, 1 7/8 (48 mm) inches long, 15/64-inch (6.0 mm) head for 5/8-inch (15.9 mm) gypsum wallboard.

[3] Two nails spaced 2 inches to 2 1/2 inches (51 mm to 64 mm) apart may be used where the pairs are spaced 12 inches (305 mm) on center except around the perimeter of the sheets.

[4] Screws shall be long enough to penetrate into wood framing not less than 5/8 inch (15.9 mm) and through metal framing not less than 1/4 inch (6.4 mm).

TABLE 25-H—APPLICATION OF TWO-PLY GYPSUM WALLBOARD[1]

FASTENERS ONLY

Thickness of Gypsum Wallboard (Each Ply) (inch) × 25.4 for mm	Plane of Framing Surface	Long Dimension of Gypsum Wallboard Sheets	Maximum Spacing of Framing Members (Center to Center) (inches) × 25.4 for mm	Base Ply Nails[2]	Base Ply Screws[3]	Base Ply Staples[4]	Face Ply Nails[2]	Face Ply Screws[3]
3/8	Horizontal	Perpendicular only	16				7	
3/8	Vertical	Either direction	16				8	
1/2	Horizontal	Perpendicular only	24	16	24	16	7	12
1/2	Vertical	Either direction	24				8	
5/8	Horizontal	Perpendicular only	24				7	
5/8	Vertical	Either direction	24				8	

FASTENERS AND ADHESIVES

Thickness	Plane of Framing Surface	Long Dimension	Maximum Spacing	Base Ply Nails[2]	Base Ply Screws[3]	Face Ply	
3/8	Horizontal	Perpendicular only	16	7	5		
Base ply	Vertical	Either direction	24	8	7		
1/2	Horizontal	Perpendicular only	24	7	5	Temporary nailing or shoring to comply with Section 2511.4	
Base ply	Vertical	Either direction	24	8	7 (12)		
5/8	Horizontal	Perpendicular only	24	7	5		
Base ply	Vertical	Either direction	24	8	7		

[1] For fire-resistive construction, see Tables 7-B and 7-C. For shear-resisting elements, see Table 25-I.

[2] Nails for wood framing shall be long enough to penetrate into wood members not less than 3/4 inch (19.1 mm), and the sizes shall comply with the provisions of Table 25-G. For nails not included in Table 25-G, use the appropriate size cooler or wallboard nails. Nails for metal framing shall comply with the provisions of Table 25-G.

[3] Screws shall comply with the provisions of Table 25-G.

[4] Staples shall not be less than No. 16 gage by 3/4-inch (19.1 mm) crown width with leg length of 7/8 inch (22.2 mm), 1 1/8 inches (28.6 mm) and 1 3/8 inches (34.9 mm) for gypsum wallboard thicknesses of 3/8 inch (9.5 mm), 1/2 inch (12.7 mm) and 5/8 inch (15.9 mm), respectively.

Courtesy of ICBO, UBC—1997 [Tables 25-G and 25-H]

Figure **10.2**

Comments

In summary, the model building code specifies that drywall shall be nailed at 7" o.c. ceilings and 8" o.c. walls using a 5d nail or with screws @ 12" o.c. The 5/8" fire separation walls and ceiling must use a 6d nail. According to UBC Table 25-G (see **Figure 10.2**)*, nails are to penetrate the wood framing 7/8" for 1/2" board and 1" for 5/8" board, unless they are ring-shanked. Screws must penetrate wood framing not less than 5/8". Fasteners must be at least 3/8" from the edge of the board. See fastener diagrams in* **Figure 10.6** *and* **Figure 10.7***.*

Nail pops are caused by wood shrinkage. Surprisingly, the longer the nail, the larger the nail pop. To avoid nail pops, the shortest acceptable nail should be used in the building construction to keep the nail-pop effect to a minimum. The project superintendent should keep a sample nail board on-site for random comparisons of the nails in use and the regulations. (For more detailed information on fastener pops, see "Effects of Site Conditions, Separation & Isolation — Lumber Shrinkage," later in this chapter.)

Industry Standards

Gypsum Construction Handbook
(United States Gypsum Company)

1. Exposure to excessive or continuous moisture and extreme temperatures should be avoided. Not recommended for use in solar or other heating systems when board will be in continuous direct contact with surfaces exceeding 125°F.

2. Must be adequately protected against wetting when used as a base for ceramic or other wall tile. Cement board or gypsum panels, water-resistant, are the recommended products for partitions in moisture-prone areas.

3. Maximum spacing of framing members: 1/2" and 5/8" gypsum panels are designed for use on framing centers up to 24"; 1/4" and 3/8" gypsum panels and 1/2" cement board, on centers up to 16". In both walls and ceilings, when 1/2" or 5/8" gypsum panels are applied across framing on 24" centers and joints are reinforced, blocking is not required. 3/8" and 1/4" Gypsum panels are not recommended for use on steel framing nor as base for water-based texturing materials.

4. Application of Gypsum panels over 3/4" wood furring applied across framing is not recommended since the relative flexibility of the furring under impact of the hammer tends to loosen nails already driven. Furring should be nom. 2" x 2" minimum (may be nom. 1" x 3" if panels are to be screw-attached).

5. The application of gypsum panels over an insulating blanket that has first been installed continuously across the face of the framing members is not recommended. Blankets should be recessed and blanket flanges attached to sides of studs or joists.

6. To prevent objectionable sag in new gypsum panel ceilings, the weight of overlaid unsupported insulation should not exceed 1.3 psf for 1/2" thick panels with frame spacing 24" o.c.; 2.4 psf for 1/2" panels on 16" o.c. framing and 5/8" panels 24" o.c.; 3/8" thick panels must not be overlaid with unsupported insulation. A vapor retarder should be installed in exterior ceilings, and the plenum or attic space should be properly vented. During periods of cold or damp weather when a polyethelene vapor retarder is installed on ceilings behind the gypsum board, it is important to install the ceiling insulation before or immediately after installing the ceiling board. Failure to follow this procedure may result in moisture condensation on the back side of the gypsum board, causing the board to sag. Water-based textures, interior finishing materials and high ambient humidity conditions can produce sag in gypsum ceiling panels if adequate vapor and moisture control is not provided. The following precautions must be observed to minimize sagging of ceiling panels:

    a) Where vapor retarder is required in cold weather conditions, the temperature of the gypsum ceiling panels and vapor retarder must remain above the interior air dew point temperature during and after the installation of panels and finishing materials.

    b) The interior space must be adequately ventilated and air circulation must be provided to remove water vapor from the structure. Most sag problems are caused by the condensation of water within the gypsum panel. The placement of vapor retarders, insulation levels and ventilation requirements will vary by location and climate and should be reviewed by a qualified engineer if in question.

7. To produce final intended results, certain recommendations regarding surface preparation, painting products and systems must be adhered to for satisfactory performance.

8. Precaution should be taken against creating a double vapor retarder by using gypsum panels as a base for highly water vapor-resistant coverings when the wall already contains a vapor retarder. Moreover, do not create a vapor retarder by such wall coverings on the interior side of exterior walls of air-conditioned buildings in hot-humid climates where conditions dictate a vapor retarder location near the exterior side of the wall. Such conditions require assessment of a qualified mechanical engineer.

Industry Standards

Plaster and Drywall Systems Manual
(BNI Publications, Inc.)

Installation of Gypsum Board

9.1.1 Method of Cutting and Installation. Cut the gypsum board by scoring and breaking or by sawing, working from the face side. When cutting by scoring, cut the face paper with a sharp knife or other suitable tool. Break the gypsum board by snapping the gypsum board in the reverse direction, or the back paper may be cut.

9.1.2 Smooth cut edges and ends of the gypsum board where necessary to obtain neat jointing when installed. Score holes for pipes, fixtures, or other small openings on the back and the face in outline before removal or cut out with a saw or special tool designed for this purpose. Where gypsum board meets projecting surfaces, scribe and cut neatly.

9.1.3 When gypsum board is to be applied to both ceiling and walls, apply the gypsum board first to the ceiling and then to the walls.

9.1.4 Space the fasteners, when used at edges or ends, not more than 1 in. (25.4 mm) from edges and not less than 3/8 in. (9.5 mm) from edges and ends of gypsum board (except where floating angles are used). Perimeter fastening into partition plate or sole at the top and bottom is not required or recommended except where the fire rating, structural performance or other special conditions require such fastening. While driving the fasteners, hold the gypsum board in firm contact with the underlying support. Application of fasteners shall proceed from the center or field of the gypsum board to the ends and edges.

9.1.5 Drive the nails with the heads slightly below the surface of the gypsum board. Avoid damage to the face and core of the board, such as breaking the paper or fracturing the core.

9.l.6 Drive the screws to provide screwhead penetration just below the gypsum board surface without breaking the surface paper of the gypsum board or stripping the framing member around the screw shank.

9.1.7 Drive the staples with the crown parallel to the framing members. Drive the staples in such a manner that the crown bears tightly against the gypsum board but does not cut into the face paper.

Note 5 — Staple attachment is restricted to the base ply of the gypsum board in a two-ply system.

9.1.8 Keep the board tight against the framing.

9.1.9 Protect the external corners with a metal bead or other suitable types of corner protection that generally are attached to supporting construction with fasteners spaced nominally 6 in. (152.4 mm) on centers. Corner beads may also be attached with a crimping tool.

Ed. Note: See "Selecting Appropriate Fasteners," later in this chapter, for more information.

Control Joints
Industry Standards
Gypsum Construction Handbook
(United States Gypsum Company)

Expansion and contraction (control) joints in ceilings exceeding 2500 sq. ft. in area and in partition, wall and wall furring runs exceeding 30 ft (9.1 m). Do not exceed a distance of 50 ft (15.2 m), in either direction, between ceiling control joints and install a control joint where ceiling framing or furring changes direction. Do not exceed a distance of 30 ft between control joints in walls or wall furring, and install a control joint where an expansion joint occurs in the base exterior wall. Wall or partition height door frames may be considered a control joint.

Control joints should be used in ceilings exceeding 2500 sq. ft. when the ceiling edges are allowed to "float." They should be used in ceilings exceeding 900 sq. ft. when the ceiling edges are screwed to framing.

Control joints should be used at all doors and windows that are less than full wall height.

Expansion (Control) Joint

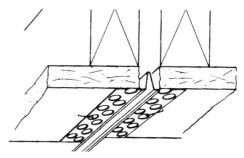

Courtesy of United States Gypsum Company, *Gypsum Construction Handbook*

Figure 10.3

Green Board (Water-Resistant Gypsum Panels)

UBC — 1997

Section 2512 — Use of Gypsum in Showers and Water Closets

When gypsum is used as a base for tile or wall panels for tub, shower, or water closet compartment walls (see Sections 807.1.2 and 807.1.3), water-resistant gypsum backing board shall be used. Regular gypsum wallboard is permitted under tile or wall panels in other wall and ceiling areas when installed in accordance with Table 25-G [see **Figure 10.2**]. Water-resistant gypsum board shall not be used in the following locations:

1. Over a vapor retarder.
2. In areas subject to continuous high humidity, such as saunas, steam rooms, or gang shower rooms.
3. On ceilings where frame spacing exceeds 12 inches (305 mm) on center.

Comments

According to the Gypsum Association, at the "Frequently Asked Questions" area of the Web site, 1/2"-thick green board may be applied to ceilings when ceiling framing, furring, or blocking does not exceed 12" on center.

Industry Standards

Gypsum Construction Handbook
(United States Gypsum Company)

Water-Resistant Gypsum Panel Application

Exposed edges and joints in areas to be tiled are treated with a coat of thinned-down ceramic tile mastic or an approved waterproof flexible sealant. Joints are treated with joint compound and joint tape.

Where water-resistant panels are used in remodeling, old wall surfaces must be removed and water-resistant panels applied to exposed studs as in new construction.

Framing— Check alignment of framing. If necessary, fur out studs around shower receptor so that inside face of lip of fixture will be flush with gypsum panel face.

Install appropriate blocking, headers, or supports for tub and other plumbing fixtures, and to receive soap dishes, grab bars, towel racks or similar items. Water-resistant gypsum panels are designed for framing 16" o.c., but not more than 24" o.c. When framing is spaced more than 16" o.c., or when ceramic tile more than 5/16" thick will be used, install suitable blocking between studs. Place blocking approximately 1" above top of tub or receptor and at midpoint between base and ceiling. Blocking is not required on studs spaced 16" o.c. or less. Vapor retarders must not be installed between water-resistant panels and framing.

Receptors — Install receptors before panels are erected. Shower pans or receptors should have an upstanding lip or flange at least 1" higher than the water dam or threshold at the entry to the shower.

Gypsum Panels— After tub, shower pan, or receptor is installed, place temporary 1/4" spacer strips around lip of fixture. Cut panels to required sizes and make necessary cut-outs. Before installing panels, apply thinned ceramic tile mastic to all cut or exposed panel edges at utility holes, joints and intersections.

Install panels perpendicular to studs with paper-bound edge abutting top of spacer strip. Fasten panels with nails 8" o.c. max. or screws 12" o.c max. Where ceramic tile more than 5/16" thick will be used, space nails 4" o.c. max., and screws 8" o.c. max.

For tile 5/16" thick or less, panels may be installed with stud adhesive (meeting ASTM C557) to wood or steel framing. Apply 3/8" bead to stud faces, two beads on studs where panels join. Do not apply adhesive to blocking where no fasteners will be used. Position panel and drive nails or screws at 16" intervals around perimeter, 3/8" from edges.

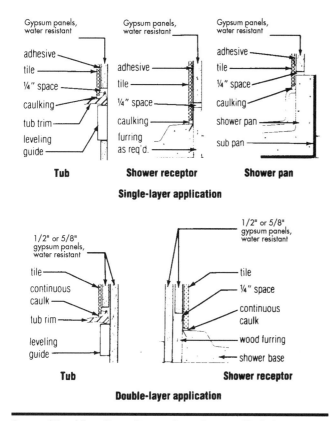

Single-layer application

Tub   **Shower receptor**   **Shower pan**

Double-layer application

Tub   **Shower receptor**

Courtesy of United States Gypsum Company, *Gypsum Construction Handbook*

Figure 10.4

For double-layer applications, both face and base layer must consist of Gypsum Panels, Water-Resistant.

In areas to be tiled, treat all fastener heads with Setting-Type or Lightweight Setting-Type Joint Compound rather than Ready-Mix Type Joint Compound. Fill tapered edges in gypsum panel completely with compound, embed Joint Tape firmly, and wipe off excess compound. When hardened, apply a second or skim coat over the taping coat, being careful not to crown the joint or to leave excess compound on panel (compound is difficult to sand and remove when dry). For butt joints and interior angles, embed Joint Tape with Setting-Type or Lightweight Setting-Type Joint Compound without crowning the joints. A fill coat is not necessary. Spot fastener heads at least once with Setting-Type or Lightweight Setting-Type Compound.

Fill and seal all openings around pipes, fittings and fixtures with a coat of thinned-down ceramic tile mastic or an approved waterproof flexible sealant. To thin water-based mastic, add one-half pint of water per quart of mastic to make a paint-like viscosity with a brush. Apply the thinned compound onto the raw gypsum panel core at cut-outs. Allow areas to dry thoroughly prior to application of tile. Before compound dries, wipe excess material from surface of gypsum panels. Remove spacer strips but do not seal gap at bottom edge of panels. Install tile down to top edge of shower floor or tub and overlapping lip or return of tub or receptor.

For areas not to be tiled, embed tape with appropriate joint compound in the conventional manner. Finish with at least two coats of joint compound to provide a treated surface for painting and wallpapering.

Comments

Ceramic tile may be applied directly over green board or cement board in a shower. However, the installation of green board requires attention to certain construction details; for example, the use of waterproof mastic (often black in color) and the priming of all open ends of board with waterproof mastic during the hanging of the board. This installation requires the site supervisor's special attention during construction.

Drywall as Shear

UBC — 1997

Section 2513 — Shear-Resisting Construction with Wood Frame

2513.1 General. Cement plaster, gypsum lath and plaster, gypsum veneer base, gypsum sheathing board, and gypsum wallboard may be used on wood studs for vertical diaphragms if applied in accordance with this section. Shear-resisting values shall not exceed those set forth in Table 25-I [see **Figure 10.5**]. The effects of overturning on vertical diaphragms shall be investigated in accordance with Section 1605.2.2.

The shear values tabulated shall not be cumulative with the shear value of other materials applied to the same wall. The shear values may be additive when the identical materials applied as specified in this section are applied to both sides of the wall.

2513.2 Masonry and Concrete Construction. Cement plaster, gypsum lath and plaster, gypsum veneer base, gypsum sheathing board, and gypsum wallboard shall not be used in vertical diaphragms to resist forces imposed by masonry or concrete construction.

2513.3 Wall Framing. Framing for vertical diaphragms shall comply with Section 2320.11 for bearing walls, and studs shall not be spaced farther apart than 16 inches (406 mm) center to center. Sills, plates and marginal studs shall be adequately connected to framing elements located above and below to resist all design forces.

2513.4 Height-to-Length Ratio. The maximum allowable height-to-length ratio for the construction in this section shall be 2 to 1. Wall sections having height-to-length ratios in excess of 1-1/2 to 1 shall be blocked.

2513.5 Application. End joints of adjacent courses of gypsum lath, gypsum veneer base, gypsum sheathing board or gypsum wallboard sheets shall not occur over the same stud.

Where required in Table 25-I [see **Figure 10.5**], blocking having the same cross-sectional dimensions as the studs shall be provided at all joints that are perpendicular to the studs.

The size and spacing of nails shall be as set forth in Table 25-I. Nails shall not be spaced less than 3/8 inch (9.5 mm) from edges and ends of gypsum lath, gypsum veneer base, gypsum sheathing board and gypsum wallboard, or from sides of studs, blocking, and top and bottom plates.

2513.5.1 Gypsum lath. Gypsum lath shall be applied perpendicular to the studs. Maximum allowable shear values shall be as set forth in Table 25-I.

2513.5.2 Gypsum sheathing board. Four-foot-wide (1219 mm) pieces may be applied parallel or perpendicular to studs. Two-foot-wide (610 mm) pieces shall be applied perpendicular to the studs. Maximum allowable shear values shall be as set forth in Table 25-I.

2513.5.3 Gypsum wallboard or veneer base. Gypsum wallboard or veneer base may be applied parallel or perpendicular to studs. Maximum allowable shear values shall be as set forth in Table 25-I.

Comments

While the UBC allows drywall for shear bracing in all seismic zones, certain cities and counties have imposed their own code restrictions disallowing this practice. These restrictions, and others, were adopted following natural disasters. Builders need to confirm the practice followed in each locale. Building officials should be aware of this item during the plan check and inspection phases.

Selecting & Using Appropriate Fasteners

Industry Standards
Construction Principles, Materials, and Methods
(John Wiley & Sons, Inc.)

Nails and screws are used to apply both single- and multi-ply finishes. Clips and staples are limited to attaching the base ply in multi-ply construction.

Nails

A variety of nails are used for applying gypsum board. Nails can be bright coated, or chemically treated. Shanks may be either smooth or annularly threaded, generally with medium or long diamond points. A nail head should be flat or slightly concave, thin at the rim and not more than 5/16 in. in diameter. Nail heads of about 1/4-in. diameter provide adequate holding power without cutting the face paper.

Either annularly threaded nails developed for wallboard, known as the GWB54, or smooth- or deformed-shank nails suitable for the application of gypsum board should be used. All nails should conform to ASTM C 514. Casing nails and common nails have heads that are too small in relation to the shank or too thick and should not be used.

Nails should be of the proper length for the wallboard thickness. Generally, recommended penetration into supporting construction for smooth-shank nails is 7/8 in. Annularly threaded nails provide more withdrawal resistance, require less penetration, and generally minimize nail popping. For fire-rated construction, however, penetration of 1 in. or more usually is required, and the longer, smooth-shank nails generally are used.

Screws

Gypsum board can be fastened to both wood and metal supporting construction with drywall screws. The usual finish for drywall screws is a zinc phosphate coating with baked-on linseed oil. These screws typically are self-drilling and have self-tapping threads and flat Phillips recessed heads for use with a power screwdriver. A special contour head design makes a uniform depression free of ragged edges and fuzz.

Screws pull gypsum board tightly to the framing without damaging the board, minimizing fastener surface defects due to loose board attachment. The use of screws generally is acceptable in fire-rated constructions.

Type W and similar screws are designed for fastening to wood framing or furring. Type W screws are diamond-pointed to provide efficient drilling action through both gypsum and wood and have a specially designed thread for quick penetration and increased holding power. Recommended minimum penetration into supporting construction is 5/8 in.,

ALLOWABLE SHEAR FOR WIND OR SEISMIC FORCES IN POUNDS PER FOOT FOR VERTICAL DIAPHRAGMS OF LATH AND PLASTER OR GYPSUM BOARD FRAME WALL ASSEMBLIES[1]

TYPE OF MATERIAL	THICKNESS OF MATERIAL × 25.4 for mm × 304.8 for mm	WALL CONSTRUCTION	NAIL SPACING[2] MAXIMUM (inches) × 25.4 for mm	SHEAR VALUE × 14.6 for N/m	MINIMUM NAIL SIZE[3] × 25.4 for mm
1. Expanded metal, or woven wire lath and portland cement plaster	$7/8''$	Unblocked	6	180	No. 11 gage, $1^1/2''$ long, $7/16''$ head No. 16 gage staple, $7/8''$ legs
2. Gypsum lath	$3/8''$ lath and $1/2''$ plaster	Unblocked	5	100	No. 13 gage, $1^1/8''$ long, $19/64''$ head, plasterboard blued nail
3. Gypsum sheathing board	$1/2'' \times 2' \times 8'$	Unblocked	4	75	No. 11 gage, $1^3/4''$ long, $7/16''$ head, diamond-point, galvanized
	$1/2'' \times 4'$	Blocked	4	175	
	$1/2'' \times 4'$	Unblocked	7	100	
4. Gypsum wallboard or veneer base	$1/2''$	Unblocked	7	100	5d cooler (0.086″ dia., $1^5/8''$ long, $15/64''$ head) or wallboard (0.086″ dia., $1^5/8''$ long, $9/32''$ head)
			4	125	
		Blocked	7	125	
			4	150	
	$5/8''$	Unblocked	7	115	6d cooler (0.092″ dia., $1^7/8''$ long, $1/4''$ head) or wallboard (0.0915″ dia., $1^7/8''$ long, $19/64''$ head)
			4	145	
		Blocked	7	145	
			4	175	
		Blocked Two ply	Base ply: 9 Face ply: 7	250	Base ply—6d cooler (0.092″ dia., $1^7/8''$ long, $1/4''$ head) or wallboard (0.0915″ dia., $1^7/8''$ long, $19/64''$ head) Face ply—8d cooler (0.113″ dia., $2^3/8''$ long, $9/32''$ head) or wallboard (0.113″ dia., $2^3/8''$ long, $3/8''$ head)

[1]These vertical diaphragms shall not be used to resist loads imposed by masonry or concrete construction. See Section 2513.2. Values shown are for short-term loading due to wind or due to seismic loading. Values shown must be reduced 25 percent for normal loading. The values shown in Items 2, 3 and 4 shall be reduced 50 percent for loading due to earthquake in Seismic Zones 3 and 4.
[2]Applies to nailing at all studs, top and bottom plates, and blocking.
[3]Alternate nails may be used if their dimensions are not less than the specified dimensions.

Courtesy of ICBO, *Uniform Building Code—1997 [Table 25-1]*

Figure 10.5

but in two-ply application when the face layer is being screw-attached, the additional holding power developed in the base ply permits reducing the penetration into supports to 1/2 in. Type W screws are available in 1-1/4-in. length. Drywall sheet metal screws, more readily available in longer sizes, may be substituted in two ply construction.

Type S and similar screws are designed for fastening gypsum board to 25-gauge metal studs or furring. Type S screws have a self-tapping thread and mill-slot drill point designed to penetrate sheet metal with little pressure. This is an important consideration because steel studs are flexible. The threads should be of adequate depth and turned within 1/4 in. of the head to eliminate stripping. They are available in several lengths, from 1 in. to 2-1/4 in. Other lengths and head profiles are available for attaching wood trim, metal trim, and metal framing components. Recommended minimum penetration through sheet metal for drywall sheet metal screws is 3/8 in.

Type G and similar screws are used for fastening gypsum board to gypsum board. Type G screws are similar to Type W screws but have a deeper special thread design. They generally are available in 1-1/2-in. length only. Drywall gypsum screws require penetration of at least 1/2 in. of the threaded portion into the supporting gypsum board. Allowing approximately 1/4 in. for the point, this results in a minimum penetration of 3/4 in. For this reason, drywall gypsum screws should not be used to attach wallboard to 3/8-in.-thick backing board. In two-ply construction with a 3/8-in.-thick base ply, nails or longer screws should be used to provide the necessary penetration into supporting wood or metal construction.

Staples are recommended only for attaching base ply to wood members in multi-ply construction. They should be of 16-gauge flattened galvanized wire with 1 minimum 7/16-in.-wide crown and divergent sheared beveled points. Staples should be long enough to provide a minimum penetration of 5/8-in. into supporting construction.

Floating Interior Angle Application

Industry Standards

Gypsum Construction Handbook
(United States Gypsum Company)

The floating interior angle method of applying gypsum panel effectively reduces angle cracking and nail pops resulting from stresses at intersections of walls and ceilings. Fasteners are eliminated on at least one surface at all interior angles both where walls and ceilings meet and where sidewalls intersect. Follow standard framing practices for corner fastening. Conventional framing and ordinary wood back-up or blocking must be provided where needed at vertical and horizontal interior angles. Apply gypsum panel to ceilings first.

Ceilings

Use conventional angle nail or screw application. Apply the first nails or screws approx. 7" from the wall and at each joist. Use conventional fastening in the remainder of the ceiling area.

Sidewalls

Apply gypsum panel on walls so that its uppermost edge or end) is in firm contact with and provides support to the perimeter of the panel already installed on the ceiling. Apply the first nails or screws approx. 8" below the ceiling at each stud. At vertical angles omit corner fasteners for the first panel applied at the angle. This panel edge will be overlapped and held in place by the edge of the abutting panel. Nail or screw-attach the overlapping panel in the conventional manner. Use conventional fastening for remainder of sidewall area.

Double Nailing

When double nailing is used with a floating interior angle, follow above spacing on first nail from intersection and use double nailing in rest of area. Conventional framing and ordinary wood back-up or blocking at vertical internal angles must be provided.

Single Nailing Application

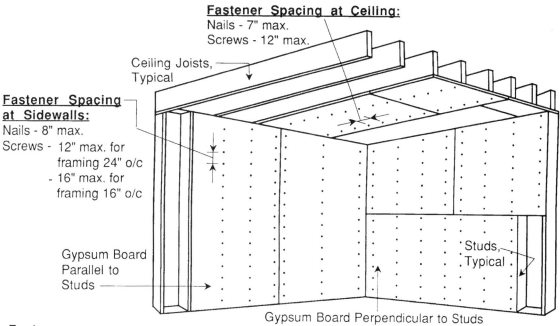

Fastener Spacing at Ceiling:
Nails - 7" max.
Screws - 12" max.

Ceiling Joists, Typical

Fastener Spacing at Sidewalls:
Nails - 8" max.
Screws - 12" max. for framing 24" o/c
      - 16" max. for framing 16" o/c

Gypsum Board Parallel to Studs

Studs, Typical

Gypsum Board Perpendicular to Studs

Fasteners:
1/2" thick Gypsum Wall Board -   No. 13 gauge, 1-3/8" long, 19/64" head; 0.098" diameter, 1-1/4" long, annular ringed; 5d, cooler or wallboard nail (0.086" dia., 1-5/8" long, 15/64" head).

5/8" thick Gypsum Wall Board -   No. 13 gauge, 1-5/8" long, 19/64" head; 0.098" diameter, 1-3/8" long, annular ringed; 6d, cooler or wallboard nail (0.0926" dia., 1-7/8" long, 1/4" head).

Courtesy of ICBO, U.B.C. *Field Inspection Workbook — 1997*

Figure 10.6

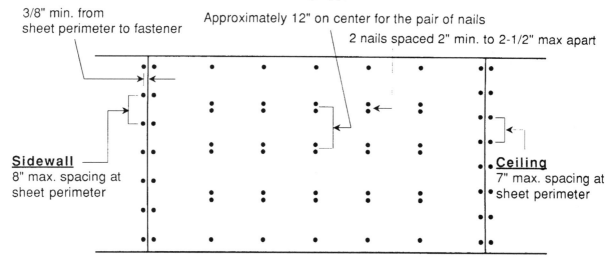

Double Nailing Application

3/8" min. from sheet perimeter to fastener

Approximately 12" on center for the pair of nails

2 nails spaced 2" min. to 2-1/2" max apart

Sidewall
8" max. spacing at sheet perimeter

Ceiling
7" max. spacing at sheet perimeter

Courtesy of ICBO, U.B.C. *Field Inspection Workbook — 1997*

Figure 10.7

Finishing Drywall

Industry Standards

Bathrooms
(Creative Homeowner Press®)

Drywall intended as a base for wallcovering or paint should be finished with drywall tape and joint compound. The compound should be sanded smooth, because even the smallest dents and ridges show through paint, especially paint with a glossy sheen. For a top-notch job, plan on applying joint compound in three stages, sanding the surface after each application. Drywall meant to receive tile simply needs to be taped with one coat of compound.

Comments

Some experts recommend one coat of primer prior to installing wallcovering.

Industry Standards

Construction Principles, Materials, and Methods
(John Wiley & Sons, Inc.)

Joint Tape

Tape used for joint reinforcement typically is a strong-fibered tape with chamfered edges. The special paper resists tensile stresses across the joint as well as longitudinally.

Joint Compounds

A topping compound is primarily a surface filler used to conceal and smooth over embedded tape, fasteners, and trim. It is a casein or casein-vinyl formulation available either in premixed or powder form. It bonds well with joint tape and compound, gypsum board, and fasteners; it sands easily and provides a surface with sufficient "tooth" and suction for painting.

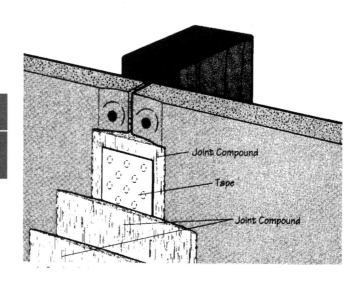

Joint Compound

Tape

Joint Compound

A finished drywall joint contains paper or fiberglass mesh tape embedded into joint compound. Two or more coats of compound, sanded smooth, ensure a seamless appearance when finished.

Courtesy of Creative Homeowner Press®, *Bathrooms*

Figure 10.8

Some manufacturers make an all-purpose compound that combines the characteristics of both adhesive and filler. It is a convenient formulation available in powder or premixed form, in either a machine or handtool consistency. All-purpose compound can be used for embedding tape, topping over tape, finishing over metal trim, and concealing fasteners. It should not be used for laminating gypsum boards unless specifically recommended by its manufacturer.

Blueboard — Gypsum Base with Veneer Plaster

Industry Standard
Gypsum Construction Handbook
(United States Gypsum Company)

Gypsum Base (Lath)
Gypsum bases finished with veneer plasters are recommended for interior walls and ceilings in all types of construction. For these interiors, a veneer of specially formulated gypsum plaster is applied in one coat (1/16" to 3/32" thick) or two coats (1/8" to 3/16" thick) over the base. The resulting smooth or textured monolithic surfaces are preferred for hard-wear locations where durability and resistance to abrasion are required.

Gypsum Bases are available in large-size gypsum board panels (4' width), rigid and fire-resistant. A gypsum core is faced with specially treated, multilayered paper (blue) designed to provide a maximum bond to veneer plaster finishes. The paper's absorbent outer layers quickly and uniformly draw moisture from the veneer plaster finish for proper application and finishing: the moisture-resistant inner layers keep the core dry and rigid to resist sagging. The face paper is folded around the long edges. Ends are square-cut and finished smooth.

Advantages
Gypsum bases, in conjunction with selected veneer plaster finishes, provide the lasting beauty of plaster walls and ceilings at a lower cost and with less weight and residual moisture than conventional plastering.

Rapid Installation — Construction schedules are shortened. Walls and ceilings can be completed in 3 to 4 days, from bare framing through decorated interiors.

Fire Resistance — Ratings of up to 4 hours for partitions, 3 hours for floor-ceilings and 4 hours for column fire protection assemblies have been obtained.

Sound Control — Gypsum-base partitions faced with veneer plaster finishes on both sides have high resistance to sound transmission. Resilient attachment of base and use of appropriate insulation further improves sound isolation.

Durability — Hard, high-strength surfaces provide excellent abrasion resistance resulting in minimum maintenance, even in high-traffic areas.

Easily decorated, smooth-surfaced interiors accept paints, texture, fabric and wallpaper. Veneer plaster finishes also may be textured. Finish plaster can be painted with breather-type paints the day following application.

Gypsum Base Limitations

Industry Standards
Gypsum Construction Handbook
(United States Gypsum Company)

1. Maximum frame and fastener spacing is dependent on thickness and type of base used.

2. Recommended for use with Basecoat and Finish Plaster, and Basecoat and Interior Finish Plaster. Do not apply gauged-lime putty finishes or portland cement plaster directly to base; bond failure is likely.

3. Not recommended for use in areas exposed to excessive moisture for extended periods or as a base for adhesive application of ceramic tile in wet areas (Gypsum Panels, Water-Resistant, or Cement Board are recommended for this use).

4. Gypsum base that has faded from the original light blue color from exposure to sunlight should be treated with either a plaster bonding agent or spray-applied alum solution before Interior Finish Plaster or any veneer plaster finish containing lime is applied. Basecoat and Finish Plaster, or Basecoat Plasters, do not contain lime and are not susceptible to bond failure over faded base.

5. Joints must be treated with Joint Tape and Setting-Type Joint Compound when framing is spaced 24" o.c. in one-layer applications.

Gypsum Wallboard: Effects of Site Conditions

Industry Standards

Gypsum Construction Handbook
(United States Gypsum Company)

Temperature

Install gypsum products, joint compounds and textures at comfortable working temperatures above 55°F (13°C). In cold weather, provide controlled, well-distributed heat to keep the temperature above minimum levels. For example, if gypsum board is installed at a temperature of 28°F (–2°C), it expands at the rate of 1/2" for every 100' when the temperature is raised to 72°F (22°C).

At lower temperatures, the working properties and performance of plasters, veneer plaster finishes, joint compounds and textures are seriously affected. They suffer loss of strength and bond if frozen after application and may have to be replaced. Ready-mixed compounds deteriorate from repeated freeze-thaw cycles, lose their workability and may not be usable. Avoid sudden changes in temperature, which may cause cracking from thermal shock.

Humidity

High humidity resulting from atmospheric conditions or from on-the-job use of such wet materials as concrete, stucco, plaster and spray fireproofing often creates situations for possible problems. In gypsum board, water vapor is absorbed, which softens the gypsum core and expands the paper. As a result, the board may sag between ceiling supports. Sustained high humidity increases chances for galvanized steel components to rust, especially in marine areas where salt air is present. High humidity can cause insufficient drying between coats of joint compounds, which can lead to delayed shrinkage and/or bond failure. Jobs may be delayed because extra time for drying is required between coats of joint compound.

Low humidity speeds drying, especially when combined with high temperatures and air circulation. These conditions may cause dryouts in veneer plaster finishes and conventional plasters. They also reduce working time and may result in edge cracking of the joint treatment. Crusting and possible contamination of fresh compound, check and edge cracking are also caused by hot and dry conditions. Under hot, dry conditions, handle gypsum board carefully to prevent cracking or core damage during erection.

Moisture

Wind-blown rain and standing water on floors increase the humidity in a structure and may cause the problems previously described. Water-soaked gypsum board and plasters have less structural strength and may sag and deform easily. Their surfaces, when damp, are extremely vulnerable to scuffing, damage and mildew.

Ventilation

Ventilation should be provided to remove excess moisture, permit proper drying of conventional gypsum plasters and joint compounds and prevent problems associated with high-humidity conditions. For veneer plaster finishes, to prevent rapid drying and possible shrinkage, poor bond, chalky surfaces and cracking, air circulation should be kept at a minimum level until the finish is set. Rapid drying also creates problems with joint compounds, gypsum plasters and finishes when they dry out before setting fully and, as a result, don't develop full strength.

Sunlight

Strong sunlight for extended periods will discolor gypsum panel face paper and make decoration difficult. The blue face paper on veneer gypsum base will fade to gray or tan from excessive exposure to sunlight or ultraviolet radiation. Applying finishes containing alkali (lime) to this degraded base may result in bond failure unless the base is treated with an alum solution or bonding agent.

Movement in Structures

Today, building frames are much lighter than former heavy masonry or massive concrete structures. Modern structural design uses lighter but stronger materials capable of spanning greater distances and extending buildings higher than ever before. While meeting current standards of building design, these frames are more flexible and offer less resistance to structural movement. This flexibility and resulting structural movement can produce stresses within the usually non-load bearing gypsum assemblies. Unless relief joints are provided to isolate these building movements, when accumulated stresses exceed the strength of the materials in the assembly, they will seek relief by cracking, buckling or crushing the finished surface.

Structural movement and most cracking problems are caused by deflection under load, physical change in materials due to temperature and humidity changes, seismic forces or a combination of these factors.

Concrete Floor Slab Deflection

Dead and live loads cause deflection in the floor slab. If this deflection is excessive, cracks can occur in partitions at the mid-point between supports. If partition installation is delayed for about two months after slabs are completed, perhaps two-thirds of the ultimate creep deflection will have taken place, reducing chances of partition cracking. This is usually a one-time, non-cyclical movement.

Wind and Seismic Forces

Wind and seismic forces cause a cyclical shearing action on the building framework, which distorts the rectangular shape to an angled parallelogram. This distortion, called racking, can result in cracking and crushing of partitions adjacent to columns, floors and structural ceilings.

Structural Movement

To resist this racking, building frames must be stiffened with shear walls and/or cross-bracing. Light steel-frame buildings are diagonally braced with steel strapping. Wood-frame structures are strengthened with let-in cross-bracing and/or shear diaphragms of structural sheathing. On larger buildings, racking is resisted by shear walls and wind-bracing without considering the strength added by finishing materials. Moreover, the partitions must be isolated from the structure to prevent cracking caused by racking movement and distortion.

Thermal Expansion

All materials expand with an increase in temperature and contract with a decrease. In tall concrete or steel-frame buildings, thermal expansion and contraction may cause cracking problems resulting from racking when exterior columns and beams are exposed or partially exposed to exterior temperatures. Since interior columns remain at a uniform temperature, they do not change in length.

Exposed exterior columns can be subjected to temperatures ranging from over 100° to O°F (38° to –18°C), and therefore will elongate or contract in length. The amount of expansion or contraction of the exposed columns depends on the temperature difference and several other factors. (Structural movement caused by thermal differentials accumulates to the upper floors.) However, the stiffness of the structure resists the movement and usually full, unrestrained expansion is not reached.

Racking, resulting from thermal movement, is greatest in the outside bays of upper floors in winter when temperature differentials are largest. To prevent major changes, as described above, apply proper insulation to exterior structural members. The design should call for control joints to relieve stress and minimize cracking of surfaces.

Hygrometric Expansion

Many building materials absorb moisture from the surrounding air during periods of high humidity and expand; they contract during periods of low humidity. Gypsum, wood and paper products are more readily affected by hygrometric changes than are steel and reinforced concrete. Gypsum boards will expand about 1/2" per 100' with a relative humidity change from 13% RH to 90% RH. Unless control joints are provided, hygrometric changes create stresses within the assembly, which result in bowed or wavy walls, sag between supports in ceilings, cracking and other problems.

Separation & Isolation — Relief Joints

Select gypsum assemblies to provide the best structural characteristics to resist stresses imposed on them. As described previously, these systems must resist internal stresses created by expansion and contraction of the components and external stresses caused by movement of the structure. The alternative solution is to provide control and relief joints to eliminate stress buildup and still maintain structural integrity of the assembly.

To control external stresses, partitions and other gypsum construction must be relieved from the structural framework, particularly at columns, ceilings and intersections with dissimilar materials. In long partition runs and large ceiling areas, control joints are recommended to relieve internal stress buildup. Relief joints for individual structures should be checked for adequacy by the design engineer to prevent cracking and other deformations.

As another annoyance, lumber shrinkage often results in subfloors and stair treads squeaking under foot traffic. This squeaking can be avoided by using adhesive to provide a tight bond between components and prevent adjacent surfaces from rubbing together.

Acoustical performance values (STC and MTC) are based on laboratory conditions. Such field conditions as lack of sealants, outlet boxes, back-to-back boxes, medicine cabinets, flanking paths, doors, windows and structure borne sound can diminish acoustical performance values. These individual conditions usually require the assessment of an acoustical engineer.

Separation & Isolation — Lumber Shrinkage

In wood-frame construction, one of the most expensive problems encountered is fastener pops, often caused by lumber shrinkage, in drywall surfaces. Shrinkage occurs as lumber dries. Even "kiln-dried" lumber can shrink, warp, bow and twist, causing boards to loosen and fasteners to fail. Gypsum surfaces can also crack, buckle or develop joint deformations when attached across the wide dimension of large wood framing members such as joists. Typically, this installation occurs in stairwells and high wall surfaces where the gypsum finish passes over mid-height floor framing, as in split-level houses.

Framing lumber, as commonly used, has a moisture content of 15% to 19%. After installation, the lumber loses about 10% moisture content and consequently shrinks, particularly during the first heating season. Wood shrinks most in the direction of the growth rings (flat grain), somewhat less across the growth rings (edge grain) and very little along the grain (longitudinally). Shrinkage tends to be most pronounced away from outside edges and toward the center of the member. When nails are driven toward the central axis, shrinkage leaves a space between the board and the nailing surface.

Based on experiments conducted by the Forest Products Laboratory and Purdue University, the use of shorter nails results in less space left between the board and nailing surface after shrinkage than with longer nails having more penetration. Using the shortest nail possible with adequate holding power will result in less popping due to shrinkage. Longer nails, however, usually are required for fire-rated construction, as specified by the experiments.

The annular drywall nail, with an overall length of 1-1/4", has equivalent holding power to a 1-5/8" coated cooler-type nail, but the shorter length of the nail lessens the chances for nail popping due to lumber shrinkage.

Contractors can take several preventive measures to minimize fastener failures and structural cracking resulting from lumber shrinkage. Type W screws are even better than the nail because they develop greater holding power and thus reduce possibilities for fastener pops. The floating interior angle system effectively reduces angle cracking and nail pops resulting from stresses at intersections of walls and ceilings. Gypsum boards should be floated over the side face of joists and headers and not attached. To minimize buckling and cracking in wall expanses exceeding one floor in height, either float the board over second-floor joists using resilient channels or install a horizontal control joint at this point.

Ed. Note: See "Control Joints" earlier in this chapter for further information on this topic.

Ceramic Tile

Comments

Ceramic tile continues to be a popular material for bathroom and kitchen surfaces despite the increased use of stone and solid surfacing materials such as Corian®. Tile offers a range of color, size and pattern, and provides a durable surface. Ceramic tile is available in glazed, decorative, mosaic and quarry. Ceramic tile used for baths and kitchen countertops is usually glazed or mosaic. Quarry tile is generally used for flooring rather than countertops. Decorative tile is best for vertical surfaces where its painted or relief pattern is not as likely to be worn off or damaged.

The 1998 Handbook for Ceramic Tile Installation, published by the Tile Council of America, Inc., provides detailed methods and standards for ceramic tile installation.

See the "Kitchen & Bathroom Countertops" section of Chapter 6, "Finish Carpentry & Cabinetry," for more information on types of ceramic tile and recommended applications.

See "Avoiding Failures in Ceramic Tile Installation" (at the end of this chapter) which identifies common causes of tile problems.

Wall Base for Ceramic Tile

Drywall

Comments

The base should be flat and solid and securely fastened to the framing members. If tile is to be installed over a plaster wall, inspect the wall first for holes and cracks, which must be patched with spackling or joint compound. Plaster that crumbles (when poked with a screwdriver) should be removed and replaced. The surface of the wall must be clean, dry and free of dust before the tile is installed.

Drywall is considered an appropriate base for wall tile exposed to moisture. See "Ceramic Tile Over Green Board" in the following section, and "Green Board (Water-Resistant Gypsum Panels)" earlier in this chapter's drywall section. Basic principles of drywall installation include:

- *Drywall is normally installed using nails or screws (see Figure 10.7 for spacing).*

- *Drywall sheets should be staggered from row to row to avoid having the joints line up.*

- *Joints should be avoided at the corners of a window or door to minimize cracking.*

- *At least 1/4" space should be allowed above the lip of bathtubs, shower pans or receptors.*

- *Fiberglass mesh tape provides stronger joints than paper tape to support ceramic tile installation.*

- *After applying the joint compound, it is not necessary to provide a finish coat, though the nail or screw heads and the metal corner bead should be covered.*

- *Joints should be allowed to set before installing the tile.*

See the Gypsum Wallboard sections in the first half of this chapter for more on correct drywall installation procedures.

Cement/Concrete Board Backing

Comments

Concrete board backing, or backerboard, is comprised of a solid concrete core, faced with fiberglass on both sides. It is recommended as an underlayment for wet areas such as bathtub surrounds and shower walls.

Since backerboard can be thinner than drywall, it may be necessary to fur out the studs with felt to create a flush surface where the backerboard meets the drywalled surface. Furring should also be done in a shower with a shower pan running up the sides to make the surface even for the backerboard. (The backerboard is supported with small blocks until the mortar bed has been poured over the shower pan.)

Cement backerboard can be more effective than green board in resisting moisture effects, and does not require priming or the application of waterproof mastic. However, it can be more time-consuming to install.

Industry Standards

1998 Handbook for Ceramic Tile Installation
(Tile Council of America, Inc.)

Recommended Uses:

1. over wood or concrete subfloors.

2. in showers over dry, well-braced wood studs, furring or metal studs.

Requirements:

- to be used in conjunction with Method W244.

- form slope for waterproof membrane with portland cement mortar.

- slope waterproof membrane 1/4" per ft. to weep holes in drain.

- turn waterproof membrane up walls a minimum of 3" above shower curb (6" above floor in showers without curbs).

- fur studs with 1-1/4", or thicker, furring strips above the top of the waterproof membrane to allow the top of the membrane to be flush with the face of the furring strips.

- shower floor membrane, as required by local authority having jurisdiction.

Materials:

- cementitious backer units — ANSI A118.9 or ASTM C1325.

- fiber cement underlayment — ASTM C1288.

- 2" wide glass fiber mesh tape.

- dry-set mortar — ANSI A118.1.

- latex-portland cement mortar — ANSI A118.4.

- grout — ANSI A118.6 specify type.

- metal studs — ASTM C-645.

- wall membrane (when required.)—15 lb. roofing felt or 4 mil polyethelene film, moisture resistant, not waterproof.

Preparation by Other Trades:

- over metal studs — see Method W244.

- studs — install square and plumb.

- provide a 1/8" spacing at horizontal and vertical joints and corners of cementitious backer units and fill space solid with dry-set or latex-portland cement mortar.

- embed 2" wide glass fiber mesh tape in a skim coat of the same mortar over joints and corners.

Preparation by Tile Trade:

- surround drain with broken pieces of tile or crushed stone to prevent mortar from blocking weep holes.

Installation Specifications:

- cementitious backer units — ANSI A108.11.

- tile — ANSI A108.5.

- grout — A108.10.

Cement Backer Board/Underlayment

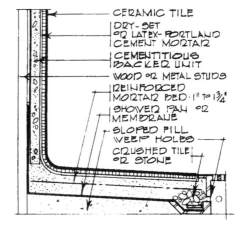

Courtesy of Tile Council of America, Inc., *1998 Handbook for Ceramic Tile Installation*

Figure 10.9

Ceramic Tile Over Green Board

Ed. Note: Green board is used as a base for ceramic tile and other applications where moisture will be present. Although UBC Section 2512 appears earlier (in the drywall section of this chapter), we have reprinted it here for convenient reference.

UBC — 1997

Section 2512 — Use of Gypsum in Showers and Water Closets

When gypsum is used as a base for tile or wall panels for tub, shower or water closet compartment walls (see Sections 807.1.2 and 807.1.3), water-resistant gypsum backing board shall be used. Regular gypsum wallboard is permitted under tile or wall panels in other wall and ceiling areas when installed in accordance with Table 25-G [see **Figure 10.2**]. Water-resistant gypsum board shall not be used in the following locations:

1. Over a vapor retarder.

2. In areas subject to continuous high humidity, such as saunas, steam rooms or gang shower rooms.

3. On ceilings where frame spacing exceeds 12 inches (305 mm) on center.

807.1.2 Walls. ...In all occupancies, accessories such as grab bars, towel bars, paper dispensers and soap dishes, provided on or within walls, shall be installed and sealed to protect structural elements from moisture.

807.1.3 Showers. ...Showers in all occupancies shall be finished as specified in Sections 807.1.1 and 807.1.2 to a height of not less than 70 inches (1778 mm) above the drain inlet. Materials other than structural elements used in such walls shall be of a type which is not adversely affected by moisture. See Section 2512 for other limitations.

Industry Standards

1998 Handbook for Ceramic Tile Installation
(Tile Council of America, Inc.)

Ed. Note: In its publication 1998 Handbook for Ceramic Tile Installation, *the Tile Council of America, Inc. makes the following recommendations and issues a caution that should be noted.*

From Methods W223-96, B413-96 & B416-96:

- Apply water-resistant gypsum backing board horizontally with the factory paperbound edge spaced a minimum of 1/4" above the lip of the tub or the lip of the shower pan. Water-resistant gypsum backing board single layer thickness shall be a minimum 1/2"-thick over studs spaced at maximum 16" o.c.

- All openings cut in backing board for plumbing and all cut joints between adjoining pieces shall be sealed with adhesive or other materials recommended by manufacturer of backing board.

- Gypsum backing board joints treated with tape and joint compound bedding coat only (no finish coats). Nail heads one coat only.

Ed. Note: See the ANSI requirement for water-resistant joint compound and tape following this excerpt.

Wood or Metal Studs:
Gypsum Board Organic Adhesive

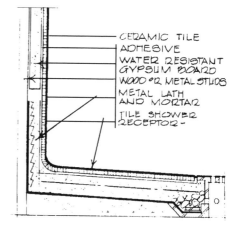

CERAMIC TILE
ADHESIVE
WATER RESISTANT GYPSUM BOARD
WOOD OR METAL STUDS
METAL LATH AND MORTAR
TILE SHOWER RECEPTOR

See "Caution" on the following page.

Courtesy of Tile Council of America, Inc., 1998 *Handbook for Ceramic Tile Installation*

Figure 10.10

Tile Over Water-Resistant Gypsum Board

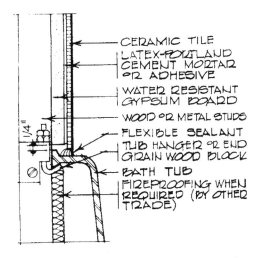

CERAMIC TILE
LATEX-PORTLAND CEMENT MORTAR OR ADHESIVE
WATER RESISTANT GYPSUM BOARD
WOOD OR METAL STUDS
FLEXIBLE SEALANT
TUB HANGER OR END GRAIN WOOD BLOCK
BATH TUB
FIREPROOFING WHEN REQUIRED (BY OTHER TRADE)
1/4"

See "Caution" on this page.

Courtesy of Tile Council of America, Inc., *1998 Handbook for Ceramic Tile Installation*

Figure 10.11

Caution

Substrate Limitations: The performance of a properly installed thin-set ceramic tile installation is dependent upon the durability and dimensional stability of the substrate to which it is bonded. The user is cautioned that certain substrate materials used in wet areas are subject to deterioration from moisture penetration.

ANSI A108.1A
(American National Standards Institute/Tile Council of America, Inc.)

AN–2.5.2.1 Suitable Backings: ...Water-resistant gypsum backing board is suitable backing for latex-portland cement mortars in wet areas such as tub-shower recesses, residential showers or other locations subject to similar wetting conditions.

AN–2.5.3.2 Suitable Backings: ...or water-resistant gypsum backing board for walls only.

AN–3.5.2 Wet areas: Install water-resistant gypsum backing board in accordance with GA-216-89, except that joints shall be filled with water-resistant joint compound and tape.

AN–3.5.3... A 1/4" gap shall be left between the paper edge and tub or shower receptor. The gap shall be caulked with a flexible sealant.

Expansion Joints in Tile

Industry Standards
Gypsum Construction Handbook
(United States Gypsum Company)

Exposed edges and joints in areas to be tiled are treated with a coat of thinned down ceramic tile mastic or an approved waterproof flexible sealant. Joints are treated with joint compound and joint tape.

Industry Standards
1998 Handbook for Ceramic Tile Installation
(Tile Council of America, Inc.)

Recommendations:

- interior — 24' to 36' in each direction.
- exterior — 12' to 16' in each direction.
- interior tilework exposed to direct sunlight or moisture — 12' to 16' in each direction.
- where tilework abuts restraining surfaces such as perimeter walls, dissimilar floors, curbs, columns, pipes, ceilings, and where changes occur in backing materials.
- all expansion, control, construction, cold and seismic joints in the structure should continue through the tilework, including such joints at vertical surfaces.
- joints through tilework directly over structural joints must never be narrower than the structural joint.

Expansion Joint Width (Vertical and Horizontal):

- exterior (all tile) — minimum 3/8" for joints 12' on center, minimum 1/2" for joints 16' on center. Minimum widths must be increased 1/16" for each 15°F tile surface temperature change greater than 100°F between summer high and winter low. (Decks exposed to the sky in northern U.S.A. usually require 3/4" wide joints on 12' centers.)
- interior for quarry tile and paver tile — same as grout joint, but not less than 1/4".
- glazed wall tile — preferred not less than 1/4", but never less than 1/8".

Comments

The UBC does not directly address expansion joints in ceramic tile.

Many instances of ceramic tile buckling up off the substrata are due to the omission of expansion joints. In its publication 1998 Handbook for Ceramic Tile Installation, the Tile Council of America, Inc. recommends installation procedures for sealing expansion joints.

American National Standards Institute
(ANSI/Tile Council of America, Inc.)

AN–3.7 Requirements For Expansion Joints.

AN–3.7.1 It is not the intent of these specifications to make expansion joint recommendations for specific projects. Specifier must specify expansion joints and show locations.

AN–3.7.2 Exterior Work. Locate expansion joints in exterior tilework on walls and floors not more than 16 feet (5 m) on center both ways on horizontal and vertical surfaces, over all construction or expansion joints in the backing, and where backing materials change, or change directions.

AN–3.7.3 Interior Work. Locate expansion joints in the tilework over all construction or expansion joints in the backing and where backing materials change. Where tile floors abut rigid walls and at intervals of 24 to 36 feet (7 to 11 m) in large floor areas, expansion joints are mandatory for quarry tile, and paver tile, but may be omitted in other tile on dimensionally stable backing at the discretion of the architect.

Tile Mortar

Mastic (Organic Adhesive)

Industry Standards

NKBA Kitchen and Bathroom Installation Manual, Volume 1
(National Kitchen & Bathroom Association)

In this method, tile is directly applied to the substrate material with troweled-on mastic. The countertop will only be raised the thickness of the tile. This is generally referred to as thin-set installation. Mastic manufacturers state that installation may be done over any of the following substrate surfaces: existing tile, fiberglass, wood, paneling, brick, masonry, concrete,

---

Vertical and Horizontal Joint Design Essentials

Use These Details for Control, Contraction, and Isolation Joints
Note: Preparation of openings left by the tile contractor and installation of back-up strip and sealant should be specified in the Caulking and Sealant section of the job specification.

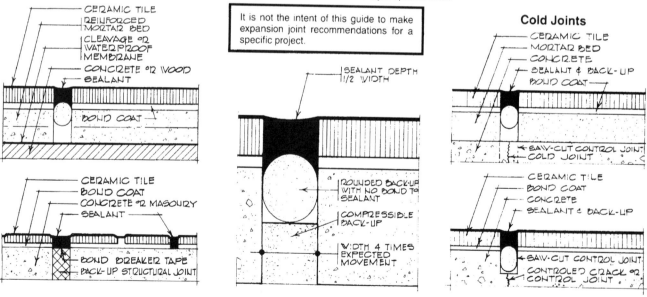

Courtesy of Tile Council of America, Inc., *1998 Handbook for Ceramic Tile Installation*

Figure 10.12

plywood, or vinyl. Most countertop installations are done over plywood. The surface must be dry, flat, and free of dirt and grease. This installation cannot hide any dips or bows in the substrate material, so any imperfections in the substrate will show up in the finished tile installation.

Conventional Mortar Bed (Mud)

In this method, the tile is installed on a bed of mortar 3/4" to 1-1/4" (1.91 cm to 3.2 cm) thick.

Thin-Set Over Backerboard

A glass mesh concrete backerboard may take the place of a conventional mortar bed. It is unaffected by moisture and has one of the lowest coefficients of expansion of all building panels. Additionally, the boards are only one-half the weight of conventional mortar installations.

A successful ceramic tile countertop installation is only as good as what is installed below the tile surface. The cabinets must be level and plumb, and the substrate set level as well. If this is not done, the backsplash grout will not be straight. A tolerance of 1/8" (.32 cm) in a 10' (304.80 cm) run of countertop is considered acceptable. (A 4' to 6' (121.92 cm to 182.88 cm) level should be used to verify this. For longer runs, a 4' (121.92 cm) level and an 8' (243.84 cm) straight edge should be used.

While plywood decking is the most common substrate material for countertops, some installers prefer traditional lumber decking. Traditional decking is often used to provide flexibility under the tile. Generally, grade-one or grade-two kiln dried Douglas fir, 1" x 4" (2.54 cm x 10.16 cm) or 1" x 6" (2.54 cm x 15.24 cm) spaced 1/4" (.64 cm) apart, is used. It may be installed perpendicular to the backsplash (from the front of the counter to the back) or running parallel with the cabinet space.

The decking should be delivered to the project site several days before the installation to allow the wood to reach the relative humidity of the room. The decking should overhang the cabinets and be flush with the face of the drawers.

Whenever possible, any cutout should be a minimum of 2" (5.08 cm) away from a wallboard or plastered backsplash.

Elimination of stress is critical when countertop overhangs are planned. The tile must have a solid base. If any movement occurs when pressure is placed on top, the tile and/or grout will crack. The underside of the decking should be finished to match the cabinets or correspond with other products used in the project.

Installation of Mortar Bed

Industry Standards

1998 Handbook for Ceramic Tile Installation
(Tile Council of America, Inc.)

Ed. Note: In its 1998 Handbook for Ceramic Tile Installation, the Tile Council of America, Inc., *describes the installation of the mortar bed used as a substrata to which ceramic tile is adhered.*

Absorptive ceramic tile must be soaked before setting on a mortar bed that is still workable when using a neat portland cement bond coat. The other method is to allow the mortar bed to cure and adhere the tile to it with Dry-Set (Thin-Set on West Coast) Mortar, Latex-Portland Cement Mortar or Epoxy Mortar. Epoxy Adhesive may be used for high bond strength and Organic Adhesive is used for interior work only.

Dry-Set Mortar: On the West Coast known as Thin-Set Mortar. This material is used to bond dry tile to masonry, gypsum board, cement backer boards, mortar beds, brick, ceramic tile and dimension stone. Not affected by prolonged contact with water but is not a water barrier and is not intended to be used to level or fill the work of others.

Latex-Portland Cement Mortar: Similar uses as Dry-Set but is less rigid and has superior bonding strength. It is recommended for the installation of large unit porcelain bodied tile.

Epoxy Mortar: Used where high bond strength, impact resistance and chemical resistance is required. With manufacturer's approval may be used over steel, wood, concrete and other substrata.

Epoxy Adhesive: Used where high bond strength and ease of application are required but not optimum for chemical resistance.

Organic Adhesive: Interior use for bonding tile to gypsum board, gypsum plaster, portland cement mortar, formed concrete and masonry. In wet areas suitable for bonding tile to properly prepared portland cement mortar, formed concrete, masonry and, for walls only, water resistant gypsum board. Not suitable for swimming pools or exterior.

Comments

ANSI specifications A-108.1A through A-108.11, A-118.1 through A-118.9, and A-136.1 detail construction methods and recommended areas of use of each type of tile bonding agent. These specifications are detailed and parallel the recommendations of the Tile Council of America, Inc.

UBC — 1997

1403.5.5 Ceramic tile. Portland cement mortars for installing ceramic tile on walls, floors and ceilings shall be as set forth in Table 14-A. [See **Figure 10.13.**]

Comments

*The word **mortar** is commonly used to describe (1) the backing substrata to which tile is adhered or (2) the material that bonds the tile to the substrata. A **mortar bed** is a layer of fresh mortar into which a structural member or flooring is set. Mortar has a Portland cement content; however, adhesives contain no Portland cement.*

*The UBC **does** provide specifications for materials needed to construct a mortar bed, to which ceramic tile is adhered. However, the UBC **does not** provide specifications for mortar used to adhere the tile to the mortar bed.*

***Caution:** Read and follow manufacturers' directions for installation of all tile-adhering mortars and adhesives.*

Tile Grout

Industry Standards
NKBA Kitchen & Bathroom Installation Manual, Volume 1
(National Kitchen & Bathroom Association)

Generally, there are four broad categories of grout that are specified for kitchen and bathroom installations:

Epoxy Grouts are made up of an epoxy resin and hardener, and are used when superior strength and chemical resistance are necessary. New formulas produce nearly flush joints in backsplashes and cover base trim. They are not stain resistant, and are offered in a limited range of colors. Epoxy grouts are more expensive than other types of grouts, and require careful installation procedures.

Silicone Rubber Grouts, after curing are resistant to staining, moisture, mildew, cracking, crazing, and shrinking. They are used where great elasticity and moisture resistance are required. They're ideal for bathroom application (walls, floors, or vanity tops). Silicone rubber grouts are not recommended for kitchen countertops because they are unsuitable for food preparation areas.

Dry-Set Grouts, also referred to as non-sanded grouts, are suitable for grout joints that do not exceed 1/8" (.32 cm). The grout is smooth in texture, and is often used with soft glazed tiles that could be scratched by abrasive sand. While this grout is generally mixed with water, a latex additive used in place of the water improves stain resistance and bonding ability. It also reduces water absorption, making it ideal for use in wet areas such as kitchen and bathroom countertops. The latex additive also eliminates the necessity of damp curing in some installations.

Sanded Grouts are used with wider joints, up to 3/8" (.96 cm), and have a rougher texture than non-sanded grouts. The sand is added to ensure proper strength of the wider joint. Like dry-set grouts, sanded grouts may be enhanced by a latex additive. Sanded grouts are most often used for floors and ceramic mosaic tiles.

Sealers are often specified for application on grout joints once the grout has thoroughly set. Several coats are often required in heavy use areas such as countertops.

Ceramic Tile Setting Mortars

COAT		VOLUME TYPE 1 PORTLAND CEMENT	VOLUME TYPE S HYDRATED LIME	VOLUME SAND		MAXIMUM THICKNESS OF COAT (inches)	MINIMUM INTERVAL BETWEEN COATS (hours)
				Dry	Damp	× 25.4 for mm	
1. Walls and ceilings over 10 square feet (0.93 m²)	Scratch	1	1/2	4	5	3/8	24
		1	0	3	4	3/8	24
		1	1/2	4	5	3/4	24
	Float or leveling	1	1	6	7	3/4	24
2. Walls and ceilings 10 square feet (0.93 m²) or less	Scratch and float	1	1/2	2 1/2	3	3/8 3/4	24
3. Floors	Setting bed	1	0	5	6	1 1/4	—
		1	1/10	5	6	1 1/4	—

Courtesy of ICBO, UBC — 1997 [Table 14-A]

Figure 10.13

Cement Backer Board/Underlayment

Dry-Set Mortar or
Latex-Portland Cement

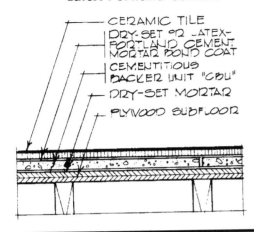

- CERAMIC TILE
- DRY-SET OR LATEX-PORTLAND CEMENT MORTAR BOND COAT
- CEMENTITIOUS BACKER UNIT "CBU"
- DRY-SET MORTAR
- PLYWOOD SUBFLOOR

Courtesy of Tile Council of America, Inc., *1998 Handbook for Ceramic Tile Installation*

Figure 10.14

Uneven grout colors can result if the grout is allowed to dry unevenly. This is most often caused because of a nearby source of heat or cooling such as a heat duct, hot air vent, or an air conditioner. This can be prevented by shutting off the source of air or wetting the grout frequently in that area.

Ceramic tile countertops are installed directly on a deck or substrate by one of three installation methods: **mastic** (organic adhesive), **conventional mortar bed** (mud), or **thin set** over a backerboard.

Ed. Note: See also "Wall Base for Ceramic Tile" earlier in this chapter.

Comments

It is very difficult to maintain light-colored grout on floors that will be exposed to traffic entering from outside.

Examples of Typical Tile Installations

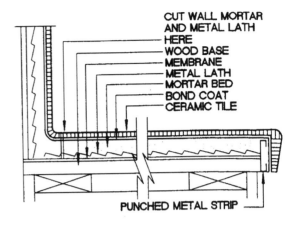

- CUT WALL MORTAR AND METAL LATH HERE
- WOOD BASE
- MEMBRANE
- METAL LATH
- MORTAR BED
- BOND COAT
- CERAMIC TILE

PUNCHED METAL STRIP

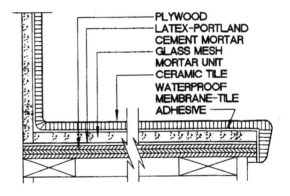

- PLYWOOD
- LATEX-PORTLAND CEMENT MORTAR
- GLASS MESH MORTAR UNIT
- CERAMIC TILE
- WATERPROOF MEMBRANE-TILE ADHESIVE

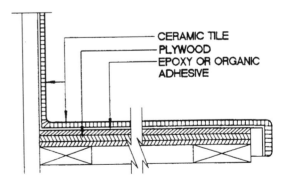

- CERAMIC TILE
- PLYWOOD
- EPOXY OR ORGANIC ADHESIVE

Courtesy of National Kitchen & Bath Association, *Kitchen & Bathroom Installation Manual, Volume 1*

Figure 10.15

Waterproofing Showers & Tubs

Sloped Substrata

Industry Standards
1998 Handbook for Ceramic Tile Installation
(Tile Council of America, Inc.)

Ed. Note: In its publication 1998 Handbook for Ceramic Tile Installation, the Tile Council of America, Inc. provides installation details for shower receptors and walls (details B414, B415, and B416). It includes other details for roof decks, tubs, fountains, and steam. Recommended installation details for all these items share a common method — placement of the waterproof membrane over substrata sloped toward the drain.

American National Standards Institute (ANSI)
AN–3.62 Prior to applying waterproof membranes, most plumbing codes require that floors or showers and roman tubs be sloped, by means of a smooth and solidly formed sloping sub-base, to weep holes located in clamp stile drains.

*Ed. Note: See **Figure 10.4** for gypsum wallboard installation around tubs and showers.*

Drains

Comments

The UBC does not address the installation of floor drains and waterproofing.

Tile installation for floor drains should utilize a two-part drain. The lower portion of the drain should be set to accept water off the waterproof membrane, and the top section should be set to receive water off the surface of the tile. Failure to slope the substrata under the waterproofing and toward the drain is a common installation error.

Hot mop is not an acceptable membrane, because when it cools, the material tends to be brittle and inflexible. Tile suppliers sell a vinyl sheet that uses contact cement on the joints, which is an effective alternative.

The vinyl pan must be installed first and must terminate up the wall 3" above the flood level or 6" above the floor. In a shower, the vinyl pan must terminate 3" above the dam height. Then, the wall membrane is installed overlapping the vertical vinyl pan membrane.

Cement Mortar

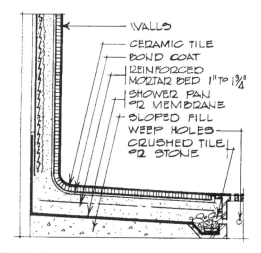

WALLS
CERAMIC TILE
BOND COAT
REINFORCED MORTAR BED 1" TO 1¾"
SHOWER PAN OR MEMBRANE
SLOPED FILL
WEEP HOLES
CRUSHED TILE OR STONE

Courtesy of Tile Council of America, Inc., *1998 Handbook for Ceramic Tile Installation*

Figure 10.16

As they work, installers have a tendency to drop nails and screws onto the vinyl pan. These materials will puncture the membrane if they are stepped on during the installation process. To avoid ruptures from dropped nails and screws, flood the pan for 24 hours just prior to floating the sloped-fill mortar.

Ceramic Floor Tile: Over Wood

Recommended Installation
UBC — 1997

2312.1 Structural Floor Sheathing ...Flooring, including the finish floor, underlayment and subfloor, where used, shall meet the following requirements [for the installation of ceramic tile over wood floor]:

1. Deflection under uniform design load limited to 1/360 of the span between supporting joists or beams.

Industry Standards
1998 Handbook for Ceramic Tile Installation
(Tile Council of America, Inc.)

Design floor areas over which tile is to be applied to have a deflection not greater than 1/360 of the span. Make allowance for live load, including weight of the tile and setting bed.

Comments

The Handbook details four types of installations over wood subfloor. One installation includes a minimum 1-1/4" mortar bed, two uses another layer of plywood properly gapped between sheets and at walls, and the last one involves cementitious backer units.

American National Standards Institute
(ANSI/Tile Council of America, Inc.)

ANSI A108.4: Where ceramic tile is to be bonded directly to plywood floors with organic adhesive, include the following requirements in the carpentry section of the project specifications.

AN–3.4.1 Requirement for Carpentry for Organic Adhesive or Epoxy Adhesive.

AN–3.4.1.1 Floor Framing. Maximum spacing 16" on center with framing size and span in accordance with applicable building code provisions for floors and floor loading.

AN–3.4.1.2 Subfloor — Exposure 1 or Exterior plywood conforming to provisions of Product Standard PS 1–83 for Construction and Industrial Plywood, or plywood APA Rated Sheathing, or APA Rated Sturd-I-Floor conforming to provisions of Manufacturing and Performance Standard for APA Rated Sheathing panels, or 1" nominal boards.

Underlayment — Plywood Underlayment, Exposure 1 or C-C plugged Exterior, or sanded plywood grades with special innerply construction conforming to underlayment provisions of Product Standard PS 1-83 for Construction and Industrial Plywood, or plywood APA Rated Sturd-I-Floor conforming to provisions of Manufacturing and Performance Standard for APA Rated Sturd-I-Floor panels. Each panel of subfloor and underlayment shall be identified with a trademark of the approved testing agency.

AN–3.4.1.3 Over 19/32 inch (15 mm) thick structural subflooring or 1-by-6 inch (19 x 140 mm) tongue and grooved boards, or other structural subflooring, secure 11/32 inch (9 mm) thick underlayment with adhesive or 3d ring shank nails; locate nails at 6 inch (152 mm) centers along panel edges and 8 inch (203 mm) centers each way throughout the panel; offset joints of subfloor and underlayment.

AN–3.4.1.4 Allow 1/8 inch (3 mm) between panels and 1/4 inch (6 mm) between panel and wall for expansion. Floor surfaces along adjacent edges of sheets shall not be more than 1/32 inch (1 mm) above or below each other.

Comments

Means Illustrated Construction Dictionary defines **slip sheet** *as "protective paper placed over the faces of prefinished plywood paneling to protect them during transport." In the ceramic tile industry, a slip sheet is known as a* **cleavage membrane.** *(See* **Figure 10.17.***)*

Installation of this type of membrane separates the minor movements of the substrate from the tile panel. It prevents the tile sawtooth cracking of grout joints over slab cracks, as well as loosening of grout joints over plywood joints on wood decks. Tile manufacturers provide vinyl slip sheet in rolls.

We have seen installations with 15# felt slip sheets glued to the slab with a latex adhesive and the tile set in thinset over the building paper that have performed well over slab cracks.

Floors (Interior): Wood Subfloor
Cement Mortar Metal Lath

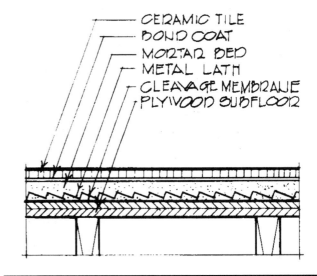

Courtesy of Tile Council of America, Inc., *1998 Handbook for Ceramic Tile Installation*

Figure 10.17

Avoiding Failures in Ceramic Tile Installation

Comments

- The tile installer should check all corners — inside and outside — for square and plumb prior to starting a job. The surface should be flat and free of any imperfections that could cause the tile to be out of line or prevent it from laying flat.

- Exterior corners should be square to ensure the proper appearance of the finished tile surface. Wall preparation is critical in this area. Corner bead or buildup of compound and adhesive may cause the corner to be out of square.

- In laying out tile, the object is to have full tiles showing in the most visible parts of the room, and cut tiles in the less noticeable areas. Layout each wall or section of wall separately. For expansion joints, allow approximately 1/4" between the perimeter tile and the wall and right above bathtubs, floors, and fixtures. The last tile should not be less than one-half the width of a full tile.

- The wall surface should be completely free of dust, debris and foreign substances before beginning the tile installation.

- Before grouting, all excess adhesive should be removed from the joints.

- Latex additives can be used with joint filler material to add to its flexibility and strength. It is important to fill the joints completely, leaving no gaps at the bottom. Tiles in moist areas should be grouted with mildew-resistant grout with a latex additive.

- Proper sealing of grout joints should make them stain-resistant. There are also grout formulations that include stain-inhibitors.

- Some water may contain high iron or other chemicals that can stain grout. Colored grout may be a consideration in these situations.

- Proper caulking when grout has cured (a few days after application) should be done at expansion joints in tile surfaces, thereby preventing cracks in areas where movement is likely (where floor tile meet cabinet toekick, where tile meets wall tile, or where two walls meet, as well as around faucets, valves and sinks).

- Tile should be cut as neatly as possible around wall penetrations such as supply pipes and valves. Care should be taken to properly caulk around wall penetrations prior to installing the finish trim.

- When applying finish trim and accessories, care should be taken not to place uneven or excess pressure on tiled surfaces — this could cause cracking of tile or joints.

- Tile should be from the same run or kiln, and the color should be consistent.

- Tile with edge defects should not be used.

- Special tile (for example, bullnose or corners) should be used in lieu of cut tile whenever possible.

- Tile should lay flat on floors or walls. Causes of problems include:
  - Uneven application of adhesive mortar or mastic.
  - A particle of dried adhesive, dirt, or a tile chip may become lodged under the tile.
  - A popped nail or screw.
  - Sloppy flash patching.
  - Placing a tile over an uneven wallboard joint. **(Ceramic tile does not bend.)**

- Because tile has no flexibility, it is imperative (particularly with floor tile) to provide a uniform subsurface that is free of voids. The structural support under the underlayment should be rigid and designed to support the weight of the tile flooring.

- Premixed adhesives are suitable for most applications, but some of these formulas should not be used in moisture areas.

Coefficient of Friction

Industry Standards

1998 Handbook for Ceramic Tile Installation
(Tile Council of America, Inc.)

Ed. Note: The floor tiling installation section of the Handbook provides the following guidance.

Consideration must also be given to (1) wear properties of surface of tile selected, (2) fire-resistance properties of installation and backing, (3) coefficient of friction.

Glazed tile or soft body decorative unglazed tile should have the manufacturer's approval for intended use.

Ed. Note: ANSI issues the same cautions on the use of tile. Information specific to a particular type of tile is found in the standards section referring to it. The statement in the following excerpt addresses coefficient of friction.

American National Standards Institute
(ANSI/Tile Council of America, Inc.)

ANSI A137.1 — Coefficient of Friction. When coefficient of friction (COF) data are required for a specific project, testing shall conform to ASTM C 1028. However, because area of use and maintenance by the owner of installed tile directly affect coefficient of friction, the COF of the manufactured product shall be as agreed upon by manufacturer and purchaser.

Comments

The UBC does not address the slipperiness of tile shower floors. Within the industry, however, there is some concern — but not much scientific data — about the required coefficient of friction for floor tile in general, and wet areas, specifically. Manufacturers provide data through their suppliers about the characteristics of their products, including the coefficient of friction.

Occupational Safety and Health Administration

OSHA (Occupational Safety and Health Administration) has established a recognized industry standard of 0.50 (wet and dry) for slip-resistant surfaces.

Americans with Disabilities Act (ADA)

ADA recommends "a static coefficient of friction of 0.60 for accessible routes and 0.80 for ramps." ADA does not specifically state that 0.60 is both a dry and a wet requirement.

CHAPTER 11 FLOOR COVERING & ACOUSTICAL CEILINGS

Table of Contents

(continued on next page)

FLOOR COVERING & ACOUSTICAL CEILINGS

Common Defect Allegations

Floor Covering

- *Imperfections in the underlayment can show through any floorcovering. Sources include buildup where flash patches were not properly sanded, nails or screws that should have been set flush, and dirt/debris that should have been cleaned or removed.*

- *Floor covering is affected by extreme moisture variations. If carpet, vinyl, or wood are to be installed over a concrete slab, and there is any reason to suspect moisture problems, testing is recommended. The calcium chloride test, also referred to as a "dome test," is based upon the amount of water vapor emission over a 72 hour period. A dish of premeasured dry calcium chloride is opened and set inside a clear plastic dome that is 12" square and is taped to the floor. Flooring should not be placed over slabs that are emitting 5 lbs. or more of water vapor unless special mechanical lock waterproof coatings are applied in advance.*

- *Hardwood floors are very susceptible to moisture damage. The wood flooring material should be delivered to the site where it will be installed 72 hours in advance to allow it to acclimate to the conditions in the structure. If a wood floor is to be installed over concrete, sleepers should be installed first over moisture barriers to keep the wood from coming in contact with the floor.*

- *Wood flooring can fail when the edges come in contact with high wet grade against the exterior wall, even though the floor has a good horizontal membrane. Floors can also fail from over cleaning. The side of the wood that is swelling from moisture expands more than the side that is not exposed to moisture. Therefore, if the water is coming from below, the wood will cup. Water from the top will usually cause the wood to crown. Note that when the wood expands, it shoves the outer strips away from the center, and when it dries, it shrinks, leaving gaps. If the gaps are not too large, a color caulk filler can be applied. Otherwise, the wood needs total replacement.*

- *Other installation problems that occur with hardwood flooring include:*

    - *joints staggered in a way that is not visually pleasing.*
    - *excess shrinkage, causing wider than acceptable gaps between boards or flooring strips.*
    - *buckling of floorboards due to expansion from moisture penetration.*
    - *poor layout, resulting in narrow pieces at the wall or against the base.*
    - *uneven staining, or flashing of finish from uneven application.*
    - *excessive chipping at cuts.*
    - *hammer or other distress marks.*
    - *exposed fasteners.*
    - *excess face nailing on tongue and groove flooring (on strip next to wall).*

- *Vinyl and tile floor defects include joint lifts (vinyl) due to inadequate adhesive application, excess mastic oozing through joints, failure to align tiles properly for pattern, and poor layout with very narrow tile pieces around perimeter of room.*

- *Like wood, carpet will also deteriorate from moisture. Prolonged exposure to moisture can cause the latex adhesive to break down, allowing the backing to delaminate from the woven carpet.*

- *The majority of the claims on carpet are from improper installation, resulting in excessive stretching or seaming. Pre-installation planning should include preparation of a seaming diagram with the goal of keeping seams away from high-traffic areas. Carpet may stretch after it is installed, and may need to be re-stretched and cut to fit. Another complaint is poor fit around jambs and other protrusions.*

Acoustical Ceilings

- *In high seismic areas the suspended ceilings require 45 degree splay wires to stabilize the grid in earthquakes. Compression struts are also required. These struts are usually made from metal studs that are screwed to the ceiling and the grid in a predetermined pattern. The struts prevent the ceiling from shifting upwards in an earthquake.*

- *In airtight rooms, especially where a positive air system is in use, just opening a door will often cause the tiles to raise. This can cause loose fibers or particles of the acoustic panels to drop. To prevent this problem, install retainer clips to hold the tiles in place.*

> • *White tiles should be handled with disposable gloves. Chrome paracube diffusers must also be handled with disposable gloves. Once they are contaminated, they cannot be cleaned well enough to use again.*

Introduction

The first part of this chapter addresses floor coverings. There are sections on vinyl and rubber, carpet, hardwoods and softwoods, parquets, and floating laminate floors, with guidelines for preparation and installation, as well as some allowable tolerances for installations. (See Chapter 10, "Drywall & Ceramic Tile," for information on ceramic tile flooring.) The kinds of problems that lead to defect claims related to floor coverings include cracks between wood floorboards or stretched or detached carpet; and bubbles, ridges or depressions in vinyl sheet flooring.

The second part of this chapter covers suspended ceilings. The use of a suspended acoustical ceiling system is predominantly found in commercial office and retail applications. One of the primary functions of a suspended acoustical ceiling is to provide a space to conceal HVAC ducting, plumbing pipe, electrical conduit, light fixtures, communications and computer cabling, insulation and other utilities.

A suspended acoustical ceiling is also a method of providing a finished architectural surface. A wide range of styles and colors of the metal grid system and the lay-in tiles can be used, from simple white to contrasting accents.

Inspectors will most likely look for proper fasteners and spacing of hanging wire attachments, proper number of turns of the hanging wire attachments, proper sizing of the hang wire, and proper installation of any additional seismic supports. Installers should strictly adhere to the design specifications and any local building code requirements regarding suspended ceiling systems. While elements within the support system can be changed fairly easily, any modification to the grid system itself after it has been installed is usually costly and time-consuming.

The following organizations may be helpful in providing information on floor coverings & acoustical ceilings:

Acoustical Society of America
500 Sunnyside Boulevard
Woodbury, NY 11797
Telephone: 516-576-2200
www.asa.aip.org

Association of the Wall & Ceiling Industries — International (AWCI)
803 West Broad Street, Suite 600
Falls Church, VA 22046
Telephone: 703-534-8300
www.awci.org

Carpet & Rug Institute
P.O. Box 2048
310 South Holiday Avenue
Dalton, GA 30720
Telephone: 706-278-3176
www.carpet-rug.com

Ceilings & Interior Systems Construction Association (CISCA)
1500 Lincoln Highway
Suite 202
St. Charles, IL 60174
Telephone: 630-584-1919
www.cisca.org

Floor Covering Installation Contractors Association
P.O. Box 948
Dalton, GA 30722-0948
Telephone: 706-226-5488

Maple Flooring Manufacturers Association
60 Revere Drive
Suite 500
Northbrook, IL 60062
Telephone: 847-480-9138
www.maplefloor.com

National Oak Flooring Manufacturers Association
22 North Front Street
Suite 660
Memphis, TN 38103
Telephone: 901-526-5016
www.nofma.org

National Wood Flooring Association (NWFA)
16388 Westwoods Business Park
Ellisville, MO 63021
Telephone: 314-391-5161
www.woodfloors.org
NWFA represents all segments of the wood flooring industry
(manufacturers, retailers, and installers). It provides expert information
to its members and to consumers. The NWFA Web site features a section
called "Consult a Wood Flooring Professional," which enables users to
e-mail questions. NWFA also maintains an information hotline, with
a charge of $.25/minute (1-500-443-WOOD [9663]).

Paint & Decorating Retailers Association (PDRA)
403 Axminister Drive
St. Louis, MO 63026-2941
Telephone: 314-326-2636
info@pdra.org

Resilient Floor Covering Institute
966 Hungerford Drive, #12B
Rockville, MD 20850
Telephone: 301-340-8580

*Ed. Note: Comments and recommendations within this chapter are not intended
as a definitive resource for construction activities. For building projects, contractors
must rely on the project documents and any applicable code requirements pertaining
to their own particular locations.*

Sheet Vinyl Flooring

Industry Standards

Construction Principles, Materials, and Methods
(John Wiley & Sons, Inc.)

9.10.1.2 Vinyl Sheet

Vinyl sheet products are made with a vinyl wear surface bonded to a backing. The backing may be vinyl, polymer impregnated mineral fibers, asphalt or resin saturated felt, nonfoam plastic, or foamed plastic. Some vinyl products have a layer of vinyl foam bonded either to the backing or between the wear surface and the backing. Backings are classified in ASTM Standard F 1303 as Class A, fibrous formulations; B, nonfoamed plastics; and C, foamed plastics.

In addition to PVC resins, the wear surface of vinyl-surfaced sheets may contain decorative vinyl chips, filler, pigments and other ingredients. Powdered vinyl resins, fillers, plasticizers, stabilizers, and pigments are mixed, rolled into sheets, and chopped to form these vinyl chips. Vinyl chips of various colors are mixed with additional resins and spread evenly over the backing and bonded to it under high heat and pressure. The vinyl resins and plasticizers together are called the binder.

Until recently, the wear surface of sheet vinyl was classified as filled or clear. Clear meant that the wear layer contained mostly binder and that when decorative elements occurred they were beneath a layer of clear vinyl. Filled meant that the wear layer was mostly vinyl chips (fillers). However, because even clear vinyl wear surfaces have some fillers, these designations have always been somewhat misleading. Therefore, the industry no longer uses the designations clear and filled. Instead, ASTM Standard F 1303 classifies vinyl sheet flooring as Type I or Type II. In Type I flooring the binder constitutes at least 90% of the wear layer; in Type II, it is at least 34%.

In addition, ASTM Standard F 1303 designates three grades within each type. The grades define wear layer thickness. Grade 1 is to be used for commercial, light-commercial, and residential projects. It requires a 0.020-in. wear layer in Type I and a 0.050-in. wear layer in Type II. Grade 2 is to be used for light commercial and residential projects. It designates a 0.014-in. wear layer in Type I and a .030-in. wear layer in Type II. Grade 3 is for residential projects only. It requires a 0.010-in. wear layer in Type I and a 0.020-in. wear layer in Type II.

Greater thicknesses are required in Type II than in Type I because the abrasion resistance and durability per unit of thickness of a wear layer are greater in the binder than in the fillers. The more binder, the thinner the wear layer can be for the same service.

Sheet products with vinyl backings may have a design imprinted on top of the backing or on the underside of the wear surface. They are usually printed with vinyl inks. A clear PVC wear surface is then calendered to the desired thickness and laminated to the backing with heat and pressure.

Concrete Subfloor Moisture Vapor Emission

9.10.2.1 Subfloor Moisture.
Concrete subfloors and mastic underlayments mixed with water release large amounts of moisture as they cure. With lightweight aggregate concrete (weighing less than 90 Ib./cu. ft.), or under conditions that retard the curing process, moisture may be released over long periods of time. Field tests described under "Concrete Subfloors" in Section 9.10.5. should be used to establish that the subfloor is sufficiently dry to receive the intended product. Since it originates in the original mix of the concrete, subfloor moisture may be present in below grade, on grade, and suspended subfloors.

Preparation for Installation

9.10.6.1 Preparation for Flooring. The effectiveness of a flooring installation greatly depends on the proper selection and preparation of the elements that make up the installation. Subfloors that are to receive flooring directly must be firm, smooth, and dense and must possess good bonding properties. When these properties are lacking, it may be necessary to prepare the subfloor by grinding, sanding, or using an underlayment. Adhesives should be selected that are compatible with all elements, including the flooring itself.

Application of Flooring. The installation of sheet materials should be planned to minimize the number and the total length of seams. Necessary seams should be placed in inconspicuous locations, out of the path of heavy foot traffic. In a rectangular room, running the flooring strips parallel to the side walls generally results in an economical installation with a minimum of seams. However, sheet flooring installed directly over wood strip floors should run perpendicular to the floor joints and may result in seams running the short dimension, parallel to end walls.

Comments

Common Problems with Vinyl Flooring

The following problems can sometimes be corrected with a repair, but may require replacement of the vinyl flooring. Exactly matching for color and pattern with material from a new lot is not always possible.

• *Bubbles, ridges, or depressions in the floor surface can be caused by inadequate preparation of the subfloor, or by improper installation (e.g., irregularities in use of adhesive or failure to roll the floor). Generally, 1/8" is considered the maximum height or depth acceptable for raised areas or depressions in finished vinyl sheet flooring. Bubbles should not be more than 1/16" high. (For more information on tolerances for vinyl sheet flooring, see Residential Construction Performance Guidelines, published by the National Association of Home Builders [Telephone: 800-368-5242].)*

• *Lifting of the vinyl flooring (failure to adhere) may be caused by moisture or the presence of foreign material such as oil or grease between the flooring material and the subfloor, inadequate preparation of the subfloor, or a failure to apply adhesive correctly.*

Vinyl & Rubber Tile Flooring

Comments

Resilient vinyl tile may be used to help hide irregularities in the surface. Textured and grained surface tiles may be more durable and easier to maintain because the dirt collects in the recessed areas rather than lying on the surface where they can be ground into the tile.

Industry Standards

Construction Principles, Materials, and Methods
(John Wiley & Sons, Inc.)

9.10.1.2 Vinyl Tile. Vinyl tile may be of homogeneous solid composition or backed with other materials such as organic felts, mineral fibers or scrap vinyl.

Ingredients for solid vinyl tiles are mixed at high temperature and hydraulically pressed or calendered into homogeneous sheets of required thickness, and the sheets are cut into tile sizes. Backed products are essentially vinyl sheet flooring cut into tile sizes. Some tiles are made with a self-adhesive back.

9.10.1.3 Rubber Tile. Natural or synthetic rubber is the basic ingredient of rubber flooring. Clay and fibrous talc or mineral fillers provide the desired degree of reinforcement; oils and resins are added as plasticizers and stiffening agents. Color is achieved by non-fading organic pigments, and chemicals are added to accelerate the curing process.

The ingredients are mixed thoroughly and rolled into colored sheets. The sheets are calendered to uniform thickness and vulcanized in hydraulic presses under heat and pressure into compact, flexible sheets with a smooth, glossy surface. The backs then are sanded to gauge, ensuring uniform thickness, and sheets are cut into tiles.

Comments

Guidelines for Professional Installation

- *Conduct a trial layout before any installation, placing the cuts equally on either side of the room. The layout design should discourage patterns that have less than one-half tile at the border edge. Seams should not be placed directly over a plywood joint in the subfloor.*

- *Properly prepare the underlayment, ensuring that there are no voids or raised irregularities. Flash patch knotholes in plywood. Eliminate any blemishes in a concrete subsurface and ensure that there will be no moisture penetration. Thoroughly clean the underlayment using a substance recommended for use with the tile and adhesive. Make sure to allow enough time for the flash-patching to set before adhering the tile. If the tile is applied too soon, the adhesive will not bond properly.*

- *Work off a centerline.*

- *Position tiles so that smaller cut pieces are in inconspicuous locations.*

- *Follow manufacturer's instructions for the tile and adhesive used. (For example, use the correct size notch on the trowel to ensure the proper thickness of adhesive.)*

- *Allow for expansion and contraction of the subfloor by leaving a space of 1/4" between the tile and the walls.*

- *Remove any adhesive that seeps between the joints of the tile right away.*

- *Protect the finish floor while the remainder of the job is completed. If an individual tile is chipped, scratched or scuffed, it may have to be removed and replaced. Keep extra tiles for this purpose, as it may be difficult to exactly match color in a new batch of tile.*

- *Transition properly from one room to another where the height of the surface floor changes.*

Vinyl & Rubber Flooring: Resistance to Damage

Industry Standards

Construction Principles, Materials, and Methods
(John Wiley & Sons, Inc.)

9.10.2.3 Resilience. Resilience is a measure of the instantaneous yielding and recovery of a surface from impact. Indentation resistance, quietness, and underfoot comfort are closely related to resilience.

9.10.2.3 Indentation Resistance. In assessing indentation resistance, the momentary indentation produced from foot traffic and dropped objects is of primary importance. These impact pressures sometimes are quite high and demanding. A 105-lb. woman in spike heels, for example, exerts a pressure on the floor of approximately 2000 psi, while a 225-lb. man with his weight spread over 3 in. by 3 in. heels exerts only 25 psi.

Permanent indentation from heavy stationary objects, such as a piano or a desk, may be minimized by using floor protectors to distribute the load. Indentation resistance of thinner flooring materials is greatly affected by the subfloor or underlayment and may be increased by selection of harder subsurface materials. Homogeneous vinyl tile and foam-cushioned vinyls have the highest indentation resistance.

Permanent indentation in some flooring types and under certain conditions cannot be entirely prevented. However, these indentations may be less conspicuous in patterned, textured, and low-luster floors.

9.10.2.4 Resistance to Sunlight. The actinic rays in strong sunlight may affect some resilient floors by causing fading, shrinking, or brittleness. Linoleum and vinyl products are most resistant to such deterioration. Color pigments are the critical factor in fade-resistant properties. Neutral colors show the best light resistance; pastel tones, especially yellows, blues, and pinks, are least effective in retaining colors under prolonged exposure to sunlight.

Vinyl & Rubber Flooring: Slip Resistance, Mastics, and Underlayment

Industry Standards

Construction Principles, Materials, and Methods
(John Wiley & Sons, Inc.)

9.10.2.7 Slip Resistance. The Americans with Disabilities Act of 1990 requires designers to specify flooring materials that have a static coefficient of friction of not less than 0.60 for level surfaces and 0.80 for ramps. Some manufacturers currently publish these data for their flooring products, even though there is no consensus in the industry concerning the test methods needed to ensure compliance. It would be prudent to verify the current status of slip-resistance requirements before selecting a resilient flooring for any project.

9.10.4.1 Mastic. Suitable mastic underlayments contain a chemical binder such as latex, asphalt, or polyvinyl-acetate resins and portland, gypsum, or aluminous cement. Mixtures consisting of powdered cement and sand to which only water has been added function only as crack fillers; when applied in thin coats, they break down under traffic.

Latex underlayments are most suitable for applications that require a thin layer (3/8 in. or less), for skim coating, and for patching where the fill must be featheredged. Skim coating does not attempt to raise the elevation of the floor, but merely smooths over surface irregularities.

Asphaltic and polyvinyl-acetate underlayments are used for installations that require thicker underlayments (more than 3/8 in.). Mastic underlayments should be troweled smooth and true, with not more than a 1/8-in. variation from a straight line in 10 ft. Subfloors should be free of wax, oil, and surface coatings, such as concrete curing compounds, before mastic underlayment is applied.

Carpet

Comments

A tremendous amount of technical information has been generated on the subject of carpeting. While such coverage is beyond the scope of this book, we will focus on the basic issues that may be pertinent in an average installation application or in a claim of defect. Resolving any dispute will involve consideration of the manufacturers' specifications and installation recommendations.

Acoustic Value

Industry Standards

Construction Principles, Materials, and Methods
(John Wiley & Sons, Inc.)

9.11 Carpet. Carpet is often selected for its comfort and decorative values, but it is also extremely effective in reducing impact sound transmission through floor and ceiling assemblies. Therefore, its acoustical performance should be a prime consideration in flooring selection. Many common installations will provide a performance considerably higher than the range of -5 to +10 on the Impact Noise Reduction (INR) scale. Specially selected combinations of carpet and cushioning may be rated as high as +17 over wood floors, and +29 over concrete slabs.

Carpet is also capable of absorbing sound and reducing sound reflection within a room, much like acoustical ceiling tile. The Noise Reduction Coefficient (NRC) of most carpet ranges between 0.35 and 0.55, which compares favorably with a range of 0.55 to 0.75 for acoustical ceiling tile. Properly selected carpet may achieve absorption coefficients equal to acoustical tile. However, carpet is not particularly effective in controlling the transmission of airborne sound; where this consideration is important, special sound-isolating construction should be used.

This section describes carpet suitable for long-term wall-to-wall installation, as distinguished from rugs, which usually have bound edges and are laid loose over a finished flooring.

Carpet Construction

9.11.1 Carpet Construction. Most carpet consists of pile yarns, which form the wearing surface, and backing yarns, which interlock the pile yarns and hold them in place. Carpet can be identified according to the carpet construction, which describes the method of interlocking the backing and the pile yarns. Comparative factors related to carpet construction, such as pile yarn weight, pile thickness, and number of tufts per square inch, may be useful in comparing carpet of similar construction.

Carpet can also be identified by the material of the pile fibers of which the pile yarns are made, including wool, nylon, acrylic, polyester, and polypropylene. The various fibers have unique characteristics that may affect carpet performance and styling. Both carpet construction and fiber properties influence the selection of dyeing methods.

Carpeting Materials

9.11.1.2 Wool. The outstanding characteristic of wool is resilience, which, in combination with moderate fiber strength and good resistance to abrasion, produces excellent appearance retention. Wool's relatively high specific gravity contributes to greater pile density.

.11.1.2 Nylon. Nylon comprises about 85% of the commercial carpet market and a large portion of the housing market as well. The extensive use of nylon can be attributed to its lower cost, availability in many bright colors, exceptional resistance to abrasion, and high fiber strength.

9.11.1.2 Acrylics and Modacrylics. Acrylics and modacrylics (modified acrylics) are synthetic fibers that closely resemble wool in abrasion resistance and texture.

Fibers of the acrylic family are now available only in staple form and are characterized by an appearance and high durability comparable to that of wool. Acrylics often are blended with modacrylics in commercial carpet to reduce potential flammability. However, with substantial improvement in acrylic fibers, the trend is toward 100% acrylic fiber.

9.11.1.2 Polyester. Polyester is a fiber-forming thermoplastic polymer. It is made from terephthalic acid and ethylene glycol. Polyester fibers are staple fibers, and polyester yarns are spun yarns.

9.11.1.2 Polypropylene Olefin. There are two classes of olefin, polyethylene and polypropylene. Only polypropylene has been produced in a fiber suitable for carpet construction.

Polypropylene has the lowest moisture absorption rate of any carpet fibers, which gives it superior stain resistance as well as excellent wet cleanability. Its low specific gravity results in superior covering power, and its high fiber strength contributes to good wear resistance.

Resistance to Damage

9.11.2 Selection Criteria. Carpet performance cannot be attributed to any single element of carpet construction or physical property of the pile fiber. Installed performance is rather the combined effect of many variables such as surface texture and carpet construction, backing, cushioning, and pile thickness, weight, and density. Of these, pile weight and pile density are the most uniformly significant, regardless of fiber type or carpet construction.

Although pile fibers differ in their physical properties, all fibers included in this discussion will provide adequate service when used in a carpet construction suitable for the traffic exposure. The variables of carpet construction are so great that it is difficult to assess their individual effects on performance and selection criteria. Therefore, selection criteria are outlined for fibers only, and the effects of carpet construction are described where appropriate in the following discussion.

Individual selection criteria may be useful in carpet selection for special conditions of traffic or exposure to special hazards. For example, *alkali, acid,* and *stain resistance* may be important in food preparation and serving areas. *Soiling resistance* and *wet cleanability* may be a factor in entry areas. *Insect* and *fungus resistance* may require consideration in potentially damp locations, and the possibility of *static build-up* should be considered in areas of prevailing low humidity and where such build-up might affect equipment or activities, such as in computer rooms. These and other criteria have been combined into composites such as *durability, texture retention,* and *ease of maintenance* for average conditions.

9.11.2.1 Durability. Pile weight and density, backing and cushioning firmness, quality of installation, and maintenance significantly affect the durability of carpet. In addition, durability is affected by hazards that tend to destroy the pile fibers. The resistance of fibers to these hazards is shown in ratings for resistance to abrasion, alkalies, acids, insects, fungi, and burns. The rating for durability is a composite that reflects overall resistance to destruction or loss of pile fibers and is a measure of the service life of a carpet.

9.11.2.1 Abrasion Resistance. Abrasion resistance is the resistance of the fiber to wearing away caused by foot traffic or other moving loads. It is measured in terms of the actual loss of fiber when exposed to a laboratory machine that simulates the abrasive forces of foot traffic. Since loss of fiber occurs as a result of breaking, fiber strength is one of the physical properties that influences abrasion resistance. Nylon and polypropylene have superior fiber strength and hence excellent abrasion resistance.

9.11.2.1 Alkali and Acid Resistance. Foods and beverages are generally mildly alkaline or acid in nature; many soaps and detergents are strongly alkaline. If alkaline or acid solutions are not promptly removed when spilled, they may attack the pile fibers. Wool fibers are more vulnerable to such attacks because they have a higher moisture absorption rate and are less inert chemically than the synthetic fibers.

9.11.2.1 Insect and Fungus Resistance. The synthetic fibers in modern carpets contain no organic nutritive value and are, therefore, immune to attack by insects, such as carpet beetles and moths, and to fungi, such as mold and mildew. To render wool carpet resistant to these hazards, most manufacturers treat wool yarn in a dye bath with a chemical preservative that provides long-term protection from insect attack, even after wet and dry cleaning. Since many carpets intended for interior use employ at least some organic fibers in the backing, some fungus hazard exists with most carpets, even those with synthetic fiber piles.

In general, the hazard of insect and fungus attack can be reduced by regular vacuuming and exposing the carpet to light and air. This is particularly important where large or heavy pieces of furniture make part of the carpet inaccessible to regular cleaning and ventilation. In such areas, greater insect protection can be provided for wool carpets by periodic spraying with mothproofing agents.

9.11.2.1 Burn Resistance. Most synthetic carpet fibers are flame resistant to some degree, but they will melt and fuse when exposed to the heat of a burning cigarette or glowing ash that produces more than 500°F. Prolonged exposure to such concentrated heat may result in complete local loss of fiber or a slightly fused spot. The fused spot is more resistant to wear and abrasion than the surrounding area, and this causes a visible discoloration in the carpet surface.

Although wool fiber will actually burn by charring, the damage from a lit cigarette usually is less severe, and the charred spot will wear off readily or can be removed with fine sandpaper. The fused spot on synthetic carpets similarly can be snipped off if it is not too severe, and, if followed by brushing, an acceptable appearance usually will result. If the burn is severe, replacement of the burnt area may be necessary.

The behavior of a carpet in a fully developed fire is controlled by building codes and laws. *All carpet manufactured in the United States must pass a methenamine "pill" test* in accordance with ASTM Standard D 2859, "Test Method for Flammability of Finished Textile Floor Covering Materials." This same test is described in Federal Standard Document FF 1-70,

"Methenamine Pill Test." In this test, a carpet is exposed to the burning of a methenamine tablet. The medium flame spread index or critical radiant flux must be 0.04 watts/sq. cm. Often, a carpet will be required by code to have a higher rating than the pill test minimum. The National Institute of Standards and Technology recommends that carpet used in corridors and exit ways have a radiant flux of at least 0.22 watts/sq. cm in commercial occupancies and of 0.45 in institutional occupancies.

A carpet's flame spread during a fully developed fire is usually measured by the Flooring Radiant Panel Test of ASTM E 648, "Test Method for Critical Radiant Flux of Floor Covering Systems Using a Radiant Heat Source," or NFPA 253, "Test Method for Critical Radiant Flux of Floor Covering Systems Using a Radiant Heat Energy Source," which are essentially the same test. This name spread index is called the critical radiantpux. It represents the minimum energy necessary to sustain flame. The higher the number, the more resistant the carpet to flame propagation.

Sometimes, a carpet's flame spread index is required to be measured by the Smoke Chamber Test in UL 992, "Smoke Chamber Test." This test measures the length of spread and time of travel of a flame. The range is from O to 25.

9.11.2.2 Appearance Retention. Appearance retention depends on factors that change original carpet color, texture, or pattern, such as fading, soiling, and staining, and compression and crush resistance. Other factors common to many types of fiber and carpet construction that affect appearance without impairing serviceability are pilling, shedding, sprouting, and shading. Ratings for appearance retention are composites of these factors.

9.11.2.2 Compression Resistance. The extent to which the pile will be compressed under heavy loads or by extensive foot traffic is called compression resistance. For instance, of two samples tested under the same conditions, the one that compresses less is said to have better compression resistance. With the exception of polypropylene, which is rated somewhat lower, all fibers are approximately equal in their ability to resist

Selection Criteria for Carpet Pile Fibers[a]

Criteria	Wool	Nylon	Acrylic	Modacrylic	Polypropylene
Resistance to: Abrasion	Good	Excellent	Good	Good	Excellent
Alkalies	Fair	Good to Excellent	Good to Excellent	Good to Excellent	Good to Excellent
Acids	Fair	Good to Excellent	Good	Good	Good to Excellent
Insects and fungi	Excellent[b]	Excellent	Excellent	Excellent	Excellent
Burns	Good	Fair	Fair	Fair	Fair
Compression	Good	Good	Good	Good	Fair
Crushing	Excellent	Good	Good to Excellent	Good	Fair to Good
Staining	Good	Good to Excellent	Good to Excellent	Good to Excellent	Excellent
Soiling	Good	Fair to Good	Good to Excellent	Good to Excellent	Excellent
Static buildup	Fair to Good	Fair	Good	Good	Excellent
Texture retention	Excellent	Good to Excellent	Good to Excellent	Good	Fair to Good
Wet cleanability	Fair to Good	Good	Good to Excellent	Good to Excellent	Excellent
Durability	Good to Excellent	Excellent	Good to Excellent	Good to Excellent	Good
Appearance retention	Excellent	Good to Excellent	Good to Excellent	Good to Excellent	Good
Ease of maintenance	Good to Excellent	Good	Good to Excellent	Good to Excellent	Excellent

[a]In each case, criteria vary depending on the properties of the specific fiber type used, carpet construction, and installation procedures.

[b]When chemically treated.

Courtesy of John Wiley & Sons, Inc., *Construction Principles, Materials, and Methods*

Figure 11.1

compression loads. Of greater importance in resisting such forces are the cushioning, the pile height and the pile density. Looped-pile construction with closely spaced tufts and tightly twisted yarns is more resistant to compression.

Compressed fibers in a small area may be restored by dampening the pile with sponge or steam iron and brushing the pile erect. If a larger area becomes matted down by excessive traffic, it can be restored by vacuuming with a beater bar machine, using a pile lifter machine, or wet cleaning.

9.11.2.2 Crush Resistance. Crush resistance depends on the ability of the fibers to recover from short- and long-term compression loads. This property is measured by the extent to which the fiber springs back after a load has been removed, as a percentage of the original height. Wool and acrylic have the highest crush resistance, nylon and modacrylic moderate, and polypropylene, somewhat lower. Pile density, spacing of tufts, and tightness of yarns affect crush resistance more than the relative rating of the fibers.

9.11.2.2 Texture Retention. The ability of carpets to retain the surface texture imparted during manufacture is related to the compression and crush resistance of the fibers, as well as the density of the pile and the tightness of the yarns. Generally, all fibers have adequate texture retention, with wool rated highest and polypropylene somewhat lower than the other synthetic fibers. Within this range, special fiber types such as heat-set nylon and bicomponent acrylic (mushroom cross section) have improved texture retention .

In areas where the texture has been conspicuously damaged by continuous traffic or heavy loads, the surface can be partially restored by the methods suggested above under "Compression Resistance."

Static Resistance & Cushioning Requirements

9.11.2.4 Static Generation. Static electricity is an annoyance in every carpeted space, but it actually can become harmful in areas housing computers or other electrically sensitive equipment. Static occurs whenever two different materials come into contact with each other. People usually do not become aware of static until it reaches about 3.5 kilovolts (kv). The normal carpet requirements for solely human occupancy require a level of 3 kv or less. Computers require 2 kv or less.

Of the three factors regarding static electricity—static generation, static dissipation (conductivity), and static decay time—only the first is usually limited in the selection of carpets in nonsensitive locations. Static generation in carpet is measured by the American Association of Textile Colorist and Chemists' "Step Method," which simulates conditions of actual use and measures the charge generated by someone walking across the carpet.

Static dissipation may be also limited in spaces that will house computers. It is measured by a method recommended by IBM Corp.

Nylon is inherently high in static buildup. To fight this fact, some nylon carpet manufacturers include carbon-loaded nylon fibers that carry a lifetime antistatic guarantee.

9.11.2.7 Cushioning Requirements All carpet should be installed over cushioning to increase resilience and durability. Some carpets, especially those used in direct glue-down installation, have an integral secondary backing that serves this function. In loomed carpets, cellular (foam or sponge) rubber cushioning usually is bonded directly to the carpet at the mill. For most carpets, however, cushioning is provided in the form of a separate padding. Currently available paddings include felted hair, rubberized fibers, cellular rubber, and urethane foam.

Cushioning should meet or exceed the requirements of the following listed standards:

- Cushioning bonded to a carpet: Federal Specification DDD-C-0085, "Carpets and Rugs, Wool, Nylon, Acrylic, Modacrylic."
- Separate cushioning made of cellular rubber, jute and hair, or hair felt: Federal Specifications ZZ-C-00811b, "Cellular Rubber Carpet and Rug Cushion" and DDD-C-001023, "Carpet and Rug Cushion (Hair Felt and Rubber Coated Jute and Animal Hair or Fiber)."
- Bonded urethane cushion: Federal Specification L-C-001369, "Bonded Urethane Carpet and Rug Cushion."
- Virgin urethane cushion: Federal Specification L-C-001676, "Virgin Urethane Carpet and Rug Cushion."

9.11.2.7 Felted Hair. The most economical traditional type of conventional padding is made of felted animal hair. This padding has a waffle design to provide a skid-proof surface and improve resiliency. It is sometimes reinforced with a jute backing or a burlap center liner.

When reinforced with burlap, the hair is punched through the burlap fabric and compressed to a uniform thickness. Sizing (adhesive) sometimes is used to strengthen the bond between the fibers and the burlap core. Many manufacturers also sterilize and mothproof hair padding.

Felted padding of hair or hair and jute may mat down in time or may develop mildew, especially if the fibers become wet, as during cleaning. However, when properly cleaned, sterilized, and treated, hair padding is suitable for reasonably dry floors at all grade levels and on conventional radiant-heated floors.

9.11.2.7 Rubberized Fibers. Some padding made of jute or hair is coated with rubber on one or both sides to hold the fibers together and provide additional resilience. Sometimes this padding has an animal hair waffle top and a jute back reinforced with a patterned, rubberized application.

9.11.2.7 Sponge Rubber. In addition to cushioning bonded directly to the carpet, foam or sponge rubber is produced in sheet form with waffle, ripple, grid, or V-shaped rib designs. A scrim of burlap fabric usually is bonded to the rubber sheet to facilitate installation of the carpet. When laid with the fabric side up, this permits a taut and even stretch of the carpet.

Rubber padding is more expensive, but it retains its resilience longer than hair padding. It is highly resistant to decay and mildew and is non-allergenic. It can be used at all grade levels, but the denser cushionings are not recommended for radiant-heated floors.

9.11.2.7 Polyurethane Foam. Urethane foam padding is a high-density polymeric foam available in two major types: prime and bonded. Prime urethane foam padding is available as either prime or densified prime. The latter is modified chemically to make it wear better.

Carpet Emissions
Industry Standards
Building Materials Technology, Structural Performance & Environmental Impact
(The McGraw-Hill Companies)

10.10 Carpets. Most carpeting comes with manufacturers' specifications, including flammability and smoke-density ratings by the American Society for Testing and Materials (ASTM).

Wall-to-wall carpeting may cause health problems because of the chemicals used in the fibers, backing, pads, and adhesives. When buying new carpeting, look for the Carpet and Rug Institute indoor air quality label that indicates the product has passed tests for low emission levels of chemical pollutants. The U.S. Consumer Product Safety Commission receives many complaints of health problems after the installation of new carpeting in offices, schools, and homes because of chemicals outgassing from the carpet.

Other options to use include carpets with jute or recycled backing that is tacked down, not glued, and carpeting made from recycled plastic soda bottles.

While installation is going on, and for three days afterward, make sure there is plenty of ventilation. Then, regularly use a vacuum cleaner.

When removing old and installing new carpeting, workers should wear a dust mask and ventilate the area for at least 3 days.

In the home, instead of vacuuming throw rugs, shake them outdoors. Use doormats at entrances to prevent tracking in dirt and contaminants from outdoor soil. Dust mites, those microscopic creatures thriving in wall-to-wall carpeting, can cause allergic reactions. Since vacuuming does not eliminate them, nonslip and easily washed scatter rugs are recommended for sensitive people.

Guidelines for Avoiding Carpet Problems

Comments

Problems with installed carpet usually involve improper fit (carpet has detached or is stretched), failure to provide continuous padding under the entire carpet surface, or visible gaps at seams. None of these conditions is acceptable. Also —

- *The direction (knap) of the carpet should match.*
- *The floor should be prepped, including flash patching to eliminate bumps or depressions.*
- *Humidity and change in temperature can have an effect on materials during installation.*
- *If carpet tacks are used, they should be of correct length and color.*
- *Seams should be avoided in high-traffic areas.*

Wood Floors

Materials Handling
Industry Standards
Construction Principles, Materials, and Methods
(John Wiley & Sons, Inc.)

To maintain proper moisture content, flooring products should not be transported or unloaded in rain, snow, or excessively humid weather. Flooring should not be delivered to a construction site until the building is enclosed, concrete and plaster work has been completed, and all building materials are dry. In winter, an interior temperature of 65° to 70°F should be maintained for at least 5 days before flooring is delivered. Flooring should be stored for several days in the rooms where it will be installed to allow it to become acclimated to local conditions.

387

Ventilation Requirements

In crawl space construction, adequate cross-ventilation should be provided under the floor. The total area of vent openings should equal 1.5 % of the first floor area.

A groundcover of 4- to 6-mil polyethylene film is essential as a moisture retarder. Inadequate moisture control can harm any floor installation by contributing to warping or discoloration of the flooring.

Terminology

9.9.1 Materials. The terms hardwood and softwood, popularly applied to the two major groups of trees cut for lumber, actually have no bearing on the degree of hardness of the wood. In fact, many softwoods are harder than some of the hardwoods. The terms are used primarily to distinguish the botanical characteristics of the trees. Arbitrarily, trees having broad leaves are known as hardwoods, while coniferous trees— those bearing needles and cones—are known as softwoods.

About 12 types of woods are regularly manufactured into flooring. Of these, the hardwoods account for about 80% of wood flooring. The greater popularity of hardwoods can be attributed to their appearance and, in the species used, substantially greater hardness and wear resistance.

Industry Standards

National Wood Flooring Association
(NWFA Internet Web Site: www.woodfloors.org)

Unfinished wood flooring: A product that must be jobsite sanded and finished after installation.

Pre-finished wood flooring: Factory sanded and finished flooring that only needs installation.

Solid wood flooring: Completely lumber, it is available in unfinished and pre-finished. Solid wood flooring is produced in:

- Strip-in thicknesses of 1/2" or 3/4" in widths of 1-1/2", 2", and 2-1/4".
- Plank-in thicknesses of 1/2" or 3/4" and widths of 3" to 8".
- Parquet (geometrical patterns composed of individual wood slats held in place by mechanical fastening or an adhesive).

Solid wood flooring can be used on grade and above grade, but not below grade. Solid wood should be in a moisture controlled environment. Solid wood strip or plank is nail down only and requires a wood subfloor. Solid wood parquet can be glued to a variety of subfloor materials.

Engineered wood flooring: Produced by bonding layers of veneer and lumber with an adhesive. Engineered wood flooring is available in pre-finished and unfinished. These products are more dimensionally stable and are ideal for glue-down installation or float-in installation above grade, on grade or below grade, including basements and humid climates. Engineered wood flooring is produced in:

- Strip — thicknesses of 5/16", 3/8", 1/2" or 5/8" and in widths of 2" and 2-1/4".
- Plank — thicknesses of 5/16", 3/8", 1/2" or 5/8" and in widths of 3" to 8".
- Parquet — one-piece wood tile available in 9" x 9" or 8" x 8" and other patterns.

Acrylic impregnated wood flooring: A pre-finished wood flooring product. Through a high-pressure treatment, acrylic and color are forced into the pores throughout the thickness of the wood. The "finish" is inside the wood, creating a resistance to moisture. These materials appeal most often to commercial customers, but are also used residentially. Acrylic impregnated floors are available in the same styles as laminate floors.

Engineered wood: Can be used on grade, above and below grade. Engineered wood is more dimensionally stable so it can be installed in areas where solid wood is not compatible due to moisture. Engineered strip, plank and parquet are glue down applications over various subfloor materials. Some engineered strip and plank can be nailed down which requires a wood subfloor. Engineered includes floating floors where tongue and grove are glued together, but the floor is not anchored to the subfloor. This is a good choice for going over existing vinyl flooring.

Hardwoods

Industry Standards

Construction Principles, Materials, and Methods
(John Wiley & Sons, Inc.)

9.9.1.1 Of all hardwood flooring produced in a typical year, oak of various commercial species supplies more than 90%, as compared with 6% or so for maple.

The balance consists largely of beech, birch, pecan, and several other hardwoods in limited quantities.

9.9.1.1 Oak. There are about 20 species of oak in the United States that are considered commercially important in lumber production. Of these, about half are classed as red oak and half as white oak. As growing trees, the several species within each group are readily distinguishable, but in lumber form, the differences are fairly inconspicuous. Therefore, precise separation of the various species within each group of oaks is impractical and unnecessary in flooring manufacture.

Oak is lumbered throughout the southern, eastern, and central states, in forests of the Atlantic Plain and the Appalachian Mountains. In these regions, species of oak grow under a wide range of climatic conditions in many different kinds of soil. There is, accordingly, much variation in the color of the wood, especially the heart wood; the sapwood usually shades from white to cream color in all species of oak. In the standard grading rules for oak flooring, color is entirely disregarded except in the amount of light-colored sapwood allowed. Sapwood is limited only in the top grade of flooring, clear grade.

Red oak and white oak are about equal in mechanical properties. Both make a very satisfactory floor of attractive appearance when properly finished. A special feature of white oak is the prominence of large rays that make an interesting flake pattern in quarter-sawn flooring.

Although grading rules do not differentiate between red oak and white oak, practically all manufacturers supply either all red or all white oak flooring except in the lowest grades. Red oak flooring generally is higher in price and more uniform in color than white oak.

9.9.1.1 Maple. Maple flooring is made from sugar maple, logged largely in the Northeast, the Appalachians, and the Great Lakes states (Minnesota, Michigan, and Wisconsin). In the lumber trade, sugar maple is known as hard maple or rock maple. This species is extremely strong, hard, and abrasion resistant, making it particularly suitable for hard-use locations, such as factories and gymnasiums, as well as residences.

The so-called soft maples — silver maple, red maple, and bigleaf maple — are not as hard, heavy, or strong as hard maple and therefore are not used commonly for flooring. The heartwood of both sugar maple and black maple is light reddish-brown, and the sapwood, which in mature trees is several inches thick, is creamy white, slightly tinged with brown. The contrast in color between heartwood and

sapwood in maple is much less pronounced than in oak, and the standard grading rules permit natural color variation in the wood.

9.9.1.1 Beech and Birch. Beech and birch are lumbered in the northeastern part of the country and around the Great Lakes. In comparison with hard maple, beech and birch are used only sparingly in the manufacture of flooring.

Softwoods

9.9.1.2 Softwoods. In a typical year, more than 50% of the softwood flooring produced is southern pine, more than 40% is Douglas fir, and the balance is western hemlock, eastern white pine, ponderosa pine, western larch, eastern hemlock, redwood, spruce, cypress, and the true firs. Western larch is similar to Douglas fir in strength properties and often is sold in mixture with Douglas fir of the northern interior region of the western states. Ponderosa pine, eastern white pine, and redwood are softer than desirable where wear is a prime factor. However, the formidable decay resistance of redwood in the all-heartwood grade has prompted its use for porch and deck flooring.

9.9.1.2 Southern Pine. Southern pine is a commercial name applied to a group of yellow pines that grow principally in the southeastern states. The group includes longleaf, shortleaf, loblolly, slash pines, and several others of minor importance. Except in dimension lumber and structural timbers, no differentiation between the species is made in marketing the products of this group.

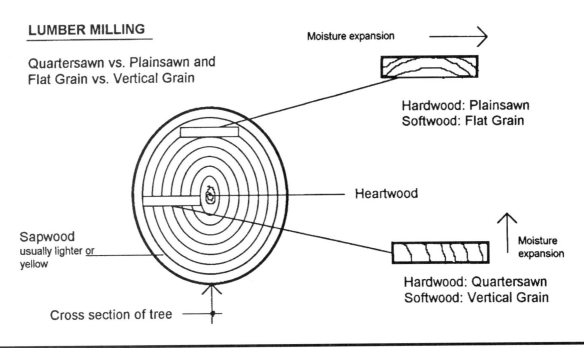

LUMBER MILLING

Quartersawn vs. Plainsawn and
Flat Grain vs. Vertical Grain

Moisture expansion

Hardwood: Plainsawn
Softwood: Flat Grain

Heartwood

Sapwood
usually lighter or
yellow

Moisture
expansion

Hardwood: Quartersawn
Softwood: Vertical Grain

Cross section of tree

Drawing by contributing editors

Figure 11.2

The wood of all southern pines is much alike in appearance. The sapwood and the heartwood often are different in color, the former being yellowish-white and the latter a reddish-brown. However, the contrast in color between sapwood and heartwood in southern pine generally is not conspicuous in a finished floor, and the standard grading rules permit sapwood in all grades of southern pine flooring unless otherwise specified.

When flooring of uniform color is essential, the standard flooring specifications can be amended to require all-sapface stock (for a light color) or all heartface material (for a reddish-brown color). Special selection of stock for color increases the cost somewhat over the established grade.

9.9.1.2 Douglas Fir. Red fir, yellow fir, coast Douglas fir, and Oregon pine are other names by which Douglas fir is known in the western parts of the United States and Canada, where it grows. Douglas fir occupies the same important position in the western and Pacific Coast states as southern pine does in the southeastern states.

The sapwood of Douglas fir is creamy white. The heartwood is reddish-brown, and, as in southern pine, the contrast in color between the two is not so pronounced as to be objectionable in a finished floor. Pieces containing both heartwood and sapwood are permitted in all grades.

9.9.1.2 West Coast Hemlock. Western hemlock grows along the Pacific coast from northern California to Alaska and as far inland as northern Idaho and northwestern Montana. The bulk of hemlock lumber being produced comes from Oregon, Washington, and California and is referred to commercially as West Coast hemlock.

Both the heartwood and the sapwood of western hemlock are almost white with a pinkish tinge and with very little contrast, although the sapwood may sometimes be lighter in color.

Western hemlock has light, clear color and good finishing qualities, which account for its use in moderate-wear areas, such as bedrooms, where good appearance is the principal requirement. Western hemlock flooring is relatively free from warping and is easy to cut and nail, but it is not as hard and wear-resistant as Douglas fir or larch.

Flooring Grading Rules

Industry Standards

National Oak Flooring Manufacturers Association
(NOFMA Internet Web Site: www.nofma.org)

Ed. Note: The principal function of the National Oak Flooring Manufacturers Association (NOFMA) is to formulate and administer industry standards on hardwood flooring. Establishing grading rules for flooring is a major part of these standards. The following official flooring rules were published in November 1997. NOFMA updates these standards regularly and posts information on its Web site (www.nofma.org).

Oak Flooring Grading Rules
(Note: Characteristics included in a higher grade are automatically accepted in lower grades.)

Clear Oak: A flooring product of mostly heartwood with a minimum number of character marks and discoloration, providing a uniform appearance while allowing for all heartwood natural color variations.

Will admit the following:

- 3/8" bright sapwood entire length of strip or equivalent if not extending further than 1" for 1/3 length of piece.
- Small burls and fine pinworm holes.
- Equivalent characters such as small tight checks.
- In the absence of these, one thin brown streak 3" long to be allowed every 6'.

Select Oak: A flooring product with coloration variations produced by differences of natural heartwood and sapwood, along with characters described.

The face may contain:

- Unlimited sound sapwood.
- Slight imperfections in milling; a small tight knot every 3'.
- Pinworm holes.
- Burls and a reasonable amount of slightly open checks.

Brown streaks should be extended the entire length of a piece. Two flay worm holes to every 8' are permitted. Slight imperfections in face work (torn grain) admitted. An intermittent, brown burn across the face not exceeding 1/4" width admitted. Also, a slight quantity of bark on the back or sides admitted. Will admit pieces with 1/2 tongue. Spot filling is generally required for open characters.

No. 1 Common Oak: A flooring product which contains prominent variations in coloration and varying characters.

The following are not admitted:

- Broken knots over 1/2" in diameter.
- Large grub worm holes.
- Splits extending through the piece.

Open characters such as checks and knot holes are admitted, but must be sound and readily filled. Not more than 20" scant stock in thickness allowed to every 5'. Minor imperfections in machining permitted. Shall admit sticker stain; varying wood characteristics, such as flag worm holes, heavy streaks, checks, and worm holes; and an occasional dark machine burn across the face not exceeding 1/2" wide, 1/64" deep and not more than two each 3'. One-quarter tongue allowed. Extremely dark pieces are not to be included.

No. 2 Common Oak: May contain sound natural variations of the forest product and manufacturing imperfections. The purpose of this grade is to furnish a floor suitable for homes, general utility use, or where character marks and contrasting appearance is desired.

The following are not admitted:

- Shattered or rotten ends.
- Large broken knots.
- Excessive bad millwork.
- Shake.
- Advanced rot.
- Similar unsound defects.

Dark machine burns exceeding 3/64" deep not admitted. Knot holes and open characters which will readily fill are admitted. A limited number of pieces with no tongue which may be face nailed are admitted.

Prefinished Oak Grading Rules

White Oak and Red Oak in *Standard & Better* Grades with a natural coloration, to be separated. All other colors and grades may be mixed Red Oak and White Oak. Grades are established after the flooring has been sanded and finished.

Prime Prefinished Oak: This is the top grade and the overall appearance shall be good. The face of strips shall be selected for appearance after finishing. This grade includes characteristics found in the unfinished grades of *Clear* and *Select* grade.

The following characters are admitted:

- Unlimited Sapwood and the natural variations of color.
- Occasional small Burls.
- Light brown streaks not more than 1/8" in width and 6" in length or the equivalent.
- An occasional very small, tight 1/8" Knot.
- Limited 1/32" fine Pinworm Holes, may be included in any one piece when properly filled.
- Will not admit pieces with less than 3/4 full tongue.

Standard Prefinished Oak: The face of strips may contain sound wood characteristics which are even and smooth after filling and finishing. This grade includes some characteristics found in the unfinished grades *Select*, *No. 1 Common*, and *No. 2 Common*.

The following characters are admitted:

- Worm holes.
- Season and Kiln Checks.
- Broken Knots up to 3/8" in diameter, minor imperfections in machining.
- Torn Grains.
- Burns.

Other characters will be admitted if they do not impair the soundness of the floor. All larger admitted open characters are to be properly filled and finished. Limited unfinished/unfilled small open grade characters permitted.

Large Grub Worm Holes, Splits extending through the piece, Shake and similar unsound defects not admitted.

For naturally finished coloration: All the varying color characteristics of the wood admitted to include Sticker Stain, and Dark Streaks up to 3/8" in width not to exceed 1" in length for each lineal foot.

For stained finishes: All varying colorations and streaks permitted, predominantly dark boards not permitted.

Tavern Prefinished Oak: Should lay a serviceable floor.

A limited amount of unfilled/unfinished open characters admitted. A limited amount of pieces with finish irregularities such as bubbles, small skips, lines, stain/color variation, surface handling scratches, minor trash, and the like are allowed.

The following characters are *not* admitted:

- Mismanufactured boards.
- Shattered or rotten ends.
- Large open knots and other unsound defects of a similar nature.
- Pieces with less than 1/4 full tongue.

Beech, Birch & Hard Maple Grading Rules

First Grade — Beech, Birch & Hard Maple: Shall have the face practically free of all defects, but the natural color of the wood shall not be considered a defect. The highest standard grade, combines appearance and durability.

Will admit the following:

- Variations in the Natural Color of the wood (with use of some finishes, slight shadows and color variation may appear).
- An occasional small, firm Pin Knot, not over 1/8" in diameter, provided it does not occur on edges or ends of strips.
- Occasional dark Green or Black Spots or Streaks not over 1/4" wide and 3" long (or its equivalent) which may contain a tight check not over 1/2" long, provided it is boxed within the piece.
- Birds' Eyes and small Burls.
- Slightly Torn Grain.
- Similar defect, which can be readily removed by the ordinary method of sanding the floor after it is laid.
- A slightly Shallow Place not over 12" long on underside of the flooring if it does not extend to either end of the piece.

Pieces with 1/2 Tongue for no more than 25% of the length are allowed. The wood must be sound and free of Shake. Bark Streaks shall not be permitted.

Second Grade — Beech, Birch & Hard Maple: A floor with varying wood characteristics and colors to include distinct color variations, numerous Streaks, stained Sapwood, sound Knots, and Checks. All defects must readily fill.

Will admit the following:

- Sound, tight Knots, provided they do not occur on edges or ends of strips.
- Slight Imperfections in machining.
- Distinct Color Variations.
- Sticker Stain/Shadow.
- Numerous dark Green or Black Spots or Streaks, provided they do not occur in combination with predominantly dark heartwood.
- Slight Checks not exceeding 3" in length (may be slightly open) and running parallel with and well inside the edges and ends of the strips.
- Dark Spots and Streaks with slight Checks in center.
- Small Rough Spots (Torn Grain) which cannot be wholly removed by ordinary method of sanding the floor after it is laid.
- Slightly Torn Edges.
- Short Tongue if sufficient to hold properly in the floor.
- Shallow or Waney Back, if piece has sufficient bearing of full thickness to support it in the floor.
- Small bark Streaks where bark is as sound as surrounding wood.
- Slight variation in Angle of End Matching.
- The face shall be free of Shake and wood must be sound.

Third Grade — Beech, Birch & Hard Maple: Must be of such character as will lay and give a good serviceable floor. The wood must be firm, serviceable, and may contain all defects common to Maple. Pieces with 1/4 full Tongue admitted.

Third Grade will not admit:

- Knot Holes over 3/8" in diameter or unsound Knots where the unsound portion is over 1" in diameter.
- Voids on Ends or Edges.
- Shake.
- Heart Checks.
- Badly Split Ends and Imperfections in Manufacture which would materially impair the serviceability of the floor.

Special Grades for Beech, Birch & Hard Maple

First Grade White — Hard Maple: Special stock, selected for uniformity of color. It is almost ivory white and is the finest grade of Hard Maple flooring that can be produced. Sapwood/Heartwood pieces must have 95% Sapwood on the face. Strips must be free from stain and Heartwood portion must be nearly white. All *First Grade* rules apply.

Exceptions:

1. Streaks — should be light brown or light green, not over 1/4" wide and 3" long (or equivalent), one per 3'.
2. Black Spots, Sticker Stain/Shadow — not admitted.

First Grade Red — Beech & Birch: Special grades produced from all red faced stock, and are specially selected for color. The color is rich, being a soft tint which lends these two woods an individuality found in no other species. Strips must have 95% red faced characteristics. All *First Grade* rules apply.

Exceptions:

1. Streaks — Should be light brown.
2. Black Spots, Sticker Stain/Shadow — not admitted.
3. Hickory/Pecan Grading Rules.

First Grade — Hickory/Pecan: Shall have the face practically free of all defects, but the natural color of the wood shall not be considered a defect. The highest standard grade, combines a nearly uniform appearance with exceptional durability.

The following characters are admitted:

- Variations in the Natural Color of the wood, Heartwood and Sapwood.
- An occasional small, firm Pin Knot or Bird Peck, not over 1/8" diameter, provided it does not occur on edges or ends of strips.
- Dark Streaks not over 1/4" wide and 3" long (or its equivalent), one for every 3' in length.
- Slight Checks not over 1/2" long, provided Check is boxed within the piece.
- Small Burls.
- Slight Torn Grain or slight intermittent Machine Burn.
- Similar defect which can be readily removed by the ordinary method of sanding the floor after it is laid.
- A slightly Shallow Place not over 12" long on underside of the flooring if it does not extend to either end of the piece.

Pieces with 1/2 tongue for no more than 25% of the length are allowed. The wood must be free of Shake. Bark Streaks shall not be permitted.

Second Grade — Hickory/Pecan: A floor with varying wood characteristics and colors to include heavy Streaks, stained Sapwood, sound Knots, Checks and Small Splits. All defects must readily fill and be sound.

The following characteristics are admitted:

- Broken Knots up to 1/2" in diameter.
- Distinct Color Variations (predominantly dark, discolored pieces not allowed).
- Sticker Stain/Shadow.
- Numerous dark Streaks or black spots.
- Checks to 1/16" not exceeding 3" in length, and running parallel and well inside the strip edges.
- Small End Split 1/16" x 1/2" showing no movement.
- Bird Pecks to 1/2" where bark is sound and as hard as surrounding wood.

Minor imperfections in machining permitted:

- Torn Grain (less than 1/16" deep and 3" long for full width).
- Slightly Torn Edges.
- An occasional dark Machine Burn 1/2" in width (1 per 3).

Will admit pieces with 1/2 full Tongue entire length of piece.

Third Grade — Hickory/Pecan: Must be of such character as will lay and give a good serviceable floor. The wood must be firm, and may contain defects of every character. This grade is intended to give a "rustic" appearance.

The following defects are ***not*** allowed:

- Knot Holes over 3/8" in diameter or unsound Knots, where the unsound portion is over 1" in diameter (the unsound portion cannot extend through piece).
- Shake.
- Soft Rot.
- Splits and open defects which extend through piece or show movement.
- Torn Grain more than 1/4" deep.
- Edge Splinters.
- Imperfections in Manufacture which would materially impair the serviceability of the floor.

Knot Holes, Bird Pecks, Worm Holes, and the like which will readily fill are admitted. Pieces with 1/4 full tongue admitted.

Special Grades — Hickory/Pecan

First Grade Red — Hickory/Pecan: A special stock selected for its deep red/brown color with the minimal contrast of the lighter Sapwood.

Face of pieces shall be Heartwood (95%). All First Grade rules apply.

First Grade White — Hickory/Pecan: Special stock selected for its creamy color with the minimal contrast of the darker Heartwood. The face of pieces shall be bright Sapwood (95%). All First Grade rules apply.

Exceptions:

1. Streaks should be light brown, not over 1/4" wide and 3" long (or equivalent), one per 3'.
2. Black Spots not allowed.
3. Sticker Stain/Shadow not allowed.

Second Grade Red — Hickory/Pecan: Special stock selected for minimal contrasting lighter Sapwood. The face of pieces shall be Heartwood (85%). All Second Grade rules apply.

Ash Grading Rules

Clear Ash: The face shall be practically free of defects.

The following characters are admitted:

- Small burls (less than 1/8" in diameter).
- Fine pinworm holes with no discoloration (1 for every 3' in length).

In the absence of these, one (1) thin light brown streak (3" long to be allowed for every 6' of length or equivalent).

Brown Heartwood is allowed as follows: 3/8" entire length or 1" for one-third the length of the strip.

Select Ash: The face shall contain mostly Sapwood, unstained.

The following characters are admitted:

- Narrow streaks not running entire length of the strip
- Pin worm holes (up to 3 every 3' in length)
- Imperfection in milling (Torn Grain) which will sand out
- One (1) small tight knot (1/4" in diameter) to every 3' in length
- Small pith fleck (less than 1/4" diameter)
- An intermittent brown machine burn across the face not exceeding 1/4" in width
- Unlimited cambium miners

Brown Heartwood is allowed as follows: 3/8" entire length or 1" for one-third the length of the strip.

Will admit pieces with 1/2 tongue. Most defects are lost sight of after the floor is laid and finished, giving a good appearance.

No. 1 Common Ash: A floor with varying wood characteristics such as Heavy streaks, Stained sapwood, and Sound knots typical of this grade. All defects must readily fill and be sound.

Partial Nail Schedule		Type of Flooring	Fasteners	Spacing
Strip T & G	3/8 x 1 1/2 3/8 x 2		1 1/4-in. machine driven fasteners, or 4d or 5d bright casing nails or finish nails	8 in O.C. or closer
	1/2 x 1 1/2 1/2 x 2		1 1/2-in. to 1 3/4-in. machine driven fasteners or 5d or 6d cut-steel or finish nails	8 in. to 10 in.O.C. or closer
	3/4 up to 3 1/4 strip		2-in. machine driven fasteners or cut nails or 7d or 8d flooring nails.	8 in. to 10 in.O.C. or closer
Plank T&G	3/4 up to 4		2-in. machine driven fasteners or cut nails or 7d or 8d flooring nails.	8 in. O.C. into & between joists

Courtesy of The Taunton Press, *Hardwood Floors: Laying, Sanding, and Finishing*

Figure 11.3

The following characters are admitted:

- Broken knots up to 1/2" in diameter.
- Pith flecks less than 3/16" in diameter.
- Worm holes up to 3/16".
- Checks and End splits less than 1/16" wide and not extending through the piece.
- Sticker stain.

Minor imperfections in machining permitted; Torn grain (not over one-fourth [1/4] of the surface, less than 1/26" in depth); One (1) dark machine burn across the face for every 3' of length, not exceeding 1/2" in width, 1/64" in depth.

Will admit pieces with 1/4 tongue.

No. 2 Common Ash: Defects of every character admitted, but should lay a serviceable floor.

The following defects are *not* allowed:

- Soft rot.
- Broken knots where the unsound portion extends through piece.
- Torn grain over 3/16" in depth.
- Splits and Open defects extending through the piece.
- Shake and Pith flecks that are soft if over 1/4" in diameter.

Knot holes and defects which will readily fill are admitted.

A limited number of pieces with no tongue and limited number of pieces that are thin (scant) in thickness but will End Match admitted.

Wood Floor Installation
Industry Standards
Hardwood Floors: Laying, Sanding, and Finishing
(The Taunton Press)
Plywood-on-Slab and Screed Systems

As explained earlier, parquet, laminated strip and plank, and floating plank systems are the only kinds of flooring that should be applied directly to concrete slabs. Conventional strip and plank over concrete will have to be fastened to plywood underlayment or solid-wood screeds. The plywood-on-slab method is basically just another form of underlayment.

To create a vapor barrier that will protect both the underlayment and finish flooring from moisture, cover the slab with 4-mil to 6-mil polyethylene. First, lay a bed of adhesive on the slab. Then roll the poly into it. The plastic should be large enough to overlap the baseboards. The excess can be trimmed later. Next, install underlayment as described above. Regular masonry nails or concrete fasteners will do, but powder-actuated fasteners are easier and faster, even if you have to rent the tool. In any case, be certain the plastic is sealed at the seams (a 6-in. overlap should be sufficient) and that the plywood is flat.

Fasten the sheets in the center first, then work toward the edges of each sheet. If you use lead or sleeve-type concrete anchors, I suggest pouring a small amount of asphalt mastic or construction adhesive into each hole to prevent water seepage. Another vapor-barrier method (or when working over lightweight concrete) is to score the back of the underlayment with a 12-in. grid ⅛ in. deep, then bed the sheets in a coat of cut-back asphalt mastic troweled onto the slab. Use an adhesive that will remain fairly elastic over time, such as a "cold-tar" mastic. By "cut back," I mean an asphalt adhesive that has been thinned somewhat with the appropriate solvent, generally paint thinner. Trowel the mastic evenly over the entire slab, then allow it to set for 12 hours or longer before laying the underlayment.

Screeds are another common way of setting a wooden floor over a slab. Screeds are basically treated 1x3s or 1x4s over which strip or plank flooring is laid. They provide a nailing surface and keep the flooring from direct contact with the slab, thereby reducing moisture exchange.

Screeds are set in a mastic bed between two layers of polyethylene vapor barrier. Fastening the screeds to the slab is optional. It's acceptable just to bed them in mastic on top of the lower vapor barrier.

If you do decide to fasten the screeds to the slab, use powder-actuated fasteners or concrete anchors. I use pressure-treated 1x3s or 1x4s for the screeds. Lay the first layer of plastic, spread the mastic and place the screeds on 9-in. centers for strip and plank flooring up to 4 in. wide. In order to have adequate nailing surface, flooring wider than 4 in. will require a subfloor over the screeds or plywood-on-slab underlayment.

Now and then, I encounter a slab with an embedded radiant-heat system, in which case I trowel mortar, Gypcrete or plasticized cement between the screeds, flush with their tops. Once set, the mortar can be sanded flush to the screeds. Besides providing additional support for the flooring, the mortar adds thermal mass for the heating system.

Another version of the screed and radiant heat system that's a popular retrofit method consists of 2x4s installed on 9-in. to 12-in. centers on top of the slab. The radiant coils are intertwined between and around these, then covered with another layer of concrete, Gypcrete or other heavy-mass substance. The flooring is then nailed to the screeds or to 3/4-in. plywood underlayment installed over the screeds.

Adhesives

The most common wood-flooring adhesives in use today can be grouped into one of three categories: cold-tar mastics or "cutback," water-based mastics, latex or emulsions, and chlorinated solvent mastics. Each of these has advantages and disadvantages, but as far as working qualities go, you're looking for an adhesive to "flash" quickly, which means that it initially cures enough to become tacky. An adhesive's open working time — specified in minutes or hours — is a measure of how long the exposed surface will remain tacky enough to work with.

Cold-tar mastic or "cutback" is the traditional adhesive for parquet and other floors and is still widely used today, especially for 3/4-in. parquet. It's inexpensive and is a good choice where a polyethylene film is required as a vapor barrier. It's also flammable, smelly and messy to use and clean up, and has a tendency to bleed up between pieces or through porous wood fibers. There's also some concern over the toxicity of the solvents used to thin the mastic, so be sure to wear a respirator and gloves. Let it flash off at least four to six hours before installing over it.

I like the chlorinated solvent mastics best because they offer the most favorable combination of flash time, open working time, elasticity and longevity, even when exposed to excess moisture. They do require good ventilation and cleanup with a compatible solvent, usually paint thinner. If you happen to be using a chlorinated solvent over vinyl flooring, be sure you use a plasticizer-blocking sealer first, or the bond may be substantially weakened.

Water-based adhesives are by far the safest. They're nearly odorless, non-flammable and flash almost instantly. But, in my opinion, water-based adhesives aren't as durable as solvent-based adhesives, especially in moist conditions, such as you'd encounter over a concrete slab. One other type of adhesive, epoxy, is also occasionally used for flooring. Although it's moisture resistant, it's also messy and sets up too quickly into a brittle bond. This can cause a loose or noisy floor later on.

Whichever adhesive you pick, be sure to use the required protective equipment, especially an organic-vapor respirator with solvent and epoxy adhesives. Epoxy is a skin irritant for many people, so use thin plastic or rubber gloves when handling it. Always extinguish gas-range and water-heater pilot lights before spreading flammable adhesives or chlorinated solvent adhesives. Arrange the ventilation so that air near the floor, where vapors tend to settle, will be kept constantly moving.

The label on the adhesive can should give specifics on how to apply the material. It should also tell what size and type of trowel to use. I spread the solvent-based adhesives with a 5/32-in. V-notch trowel. A notched trowel is more effective than a flat one because the notches automatically meter the amount of adhesive being applied and the proper ridge depth. If you spread too much, the tiles won't seat flat and the excess adhesive will ooze up between the joints, a real mess that will take forever to dry. Too little adhesive creates an inferior bond, resulting in loose tiles, another real mess since it's not easy to reset a tile later.

Wood Floor Finishes
Industry Standards
National Wood Flooring Association
(NWFA Internet Web Site: www.woodfloors.org)

The specific needs of the project may dictate the best finish. Following are some general comparisons.

Water Base Urethane	Swedish Finish (acid curing)
Durability Very Good	Durability Excellent
Mild Odor	Strong Odor
Clear in Color	Clear in Color
Easy to Recoat	Recoatable
Fast Drying	Fast Drying
Not Flammable	Combustible
Environmentally Safe	

Oil Modified Urethanes (solvent evaporates to cure)

Durability Very Good
Moderate Odor
Amber in Color
Easy to Recoat
Slow Drying
Combustible
Commonly Available

Moisture-Cured Urethane (absorbs moisture to cure)

Durability Excellent
Strong Odor
Clear to Dark Amber Color
Recoatable
Dries Quickly with High Humidity
Flammable

Seal and Wax or Oil Finish

Durability Good
Mild Odor
Amber in Color
Renewable by Consumer
Dry Time Varies with Product
Combustible
Low Luster
Water Spots

Consult your wood flooring professional for recoats. Use finish products designed for hardwood floors. Use manufacturer's recommendation for proper amount of coats. Use respirator as required by manufacturers.

Wood Flooring: Moisture Effects

Comments

All wood flooring installations and/or installation failure analysis must include the proper method of testing for moisture and water migration. Most hardwood failures are the result of water intrusion above the membrane.

Industry Standards

Hardwood Floors: Laying, Sanding, and Finishing
(The Taunton Press)

Water & Wood: A Troublesome Pair

It's amusing to read the advertising hype for furniture polishes. Some insist that wood is a "living" material that needs to "breathe" or be "nourished" by whatever concoction the ad happens to be pushing. The fact is, once it's felled and sawn, a tree and the wood in it are forever dead. That's not to say wood is static: it's just no longer alive.

Much as the human body has veins and arteries to deliver nutrients to its cells, so too does the living tree have a cell structure through which nutrients flow to its various parts. In the living tree, these cells are saturated with sap, which is mostly water with some dissolved minerals from the soil. After the wood is sawn and air or kiln dried, the sap evaporates, leaving the cells and their walls slightly shrunken but dry and porous. Because the cell walls will reabsorb water and expand in moist conditions, wood is said to be hygroscopic— it responds to changes in atmospheric moisture.

If not accounted for, wood's hygroscopic nature may cause a lot of grief, particularly if dry wood is exposed to liquid water. As wood cells absorb and lose moisture, a board swells and shrinks more across the grain than it does parallel to the grain. This means that with seasonal variations in moisture, a plainsawn board will change far more in width than it will in length or thickness. In contrast, a quartersawn board swells and shrinks more in thickness than in width. Therefore quartersawn stock is considered more moisture stable.

The width of a piece of 2-1/4-in. oak flooring is affected by changes in its moisture content. Here, I should explain what's meant by moisture content in wood. As I explained earlier, wood constantly absorbs and desorbs moisture from the air. However, when a dried board is not giving off or absorbing moisture from the air, it's said to be at equilibrium moisture content (EMC). EMC is expressed as a percentage of the wood's dry weight, so an EMC of 5% really means that 5% of the board's weight is water.

EMC is related to relative humidity (RH). Wood technologists have graphs that precisely tie the two together, but as a rule of thumb, a relative humidity of 25% gives an EMC of 5%, and a relative humidity of 75% gives on EMC of 14%. A 50% swing in relative humidity produces an EMC gradient of 10%. This, in turn, translates to a width variation of 1/16-in. Not much in a single board but in a floor, all of the boards expand and contract, pushing against each other. Over the width of a 10-ft. wide floor, that amounts to more then 3 in. of total expansion or contraction.

In most houses, at least ones that are heated in the winter and cooled in the summer, the relative-humidity swing will be less than 50%. You will have to allow for expansion and contraction, but most of the time no moisture-related damage will occur. When it does, the results can be spectacular. Flooding caused by broken pipes or seepage through wells is the worst. I've seen swollen floors buckle like hot pavement. In extreme cases, the swelling will actually push the walls out. The opposite extreme is wood heat, which is so dry that it tends to shrink the flooring, opening up cracks.

There are several ways to avoid moisture damage. First, buy dry flooring. Purchase a moisture meter or borrow one from your supplier (most have them) and make sure your flooring is between 6% and 9% moisture content. A $100 moisture meter is cheap insurance against the potential disaster of not recognizing and correcting moisture problems. Don't allow flooring to get rained on. You'd be surprised what even a light rain will do to flooring.

Test the moisture content of the subfloor, too, including concrete floors. The difference between subfloor and flooring shouldn't be greater than 4%. Don't bring flooring into the house until the drywall is well cured. Allow your material to acclimate uncovered in the house for three to six weeks. This should give it plenty of time to reach EMC. Finally, leave an expansion gap between the flooring and the wall, 1/16-in. of expansion gap for every cross-grain running foot of flooring. The gap will be hidden by the baseboard. Very wide floors will need more of a gap than the baseboard can cover. In this case, undercut the baseboard and/or add a wider shoe molding.

Wood Floor Maintenance

Comments

Proper maintenance is required to keep wood floors looking their best over time. The following are some basic guidelines from the National Wood Flooring Association.

Industry Standards
National Wood Flooring Association
(NWFA Internet Web Site: www.woodfloors.org)

For Waxed Floors
Keep grit off the floor, dust mop or vacuum regularly and keep doormats clean. Wipe up spills promptly with a dry cloth or dry paper towel, use a slightly dampened cloth for sticky spills and buff with a dry cloth to restore luster. When the floor looks dull, buff first to see if luster will be restored before waxing. When areas of heavy use no longer respond to buffing, wax only those areas and buff all the floor to an even luster. When the whole floor needs attention, clean the floor with a solvent based wood floor cleaner and then wax. Your floor should only need to be completely rewaxed once or twice a year depending on traffic.

For Surface Finishes (Including Urethanes)
Keep grit off the floor, dust mop or vacuum regularly and keep doormats clean. Wipe up spills promptly with a dry cloth. Use a slightly dampened cloth for sticky spills.

For general cleaning, there are good generic wood floor cleaners or use a mild solution of white vinegar and warm water (1/4 cup of vinegar to 1 quart of warm water), and with a spray bottle, spritz a small amount on a mop or cloth and go over a small area with the mop or cloth. Buff dry. When luster does not return to traffic areas, the floor may require recoating. Consult your wood floor professional.

Do not wax a surface finish. Wax will, in most cases, be slippery. If you wax a surface finish, the floor will not be merely recoated to rejuvenate it, it will have to continue to be waxed as a maintenance procedure.

Acrylic impregnated floors require a spray and buff system as recommended by the manufacturer.

Allowable Tolerances in Wood Flooring

Industry Standards
Handbook of Construction Tolerances
(The McGraw-Hill Companies)

Wood Flooring
For strip flooring and parquet flooring, the subfloor should be level to within 1/4 in. in 10 ft. with no abrupt projections or depressions.

Wood Floor Framing and Subflooring
In general, a level tolerance of ±1/4 in. in 10 ft. for new construction is a reasonable expectation and is less than the maximum allowable deflection (L/240 for dead and live load) stated by the *Uniform Building Code*.

Ed. Note: See Residential Construction Performance Guidelines, *published by the National Association of Home Builders (Telephone: 800-368-5242), for more information on strip oak flooring tolerances.*

Comments

This discussion on tolerances by various sources reflects the best information on this subject relating to new construction and remodeling.

Disasters result in a broader tolerance. Building officials will generally loosen the minimums for occupancy, as they did after the Northridge Earthquake. During that disaster, slab floors settled as much as 10" at one corner of a building, and the "mudjacking" contractors contracted to bring the floor to "Liveable Straight Line Level," which is 1" in 20'.

Mudjacking *is the process of pumping a relatively stiff concrete mixture at the end of a metal pipe driven into the loose soil according to a predetermined grid (usually 6' on center each way in the horizontal plane and 2' on center in the vertical dimension), effectively compacting and raising the soil.*

Pressure grouting *is a similar process that uses a wet slurry-type mixture to fill cracks and voids in fractured soil or under slab voids.*

Common Problems in Wood Floors

Industry Standards

National Wood Flooring Association
(NWFA Internet Web Site: www.woodfloors.org)

Because wood is a natural product it will react to changes in its environment. Normal cracks are not uncommon if there are separations between individual flooring pieces and are uniform and general throughout the floor.

The most common causes of separations are Mother Nature and dryness. The loss of moisture results in the most frequent reason for shrinkage of individual pieces and cracks. Most cracks are seasonal — they appear in dry months, or the cold season when heating is required, and close during humid periods. This type of separation and close is considered normal. In solid 2-1/4" wide strip oak floors, dry time cracks may be the width of a dime's thickness (1/32"). Wider boards will have wider cracks and the reverse is true.

The cure is to minimize changes by adding moisture to the air space during dry periods. A constant Relative Humidity (RH) of 50% works in concert with the manufacture of wood floors to provide stability in the floor. You must live with normal cracks or add humidity — it's your choice.

Parquet and Block Flooring

Comments

As with other types of tile flooring, it is important to plan the layout carefully, squaring off the room and establishing a center line. Follow the manufacturer's instructions and details, such as the correct size of notched trowel, and the proper solvent to use for cleaning any adhesive that seeps between the tile joints.

Industry Standards

Construction Principles, Materials, and Methods
(John Wiley & Sons, Inc.)

9.9.5 Parquet Flooring

Parquet (pattern) floors consist of individual strips of wood (single slats) or larger units (blocks) installed to form a decorative geometric pattern. Blocks may be made of laminating several hardwood veneers or by gluing a number of solid hardwood pieces into a unit to facilitate installation. Unlike strip-and-plank flooring, parquet flooring usually is installed with mastic.

Oak is by far the most predominant species used in all types of pattern flooring. Other species, such as maple, walnut, cherry,

and East Indian teak, also are available. Sometimes a mixture of hardwoods, such as hickory, ash, elm, pecan, sycamore, beech, and hackberry, are used at random in a single block.

9.9.5.1 Block Flooring

Block flooring is manufactured in several basic types. In unit block (also known as solid unit block), short lengths of strip flooring are joined together edgewise to form square units. In laminated (plywood) block, three or more plies of veneer are bonded with adhesive to obtain the desired thickness. Slat block (sometimes called mosaic parquet hardwood slat) flooring utilizes narrow slats or "fingers" of wood preassembled into larger units to facilitate installation.

Most unit-block and laminated-block flooring is tongued on two adjoining or opposing edges and grooved on the other two to ensure alignment between adjoining blocks. Some manufacturers produce square-edged blocks, while others include grooves on all four block edges and furnish splines for insertion between adjoining blocks. Both types are designed to be installed with mastic over a wood subfloor or concrete slab. Prefinished blocks usually have eased or beveled edges.

Unit blocks typically consist of several 3/4-in. T&G strips, all laid parallel or alternating in each quarter of the block checkerboard fashion. Consequently, typical block sizes are multiples of the strip width used.

9.9.5.1 Laminated Block

Laminated block is made typically 15/32 in. thick, in 9-in. squares, but other sizes, such as 8-in. and 8-1/2-in., also are available from some manufacturers. Appearance grades are Prime and Standard.

Because of its cross-laminated construction in three to five plies, shrinking and swelling of individual blocks are minimized. This type of wood flooring has good dimensional stability and often is recommended for damp locations, such as slabs on grade.

Adhesives used in the manufacture of laminated block flooring should be able to resist the temperature and humidity variations to which the flooring may be subjected. Melamine-urea resin adhesive gives good results at moderate cost and represents the typical adhesive type used for most laminated block flooring.

Highly water-resistant adhesives such as phenols, resorcinols, and melamines may also be used if the application warrants it; however, the use of these glues adds to the cost of the product. Adhesives that create high-strength dry bonds but that are adversely affected by moisture are not recommended for the manufacture of laminated-block flooring.

9.9.5.1 Slat Block

Appearance grades are based on grading rules developed by the American National Standards Institute and the American Parquet Association, ANSI/APA 1-1984, "Mosaic-Parquet Hardwood Slat Flooring," which also checks compliance with the rules through periodic inspections of member plants. These products are suitable for installation in mastic over concrete surfaces, both above and on grade. The basic components of these products are solid, 5/16 in. thick, generally square edged slats of hardwood, 3/4 in. to 1-1/4 in. wide and 4 to 7 in. long, assembled into basic squares. These in turn are factory assembled checkerboard fashion, with the grain in each adjoining square reversed, into larger flooring blocks up to 30 in. long and wide.

Several types of slat block flooring are produced. Some are assembled into panels held together with a face paper; these generally are 9-1/2-, 18-, or 19-in. squares and are marketed unfinished. Others are made up of single basic 6-in. T&G squares, which are held together by mechanical attachments and are generally factory finished. Still others are assembled into panels held together with a backing material such as a textile webbing, asphalt saturated felt, or another type of felt or non-woven interfacing. These products generally are 9-1/2, 11, or 12 in. square; they may be square edged or grooved and splined and be either unfinished or prefinished.

Floating Laminate Floors

Comments

High-pressure melamine flooring has become popular recently for its wearability, wide range of wood grain patterns and colors, low maintenance and relatively easy installation. It comes in planks, each of which has a laminate surface, bonded to a wood-based core. A "balancing layer" is bonded to the back of the plank to provide stability. Manufacturers of this type of flooring indicate that floating laminate floors can be suitable for light commercial, as well as residential applications.

Installation

The major manufacturers of systems such as Pergo, Armstrong, and Wilsonart provide how-to books and telephone advice, and some rent tools to use for the installation. Distributors also offer guidance on their Web sites.

Floating floors can be installed over concrete or existing vinyl flooring. The floor is not anchored to the subfloor. A special underlayment (provided by the manufacturer) is placed (over polyethene film in the case of concrete). The planks are laid in rows, with spacers inserted between the flooring and all of the walls. The manufacturer's block is used to push the planks together. They are glued, row by row, in the grooves only and not along the starting wall. Small traces of excess glue that

have not been wiped away during the installation can be removed later by damp mopping or with a small amount of acetone on a cloth.

Floating floor systems can include wallbases to match or contrast with the floor, quarter round trim, end and T-moulding, stairnose and reducer strips. Special underlayment foam is available that can even out minor surface irregularities in the subfloor, while providing sound and heat insulation. Sound reduction and comfort can also be enhanced using special underlayment boards designed by the manufacturer for this purpose.

Acoustical Ceilings: Characteristics & Use

Comments

Acoustical ceilings are often used in office and commercial space to reduce unwanted noise while providing the desired aesthetic appearance. This type of ceiling is also frequently used in residential finished basements. Use of acoustical ceilings allows access to wiring, piping and ductwork, and makes it easier to reconfigure space in the future.

One of the biggest challenges with acoustic tile installations is coordinating all of the other trades, such as HVAC and electrical, that will be installing related items.

Acoustical ceilings can act as a support element for these items:

- *fire sprinklers (supported on grid or by independent means)*
- *light fixtures (recessed lights within the framework or independently; check your local electrical code)*
- *speakers (supported on the grid system or independently)*
- *signs (supported on the grid or independently)*

Signs, light fixtures, and speakers can all be relocated with relative ease in the event of future reconfiguration of the space.

Selecting Ceiling Tiles

The type of ceiling tile that is installed is usually predetermined by the architect, designer or owner. Many types of ceiling tiles are manufactured, some with stringent design specifications. The room or building use will dictate whether any building code requirements apply. Some design considerations in selecting a specific ceiling tile are:

Fire Rating: There are applications where a specific fire rating is required. Standardized tests for flame spread specifications are given for each type of ceiling tile. Ceiling installers should check that the properly rated ceiling tile is received prior to installation, keeping in mind that many ceiling tile finish patterns are standardized and look the same on the surface. Installers should also check to see if hold-down clips are required in order to provide a fire-rated ceiling. These clips prevent inadvertent removal of tiles that would then cause a breech in the fire-rated ceiling.

Acoustical ceilings are rated for fire performance as follows:

- Surface burning characteristics (flame spread and smoke ratings).

- Fire resistance (may be designated in Fire-Rated Assemblies certified by Underwriters Laboratories, Inc.).

- Flash Over (see Full-Room test procedure of UBC Standard 42-2).

Restaurant Kitchens: Commercial kitchens require a ceiling system that can be washed. The ceiling tiles are manufactured with a surface that can be cleaned without causing damage to the tile.

Light Reflectance: The use of the room or building will have different requirements for the amount of lighting that may be required. Use of tiles with high light reflectance will decrease the required number of light fixtures in a room or building.

Sound Transmission: Ceiling tiles are used for their acoustical property of reducing the amount of noise in a room or building. There are standardized tests for sound transmission specifications that are given for each type of ceiling tile. This is measured in Sound Transmission Class (STC).

Acoustical performance is also described in terms of NRC (sound absorption reduced reverberation) and CAC (Ceiling Articulation Class, or reduced sound transmission from adjacent spaces, such as the activity on the floor above or from noise from pipes and ducts, electronic devices, etc.).

Impact Resistance: Some applications may have a high probability of impact, such as a school or gym.

There are ceiling tiles that are designed to withstand this type of use.

Architectural Design: Ceiling systems can be very plain and inexpensive, or can be elaborate and cost many times more than a standard fissured tile system.

Generally, the product manufacturer will be able to provide a catalog of products.

Among the more common alternatives:

Tegular Tiles: Notched at the perimeter edges so that the center drops below the grid to reveal a nice shadow effect.

Concealed Spline: Slotted so that the grid slips into the notch and the grid metal disappears. These systems do not respond well in situations in which maintenance workers randomly remove panels for access.

Fire-Rated and Clean Room systems: Usually require retainer clips to prevent the tiles from lifting during air pressure changes.

Food Processing and Food Serving areas: Usually require a washable surface on the tile face.

Acoustical Ceilings

Suspended Ceilings

Industry Standards

Fundamentals of the Construction Process
(R. S. Means Co., Inc.)

Suspended ceilings consist of a ceiling board or tile and/or a suspension system. One component of the suspension system is the main runner, consisting of a 1-1/2" channel, spaced 2 to 3 feet apart and hung from the supporting structure. From the main runner, cross members are supported by clips, 1 to 2 feet apart, to suit the modular tile size. For a concealed spline ceiling, with 1 foot square tiles, the spline is, in turn, supported by the cross members.

Suspended ceiling boards can be sealed in place to create an isolated air space between them and the next level, called a plenum, which acts in the heating system as a return air reservoir. This design saves on return air ductwork costs. However, most building codes require that a plenum ceiling contain fire-rated components.

On commercial projects, installation of the suspension system or ceiling grid is usually coordinated with several subcontractors whose work is related to the ceiling finishes. First, the ceiling grid must be centered within the perimeter partitions of the individual room. Next, the sprinkler heads are centered, in rows, in the individual ceiling tiles. The light fixtures are usually the same size (modular) as the ceiling tiles and the layout is as symmetrical as their positioning will allow. Finally, the diffusers for the heating system are placed in rows occupying full or half modules within the grid. Although the ceiling drawings in the plans address some of these problems, the final layout is a result of the coordination of several subcontractors' shop drawings.

Comments

Lighting

Lighting in suspended ceilings can be standard ceiling grid fixtures, fluorescent fixtures mounted on the ceiling joists (with translucent panels installed in the ceiling grid below), or a luminous ceiling comprised of fluorescent tubing with translucent panels (over the entire ceiling area). For the overall luminous ceiling, fluorescent lamps (4', 40 watt) should be spaced between 18-24" apart.

Grid System

The grid system for a suspended acoustical ceiling must be hung from the structural ceiling surface. Galvanized wire is attached to the structural ceiling surface by various types of fasteners.

"Eye" lag bolts are used most often in constructing suspended ceilings for wood-framed buildings. Various manufacturers have designed fastening systems that utilize a drill (with a special tip) that is secured to the end of a pole. While standing on the floor, the installer first drills the lag bolt into the ceiling joist, and then pulls the pole off the lag bolt while it is still on the hanging wire. Another quick pull of the drill trigger twists the end of the hanging wire around itself. **A minimum of 3 to 4 tight turns are required.**

There are several common methods of wire attachment for concrete ceiling surfaces. In new, multiple-story construction, the hanging wires can be installed through the sheet metal form prior to the pouring of concrete for the floor at each level. This is done very early in the construction schedule, and the installer may still need to add hanging wires when the acoustical ceiling is installed during the finish portion of the construction schedule.

The most efficient method, in applications of existing concrete ceilings, utilizes a power-actuated pin fastener, with the hanging wire pre-attached to the fastener. There are various pole systems that allow the installer to stand on the floor to attach the hanging wire.

Another and more time-consuming method requires the use of a ladder or scaffold. The installer drills a hole into the concrete, and then attaches an anchor and tie to the hanging wire.

In many regions, additional seismic support is required. This additional support limits the amount of buckling and sway that may occur during an earthquake, thereby preventing possible injuries from collapsing suspended ceilings. During installation of the supplementary seismic support, additional hanging wire is attached to various points in the grid system. Wires are splayed at 45° angles to the supporting structure, and a compression strut system is installed at the central point of the splayed wires. See **Figure 11.4** *and* **Figure 11.5.**

The grid system layout must be carefully planned prior to the installation of the hanging wire. Within the industry, it is an accepted standard that ceiling tiles at the perimeter of the room shall not be less than 1/2 the width or length of the tile. The hanging wire should be installed as close to perpendicular to the ceiling system as possible.

Acoustic Tile Ceiling

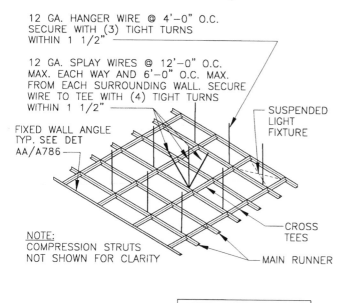

12 GA. HANGER WIRE @ 4'-0" O.C.
SECURE WITH (3) TIGHT TURNS
WITHIN 1 1/2"

12 GA. SPLAY WIRES @ 12'-0" O.C.
MAX. EACH WAY AND 6'-0" O.C. MAX.
FROM EACH SURROUNDING WALL. SECURE
WIRE TO TEE WITH (4) TIGHT TURNS
WITHIN 1 1/2"

FIXED WALL ANGLE
TYP. SEE DET
AA/A786

SUSPENDED
LIGHT
FIXTURE

CROSS
TEES

MAIN RUNNER

NOTE:
COMPRESSION STRUTS
NOT SHOWN FOR CLARITY

NOTE:
WIRES SHALL BE TAUT
WITHOUT CAUSING LIFT

Drawings by SH₂A, Inc., Architects

Figure 11.4

Compression Strut

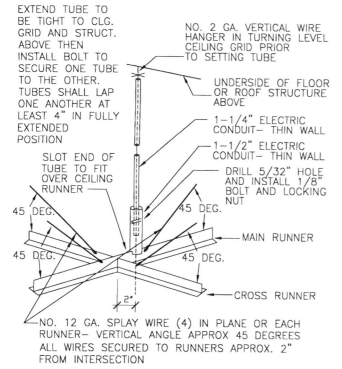

EXTEND TUBE TO
BE TIGHT TO CLG.
GRID AND STRUCT.
ABOVE THEN
INSTALL BOLT TO
SECURE ONE TUBE
TO THE OTHER.
TUBES SHALL LAP
ONE ANOTHER AT
LEAST 4" IN FULLY
EXTENDED
POSITION

SLOT END OF
TUBE TO FIT
OVER CEILING
RUNNER

NO. 2 GA. VERTICAL WIRE
HANGER IN TURNING LEVEL
CEILING GRID PRIOR
TO SETTING TUBE

UNDERSIDE OF FLOOR
OR ROOF STRUCTURE
ABOVE

1-1/4" ELECTRIC
CONDUIT— THIN WALL

1-1/2" ELECTRIC
CONDUIT— THIN WALL

DRILL 5/32" HOLE
AND INSTALL 1/8"
BOLT AND LOCKING
NUT

45 DEG.   45 DEG.

45 DEG.   45 DEG.

MAIN RUNNER

CROSS RUNNER

2"

NO. 12 GA. SPLAY WIRE (4) IN PLANE OR EACH
RUNNER— VERTICAL ANGLE APPROX 45 DEGREES
ALL WIRES SECURED TO RUNNERS APPROX. 2"
FROM INTERSECTION

Drawings by SH₂A, Inc., Architects

Figure 11.5

UBC — 1997

Section 2504 — Horizontal Assemblies

2504.1 General. In addition to the requirements of this section, supports for horizontal assemblies of plaster or gypsum board shall be designed to support all loads as specified in Chapter 16 of this code.

Exception: Wood-framed assemblies meeting the requirements of Section 2320 need not be designed.

2504.2 Wood Framing. Wood stripping or suspended wood systems, where used, shall not be less than 2 inches (51 mm) nominal thickness in the least dimension, except that furring strips not less than 1-inch-by-2-inch (25 mm by 51 mm) nominal dimension may be used over solid backing.

2504.3 Hangers. Hangers for suspended ceilings shall not be less than the sizes set forth in Table 25-A [see **Figure 11.6**], fastened to or embedded in the structural framing, masonry or concrete.

Hangers shall be saddle-tied around main runners to develop the full strength of the hangers. Lower ends of flat hangers shall be bolted with 3/8-inch (9.5 mm) bolts to runner channels or bent tightly around runners and bolted to the main part of the hanger.

2504.4 Runners and Furring. The main runner and cross-furring shall not be less than the sizes set forth in Table 25-A [see **Figure 11.6**], except that other steel sections of equivalent strength may be substituted for those set forth in this table. Cross-furring shall be securely attached to the main runner by saddle-tying with not less than one strand of 0.051-inch (1.30 mm) (No. 16 A.W. gage) or two strands of 0.040-inch (1.02 mm) (No. 18 A.W. gage) tie wire or approved equivalent attachments.

TABLE 25-A—SUSPENDED AND FURRED CEILINGS[1]
[For support of ceilings weighing not more than 10 pounds per square foot (4.89 kg/m²)]

MINIMUM SIZES FOR WIRE AND RIGID HANGERS			Maximum Area Supported (square feet)	Size
Size and Type			× 0.09 for m²	× 25.4 for mm
Hangers for suspended ceilings			12.5	0.148-inch (3.76 mm) (No. 9 B.W. gage) wire
			16	0.145-inch (4.19 mm) (No. 8 B.W. gage) wire
			18	$^3/_{16}$" diameter, mild steel rod[2]
			20	$^7/_{32}$" diameter, mild steel rod[2]
			22.5	$^1/_4$" diameter, mild steel rod[2]
			22.0	1" × $^3/_{16}$" mild steel flats[3]
Hangers for attaching runners and furring directly to beams and joists	For supporting runners	Single hangers between beams[4]	8	0.109-inch (2.77 mm) (No. 12 B.W. gage) wire
			12	0.134-inch (3.40 mm) (No. 10 B.W. gage) wire
			16	0.165-inch (4.19 mm) (No. 8 B.W. gage) wire
		Double wire loops at beams or joists[3]	8	0.083-inch (2.11 mm) (No. 14 B.W. gage) wire
			12	0.109-inch (2.77 mm) (No. 12 B.W. gage) wire
			16	0.120-inch (3.05 mm) (No. 11 B.W. gage) wire
	For supporting furring without runners[4] (wire loops at supports)	Type of support: Concrete Steel Wood	8	0.083-inch (2.11 mm) (No. 14 B.W. gage) wire 0.065-inch (1.65 mm) (No. 16 B.W. gage) wire (2 loops)[5] 0.065-inch (1.65 mm) (No. 16 B.W. gage) wire (2 loops)[5]

MINIMUM SIZES AND MAXIMUM SPANS FOR MAIN RUNNERS[6,7]		
Size and Type	Maximum Spacing of Hangers or Supports (Along Runners)	Maximum Spacing of Runners (Transverse)
× 25.4 for mm × 1.49 for kg/m	× 304.8 for mm	
$^3/_4$" — 0.3 pound per foot, cold- or hot-rolled channel	2'	3'
$1^1/_2$" — 0.475 pound per foot, cold-rolled channel	3'	4'
$1^1/_2$" — 0.475 pound per foot, cold-rolled channel	3.5'	3.5'
$1^1/_2$" — 0.475 pound per foot, cold-rolled channel	4'	3'
$1^1/_2$" — 1.12 pounds per foot, hot-rolled channel	4'	5'
2" — 1.26 pounds per foot, hot-rolled channel	5'	5'
2" — 0.59 pounds per foot, cold-rolled channel	5'	3.5'
$1^1/_2$" × $1^1/_2$" × $^3/_{16}$" angle	5'	3.5'

MINIMUM SIZES AND MAXIMUM SPANS FOR CROSS FURRING[6,7]		
Size and Type of Cross-furring	Maximum Spacing of Runners or Supports	Maximum Spacing of Cross-furring Members (Transverse)
× 25.4 for mm × 1.49 for kg/m	× 304.8 for mm	× 25.4 for mm
$^1/_4$" diameter pencil rods	2'	12"
$^3/_8$" diameter pencil rods	2'	19"
$^3/_8$" diameter pencil rods	2.5'	12"
$^3/_4$" — 0.3 pound per foot, cold- or hot-rolled channel	3'	24"
	3.5'	16"
	4'	12"
1" — 0.410 pound per foot, hot-rolled channel	4'	24"
	4.5'	19"
	5'	12"

[1]Metal suspension systems for acoustical tile and lay-in panel ceiling systems weighing not more than 4 pounds per square foot (19.5 kg/m²), including light fixtures and all ceiling-supported equipment and conforming to UBC Standard 25-2, are exempt from Table 25-A.

[2]All rod hangers shall be protected with a zinc or cadmium coating or with a rust-inhibitive paint.

[3]All flat hangers shall be protected with a zinc or cadmium coating or with a rust-inhibitive paint.

[4]Inserts, special clips or other devices of equal strength may be substituted for those specified.

[5]Two loops of 0.049-inch (1.24 mm) (No. 18 B.W. gage) wire may be substituted for each loop of 0.065-inch (1.65 mm) (No. 16 B.W. gage) wire for attaching steel furring to steel or wood joists.

[6]Spans are based on webs of channels being erected vertically.

[7]Other sections of hot- or cold-rolled members of equivalent strength may be substituted for those specified.

Figure 11.6

Comments

The wall angle and main runners are the first components of the grid system to be installed. Proper steps must be taken to be sure that the grid system is as horizontally level as possible. String levels, water levels and lasers are the most common tools utilized to level the grid system. The hanging wire should be laid out to be directly perpendicular to the main runner locations. Once the wall angle and main runners are in place, the cross tees are snapped in place at specified intervals to fit the ceiling tiles. The most common tile sizes are 2' x 2' or 2' x 4'.

Any other items that will be installed into the grid system, such as light fixtures and HVAC registers, should be installed and connected at this time. These items will require their own seismic hanging wires; usually one at each diagonal corner.

The ceiling installer should carefully check the contract specifications to determine who is responsible for the seismic hanging wires for light fixtures, HVAC registers, and any other items that are placed in the ceiling grid.

Installation Terminology

On Center (o.c.): On center in suspended ceiling installations refers to the distance from the center of one tee to the center of the next.

Patterns: The two most common tee patterns or layouts are 2' x 2' and 2' x 4'. The 2' x 4' pattern is more economical, easier to plan, and faster to install.

   2 x 4-ft. Tee Layout: Using 2' x 4' acoustical panels, full-length main tee sections are spaced 4' o.c., with 4' cross tees at 2' o.c., spanning between them.

   2 x 2-ft. Tee Layout: Using 2' x 2' acoustical panels, 2' cross tees are added to a 2' x 4' grid, spanning between centers of the 4' cross tees.

Tees: The metal framing members of the ceiling grid.

   Main Tees: Main tees run from wall to wall (between the wall angles) as the primary support for the ceiling's weight. They are hung by hanger wire from joists or other supports above.

   Cross Tees: Cross tees snap into main tees as secondary support members for individual ceiling panels. They come in two lengths: 4 ft. (used for both 2 x 4-ft. and 2 x 2-ft. grid patterns), and 2 ft. (used for 2 x 2-ft. grid patterns only).

Wall Angle: An L-shaped metal strip, the continuous finished edge around the perimeter of the ceiling where it meets the wall.

Adhered Ceilings
Industry Standards
Fundamentals of the Construction Process
(R. S. Means Co., Inc.)

Ceiling tiles, 12" x 12", can also be mounted on a flat substrate with adhesive. These are usually in acoustical (sound absorbing) material made of mineral fiber, sometimes having plastic or metal facing (see **Figure 11.7**).

Ceiling tiles are commonly found in sizes from 1' square to 2' x 4' rectangles, almost always acoustical. The exposed face may be perforated, fissured, textured, or plastic covered. Acoustical ceiling tiles (shown in **Figure 11.7**) are available in mineral fiber in many patterns and textures.

Comments

Plan ceiling tile layout so that equal-sized tiles are used on opposing borders. Ensure a level ceiling by shimming the furring strips as necessary. Cover the gap between ceiling tile and the wall with cove molding.

Mineral Fiber Tile Applied with Adhesive

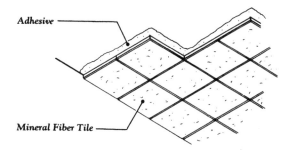

Adhesive

Mineral Fiber Tile

Fiberglass Board on Suspended Grid System

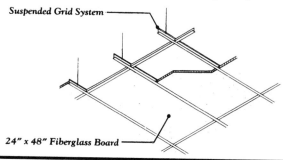

Suspended Grid System

24" x 48" Fiberglass Board

R.S. Means Co., Inc., *Fundamentals of the Construction Process*

Figure 11.7

CHAPTER

12 PAINTING & WALLCOVERING

Table of Contents

(continued on next page)

Text in blue print indicates excerpts from model building code(s). "Comments" (in solid blue boxes) were written by the editors, based on their own experience.

For building product information, use this book's special Internet gateway to thousands of manufacturers:
www.rsmeans.com/prodsupp/rlstand.html

CHAPTER 12
PAINTING & WALLCOVERING

Common Defect Allegations

Most defect claims on painting involve the building exterior. Claims on interior painting usually relate to drywall taping and/or mud showing through the paint, which appears dull in those areas. This condition is sometimes referred to as "flashing," and may result from insufficient paint thickness or use of a quickset compound or "hot mud."

According to the National Association of Home Builders' Residential Construction Performance Guidelines, "setting nails and filling nail holes are considered part of painting and finishing." Complaints of this type are also common.

Exterior claims often result from deferred maintenance. In some regions oil-based paints are prohibited, and exterior painting (with latex paint) is required every two years. Complaints may be raised regarding paint fading, but fading is generally considered a normal occurrence. (Consult the manufacturer's product warranty information.) Paint peeling before the end of the contractor's warranty constitutes a defect.

Wood window warranties require that paint be applied 1/8" onto the glass pane to make a weather seal. Even when the paint is properly applied, cleaning personnel will often take a razor and cut that weather seal, allowing water to enter the assembly. (Claims are also made on scratched glass.) Many times the panes will need to be replaced, requiring painting, and the cycle starts all over again. The painter needs to mask the entire window, not just a border, and residual tape adhesive must be removed chemically.

Another complaint is that tops and bottoms of doors are not painted. Sealing these surfaces is an absolute must to preserve the doors from warping. Hardware should be removed, and escutcheons should fit tightly into the paint or be caulked to prevent water entry into the interior of the weather-exposed door.

> *Backpriming is required on all exterior carpentry, including siding. Siding shingles and boards should never be allowed to weather without some form of protection. Cedar and redwood have an inherent resistance to dryrot in the form of a natural insecticide that stops fungal growth, but this does not protect the wood from deterioration from lignin removal during the wetting/drying process.*

Introduction

This chapter summarizes some common standards for painting and the installation of wallcoverings. We must stress that these are guidelines, and are not a substitute for researching individual products and local custom. Read the product label and follow the manufacturer's directions regarding temperature and other requirements for storage and application.

The *Uniform Building Code* (UBC) does not address painting and wallcovering. The recommendations in this chapter are from respected industry sources, with additional *Comments* from the editors based on their experience and knowledge of accepted practice in the field.

Oil-based paints are banned in some states due to the air quality laws. The warranties on water-based paints tend to be of shorter duration than those on oil-based paints. It is important to be aware of the limitations of the paint product and the frequency of painting required to preserve building components.

As a further resource, we recommend the *Builders Guide to Paints and Coatings*, published by the NAHB Research Center. This book, excerpts of which are included in this chapter, addresses the characteristics of paint coatings, color usage, substrate preparation, application, causes of and solutions to problems, and safety rules and regulations. It also includes a sample set of specifications. This publication is available for purchase from the NAHB Research Center (Telephone: 800-638-8556).

Wallcoverings are often included in the construction budget for a residential or light commercial project. It is important that the desired items are clearly specified, since the cost differences between products can be extreme. The owner or interior designer generally selects the materials, passing this information on to the architect or contractor to be included on the finish plans. Requirements for materials and workmanship may be stated in the specifications. These may include: product specification, surface preparation, method of application, workmanship, and inspection. **Figure 12.1** is a sample specification for paint and wallcoverings.

Warranties should be written into the contract with a professional paperhanger. A *Full Warranty* indicates that all faulty products will be repaired or replaced, or the fee refunded. A *Limited Warranty* may be restricted to the cost of materials only, or be limited in some other way. The warranty's duration should also be clear.

Professional paperhangers can be located through organizations such as the **National Guild of Professional Paperhangers, Inc.** and the **Painting and Decorating Contractors of America.**

The following organizations offer information on paint and wallcoverings.

Painting and Decorating Contractors of America (PDCA)
3913 Old Lee Highway, Suite 33B
Fairfax, VA 22030-2433
Telephone: 703-359-0826 or 800-332-7322
www.pdca.org
The PDCA has a technical division that develops industry standards and specifications for the application of paints, coatings and wallcoverings. PDCA collects, develops and distributes educational information in the form of seminars, videos, and publications, including *Painting and Decorating Craftsman's Manual and Textbook, Wallcovering and Paint Problem Solver(s), Third-Party Inspection Standard,* and *Touch Up/Damage and Repair Standard.*

National Guild of Professional Paperhangers
910 Charles Street
Fredericksburg, VA 22401
Telephone: 540-370-0012
www.ngpp.org
The NGPP is devoted exclusively to wallcovering installation professionals. The organization has 35 chapters nationwide and works to establish standards for the wallcoverings industry. The NGPP provides product testing, a lending library of installation references and videotapes for members, and sells *The Complete Guide to Wallpapering.*

Paint & Decorating Retailers Association (PDRA)
403 Axminister Drive
Fenton, MO 63026-2941
Telephone: 314-326-2636
info@pdra.org
The PDRA, an association of paint and decorating stores, offers professional advice on paint, wallcovering, window treatment and floor covering.

National Wood Window & Door Association (NWWDA)
1400 East Touhy Avenue, Suite 470
Des Plaines, Illinois 60018
Telephone: 847-299-5200
www.nwwda.org
The NWWDA is included in this chapter because window and door manufacturers' warranties often require specific finish procedures and products.

Ed. Note: Comments and recommendations within this chapter are not intended as a definitive resource for construction activities. For building projects, contractors must rely on the project documents and any applicable code requirements pertaining to their own particular locations.

Sample Wall Finishes Plan

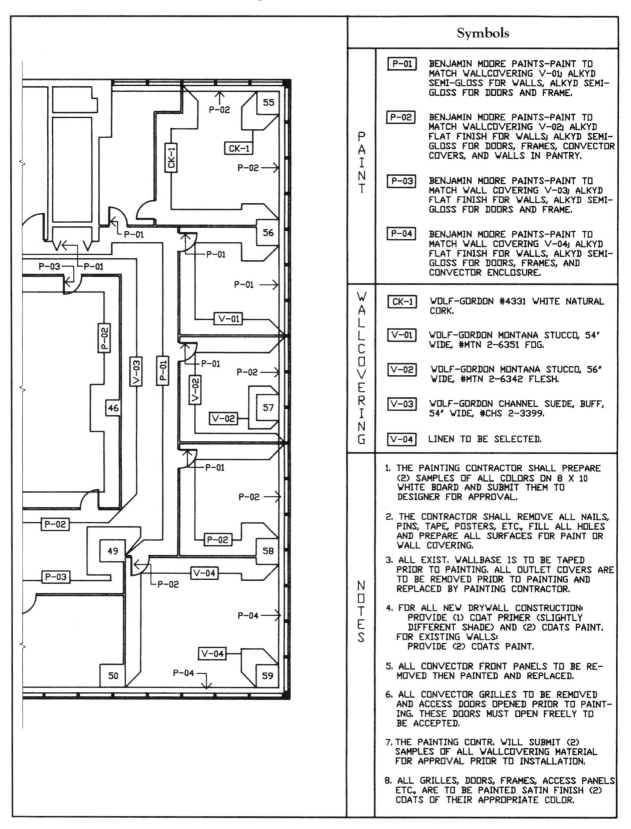

Figure 12.1

Types of Paint

Industry Standards

Fundamentals of the Construction Process
(R.S. Means Co., Inc.)

The four main groupings for painting and coating are *transparent finishes*, *primers*, *undercoating*, and *finish coats*.

Transparent Finishes: The first group includes shellac, lacquer, and varnish, primarily to protect natural wood used in finishes such as for floors, stairs, doors, and furniture.

Primers: The two main types of primers are oil-based primer and latex. Oil-based primer is compatible with both oil (solvent) and latex-based finish paints, but latex primer can only be used with latex finish paint. A primer's functions are to seal the substrate and give the surface a uniform opacity. Other primers have been developed for highly specific substrates such as masonry, metal, or previously varnished surfaces. Concrete block surfaces must be filled, rather than primed, prior to painting.

Undercoating: Undercoating is the preferred first coat under enamel paint finish coats.

Finish Coats: The two main formulations for finish paint are latex (water) or solvent (oil) based. Latex paints are emulsions and dry through the evaporation of water. Drying is fast under normal conditions and in hot climates may be so rapid as to inhibit brushing. Latex paints do not penetrate the surface, so surface preparation is critical to a good bond. Mechanical methods such as wire brushing are employed to remove chalk, flaking paint, and loose dirt. Chemical methods such as bleach and detergents are used to remove oil, grease, and mildew.

Solvent paints dry through the solvent evaporation. Neither formulation is good for immersion in water, but solvent paints develop a tighter film than latex paints and are superior in abnormally wet environments. Solvent paint surfaces deteriorate through oxidation which a film of fresh solvent paint can arrest. A latex paint film is "breathable," and old solvent painted surfaces underneath will continue to oxidize and peel.

Paints get their color through pigments and their spreadability through the "vehicle." The vehicle component in latex paint is a man-made resin and in solvent paint is oil. Enamels are solvent-based paints in which the pigments are more finely ground and the vehicle is varnish, a combination of resins and oil. This premium finish spreads much more smoothly than paint, is self-leveling, and has considerable hiding power. The resulting film has a high gloss and retains the gloss for an extended period.

Latex vs. Alkyd Paints

Industry Standards

WIC Manual of Millwork
(Woodwork Institute of California)

Latex paint has become popular because of the environmental necessity to reduce VOCs (Volatile Organic Compounds). Alkyd paint is a synthetic resin modified with oil and diluted with a petroleum solvent. This is very similar to the old oil based paints. Alkyd resins help enhance the flexibility of the paint. True oil based paints have almost disappeared off the market.

There is no universal correct answer as to which is best, latex or alkyd. The three P's will determine which to use. Project, what is the surface you are coating? Price, what can you afford? Preference, what look are you trying to achieve?

Each of the paints has qualities that make it appropriate for different uses. Here is a comparison of some of those qualities.

Durability — Latex has better elasticity, and alkyd has better adhesion on heavily chalked surfaces.

Versatility — Both with appropriate pre-treatment or undercoat will cover a wide range of projects.

Application — Alkyd has better hide and one coat coverage.

Color Retention — Alkyd is more likely to fade and chalk when exposed to sun.

Drying Time — Latex will dry to recoat in one to six hours while alkyd takes eight to 24 hours.

Odor — Latex wins this contest with low odor.

Applications for Paint Finishes
Industry Standards
Paint & Decorating Retailers Association (PDRA)
(PDRA Internet Web Site: info@pdra.org)

High Gloss (70+ on a 60 degree gloss meter)

Where to Use

For kitchen & bathroom walls, kitchen cabinets, banisters & railings, trim, furniture, door jambs & windowsills.

Comments

More durable, stain resistant & easier to wash. However, the higher the gloss, the more likely surface imperfections will be noticed.

Semigloss (35 to 70 on a 60 degree gloss meter)

Where to Use

For kitchen & bathroom walls, hallways, children's rooms, playrooms, doors, woodwork & trim.

Comments

More stain-resistant & easier to clean than flat paints. Better than flat for high-traffic areas.

Satin or Silk (range overlapping eggshell & semigloss)

Similar characteristics to Semigloss & Eggshell.

Eggshell (20 to 30 on a 60 degree gloss meter)

Where to use

Can be used in place of flat paints on wall surfaces especially in halls, bathrooms & playrooms. Can be used in place of semigloss paints on trim for less shiny appearance.

Comments

It resists stains better than flat paint & gives a more lustrous appearance.

Flat (less than 15 on a 60 degree gloss meter)

Where to use

For general use on walls & ceilings.

Comments

Hides surface imperfections. Stain removal can be difficult. Use for uniform, nonreflecting appearance. Best suited for low-traffic areas.

Special Paints
Industry Standards
Fundamentals of the Construction Process
(R.S. Means Co., Inc.)

Special Paints: Special paints have been developed for as many specific applications as there are surfaces or conditions, some of which bear mentioning. Paints with improved "hiding" power, that of obscuring the undercoat, are referred to as "one coat" and "high hiding." These paints can be applied in thick coats, without sagging (running), and are used for exterior, rapid interior and acoustical repainting.

Solvents in dry fog paint are used for spraying interior walls and ceilings. These paints dry before they fall to the floor, eliminating damage caused by overspray.

Fire retardant paints have been developed in several formulations, both latex and solvent, which significantly reduce flame spread through swelling (intumescence), to form a honeycomb structure to protect the surface.

A few paints have been developed for immersion in water (for swimming pools and exterior masonry), among them cement and rubber-based types. Rubber-based paints, when used along with aluminum paints, are excellent for protecting metals in roofing, window, railing, and heating systems.

Brushwork is used for most types of painting and is the method over which the worker has the most control. It is required for narrow surfaces, accent striping, curved and irregular surfaces such as piping and millwork, and ornamental work. Some paints, like some types of machinery enamel, must be brush-applied.

Paint Types

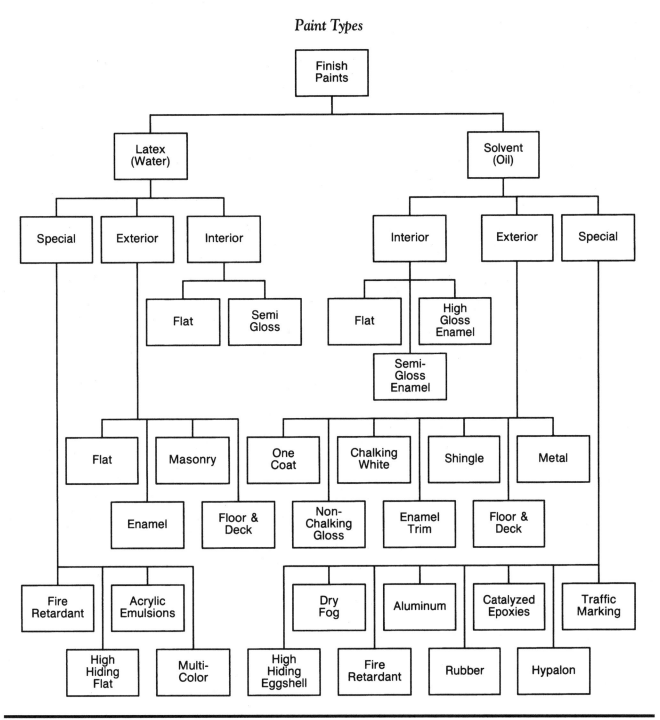

Figure 12.2

Elastomeric Paints

Comments

New technologies in paint manufacture have solved a series of problems. Elastomeric paints are, however, not appropriate for all projects.

Elastomeric paint creates an elastic film over the material it is covering. When walls have a high moisture emission, blisters can be created when the sun strikes the wall causing water vapor to expand.

Plaster or wood-sided and drywall walls experience severe temperature differentials. The result is condensation in the wall cavity. If this situation is compounded by high humidity levels or minor water intrusion, the walls can absorb large quantities of water vapor.

Most building wraps are designed to allow moisture to transfer out of the wall to a point of equilibrium over extended periods. Elastomeric paint prevents that process and all moisture must evaporate through the conditioned space. When molds develop, the air transfer will sometimes contaminate the interior space of a building.

Another complaint is the inability of the elastomeric paint to receive an overcoat when a color change is preferred or when weathering and fading have occurred. Some paints require a sandblasting before another coat can be applied.

Paint Film Thickness

Comments

Content

Latex and solvent-based paints have similar components; however latex paint is diluted with water, and solvent paint is diluted with a petroleum product. The main constituents of paint are **pigments**, **surfactants**, and **dilutants.**

The primary pigment ingredient is titanium dioxide, which is white. This provides the opaque barrier that creates the "hide" ability. Deeper-color paints have reduced titanium dioxide content and rely more on the colored pigments for hiding power. They may require additional coats.

Pigment durability is an issue with paints. Yellow, orange, lavender, purple, light blue, pink, peach, and salmon are a poorer choice for exterior use because they fade faster and require more coats to cover.

Surfactants, or "surface active agents," include wetting agents, dispersants, defoamers, and emulsifiers. These chemicals help keep pigments and other ingredients in suspension until after application. As the surfactants dry off, a film is formed.

As stated above, paint is diluted with a solvent — either water or petroleum. The solvent will precipitate, or separate from the solution, leaving a dried paint film.

Film Thickness

Manufacturers offering paint warranties usually base the warranty on paint film thickness. Dry paint film thickness, which is measured in mils (1 mil = 1/1000 of an inch), is most accurately determined as follows. The liquid in 1 gallon of paint can be spread 1-mil thick to cover 1,604 sq. ft. Paint manufacturers typically recommend a gallon to square foot ratio of 400 sq. ft. per gallon. If we divide 1,604 by 400, we realize that the manufacturers are recommending 4 mils of wet coat film. A manufacturer's product data on the paint can label should reveal the volume solids. If the volume solids are 25% of the product volume, the dry film thickness will be 1 mil.

Paint is applied bound up in a solvent, and when the solvent dries off, a film is left. The solids are entirely responsible for the dry film thickness and its durability. Multiple coats are preferable, as the laminated paint is more durable. A good quality undercoat is important, as this is the anchor for future coats of paint. Undercoat and topcoat of paints are better purchased from the same manufacturer, since the products are formulated to work together.

Determining Paint or Coating Quality

Industry Standards

Builders Guide to Paints and Coatings
(NAHB Research Center)

Ed. Note: The full publication, Builders Guide to Paints and Coatings, is available for purchase from the NAHB Research Center (Telephone: 800-638-8556).

What Is a Quality Paint or Coating?

There are a number of ways in which paints differ substantially in their performance, depending on the amount and quality of ingredients that they contain. These include:

- durability.
- longevity of the color and freshness of the finish.
- washability.
- hiding power.
- good bonding with previous coatings.
- uniformity of color and surface finish.
- for exterior finishes, elasticity to accommodate to substantial temperature and humidity changes and expansion and contraction of the substrate, and resistance to ultra-violet rays and environmental pollutants.
- batch-to-batch consistency of color and appearance.

Characteristics of a Good Coating

Qualities to look for in a good coating include the following:

- Resistance to damage by moisture.
- Resistance to alkali damage.
- High gloss retention.
- Excellent color retention.
- Good hiding capability.
- Scrub resistance.
- Stain and dirt resistance; washability.
- Mildew resistance.
- Good adhesion.
- Crack resistance.
- Good touch-up capability.

Interior and Exterior Coatings

Exterior coatings must provide weather protection. This requirement is prominently represented in types of extenders, binder, and additives that exterior paints contain, and the ways in which they perform.

Interior finishes must be dirt and stain resistant, and must have good ease of stain removal, or must be scrub resistant: to allow for cleaning. A prominent cause of home buyer dissatisfaction arises from the experience of trying to scrub or clean an interior surface that has been soiled by the presence and activities of children, within months after buying the home, and discovering that the scrubbing produces undesirable and unattractive change in the appearance of the surface that has been cleaned. This problem can arise from one or both of two causes. One cause can be failure to exercise enough foresight to use a paint with a hard finish and at least some gloss, in areas where children's hands are likely to come into contact with the surfaces. A second cause can be use of a lower-quality paint, regardless of type.

Properly Painted Surface

Ed. Note: The Painting and Decorating Contractors of America (PDCA) publishes Standard PDCA P5-92, "Benchmark Sample Procedures," in order to "outline procedures for on-site demonstration of achievable quality from the specified paint and/or decorative coating systems." This document is recommended for projects whose scope makes it "advisable to establish achievable levels of quality before beginning." It involves taking and evaluating samples from a Benchmark Sample area. The following excerpt from Standard P5-94 defines "Properly Painted Surface."

Industry Standard

Standard PDCA P5-94, Benchmark Sample Procedures for Paint and Other Decorative Coating Systems
(Painting and Decorating Contractors of America)

5.6 Properly Painted Surface: One that is uniform in appearance, color and sheen. It is one that is free of foreign material, lumps, skins, runs, sags, holidays, misses, strike-through, or insufficient coverage. It is a surface which is free of drips, spatters, spills or overspray which were caused by the contractor's workforce. Compliance to meeting the criteria of a "properly painted surface" shall be determined when viewed without magnification at a distance of five feet or more, under normal lighting conditions and from a normal viewing position. Normal lighting conditions are described as those in place when the project is finished. This includes, but is not limited to, design lighting (e.g., wall washers, spots and floods, etc.) and natural lighting (e.g., skylights, clear view windows, window walls and window treatments, etc.).

Ed. Note: PDCA also publishes Standard P2-92, which establishes the qualifications and responsibilities of a third-party inspection, and proper inspection procedures. PDCA Standard P3-93 establishes the number and placement of paint colors prior to bidding.

Industry Standards

WIC Manual of Millwork
(Woodwork Institute of California)

Paint is the final finish product that is the first thing people see when viewing a home. It has been said that beauty is in the eye of the beholder. Disputes over the quality of a paint job are often subjective. We can offer little help with arguments over color tinting or shades of color. These problems are best handled by having the customer view a test area and approve the color and sheen before the project proceeds.

Ed. Note: See "Finishing Doors & Windows" later in this chapter for WIC's specific recommendations.

Responsibility for Touch-up & Damage Repair

Industry Standard
PDCA Standard P1-92
(Painting and Decorating Contractors of America)

Ed. Note: PDCA Standard P1-92, "Touch-Up Painting and Damage Report — Financial Responsibility," defines and categorizes the term "touch-up" and establishes financial responsibility for repair or correction of damage to finished painted surfaces by individuals other than those employed by the painting contractor.

2. Description

2.1 This standard includes the repair and repaint of finished painted surfaces which have been damaged by individuals other than those employed by the painting contractor. This type of damage is known as *damage caused by others*. The painting contractor will correct the *damage caused by others* after receiving a separate work directive from the contracting or agreement entity. A time and/or price adjustment will then be submitted by the painting contractor.

The work may be done for a lump sum or time and material depending on the most reasonable individual scenario. The painting contractor will repair and/or repaint the damaged area after receiving acceptance of his submittal and authorization to proceed.

2.2 *Latent damage* is due to conditions beyond the control of the painting contractor. They are caused by conditions not apparent at the time of initial painting or decorating. The painting contractor will correct *latent damage* after receiving a separate work directive from the contracting or agreement entity. A time and/or price adjustment will then be submitted by the painting contractor.

The work may be done for a lump sum or time and material depending on the most reasonable individual scenario. The painting contractor will repair and/or repaint the damaged area after receiving acceptance of his submittal and authorization to proceed.

2.3 The contractual work is job and item specific. In no case shall the painting contractor be responsible for *damage caused by others* or *latent damage* as herein described.

2.4 The painting contractor will produce a "properly painted surface."

Ed. Note: See the definition of "properly painted surface" in the excerpt from PDCA P5-94 in the preceding section.

Preparing the Surface for Paint

Industry Standards
Builders Guide to Paints and Coatings
(NAHB Research Center)

Ed. Note: The full publication, Builders Guide to Paints and Coatings, is available for purchase from the NAHB Research Center (Telephone: 800-638-8556).

Surface preparation is critical to the proper adhesion of coatings. *Regardless of the type of substrate, all contamination must be removed prior to coating of the surface.*

New Interior Wood
Sand new wood smooth with a fine sandpaper and prime with an alkyd primer. Sanding should always be done in one direction; circular motion should not be used.

Comments
Moulded urethane millwork items are available prefinished. Other finishes should be applied in accordance with manufacturer's instructions. Cut surfaces should be primed and painted within a few days of installation.

Drywall
Before a primer is applied to drywall, the surface must be clean and dry. Nail heads must be spackled, and joints must be taped and covered with joint compound. Spackled nail heads and tape joints should be sanded smooth and all dust should be removed with a damp cloth or sponge.

With drywall whose surface is made of recycled paper, the use of a high quality primer is especially important.

Latex primers should be used on drywall. Solvent-based primers will penetrate the paper and raise the nap. An exception is drywall to which wallpaper is to be applied. A rough surface is desirable for adherence of the wallpaper, and an alkyd primer should therefore be used.

Existing Houses and Surfaces

For interior coating of an existing house, all surfaces should be cleaned thoroughly with a strong household detergent. Remove oil, dirt, grease, wallpaper paste, wall sizing, pencil marks, wax, chalk, and water-soluble materials before any coating is applied. Special attention should be paid to stove areas, ceilings, vent areas, bathroom areas (especially sinks and shower stalls), kitchen sink areas, fingerprints on corners, and switches.

Grease that is not removed can cause premature peeling. Test suspected areas by splashing water onto the surface. If the water beads, rewash the area. Do **not** use degreasers such as oven cleaners; they can damage the old paint film, and any degreaser that remains can attack the new top coat from underneath.

Fill all cracks and nail holes with spackling plaster and sand smooth. Cover cracks and nail holes with spackling plaster. Remove all cracking, peeling, and blistering paint with a scraper and/or sandpaper, and sand smooth.

Scruff glossy finishes with fine sandpaper. Wash with a household detergent in water to remove all dust and to dull the gloss. Do **not** use solvent-type sanding aids. Always sand in one direction. Scratches caused by circular motion can show through a topcoat and give the finish an undesired textured effect.

Either remove old wallpaper or reglue loose sections and allow to dry. Old wallpaper can be removed with steam if an alkyd primer was used as a seal coat. But if latex was used, steam will penetrate and cause the drywall to delaminate. Such wallpapered surfaces must be painted.

Before painting wallpaper, test a small area to determine if the pattern inks bleed into the paint. If so, use an alkyd primer as a seal coat.

Paint & Wood Damage

If the grain of the wood is raised as a result of water saturation or if old coats of paint are blistered or peeling, surface preparation is necessary. This involves scraping with scrapers or removal with electricity heated paint removers.

When this operation is completed, the area should be sanded smooth. Sanding should be done with the grain only. A medium grit paper should first be used, followed by finer paper as the surface becomes smoother. After sanding is completed, all dust should be removed.

Plaster

Allow bare new plaster to cure for 60 days, by which time it will be dry and hard. If a new or old plaster surface is textured, soft, porous, or powdery, wash with a mixture of one pint of vinegar in one gallon of water. Repeat until the surface is hard. Rinse thoroughly with clean water, allow to dry, and apply a wall and wood primer.

Exterior Surface Preparation

In new construction, exterior wood should be covered with coating as quickly as possible. Even relatively brief exposure of unpainted wood to sunlight will cause the lignin in the wood to degrade, creating "straw" on the surface. This can result in poorer adhesion of the coating.

Apart from this consideration, exterior wood in new construction ordinarily involves little more preparation than interior wood. Dirt must be removed, and cracks and open joints in siding should be sealed. Species and grades of wood are important in exterior paint performance.

In existing construction, it has been estimated that 80% of coating failure is the result of inadequate preparation of the surface. The most common causes of exterior paint failure are the following:

- Moisture. This is by far the biggest culprit.
- Salt build-up.
- Chalking paint.
- Dirt.
- Old cracking and peeling paint.
- Mildew.

Structural deficiencies and improper application techniques also play a role.

Concrete & Masonry

Concrete and mortar joints in concrete masonry block require 30 days to cure and dry before any coating can be applied. Coatings used over masonry must be alkali-resistant.

Repair cracks and breaks in masonry, and remove all loose stone and efflorescence with a wire brush. Efflorescence consists of highly alkali chemicals that build up on the surface in white crystalline form as water reaches the surface. These crystals can push off the topcoat. After removing efflorescence, a masonry conditioner should be applied.

Use of a primer coat is highly important to successful coating of masonry surfaces. Primers must be used that will not cause alkali activation. Special primers are made for use on masonry; these should be employed, and manufacturer's instructions should be carefully followed.

Comments

The problems arising from painting concrete products are related to moisture and alkalinity.

It is easy to understand the difficulty that can arise when moisture is trapped behind a paint film. Generally, the result is paint failure. The Plastic Sheet Method can assist the contractor in determining whether the concrete is dry enough to paint. To use this technique, tape the perimeter of a 4-mil-thick clear plastic sheet 18" square, securing it to the floor, wall, or ceiling. Allow it to remain in place for at least 16 hours. Then, make a visual check of the plastic over the concrete or masonry surface for moisture. A good time to check the test area is early morning, when the environment is cool.

Alkalinity is a common cause of paint failure on concrete products, and it is the least understood. The pH scale runs from acidic 0 to 6, 7 neutral, and alkali 8 to 14. Each number in the scale represents a tenfold change from its neighbor. A rating of 12 is 10 times more alkaline then 11. Most paint products require a pH of 10 or less before coating is applied. All manufacturers recommend that concrete be allowed to weather and cure for 30 days prior to painting. This allows the concrete to dry and also allows the alkaline level to recede. After this waiting period, it is best to test the pH level of the concrete and use an alkali-resistant primer. Concrete can be reduced in alkaline level by washing it with a clean water rinse and allowing it to dry. Repeating this cycle will reduce the alkali level.

Brick

Brick should be allowed to cure for at least one year, and should be wire brushed to remove efflorescence before being coated. Large areas may require flushing with muriatic acid and water. Glazed brick will not hold typical alkyd paint, latex paint, or enamel.

Stucco

Stucco surfaces that are to be coated must be clean and free of loose pieces. Under normal drying conditions, new stucco surfaces can be coated after about 30 days of curing time. Drying conditions vary in different locations.

Metal

Conventional finish coats are not designed for use on unprimed metal. Primers designed for use on specific metallic substrates must always be used. Iron and steel require primers that are formulated for rust inhibition. Galvanized metal requires another type of primer.

Aluminum siding is normally provided with a coating in the desired color. This coating is meant to chalk and clean itself. If painting of any portion of the siding in a different color is desired, the siding should be power-washed to remove chalking before a new coating is applied.

Inspecting Surfaces Before Painting

Industry Standards
Standard PDCA P4-94
(Painting and Decorating Contractors of America)

1. Scope

1.1 The purpose of this standard is to establish the responsibilities for inspection and approval of surfaces prior to painting and decorating.

1.2 This standard is intended for use on construction projects where the painting and decorating contractor applies paints, coatings or wallcoverings over a surface assembled, constructed and/or prepared by another contractor or trade not under the painting and decorating contractor's control.

2. Significance & Use

2.1 The owner or the owner's delegated agent, such as but not limited to the architect, is the final judge in all matters relating to the "Quality of Appearance" and acceptance of surfaces.

2.2 "Quality of Appearance" is a subjective term governed by the owner or their delegated agents, and established by specification and reference standards. It is controlled by sample review and/or mock up approval along with periodic jobsite inspections and approvals.

2.3 The painting and decorating contractor is not obligated to render any final professional opinion regarding the "Quality of Appearance" of work performed by others.

5. Standard Specification

5.1 Acceptance of Surfaces

> 5.1.1 The painting and decorating contractor is required to inspect surfaces to be finished only to determine, by reasonable and visible evidence, that the finish will satisfactorily adhere to surfaces provided by others and perform as specified.

> 5.1.2 The owner or the owner's designated agents have the responsibility to determine that a surface is complete and ready to finish painting or wallcovering.

> 5.1.3 When a trade has left its work without notification to the contrary; or notification to proceed has been given,

such action will be construed as tacit evidence that all work has been inspected, and that it is warrantable, complete and ready for finishing.

5.1.4 If "Quality of Appearance" of a surface prior to finishing is judged marginal or unacceptable by others conducting essential inspection, such alleged defective work must be corrected prior to priming and finishing so that all surfaces are made complete and ready for finishing. If the unacceptable work is not made complete and ready for finishing, the painting contractor will be duly informed, ordered to stop work and told to proceed only as directed.

5.1.5 Once finishing has begun, as scheduled or as directed, the correction of "Defects and/or Latent Damage" is considered "Damage Repair" as per PDCA Standard P1-92, "Touch-Up Painting and Damage Repair — Financial Responsibility."

Ed. Note: See page 416.

6. Comments

6.2 Quality of Appearance is achieved through quality control. Inspecting work in progress and taking necessary action at the appropriate time to make required corrections is imperative to ensure Quality of Appearance. This standard encourages periodic inspection and corrective actions.

Applying Coatings

Industry Standards
Builders Guide to Paints and Coatings
(NAHB Research Center)

Number of Coats

A primer and two topcoats are ideal for external applications. Although only one topcoat is generally employed, two topcoats will give the greatest longevity for the coatings and the greatest satisfaction to the owner.

Two coats consisting of a quality primer and topcoat should be regarded as minimum external coating protection for the home.

Weather Conditions

Most exterior coatings perform best when applied at 60–80 degrees F.

For both alkyd and latex paints, the minimum application temperature is 50 degrees F.

Certain coatings may not reach full serviceability until several days after they are applied. For example, an enamel or clear coating subjected to abrasion or pressure, such as a walking surface, should be allowed to cure for three days before being subjected to use.

Comments

Hot Weather

It is important to know what the manufacturer requires for a specific paint. There are, however, some common-sense work methods that hold true for most paints. Never paint an exterior wall that has been in full sun for even a moderate period of time. Start work on the shady side of the home and work around the home staying in the shade if possible. House paints applied to very hot surfaces will dry too quickly which may result in application problems such as color streaking and uneven mill thickness.

Storage of paint products in direct sun will cause partially used containers to dry out with the resulting loss of product. There is a chance overheating will cause a container to rupture.

Cold Weather

Once again, it is important to read the product label and follow directions.

Paint application is restricted to where the surface and ambient temperatures are above 50 degrees. Do not apply these paints late in the day where the overnight temperature will fall below 50 degrees. Paint manufacturers that supply the colder climates have produced paints that tolerate lower temperatures. Check with your supplier and always read the label.

Applying paints in too low temperatures can result in improper film formation. This is more likely in latex paints. The surfactants that help hold the dissimilar liquids and solids together can, in cold weather, exude them. This is most likely to occur when the temperature is low and the humidity is rising or dew has formed. This slows the drying process and allows large quantities of the surfactants to collect on the surface. The appearance of the painted surface is variations in sheen and streaking. Latex paints can be carefully washed to remove the surfactant buildup, ask your supplier or manufacturer's representative. Alkyd paint surfactant exudation is more difficult to correct. Consult the manufacturer. The paint film is not damaged by the surfactant exudation. This is only an appearance issue.

Paint that has frozen must be examined carefully. Check with the manufacturer about the specific paint to determine its resistance to damage from freezing. Inspect the paint; if it has a sour smell, the consistency of cottage cheese, or (after remixing) remains very thick, it cannot be used. If the paint will remix and return to its homogenous pre-freezing consistency, then it can be used. Many paints can survive a single freeze-thaw cycle.

Doors & Wood Windows

Ed. Note: Painting and coatings for doors and windows is a frequent subject of defect claims. It is covered here as well as in Chapter 9, "Windows & Doors."

Comments

Doors will have a manufacturer recommendation for painting, which must be followed to maintain the warranty.

Wood Doors

Remember that a door has six sides. Most frequently missed are the top and bottom. Failure to paint these surfaces within a specified time period will result in loss of warranty. Moisture uptake from an unpainted door bottom or top edge will frequently cause the door to warp after installation. Painting under door butts or door edge lock hardware is not required.

Metal Doors

A word of caution here about factory-primed galvanized doors. The usual primer coat is very thin, significantly less than 1/2 mil. Carefully follow the manufacturer recommendations for painting. Note that latex paints are generally specified. Oil-based or solvent thinned paints can strike through the factory primer. Alkyd resins can react with the zinc in the galvanized coating. The reaction is called "saponification," which is the hydrolysis of the ester in the alkyd resin by the alkali in the zinc, resulting in the formation of a soap compound. This will cause the loss of adhesion and will result in peeling.

Industry Standards

Specifiers Guide to Wood Windows & Doors

(National Wood Window & Door Association)

Exterior Use

In exterior use, temperature and humidity are not controlled on both sides of the door. Care must be taken when specifying Architectural wood flush doors in exterior openings. Consult individual manufacturers for specific recommendations and warranty limitations.

G–19: Job Site Finishing

Because of the many uncontrollable variables that exist at a site, such as temperature and moisture variation, dust and other factors, door manufacturers' warranties do not cover the appearance of finishes applied at the job site.

For additional information, see the NWWDA publication *How to Store, Handle, Finish, Install, and Maintain Wood Doors.*

8. Finishing

Wood is hygroscopic and dimensionally influenced by changes in moisture content caused by changes within its surrounding environment. To assure uniform moisture exposure and dimensional control all surfaces must be finished equally.

Doors may not be ready for finishing when initially received. Before finishing, remove all handling marks, raised grain, scuffs, burnishes and other undesirable blemishes by block sanding all surfaces in a horizontal position with a 120, 150 or 180 grit sandpaper. To avoid cross-grain scratches, sand with the grain.

Certain species of wood, particularly oak, contain chemicals which react unfavorably with foreign materials in the finishing system. Eliminate the use of steel wool on bare wood, rusty containers or any other contaminate in the finishing system.

A thinned coat of sanding sealer should be applied prior to staining to promote a uniform appearance and avoid sharp contrasts in color or a blotchy appearance.

All exposed wood surfaces must be sealed including top and bottom rails. Cutouts for hardware in exterior doors must be sealed prior to installation of hardware and exposure to weather. Dark-colored finishes should be avoided on all surfaces if the door is exposed to direct sunlight, in order to reduce the chance of warping or veneer checking. Oil-based sealers or prime coats provide the best base coat for finishing. If a water-based primer is used, it should be an exterior grade product.

Note: Water-based coatings on unfinished wood may cause veneer splits, highlight joints and raise wood grain and therefore should be avoided. If a water-based primer is desired, please contact the finish supplier regarding the correct application and use of these products.

Be sure the door surface being finished is satisfactory in both smoothness and color after each coat. Allow adequate drying time between coats. Desired results are best achieved by following the finish manufacturer's recommendations. Do not finish door until a sample of the finish has been approved.

Finishes on exterior doors may deteriorate due to exposure to the environment. In order to protect the door it is recommended that the condition of the exterior finish be inspected at least once a year and re-finished as needed.

Note: Certain wood fire doors have fire-retardant salts impregnated into various wood components that makes the components more hygroscopic than normal wood. When exposed to high moisture conditions, these salts will concentrate on exposed surfaces and interfere with the finish. Before finishing, reduce moisture content in the treated wood below 11% and remove the salt crystals with a damp cloth, followed by drying and light sanding. For further information on fire doors, see NWWDA publications regarding installing, handling and finishing fire doors.

Finishing Doors & Windows

Industry Standards

WIC Manual of Millwork
(Woodwork Institute of California)

Doors — Finishing

A. Prior to finishing, make sure that the building atmosphere is dried to a normal, interior relative humidity, and that the doors have been allowed to equalize to a stable moisture content.

B. Before finishing, remove handling marks or effects of exposure to moisture with a complete, thorough, final block, sanding over all surfaces of the door, using at least 150 grit sandpaper, and clean before applying sealer or finish. Deep scratches must be steamed out before sanding. Sharp edges must be eased by sanding.

C. Certain species of wood, particularly oak, contain chemicals which react unfavorably with certain finishes causing dark stain spots. Where possible, the species/finish combination should be tested prior to finishing the doors. Notify your finish supplier or door supplier immediately if any undesirable reaction is noticed. Do not continue with the finishing until the problem is resolved.

D. In order not to induce warpage, avoid dark stains or dark colored paints on door surface exposed directly to sunlight.

E. In order to prevent blemish magnification, avoid extremely dark stains in light colored wood species.

F. Water based sealer or prime coats should not be used. Water based top coats should only be used over surfaces that have been completely sealed with a non-water based sealer or primer.

G. A first coat of a thinned clear sanding sealer, followed by light block sanding, will minimize subsequent handling marks and promote the uniformity of subsequent stain coats.

H. All exposed wood surfaces must be sealed, including top and bottom rails.

I. To achieve the desired results of color uniformity, finish build, gloss and reduce the frequency of refinishing, obtain and follow finish manufacturer's recommendations. Be sure the door surface being finished is satisfactory in both smoothness and color after each coat before applying the next coat.

K. Certain wood fire doors have edges, and possibly crossbands under the face veneer, which contain fire retardant salts. These salts are usually hygroscopic and will take on excess moisture in a damp atmosphere. The salts will concentrate at the surface and form whitish crystals that can interfere with the finish. Before finishing, remove the salt crystals with a damp cloth, followed by drying and light sanding.

Windows — Finishing

5.7.2 Field-applied protective coatings can damage window sealants and gaskets and are not recommended. Contact the window manufacturer before applying any such coatings.

5.7.3 Masking tapes shall not be used on window surfaces as they may cause damage when they are removed.

Comments

Many manufacturers of wood windows utilize varying versions of the WIC recommendations for warranty compliance.

These warranty conditions usually include the following:

1. *Painting of wood windows must be accomplished on all sides of the windows within 48 hours of delivery to the construction site or immediately upon installation and repainted periodically to avoid damage to the wood parts.*

2. *Lap the finish coat 1/16" onto the glass for a proper moisture seal.*

3. *Primers usually are not compatible with lacquer and varnishes. Primer paints must be designated to prevent the application of dissimilar products.*

4. *Abrasive cleaners or solutions containing solvents should not be used.*

Cabinet Finishing

Ed. Note: Wood cabinetry, which is categorized under Finishes and Furnishings, is not usually associated with the structural integrity of a building. Therefore, standards for finishing cabinets are usually determined by professional associations and published reference books rather than by building codes. Detailed information about cabinet finishing is included in Chapter 6, "Finish Carpentry & Cabinetry," in the "Finishing of Millwork" section.

Wallcovering

Types of Wallcovering

Comments

*The five basic types of wallcoverings are **wallpaper** (mostly paper, with a printed design), **vinyl** (a sheet of PVC with a structural material), **fiber products** (yarn or tufted material laminated to a backing), **rigid**, and **specialties** such as acoustical and wood.*

Ed. Note: Wood paneling is addressed in Chapter 6, "Finish Carpentry & Cabinetry."

Surface Preparation

Industry Standards

Fundamentals of the Construction Process
(R.S. Means Co., Inc.)

Surfaces to receive wallcovering must be prepared by sizing or sealing the surface. Mildew must be treated with bleach. "Hot spots," or highly alkaline concentrations on the surface, will discolor the wallpaper and must be treated with zinc sulfate. Holes and cracks must be filled and the surface should be left uniformly smooth. If wallcovering is to be hung over paneling, be sure to apply lining paper first. This material provides a smooth surface on which to place the final wallcovering.

Installation of Wallcovering

Comments

Open and inspect wallcovering materials when they are delivered to the site. It is important to make sure that all rolls of wallpaper and borders are from the same dye lot. The materials should include specific instructions for hanging.

Fresh plaster should be permitted to cure for 90 days before it is primed.

Bleaching, if necessary to prevent or eliminate mold and mildew, should be done prior to the application of primer or sizing by washing walls with a solution of one part bleach to four parts water.

Material Quantities

Each room to be papered should be measured in feet, rounding off to the next highest foot or half foot. Determine the square footage of each wall, subtracting for the areas that will not be covered. This number can be divided by 25 (the square feet in one single roll of metric wallcovering). The result is the number of rolls needed. Pattern requirements or other special conditions can affect this formula. The manufacturer or distributor should be able to offer guidance on any necessary adjustments.

Installation

Hanging the wallcovering begins by dropping a plumbline on each wall and correctly lining up the first strip. In planning and cutting, allow for the proper pattern match. Air bubbles and wrinkles should be removed with a smoothing brush or soft sponge. The edges of the strips should butt and lie flat and smooth. Wallpaper should not be wrapped around an inside corner, but cut such that two pieces butt up to the corner. If the ceiling is to be covered, it should be done before the walls.

It is a good idea to inspect the wallcovering strips after hanging a few strips, in the event there is a manufacturer defect. While manufacturers will replace defective materials, they will not reimburse labor costs.

Pattern Matches

Patterns can be **random** *(no specific points of match),* **free** *(separated by the trim between strips, but possibly aligned for overall consistency),* **drop** *(a diagonal pattern where every other strip is the same at the ceiling line), or* **straight across** *(the same elements are repeated at an equal distance from the ceiling in each strip).*

Problems

Pattern mismatches are generally not accepted in new construction. In remodeling, out of plumb walls or trim out of square may lead to some unavoidable misalignment of patterns. Wallpaper with defects in pattern should be replaced by the manufacturer.

Peeling wallpaper is a defect that should be addressed by the installing contractor. It can be reattached if the result shows no evidence of repair. Otherwise, the strip should be replaced.

Repairs

Repairs can be made to wallcovering using the following method:

- *Cut out a piece of wallcovering (larger than the damaged area) to use for a patch.*
- *Paste the patch over the damaged spot, positioned to match the underlying pattern.*
- *Cut through both layers of wallcoverings using a straight edge and safety knife.*
- *Remove the excess covering and place the patch exactly in the opening.*

Ed. Note: Refer to the Introduction to this chapter for information on wallcovering associations and resources.

CHAPTER
13
SPECIALTIES

Table of Contents

(continued on next page)

Text in blue print indicates excerpts from model building code(s). "Comments" (in solid blue boxes) were written by the editors, based on their own experience.

For building product information, use this book's special Internet gateway to thousands of manufacturers: www.rsmeans.com/prodsupp/rlstand.html

CHAPTER 13 SPECIALTIES

Introduction This chapter includes prefinished (and often preassembled) manufactured items that are installed near the end of a project when other finish work is complete. Included in this category are bathroom accessories (including shower compartments, medicine cabinets, and grab bars for handicapped residents or building users), partitions used for commercial applications (such as office and toilet partitions), signs and directories, bulletin and chalk boards, access panels, lockers, prefabricated fireplaces and wood stoves, cupolas and fire extinguishers. Some distributors specialize in all or most of these items.

The project drawings must be reviewed carefully for these items, which may appear in only one reference. A general note on the drawings may describe the item, or detailed information may be given, such as the vendor's name and contact information. Substitutions may be restricted.

Contractors who are installing specialty items obtain detailed information from the manufacturer regarding installation procedures and will need to plan for any special equipment that might be required. It is also important to plan for related work when installing specialties on the project. Examples include concrete bases for lockers, wood blocking for toilet partitions, anchor bolts, inserts and sleeves for equipment, pads, and box-outs for water fountains or fire extinguishers.

The items in this chapter are often supplied and installed by the distributor, or by one or more subcontractors. As a result, it is difficult to find published standards for quality installation for several of these items. In those cases, the editors have provided some general guidelines for what would be expected in a professional installation.

The following organizations may be helpful in locating further information on specialties:

For bathroom fixture and accessory standard spacing:

National Kitchen & Bath Association (NKBA)
687 Willow Grove Street
Hackettstown, NJ 07840-9988
www.nkba.org

For ADA-compliant bathroom accessories, toilet partitions, grab bars, stair rails, and signage:

ADA Technical Assistance Center
Telephone: 800-949-4232
The ADA Technical Assistance Center provides local disability and business technical assistance and information about the *Americans with Disabilities Act — Act Guidelines*. The guidelines are available at no cost from the ADA Technical Assistance Center as well as the U.S. Department of Justice (Telephone: 800-514-0301; Web Site: **www.usdoj.gov/crt/ada**).

For fire extinguishers:

National Fire Protection Association
1 Batterymarch Park
P.O. Box 9101
Quincy, MA 02269-9101
Telephone: 617-770-3000
www.nfpa.org

For de-mountable partitions:

Ceilings & Interiors Systems Construction Association (CISCA)
1500 Lincoln Hwy., Suite 202
St. Charles, IL 60174
Telephone: 708-584-1919

Ed. Note: Comments and recommendations within this chapter are not intended as a definitive resource for construction activities. For building projects, contractors must rely on the project documents and any applicable code requirements pertaining to their own particular locations.

Bathroom Accessories

Shower Stalls

Comments

The category of bathroom accessories may include prefabricated shower stalls, medicine cabinets, towel bars and related items. We will begin with shower stalls, which can be constructed and finished with tile, or installed as prefabricated units. If a one-piece unit is to be installed, it is important to consider access to the bathroom for this large item, which may not fit through standard doorways or windows. The unit's manufacturer should provide detailed instructions, including requirements to maintain the warranty. Following are some basic guidelines.

- According to guidelines published by the National Kitchen & Bath Association in the **Kitchen & Bathroom Installation Manual, Volume 1**, shower stalls' interior dimensions should be a minimum of 34" x 34" (although job site limitations may make it necessary to reduce this dimension to 32" x 32"). For disabled users, shower stalls should include grab bars, a seat (17"-19" above the shower floor and at least 15" deep), and a door opening that allows adequate wheelchair entry and turning space (32"-36" depending on the interior space). Shower doors should open into the bathroom.

- The shower valve should be approximately 48" above the shower floor. The rough-in plumbing for this unit involves supplying both cold and hot water, and installing the drain, connected to a p-trap. Building codes generally require that the shower drain be a minimum of 12" from the nearest wall. If the shower drain is placed more than 6' from the main soil stack, the building code may require a separate vent.

- Prefabricated shower units are watertight and therefore do not require cement board on the surrounding walls. Once the unit has been put in place using manufacturer-recommended adhesive, it is difficult to remove in order to make plumbing adjustments. Plumbing should be carefully planned and executed to avoid leaks before adhering the shower unit.

- According to the National Kitchen & Bathroom Association's **Kitchen & Bathroom Installation Manual, Volume 1**, glass used for a shower enclosure within 18" of the floor should be safety glazing — laminated with a plastic interlayer, tempered glass, or approved plastics such as those found in the model safety code.

- Barrier-free shower units are available with options such as shower doors, fold-up seats, hand-held shower sprays, grab bars, soap dishes, and lights, as well as custom support blocking. Following are the Americans with Disabilities Act requirements for roll-in showers in public access facilities. (The ADA guidelines and technical assistance on ADA compliance are available from the ADA Technical Assistance Center at 800-949-4232 or from the U.S. Department of Justice at 800-514-0301 or **www.usdoj.gov/crt/ada**.)

(Ed. Note: More information on showers can be found in Chapter 14, "Plumbing.")

Roll-in Showers for ADA Compliance

Industry Standards

Means ADA Compliance Pricing Guide
(R.S. Means Co., Inc.)

ADAAG Reference Number: 4.21 Shower Stalls
Where Applicable
Accessible public bathing facility.

Design Requirements
- On accessible route.
- No lip at entry.
- 36" x 60" clear floor space in front, 33" to 36" a.f.f., 1-1/4" to 1-1/2" in diameter, 1-1/2" from wall, on side and rear walls.
- Shower head adjustable and hand held with flexible hose at least 60" long on rear wall, 27" maximum from corner.
- Accessible controls, 48" a.f.f. maximum.

Design Suggestions
Recessing the floor pan below floor level allows for smooth roll-in. This can be very difficult as a retrofit, but is easier to do in new construction, since it requires strengthening the existing floor structure.

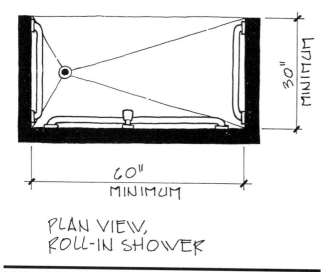

PLAN VIEW,
ROLL-IN SHOWER

R.S. Means Co., Inc., *Means ADA Compliance Pricing Guide*

Figure 13.1

Grab Bars for ADA Compliance

ADAAG Reference Numbers

4.26 Handrails, Grab Bars, and Tub and Shower Seats
4.16 Water Closets
4.17 Toilet Stalls
4.20 Bathtubs
4.21 Shower Stalls

Where Applicable:

All accessible toilets, tubs, and showers.

Design Requirements

- 1-1/4" to 1-1/2" diameter, 1-1/2" from wall.

- Capable of resisting 250 lbs. of force (as specified in 4.26.3).

- For toilet stalls, 33" to 36" a.f.f., 36" long on rear wall, 12" from corner; 42" long on side wall, 12" from corner. In 36" wide stalls, two 42" long grab bars on either side. *(See illustrations in ADAAG Sections 4.17, 4.20, and 4.21 for exact configurations.)*

- In roll-in showers:

    a. in 36" x 36" stalls, grab bars on side wall and wall opposite seat.

    b. in 30" x 60" stall, on both side wall and rear wall.

- In tubs:

    a. For 60" tub with in-tub seat: two grab bars on rear wall, 24" long, top bar 33" to 36" a.f.f., bottom 9" above rim of tub. One 24" grab bar on side wall; one 12" grab bar on side wall opposite controls.

    b. For 60" tub with in-tub seat: two grab bars on rear wall, 48" long for tub with end seat, top bar 33" to 36" a.f.f., bottom 9" above rim of tub. One 24" long grab bar on side wall with controls.

Design Suggestions

Textured grab bars provide a better gripping surface than smooth bars. If studs or blocking are insufficient or difficult to locate in a remodeling project, it might be possible to attach a painted wood 1 x 6 on the face of the wall to the studs, and attach the grab bar to that. In tight spaces, a fold-down grab bar allows flexibility in use, but only in addition to the required fixed grab bars. Grab bars are vital for safety, however, and it should be determined that any grab bar or installation method meets the strength requirements in ADAAG 4.26.3.

Comments

Even if grab bars are not necessary for the current or anticipated owners of a new or remodeled home, installation of blocking (reinforcement) in bathroom walls can still be a good idea in new construction, in the event there is a future need to add grab bars.

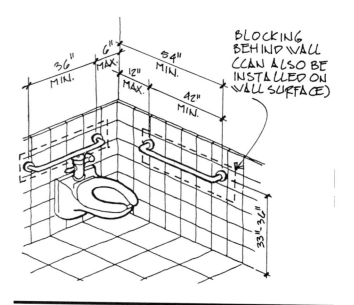

R.S. Means Co., Inc., *Means ADA Compliance Pricing Guide*

Figure 13.2

Medicine Cabinets

Comments

Medicine cabinets can be recessed or surface-mounted. The top of the cabinet is usually 6' above the finished floor (and the bottom no higher than 40" for public access bathrooms), although the height can be adjusted to the requirements of individual homeowners. (Mirrors in public access bathrooms can be 48" high maximum, if tilted.) Surface-mounted cabinets should be attached (with a minimum of two screws, near each edge of the cabinet) to the wall studs. Some cabinets fit between two studs, in which case head and sill blocking is installed with L-clips. If the studs are not lined up with the desired location of the medicine cabinet, some studs will have to be cut, and new ones added. The cabinet is attached at its sides, with screws through the sides and into the studs.

Towel Bars, Dispensers and Storage

Comments

According to the standards for universal access in NKBA's Kitchen & Bathroom Installation Manual, Volume 1, there should be a minimum of 16" clearance from the centerline of the toilet or bidet to any obstruction. The toilet paper holder should be 26" above the floor, within reach of a person seated on the toilet.

Storage of toiletries and general bathroom supplies should be provided at a height in the range of 15"-48" above the floor.

The height of towel bars is generally in the range of 34"-48". This decision may be affected by the wall finishes and owner's preference. (For example, if the brackets are to be a ceramic material incorporated into a tiled wall, the height of the tile will affect the placement.)

Toilet Room Dispensers for ADA Compliance

Industry Standards

Means ADA Compliance Pricing Guide
(R.S. Means Co., Inc.)

ADAAG Reference Numbers
4.27 Controls and Operating Mechanisms

Where Applicable
At least one of each type of dispenser must be accessible in accessible public toilet rooms.

Design Requirements
- Dispensers to be on an accessible route.
- Dispensers to be within reach range 48" for front reach, 54" for side reach.
- Controls must be accessible (operable with a closed fist).
- 30" x 48" clear floor space in front of dispensers.

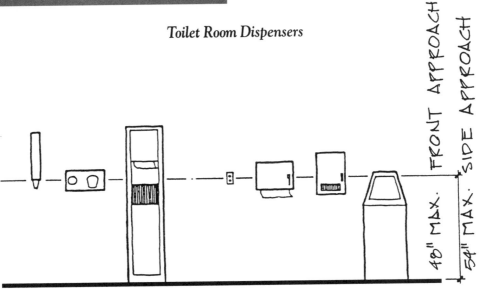

Toilet Room Dispensers

Design Suggestions

Specify dispensers with easy-to-operate controls. Locate all dispensers as close as possible to accessible fixtures (but still within easy reach) and at least 18" from an inside corner.

Toilet Partitions

Comments

Toilet partitions are available in a variety of installation configurations. The methods of vertical support include ceiling-hung, floor-anchored, overhead-braced, and floor-to-ceiling anchored.

The economy grade partitions are composed of particleboard with steel frame supports and laminated with plastic laminate. In wet applications or where a premium grade is desired, there are other options, such as a solid phenolic core with laminate cover or high density polyethylene.

Also available is a fiberglass-reinforced panel (FRP) in lieu of plastic laminate. The advantage of the FRP is that it is almost vandal-proof. The surface is textured and discourages graffiti.

Hardware options also go from chrome-plated steel to stainless steel, depending on the intended use, with available plastic or aluminum wall brackets and plastic pilaster shoes.

The phenolic core panels have a relatively high fire rating. This is critical in fire-resistive construction, especially in medical facilities.

The Americans with Disabilities Act (ADA) requires specific dimensions between the water closet and the side walls, as well as clearance between the front of the fixture and the partition door or wall. These are considerations when ordering and installing the enclosure. Many building departments now require that a percentage of the Tenant Improvement cost be applied toward ADA compliance.

Multiple-Stall Toilet Rooms for ADA Compliance

Industry Standards

Means ADA Compliance Pricing Guide
(R.S. Means Co., Inc.)

ADAAG Reference Number: 4.22 Toilet Rooms

Where Applicable:

All public and common-use, multiple-use, toilet rooms.

Design Requirements

- Located on an accessible route.
- Accessible doors compliant with all width, hardware, pull weight, and space requirements.

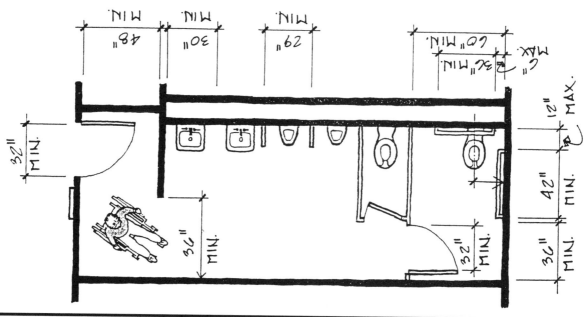

R.S. Means Co., Inc., *Means ADA Compliance Pricing Guide*

Figure 13.4

- At least one fully accessible toilet stall, 60" x 56" minimum with out-swinging door, 32" clear door opening, toilet seat 17" to 19" a.f.f., centerline 18" from wall, flush valve on open side, grab bars 33" to 36" a.f.f., 1-1/2" diameter, 1-1/2" from wall, 42" long minimum at side wall, 36" long minimum at rear wall, toilet paper dispenser below grab bar within 36" of rear wall, 19" a.f.f. minimum.

- If there are six or more stalls, one 36"-wide stall with out- swinging door and grab bars on sides of stall.

Fire Extinguishers

Comments

Fire extinguishers should, according to NKBA's Kitchen & Bathroom Installation Manual, Volume 1, be "visibly located in the kitchen, away from cooking equipment and 15" to 48" above the floor. NFPA and most building codes recommend one fire extinguisher for each 3000 sq. ft. of floor area. Smoke alarms should be included near the kitchen." In commercial projects, fire extinguisher cabinets are generally #18 gauge steel with metal, glass, wood or mirror doors. Cabinets may be surface-mounted, recessed, or semi-recessed. Residential fire extinguisher cabinets are generally 1'5" x 7'2".

Fire extinguishers themselves are classified by type of fire (e.g., Class A: fires of wood, paper, textile, rubbish; Class B: gasoline, oil, grease, fat; and Class C: electrical) and by occupancy (light hazard: schools, offices, public buildings; ordinary hazard: dry goods shops and warehouses; and extra hazard, such as paint shops).

There are maximum distances allowed between the fire extinguisher(s) and any point in the building, depending on the occupancy and use of the building. Consult your local building officials and/or fire department for more information.

Ed Note: Refer to Chapter 16, "Electrical," for more on smoke detector requirements.

Signage

Comments

Signage may be a part of light commercial projects, and is usually specified in the project documents and installed by the contractor. For public access buildings, signage must be compliant with the Americans with Disabilities Act and should be shown on the drawings where required. **ADA signage information is provided after the UBC signage requirements in this section.** *For detailed ADA requirements, review the ADA Act Guidelines, which are available from the ADA Technical Assistance Center at 800-949-4232 or the U.S. Department of Justice at 800-514-0301 or* **www.usdoj.gov/crt/ada/adahom1.htm**. *Contact the ADA Technical Assistance Center with any questions about implementing requirements of the ADA.*

Following are signage requirements from the 1997 UBC that specifically cover Exit Signs, Fire Door Signs, Maximum Room Capacity and Live Load Signs, and Marquees.

Exit Signs
UBC — 1997
1003.2.8 Means of egress identification

1003.2.8.1 General. For the purposes of Section 1003.2.8, the term "exit sign" shall mean those required signs that indicate the path of exit travel within the means of egress system.

1003.2.8.2 Where required. The path of exit travel to and within exits in a building shall be identified by exit signs conforming to the requirements of Section 1003.2.8 Exit signs shall be readily visible from any direction of approach. Exit signs shall be located as necessary to clearly indicate the direction of egress travel. No point shall be more than 100 feet (30 480 mm) from the nearest visible sign.

Exceptions:

1. Main exterior doors that obviously and clearly are identifiable as exit doors need not have exit signs when approved by the building official.

2. Rooms or areas that require only one exit or exit access.

3. In Group R, Division 3 Occupancies and within individual units of Group R, Division 1 Occupancies.

4. Exits or exit access from rooms or areas with an occupant load of less than 50 where located within a Group 1, Division 1.1, 1.2 or 2 Occupancy or a Group E, Division 3 day-care occupancy.

1003.2.8.3 Graphics. The color and design of lettering, arrows and other symbols on exit signs shall be in high contrast with their background. Exit signs shall have the word "EXIT" on the sign in block capital letters not less than 6 inches (152 mm) in height with a stroke of not less than 3/4 inch (19 mm). The word "EXIT" shall have letters having a width of not less than 2 inches (51 mm) except for the letter "I" and a minimum spacing between letters of not less than 3/8 inch (9.5 mm). Signs with lettering larger than the minimum dimensions established herein shall have the letter width, stroke and spacing in proportion to their height.

1003.2.8.4 Illumination. Exit signs shall be internally or externally illuminated. When the face of an exit sign is illuminated from an external source, it shall have an intensity of not less than 5 footcandles (54 1x) from either of two electric lamps. Internally illuminated signs shall provide equivalent luminance and be listed for the purpose.

Exception: Approved self-luminous signs that provide evenly illuminated letters that have a minimum luminance of 0.06 foot lambert (0.21 cd/m²).

1003.2.8.5 Power source. All exit signs shall be illuminated at all times. To ensure continued illumination for a duration of not less than 1-1/2 hours in case of primary power loss, the exit signs shall also be connected to an emergency electrical system provided from storage batteries, unit equipment or an on-site generator set, and the system shall be installed in accordance with the Electrical Code. For high-rise buildings, see Section 403.

Exception: Approved self-luminous signs that provide continuous illumination independent of an external power source.

1003.2.9 Means of egress illumination.
1003.2.9.1. General. Any time a building is occupied, the means of egress shall be illuminated at an intensity of not less than 1 footcandle (10.76 1x) at the floor level.

Exceptions:

1. In Group R, Division 3 Occupancies and within individual units of Group R, Division Occupancies.

2. In auditoriums, theaters, concert or opera halls, and similar assembly uses, the illumination at the floor level may be reduced during performances to not less than 0.2 footcandle (2.15 1x), provided that the required illumination be automatically restored upon activation of a premise's fire alarm system when such system is provided.

1003.2.9.2 Power supply. The power supply for means of egress illumination shall normally be provided by the premises' electrical supply. In the event of its failure, illumination shall be automatically provided from an emergency system for Group I, Divisions 1.1 and 1.2 Occupancies and for all other occupancies where the means of egress system serves an occupant load of 100 or more. Such emergency systems shall be installed in accordance with the Electrical Code.

Fire Door Signs
UBC — 1997

713.13 Signs When required by the building official, a sign shall be displayed permanently near or on each required fire door in letters not less than 1 inch (25 mm) high to read as follows:

**FIRE DOOR
DO NOT OBSTRUCT**

Maximum Room Capacity Signs
UBC — 1997

1007.2.6 Posting of room capacity. Any room that is used for an assembly purpose where fixed seats are not installed shall have the capacity of the room posted in a conspicuous place on an approved sign near the main exit or exit-access doorway from the room. Such signs shall indicate the number of occupants permitted for each room use.

Live Load Signs
UBC — 1997
Section 1607 — Live Loads

1607.3.5 Live loads posted. The live loads for which each floor or portion thereof of a commercial or industrial building is or has been designed shall have such design live loads conspicuously posted by the owner in that part of each story in which they apply, using durable metal signs, and it shall be unlawful to remove or deface such notices. The occupant of the building shall be responsible for keeping the actual load below the allowable limits.

Ed. Note: Live load signage requirements differ in various regions. Check your local building code.

Marquees
UBC — 1997

3205.1 General. For the purpose of this section, a marquee shall include any object or decoration attached to a part of said marquee.

Projection and Clearance. The horizontal clearance between a marquee and the curb line shall not be less than 2 feet (610 mm).

A marquee projecting more than two thirds of the distance from the property line to the curb line shall not be less than 12 feet (3658 mm) above the ground or pavement below.

A marquee projection less than two thirds of the distance from the property line to the curb line shall not exceed 25 feet (7620 mm) in length along the direction of the street.

Length. A marquee projecting more than two thirds of the distance from the property line to the curb line shall not exceed 25 feet (7620 mm) in length along the direction of the street.

Thickness. The maximum height or thickness of a marquee measured vertically from its lowest to its highest point shall not exceed 3 feet (914 mm) when the marquee projects more than two thirds of the distance from the property line to the curb line and shall not exceed 9 feet (2743 mm) when the marquee is less than two thirds of the distance from the property line to the curb line.

Construction. A marquee shall be supported entirely by the building and constructed of noncombustible material or, when supported by a building of Type V construction, may be of one-hour fire-resistive construction.

Roof Construction. The roof or any part thereof may be a skylight, provided glass skylights are of laminated or wired glass complying with Section 2409. Plastic skylights shall comply with Section 2603.7.

Every roof and skylight of a marquee shall be sloped to downspouts that shall conduct any drainage from the marquee under the sidewalk to the curb.

3205.7 Location Prohibited. Every marquee shall be so located as not to interfere with the operation of any exterior standpipe or to obstruct the clear passage of a means of egress from the building or the installation or maintenance of electroliers.

Signage for ADA Compliance
Industry Standards
Means ADA Compliance Pricing Guide
(R. S. Means Co., Inc.)

ADAAG Reference Number: 4.30 Signage
Where Applicable

Signs are required at all entrances and rest rooms when not all are accessible, and at parking spaces, volume control telephones, text telephones, and assistive listening systems. Any signs designating permanent spaces (such as room numbers, exit signs, and bathroom designations) must have tactile and Braille lettering and be mounted at the door. If provided, signage conveying directions to a facility and information about spaces inside must comply with ADA requirements for contrast, character height, font, and proportion. Temporary signage, such as building directories and menus, is not required to comply.

Design Requirements
For all permanent signs:

- High contrast between characters/pictures and background (dark on light, or light on dark).
- Simple-serif or sans-serif font.
- Matte or other non-reflective surface.
- Character width-to-height ratio between 3:5 and 1:1.
- Stroke width-to-height ratio between 1:5 and 1:10.
- Overhead signs that are above 80" a.f.f. must have letters no less than 3" high.
- International symbol of accessibility at entrances if all are not accessible, with directions to the nearest accessible entrance; similar for rest rooms. All symbols pictograms to have 6" border height minimum (no size requirement for the symbol itself).

For signs at permanently identified rooms and spaces:

- Characters raised at least 1/32", with upper case characters 5/8" to 2" high.
- Grade II Braille (an abbreviated version).
- Signs to be located on wall adjacent to the door, on the latch side, 60" a.f.f. A person must be able to approach within 3" of the sign.

Design Suggestions

Regarding contrast, evidence suggests that light characters on a dark background are more easily read. Since there is no firm definition of high contrast, choose colors that leave as little doubt as possible, e.g., white characters on a red background. Although room signs have been customarily placed on doors, this practice is not effective for people who must read the sign by touch or be able to approach within inches of the sign to see letters. If a sign exists on a door, keeping it and adding an accessible sign adjacent to the door can be effective for both groups of users. Raised characters and Braille are not required for informational or directional signs, but if possible, some method of wayfinding should be provided for people with severe visual impairments, such as audible signs at decision points or information booths. Temporary signs (e.g., menus or prices) are not required to comply with ADA Standards, but the *effective communications* requirement of ADA does require some method of conveying the information, such as a Braille menu or having the choices read to a customer. The Appendix of ADAAG provides some very useful information on making signage as helpful as possible.

De-mountable or Movable Partitions

Comments

Movable partitions, often called "operable" panels or partitions, are manufactured by office furniture and specialties companies, and are usually installed (and serviced) by those firms. De-mountable partitions are used for applications such as in-plant offices, security stations and guardhouses, smoking enclosures, reception areas, hotel meeting rooms, computer and other workstations, additional/flexible office areas, mini storage buildings, and convention halls.

Partitions are available in full and partial height in a variety of finishes including vinyl-clad, gypsum panels, and fabric, in a choice of colors. They can be obtained in styles without visible fasteners for visual continuity. Some manufacturers offer wall units that incorporate power, voice and data wiring to simplify future reconfigurations of office space.

Movable walls often have available glazing, which allows light and aesthetic benefits, while providing the function of a separate area. De-mountable partitions are fire-rated, and also must meet seismic and sound control requirements per local building code.

UBC — 1997

601.5.3 Folding, portable or movable partitions. Approved folding, portable or movable partitions need not have a fire-resistive rating, provided:

1. They do not block required exits or exit-access doors (without providing alternative conforming exits or exit-access doors) and they do not establish a corridor.

2. Their location is restricted by means of permanent tracks, guides or other approved methods.

3. Flammability shall be limited to materials having a flame-spread classification as set forth in Table 8-B for rooms or areas.

Comments

While de-mountable partitions are usually installed by the manufacturer or distributor, the following guidelines may be helpful in ensuring a quality installation.

- *Finishes must be correct as specified, and shading of fabric or other finish should match between panels.*

- *Existing finishes in surrounding space should be protected during the installation of de-mountable partition walls.*

- *De-mountable partitions should not be fastened to ceiling or floors at any point.*

- *Wands used to connect to a power source in the ceiling should be carefully anchored.*

- *Associated cabinetry and countertops should be level and have no scratches or other damage to finishes.*

Lockers

Comments

Lockers are manufactured by specialty companies, which usually offer installation if the contractor will not be responsible for this item. Lockers are available in institutional and deluxe sports club models, single-, double- and multi-tier, and with double doors for limited swing space. The contractor on a project involving lockers will be concerned with preparation of the area where the lockers will be installed. This may involve installation of concrete, wood or metal supports. Supports should be in alignment with the project design requirements for the locker installation. All edges and exposed surfaces, including end units, should be finished, with no defects such as scratches or chips in the finish. Doors and hardware should operate freely, without chafing or binding. There should be no obstructions in the free swing of the locker doors (90 degrees). Consideration should be made for space allowance between benches and open locker doors.

Prefabricated Fireplaces

Comments

Prefabricated fireplaces are available from specialty woodstove and fireplace distributors. They can be installed by the distributor or by the general contractor, according to the manufacturer's instructions and with manufacturer-supplied or recommended fireplace and chimney materials. These units are available in gas, woodburning or wood pellet-burning varieties, as well as gas log-type heaters that resemble fireplaces. They can be purchased with various masonry facings including stone, brick, marble, and tile, and with prefabricated wood mantles and surrounds.

Defects related to fireplaces usually involve the ability of the fireplace to draw and exhaust smoke properly. In addition to correct installation, proper fireplace function is influenced by flue size, number of bends, height of discharge in relationship to roof lines, and prevailing winds.

See **Figures 13.5** *and* **13.6** *for masonry and concrete chimney construction, clearance and termination requirements, and correct flue sizes for the chimney height and fireplace opening area.*

Construction, Clearance and Termination Requirements for Masonry and Concrete Chimneys

CHIMNEYS SERVING	THICKNESS (min. inches) × 25.4 for mm		HEIGHT ABOVE ROOF OPENING (feet) × 304.8 for mm	HEIGHT ABOVE ANY PART OF BUILDING WITHIN (feet) × 304.8 for mm			CLEARANCE TO COMBUSTIBLE CONSTRUCTION (inches) × 25.4 for mm	
	Walls	Lining		10	25	50	Int. Inst.	Ext. Inst.
1. **RESIDENTIAL-TYPE APPLIANCES**[1,2] (Low Btu input) Clay, shale or concrete brick Reinforced concrete Hollow masonry units Stone	4[3] 4[3] 4[4] 12	$5/8$ fire-clay tile or 2 firebrick	2	2			2	1 or $1/2$ gypsum[5]
Unburned clay units	8	$4^1/_2$ firebrick						
2. **BUILDING HEATING AND INDUSTRIAL-TYPE LOW-HEAT APPLIANCES**[1,2] [1,000°F (538°C) operating temp.—1,400°F (760°C) maximum] Clay, shale or concrete brick Hollow masonry units Reinforced concrete Stone	8 8[4] 8 12	$5/8$ fire-clay tile or 2 firebrick	3	2			2	2
3. **MEDIUM-HEAT INDUSTRIAL-TYPE APPLIANCES**[1,6] [2,000°F (1093°C) maximum] Clay, shale or concrete brick Hollow masonry units (Grouted solid) Reinforced concrete Stone	8 8 8 12	$4^1/_2$ medium-duty firebrick	10		10		4	4
4. **HIGH-HEAT INDUSTRIAL-TYPE APPLIANCES**[1,6] [Over 2,000°F (1093°C)] Clay, shale or concrete brick Hollow masonry units (Grouted solid) Reinforced concrete	16[7] 16[7] 16[7]	$4^1/_2$ high-duty firebrick	20			20	8	8
5. **RESIDENTIAL-TYPE INCINERATORS** Same as for residential-type appliances as shown above.								
6. **CHUTE-FED AND FLUE-FED INCINERATORS WITH COMBINED HEARTH AND GRATE AREA 7 SQ. FT. (0.65 m[2]) OR LESS** Clay, shale or concrete brick or hollow units Portion extending to 10 ft. (3048 mm) above combustion chamber roof Portion more than 10 ft. (3048 mm) above combustion chamber roof	4 8	$4^1/_2$ medium-duty firebrick $5/8$ fire-clay tile liner	3	2			2	2
7. **CHUTE-FED AND FLUE-FED INCINERATORS—COMBINED HEARTH AND GRATE AREAS LARGER THAN 7 SQ. FT. (0.65 m[2])** Clay, shale or concrete brick or hollow units grouted solid or reinforced concrete Portion extending to 40 ft. (12 192 mm) above combustion chamber roof Portion more than 40 ft. (12 192 mm) above combustion chamber roof Reinforced concrete	4 8 8	$4^1/_2$ medium-duty firebrick $5/8$ fire-clay tile liner $4^1/_2$ medium-duty firebrick laid in medium-duty refract mortar			10		2	2
8. **COMMERCIAL OR INDUSTRIAL-TYPE INCINERATORS**[2] Clay or shale solid brick Reinforced concrete	8 8	$4^1/_2$ medium-duty firebrick laid in medium-duty refract mortar			10		4	4

[1]See Table 8-B of the Mechanical Code for types of appliances allowed with each type of chimney.
[2]Lining shall extend from bottom to top of chimney.
[3]Chimneys having walls 8 inches (203 mm) or more in thickness may be unlined.
[4]Equivalent thickness including grouted cells when grouted solid. The equivalent thickness may also include the grout thickness between the liner and masonry unit.
[5]Chimneys for residential-type appliances installed entirely on the exterior of the building. For fireplace and barbecue chimneys, see Section 3102.7.8.
[6]Lining to extend from 24 inches (610 mm) below connector to 25 feet (7620 mm) above.
[7]Two 8-inch (203 mm) walls with 2-inch (51 mm) airspace between walls. Outer and inner walls may be of solid masonry units or reinforced concrete or any combination thereof.
[8]Clearance shall be approved by the building official and shall be such that the temperature of combustible materials will not exceed 160°F (710°C).

Courtesy of ICBO, UBC — 1997 [Table 31-B]

Figure 13.5

Flue Sizes for Masonry Chimneys[1]

MINIMUM CROSS-SECTIONAL
FLUE AREA (SQ. IN.)

ROUND FLUES	SQUARE OR RECTANGULAR FLUES
NOMINAL FLUE SIZE DIAMETER, IN.	NOMINAL FLUE SIZE, IN.

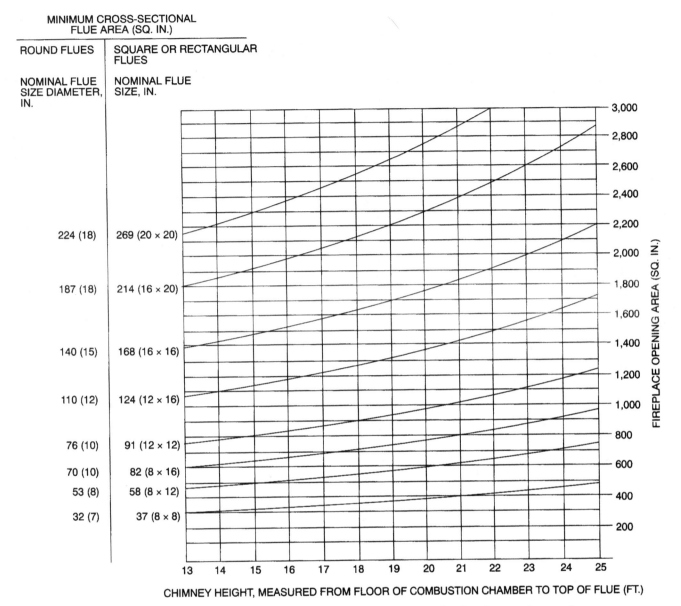

224 (18)	269 (20 × 20)
187 (18)	214 (16 × 20)
140 (15)	168 (16 × 16)
110 (12)	124 (12 × 16)
76 (10)	91 (12 × 12)
70 (10)	82 (8 × 16)
53 (8)	58 (8 × 12)
32 (7)	37 (8 × 8)

CHIMNEY HEIGHT, MEASURED FROM FLOOR OF COMBUSTION CHAMBER TO TOP OF FLUE (FT.)

FIREPLACE OPENING AREA (SQ. IN.)

[1]The smaller flue area shall be utilized where the fireplace opening area and the chimney height selected intersect between flue area curves.

For **SI:** 1 inch = 25.4 mm, 1 square inch = 654.16 mm^2, 1 foot = 304.8 mm.

Courtesy of ICBO, *UBC* — *1997* [Figure 31-1]

Figure 13.6

Cupolas and Flagpoles

Comments

Cupolas can be used as part of the calculation for venting attic space, or they can be nonfunctioning and purely decorative. If functional, cupolas must be flashed properly. Cupolas are often available at lumberyards, but can also be purchased in special and custom designs from firms that manufacture architectural sheet metal products and other specialties. Cupolas are generally made of cedar, redwood or unfinished or painted pine, and may have copper roofs. They may come with skirt flashing and a roof template to help the contractor with the installation. The 1997 UBC contains no requirements for cupolas.

The only UBC reference to flagpoles is in the Penthouses and Roof Structures section (1511). It states that the height and other restrictions of the section "shall not prohibit the placing of wood flagpoles or similar structures on the roof of any building."

Flagpoles are also manufactured by specialty companies for attachment to buildings or installation on the ground. Flagpoles can be fiberglass, aluminum, steel or bronze. Electrical models offer remote switches and self-storing operation. Installation should be performed in accordance with manufacturers' instructions. Some basic guidelines follow:

Flagpoles on roofs can be braced several different ways: corner brace, side brace, three-legged tripod type brace, or four-legged brace. The flag length should be roughly one third the length of the pole.

Flagpoles set in the ground are usually embedded in concrete topped with dry sand, with a metal collar and caulking at the ground level. Lightning protection is embedded in the ground beneath the flagpole's foundation. The length of pole below the ground is typically 10% of the pole height. The flag length should be approximately one-fourth of the flag pole height.

Outrigger flagpoles (for building fronts) are normally at a 45° or more angle. If the pole is longer than 13', bracing is required. The flag width should be roughly 3/8-1/2 the length of the outrigger flagpole.

Ed. Note: Architectural Graphic Standards, published by John Wiley & Sons, Inc., contains further information and illustrations on flagpole heights, sizes and placements.

CHAPTER
14 PLUMBING

Table of Contents

(continued on next page)

Text in blue print indicates excerpts from model building code(s). "Comments" (in solid blue boxes) were written by the editors, based on their own experience.

For building product information, use this book's special Internet gateway to thousands of manufacturers: www.rsmeans.com/prodsupp/rlstand.html

CHAPTER
14 PLUMBING

Common Defect Allegations

Potential defects in plumbing work can be extensive and corrections costly. The following items are often topics of defect claims.

- *Insufficient slope in the sewer system can cause the system to back up. Proper flushing of the new low-flow toilets is affected by improper pipe pitch. The flow line needs 1/4" per foot of fall. Pipe should be set on sand beds properly prepared to achieve correct drainage after soil settlement. If the base soil is uncompacted, when the upper backfill is compacted, the pipe will settle improperly and takes some negative flow. Investigators often run cameras down the pipe and show video tapes of the solids accumulation in the flat areas.*

- *Water heaters may not be properly strapped in in seismic zones.*

- *Combustion air vents above water heaters should be sloped; failure to do so constitutes a defect.*

- *Hot water lines should be insulated, but we find that oftentimes they are not or are only partially insulated.*

- *"Water hammer" occurs when you shut off the faucet suddenly and hear a clunk from the pipe reaction. Installing a water hammer arrester on each line will absorb the shock.*

- *There have been many recent claims of galvanic action on circulating hot water systems, as the number of installations to loop the water system for instant hot water increases. There are two types of water line damage on circulating systems. One is from having too large a pump where the particulates in the water wear out the insides of the fittings. The other is from galvanic action where there is a microcurrent of electricity that is actually taking particulates from the hot water pipe underground and moving them to the cold water pipe. This can result in green fuzzy growth around the valves serving the system. There are different theories on the best way to prevent this action. It is suggested that dielectric fittings will solve the problem, others say that a zinc block will save the copper, allowing the zinc to fill this action. It is generally agreed that the copper should be wrapped, not just through the concrete, but through the entire burial run under soil.*

- *Second-story noise through the ceiling of the first floor when toilets are flushed is a common complaint, particularly when PVC is used instead of cast iron pipe. Cast iron, no-hub pipes in that area will help to reduce this noise substantially. Offsetting the vertical line in the wall slightly will cause the flow to swirl as opposed to dropping. See the "Soundproofing" section in Chapter 7 for framing and insulation approaches to the plumbing noise problem.*

- *Undersized pipes are a defect and can cause problems such as backed-up sewer pipes, unacceptably low volume of water from faucets or showers, and inadequate volume for outdoor sprinklers.*

- *Other complaints include garbage disposals that failed after 8 years, chips in enamel sinks, and deteriorated faucet finishes. Most of these items relate to the product manufacturer's warranty, rather than any defect in installation.*

Introduction

While there are usually no written specifications or detailed drawings prepared for the plumbing systems of individual homes, light commercial installations typically have plans and specifications for the plumbing incorporated into the general bid or construction documents. Whether or not such documents are available at bidding time, it is understood that the installation will have to be governed by local and/or national plumbing codes.

Plumbing codes regulate the minimum number of fixtures based on use of the building and anticipated number of occupants. Codes further regulate the potable water supply and distribution, and the collection and disposal of sanitary waste and waste water. Other code regulated items might be special laboratory wastes, gray water systems, gas piping, and fire protection systems.

There are several national plumbing codes, including the *Uniform Plumbing Code*, the *Standard Plumbing Code*, and the *International Plumbing Code*. Plumbing code requirements are also included in the major regional building codes — BOCA, SBCCI, ICBO, and the *International One- and Two-Family Dwelling Code* (IOTFDC), formerly CABO. (The UBC references the *International Plumbing Code*, which was developed by a committee appointed by and consisting of representatives of BOCA, ICBO, and SBCCI, using the code format established by CABO.) There are many similarities in the requirements of these codes; all are concerned with the protection of public health, safety and welfare.

This chapter includes excerpts from major regional building codes. Because plumbing codes tend to be difficult to read and decipher, some IOTFDC excerpts (themselves based on other national codes) are provided because they state requirements in a simpler way. Note that as of November 1997, the International Code Council (ICC) assumed responsibility for the development and maintenance of the *International One- and Two-Family Dwelling Code* (IOTFDC), formerly CABO.

Most states have adopted one of the major codes mentioned above and the choice of codes seems to be in large part by region of the country. All of the western states from Montana south to New Mexico and across to the West Coast have adopted the *Uniform Plumbing Code*, with the exception of Utah. Iowa, however, decided to go with the western states. Utah along with most of the Northeast, Midwest, Oklahoma, and Kansas have adopted the *International Plumbing Code*. The South, from North Carolina west to Arkansas and Texas and south along the coast, have all chosen the *Standard Plumbing Code* (an SBCCI version of the *International Plumbing Code*). North and South Dakota, New Jersey and Maryland have all selected the *National Standard Plumbing Code*. Nebraska is alone in adopting the *A40 1993 Safety Standard for Plumbing*. Kentucky, Wisconsin, Minnesota, and Massachusetts have currently not chosen a national code.

Several states, such as Massachusetts, have developed their own more stringent codes. Many cities have their own specific code requirements as well. Code information in this chapter, as in Chapter 15, "HVAC," is included for easy reference to common defect problems, but it is not intended to replace your local code. For instance, it is important to determine approval and installation requirements for CPVC hot and cold water distribution systems from the appropriate local authority. Anyone who performs installations of plumbing must be qualified, experienced, licensed (in many locations) and have a full knowledge of the prevailing code and practices for their locale.

Following is a list of resources that can provide further information on plumbing codes and industry standards.

International Association of Plumbing and Mechanical Officials (IAPMO)

20001 East Walnut Drive South
Walnut, CA 91789
Telephone: 909-595-8449
www.iapmo.org
Note: The *Uniform Plumbing Code* is available from this organization.

Plumbing · Heating · Cooling · Contractors National Association (PHCC-NA)
180 South Washington St.
P.O. Box 6808
Falls Church, VA 22046
Telephone: 703-237-8100
www.naphcc.org
Note: The *National Standard Plumbing Code* is available from this organization.

National Fire Protection Association (NFPA)
1 Batterymarch Park
Quincy, MA 02269
Telephone: 617-770-3000
www.nfpa.org

American Fire Sprinkler Association (AFSA)
1259 Jupiter Road, Suite 142
Dallas, TX 75238-3200
Telephone: 214-349-5965
The American Fire Sprinkler Association is a non-profit international organization offering educational and technical information on sprinklers, and representing open shop fire sprinkler contractors.

National Fire Sprinkler Association (NFSA)
P.O. Box 1000
Patterson, NY 12563
Telephone: 914-878-4200
The National Fire Sprinkler Association promotes the use of sprinklers and offers educational opportunities and technical advice. It is also involved with labor relations for sprinkler fitters.

Note: The *International Plumbing Code* is jointly copyrighted by and available through the International Code Council, Inc. (ICC), the Building Officials and Code Administrators International, Inc. (BOCA), the International Conference of Building Officials (ICBO), and the Southern Building Code Congress International, Inc. (SBCCI).

The BOCA *National Plumbing Code* is available from BOCA.

The *Standard Plumbing Code* is available from the Southern Building Code Congress International, Inc. (SBCCI).

(See "Understanding Building Codes & Other Standards" at the beginning of this book for information on contacting these organizations.)

Ed. Note: Comments and recommendations within this chapter are not intended as a definitive resource for construction activities. For building projects, contractors must rely on the project documents and any applicable code requirements pertaining to their own particular locations.

General Installation Requirements

Comments

*Residential hot and cold water systems typically include water distribution piping, fittings, control valves, boilers and/or hot water heaters, and pumps. The cold water supply begins once it enters the building, typically through a water meter. The hot water supply system starts at the hot water generating equipment. The distribution system then delivers **potable water** throughout the building. Potable water is suitable for human consumption and free of impurities that may cause disease. The following codes regulate the minimum number of plumbing fixtures required based on use and building occupancy. They also regulate the potable water supply and its distribution, as well as the collection and disposal of sanitary waste and waste water.*

International One- and Two-Family Dwelling Code (IOTFDC) — 1998

Copyright 1998, International Code Council, Inc. — *International One- and Two-Family Dwelling Code*, 5203 Leesburg Pike, Suite 708, Falls Church, Virginia 22041.

3102.1 General. The water-distribution and drainage system of any building or premises where plumbing fixtures are installed shall be connected to a public water-supply or sewer system, respectively, if available. When either a public water-supply or sewer system, or both, are not available, or connection thereto is not feasible, an individual water-supply or individual (private) sewage-disposal system, or both, shall be provided.

3103.1 General. In the process of installing or repairing any part of a plumbing and drainage installation, the finished floors, walls, ceilings, tile work or any other part of the building or premises which must be changed or replaced shall be left in a safe structural condition in accordance with the requirements of the building portion of this code.

3103.2 Drilling and notching. Wood-framed structural members shall not be drilled, notched or altered in any manner except as provided in Sections 502.6, 602.6, and 802.6. Holes in cold-formed steel-framed load-bearing members shall only be permitted in accordance with Sections 506.2, 603.2 and 804.2. In accordance with Sections 506.3.5, 603.3.4 and 804.3.5, cutting and notching of flanges and lips of cold-formed steel-framed load-bearing members shall not be permitted.

3103.3 Breakage and protection. Pipes passing under or through walls shall be protected from breakage. Pipes passing through or under cinder, concrete, cold-formed steel framing or other corrosive material shall be protected against external corrosion by protective coating, wrapping, grommets or other means which prevent such corrosion.

3103.4 Sleeves. Annular spaces between sleeves and pipes shall be filled or tightly caulked as approved by the building official. Annular spaces between sleeves and pipes in fire-rated assemblies shall be filled or tightly caulked in accordance with Chapters 2 through 10.

3103.5 Pipes through footings or foundation walls. A soil or waste pipe, or building drain passing under a footing or through a foundation wall shall be provided with a relieving arch; or there shall be built into the masonry wall an iron pipe sleeve two pipe sizes greater than the pipe passing through as approved by the building official.

3103.6 Freezing. Water, soil or waste pipe shall not be installed outside of a building or in an exterior wall unless adequate provision is made to protect such pipe from freezing.

3103.7 Depth. Piping installed deeper than and parallel to footings or load-bearing walls shall be 45 degrees (0.79 rad) therefrom.

3104.1 Trenching and bedding. Piping shall be installed in trenches so that it rests on a solid and continuous bearing surface. When overexcavated, the trench shall be backfilled to the proper grade with compacted earth, sand, fine gravel or similar granular material. Piping may not be supported on rocks or blocks at any point. Rocky or unstable soil shall be overexcavated by two or more pipe diameters and brought to the proper grade with suitable compacted granular material.

Uniform Plumbing Code — 1997

609.1 Installation. All water piping shall be adequately supported to the satisfaction of the Administrative Authority. Burred ends shall be reamed to the full bore of the pipe or tube. Changes in direction shall be made by the appropriate use of fittings, except that changes in direction in copper tubing may be made with bends, provided that such bends are made with bending equipment which does not deform or create a loss in the cross-sectional area of the tubing. Provisions shall be made for expansion in hot water piping. All piping, equipment, appurtenances, and devices shall be installed in a workmanlike manner in conformity with the provisions and intent of the Code. All water service yard piping shall be at least twelve (12) inches (305 mm) below the average local frost depth. The minimum cover shall be twelve (12) inches (305 mm) below finish grade.

609.2 Water pipes shall not be run or laid in the same trench as building sewer or drainage piping constructed of clay or materials which are not approved for use within a building unless both of the following conditions are met:

609.2.1 The bottom of the water pipe, at all points, shall be at least twelve (12) inches (305 mm) above the top of the sewer or drain line.

609.2.2 The water pipe shall be placed on a solid shelf excavated at one side of the common trench with a minimum clear horizontal distance of at least twelve (12) inches (305 mm) from the sewer or drain line.

Water pipes crossing sewer or drainage piping constructed of clay or materials which are not approved for use within a building shall be laid a minimum of twelve (12) inches (305 mm) above the sewer or drain pipe.

609.3 Water piping installed within a building and in or under a concrete floor slab resting on the ground shall be installed in accordance with the following requirements:

609.3.1 Ferrous piping shall have a protective coating of an approved type, machine applied and conforming to recognized standards. Field wrapping shall provide equivalent protection and is restricted to those short sections and fittings necessarily stripped for threading. Zinc coating (galvanizing) shall not be deemed adequate protection for piping or fittings.

Approved non-ferrous piping need not be wrapped.

609.3.2 Copper tubing shall be installed without joints where possible. Where joints are permitted, they shall be brazed and fittings shall be wrought copper.

720.0 Sewer and Water Pipes. Building sewers or drainage piping of clay or materials which are not approved for use within a building shall not be run or laid in the same trench as the water pipes unless both of the following requirements are met:

(1) The bottom of the water pipe, at all points, shall be at least twelve (12) inches (305 mm) above the top of the sewer or drain line.

(2) The water pipe shall be placed on a solid shelf excavated at one side of the common trench with a minimum clear horizontal distance of at least twelve (12) inches (305 mm) from the sewer or drain line.

Water pipes crossing sewer or drainage piping constructed of clay or materials which are not approved for use within a building shall be laid a minimum of twelve (12) inches (305 mm) above that sewer or drain pipe.

International Plumbing Code — 1997

Copyright 1997, International Code Council, Inc., Falls Church, Virginia. *International Plumbing Code.* Reprinted with permission of author. All rights reserved.

704.1 Slope of horizontal drainage piping. Horizontal drainage piping shall be installed in uniform alignment at uniform slopes. The minimum slope of a horizontal drainage pipe shall be in accordance with Table 704. 1.

704.2 Change in size. The size of the drainage piping shall not be reduced in size in the direction of the flow. A 4-inch by 3-inch (102 mm by 76 mm) water closet connection shall not be considered as a reduction in size.

704.3 Connections to offsets and bases of stacks. Horizontal branches shall connect to the bases of stacks at a point located not less than 10 pipe diameters downstream from the stack.

Except as prohibited by Section 713.2, horizontal branches shall connect to horizontal stack offsets at a point located not less than 10 pipe diameters downstream from the upper stack.

704.4 Future fixtures. Drainage piping for future fixtures shall terminate with an approved cap or plug.

704.5 Dead ends. In the installation or removal of any part of a drainage system, dead ends shall be prohibited. Cleanout extensions and approved future fixture drainage piping shall not be considered as dead ends.

Pipe Support
Industry Standards
Plumbing Estimating Methods
(R.S. Means, Co., Inc.)

Pipe supports fasten and support piping systems to walls, ceilings, floor slabs, or structural members within a building. Some supports carry single pipelines, such as *band hangers, clevis hangers, single or double rod roll hangers,* and *riser clamps.* Other supports carry multiple pipe runs, such as *trapeze hangers* and *pipe racks.*

IOTFDC — 1998 (formerly CABO)
3105.1 General. Support for piping shall be provided in accordance with the following:

1. Piping shall be supported so as to ensure alignment and prevent sagging.
2. Piping in the ground shall be laid on a firm bed for its entire length, except where support is otherwise provided.
3. Hangers and anchors shall be of sufficient strength to maintain their proportional share of the weight of pipe and contents.
4. Piping shall be supported at distances not to exceed those indicated in Table 3105.1 (see **Figure 14.1**).

Piping Support

PIPE MATERIAL	MAXIMUM HORIZONTAL SPACING	MAXIMUM VERTICAL SPACING
Cast-iron soil pipe	5' except may be 10' where 10' lengths of pipe are installed.	Base and each story height but not to exceed 15'0"
Threaded-steel pipe	$^3/_4$" diameter and under—10'0" 1" diameter and over—12'0"	15'0"
Copper tube and Copper pipe	$1^1/_4$" diameter and under—6'0" $1^1/_2$" diameter and over—10'0"	Each story height but not to exceed 10'0"
Lead pipe	Continuous support	4'0"
Plastic parallel water distribution manifold bundles	4'0"	Each story height and piping shall have a midstory guide.
Plastic pipe (DWV)	4'0"	Each story height and piping shall have a midstory guide.
Plastic pipe and tube, hot- and cold-water, rigid	3'0"	Each story height and piping shall have a midstory guide.
Plastic pipe and tube, hot- and cold-water, flexible	32"	Each story height and piping shall have a midstory guide.

For SI: 1 inch = 25.4 mm, 1 foot = 304.8 mm.

Courtesy of ICC, IOTFDC — 1998 (formerly CABO) [Table 3105.1]

Figure 14.1

Uniform Plumbing Code — 1997

221.0 Supports. Supports, hangers and anchors are devices for properly supporting and securing pipe, fixtures, and equipment.

314.0 Hangers and Supports.

314.2 All piping shall be supported in such a manner as to maintain its alignment, and prevent sagging.

314.3 Piping in the ground shall be laid on a firm bed for its entire length. Where support is otherwise provided, it shall be acceptable to the Administrative Authority.

Minimum Hanger Rod Sizes

Pipe and Tube Size		Rod Size	
Inches	mm	Inches	mm
1/2 – 4	12.7 – 102	3/8	9.5
5 – 8	127 – 203	1/2	12.7
10 – 12	254 – 305	5/8	15.9

314.8 Horizontal cast iron hubless piping that exceeds four (4) feet (1219 mm) in length shall be supported on each side of the coupling within eighteen (18) inches (203 mm) of the joint.

Courtesy of IAPMO, Uniform Plumbing Code — 1997 [Table 3-1]

Figure 14.2

314.4 Hangers and anchors shall be of sufficient strength to support the weight of the pipe and its contents. Piping shall be isolated from incompatible materials.

314.5 All piping, fixtures, appliances, and appurtenances shall be adequately supported to the satisfaction of the Administrative Authority.

314.6 Hanger rod sizes shall be no smaller than those shown in Figure 14.2.

1211.8 All gas piping shall be adequately supported by metal straps or hooks at intervals not to exceed those shown in Figure 14.3. Gas piping installed below grade shall be effectively supported at all points on undisturbed or well compacted soil or sand.

International Plumbing Code — 1997

308.1 General. All plumbing piping shall be supported in accordance with this section.

308.2 Piping seismic supports. Where earthquake loads are applicable in accordance with the building code, plumbing piping supports shall be designed and installed for the seismic forces in accordance with the building code.

Minimum Support Intervals

	Size of Pipe			
	Inches	mm	Feet	mm
	1/2	12.7	6	1829
	3/4 or 1	19.1 or 25.4	8	2438
Horizontal	1-1/4 or larger	32 or larger	10	3048
Vertical	1-1/4 or larger	32 or larger	Every floor level	

Courtesy of IAPMO, Uniform Plumbing Code — 1997 [Table 12-2]

Figure 14.3

Hanger Spacing

PIPING MATERIAL	MAXIMUM HORIZONTAL SPACING (feet)	MAXIMUM VERTICAL SPACING (feet)
ABS pipe	4	4
Aluminum tubing	10	15
Brass pipe	10	10
Cast-iron pipe[a]	5	15
Copper or copper-alloy pipe	12	10
Copper or copper-alloy tubing, 1¼-inch diameter and smaller	6	10
Copper or copper-alloy tubing, 1½-inch diameter and larger	10	10
CPVC pipe or tubing, 1 inch or smaller	3	5[b]
CPVC pipe or tubing, 1¼ inches or larger	4	6[b]
Steel pipe	12	15
Lead pipe	Continuous	4
PB pipe or tubing	2⅔ (32 inches)	4
PVC pipe	4	4

For SI: 1 inch = 25.4 mm, 1 foot = 304.8 mm.

[a] The maximum horizontal spacing of cast-iron pipe hangers shall be increased to 10 feet where 10-foot lengths of pipe are installed.

[b] Mid-story guide.

Courtesy of ICC, International Plumbing Code — 1997 [Table 308.5]

Figure 14.4

308.3 Materials. Hangers, anchors and supports shall support the piping and the contents of the piping. Hangers and strapping material shall be of approved material that will not promote galvanic action.

308.4 Structural attachment. Hangers and anchors shall be attached to the building construction in an approved manner.

308.5 Interval of support. Pipe shall be supported in accordance with Figure 14.4.

Plumbing Administration and Testing

Ed. Note: Drainage, waste and vent piping (DWV) refers to the piping that routes waste to the sewer or septic system, and vents plumbing fixtures to outside air. The various waste lines contain a curved section of pipe near each fixture to trap water, and prevent odors and sewer gas from entering. Waste piping from sinks, tubs, showers, and so forth is pitched to carry the waste by gravity to the soil stack. The soil stack is a large pipe, usually located in the wall behind the toilet, that vents through the roof and brings waste to the sewer.

IOTFDC — 1998 (formerly CABO)

2903.5 DWV systems testing. Rough and finished plumbing installations shall be tested in accordance with Sections 2903.5.1 and 2903.5.2.

2903.5.1 Rough plumbing. DWV systems shall be tested on completion of the rough piping installation by water or air with no evidence of leakage. Either test shall be applied to the drainage system in its entirety or in sections after rough piping has been installed, as follows:

1. **Water Test** — Each section shall be filled with water to a point no less than 10 feet (3048 mm) above the highest fitting connection in that section, or to the highest point in the completed system. Water shall be held in the section under test for 15 minutes before inspection. The system shall prove leak free by visual inspection.

2. **Air Test** —The portion under test shall be maintained at a gage pressure of 5 pounds per square inch (psi) (34 kPa) or 10 inches mercury column (2488 Pa). This pressure shall be held without introduction of additional air for a period of 15 minutes.

2903.5.2 Finished plumbing. After the plumbing fixtures have been set and their traps filled with water, their connections shall be tested and proved gas tight and/or water tight as follows:

1. **Water tightness** — Each fixture shall be filled and then drained. Traps and fixture connections shall be proven water tight by visual inspection.

2903.6 Water-supply system testing. Upon completion of a section or of the entire water supply system, the system, or portion completed, shall be tested and proved tight under a water pressure not less than the working pressure of the system; or, for piping systems other than plastic, by an air test of not less than 50 psi (344 kPa). The water used for tests shall be obtained from a potable water source.

Uniform Plumbing Code — 1997

609.4 Testing. Upon completion of a section or of the entire hot and cold water supply system, it shall be tested and proved tight under a water pressure not less than the working pressure under which it is to be used. The water used for tests shall be obtained from a potable source of supply. A fifty (50) pound per square inch (344.5 kPa) air pressure may be substituted for the water test. In either method of test, the piping shall withstand the test without leaking for a period of not less than fifteen (15) minutes.

712.1 Media. The piping of the plumbing, drainage, and venting systems shall be tested with water or air.

The Administrative Authority may require the removal of any cleanouts, etc., to ascertain if the pressure has reached all parts of the system. After the plumbing fixtures have been set and their traps filled with water, they shall be submitted to a final test.

712.3 Air Test. The air test shall be made by attaching an a3.r compressor testing apparatus to any suitable opening, and, after closing all other inlets and outlets to the system, forcing air into the system until there is a uniform gage pressure of five (5) pounds per square inch (34.5 kPa) or sufficient to balance a column of mercury ten (10) inches (254 mm) in height. The pressure shall be held without introduction of additional air for a period of at least fifteen (15) minutes.

Comments

Alternative Air Test

Another method that may be used when performing a 5 P.S.I. air test on a DWV system (in addition to using a mercury manometer) is to use a pressure gauge calibrated in 1/10 lb. increments for 15 minutes. This method provides a faster way to detect a leak.

International Plumbing Code — 1997

312.1 Required tests. The permit holder shall make the applicable tests prescribed in Sections 312.2 through 312.9 to determine compliance with the provisions of this code. The permit holder shall give reasonable advance notice to the code official when the plumbing work is ready for tests. The equipment, material, power and labor necessary for the inspection and test shall be furnished by the permit holder and the permit holder shall be responsible for determining that the work will withstand the test pressure prescribed in the following tests. All plumbing system piping shall be tested with either water or air.

After the plumbing fixtures have been set and their traps filled with water, the entire drainage system shall be submitted to final tests. The code official shall require the removal of any cleanouts if necessary to ascertain if the pressure has reached all parts of the system.

Plumbing Fixtures

IOTFDC — 1998 (formerly CABO)

Section 3201 — Fixtures, Faucets and Fixture Fittings

3201.1 General. Plumbing fixtures, faucets and fixture fittings shall be constructed from approved materials, have smooth impervious surfaces, be free from defects and concealed fouling surfaces, and except as permitted elsewhere in this code, shall conform to the standards specified in Table 3201.1 and shall be provided with an adequate supply of potable water to flush and keep the fixtures in a clean and sanitary condition without danger of backflow or cross-connection.

ADA Requirements

Comments

*The Americans with Disabilities Act requires accessible toilet facilities in buildings open to the public. (This does not apply to residential construction.) Light commercial contractors should acquaint themselves with the Act. "ADAAG" stands for Americans with Disabilities Act — Act Guidelines. To order ADA material or ask questions about the Act, call the ADA Technical Assistance Center at 1-800-949-4232 or the U.S. Department of Justice at 1-800-514-0301. The Department of Justice has created an ADA Information File which they make available at the reference desk of public libraries throughout the country. The ADA Web site is **www.usdoj.gov/crt/ada/adahom1.htm**.*

Industry Standards

Means ADA Compliance Pricing Guide
(R. S. Means Co., Inc.)

Section 4.7 Toilet Stalls. Applicable to all accessible toilet rooms with at least one stall.

Design requirements:

- Located on an accessible route.
- Slip-resistant flooring.
- Stall door with 32" clear opening with accessible hardware.
- 60" x 56" minimum clear inside dimension for wall-mounted toilet (60" x 59" for floor mounted toilet), with outswinging door where possible. Alternate configurations for smaller spaces allowable for compliance: 48" x 54" stall or a 36" x 69" stall if only a 42" wide approach is possible from the latch side of the door, or if a 48" wide approach is possible from the latch side of the door, or if a 48" wide approach is possible from the hinged side of the door.
- 9" toe clearance under partitions, if stall is less than 60" deep.
- Toilet: seat 17" to 19" above finished floor, centerline 18" from wall, flush valve on open side
- Grab bars 33" to 36" a.f.f., 1-1/2" diameter, 1-1/2" from wall, 42" long minimum at side wall, 36" long minimum at rear wall.
- Toilet paper dispenser below grab bar, within 36" of rear wall, 19" a.f.f. minimum, freely dispenses paper.
- Coat hook within reach range (48" a.f.f. for forward reach).

Design Suggestions: It is usually recommended that the end toilet be used for the accessible stall, so grab bars can be attached to the wall rather than to a partition. Be sure that grab bars are anchored to either framing or blocking, so that they meet the minimum structural strength requirements (250 lbs. pressure minimum).

4.19 Lavatories and Mirrors. Requires at least one sink in all public toilet rooms.

Design Requirements:

- 34" maximum to rim, 29" minimum clear knee space below rim, 27" clear below bowl.

- Bowl 6-1/2" deep maximum.

- Pipes wrapped with insulation.

- No sharp or abrasive surfaces under sink.

- Faucets operable with closed fist (electronic sensor faucets acceptable); self-closing faucets to remain open for at least 10 seconds.

- Mirror 40" a.f.f. maximum.

- Dispensers (such as soap dispensers) operable with a closed fist, and within reach range (48" a.f.f. for front approach, 54" for side approach).

Ed. Note: Chapter 13, "Specialties," contains more information on accessible showers, grab bars and accessories.

ADA-Compliant Rest Room

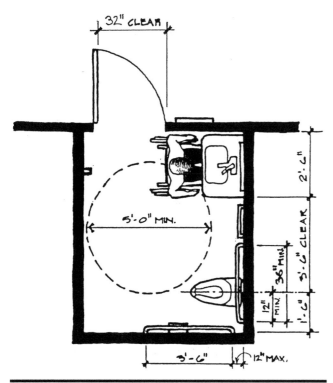

Figure 14.5

Installation
IOTFDC — 1998 (formerly CABO)

3205.1 General. The installation of fixtures shall conform to the following:

1. Floor-outlet or floor-mounted fixtures shall be secured to the drainage connection and to the floor, when so designed, by screws, bolts, washers, nuts and similar fasteners of copper, brass or other corrosion-resistant material.

2. Wall-hung fixtures shall be rigidly supported so that strain is not transmitted to the plumbing system.

3. Where fixtures come in contact with walls or floors, the contact area shall be water tight.

4. Plumbing fixtures shall be functionally accessible.

5. The center line of water closets or bidets shall be a minimum of 15 inches (381 mm) from adjacent walls or partitions or a minimum of 30 inches (762 mm) center to center from an adjacent water closet or bidet.

6. The location of piping, fixtures or equipment shall not interfere with the operation of windows or doors.

Receptors

3206.1 General. Plumbing fixtures or other receptors receiving the discharge of indirect waste pipes shall be shaped and have a capacity to prevent splashing or flooding and shall be readily accessible for inspection and cleaning.

Comments

If the plumber purchases and installs the plumbing fixtures, the installation is much more likely to be guaranteed than if the homeowner purchases the fixtures.

Showers
IOTFDC — 1998 (formerly CABO)

3209.1 General. Shower compartments shall have a minimum of 900 square inches (0.581m²) of floor area and be of sufficient size to inscribe a circle with a diameter not less than 30 inches (762 mm). Hinged shower doors shall open outward. The wall area above built-in tubs having installed shower heads and in-shower compartments shall be constructed as per Section 702.4. Such walls shall form a water-tight joint with each other and with the tub, receptor or shower floor.

Exception: Fold-down seats shall be permitted in the shower, provided the required 900-square-inch (0.581 m²) dimension is maintained when the seat is in the folded-up position.

3209.2 Water-supply riser. The water-supply riser from the shower valve to the shower head outlet shall be secured to the permanent structure.

3209.3 Shower heads. Shower heads shall be of the water-conserving type, which will deliver a maximum flow rate of 2-1/2 gpm at 80 psi (9.5 L/m at 551 kPa).

3209.4 Shower control valves. All showers and combination tub/showers shall be equipped with control valves of the pressure balance, the thermostatic mixing or the combination pressure balance/thermostatic mixing valve type with high limit stops in accordance with ASSE 1016. The high limit stops shall be set to limit water temperature to a maximum 120°F. (49°C.).

Exception: Pressure balance, thermostatic or combination mixing valves shall not be required for showers, provided the hot water supply for such showers is controlled by an approved master thermostatic mixing valve complying with ASSE 1016 and capable of delivering the combined flow of all fixtures downstream installed in accordance with the manufacturer's installation instructions and adjusted to a maximum hot water setting of 120°F. (49°C.).

3210.1 Construction. Shower receptors shall have a finished curb threshold not less than 1 inch (25 mm) below the sides and back of the receptor. The curb shall not be less than 2 inches (51 mm) or more than 9 inches (229 mm) in depth when measured from the top of the curb to the top of the drain. The finished floor shall slope uniformly toward the drain not less than one-fourth unit vertical in 12 units horizontal (2-percent slope) nor more than 1/2 inch (12.7 mm), and floor drains shall be flanged to provide a water-tight joint in the floor.

3210.2 Lining required. The adjoining walls and floor framing, enclosing on-site built-up shower receptors shall be lined with sheet lead, copper or a plastic liner material that complies with ASTM D 4068. The lining material shall extend a minimum of 3 inches (76 mm) beyond or around the rough jambs and not less than 3 inches (76 mm) above finished thresholds. Hot-mopping shall be permitted in accordance with Section 3210.2.1.

Comments

Hot mop materials are not recommended due to their brittleness and lack of flexibility — both in showers and on exterior decks (on wood framing) where high water levels can migrate into structural components.

Prefabricated Showers and Shower Compartments
International Plumbing Code — 1997

417.1 Approval. Prefabricated showers and shower compartments shall conform to ANSI Z124.2, ASME A112.19.9 or CSA B45.5. Shower valves for individual showers shall con- form to the requirements of Section 424.4.

417.2 Water supply riser. Every water supply riser from the shower valve to the shower head outlet, whether exposed or not, shall be attached to the structure in an approved manner.

417.3 Shower waste outlet. Waste outlets serving showers shall be at least 2 inches (51 mm) in diameter and, for other than waste outlets in bathtubs, shall have removable strainers not less than 3 inches (76 mm) in diameter with strainer openings not less than 1/4 inch (6.4 mm) in minimum dimension. Where each shower space is not provided with an individual waste outlet, the waste outlet shall be located and the floor pitched so that waste from one shower does not flow over the floor area serving another shower. Waste outlets shall be fastened to the waste pipe in an approved manner.

417.4 Shower compartments. All shower compartments shall have a minimum of 900 square inches (0.58 m²) of interior cross-sectional area. Shower compartments shall not be less than 30 inches (762 mm) in minimum dimension measured from the finished interior dimension of the compartment, exclusive of fixture valves, showerheads, soap dishes, and safety grab bars or rails. The 30-inch (762 mm) minimum dimension shall be measured as the side of a rectangle, altitude of a triangle or diameter of a circle. Except as required in Section 404.3.1.4, the minimum required area and dimension shall be measured from the finished interior dimension at a height equal to the top of the threshold and at a point tangent to its centerline.

417.4.1 Square shower units. Square shower units designed to accommodate a 32-inch by 32-inch (813 mm by 913 mm) nominal rough-in opening shall be permitted, provided that such units conform in material composition to the applicable standards and provided that any exterior base side measures not less than 31-1/2 inches (800 mm).

417.4.2 Wall area. The wall area above built-in tubs with installed shower heads and in shower compartments shall be constructed of smooth, noncorrosive and nonabsorbent waterproof materials to a height not less than 6 feet (1829 mm) above the room floor level, and not less than 70 inches (1778 mm) where measured from the compartment floor at the drain. Such walls shall form a water-tight joint with each other and with either the tub, receptor or shower floor.

417.5 Shower floors or receptors. Floor surfaces shall be constructed of impervious, noncorrosive, nonabsorbent and waterproof materials.

417.5.1 Support. Floors or receptors under shower compartments shall be laid on, and supported by, a smooth and structurally sound base.

417.5.2 Pans. Floors under shower compartments, except where prefabricated receptors have been provided, shall be lined and made water tight by the provision of suitable shower pans of approved material. Such pans shall turn up on all sides at least 2 inches (51 mm) above the finished threshold level. Pans shall be securely fastened to the waste outlet at the seepage entrance, making a water-tight joint between the pan and the outlet.

Exception: Floor surfaces under shower heads provided for rinsing laid directly on the ground are not required to comply with this section.

417.6 Glazing. Windows and doors within a shower enclosure shall conform to the safety glazing requirements of the building code.

Lavatories (Bathroom Sinks)

IOTFDC — 1998 (formerly CABO)

Section 3212—Lavatories

3212.1 Lavatory waste outlets. Lavatories shall have waste outlets not less than 1-1/4 inch (32 mm) in diameter. A strainer, pop-up stopper, crossbar or other device shall be provided to restrict the clear opening of the waste outlet.

3212.2 Lavatory faucets. Faucets on lavatories shall have a maximum flow rate of 2.5 gpm (9.5 L/m) at 80 psi (552 kPa).

Water Closets (Toilets)

Uniform Plumbing Code — 1997

Ed. Note: See also "ADA Requirements" earlier in this section.

402.3 Water Closets. Water closets, either flush tank, flushometer tank, or flushometer valve operated, shall have an average consumption of not more than 1.6 gallons (6.1 liters) of water per flush.

402.9 Installation. Water-conserving fixtures shall be installed in strict accordance with the manufacturers' instructions to maintain their rated performance.

411.6 Overflows in Flush Tanks. Flush tanks shall be provided with overflows discharging into the water closet or urinal connected thereto and shall be of sufficient size to prevent tank flooding at the maximum rate at which the tank is supplied with water.

International Plumbing Code — 1997

420.1 Approval. Water closets shall conform to the water consumption requirements of Section 604.4 and shall conform to ANSI Z124.4, ASME A112.19.2, CSA B45. 1, CSA B45.4 or CSA B45.5. Water closets shall conform to the hydraulic performance requirements of ASME A112.19.6. Water closet tanks shall conform to ANSI Z124.4, ASME A112.19.2, ASME A112.19.9, CSA B45. 1, CSA B45.4 or CSA B45.5.

420.2 Water closets for public or employee toilet facilities. Water closet bowls for public or employee toilet facilities shall be of the elongated type.

420.3 Water closet seats. Water closets shall be equipped with seats of smooth, nonabsorbent material. All seats of water closets provided for public or employee toilet facilities shall be of the hinged open-front type. Integral water closet seats shall be of the same material as the fixture. Water closet seats shall be sized for the water closet bowl type.

420.4 Water closet connections. A 4-inch by 3-inch (102 mm by 76 mm) closet bend shall be acceptable. Where a 3-inch (76 mm) bend is utilized on water closets, a 4-inch by 3-inch (102 mm by 76 mm) flange shall be installed to receive the fixture horn.

IOTFDC — 1998 (formerly CABO)

3213.1 Prohibited water closets. Water closets which have an invisible seal and unventilated space or walls which are not thoroughly washed at each discharge shall be prohibited. Water closets which could permit backflow of the contents of the bowl into the flush tank shall be prohibited.

3213.2 Flushing devices required. Water closets shall be of the low consumption 1.6 gallons per flush (gpf) (6.1 Lpf) type and shall be provided with a flush tank or similar device designed and installed to supply water in sufficient quantity and flow to flush the contents of the fixture, to cleanse the fixture and refill the fixture trap in accordance with ASME A112.19.2 and ASME A112.19.6.

3213.5 Overflows in flush tanks. Flush tanks shall be provided with overflows discharging to the water closet connected thereto and of sufficient size to prevent flooding the tank at the maximum rate at which the tanks are supplied with water.

3213.6 Water closet seats. Water closets shall be equipped with seats of smooth, nonabsorbent material and shall be properly sized for the water-closet-bowl type.

Bathtubs

IOTFDC — 1998 (formerly CABO)

3214.1 Bathtub waste outlets and overflows. Bathtubs shall have outlets and overflows at least 1-1/2 inches (38 mm) in diameter, and the waste outlet shall be equipped with an approved stopper.

Sinks (Kitchen)

IOTFDC — 1998 (formerly CABO)

3215.1 Sink waste outlets. Sinks shall be provided with waste outlets that are a minimum of 1-1/2 inches (38 mm) in diameter. A strainer, crossbar or other device shall be provided to restrict the clear opening of the waste outlet. Sinks on which a waste grinder is installed shall have a minimum waste opening of 3-1/2 inches (89 mm) in diameter.

3215.2 Sink faucets. Sink faucets shall have a maximum flow rate of 2.5 gpm (9.5 L/m) at 80 psi (552 kPa).

Dishwashing Machines
IOTFDC — 1998 (formerly CABO)

3218.1 Protection of water supply. Each unit shall have integral backflow protection of the water supply to the appliance.

3218.2 Sink and dishwasher. A sink and dishwasher shall be permitted to discharge through a single 1-1/2 inch (38 mm) trap. The discharge from the dishwasher shall be increased to a minimum of 3/4 inch (19 mm) and be connected with a wye fitting to the sink tail piece. The dishwasher waste line shall rise and be securely fastened to the underside of the counter before connecting to the sink tail piece.

Clothes Washers
IOTFDC — 1998 (formerly CABO)

3219.1 Backflow protection. Each unit shall have integral backflow protection of the water supply to the appliance. The discharge from such a machine shall be through an air break.

Clothes Dryers
IOTFDC — 1998 (formerly CABO)

1801.1 General. Dryer exhaust systems shall be independent of all other systems and shall convey the moisture to the outdoors. Exhaust ducts shall not be connected with sheet metal screws or fastening means which extend into the duct. Exhaust ducts shall be equipped with a backdraft damper. Exhaust ducts shall be constructed of rigid metal having a minimum thickness of 0.016 inches (0.406 mm) and shall have smooth interior surfaces with joints running in the direction of air flow. Clothes dryer transition ducts shall be limited to single lengths not to exceed 8 feet (2438 mm) in length and shall be listed and labeled. Transition ducts shall not be concealed within construction.

1801.2 Exhaust duct size. The minimum diameter of the exhaust duct shall be as recommended by the manufacturer or shall be in accordance with Section 1801.3, but shall be at least the diameter of the appliance outlet.

1801.3 Length limitation. The maximum length of a 4-inch-diameter (102 mm) exhaust duct shall not exceed 25 feet (7620 mm) from the dryer location to a wall or roof termination, and shall terminate with a full opening exhaust hood. A reduction in maximum length of 2.5 feet (762 mm) for each 45-degree (0.79 rad) bend and 5 feet (1524 mm) for

each 90-degree (1.57 rad) bend shall apply. Installations when this length is exceeded shall be in accordance with the manufacturer's installation instructions.

Section 2204 — Clothes Dryers

2204.1 General. Clothes dryers shall be listed and labeled and shall be installed in accordance with the manufacturer's installation instructions. Gas clothes dryers shall conform to ANSI Z21.5.1.

2204.2 Closet installation. Gas clothes dryers installed in closets shall be listed and labeled for such installations and no other fuel-burning appliance shall be installed in the same closet.

NFPA 54: National Fuel Gas Code
Clothes Dryers
6.4.1 Clearance.

(a) Listed Type 1 clothes dryers shall be installed with a minimum clearance of 6 in. (15 cm) from adjacent combustible material, except that clothes dryers listed for installation at lesser clearances shall be permitted to be installed in accordance with their listing. Type 1 clothes dryers installed in closets shall be specifically listed for such installation.

6.4.2 Exhausting to the Outside Air.

(a) Type 1 clothes dryers installed in closets shall be exhausted to the outside air, and no other fuel-burning appliance shall be installed in the same closet. Type 1 clothes dryers shall not be installed in bathrooms or bedrooms unless exhausted to the outside air.

6.4.3 Provisions for Make-Up Air.

(a) Make-up air shall be provided for closet-installed Type 1 clothes dryers in accordance with manufacturers' installation instructions.

6.4.4 Exhaust Ducts for Type 1 Clothes Dryers.

(a) A clothes dryer exhaust duct shall not be connected into any vent connector, gas vent, chimney, crawl space, attic, or other similar concealed space.

(b) Ducts for exhausting clothes dryers shall not be assembled with screws or other fastening means that extend into the duct and that would catch lint and reduce the efficiency of the exhaust system.

Whirlpool Tubs
Uniform Plumbing Code — 1997

415.0 Whirlpool Bathtubs. Unless otherwise listed, all whirlpool bathtubs shall comply with the following requirements:

415.1 A removable panel of sufficient dimension shall be provided to access the pump.

415.2 The circulation pump shall be located above the crown weir of the trap.

415.3 The pump and the circulation piping shall be self-draining to minimize water retention.

415.4 Suction fittings on whirlpool bathtubs shall comply with the listed standards.

416.0 Installation of Fixture Fittings. Faucets and diverters shall be installed so that the flow of hot water from the fittings corresponds to the left hand side of the fitting.

421.1 Approval. Whirlpool bathtubs shall comply with ASME Al 12.19.7 or with CSA B45.5 and CSA CAN/CSA-B45 (Supplement 1).

421.2 Installation. Whirlpool bathtubs shall be installed and tested in accordance with the manufacturer's installation instructions. The pump shall be located above the weir of the fixture trap. Access shall be provided to the pump.

421.3 Drain. The pump drain and circulation piping shall be sloped to drain the water in the volute and the circulation piping when the whirlpool bathtub is empty.

421.4 Suction fittings. Suction fittings for whirlpool bathtubs shall comply with ASME Al 12.19.8.

Comments

Hand-held Showers in Whirlpools

Personal hand-held showers installed in whirlpool tubs and used as a washdown only, are connected to cold water only. If connected to both hot and cold, it is likely to be used as a shower head. Since whirlpool tubs generally are not protected by an anti-scald temperature-balanced device, use of hand-held showers in these circumstances increase the user's risk of being scalded.

Water Heaters

IOTFDC — 1998 (formerly CABO)
Section 2307—Water Heaters

2307.1 General. Water heaters shall be listed and labeled as conforming to ANSI Z21.10.1, ANSI Z21.10.3, or UL174 and shall be installed in accordance with manufacturer's installation instructions and the requirements of this code.

2307.1.1 Vent. Water heaters designed to be vented shall be connected to a venting system and such system shall be installed in accordance with Chapter 21.

2307.1.2 Combustion air. Water heaters that depend on the combustion of fuel for heat shall be provided with a sufficient

Hot Water Consumption Rates

Type of Building	Size Factor	Maximum Hourly Demand	Average Day Demand
Apartment Dwellings	No. of Apartments: Up to 20 21 to 50 51 to 75 76 to 100 101 to 200 201 up	12.0 Gal. per apt. 10.0 Gal. per apt. 8.5 Gal. per apt. 7.0 Gal. per apt. 6.0 Gal. per apt. 5.0 Gal. per apt.	42.0 Gal. per apt. 40.0 Gal. per apt. 38.0 Gal. per apt. 37.0 Gal. per apt. 36.0 Gal. per apt. 35.0 Gal. per apt.
Dormitories	Men Women	3.8 Gal. per man 5.0 Gal. per woman	13.1 Gal. per man 12.3 Gal. per woman
Hospitals	Per bed	23.0 Gal. per patient	90.0 Gal. per patient
Hotels	Single room with bath Double room with bath	17.0 Gal. per unit 27.0 Gal. per unit	50.0 Gal. per unit 80.0 Gal. per unit
Motels	No. of units: Up to 20 21 to 100 101 Up	6.0 Gal. per unit 5.0 Gal. per unit 4.0 Gal. per unit	20.0 Gal. per unit 14.0 Gal. per unit 10.0 Gal. per unit
Nursing Homes		4.5 Gal. per bed	18.4 Gal. per bed
Office buildings		0.4 Gal. per person	1.0 Gal. per person
Restaurants	Full meal type Drive-in snack type	1.5 Gal./max. meals/hr. 0.7 Gal./max. meals/hr.	2.4 Gal. per meal 0.7 Gal. per meal
Schools	Elementary Secondary & High	0.6 Gal. per student 1.0 Gal. per student	0.6 Gal. per student 1.8 Gal. per student

For evaluation purposes, recovery rate and storage capacity are inversely proportional. Water heaters should be sized so that the maximum hourly demand anticipated can be met in addition to allowance for the heat loss from the pipes and storage tank.

R.S. Means Co., Inc., 1999 *Plumbing Cost Data* [Table R151-110]

Figure 14.6

supply of combustion air and shall be installed in accordance with Chapter 20.

2307.2 Prohibited locations. Fuel-burning water heaters shall not be installed in a room used as a storage closet. Water heaters located in a bedroom or bathroom shall be installed in a sealed enclosure such that combustion air will not be taken from the living space. Direct vent water heaters are not required to be installed within an enclosure.

2307.2.1 Water heater access. Access to water heaters that are located in an attic or underfloor crawl space shall be permitted to be through a closet located in a sleeping room or bathroom when ventilation of those spaces is in accordance with this code.

Section 3301 — General

3301.1 Required. Each dwelling shall have an approved automatic water heater or other type domestic water-heating system sufficient to supply hot water to plumbing fixtures and appliances intended for bathing, washing or culinary purposes. Storage tanks shall be constructed of noncorrosive metal or be lined with noncorrosive material.

3301.2 Installation. Water heaters shall be installed in accordance with this chapter and Chapter 23.

3301.3 Prohibited locations. Water heaters shall be located as required by Sections 2307.2 and 2307.3.

Exception: Direct vent-type water heaters.

Uniform Plumbing Code — 1997

502.13 Water Heater. An appliance designed primarily to supply hot water and is equipped with automatic controls limiting water temperature to a maximum of two hundred ten degrees (210°F.) (99°C.).

507.1 Fuel burning water heaters shall be assured a sufficient supply of air for proper fuel combustion and ventilation.

507.2 In buildings of unusually tight construction, combustion air shall be obtained from outside. In buildings of ordinary tightness insofar as infiltration is concerned, all or a portion of the combustion air for fuel burning water heaters may be obtained from infiltration if the enclosure volume equals at least fifty (50) cubic feet per 1,000 Btu/h input of the water heater.

507.4 Louvers and Grilles. In calculating free area of all louvers and grilles, consideration shall be given to the blocking effect of louvers, grilles or screens protecting openings. Screens used shall not be smaller than one-fourth (1/4) inch (6.4 mm) mesh. The free area through a design of louver or grille shall be used in calculating the size opening required to provide the free area specified.

509.0 Prohibited Locations. Water heaters which depend on the combustion of fuel for heat shall not be installed in a room used or designed to be used for sleeping purposes, bathrooms,

clothes closets or in a closet or other confined space opening into a bath or bedroom

Exception: Direct vent water heaters.

Where not prohibited by other regulations, water heaters may be located under a stairway or landing.

International Plumbing Code — 1997

502.1 General. Water heaters shall be installed in accordance with the manufacturer's installation instructions. Gas- and oil-fired water heaters shall conform to the requirements of this code and the mechanical code or gas code. Electric water heaters shall conform to the requirements of this code and the provisions of NFPA 70 listed in Chapter 14.

502.2 Water heaters installed in garages. Water heaters having an ignition source shall be elevated such that the source of ignition is not less than 18 inches (457 mm) above the garage floor.

502.3 Rooms used as a plenum. Water heaters using solid, liquid or gas fuel shall not be installed in a room containing air-handling machinery when such room is used as a plenum.

502.4 Prohibited location. Fuel-fired water heaters shall not be installed in a sleeping room, bathroom or a closet accessed through a sleeping room or bathroom.

Exception: A sealed combustion chamber or direct vent water heater may be installed in a sleeping room, bathroom or closet accessed through a sleeping room or bathroom.

502.5 Water heaters installed in attics. Attics containing a water heater shall be provided with an opening and unobstructed passageway large enough to allow removal of the water heater. The passageway shall not be less than 30 inches (762 mm) high and 22 inches (559 mm) wide and not more than 20 feet (6096 mm) in length when measured along the centerline of the passageway from the opening to the water heater. The passageway shall have continuous solid flooring not less than 24 inches (610 mm) wide. A level service space at least 30 inches (762 mm) deep and 30 inches (762 mm) wide shall be present at the front or service side of the water heater. The clear access opening dimensions shall be a minimum of 20 inches by 30 inches (508 mm by 762 mm) where such dimensions are large enough to allow removal of the water heater.

Water Heater Relief Valve

IOTFDC — 1998 (formerly CABO)

3303.2 Relief valves. Relief valves shall have a minimum-rated capacity for the equipment served and shall conform to ANSI Z21.22.

International Plumbing Code — 1997

504.5 Relief valve. All storage water heaters operating above atmospheric pressure shall be provided with an approved, self-closing (levered) pressure relief valve and temperature relief valve or combination thereof. The relief valve shall conform to ANSI Z21.22. The relief valve shall not be used as a means of controlling thermal expansion.

504.5.1 Installation. Such valves shall be installed in the shell of the water heater tank. Temperature relief valves shall be so located in the tank as to be actuated by the water in the top 6 inches (153 mm) of the tank served. For installations with separate storage tanks, the valves shall be installed on the tank and there shall not be any type of valve installed between the water heater and the storage tank. There shall not be a check valve or shutoff valve between a relief valve and the heater or tank served.

504.6 Relief valve approval. Temperature and pressure relief valves, or combinations thereof, and energy cutoff devices shall bear the label of an approved agency and shall have a temperature setting of not more than 210° F (99°C) and a pressure setting not exceeding the tank or water heater manufacturer's rated working pressure or 150 psi (1035 kPa), whichever is less. The relieving capacity of each pressure relief valve and each temperature relief valve shall equal or exceed the heat input to the water heater or storage tank.

504.7 Relief outlet waste. The outlet of a pressure, temperature or other relief valve shall not be directly connected to the drainage system.

504.7.1 Discharge. The discharge from the relief valve shall be piped full-size separately to the outside of the building or to an indirect waste receptor located inside the building. In areas subject to freezing, the relief valve shall discharge through an air gap into an indirect waste receptor located within a heated space, or by other approved means. The discharge shall be installed in a manner that does not cause personal injury or property damage and that is readily observable by the building occupants. The discharge from a relief valve shall not be trapped. The diameter of the discharge piping shall not be less than the diameter of the relief valve outlet. The discharge pipe shall be installed so as to drain by gravity flow and shall terminate atmospherically not more than 6 inches (153 mm) above the floor. The end of the discharge pipe shall not be threaded.

Automatic Fire Sprinklers

Comments

Residential automatic sprinklers are not mandatory in many jurisdictions for one- and two-family residences.

While sprinklers are not usually required in private residences, they are typically required for many light commercial buildings. Depending on local requirements, buildings such as small office buildings, shops, educational, day-care or health-care buildings, taverns, restaurants or other similar establishments may need sprinklers. The requirements of the 1997 Uniform Building Code delineates what is required for specific usages in Section 904 — Fire Extinguishing Systems. Details on smoke detectors may be found in Chapter 16, "Electrical."

There are basically five types of sprinkler systems: Wet Pipe, Dry Pipe, Pre-Action, Deluge, and Firecycle. **Wet-pipe systems** *are by far the most common, and work by using automatic sprinklers attached to piping containing water under pressure. When the heat from a fire melts a fusible link, the water is released onto the fire. This system is used where there is no danger of freezing.* **Dry-pipe systems** *are used in unheated areas, such as parking garages, and have automatic sprinklers with piping containing air under pressure. When the sprinkler head opens, the air is released and water flows from the piping.*

Pre-action systems *are used where the accidental discharge of water would be very damaging. The piping is dry, containing low pressure air, and operates quickly to minimize fire and water damage. The water supply valve is opened by fire detection equipment, and not by a fusible link.* **Deluge systems** *are very similar to pre-action systems in that they both use fire detection equipment and a main valve. However, deluge systems use open sprinklers instead of closed ones. They are used where flammable material can cause fire to spread quickly.* **Firecycle systems** *cycle on and off while controlling a fire by utilizing heat detectors and an electrical control panel. Water cannot flow until the heat detector activates, so these systems are used where water damage must be kept to a minimum.*

Wet Pipe Sprinkler System

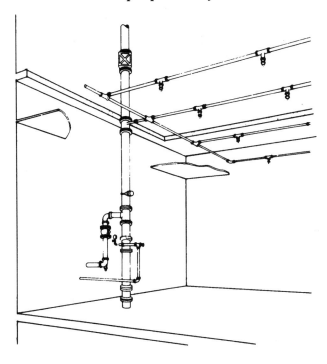

R.S. Means Co., Inc., *Plumbing Estimating Methods*

Figure 14.7

NFPA 13D: Installation of Sprinkler Systems in One- and Two-Family Dwellings and Manufactured Homes

Section 1-1 Scope. This standard covers the design and installation of automatic sprinkler systems for protection against the fire hazards in one- and two-family dwellings and manufactured homes.

1-2 Purpose. The purpose of this standard is to provide a sprinkler systems that aids in the detection and control of residential fires and thus provides improved protection against injury, life loss, and property damage. A sprinkler system designed and installed in accordance with this standard is expected to prevent flashover (total involvement) in the room of fire origin, where sprinklered, and to improve the chance for occupants to escape or be evacuated.

Guidelines have been established for the design and installation of sprinkler systems for one- and two-family dwellings and manufactured homes. Nothing in this standard is intended to restrict new technologies or alternative arrangements, provided that the level of safety prescribed by the standard is not reduced.

1-4 Maintenance. The owner is responsible for the condition of a sprinkler systems and shall keep the system in normal operating condition.

1-5 Devices, Materials, Design, and Installation.

1-5.1 Only new residential sprinklers shall be employed in the installation of sprinkler systems.

1-5.2 Only listed and approved devices and approved materials shall be used in sprinkler systems.

Exception: Listing shall be permitted to be waived for tanks, pumps, hangers, waterflow detection devices, and waterflow valves.

Section 2 — Water Supply

2-1 General Provisions. Every automatic sprinkler system shall have at least one automatic water supply. Where stored water is used as the sole source of supply, the minimum quantity shall equal the water demand rate times 10 minutes. (See 4-1.3.)

Exception: For dwelling units that are one story in height and less than 2000 ft^2 (186 m^2) in area, the water supply shall be at least 7 minutes for the two-sprinkler demand.

4-1 Design Criteria.

4-1.1 Design Discharge. The system shall provide a discharge of not less than 18 gpm (68 L/min) to any single operating sprinkler and not less than 13 gpm (49 L/min) per sprinkler to the number of design sprinklers, but the discharge shall not be less than the listing of the sprinkler. The minimum operating pressure of any residential sprinkler shall be 7 psi (0.5 bar).

4-1.2 Number of Design Sprinklers. The number of design sprinklers shall include all sprinklers within a compartment, up to a maximum of two sprinklers, under a slat, smooth, horizontal ceiling. For compartments containing two or more sprinklers, calculations shall be provided to verify the single operating sprinkler criteria and the multiple (two) operating sprinkler criteria.

The definition of "compartment" as used in 4-1.2 for determining the number of design sprinklers is a space that is completely enclosed by walls and a ceiling. The compartment enclosure shall be permitted to have openings to and adjoining space, provided the openings have a minimum lintel depth of 8 in. (203 mm) from the ceiling.

4-1.3 Water Demand. The water demand for the system shall be determined by multiplying the design discharge specified in 4-1.1 by the number of design sprinklers specified in 4-1.2.

4-1.4 Sprinkler Coverage. Residential sprinklers shall be spaced so that the maximum area protected by a single sprinkler does not exceed 144 ft^2 (13.4 m^2).

The maximum distance between sprinklers shall not exceed 12 ft (3.7 m) on or between pipelines, and the maximum distance to a wall or partition shall not exceed 6 ft (1.8 m). The minimum distance between sprinklers within a compartment shall be 8 ft (2.4 m).

4-2 Position of Sprinklers.

4-2.1 Pendent and upright sprinklers shall be positioned so that the deflectors are within 1 in. to 4 in. (25.4 mm to 102 mm) from the ceiling.

Exception: Special residential sprinklers shall be installed in accordance with the listing limitations.

4-2.2 Sidewall sprinklers shall be positioned so that the deflectors are within 4 in. to 6 in. (102 mm to 152 mm) from the ceiling.

Exception: Special residential sprinklers shall be installed in accordance with the listing limitations.

4-2.3 Sprinklers shall be positioned so that the response time and discharge are not unduly affected by obstructions such as ceiling slope, beams, or light fixtures.

4-2.4 In basements where ceilings are not required for the protection of piping or where metallic pipe is installed, residential sprinklers shall be permitted to be positioned in a manner that anticipates future installation of a finished ceiling.

4-2.5 In closets and storage areas that are required to be protected in accordance with Section 4-6 and are less than 5 ft. (1.5 m) in height at the lowest ceiling, a single sprinkler located at the highest ceiling shall be permitted to protect a volume not larger than 300 ft³ (3.93 m³).

Water Supply and Distribution

International Plumbing Code — 1997
Section 602 — Water Required

602.1 General. Every structure equipped with plumbing fixtures and utilized for human occupancy or habitation shall be provided with a potable supply of water in the amounts and at the pressures specified in this chapter.

Section 603 — Water Service

603.1 Size of water service pipe. The water service pipe shall be sized to supply water to the structure in the quantities and at the pressures required in this code. The minimum diameter of water service pipe shall be 3/4 inch (19.1 mm).

Comments
Water Service Pipe

The water service pipe should not only be a minimum of 3/4", but also should not be smaller than the largest portion of the water main after the outlet of the metering device (or main shut-off valve if a meter is not provided). It makes no sense to have a 1" or 1-1/2" inside main if supply piping is only 3/4".

IOTFDC — 1998 (formerly CABO)
Section 3402 — Protection of Potable Water Supply

3402.1 Connections. Connections shall not be made to a potable water supply in a manner which is capable of contaminating the water supply or provide a cross-connection between the supply and source of contamination unless an approved backflow-prevention device is provided. Cross-connections between a private water supply and potable public supply shall be prohibited.

3402.2 Backflow protection. A means of protection against backflow shall be provided in accordance with Sections 3402.2.1 through 3402.2.6.

3402.2.1 Air gaps. Air gaps shall comply with ASME A112.1.2 or the requirements of this section. The minimum air gap shall be measured vertically from the lowest end of a water supply outlet to the flood level rim of the fixture of receptor into which such potable water outlets discharge. The minimum required air gap shall be twice the diameter of the effective opening of the outlet, but in no case less than the values specified in Table 3402.2.1. An air gap is required at the discharge point of a relief valve or piping. Air gap devices shall be incorporated in dishwasher and clothes washer equipment.

3402.2.2 Atmospheric vacuum breakers. Pipe applied atmospheric vacuum breakers shall conform to ASSE 1001. Hose connection vacuum breakers shall comply with ASSE 1011 or ASSE 1019. Theses devices shall operate under normal atmospheric pressure. Except deck-mounted and integral vacuum breakers, the critical level of an atmospheric-type vacuum breaker shall be set a minimum of 6 inches (152 mm) above the flood level rim of the fixture, device or highest point of usage. The vacuum breaker shall be installed in accordance with the manufacturers' installation instructions.

International Plumbing Code — 1997

602.4 No water piping supplied by any private water supply system shall be connected to any other source of supply without the approval of the Administrative Authority, Health Department, or other department having jurisdiction.

603.0 Cross-Connection Control. Cross-connection control shall be provided in accordance with the provisions of this chapter.

No person shall install any water operated equipment or mechanism, or use any water treating chemical or substance, if it is found that such equipment, mechanism, chemical or substance may cause pollution or contamination of the domestic water supply. Such equipment or mechanism may be permitted only when equipped with an approved backflow prevention device or assembly.

603.1 Approval of Devices or Assemblies. Before any device or assembly is installed for the prevention of backflow, it shall have first been approved by the Administrative Authority. Devices or assemblies shall be tested for conformity with recognized standards or other standards acceptable to the Administrative Authority which are consistent with the intent of this Code.

All devices or assemblies installed in a potable water supply system for protection against backflow shall be maintained in good working condition by the person or persons having control of such devices or assemblies. The Administrative Authority or other department having jurisdiction may inspect such devices or assemblies and, if found to be defective or inoperative, shall require the repair or replacement thereof. No device or assembly shall be removed from use or relocated or other device or assembly substituted, without the approval of the Administrative Authority.

603.4.6 Protection from Lawn Sprinklers and Irrigation Systems.

603.4.6.1 Potable water supplies to systems having no pumps or connections for pumping equipment, and no chemical injection or provisions for chemical injection, shall be protected from backflow by one of the following devices:

1. Atmospheric vacuum breaker
2. Pressure vacuum breaker
3. Reduced pressure backflow preventer

603.4.6.2 Where sprinkler and irrigation systems have pumps, connections for pumping equipment, auxiliary air tanks or are otherwise capable of creating back-pressure, the potable water supply shall be protected by the following type of device if the backflow device is located upstream from the source of back-pressure.

1. Reduced pressure backflow preventer

603.4.7 Potable Water Outlets with Hose Attachments, other than water heater drains, boiler drains, and clothes washer connections, shall be protected by a listed non-removable hose bibb type backflow preventer or by a listed atmospheric vacuum breaker installed at least six (6) inches (152 mm) above the highest point of usage and located on the discharge side of the last valve. In climates where freezing

temperatures occur, a listed self-draining frost proof hose bibb with an integral backflow preventer shall be used.

603.4.15 Backflow Preventers shall not be located in any area containing fumes that are toxic, poisonous or corrosive.

603.4.17 Faucets with Hose-Attached Sprays shall vent to atmosphere under back-siphonage conditions.

603.4.18 — Protection from Fire Systems

603.4.18.1 Except as provided under Sections 603.4.18.2 and 603.4.18.3 below, potable water supplies to fire protection systems, including but not limited to standpipes and automatic sprinkler systems, shall be protected from back-pressure and back-siphonage by one of the following testable devices:

1. Double check valve assembly
2. Double check detector assembly
3. Reduced pressure backflow preventer
4. Reduced pressure detector assembly

608.6.1 Private water supplies. Cross-connections between a private water supply and a potable public supply shall be prohibited.

608.8 Identification of potable and nonpotable water. In all buildings where two or more water distribution systems, one potable water and the other nonpotable water, are installed, each system shall be identified either by color marking or metal tags as required by ASME A13.1.

Water Distribution

Comments

It is good engineering practice to supply each bathroom group with 3/4" service and 1/2" to each fixture.

IOTFDC — 1998 (formerly CABO)
Section 3403 — Water Supply System

3403.2 Minimum pressure. Minimum static pressure (as determined by the local water authority) at the building entrance for either public or private water service shall be 40 pounds per square inch (psi) (276 kPa).

3403.3 Maximum pressure. The maximum static pressure shall be 80 psi (551 kPa). When the main pressure exceeds 80 psi (551 kPa), an approved pressure-reducing valve complying with ASSE 1003 shall be installed on the domestic water branch main or riser at the connection to the water service pipe.

3403.5 Determining water-supply fixture units. Supply load in the building water-distribution system shall be determined by total load on the pipe being sized, in terms of water-supply fixture units (w.s.f.u.), as shown in Table 3409.2. For fixtures not listed, choose a w.s.f.u. value of a fixture with similar flow characteristics.

Example: Add up the total number of fixture units for various fixture groupings plus any individual fixtures that are in addition to a grouping. For example: The w.s.f.u. load on the water-service and hot- and cold-water main distribution piping for a two-and-one-half bath house with an additional lavatory in a dressing room, kitchen sink with dishwasher, and standpipe for clothes washer is calculated as follows:

	Hot Main	Cold Main	Combined Service
2-1/2 bath group	2.8	4.2	5.6
Extra lavatory	0.5	0.5	0.7
Kitchen group	1.9	1.0	2.5
Clothes washer	1.0	1.0	1.4
TOTAL	6.2	6.7	10.2

3403.6 Estimating supply demand. Maximum supply demand in gallons per minute (gpm) (L/m) in the service pipe or in various parts of the water distribution system shall be determined from Table 3403.6 after computing water supply fixture unit loads from Table 3403.5. Where supply outlets impose a continuous demand, such as a hose bibb or lawn sprinkler system, estimate this continuous supply separately and add to the gpm (L/m) demand for fixtures supplied by the pipe to be sized.

Ed. Note: Table 3403.6 provides the demand flow rate as a function of fixture unit load. Table 3403.5 supplies information about water supply fixture unit values for various plumbing fixtures and fixture groups.

Drainage System

IOTFDC — 1998 (formerly CABO)
Section 3505 — Drainage System

3505.1 Drainage fittings and connections. Changes in direction in drainage piping shall be made by the appropriate use of sanitary tees, wyes, sweeps, bends or by a combination of these drainage fittings.

3505.1.2.1 Prohibited connection. A kitchen sink and water closet shall not be connected to a stack at the same level directly opposed, nor shall either of these fixtures be installed directly opposed to other types of waste fixtures. Double sanitary tee patterns shall not receive the discharge of back-to-back water closets and fixtures or appliances with pumping action discharge.

3505.1.7 Water closet connection between flange and pipe. A 3-inch (76 mm) 1/4 bend or bends shall be acceptable for water closet or similar connections, provided a 4-inch-by-

3-inch (102 mm by 76 mm) flange is installed to receive the closet fixture horn. Alternately, a 4-inch-by-3-inch (102 mm by 76 mm) elbow shall be acceptable with a 4-inch (102 mm) flange.

3505.2 Drainage pipe cleanouts. Drainage pipe cleanouts shall comply with Sections 3505.2.1 through 3505.2.11.

3505.2.2 Spacing. Cleanouts shall be installed not more than 100 feet (30 480mm) apart in horizontal drainage lines.

3505.2.5 Access. Cleanouts shall be accessible. Minimum clearance in front of cleanouts shall be 18 inches on 3 inches (457 mm on 76 mm) and larger pipes, and 12 inches (305 mm) on smaller pipes. Concealed cleanouts shall be provided with access of sufficient size to permit removal of the cleanout plug and rodding of the system. Cleanout plugs shall not be concealed with any permanent finishing material.

3505.2.9 Cleanout size. Cleanouts shall be sized in accordance with Table 3505.2.9.

Indirect Waste

IOTFDC — 1998 (formerly CABO)
Section 3207 — Prohibited Receptors

3207.1 Indirect waste. No plumbing fixture which is used for domestic or culinary purposes shall be used to receive the discharge of an indirect waste.

Exceptions:

1. A kitchen sink trap shall be permitted to be used as a receptor for a dishwasher.
2. A laundry tray shall be permitted to be used as a receptor for a clothes washer.

Uniform Plumbing Code — 1997

801.1 Airgap or Airbreak Required. All indirect waste piping shall discharge into the building drainage system through an airgap or airbreak as set forth in this Code. Where a drainage airgap is required by this Code, the minimum vertical distance as measured from the lowest point of the indirect waste pipe or the fixture outlet to the flood level rim of the receptor shall be not less than one (1) inch (25.4 mm).

815.0 Air-Conditioning Equipment. If discharged into the drainage system, any evaporative cooler, airwasher, or similar air-conditioning equipment shall drain by means of an indirect waste pipe.

815.1 Size. Air-conditioning condensate waste pipes shall be independent of any drainage and waste system.

Comments

Storm systems are not a plumbing concern in one- and two-family homes with pitched roofs that funnel rainwater into exterior gutters and downspouts. However, a light commercial or any flat roof building often requires a system of roof drains connected by interior piping, then piped out through the foundation to a municipal/or other storm system. Local code will determine if this system is kept separate from the sanitary waste disposal system.

Vents

Industry Standards
Plumbing Estimating Methods
(R.S. Means Co., Inc.)

The vent piping shown in **Figure 14.8** is installed as part of the sanitary system, primarily to provide:

A flow of air to or from a drainage system.

A circulation of air within such a system to protect trap seals from siphonage and back pressure.

The vent stack, also shown in **Figure 14.8**, is any vertical vent pipe extending floor to floor, connected to the vent system to provide circulation of air to and from any part of the drainage system. The vent stack ends at a minimum of two feet above the roof. This is called the *vent terminal* or *extension*. The vent terminal is flashed with lead or copper sheet flashing to make it weather-tight. In areas of the country where freezing poses a problem, vent terminals should be at least four inches in diameter to prevent frost or snow from clogging the vent opening.

IOTFDC — 1998 (formerly CABO)
Ed. Note: IOTFDC Chapter 36, "Vents," and Chapter 37, "Traps," provide detailed requirements for the installation of vent systems and traps.

Section 3601 — Vent Systems
3601.1 General. This chapter shall govern the selection and installation of piping, tubing and fittings for vent systems. This chapter shall control the minimum diameter of vent pipe, circuit vents, branch vents and individual vents, and the size and length of vents and various aspects of vent stacks and stack vents. Additionally, this chapter regulates vent grades and connections, height above fixtures and relief vents for stacks and fixture traps, and the venting of sumps and sewers.

3602.1 Trap seal protection. The plumbing system shall be provided with a system of vent piping which will permit the admission or emission of air so that the seal of any fixture trap

Typical Waste and Vent Installation for Water Closet, Lavatory, and Bathtub

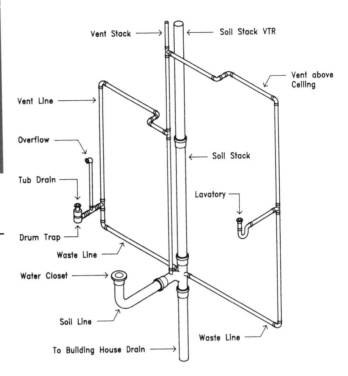

R.S. Means Co., Inc., *Plumbing Estimating Methods*

Figure 14.8

shall not be subjected to a pneumatic pressure differential of more than 1 inch of water (249 Pa).

3601.2.1 Venting required. Every trap and trapped fixture shall be vented in accordance with one of the venting methods specified in this chapter.

3601.3 Use limitations. The plumbing vent system shall not be utilized for purposes other than the venting of the plumbing system.

3601.4 Extension outside a structure. In climates where the 97-1/2-percent value for outside design temperature is less than 0°F. (–18°C.) (ASHRAE 97.5-percent column, winter, see Chapter 3), vent pipes installed on the exterior of the structure shall be protected against freezing by insulation, heat or both. Vent terminals shall be protected from frost closure in accordance with Section 3603.2.

Section 3602 — Vent Stacks and Stack Vents
3602.1 Main vent required. Every building shall have a main vent that is either a vent stack or a stack vent. Such vent shall run undiminished in size and as directly as possible from the building drain through to the open air above the roof.

3602.2 Vent connection to drainage system. Every vent stack shall connect to the base of the drainage stack. The vent stack shall connect at or below the lowest horizontal branch.

Where the vent stack connects to the building drain, the connection shall be located within ten pipe diameters downstream of the drainage stack. A stack vent shall be a vertical extension of the drainage stack.

3602.3 Vent termination. Every vent stack or stack vent shall extend outdoors and terminate to the open air.

Section 3603 — Vent Terminals

3603.1 Roof extension. All open vent pipes which extend through a roof shall be terminated a minimum of 6 inches (152 mm) above the roof, except that where a roof is to be used for any purpose other than weather protection, the vent extensions shall be run a minimum of 7 feet (2134 mm) above the roof.

3603.2 Frost closure. Where the 97-1/2-percent value for outside design temperature is less than 0°F. (–18°C.) (ASHRAE 97.5-percent column, winter, see Chapter 3), every vent extension through a roof or wall shall be a minimum of 3 inches (76 mm) in diameter. Any increase in the size of the vent shall be made inside the structure a minimum of 1 foot (305 mm) below the roof or inside the wall.

3603.3 Flashings and sealing. The juncture of each vent pipe with the roof line shall be made water tight by an approved flashing. Vent extensions in walls and soffits shall be made weather tight by caulking.

3603.4 Prohibited use. Vent terminals shall not be used as a flag pole or to support flag poles, TV aerials, or similar items, except when the piping has been anchored in an approved manner.

3603.5 Location of vent terminal. An open vent terminal from a drainage system shall not be located directly beneath any door, openable window, or other air intake opening of the building or of an adjacent building, nor shall any such vent terminal be within 10 feet (3048 mm) horizontally of such an opening unless it is a minimum of 2 feet (610 mm) above the top of such opening.

3603.6 Extension through the wall. Vent terminals extending through the wall shall terminate a minimum of 10 feet (3048 mm) from the lot line and 10 feet (3048 mm) above average ground level. Vent terminals shall not terminate under the overhang of a structure with soffit vents. Side wall vent terminals shall be protected to prevent birds or rodents from entering or blocking the vent opening.

Section 3604 — Vent Connections and Grades

3604.1 Connection. All individual, branch and circuit vents shall connect to a vent stack, stack vent or extend to the open air.

Exception: Individual, branch and circuit vents shall be permitted to terminate at an air admittance valve in accordance with Section 3614.

3604.2 Grade. All vent and branch vent pipes shall be so graded, connected and supported as to allow moisture and condensate to drain back to the soil or waste pipe by gravity.

3604.3 Vent connection to drainage system. Every dry vent connecting to a horizontal drain shall connect above the centerline of the horizontal drain pipe.

3604.4 Vertical rise of vent. Every dry vent shall rise vertically to a minimum of 6 inches (152 mm) above the flood-level rim of the highest trap or trapped fixture being vented.

3604.5 Height above fixtures. A connection between a vent pipe and a vent stack or stack vent shall be made at least 6 inches (152 mm) above the flood level rim of the highest fixture served by the vent. Horizontal vent pipes forming branch vents or loop vents shall be a minimum of 6 inches (152 mm) above the flood level rim of the highest fixture served.

3604.6 Vent for future fixtures. Where the drainage piping has been roughed-in for future fixtures, a rough-in connection for a vent shall be installed a minimum of one-half the diameter of the drain. The vent rough-in shall connect to the vent system. The connection shall be identified to indicate that the connection is a vent.

Section 3614 — Air Admittance Valves

3614.1 General. Vent systems utilizing air admittance valves shall comply with this section. Individual- and branch-type air admittance valves shall comply with ASSE 1051.

3614.2 Installation. The valves shall be installed in accordance with the requirements of this section and the manufacturer's installation instructions. Air admittance valves shall be installed after the DWV testing required by Section 2903.5.1 or 2903.5.2 has been performed.

3614.3 Where permitted. Individual, branch and circuit vents shall be permitted to terminate with a connection to an air admittance valve. The air admittance valve shall only vent fixtures that are on the same floor level and connect to a horizontal branch drain.

3614.4 Location. The air admittance valve shall be located a minimum of 4 inches (102 mm) above the horizontal branch drain or fixture drain being vented. The air admittance valve shall be located within the maximum developed length permitted for the vent. The air admittance valve shall be installed a minimum of 6 inches (152 mm) above insulation materials where installed in attics.

3614.5 Access and ventilation. Access shall be provided to all air admittance valves. The valve shall be located within a ventilated space that allows air to enter the valve.

3614.6 Size. The air admittance valve shall be rated for the size of the vent to which the valve is connected.

3614.7 Vent required. Within each plumbing system, a minimum of one stack vent or vent stack shall extend outdoors to the open air.

Uniform Plumbing Code — 1997
901.0 — Vents Required

Each plumbing fixture trap, except as otherwise provided in this Code, shall be protected against siphonage and back-pressure, and air circulation shall be assured throughout all parts of the drainage system by means of vent pipes installed in accordance with the requirements of this chapter and as otherwise required by this Code.

904.1 The size of vent piping shall be determined from its length and the total number of fixture units connected thereto, as set forth in Figure 14.8. The diameter of an individual vent shall not be less than one and one-fourth (1-1/4) inches (32 mm) nor less than one-half (1/2) the diameter of the drain to which it is connected. In addition, the drainage piping of each building and each connection to a public sewer or a private sewage disposal system shall be vented by means of one or more vent pipes, the aggregate cross-sectional area of which shall not be less than that of the largest required building sewer, as determined from Figure 14.8.

Exception: When connected to a common building sewer, the drainage piping of two (2) or more buildings located on the same lot and under one (1) ownership may be vented by means of piping sized in accordance with Figure 14.8, provided the aggregate cross-sectional area of all vents is not less than that of the largest required common building sewer.

904.2 No more than one-third (1/3) of the total permitted length, per Figure 14.8, of any minimum sized vent shall be installed in a horizontal position.

905.1 All vent and branch vent pipes shall be free from drops or sags and each such vent shall be level or shall be so graded and connected as to drip back by gravity to the drainage pipe it serves.

906.4 Vent pipes for outdoor installations shall extend at least ten (10) feet (3048 mm) above the surrounding ground and shall be securely supported.

906.5 Joints at the roof around vent pipes shall be made watertight by the use of approved flashings or flashing material.

908.1 Wet venting is limited to vertical drainage piping receiving the discharge from the trap arm of one (1) and two (2) fixture unit fixtures that also serves as a vent for not to exceed four (4) fixtures. All wet vented fixtures shall be within the same story; provided, further, that fixtures with a continuous vent discharging into a wet vent shall be within the same story as the wet vented fixtures. No wet vent shall exceed six (6) feet (1829 mm) in developed length.

909.0 Special Venting for Island Fixtures. Traps for island sinks and similar equipment shall be roughed in above the floor and may be vented by extending the vent as high as possible, but not less than the drainboard height and then returning it downward and connecting it to the horizontal sink drain immediately downstream from the vertical fixture drain. The return vent shall be connected to the horizontal drain through a wye-branch fitting and shall, in addition, be provided with a foot vent taken off the vertical fixture vent by means of a wye-branch immediately below the floor and extending to the nearest partition and then through the roof to the open air or may be connected to other vents at a point not less than six (6) inches (152 mm) above the flood level

Maximum Unit Loading and Maximum Length of Drainage and Vent Piping

Size of Pipe, inches (mm)	1-1/4 (32)	1-1/2 (38)	2 (51)	2-1/2 (64)	3 (76)	4 (102)	5 (127)	6 (152)	8 (203)	10 (254)	12 (305)
Maximum Units											
Drainage Piping[1]											
Vertical	1	2[2]	16[3]	32[3]	48[4]	256	600	1380	3600	5600	8400
Horizontal	1	1	8[3]	14[3]	35[4]	216[5]	428[5]	720[5]	2640[5]	4680[5]	8200[5]
Maximum Length											
Drainage Piping											
Vertical, feet	45	65	85	148	212	300	390	510	750		
(m)	(14)	(20)	(26)	(45)	(65)	(91)	(119)	(155)	(228)		
Horizontal (Unlimited)											
Vent Piping (See note)											
Horizontal and Vertical											
Maximum Units	1	8[3]	24	48	84	256	600	1380	3600		
Maximum Lengths, feet	45	60	120	180	212	300	390	510	750		
(m)	(14)	(18)	(37)	(55)	(65)	(91)	(119)	(155)	(228)		

Courtesy of IAPMO, Uniform Plumbing Code — 1997 [Table 7-5]

Figure 14.9

rim of the fixtures served. Drainage fittings shall be used on all parts of the vent below the floor level and a minimum slope of one-quarter (1/4) inch per foot (20.9 mm/m) back to the drain shall be maintained. The return bend used under the drainboard shall be a one (1) piece fitting or an assembly of a forty-five (45) degree (0.79 rad), a ninety (90) degree (1.6 rad) and a forty-five (45) degree (0.79 rad) elbow in the order named. Pipe sizing shall be as elsewhere required in this Code. The island sink drain, upstream of the returned vent, shall serve no other fixtures. An accessible cleanout shall be installed in the vertical portion of the foot vent.

UBC — 1997

901.2.1 Venting required. Every trap and trapped fixture shall be vented in accordance with one of the venting methods specified in this chapter.

901.4 Use limitations. The plumbing vent system shall not be utilized for purposes other than the venting of the plumbing system.

903.1 Main vent required. Every sanitary drainage system receiving the discharge of a water closet shall have a main vent that is either a vent stack or a stack vent. Such vent shall run undiminished in size and as directly as possible from the building drain through to the open air above the roof.

903.2 Vent stack required. A vent stack shall be required for every drainage stack that is five branch intervals or more.

904.2 Frost closure. Where the 97-1/2 % value for outside design temperature is less than 0°F (–18°C), every vent extension through a roof or wall shall be a minimum of 3 inches (76 mm) in diameter. Any increase in the size of the vent shall be made inside the structure a minimum of 1 foot (305 mm) below the roof or inside the wall.

904.4 Prohibited use. Vent terminals shall not be used as a flag pole or to support flag poles, TV aerials or similar items, except when the piping has been anchored in an approved manner.

904.5 Location of vent terminal. An open vent terminal from a drainage system shall not be located directly beneath any door, openable window, or other air intake opening of the building or of an adjacent building, and any such vent terminal shall not be within 10 feet (3048 mm) horizontally of such an opening unless it is at least 2 feet (610 mm) above the top of such opening.

904.6 Extension through the wall. Vent terminals extending through the wall shall terminate a minimum of 10 feet (3048 mm) from the lot line and 10 feet (3048 mm) above average ground level. Vent terminals shall not terminate under the overhang of a structure with soffit vents. Side wall vent terminals shall be protected to prevent birds or rodents from entering or blocking the vent opening.

Maximum Distance of Fixture Trap from Vent

SIZE OF TRAP (inches)	SIZE OF FIXTURE DRAIN (inches)	SLOPE (inch per foot)	DISTANCE FROM TRAP (feet)
1 1/4	1 1/4	1/4	3 1/2
1 1/4	1 1/2	1/4	5
1 1/2	1 1/2	1/4	5
1 1/2	2	1/4	8
2	2	1/4	6
3	3	1/8	10
4	4	1/8	12

For SI: 1 inch = 25.4 mm, 1 inch per foot = 0.0833 mm/m, 1 foot = 304.8 mm.

Courtesy of IAPMO, Uniform Plumbing Code — 1997 [Table 906.1]

Figure 14.10

906.1 Distance of trap from vent. Each fixture trap shall have a protecting vent located so that the slope and the developed length in the fixture drain from the trap weir to the vent fitting are within the requirements set forth in Table 906.1.

908.1 Individual vent as common vent. An individual vent is permitted to vent two traps or trapped fixtures as a common vent. The traps or trapped fixtures being common vented shall be located on the same floor level.

909.1 Wet vent permitted. Any combination of fixtures within two bathroom groups located on the same floor level are permitted to be vented by a wet vent. The wet vent shall be considered the vent for the fixtures and shall extend from the connection of the dry vent along the direction of the flow in the drain pipe to the most downstream fixture drain connection to the horizontal branch drain. Only the fixtures within the bathroom groups shall connect to the wet-vented horizontal branch drain. Any additional fixtures shall discharge downstream of the wet vent.

913.1 Limitation. Island fixture venting shall not be permitted for fixtures other than sinks and lavatories. Residential kitchen sinks with a dishwasher waste connection, a food waste grinder, or both, in combination with the kitchen sink waste, shall be permitted to be vented in accordance with this section.

Trap Arms

IOTFDC — 1998 (formerly CABO)

Section 3605 — Fixture Vents

3605.1 Distance of trap from vent. Each fixture trap shall have a protecting vent located so that the slope and the developed length in the fixture drain from the trap weir to the vent fitting comply with Table 3605.1 (see **Figure 14.11**).

Maximum Distance of Fixture Trap From Vent

SIZE OF TRAP (inches)	SLOPE (inch per foot)	DISTANCE FROM TRAP (feet)
1-1/4	1/4	5
1-1/2	1/4	6
2	1/4	8
3	1/4	12
4	1/8	16

For SI: 1 inch = 25.4 mm, 1 inch per foot = 0.0833 mm/m
1 foot = 304.8 mm.

Courtesy of ICC, IOTFDC — 1998 (formerly CABO) [Table 3605.1]

Figure 14.11

3605.2 Fixture drains. The total fall in a fixture drain due to pipe slope shall not exceed one pipe diameter, nor shall the vent pipe connection to a fixture drain, except for water closets, be below the weir of the trap, except as provided in Section 3605.3.

3605.3 Vertical leg for waste fixture drains. A vertical leg (see **Figure 14.12**) shall be permitted within a fixture drain of a waster fixture in accordance with the following criteria:

1. Minimum trap diameter shall be in accordance with Table 3701.7.
2. The diameter of Section A shall be equal to the diameter of the trap.
3. The length of Section A shall be a minimum of 8 inches (203 mm) and in accordance with Table 3605.1.
4. The diameter of Section B shall be one pipe size larger than the diameter of Section A.
5. The length of Section B shall be a maximum of 36 inches (914 mm).
6. The diameter of Section C shall be one pipe size larger than the diameter of Section B.
7. There is no restriction on the length of Section C.
8. Bends shall be the diameter of the largest connected section.

3605.4 Crown Vent. A vent shall not be installed within two pipe diameters of the trap weir.

Vertical Leg Trap Arm Schematic

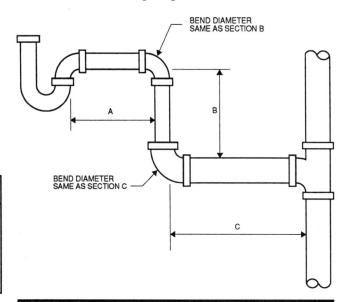

Courtesy of ICC, IOTFDC — 1998 (formerly CABO) [Figure 3605.3]

Figure 14.12

Traps

Uniform Plumbing Code — 1997

1001.1 Each plumbing fixture, excepting those having integral traps, shall be separately trapped by an approved type waterseal trap. Not more than one (1) trap shall be permitted on a trap arm.

1002.1 Fixture traps. Each plumbing fixture shall be separately trapped by a water-seal trap, except as otherwise permitted by this code. The trap shall be placed as close as possible to the fixture outlet. The vertical distance from the fixture outlet to the trap weir shall not exceed 24 inches (610 mm). The distance of a clothes washer standpipe above a trap shall conform to Section 802.4. A fixture shall not be double trapped. An automatic clothes washer or laundry tub shall not discharge to a trap serving a kitchen sink.

Exceptions:

1. This section shall not apply to fixtures with integral traps.
2. A combination plumbing fixture is permitted to be installed on one trap provided that one compartment is not more than 6 inches (152 mm) deeper than the other compartment and the waste outlets are not more than 30 inches (762 mm) apart.

1003.1 Each trap, except one for an interceptor or similar device shall be self-cleaning. Traps for bathtubs, showers, lavatories, sinks, laundry tubs, floor drains, hoppers, urinals, drinking fountains, dental units, and similar fixtures shall be of standard design and weight and shall be of ABS, cast brass, cast iron, lead, PVC, or other approved material. An exposed and readily accessible drawn brass tubing trap, not less than 17 B&S Gauge (0.045 inch) (1.1 mm), may be used on fixtures discharging domestic sewage but shall exclude urinals. Each trap shall have the manufacturer's name stamped legibly in the metal of the trap and each tubing trap shall have the gauge of the tubing in addition to the manufacturer's name. Every trap shall have a smooth and uniform interior waterway.

1003.2 No more than one (1) approved slip joint fitting may be used on the outlet side of a trap, and no tubing trap shall be installed without a listed tubing trap adapter.

Comments

Slip Joints

Slip Joints should not be allowed on the outlet (street side) of the trap. The packing may dry out, thus allowing the emittance of sewer gases into the building.

1003.3 The size (nominal diameter) of a trap for a given fixture shall be sufficient to drain the fixture rapidly, but in no case less than nor more than one (1) pipe size larger than given in Table 7-3. The trap shall be the same size as the trap arm to which it is connected.

1004.0 Traps — Prohibited. No form of trap which depends for its seal upon the action of movable parts shall be used. No trap which has concealed interior partitions shall be used. "S" traps, bell traps, and crown-vented traps shall be prohibited. No fixture shall be double trapped.

Drum and bottle traps may be installed only when permitted by the Administrative Authority for special conditions. No trap shall be installed without a vent, except as otherwise provided in this Code.

1005.0 Trap Seals. Each fixture trap shall have a water seal of not less than two (2) inches (51 mm) and not more than four (4) inches (102 mm) except where a deeper seal is found necessary by the Administrative Authority for special conditions or for special designs relating to handicapped accessible fixtures. Traps shall be set true with respect to their water seals and, where necessary, they shall be protected from freezing.

1008.0 Building Traps. Building traps shall not be installed except where required by the Administrative Authority. Each building trap when installed shall be provided with a cleanout and with a relieving vent or fresh air intake on the inlet side of the trap which need not be larger than one-half the diameter of the drain to which it connects. Such relieving vent or fresh air intake shall be carried above grade and terminate in a screened outlet located outside the building.

Private Sewage Disposal

IOTFDC — 1998 (formerly CABO)

Section 3801 — General

3801.2 Mandatory connection to public sewer. A permit shall not be issued for the installation, alteration or repair of a private sewage disposal system or part thereof when a connection with a public sewer is available. "Available" shall be deemed to be a parcel of land abutting on a street, alley or easement.

3801.3 Mandatory connection to a sewage system. Plumbing fixtures and drainage piping shall be connected to a public sewer or an approved private or individual sewage disposal system.

3801.5 Prohibited Connections. Rain, surface or subsurface water shall not be connected to or discharge into a drainage system, sanitary sewer system or individual sewage disposal system. Cesspools, septic tanks, seepage pits and drain fields shall not be connected to public sewers or to building sewers leading to public sewers.

Section 3803 — Disposal Systems

3803.1 General. The type of private sewage disposal system shall be determined on the basis of location, soil porosity and groundwater level as determined by the local jurisdiction.

Location of Sewage Disposal System

MINIMUM HORIZONTAL DISTANCE IN CLEAR REQUIRED FROM	BUILDING SEWER	SEPTIC TANK	DISPOSAL FIELD	SEEPAGE PIT OR CESSPOOL
Buildings or structures[1]	2 feet	5 feet	8 feet	8 feet
Property line adjoining private property	Clear	5 feet	5 feet	8 feet
Water-supply wells	50 feet[2]	50 feet	50 feet	100 feet
Streams	50 feet	50 feet	50 feet	100 feet
Large trees		10 feet		10 feet
Seepage pits or cesspools		5 feet	5 feet	12 feet
Disposal field		5 feet	4 feet[3]	5 feet
Domestic water line	1 foot	5 feet	5 feet	5 feet
Distribution box		5 feet	5 feet	5 feet

For **SI:** 1 foot = 304.8 mm.

NOTE: When disposal fields and/or seepage pits are installed in sloping ground, the minimum horizontal distance between any part of the leaching system and ground surface shall be 15 feet.

[1] Including porches and steps whether covered or uncovered, breezeways, roofed porte cocheres, roofed patios, carports, covered walks, covered driveways and similar structures or appurtenances.

[2] All nonmetallic drainage piping shall clear domestic water-supply wells by at least 50 feet. This distance may be reduced to not less than 25 feet when approved-type metallic piping is installed.

Where special hazards are involved, the distance required shall be increased as may be directed by the building official or public health authority.

[3] Plus 2 feet for each additional foot or depth in excess of 1 foot below the bottom of the drain line.

Courtesy of ICC, IOTFDC — 1998 (formerly CABO) [Figure 3804.1]

Figure 14.13

3803.4 Additional capacity. Private sewage disposal systems shall be designed so that additional seepage pits or subsurface drain field, equivalent to at least 50 percent of the required original system, shall be permitted to be installed.

Section 3804 — Location

3804.1 General. Private sewage disposal systems shall be located as set forth in Table 3804.1 (see **Figure 14.13**).

Gas Piping Installation

Industry Standards
Plumbing Estimating Methods
(R.S. Means Co., Inc.)

Natural gas serves as an energy source for items such as boilers, burners, hot water generators, unit heaters, etc. Gas is generally supplied to customers via gas mains supplied and maintained by local gas companies. In most cities, the gas service and meter to individual buildings is also provided by the gas company. However, the estimator [or contractor] should check with the local utility for a listing of the regulations for each particular project.

The gas system within a building is all the piping, valves, and devices starting from the gas meter. The plumber begins the distribution of piping within the building after the gas meter, supplying a gas regulator if required. Gas regulators are usually required if the gas supply is at a pressure in excess of 1/2 psi.

> ## Comments
> *When gas is used as a fuel for cooking, clothes drying, water heating, gas logs, heating, cooling or incineration, it is usually included as part of the plumbing installation. In many areas, the installing mechanic must be a licensed gas fitter rather than a plumber. Gas appliances such as water heaters, furnaces, boilers, incinerators and the like must not only be vented to the outside air, but also must be provided with sufficient fresh make-up air to allow for combustion.*

IOTFDC — 1998 (formerly CABO)

2607.7 Appliance connection. Gas appliances and equipment shall be connected to the building piping by rigid metallic pipes, semi-rigid metallic tubing, or a listed and labeled gas appliance connector having a diameter not less than the nominal inlet connection to the appliance in accordance with their listing and label. Labeled metal appliance connectors shall have a maximum overall length of 3 feet (914 mm), except range and domestic clothes dryer connections, which may not exceed 6 feet (1829 mm)

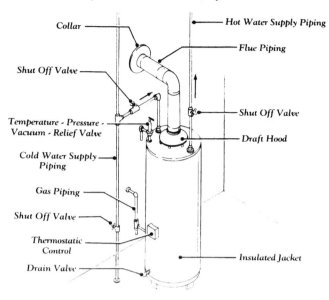

Gas-Fired Hot Water System

Collar

Hot Water Supply Piping

Flue Piping

Shut Off Valve

Temperature - Pressure - Vacuum - Relief Valve

Shut Off Valve

Draft Hood

Cold Water Supply Piping

Gas Piping

Shut Off Valve

Thermostatic Control

Drain Valve

Insulated Jacket

R.S. Means Co., Inc., *Fundamentals of the Construction Process*

Figure 14.14

in length. Connectors shall not be concealed within or extended through walls, floors or partitions. The connection of an indoor appliance with any type of gas hose is prohibited. Outdoor portable appliances shall be permitted to be connected with an approved outdoor hose connector not to exceed 15 feet (4572 mm) in length, provided it connects outdoors to approved fuel-gas piping including an approved valve at the inlet of the hose connector. Appliances may be connected to fuel-gas piping with a listed quick-disconnect device.

2608.1.5 Piping beneath buildings. Fuel-gas piping located beneath buildings shall be encased in conduit which is capable of withstanding superimposed loads. The terminal point where the conduit enters the building shall be sealed to prevent the entrance of gas leakage. The conduit shall extend at least 4 inches (102 mm) outside the building and be vented above grade to the outside. This section shall not apply to piping in ventilated crawl spaces.

2608.2 Piping in buildings. Piping within buildings shall comply with Sections 2608.2.1 through 2608.2.6.

2608.2.1 Drilling and notching. When necessary, wood-framed structural members shall be drilled or notched as provided in Sections 502.6, 602.6 and 802.6. Holes in cold-formed steel-framed load-bearing members shall only be permitted in accordance with Sections 506.2, 603.2 and 804.2. In accordance with the provisions of Sections 506.3.5, 603.3.4 and 804.3.5, cutting and notching of flanges and lips of cold-formed steel-framed load-bearing members shall not be permitted.

2608.2.3 Prohibited locations. Fuel-gas piping shall not be run in or through supply and return air ducts, clothes chutes, chimneys, vents, dumbwaiters or elevator shafts. This provision shall not apply to ducts used to provide combustion air in accordance with Chapter 20. Valves and unions shall not be located in any air plenum.

2608.2.4 Piping in concealed locations. Portions of fuel-gas piping systems installed in concealed locations shall not have unions. Concealed tubing joints shall be brazed in accordance with Section 2607.4.

2608.2.5 Piping in concrete slabs. Fuel-gas piping embedded in concrete slabs shall be surrounded with a minimum of 1-1/2 inches (38 mm) of concrete and shall not be in physical contact with reinforcing or other metallic components. Piping shall not be embedded in concrete slabs containing quickset additives or cinder aggregate. All piping, fittings and risers shall be protected against corrosion in accordance with Section 2608.1.2.

2608.2.6 Hangers and supports. Hangers and supports shall be of sufficient strength to support the piping, and shall be fabricated of materials compatible with the piping material. Piping shall be supported at intervals not exceeding the spacings specified in Table 2608.2.6.

2608.3 Aboveground outside piping. Piping installed above-ground outside of the building shall be securely supported and protected from physical damage. Piping that penetrates outside walls shall be protected against corrosion by coating or wrapping with an inert material. Where piping is encased in a protective sleeve, the annular space between the pipe and sleeve shall be sealed.

2608.8 Marking and labeling. Where other than black steel pipe is used, gas piping shall be identified by yellow labels marked "GAS" in black letters placed at 5 foot (1524 mm) intervals where exposed. This marking shall not be required on pipe in the same room as the equipment. All tubing carrying medium pressure gas shall be marked with a label at the beginning and end of each tubing section.

2608.9 Electrical bonding and grounding. Each aboveground portion of a metallic gas piping system upstream from the appliance shutoff valve shall be electrically continuous and bonded to a grounding electrode in accordance with Chapters 39 through 48. Fuel-gas piping shall not be used as a grounding electrode.

2608.9.1 Electrical circuits prohibited. Fuel-gas piping or components shall not be used as electrical circuits except that low-voltage (50 volts or less) control circuits, ignition circuits, and electronic flame detection device circuits shall be permitted to make use of piping or components for a part of an electrical circuit.

NFPA 54: National Fuel Gas Code
3.14 Electrical Bonding and Grounding.

(a) Each aboveground portion of a gas piping system upstream from the equipment shutoff valve shall be electrically continuous and bonded to any grounding electrode, as defined by the *National Electrical Code®*, ANSI/NFPA 70.

(b) Gas piping shall not be used as a grounding electrode.

Comments

Section 3.14 requires that gas piping aboveground, ahead of the equipment shutoff valve, must be electrically continuous and bonded to a grounding electrode. It also requires that the gas piping not be the grounding electrode. The National Electrical Code® (Article 250) defines a grounding electrode as a rod driven into the ground, the steel frame of a building, buried metal water piping, or a concrete encased electrode. The National Electrical Code® further requires that if more than one of these is used, they must be bonded together.

The point of these requirements is that, to avoid any electrical potential build-up that could produce a spark, the gas piping be at ground potential.

The gas piping is forbidden to be a grounding electrode, however, because it is possible for any grounding electrode to carry large currents that have a possibility of sparking if the piping should be opened for any reason. A difference of electrical potential between an ungrounded piping system and a grounded metal object could also pose an electric shock hazard to persons coming into contact with the two systems.

CHAPTER
15 HVAC

Table of Contents

(continued on next page)

Text in blue print indicates excerpts from model building code(s). "Comments" (in solid blue boxes) were written by the editors, based on their own experience.

For building product information, use this book's special Internet gateway to thousands of manufacturers: www.rsmeans.com/prodsupp/rlstand.html

Common Defect Allegations

- *Unsupported flexible plastic duct will kink after it settles over a few years.*

- *Sometimes condensate lines are either missing or installed too high, preventing gravity flow and causing the evaporator collector pan to overflow and stain the ceilings. The condensate overflow should be exposed to the exterior so that the owner can tell when the drain is not working. The basic condensate drain should drain into a sewer drain to prevent health hazards like Legionnaires disease. Condensate pipe should be at least 3/4" to reduce the chance of clogging. Many codes require condensate to drain into storm lines. Check your local code.*

- *Air flow may be insufficient due to small ducting, or heating and cooling may not have enough tonnage and BTU rating to make the building comfortable. These claims should be reviewed by a mechanical engineer who will establish calculations based on the size of the facility. Good design usually is to slightly undersize the units so that they can run without stopping for a period of time. Short starting and stopping cycles will use more energy than a continuously running system and will not properly dehumidify the air. It also creates greater temperature fluctuations and subjects the equipment to more wear and tear.*

- *Undersized exhaust fans in a shower area can cause mold buildup in bathrooms that get a lot of use. Many times a combination heat lamp/exhaust fan provides the proper air flow without the lamp installed, but will not be adequate when the lamp is in place.*

- *Gas heaters can cause fires. In bench testing the heaters after a claim is made, it is usually found that the heater worked properly and was simply running during the fire. Most heaters have a series of limit switches that shut off gas and turn on the fan when the unit overheats.*

- *Other claims items include: missing or improperly located fresh air supplies for gas appliances in closets, inadequate working space in front of equipment, and the return air plenum partially constructed from the stairs. (On lighter shades of carpeting, the edges can turn black as the carpet acts as a filter for the return air leaking through the stringer and the wall.)*

Introduction

Usually there are no written specifications or installation drawings for the heating, cooling or ventilation for individual homes. Notes on the architectural drawings would indicate the heating and/or cooling requirements for the occupied spaces. For light commercial properties a more formal set of drawings and specifications is typically incorporated into the builder's plans and bid documents.

Whether or not installation plans and specifications are available at bidding time, it is understood that the installation will be sized adequately to maintain desired temperature and humidity conditions year-round.

The materials and installation will be governed by the appropriate building codes (either national or local) for the locality as set for its prevailing standards.

The type of system required will depend primarily on geographic location and use. Some buildings might require heating only, some cooling only with an auxiliary heating backup for extraordinary weather conditions. Most locales will require a combination of heating and cooling.

Ed. Note: Refer to Chapter 14, "Plumbing," for ventilation requirements for plumbing fixtures.

The following is a list of codes, professional organizations, and other resources that are called upon to ensure that mechanical installations are adequately sized and installed to meet or surpass the standards required by the authority having jurisdiction.

Air-Conditioning and Refrigeration Institute (ARI)
4301 North Fairfax Drive, Suite 425
Arlington, VA 22203
Telephone: 703-524-8800
www.ari.org

American Petroleum Institute (API)
1220 L Street, N.W.
Washington, DC 20005
Telephone: 202-682-8000
www.api.org

American Society of Mechanical Engineers (ASME)
3 Park Avenue
New York, NY 10016-5990
Telephone: 212-591-7740
www.asme.org

American Society of Heating, Refrigerating, and Air Conditioning Engineers (ASHRAE)
1791 Tullie Circle, N.E.
Atlanta, GA 30329
Telephone: 404-636-8400
www.ashrae.org
ASHRAE writes standards that set uniform methods of testing and rating equipment, and establish accepted practices for the HVAC&R industry.

International Association of Plumbing and Mechanical Officials (IAPMO)
20001 East Walnut Drive South
Walnut, CA 91789
Telephone: 909-595-8449
www.iapmo.org

National Fire Protection Association (NFPA)
1 Batterymarch Park
P.O. Box 9101
Quincy, MA 02269
Telephone: 617-770-3000
www.nfpa.org

Plumbing · Heating · Cooling · Contractors National Association (PHCC-NA)
180 South Washington Street
P.O. Box 6808
Falls Church, VA 22046
Telephone: 703-237-8100
www.naphcc.org
Note: The *National Standard Plumbing Code* is available from this organization.

Sheet Metal & Air Conditioning Contractors' National Association (SMACNA)
4201 Lafayette Center Drive
Chantilly, VA 20153
Telephone: 703-803-2980
www.smacna.org

Note: The *International Plumbing Code* (IPC), the *International Mechanical Code* (IMC) and the *International One- and Two-Family Dwelling Code* are jointly copyrighted by and available through the International Code Council, Inc. (ICC), the Building Officials and Code Administrators International, Inc. (BOCA), the International Conference of Building Officials (ICBO), and the Southern Building Code Congress International, Inc. (SBCCI).

The BOCA *National Plumbing Code* and *National Mechanical Code* are available from that organization. The *Standard Mechanical Code* is available from the Southern Building Code Congress International, Inc. (SBCCI).

As of November 1997, the International Code Council (ICC) assumed responsibility for the development and maintenance of the *International One- and Two-Family Dwelling Code* (IOTFDC), which replaces CABO. The IOTFDC is available from any of the above code organizations.

(See "Understanding Building Codes & Other Standards" at the beginning of this book for information on contacting these organizations.)

Ed. Note: Comments and recommendations within this chapter are not intended as a definitive resource for construction activities. For building projects, contractors must rely on the project documents and any applicable code requirements pertaining to their own particular locations.

Basic HVAC Systems

Industry Standards
HVAC: Design Criteria, Options, Selection
(R.S. Means Co., Inc.)

Heating is required in a building when the ambient temperatures are low enough to demand additional warmth for comfort. Boilers or furnaces *generate* the heat for a building; solar devices *capture, store,* and *release* heat; pipes or ducts *distribute* the heat; and convectors/radiators or diffusers are the terminal units that *deliver* the heat. A typical hydronic (hot water or steam) heating system is shown in **Figure 15.1**.

Cooling systems utilize cooler outdoor air when available, a refrigeration cycle, or other heat rejection method to supply cool air to occupied spaces. Chilled water or cool air is distributed by pipes and ducts throughout the building to terminal units (diffusers or fan coils). These end units deliver the cooling to the desired spaces. While cooling is rarely required by code, it is almost universally expected in commercial environments. Cooling systems may be independent of heating systems (such as simple window air conditioner) or integrated with the heating system (such as a rooftop unit).

Ventilating systems operate to provide fresh outdoor air to minimize odors and to reduce unhealthy dust or fumes. In many spaces, simple operable windows satisfy ventilation requirements. On the other hand, ventilation may be provided to a building by exhaust fans or fresh air intakes.

Air Conditioning usually combines all of the features of heating, cooling, and ventilating systems, and may also provide additional "conditioning" of the overall environment such as noise control, air cleaning (filtration), humidity control, and energy-efficient controls (free-cooling options).

The process of producing heating or cooling from generation to distribution to terminal units is common to all systems.

Basic Hydronic Heating System

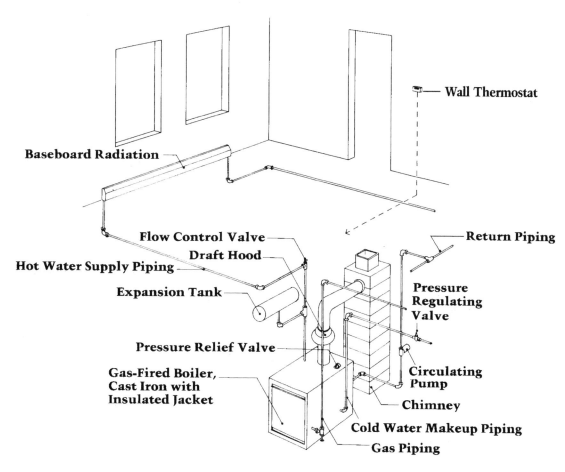

R.S. Means Co., Inc., HVAC: *Design Criteria, Options, Selection*

Figure 15.1

Generation equipment produces heat (heating) or removes heat (cooling) to or from the building. Boilers, furnaces, or supplied steam add heat; cooling towers, chillers, or heat pumps reject heat. The equipment for generation systems is the most expensive component of the HVAC system and is generally located in the mechanical equipment room.

The warm air or cold water that the various pieces of generation equipment produce is *distributed* throughout the building. A distribution system basically consists of pipes (water or steam) or ducts (air) that take the heated or cooled medium from the equipment that generated it through the building to the terminal unit. In addition, a distribution system may have valves, dampers, and fittings.

The **terminal units**, located in the conditioned spaces, include convectors (radiators), air diffusers, and fan coil units. These units receive the air or water from the distribution system and utilize it to warm or cool the air in the space.

General Mechanical System Requirements

International One- and Two-Family Dwelling Code (IOTFDC) — 1998

Copyright 1998, International Code Council, Inc. — *International One- and Two-Family Dwelling Code*, 5203 Leesburg Pike, Suite 708, Falls Church, Virginia 22041.

Section 1303 — Labeling of Equipment

1303.1 General. All appliances shall bear a permanent and legible factory-applied label which shall include the following information:

1. Name or trademark of the manufacturer.

2. The model and serial number.

3. Identity of the agency certifying compliance of equipment with approved standards.

4. Clearances from combustible construction for heat-producing appliances.

1303.2 Fuel-burning appliances. The listing and label for fuel-burning appliances, except wood stoves and fireplaces, shall also indicate:

1. The type of fuel approved for use with the appliance.

2. The input or output ratings.

3. Instructions for the lighting operation and shutoff of the appliance.

1303.3 Other than fuel-burning appliances. The listing and label for other than fuel-burning appliances shall also indicate:

1. The output rating in Btu/h or kw.

2. The electrical rating in volts, amperes (or watts) and, for other than single phase, the number of phases.

3. The electrical rating in volts, amperes (or watts) of each field-replaceable electrical component.

4. Amount and type of refrigerant, and factory test pressures or pressures applied for heat pumps and refrigeration cooling equipment.

Section 1305 — Appliance Access

1305.1 Appliance access for inspection service, repair and replacement. Appliances shall be accessible for inspection, service, repair and replacement without removing permanent construction. Thirty inches (762 mm) of working space and platform shall be provided in front of the control side to service an appliance. Room heaters shall be permitted to be installed with at least an 18-inch (457 mm) working space. A platform shall not be required for room heaters.

Section 1306 — Clearances from Combustible Construction

1306.1 Appliance clearance. Listed appliances shall be installed with at least the clearances from unprotected combustible materials as indicated on the appliance label and manufacturer's installation instructions. Unlisted appliances shall have minimum clearances to unprotected combustibles in accordance with Figure 1306.1 and Table 1306.1.

1306.2 Clearance reduction. Reduction of clearances shall be in accordance with the appliance manufacturer's instructions and Table 1306.2. Forms of protection with ventilated air space shall conform to the following requirements:

1. Not less than 1-inch (25.4 mm) air space shall be provided between the protection and combustible wall surface.

2. Air circulation shall be provided by having edges of the wall protection open at least 1 inch (25.4 mm).

3. If the wall protection is mounted on a single flat wall away from corners, air circulation shall be provided by having the bottom and top edges, or the side and top edges open at least 1 inch (25.4 mm).

4. Wall protection covering two walls in a corner shall be open at the bottom and top edges at least 1 inch (25.4 mm).

1306.2.1 Solid fuel appliances. Table 1306.2 shall not be used to reduce the clearance required for appliances listed for installation with minimum clearances of 12 inches (305 mm) or less. For appliances listed for installation with minimum clearances greater than 12 inches (305 mm), Table 1306.2 shall not be used to reduce the clearance to less than 12 inches (305 mm).

Section 1307 — Appliance Installation

1307.1 General. Installation of appliances shall conform to the conditions of their listing and label and the manufacturer's installation instructions. The manufacturer's operating instructions shall remain attached to the appliance.

1307.2 Anchorage of appliances. Appliances designed to be fixed in position shall be fastened in place. In Seismic Zones 3 and 4 in accordance with Figure 301.2(2), water heaters having nonrigid water connections and over 4 feet (1219 mm) in height from the base to the top of the tank case shall be anchored or strapped to the building to resist horizontal displacement due to earthquake motion.

1307.3 Appliances located in garage. Heating and cooling appliances located in a garage shall be protected from impact by automobiles. Appliances that generate a glow, spark or flame capable of igniting gasoline vapors and located in a garage shall be installed with burners, burner ignition devices, or heating elements and switches at least 18 inches (457 mm) above the floor level. When such appliances are enclosed in a separate compartment having access only from outside of the garage, such appliances shall be permitted to be installed at floor level, provided that the required combustion air is taken from and discharged to the exterior of the garage.

1307.4 Electrical appliances. Electrical appliances shall be installed in accordance with Chapters 15 and 39 through 48.

Section 1308 — Control Devices

1308.1 Gas appliances. Automatic gas-burning appliances shall be equipped with a listed and labeled device or devices that will shut off the fuel supply to the main burner or burners in the event of pilot or ignition failure. In addition, liquefied petroleum gas-heating appliances shall be equipped with a listed and labeled automatic device or devices that will shut off the flow of gas to the pilot in the event of ignition failure. The listed and labeled shutoff devices shall not be required on range or cooking tops, log lighters, lights or other open-burner manually operated appliances, or listed and labeled appliances not requiring such devices.

1308.2 Oil-burning appliances. Oil-burning appliances shall be provided with automatic limit devices to sense and control overheating, and primary safety controls that will shut off flow of fuel to the burners in the event of ignition failure or failure of the main burner flame. Oil-fired water boilers shall be provided with listed and labeled relief valves and temperature-limiting devices whose combined Btu/h rating shall be equal to or greater than the boiler rating.

1308.3 Forced-air furnaces. Forced-air furnaces shall be equipped with a listed and labeled limit control that will prevent outlet air temperature from exceeding 250°F. (121°C.). Such controls shall be located in the bonnet or plenum.

1308.4 Electric duct heaters. Electric duct heaters shall be equipped with an automatic reset air outlet temperature-limit control that will limit the outlet air temperature to no more than 200°F. (93°C.). The electric elements of the heater shall be equipped with fusible links or a manual reset temperature-limit control that will prevent air temperature in the immediate vicinity of the heating elements from exceeding 250°F. (121°C.).

Vented Floor, Wall and Room Heaters

IOTFDC — 1998 (formerly CABO)

Section 1601 — Vented Floor Furnaces

1601.1 General. Vented floor furnaces conforming to ANSI Z21.48 or UL 729 shall be installed in accordance with the manufacturer's installation instructions and the requirements of this code.

1601.2 Clearances. Vented floor furnaces shall be installed in accordance with their listing and the manufacturer's installation instructions.

1601.3 Location. Location of floor furnaces shall conform to the following requirements:

1. Floor registers of floor furnaces shall be installed not less than 6 inches (153 mm) from a wall.

2. Wall registers of floor furnaces shall be installed not less than 6 inches (153 mm) from the adjoining wall at inside corners.

3. The furnace register shall be located not less than 12 inches (305 mm) from doors in any position, draperies or similar combustible objects.

4. The furnace register shall be located at least 5 feet (1524 mm) below any projecting combustible materials.

5. The floor furnace burner assembly shall not project into an occupied under-floor area.

1601.4 Access. An opening in the foundation not less than 18 inches by 24 inches (457 mm by 610 mm), or a trap door not less than 20 inches by 30 inches (508 mm by 762 mm) shall be provided for access to a floor furnace. The opening and passageway shall be large enough to allow replacement of any part of the equipment.

1601.5 Installation. Floor furnace installations shall conform to the following requirements:

1. Thermostats controlling floor furnaces shall be located in the room in which the register of the floor furnace is located.

2. Floor furnaces shall be supported independently of the furnace floor register.

3. Floor furnaces shall be installed not closer than 6 inches (153 mm) to the ground. Clearance shall be permitted to be reduced to 2 inches (51 mm), provided that the lower 6 inches (153 mm) of the furnace is sealed to prevent water entry.

4. When excavation is required for a floor furnace installation, the excavation shall extend 30 inches (762 mm) beyond the control side of the floor furnace and 12 inches (305 mm) beyond the remaining sides. Excavations shall slope outward from the perimeter of the base of the excavation to the surrounding grade at an angle not exceeding 45 degrees from horizontal.

5. Floor furnaces shall not be supported from the ground.

Section 1602 — Vented Wall Furnaces

1602.1 General. Vented wall furnace construction conforming with ANSI Z21.44, ANSI Z21.49 or UL 730 shall be installed in accordance with the manufacturer's installation instructions and the requirements of this code.

1602.2 Location. The location of vented wall furnaces shall conform to the following requirements:

1. Vented wall furnaces shall be located not less than 6 inches (153 mm) from adjoining walls at inside corners.

2. Vented wall furnaces shall not be located where a door can swing within 12 inches (305 mm) of the furnace air inlet or outlet and shall not be installed less than 18 inches (457 mm) below overhead projections.

1602.3 Installation Vented wall furnace installations shall conform to the following requirements:

1. Required wall thicknesses shall be in accordance with the manufacturer's installation instructions.

2. Ducts shall not be attached to a wall furnace. Casing extensions or boots shall only be installed when listed as part of a listed and labeled appliance.

Section 1603 — Vented Room Heaters

1603.1 General. Vented Room Heaters conforming with ANSI Z21.11.1, UL 1482 or UL 896 shall be installed in accordance with the manufacturer's installation instructions and the requirements of this code.

1603.2 Clearances. Vented room heaters shall be installed in accordance with their listing and the manufacturer's installation instructions.

1603.3 Location. A room heater shall be placed so as not to cause a hazard to walls, floors, curtains and drapes, or to the free movement of persons. Heaters marked "For use in noncombustible fireplace only" shall be installed as listed and labeled.

1603.4 Installation. Room heaters shall be installed on noncombustible floors or approved assemblies constructed of noncombustible materials that extend at least 18 inches (457 mm) beyond the appliance on all sides.

1603.5 Solid-fuel-burning heaters. Solid-fuel-burning heaters installed in garages shall be installed in accordance with the manufacturer's installation instructions and the requirements of this code.

Electric Resistance Heating

IOTFDC — 1998 (formerly CABO)
Section 1501 — Baseboard Convectors

1501.1 General. Electric baseboard convectors shall be listed and labeled and shall be installed in accordance with the manufacturer's installation instructions and Chapters 39 through 48.

Section 1502 — Radiant Heating Systems

1502.1 General. Radiant heating systems shall be listed and labeled and shall be installed in accordance with the manufacturer's installation instructions and Chapters 39 through 48.

1502.2 Clearances. Clearances for radiant heating panels or elements to any wiring, outlet boxes, and junction boxes used for installing electrical devices or mounting lighting fixtures shall comply with Chapters 39 through 48.

1502.3 Installation of radiant panels. Radiant panels installed on wood framing shall conform to the following requirements:

1. Heating panels shall be installed parallel to framing members and secured to the surface of framing members or mounted between framing members.

2. Panels shall be nailed or stapled only through the unheated portions provided for this purpose and shall not be fastened at any point closer than 1/4 inch (6.4 mm) from an element.

3. Unless listed and labeled for field cutting, heating panels shall be installed as complete units.

1502.4 Installation in concrete or masonry. Radiant heating systems installed in concrete or masonry shall conform with the following requirements:

1. Radiant heating systems shall be identified as being suitable for the installation and shall be secured in place as specified in the manufacturer's installation instructions.

2. Radiant heating panels or radiant heating panel sets shall not be installed where they bridge expansion joints unless protected from expansion and contraction.

1502.5 Gypsum panels. When radiant heating systems are used on gypsum assemblies, operating temperatures shall not exceed 125°F. (52°C.).

1502.6 Finish surfaces. Finish materials installed over radiant heating panels or systems shall be installed in accordance with the manufacturer's installation instructions. Surfaces shall be secured so that nails or other fastenings do not pierce the radiant heating elements.

Section 1503 — Duct Heaters

1503.1 General. Electric duct heaters shall be listed and labeled and shall be installed in accordance with the manufacturer's installation instructions and Chapters 39 through 48.

1503.2 Installation. Electric duct heaters shall be installed so that they will not create a fire hazard. Class 1 ducts, duct coverings and linings shall be interrupted at each heater to provide the clearances specified in the manufacturer's installation instructions. Such interruptions are not required for duct heaters that are listed and labeled for zero clearance from combustible materials. Insulation installed in the immediate area of each heater shall be classified for the maximum temperature produced on the duct surface.

1503.3 Installation with heat pumps and air conditioners. Duct heaters located within 4 feet (1219 mm) of a heat pump or air conditioner shall be listed and labeled for such installations. The heat pump or air conditioner shall additionally be listed and labeled for such duct heater installations.

1503.4 Access. Duct heaters shall be accessible for servicing, and clearance shall be maintained to permit adjustment, servicing, and replacement of controls and heating elements.

Boilers

Industry Standards

HVAC: Design Criteria, Options, Selection
(R.S. Means Co., Inc.)

Heating boilers are designed to produce steam or hot water. The water in the boilers is heated by either coal, oil, gas, wood, or electricity. Some boilers have dual fuel capabilities. Boilers are manufactured from cast iron, steel, or copper.

Cast iron sectional boilers may be assembled in place or shipped to the site as a completely assembled package. These boilers can be made larger on site by adding intermediate sections. The boiler sections may be connected by push nipples, tie rods, and gaskets. Cast iron boilers are noted for their durability.

Steel boilers are usually shipped to the site completely assembled. Large steel boilers may be shipped in segments for field assembly. The components of a steel boiler consist of tubes within a shell and a combustion chamber. If the water being heated is inside the tubes, the unit is called a water tube boiler. If the water is contained in the shell and the products of combustion pass through tubes surrounded by this water, the unit is called a fire tube boiler. Water tube boilers may be manufactured with steel or copper tubes.

Electric boilers have electric resistance heating elements immersed in the water and do not fall into either category of tubular boilers. Steel boilers in the larger sizes are often slightly more efficient than cast iron and are generally constructed to be more serviceable, which with proper maintenance adds to their useful life.

IOTFDC — 1998 (formerly CABO)

Section 2301 — Boilers

2301.1 Installation. The installation of boilers shall comply with the manufacturer's installation instructions and the requirements of this code. Operating instructions shall be attached to the boiler. Boilers shall have all controls set, adjusted and tested by the installer. Fuel-burning boilers shall be provided with combustion air as required by Chapter 20.

2301.2 Clearance. Boilers shall be installed in accordance with their listing and label or Section 1306.

Section 2302 — Operating and Safety Controls

2302.1 Safety controls. Electrical and mechanical operating and safety controls for boilers shall be listed and labeled.

2302.2 Boiler gages. Boilers shall be equipped with pressure and temperature gages that indicate pressure and temperature within the normal range of operation.

2302.3 Pressure-relief valve. Boilers shall be equipped with pressure-relief valves with minimum rated capacities for the equipment served. Pressure-relief valves shall be set at the maximum rating of the boiler. Discharge shall be piped to drain by gravity to within 18 inches (457 mm) of the floor or to an open receptor.

Section 2303 — Expansion Tanks

2303.1 General. Boilers shall be provided with expansion tanks. Nonpressurized expansion tanks shall be securely fastened to the structure or boiler and supported to carry twice the weight of the tank filled with water. Provisions shall be made for draining non-pressurized tanks without emptying the system.

2303.1.1 Pressurized expansion tanks. Pressurized expansion tanks shall be consistent with the volume and capacity of the system. Tanks shall be capable of withstanding a hydrostatic test pressure of two and one-half times the allowable working pressure of the system.

2303.2 Minimum capacity. The minimum capacity of expansion tanks shall be determined from Table 2303.2.

*Ed. Note: See **Figure 15.2**, a typical boiler installation.*

Typical Boiler Installation

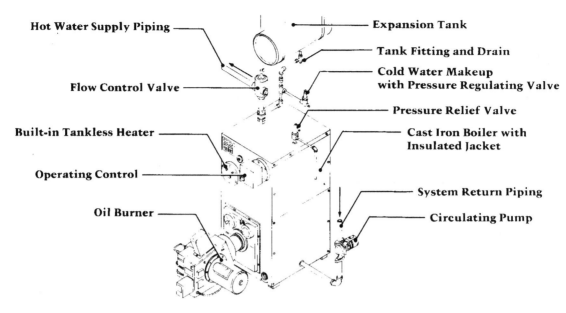

R.S. Means Co., Inc., HVAC: *Design Criteria, Options, Selection*
Figure 15.2

Expansion Tanks

Industry Standards

HVAC: Design Criteria, Options, Selection
(R.S. Means Co., Inc.)

All hydronic systems undergo changes in temperature that cause the water to expand and contract. An expansion tank is always provided on each closed loop piping system, because the tank allows the water to expand into it as the water volume increases with the temperature.

IOTFDC — 1998 (formerly CABO)
Section 2304 — Baseboard Convectors

2304.1 General. Baseboard convectors shall be installed in accordance with the manufacturer's installation instructions. Convectors shall be supported independent of the hydronic piping.

Section 2305 — Floor heating systems

2305.1 Piping materials. Piping for embedment in concrete or gypsum materials shall be standard-weight steel pipe, copper tubing, chlorinated poly (vinyl chloride) or polybutylene with a minimum rating of 100 pounds per square inch psi at 180°F. (68.9 kPa at 146°C.).

2305.2 Piping joints. Piping joints that are embedded shall be installed in accordance with the following requirements:

1. Steel pipe joints shall be welded.

2. Copper tubing shall be joined with brazing material having a melting point exceeding 1,000°F. (538°C.).

3. Polybutylene pipe and tubing joints shall be installed with socket-type heat fused polybutylene fittings.

4. CPVC tubing shall be joined using solvent cement joints.

Ed. Note: Cross-linked polyethylene (PEX) is now the accepted type.

2305.3 Testing. Piping or tubing to be embedded shall be tested by applying a hydrostatic pressure of not less than 100 psi (68.9 kPa). The pressure shall be maintained for 30 minutes, during which all joints shall be visually inspected for leaks.

Section 3302 — Water Heaters Used for Space Heating

3302.1 Protection of potable water. Piping and components connected to a water heater for space heating applications shall be suitable for use with potable water in accordance with Chapter 34. Water heaters that will be used to supply potable water shall not be connected to a heating system or components previously used with nonpotable water-heating appliances. Chemicals for boiler treatment shall not be introduced into the water heater for potable water heating.

3302.2 Scald protection. When a combination water heater/ space-heating system requires water for space heating at temperatures higher than 140°F. (60°C.), a means such as a mixing valve shall be installed to temper the water for domestic uses.

Ed. Note: See IOTFDC Section 2307 — Water Heaters in Chapter 14, "Plumbing."

Heating and Cooling Equipment

IOTFDC — 1998 (formerly CABO)
Section 1401 — General

1401.1 Installation. Heating and cooling equipment shall be installed in accordance with the manufacturer's installation instructions and the requirements of this code.

1401.2 Access. Heating and cooling equipment shall be located with respect to building construction and other equipment to permit maintenance, servicing and replacement. Clearances shall be maintained to permit cleaning of heating and cooling surfaces, replacement of filter, blowers, motors, controls, vent connections, lubrication of moving parts, and adjustments.

1401.3 Electricity required. A permanent electric outlet and lighting fixtures shall be provided in accordance with Chapter 44.

1401.4 Sizing. Heating and cooling equipment shall be sized according to ACCA Manual J.

1401.5 Heating and cooling equipment room installations. When equipment is located in an equipment room, the room shall have an opening or door that is large enough to permit removal of the largest piece of equipment, but no less than 20 inches (508 mm) wide. An unobstructed working space not less than 30 inches (762 mm) wide and not less than 30 inches (762 mm) high shall be provided along the control side of the equipment when the door of the equipment room is open.

1401.6 Attic installations When equipment is located in an attic, a minimum 22-inch-wide (559 mm) by 30-inch-wide (762 mm) passageway shall be provided from the attic opening to the equipment and its controls. The access opening shall not be smaller than 22 inches (559 mm) wide by 30 inches (762 mm) long, and may be located in a room, hall or closet. The opening and passageway shall be large enough to allow replacement of any part. The passageway shall have a minimum 22-inch-wide (559 mm) floor. Flooring shall extend a minimum of 30 inches (762 mm) in width along the control side of the equipment with a 30-inch-high (762 mm) clear working space on all sides where access is necessary for servicing.

1401.7 Crawl space installations. When equipment is installed in a crawl space, an access opening and passageway of a height and width sufficient to permit replacement of the mechanical equipment, but not less than 20 inches (508 mm) wide by 30 inches (762 mm) high, shall be provided to the working space in front of the equipment.

1401.8 Exterior installations. Equipment installed outdoors shall be listed and labeled for outdoor installation. Supports and foundations shall prevent excessive vibration, settlement, or movement of the equipment. Supports and foundations shall be level and conform to the manufacturer's installation instructions.

Section 1402 — Furnaces

1402.1 General. Warm-air furnaces shall conform to the applicable ANSI Z21.47, Z21.64 or UL 727. Fuel-burning warm-air furnaces shall not be installed in a room designed to be used as a storage closet. Furnaces located in a bedroom or bathroom shall be installed in a sealed enclosure such that combustion air will not be taken from the living space. Direct vent furnaces are not required to be installed within an enclosure.

1402.2 Clearances. Clearances shall be provided for warm-air furnaces in accordance with Table 1306.1 and in accordance with the listing and the manufacturer's installation instructions.

1402.3 Combustion air. Fuel-burning warm-air furnaces shall be supplied with combustion air in accordance with Chapter 20. Combustion air openings shall be unobstructed at least 6 inches (153 mm) in front of the openings.

1402.4 Electric furnaces. Electric furnaces shall be constructed in accordance with UL 1096. Electric furnaces shall be installed in compliance with their listing and the manufacturer's installation instructions.

Typical Warm Air Heating System

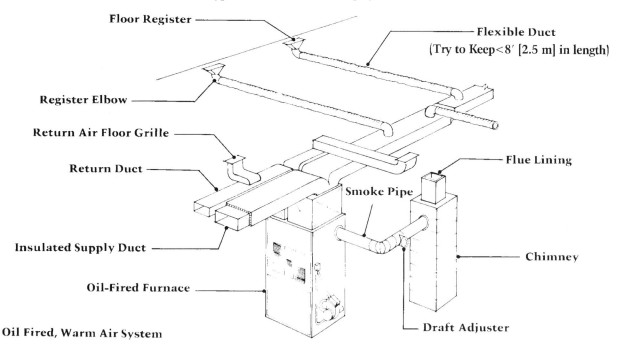

R.S. Means Co., Inc., HVAC: *Design Criteria, Options, Selection*

Figure 15.3

Section 1403 — Heat Pump Equipment

1403.1 Heating elements. Heat pump equipment utilizing supplemental electric heating elements shall have such elements constructed in accordance with UL 559.

1403.2 Foundations and supports. Supports and foundations for the outdoor unit of a heat pump shall be raised at least 3 inches (76 mm) above the ground to permit free drainage of defrost water, and shall conform to the manufacturer's installation instructions.

Section 1404 — Refrigeration Cooling Equipment

1404.1 Compliance. Refrigeration cooling equipment shall comply with Chapter 24.

Ventilation and Exhaust

Ventilation

Industry Standards

HVAC: Design Criteria, Options, Selection
(R.S. Means Co., Inc.)

Building spaces must be vented for a variety of reasons. The main purpose of ventilation is to provide fresh outdoor air for the occupants. Fresh outdoor air replenishes indoor air for breathing and most noticeably reduces odors, smoke, and fumes caused by people, cooking, and manufacturing processes. All occupied rooms (apartments, offices, stores, schools, hospitals) must be properly ventilated. There are several acceptable methods of providing ventilation: operable windows, fresh outdoor air supply, exhaust air, supply air with exhaust air, and purging. These methods are illustrated in **Figure 15.4**.

The effect of ventilation on the heating and cooling system is to increase the loads that the heating and cooling system must carry, since the outside air must be treated before it is introduced into the space.

Combustion Air

IOTFDC — 1998 (formerly CABO)

Section 2001 — General

2001.1 Air Supply. Fuel-burning equipment shall be provided with a supply of air for fuel combustion, draft hood dilution and ventilation of the space in which the equipment is installed. The methods of providing combustion air in this chapter do not apply to direct vent appliances, listed and labeled cooking appliances, refrigerators and domestic clothes dryers.

2001.1.1 Buildings of unusually tight construction.
In buildings of unusually tight construction, combustion air shall be obtained from outside the sealed thermal envelope. In buildings of ordinary tightness insofar as infiltration is

Methods of Ventilation

Types of Ventilation	Diagram	Common Uses	Comments
Operable Windows	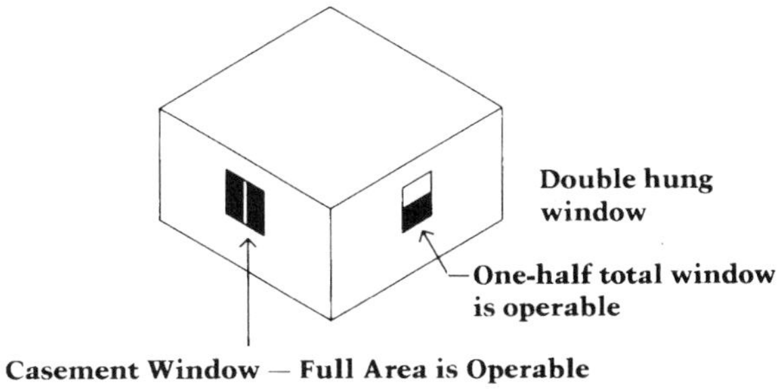 Double hung window — One-half total window is operable — Casement Window — Full Area is Operable	Residences Low-rise Offices	Operable window area should equal 4% of floor area.
Fresh Outdoor Air Supply	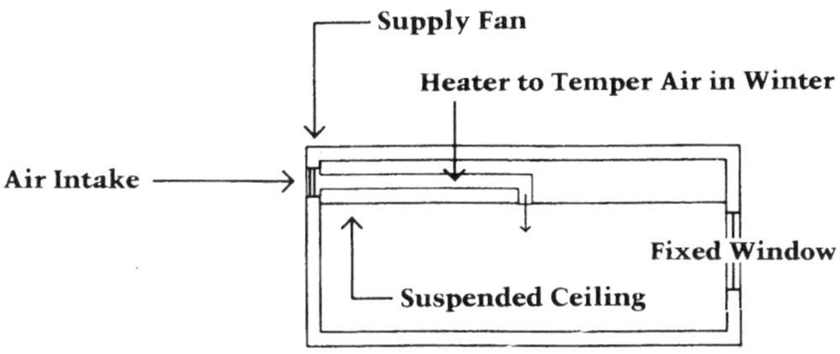 Supply Fan — Heater to Temper Air in Winter — Air Intake — Fixed Window — Suspended Ceiling	Offices Kitchens	15–25 cfm/person [11.8 L^3/s] with reheat.
Exhaust Air with No Forced Makeup Air	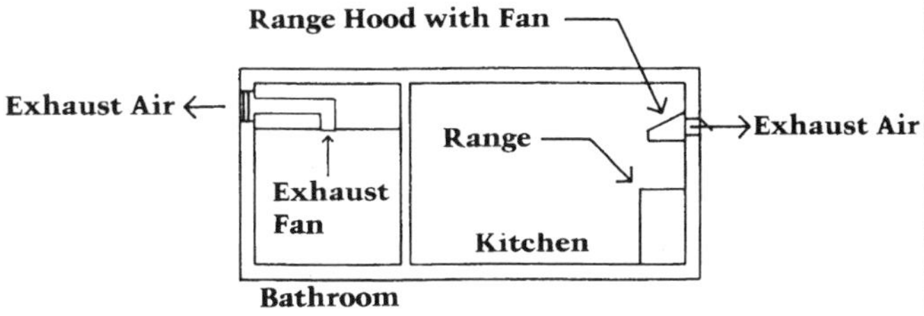 Range Hood with Fan — Exhaust Air ← — Range — → Exhaust Air — Exhaust Fan — Kitchen — Bathroom	Bathrooms Kitchens	Fire protection is sometimes required in kitchens.
Supply Air with Forced Makeup and Exhaust Air	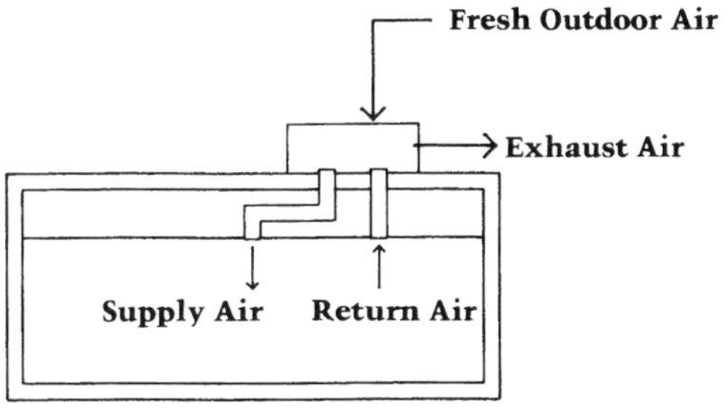 Fresh Outdoor Air — → Exhaust Air — Supply Air Return Air	Offices	Keep fresh outdoor air quantity 15-20% greater than exhaust air to "pressurize" the building.
Purging	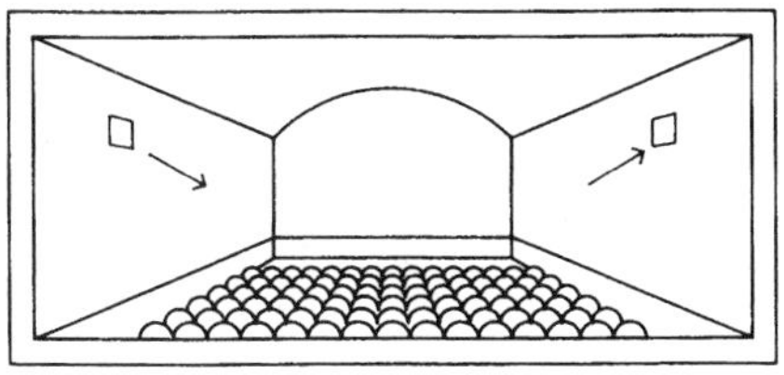	Theaters	New air is brought into the space between performances. Volume of space is large enough to provide 5 cfm/person [2.4 L^3/s] over 3 hours.

R.S. Means Co., Inc., *HVAC: Design Criteria, Options, Selection*

Figure 15.4

concerned, all or a portion of the combustion air for fuel-burning appliances shall be permitted to be obtained from infiltration when the room or space has a volume of 50 cubic feet per 1,000 British thermal units per hour (Btu/h) (4.8 m³/kW) input.

2001.2 Exhaust and ventilation system. Air requirements for operation of exhaust fans, kitchen ventilation systems, clothes dryers, and fireplaces shall be considered in determining the adequacy of a space to provide combustion air.

2001.3 Volume dampers prohibited. Volume dampers shall not be installed in combustion air openings.

2001.4 Prohibited sources. Combustion air ducts and openings shall not connect appliance enclosures with space in which the operation of a fan adversely affects the flow of combustion air. Combustion air shall not be obtained from an area in which flammable vapors present a hazard. Fuel-fired appliances shall not obtain combustion air from any of the following rooms or spaces:

Sleeping rooms.

Bathrooms.

Toilet rooms.

Exception: The following appliances shall be permitted to obtain combustion air from sleeping rooms, bathrooms and toilet rooms.

Vented gas-fired room heaters, vented decorative gas-fired appliances and decorative gas-fired appliances for installation in vented solid fuel-burning fireplaces, provided that the room is not a confined space and the building is not of unusually tight construction.

Solid fuel-fired appliances and fireplaces provided that the room is not a confined space and the building is not of unusually tight construction.

Appliances installed in an enclosure in which all combustion air is taken from the outdoors and the enclosure is equipped with a solid weatherstripped door and self-closing device.

Unvented room heaters installed in accordance with Section 1604.1.

Ed. Note: IOTFDC Section 1604.1 provides requirements for installation of unvented room heaters.

2001.5 Opening area. The free area of each opening shall be used for determining combustion air. Unless otherwise specified by the manufacturer or determined by actual measurement, the free area shall be considered 75 percent of the gross area for metal louvers and 25 percent of the gross area for wood louvers.

Section 2002 — All Air From Inside the Building

2002.1 Required volume. If the volume of the space in which fuel-burning appliances are installed is greater than 50 cubic feet per 1,000 Btu/h (4.8 m³/kW) of aggregate input rating in buildings of ordinary tightness insofar as infiltration is concerned, normal infiltration shall be regarded as adequate to provide combustion air. Rooms communicating directly with the space in which the appliances are installed through openings not furnished with doors shall be considered part of the required volume.

Air Taken from Outdoors for Equipment in Confined Space

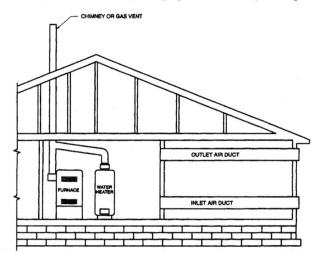

For **SI**: 1 square inch = 645.16 mm², 1 British thermal unit per hour = 0.2931 W.
Note: Each air duct opening shall have a free area of not less than 1 square inch per 2,000 Btu/h of the total input rating of all equipment in the enclosure. If the equipment room is located against an outside wall and the air openings communicate directly with the outdoors, each opening shall have a free area of not less than 1 square inch per 4,000 Btu/h of the total input rating of all equipment in the enclosure.

Courtesy of ICC, IOTFDC — 1998 (formerly CABO) [Figure 2003.2(1)]

Figure 15.5

2002.2 Confined space. Where the space in which the appliance is located does not meet the criterion specified in Section 2002.1, two permanent openings to adjacent spaces shall be provided so that the combined volume of all spaces meets the criterion. One opening shall be within 12 inches (305 mm) of the top and one within 12 inches (305 mm) of the bottom of the space, as illustrated in Figure 2002.2. Each opening shall have free area equal to a minimum of 1 square inch per 1,000 Btu/h (2201 mm^2/kW) input rating of all appliances installed within the space, but not less than 100 square inches (0.064 m^2).

Section 2003 — All Air from Outdoors

2003.1 Outdoor air. When the space in which fuel-burning appliances are located does not meet the criterion for indoor air specified in Section 2002, outside combustion air shall be supplied as specified in Section 2003.2 or 2003.3.

2003.2 Two openings or ducts. Outside combustion air shall be supplied through openings or ducts, as illustrated in Figures 2003.1, 2003.3a, 2003.3b and 2003.4. One opening shall be within 12 inches (305 mm) of the top of the enclosure, and one within 12 inches (305 mm) of the bottom of the enclosure. Openings are permitted to connect to spaces directly communicating with the outdoors, such as ventilated crawl spaces or ventilated attic spaces. The same duct or opening shall not serve both combustion air openings. The duct serving the upper opening shall be level or extend upward from the appliance space.

2003.2.1 Size of openings. When communicating with the outdoors by means of vertical ducts, each opening shall have a minimum free area of at least 1 square inch per 4,000 Btu/h (0.550 mm^2/W) of total input rating of all appliances in the space. If horizontal ducts are used, each opening shall have a free area of at least 1 square inch per 2,000 Btu/h (0.275 mm^2/W) of total input of all appliances in the space. Ducts shall be of the same minimum cross-sectional area as the required free area of the openings to which they connect. The minimum cross-sectional dimension of rectangular air ducts shall be 3 inches (76 mm).

2003.3 Single opening or duct. For an appliance with a minimum clearance of 1 inch (25.4 mm) on the sides and back and 6 inches (152 mm) on the front, outside combustion air shall be supplied through one opening or duct. The opening or duct shall be within 12 inches (305 mm) of the top of the enclosure. The opening is permitted to connect to spaces directly communicating with the outdoors, such as ventilated crawl spaces or ventilated attic spaces. A duct shall be level or extend upward from the appliance space.

2003.3.1 Size of opening. When communicating with the outdoors by means of a single opening or duct, the opening or duct shall have a free area of at least 1 square inch per 3,000 Btu/h (0.413 mm^2/W) of total input rating of all appliances in the space, but no smaller than the vent flow area. A duct shall be of the same minimum cross-sectional area

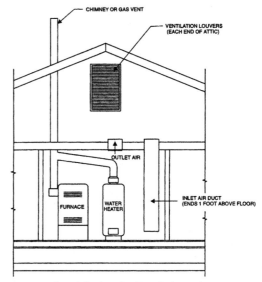

Air Through Ventilated Attic for Equipment in Confined Space

For SI: 1 square inch = 645.16 mm^2, 1 British thermal unit per hour = 0.2931 W.
Note: The inlet and outlet air openings shall have a free area of not less than 1 square inch per 4,000 Btu/h of the total input rating of all equipment in the enclosure.

Courtesy of ICC, IOTFDC — 1998 (formerly CABO) [Figure 2003.2(2)]

Figure 15.6

as the required free area of the opening to which it connects. The minimum cross-sectional dimension of a rectangular air duct shall be 3 inches (76 mm).

2003.4 Attic combustion air. Combustion air obtained from an attic area, as illustrated in Figure 2003.2(2) [**Figure 15.6**], shall be in accordance with the following:

1. The attic ventilation shall be sufficient to provide the required volume of combustion air.

2. The combustion air opening shall be provided with a metal sleeve extending from the appliance enclosure to a minimum of 6 inches (152 mm) above the top of the ceiling joists and ceiling insulation.

3. An inlet air duct within an outlet air duct shall be an acceptable means of supplying attic combustion air to an appliance room provided that the inlet duct extends a minimum of 12 inches (305 mm) above the top of the outlet duct in the attic space, as illustrated in Figure 2003.2(3).

4. The end of ducts that terminate in an attic shall not be screened.

2003.5 Under-floor combustion air. Combustion air obtained from under-floor areas, as illustrated in Figure 2003.2(4), shall have free openings areas to the outside equivalent to not less than twice the required combustion air opening.

Ideal Locations for Heating and Cooling Supply Ducts

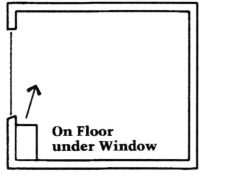

On Floor under Window

Ideal Heating Duct

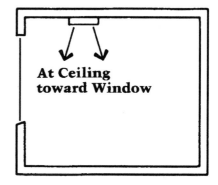

At Ceiling toward Window

Ideal Cooling Duct

R.S. Means Co., Inc., HVAC: *Design Criteria, Options, Selection*

Figure 15.7

2003.6 Opening requirements. Outside combustion air openings shall be covered with corrosion-resistant screen or equivalent protection having no less than 1/4-inch (6.4 mm) openings, and not greater then 1/2-inch (12.7 mm) openings.

Uniform Mechanical Code — 1997

Section 702 — Combustion-Air Openings

702.1 Location. One opening shall be located within the upper 12 inches (304 mm) of the enclosure and one opening shall be located within the lower 12 inches (304 mm) of the enclosure.

Exception: When all air is taken from the outdoors for an appliance with a minimum clearance of 1 inch (25 mm) on the sides and back and 6 inches (152 mm) on the front, one opening shall be permitted and located within the upper 12 inches (305 mm) of the enclosure.

Section 703 — Sources of Combustion Air

703.1 Air from Outside. Combustion air obtained from outside the building shall be supplied as follows:

1. Through permanent openings of the required area directly to the outside of the building through the floor, roof or walls of the appliance enclosure; or

2. Through continuous ducts of the required cross-sectional area extending from the appliance enclosure to the outside of the building. The required upper combustion-air duct shall extend horizontally or upwards to the outside of the building. Where not otherwise prohibited, combustion air may be obtained from an attic area, provided the attic ventilating openings are not subject to ice or snow blockage, and further provided:

2.1 The attic has not less than 30 inches (762 mm) vertical clear height to its maximum point.

2.2 Attic ventilation is sufficient for the required volume of combustion air and complies with the requirements of Section 706.

2.3 The combustion-air opening is provided with a galvanized sleeve of not less than 0.019-inch (0.48 mm) (No. 26 gage) steel or other approved material extending from the appliance enclosure to at least 6 inches (153 mm) above the top of the ceiling joists and insulation.

704.1 General. Combustion-air ducts shall:

1. Be of galvanized steel complying with Chapter 6 or equivalent corrosion-resistant material approved for this use.

Exception: In Group R, Division 3 Occupancies, unobstructed stud and joist spaces may be used, provided not more than one required fire stop is removed.

2. Have a minimum cross-sectional dimension of 3 inches (76 mm).

3. Terminate in a space at least 3 inches (76 mm) in depth open to the front or firebox side of the appliance. Such space shall extend from the floor to the ceiling of the appliance compartment.

706 Conditions Created by Mechanical Exhausting. Operation of exhaust fans, kitchen ventilation systems, clothes dryers or fireplaces shall be considered in determining combustible air requirements to avoid unsatisfactory operation of installed gas appliances.

Duct Systems

Industry Standards
HVAC: Design Criteria, Options, Selection
(R.S. Means Co., Inc.)
Ductwork

The ideal size and location of the ductwork for air-supply systems is different for heating and cooling. Even when the heating and cooling loads are approximately equal, as they are in temperate climates, the cooling ductwork is always larger. Therefore, it is difficult for one system to perfectly meet heating and cooling requirements.

Because warm air rises above cooler air, heating supply ducts should be placed low and under windows. The rising heated air will stop down-drafts and cold air spill from the windows, will help to prevent condensation on the glass, and will inject the heating supply at the source of greatest heat loss. This helps to maintain overall even room temperature.

In contrast, cooling supply ducts should be located at the ceiling and slightly away from the perimeter of the room so the cool air can mix with the warm air. The cool air will drift downward over windows and over the lights and occupants, which are other sources of heat gain.

The ideal locations of air ducts are illustrated in **Figure 15.7**.

Using a system that combines heating and cooling in the same air supply ducts involves a compromise because of the inherent conflict between heating and cooling duct sizes and locations. This can be accomplished by larger duct sizes and increased fan capacity.

IOTFDC — 1998 (formerly CABO)

1901.2.1 Duct installation materials. Duct insulation materials shall conform to the following requirements:

1. Duct coverings and linings shall have a flame-spread rating not greater than 25, and a smoke-development rating not greater than 50.

2. Duct coverings and duct linings shall withstand a test temperature of 250°F. (121°C.) minimum.

3. Fiberglass or mineral wool insulation shall be a minimum 2-inch-thick (51 mm), 3/4 pound (0.340 kg) density wrap or 1-inch-thick (25.4 mm), 1-1/2 pound (0.680 kg) liner.

4. When nonmetallic ducts or other approved insulating or lining materials are used, the material shall have a minimum thermal resistance value of R-4.2.

5. Blanket insulation and factory-insulated flexible duct shall be labeled with the R-value, flame-spread index, and smoke-developed index.

1901.2.2 Vibration isolators. Vibration isolators installed between mechanical equipment and metal ducts shall be fabricated from approved materials and shall not exceed 10 inches (254 mm) in length.

1901.3 Installation. Duct installation shall comply with Sections 1901.3.1 through 1901.3.7.

1901.3.1 Joints and seams. Joints of duct systems shall be made substantially air tight by means of tapes, mastics or gasketing. Crimp joints for round ducts shall have a minimum contact lap of at least 1-1/2 inches (38 mm) and shall be mechanically fastened by means of at least three sheet metal screws or rivets equally spaced around the joint.

1901.3.2 Support. Metal ducts shall be supported by 1-inch (25 mm) by 18-gage (0.047 inch) (1.19 mm) metal straps or 12-gage (0.048 inch) (1.2 mm) galvanized wire at intervals not exceeding 10 feet (3048 mm). Nonmetallic ducts shall be supported in accordance with the manufacturer's installation instructions.

1901.3.3 Fireblocking. Duct installations shall be fireblocked in accordance with Section 602.8.

Ed. Note: The following section (602.8) is added here for convenience and to provide further explanation of fireblocking requirements.

602.8 Fireblocking required. Fireblocking shall be provided to cut off all concealed draft openings (both vertical and horizontal) and to form an effective fire barrier between stories, and between a top story and the roof space. Fireblocking shall be provided in wood-frame construction in the following locations:

1. In concealed spaces of stud walls and partitions, including furred spaces, at the ceiling and floor level;

2. At all interconnections between concealed vertical and horizontal spaces such as occur at soffits, drop ceilings, cove ceilings, etc.;

3. In concealed spaces between stair stringers at the top and bottom of the run;

4. At openings around vents, pipes, ducts, chimneys and fireplaces at ceiling and floor level, with noncombustible materials.

1901.3.4 Duct insulation. Duct insulation shall be installed in accordance with the following requirements:

1. All ductwork installed in nonconditioned areas shall be insulated.

2. Vapor retarders with a maximum permeance of 0.05 perm [2.87 ng/(s·m²·Pa)], or aluminum foil with a minimum thickness of 2 mils (0.051 mm), shall be installed on cooling supply ducts that pass through nonconditioned spaces conducive to condensation.

3. Exterior ducts shall be protected with weatherproof covering.

4. Duct coverings shall not penetrate a fireblocked wall or floor.

1901.3.5 Ducts in slabs. Ducts shall be listed and labeled for underground installation. Metallic ducts not having an approved protective coating shall be completely encased in a minimum of 2 inches (51 mm) of concrete. Metallic ducts having an approved protective coating and nonmetallic ducts shall be installed in accordance with the manufacturer's installation instructions.

1901.3.6 Factory-made air ducts. Factory-made air ducts shall not be installed in or on the ground, in tile or metal pipe, or within masonry or concrete.

1901.3.7 Metal duct separation. Metal ducts shall be installed with at least 4 inches (102 mm) separation from earth.

Residential Ductwork

Industry Standards

Architectural Sheet Metal Manual, Fifth Edition
(Sheet Metal and Air Conditioning Contractors' National Association, Inc.)

7.2.1 Metal Gauges. Ductwork used for residential work shall not exceed 2 in. w.g. positive or negative pressures.

7.2.2 Rectangular Ducts. Minimum gauges for metal ducts not enclosed within a partition wall are listed in Table 7-1. For ducts enclosed within a partition wall, minimum gauges are listed in Table 7-2. Both tables apply to rectangular ducts.

7.2.3 Round Ducts. Minimum gauges for round ducts are listed in Table 7-3. Each joint shall be held rigidly in place by the used of mechanical fastening devices; i.e., rivets, bolts, or sheet metal screws.

Proper Duct Support

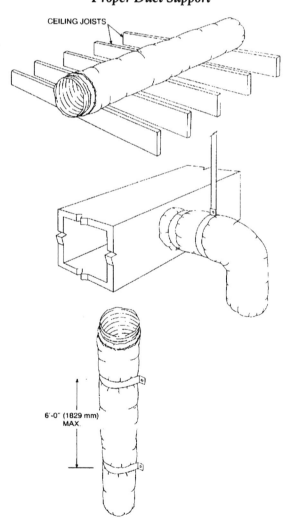

Methods of Duct Installation

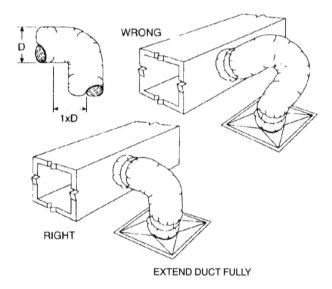

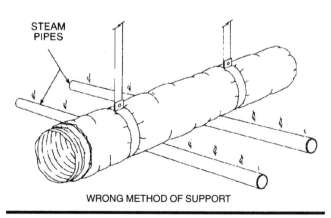

Courtesy of ICBO, Uniform Mechanical Code — 1997 [Figure A6-3-39]

Figure 15.8

Courtesy of ICBO, Uniform Mechanical Code — 1997 [Figures A6-34 and A6-35]

Figure 15.9

Combustion Air Exhaust

Chimneys and Vents

IOTFDC — 1998 (formerly CABO)

2101.1 Vent required. Fuel-burning appliances shall be vented to the outside in accordance with their listing and label and the manufacturer's installation instructions except appliances listed and labeled for unvented use. Venting systems shall consist of approved chimneys or vents, or venting assemblies which are integral parts of labeled appliances.

2101.2 Draft requirements. A venting system shall satisfy the draft requirement of the equipment in accordance with the manufacturer's installation instructions and shall be constructed and installed to develop a positive flow to convey combustion products to the outside atmosphere.

2101.3 Existing chimneys and vents. Where an appliance is permanently disconnected from an existing chimney or vent, or where an appliance is connected to an existing chimney or vent during the process of a new installation, the chimney or vent shall comply with Sections 2101.3.1 through 2101.3.4.

2101.3.1 Size. The chimney or vent shall be resized as necessary to control flue gas condensation in the interior of the chimney or vent and to provide the appliance or appliances served with the required draft. For Category I gas-fired appliances, the resizing shall be in accordance with Section 2104.

2101.3.2 Flue passageways. The flue gas passageway shall be free of obstructions and combustible deposits and shall be cleaned if previously used for venting a solid or liquid fuel-burning appliance or fireplace. The flue liner, chimney inner wall or vent inner wall shall be continuous and shall be free of cracks, gaps, perforations or other damage or deterioration which would allow the escape of combustion products, including gases, moisture and creosote.

2101.3.3 Cleanout. Masonry chimneys shall be provided with a cleanout opening complying with Section 1001.14.

2101.3.4 Clearances. Chimneys and vents shall have airspace clearance to combustibles in accordance with this code and the chimney or vent manufacturer's installation instructions.

Exception: Masonry chimneys equipped with a chimney lining system tested and listed for installation in chimneys in contact with combustibles in accordance with UL 1777, and installed in accordance with the manufacturer's instructions, shall not be required to have clearance between combustible materials and exterior surfaces of the masonry chimney. Noncombustible fireblocking shall be provided in accordance with this code.

2101.4 Space around lining. The space surrounding a flue lining system or other vent installed within a masonry chimney shall not be used to vent any other appliance. This shall not prevent the installation of a separate flue lining in accordance with the manufacturer's installation instructions and this code.

2101.5 Mechanical draft systems. A mechanical draft system shall be used only with equipment listed and labeled for such use. Provisions shall be made to prevent the flow of fuel to the equipment when the draft system is not operating. Forced draft systems and all portions of induced draft systems under positive pressure during operation shall be designed and installed so as to prevent leakage of flue gases into a building.

2101.6 Direct vent appliances. Direct vent appliances shall be listed and labeled and shall be installed in accordance with the manufacturer's installation instructions.

2101.7 Support. Venting systems shall be adequately supported for the weight of the material used.

2101.8 Duct penetrations. Vents or vent connectors shall not extend into or through supply and return air ducts or plenums.

2101.9 Fireblocking. Vent and chimney installations shall be fireblocked in accordance with Section 602.8.

Ed. Note: See "Duct Systems" earlier in this chapter for further information on fireblocking, which is provided in Section 602.8.

2101.10 Unused openings. Unused openings in any venting system shall be closed or capped.

Uniform Plumbing Code — 1997

502.12 — Venting System — Types

(1) Chimneys or vents of masonry, reinforced concrete or metal; and factory-built chimneys approved or listed for products of combustion at temperatures in excess of five hundred fifty degrees (550°F.) (288°C.).

(2) **Type B and BOW.** Factory-made gas vents listed by a nationally recognized testing agency for venting listed or approved appliances equipped to burn only gas.

(3) **Type l.** A venting system consisting of listed vent piping and fittings for use with oil-burning appliances listed for use with Type L or with listed gas appliances.

515.0 Location and Support of Venting Systems.
Combustion products' vents, vent connectors, exhaust ducts from ventilating hoods as described in Section 525.0, chimneys, or chimney connectors shall not extend into or through any air duct or plenum.

Exception: A venting system may pass through a combustion air duct. The base of every vent supported from the ground shall rest on a solid masonry or concrete base extending not less than two (2) inches (51 mm) above the adjoining ground level. The base of every vent which is not supported from the ground and is not self-supporting, shall rest on a firm metal or masonry support.

No water heater shall be vented into a fireplace or into a chimney serving a fireplace. All venting systems shall be adequately supported for the weight and the design of the material used.

516.0 Length, Pitch, and Clearance.

516.1 Vent Offsets. Except as provided for in Section 512.4, gravity vents shall extend in a generally vertical direction with offsets not exceeding forty-five (45) degrees (0.79 rad). A gravity vent may also have one (1) horizontal offset of not more than sixty (60) degrees (1.05 rad).

516.2 Every offset shall be supported for its weight and shall be installed to maintain proper clearance, to prevent physical damage and to prevent separation of the joints.

516.3 Any angle greater than forty-five (45) degrees (0.79 rad) form the vertical is considered horizontal. The total horizontal run of a vent, as described in Section 516.1 above, plus the horizontal vent connector, shall be not greater than seventy-five (75) percent of the vertical height of the vent.

516.4 Rise. Every vent connector which is a part of a gravity-tee venting system shall have a continuous rise of not less than one-fourth (1/4) inch per foot (20.9 mm/m) of length measured form the appliance vent collar to the vent.

516.5 Clearance. Single wall metal vent connectors, where permitted to be used by Section 514.0, shall be provided with clearances from combustible material of not less than six (6) inches (152 mm).

517.3 Type B. Type B gas vents with listed vent caps twelve (12) inches (305 mm) in size or smaller shall be permitted to be terminated in accordance with Table 5-2, provided they are located at least eight (8) feet (2438 mm) from a vertical wall or similar obstruction. All other Type B gas vents shall terminate not less than two (2) feet (610 mm) above the highest point where they pass through the roof and at least two (2) feet (610 mm) higher than any portion of a building within ten (10) feet (3048 mm).

517.4 Type L. No Type L venting system shall terminate less than two (2) feet (610 mm) above the roof through which it passes, nor less than four (4) feet (1219 mm) from any portion of the building which extends at an angle of more than forty-five (45) degrees (0.79 rad) upward from the horizontal.

519.0 Multiple Appliance Venting. Two (2) or more oil or listed gas-burning appliances may be connected to a common gravity-type venting system provided the appliances are equipped with an approved primary safety control capable of shutting off the burners and the venting system is designed to conform with Section 512.4 or complies with the following requirements:

519.1 Appliances which are connected to a common venting system shall be located within the same story of the building, excepting engineered venting systems as provided in Section 512.4.

519.2 Two (2) or more connectors shall not enter a common venting system unless the inlets are offset in such a manner that no portion of any inlet is opposite the other inlets.

519.4 Each vent connector of a multiple venting systems shall have the greatest possible rise consistent with the headroom available between the draft hood outlet, the barometric damper of the flue collar and the point of interconnection to a manifold, to a common vent, or to a chimney.

Uniform Mechanical Code — 1997
806.4 T type B or BW Gas Vents. Type B or BW gas vents with listed vent caps 12 inches (305 mm) in size or smaller shall be permitted to be terminated in accordance with Table 8-A, provided they are located at least 8 feet (2438 mm) from a vertical wall or similar obstruction. All other Type B gas vents shall terminate not less than 2 feet (610 mm) above the highest point where they pass through the roof and at least 2 feet (610 mm) higher than any portion of a building within 10 feet (3048 mm).

806.6 Vent Terminals. Venting systems shall terminate not less than 4 feet (1219 mm) below or 4 feet (1219 mm) horizontally from, and not less than 1 foot (305 mm) above a door, an operable window or a gravity air inlet into a building.

806.6.1 Separation from inlets. Venting systems shall terminate at least 3 feet (914 mm) above an outside- or makeup- air inlet located within 10 feet (3048 mm) and at least 4 feet (1219 mm) from a property line except a public way.

Exception: Vent termination off direct-vent appliances with inputs not exceeding 50,000 Btu/h (19kW) shall be permitted to terminate at least 2 feet (610 mm) from a property line except a public way.

NFPA 54: National Fuel Gas Code — 1996

7.6.1 Application.

(a) Gas vents shall be installed in accordance with the terms of their listings and the manufacturers' instructions.

(b) A Type B-W gas vent shall have a listed capacity not less than that of the listed vented wall furnace to which it is connected.

(c) A gas vent passing through a roof shall extend through the roof flashing, roof jack, or roof thimble.

(d) Type B or Type L vents shall extend in a generally vertical direction with offsets not exceeding 45 degrees, except that a vent system having not more than one 60- degree offset shall be permitted.
Any angle greater than 45 degrees from the vertical is considered horizontal. The total horizontal distance of a vent plus the horizontal vent connector serving draft hood-equipped appliances shall not be greater than 75 percent of the vertical height of the vent.

Exception: Systems designed and sized as provided in Part II or in accordance with other approved engineering methods.

Vents serving Category 1 fan-assisted appliances shall be installed in accordance with the appliance manufacturers' instructions and Part II or other approved engineering methods.

(e) An unused chimney flue or masonry enclosure shall be permitted to be used as a passageway for installation of a gas vent.

Air Conditioning and Refrigeration

Industry Standards

Means Mechanical Cost Data
(R.S. Means Co., Inc.)

Air Conditioning

General: The purpose of air conditioning is to control the environment of a space so that comfort is provided for the occupants and/or conditions are suitable for the processes or equipment contained therein. The several items which should be evaluated to define system objectives are:

Temperature Control

Humidity Control

Cleanliness

Odor, smoke and fumes

Ventilation

Efforts to control the above parameters must also include consideration of the degree or tolerance of variation, the noise level introduced, the velocity of air motion and the energy requirements to accomplish the desired results.

The variation in **temperature** and **humidity** is a function of the sensor and the controller. The controller reacts to a signal from the sensor and produces the appropriate suitable response in either the terminal unit, the conductor of the transporting

Air Conditioning Requirements

BTU's per hour per S.F. of floor area and S.F. per ton of air conditioning.

Type of Building	BTU per S.F.	S.F. per Ton	Type of Building	BTU per S.F.	S.F. per Ton	Type of Building	BTU per S.F.	S.F. per Ton
Apartments, Individual	26	450	Dormitory, Rooms	40	300	Libraries	50	240
Corridors	22	550	Corridors	30	400	Low Rise Office, Exterior	38	320
Auditoriums & Theaters	40	300/18*	Dress Shops	43	280	Interior	33	360
Banks	50	240	Drug Stores	80	150	Medical Centers	28	425
Barber Shops	48	250	Factories	40	300	Motels	28	425
Bars & Taverns	133	90	High Rise Office—Ext. Rms.	46	263	Office (small suite)	43	280
Beauty Parlors	66	180	Interior Rooms	37	325	Post Office, Individual Office	42	285
Bowling Alleys	68	175	Hospitals, Core	43	280	Central Area	46	260
Churches	36	330/20*	Perimeter	46	260	Residences	20	600
Cocktail Lounges	68	175	Hotel, Guest Rooms	44	275	Restaurants	60	200
Computer Rooms	141	85	Corridors	30	400	Schools & Colleges	46	260
Dental Offices	52	230	Public Spaces	55	220	Shoe Stores	55	220
Dept. Stores, Basement	34	350	Industrial Plants, Offices	38	320	Shop'g. Ctrs., Supermarkets	34	350
Main Floor	40	300	General Offices	34	350	Retail Stores	48	250
Upper Floor	30	400	Plant Areas	40	300	Specialty	60	200

*Persons per ton
12,000 BTU = 1 ton of air conditioning

R.S. Means Co., Inc., *Means Mechanical Cost Data*

Figure 15.10

medium (air, steam, chilled water, etc.), or the source (boiler, evaporating coils, etc.).

The **noise level** is a by-product of the energy supplied to moving components of the system. Those items which usually contribute the most noise are pumps, blowers, fans, compressors and diffusers. The level of noise can be partially controlled through use of vibration pads, isolators, proper sizing, shields, baffles and sound absorbing liners.

Some **air motion** is necessary to prevent stagnation and stratification. The maximum acceptable velocity varies with the degree of heating or cooling which is taking place. Most people feel air moving past them at velocities in excess of 25 FPM as an annoying draft. However, velocities up to 45 FPM may be acceptable in certain cases. Ventilation, expressed as air changes per hour and percentage of fresh air, is usually an item regulated by local codes.

Selection of the system to be used for a particular application is usually a trade-off. In some cases the building size, style, or room available for mechanical use limits the range of possibilities. Prime factors influencing the decision are first cost and total life (operating, maintenance and replacement costs). The accuracy with which each parameter is determined will be an important measure of the reliability of the decision and subsequent satisfactory operation of the installed system.

Heat delivery may be desired from an air conditioning system. Heating capability usually is added as follows: A gas fired burner or hot water/steam/electric coils may be added to the air handling unit directly and heat all air equally. For limited or localized heat requirements the water/steam/electric coils may be inserted into the duct branch supplying the cold areas. Gas fired duct furnaces are also available.

Note: When water or steam coils are used, the cost of the piping and boiler must also be added. For a rough estimate use the cost per square foot of the appropriate sized hydronic system with unit heaters. This will provide a cost for the boiler and piping, and the unit heaters of the system would equate to the approximate cost of the heating coils. The installed cost of electric and gas heaters, boilers and other heat related items on a unit basis may be located in Section 155 of *Means Mechanical Cost Data*.

IOTFDC — 1998 (formerly CABO)

Section 2401 — Refrigeration Cooling Equipment

2401.1 Approved refrigerants. Refrigerants used in direct refrigerating systems shall conform to the applicable provisions of ASHRAE 15 and ASHRAE 34.

2401.2 Refrigeration coils in warm-air furnaces. When a cooling coil is located in the supply plenum of a warm-air furnace, the furnace blower shall be rated at not less than 0.5-inch water column (124 Pa) static pressure unless the furnace is listed and labeled for use with a cooling coil. Cooling coils shall not be located upstream from heat

exchangers unless listed and labeled for such use. Conversion of existing furnaces for use with cooling coils shall be permitted provided the furnace will operate within the temperature rise specified for the furnace.

2401.3 Condensate disposal. An approved drain shall be provided to dispose of condensate from the cooling coil. Condensate drains shall terminate outside of the building, or to a floor drain, plumbing fixture, sump or an approved location.

2401.3.1 Cooling coil or air-conditioning unit. When the cooling coil or air-conditioning unit is located indoors above a living space, a water-tight pan of corrosion-resistant metal shall be installed beneath the unit to catch overflow condensate due to a clogged condensate drain. The pan shall be provided with a drain pipe of minimum 3/4-inch (19 mm) nominal pipe size which discharges at a conspicuous location to indicate that the regular drain is clogged. In lieu of a separate drain line, an approved water level detector or float switch that will shut down the equipment prior to overflow of the auxiliary pan shall be used.

Comments

Where gravity flow of condensate is not possible, use of a sump pump is recommended.

2401.4 Insulation of refrigerant piping. Refrigerant piping and fitting within a building that return refrigerant to the outdoor unit shall be insulated to prevent condensation from forming on the piping.

Section 2402 — Absorption Cooling Equipment

2402.1 Approval of equipment. Absorption systems shall be listed and labeled and installed in accordance with the manufacturer's installation instructions.

2402.2 Condensate disposal. Condensate from the cooling coil shall be disposed of as provided in Section 2401.3.

2402.3 Insulation of piping. Refrigerant piping, brine piping and fittings within a building shall be insulated to prevent condensation from forming on piping.

2402.4 Pressure-relief protection. Absorption systems shall be protected by a pressure-relief device. Discharge from the pressure-relief device shall be located so as not to create a hazard to persons or property.

2403.1 General. Cooling equipment that utilizes evaporation of water for cooling shall be installed in accordance with the manufacturer's installation instructions. Evaporative coolers shall be installed on a level platform or base not less than 3 inches (76 mm) above the adjoining ground and secured to prevent displacement. Openings in exterior walls shall be flashed in accordance with Section 703.8.

Hydronic Piping

IOTFDC — 1998 (formerly CABO)

2501.1 General. Hydronic piping shall conform to Table 2501.1. Approved piping, valves, fittings and connections shall be installed in accordance with the manufacturer's installation instructions. Pipe and fittings shall be rated for use at the operating temperature and pressure of the hydronic system. Used pipe, fittings, valves or other materials shall be free of foreign materials.

2501.2 Prohibited tees. Hot water in a system shall not enter a tee fitting through the side opening.

2501.3 System drain down. Hydronic piping systems shall be installed to permit the system to be drained. When the system drains to the plumbing drainage system, the installation shall conform to the requirements of Chapter 29 through 38.

2501.4 Protection of potable water. The potable water system shall be protected from backflow in accordance with the provisions listed in Section 3402.

2501.5 Pipe penetrations. Openings through concrete or masonry building elements shall be sleeved.

2501.6 Contact with building material. A hydronic piping system shall not be in direct contract with any building material which causes the piping material to degrade or corrode.

2501.7 Drilling and notching. Wood-framed structural members shall be drilled, notched or altered in accordance with the provisions of Sections 502.6, 602.6 and 802.6. Holes in cold-formed steel-framed load-bearing members shall only be permitted in accordance with Sections 506.2, 603.2 and 804.2. In accordance with the provisions of Sections 506.3.5, 603.3.4 and 804.3.5, cutting and notching of flanges and lips of cold-formed steel-framed load-bearing members shall not be permitted.

2501.8 Expansion, contraction and settlement. Piping shall be installed so that piping, connections and equipment shall not be subjected to excessive strains or stresses. Provisions shall be made to compensate for expansion, contraction, shrinkage and structural settlement.

2501.9 Piping support. Hangers and supports shall be of material of sufficient strength to support the piping, and shall be fabricated from materials compatible with the piping material. Piping shall be supported at intervals not exceeding the spacing specified in Table 2501.9.

Solar Systems

Active Solar Energy

Industry Standards

HVAC: Design Criteria, Options, Selection
(R.S. Means Co., Inc.)

Active solar energy systems can be used to heat or preheat domestic hot water effectively. Active solar systems also work ideally with absorption cooling systems, since the heat load in the building increases with the solar load in direct proportion to the energy captured by the solar system to run the absorber.

Active solar systems can be used with hydronic or air systems. In a hydronic system, the collectors heat water or a glycol solution and return it to a storage tank. At night the pumps will not operate and the system may drain down. Heat exchangers are used to transfer the heat from the solar loop to the heating loop, which takes the heat from the storage tank. In this way heat collected during the day can be used at night. Air systems use the sun to heat air directly, which is then distributed to the space directly or sent over the storage.

Most active solar systems (see **Figure 15.12**) use either flat plate or concentrating solar collectors, which are connected to an active pumping or fan control system. They may also contain a storage tank or thermal mass.

IOTFDC — 1998 (formerly CABO)
Section 2801 — Solar Energy Systems

2801.1 General. This section provides for construction, installation, alteration, and repair of equipment and systems utilizing solar energy to provide space heating or cooling, hot water heating, and swimming pool heating.

2801.2 Installation. Installation of solar energy systems shall comply with Sections 2801.2.1 through 2801.2.7.

Solar Collector Panel — Liquid

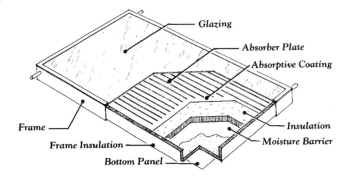

R.S. Means Co., Inc., *Means Graphic Construction Standards*

Figure 15.11

Active Solar Energy Systems

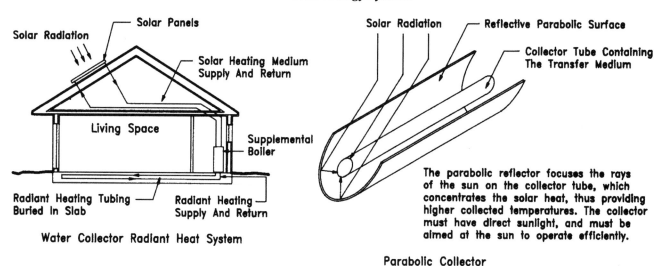

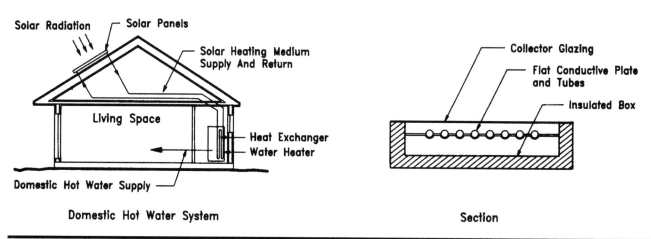

Water Collector Radiant Heat System

Parabolic Collector

Domestic Hot Water System

Section

R.S. Means Co., Inc., HVAC: *Design Criteria, Options, Selection*

Figure 15.12

2801.2.1 Access. Solar energy collectors, controls, dampers, fans, blowers, and pumps shall be accessible for inspection, maintenance, repair, and replacement.

2801.2.2 Roof-mounted collectors. The roof shall be constructed to support the loads imposed by roof-mounted solar collectors. Roof-mounted solar collectors that serve as a roof covering shall conform to the requirements for roof coverings in Chapter 9 of this code. Where mounted on or above the roof coverings, the collectors and supporting structure shall be constructed of noncombustible materials or fire-retardant-treated wood equivalent to that required for the roof construction.

2801.2.3 Pressure and temperature relief. System components containing fluids shall be protected with pressure- and temperature-relief valves. Relief devices shall be installed in sections of the system such that a section cannot be valved off or isolated from a relief device.

2801.2.4 Vacuum relief. System components that are capable of being subjected to pressure drops below atmospheric pressure during operation or shutdown shall be protected by a vacuum-relief valve.

2801.2.5 Protection from freezing. System components shall be protected from damage by freezing of heat-transfer liquids at the lowest ambient temperatures during operation.

2801.2.6 Expansion tanks. Expansion tanks in solar energy systems shall be installed in accordance with Section 2303.

2801.2.7 Roof penetrations. Roof penetrations shall be flashed and waterproofed in accordance with Chapter 9.

2801.3 Labeling. Labeling shall comply with Sections 2801.3.1 and 2801.3.2.

2801.3.1 Collectors. Collectors shall be listed and labeled to show the manufacturer's name, model, serial number, collector weight, maximum allowable temperatures and pressures, and the type of heat transfer fluids allowed.

2801.3.2 Thermal storage units. Pressurized thermal storage units shall be listed and labeled to show the manufacturer's name, model, serial number, maximum and minimum allowable operating temperatures and pressures, and the type of heat transfer fluids allowable.

2801.4 Prohibited heat transfer fluids. Flammable gases and liquids shall not be used as heat transfer fluids.

2801.5 Backflow production. All connections from the potable water supply to solar systems shall comply with Section 3402.4.3, "Lawn irrigation systems."

Special Piping, Storage and Exhaust Systems

Oil Tanks

Industry Standards

HVAC: Design Criteria, Options, Selection
(R.S. Means Co., Inc.)

Oil is normally stored in tanks which may be exposed or buried in the ground. Current laws may require containment and/or leak detection systems. Tanks may be made of single- or double-wall fiberglass or steel. Transfer pumps that supply oil to the burner reservoir or day tank are usually required on long runs.

IOTFDC — 1998 (formerly CABO)
Section 2701 — Oil Tanks

2701.1 Materials. Shop-fabricated supply tanks shall be listed and bear the label of an approved agency.

2701.2 Above-ground tanks. The maximum amount of fuel oil stored aboveground or inside of a building shall be 660 gallons (2498 L). The supply tank shall be supported on rigid noncombustible supports to prevent settling or shifting.

2701.2.1 Tanks within buildings. Supply tanks for use inside of buildings shall be of such size and shape to permit installation and removal from dwellings as whole units. Supply tanks larger than 10 gallons (38 L) shall be placed a minimum of 5 feet (1524 mm) from any fire or flame either within or external to any fuel-burning appliance.

2701.2.2 Outside above-ground tanks. Tanks installed outside above ground shall be a minimum of 5 feet (1524 mm) from an adjoining property line. Such tanks shall be suitably protected from the weather and from physical damage.

2701.3 Underground tanks. Excavations for underground tanks shall not undermine the foundations of existing

structures. The clearance from the tank to the nearest wall of basement, pit or property line shall be a minimum of 1 foot (305 mm). Tanks shall be set on and surrounded with noncorrosive inert materials such as clean earth, sand, or gravel, well tamped in place. Tanks shall be covered with not less than 1 foot (305 mm) of earth. Corrosion protection shall be provided in accordance with Section 2703.7.

2701.4 Multiple tanks. Cross connection of two supply tanks shall be permitted in accordance with Section 2703.6.

2701.5 Oil gauges. Inside tanks shall be provided with a device to indicate when the oil in the tank has reached a predetermined safe level. Glass gauges or a gauge subject to breakage that could result in the escape of oil from the tank shall not be used.

Kitchen HVAC Requirements

Kitchen Appliance Installations

IOTFDC — 1998 (formerly CABO)
Section 1802 — Range Hoods

1802.1 General. Range hoods shall be exhausted to the outdoors by a single-wall duct constructed of galvanized steel, stainless steel or copper. The duct serving the hood shall have a smooth interior surface, shall be substantially air tight and be equipped with a backdraft damper. Ducts serving range hoods shall not terminate in an attic or crawl space or areas inside the building. Listed and labeled ductless range hoods shall be installed in accordance with the terms of their listing.

Section 1803 — Installation of Microwave Ovens

1803.1 Installation of microwave oven over a cooking appliance. The installation of a listed and labeled cooking appliance or microwave oven over a listed and labeled cooking appliance shall conform to the terms of the upper appliance's listing and label and the manufacturer's installation instructions.

Comments

Adequate ventilation of microwave ovens is essential to proper operation.

Section 1804 — Overhead Ventilating Hoods

1804.1 General. Domestic open-top broiler units shall be provided with a metal ventilating hood, not less than 28 gage, with a minimum clearance of 1/4 inch (6.4 mm) between the hood and the underside of combustible material or cabinets. A minimum clearance of 24 inches (610 mm) shall be maintained between the cooking surface and the combustible material or cabinet. The hood shall be at least as wide as the broiler unit and shall extend over the entire unit. Broiler units incorporating an integral exhaust system, and listed and labeled for use without a ventilating hood, need not be provided with a ventilating hood.

Comments

A booster fan may be required for longer runs of range hood ductwork, or where there are two or more elbows.

Section 2201 — Ranges and Ovens

2201.1 Clearances. Freestanding or built-in ranges shall have a vertical clearance above the cooking top of not less than 30 inches (762 mm) to unprotected combustible material. When the underside of such combustible material is protected with non-combustible material or a metal ventilating hood, the distance shall not be less than 24 inches (610 mm). The minimum horizontal distance from the center of the burner heads of a top (or surface) cooking unit to surrounding combustible material shall not be less than that distance specified by its listing.

2201.2 Gas ranges and ovens. Gas ranges and ovens shall be listed and labeled and shall conform to ANSI Z21.1.

2201.3 Built-in units. Built-in household cooking appliances shall be listed and labeled and shall be installed in accordance with the manufacturer's installation instructions. The installation shall not interfere with combustion air or accessibility for operation and servicing.

Section 2202 — Open-top Gas Broiler Units

2202.1 General. Open-top gas broiler units shall be listed and labeled and shall be installed in accordance with the manufacturer's installation instructions. Open-top gas broiler units shall conform to ANSI Z21.1.

Commercial Kitchens

Industry Standards

HVAC: Design Criteria, Options, Selection
(R.S. Means Co., Inc.)

Commercial kitchen exhaust systems typically include the following components:

- Hood
- Grease removal device
- Exhaust duct
- Fan
- Fire extinguishing equipment

The recommended practice for these items is covered in NAPA 96 — *Standard for the Installation of Equipment for the Removal of Smoke and Grease Laden Vapors from Commercial Cooking Equipment.*

Exhaust Hoods

There are two basic types of kitchen exhaust hood systems: exhaust-only systems and exhaust-plus-makeup-air systems. The *exhaust-only system* typically consists of a hood, grease trap, filter, exhaust duct, roof curb, and fan (see **Figure 15.13**). These systems are generally used for low-intensity applications, such as delis and snack counters. They exhaust room air directly to the outside. These systems are generally less energy-efficient than make-up units because the exhaust fan removes 100% tempered air from the occupied space.

Exhaust-plus-make-up-air systems include all the features of exhaust-only systems as well as a supply air slot, supply duct, supply fan, intake extension and air-intake filter hood. See **Figure 15.14**.

NFPA recommends that hoods be installed in all applications that produce smoke or grease-laden vapors. It is also recommended that all solid-fuel-burning equipment be served by hoods that are separate from other kitchen ventilation equipment. Recommended clearances for hoods are as follows:

- 18 inches to combustible materials
- 3 inches to limited combustible materials
- 0 inches to non-combustible materials

The hood should be designed to capture a minimum amount of air. Therefore, the hood should extend at least 6 inches (152 mm) beyond the edge of the cooking surface on all sides and exhaust 100 cfm per square foot (508 L/s per square meter) for wall canopy hoods and 150 cfm per square foot (762 L/s per square meter) for island canopy hoods. Non-canopy applications must have a hood set back no more than one foot from the edge of the cooking surface and exhaust 300 cfm per linear foot (142 L/s) of cooking surface.

The gauge of metal for the hood (canopy), exhaust duct, and supply air duct is also specifically controlled. The canopy or hood for kitchen exhausts should be constructed of either 18-gauge steel or 20-gauge stainless steel. All seams, joints, and penetrations of the hood should have a liquid-tight continuous weld. Interior joints and seams do not have to be continuously welded, but they should be completely sealed. Exhaust air volume for hoods should be sufficient to remove all grease-laden vapors. Since these factors are highly dependent on the size and type of equipment being used, designers should contact equipment manufacturers to determine specific requirements.

Exhaust ducts should be designed to transport the hot flue gases outside as directly as possible. Formed of 16-gauge steel or 18-gauge stainless steel, they should be installed without dips or traps that might collect grease. Ducts should not be connected with any other duct systems; all duct joints should be completely welded to provide a continuous liquid-tight seal.

Grease Removal Devices

Grease removal devices (grease traps) should be an integral part of any kitchen exhaust system. These devices generally consist of filters, baffles, or other approved devices. NFPA recommends that mesh filters not be used.

Grease filters should have a minimum area of one square inch (6.5m²) for every two cfm (1 L/s) of exhaust air from the hood.

The distance between the grease removal system and the cooking surface should be as great as possible. For charcoal or charcoal-type broilers, the minimum distance should be four feet (1.2 m). Grease removal devices should also be protected from combustion gas outlet or from direct flame because items like deep fat fryers produce high flue gas temperatures. In cases where the minimum distance between the grease removal device and the combustion gas outlet is 18 inches (46 cm) or less, a steel baffle should be installed.

Cleaning and Inspection of Exhaust Systems

Access to ducts for cleaning purposes is essential to the proper design of a kitchen ventilation system. They should be accessible for cleaning and inspection purposes. There should be a sign placed on all duct access panels that reads: ACCESS PANEL — DO NOT OBSTRUCT. On *horizontal duct runs*, an opening 20" x 20" (50 cm x 50 cm) should be provided. If this is not possible, an opening large enough to allow thorough cleaning should be installed at 12 feet (3.654 m) on center. On *vertical duct runs*, an opening for personnel entry should be located at the top of the duct. If this is not feasible, access panels should be located at each floor. In *buildings greater than one story* in height, ducts should be enclosed in a continuous enclosure extending from the ceiling above the hood to the roof. In *buildings less than four stories*, the enclosure should have a one-hour fire rating (if it qualifies as a shaft, a two-hour enclosure is common).

Air Volumes in Exhaust Systems

Kitchen exhaust fans should provide a minimum air velocity of 1,500 feet per minute (7.6 m/s). The air volumes should be adequate to capture and remove all grease-laden cooking vapors. In the event of a fire, exhaust fans should continue to operate unless a listed component of the exhaust system requires that the fan be shut down. It is not necessary to automatically restart the exhaust fan after the extinguishing system is activated if all the cooking equipment has been shut down. Approved up-discharge fans with motors surrounded by the air flow should be hinged and supplied with flexible wiring to allow periodic cleaning.

Fire Systems for Exhaust Hoods

Approved fire extinguishing systems should be provided for all grease removal items and hoods. These extinguishing systems should encompass all duct systems and cooking equipment that could be a source of grease ignition. NFPA recommends the following methods of fire suppression for use in kitchen exhaust systems:

Dry chemical extinguishing system	NFPA 17
Wet chemical extinguishing system	NFPA 17A
Carbon dioxide extinguishing system	NFPA 12
Sprinkler system	NFPA 13
Deluge foam water sprinkler and foam spray systems	NFPA 16

Exhaust/Make-Up Air Kitchen Hood

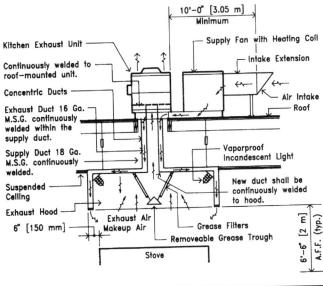

R.S. Means Co., Inc., HVAC: *Design Criteria, Options, Selection*

Figure 15.14

Exhaust-Only Type of Kitchen Hood

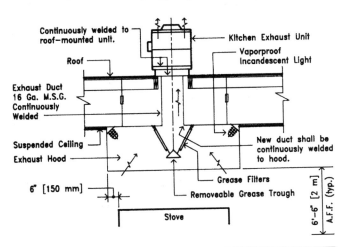

R.S. Means Co., Inc., HVAC: *Design Criteria, Options, Selection*

Figure 15.13

In the event that a fire suppression system activates, all sources of fuel and heat to the equipment should shut down. In addition, all gas appliances not requiring ventilation but located under the same hood should be shut down. All of these systems should be tied to the central fire alarm system in the building.

Special Fuel-Burning Equipment

IOTFDC — 1998 (formerly CABO)

Section 2203 — Outdoor Gas Cooking Appliances

2203.1 General. Outdoor gas cooking appliances shall be listed and labeled and shall be installed in accordance with the manufacturer's installation instructions. Outdoor gas cooking appliances shall conform to ANSI Z21.54 and Z21.58.

Section 2205 — Vented Decorative Gas Appliances

2205.1 General. Vented decorative gas appliances shall conform to ANSI Z21.50.

2205.2 Vented decorative gas appliances. Vented decorative gas appliances shall be listed and labeled and shall be installed in accordance with the manufacturer's installation instructions.

2205.2.1 Combustion air. Combustion air shall be provided in accordance with Chapter 20.

2205.3 Decorative gas appliances for installation in vented solid-fuel-burning fireplaces. Decorative gas appliances for installation in vented solid-fuel-burning fireplaces shall be listed and labeled and shall be installed in accordance with the manufacturer's installation instructions.

2205.4 Gas logs. Listed and labeled gas logs installed in solid fuel-burning fireplaces shall be in accordance with the provisions of this section, provided that:

1. The gas logs are installed in accordance with their listing and label and the manufacturer's installation instructions.

2. If the fireplace is equipped with a damper, it shall be permanently blocked open to provide the appliance manufacturer's required minimum vent opening at all times.

   Exception: Listed appliances incorporating controls to prevent operation of the appliance without an adequate vent opening shall be installed in accordance with the conditions of the listing and manufacturer's installation instructions.

3. The minimum flue passageway shall not be less than 1 square inch per 1,000 British thermal units per hour (Btu/h) (645 mm² per 293W) input.

4. Gas logs equipped with a pilot shall have listed and labeled shut-off valve.

2205.5 Gas-fired log lighters. Unlisted gas-fired log lighters shall be installed in accordance with the manufacturer's installation instructions.

Section 2206 — Gas Lights

2206.1 Clearances. Gas lights shall be listed and labeled and shall be installed in accordance with the manufacturer's installation instructions.

2206.2 Mounting on buildings. Gas lights for wall or ceiling mounting shall be attached to a substantial structure in such a manner that they are not dependent on the gas piping for support.

2206.3 Mounting on posts. Gas lights for post mounting shall be rigidly attached to a post. Posts shall be rigidly mounted. The strength and rigidity of posts greater than 3 feet (914 mm) in height shall be at least equivalent to that of a 2-1/2 inch-diameter (64 mm) post constructed of 14-gage steel, or 1 inch (25.4 mm) Schedule 40 steel pipe. Posts 3 feet (914 mm) or less in height shall not be smaller than a 3/4 inch (19 mm) Schedule 40 steel pipe. Drain openings shall be provided near the base of posts when there is a possibility of water collecting inside them.

2206.4 Gas appliance pressure regulator. When a gas appliance pressure regulator is not supplied with a gas light, a pressure regulator shall be installed in the service line of the line to the gas light. For multiple installations, one regulator used to serve several gas lights shall have the requisite capacity to supply all appliances simultaneously.

Section 2207 — Sauna Heaters

2207.1 Locations and protections. Sauna heaters shall be protected from accidental contact by persons with a guard of material having a low thermal conductivity, such as wood. The guard shall have no substantial effect on the transfer of heat from the heater to the room.

2207.2 Installation. Sauna heaters shall be listed and labeled and shall be installed in accordance with the manufacturer's installation instructions.

2207.3 Construction of gas-fired heaters. The provisions of Chapter 26 shall apply to gas connections. When access to controls is from an adjacent room, connections shall be made in that location.

2207.4 Combustion air. Combustion air for gas-fired sauna heaters shall not be taken from inside the sauna room. Combustion air and venting for a nondirect vent-type heater shall be provided in accordance with Chapters 20 and 21, respectively.

2207.5 Controls. Sauna heaters shall be equipped with a thermostat that will limit room temperature to no greater than 194°F. (90°C.). If the thermostat is not an integral part of the heater, the heat-sensing element shall be located within 6 inches (153 mm) of the ceiling.

CHAPTER
16 ELECTRICAL

Table of Contents

(continued on next page)

Text in blue print indicates excerpts from model building code(s). "Comments" (in solid blue boxes) were written by the editors, based on their own experience.

For building product information, use this book's special Internet gateway to thousands of manufacturers:
www.rsmeans.com/prodsupp/rlstand.html

CHAPTER

16 ELECTRICAL

Common Defect Allegations

- *Insufficient number of receptacles and missing GFIs in the bathrooms, kitchens, and exterior locations.*

- *Failure to provide exterior disconnects that are weathertight and rated for exterior application.*

- *Kitchen dedicated circuits for heavy load appliances wired with a 14 ga. conductor instead of 12 ga.*

- *Improper or missing labels on the panels.*

- *Wiring within 6 feet of the attic access opening. This should not be allowed, in order to prevent someone from pulling themselves up using the cable as a handgrab.*

- *Failure to weatherseal exterior lighting to the wall finish, thereby allowing rainwater into the wall cavity and the wiring.*

- *Holes in the drywall of an electrical closet where the electricians ran telephone and TV cable. If these holes are not patched, they can allow rodents and vermin to enter the wall cavity.*

Introduction   Each year it seems the number of electrical devices in our homes or offices increases. Because of the inherent danger of shock and fire from electrical power, the installation and use of electrical power is closely regulated by numerous codes — national, state, and local. Faulty electrical systems are one of the major causes of fire, after human error.

We have included many excerpts from the *National Electrical Code®* and *NEC® Handbook*, both published by the National Fire Protection Association. The *International One- and Two-Family Dwelling Code* (formerly

CABO) covers residential construction and includes electrical; a major source of the information in the IOTFDC is the *National Electrical Code*®. *NEC*® information is also included in BOCA.

The information in this chapter is provided as a basic reference for the general contractor, student, or building owner seeking a better understanding of the standards for electrical installation. It is intended to be used by supervisory personnel or consultants to check design or completed work against fundamental requirements, but it is not to be used as an instruction manual for the installation. An electrical contractor or installer must be experienced and licensed (where required) with full knowledge of local and applicable national codes before performing any electrical work.

The following professional organizations may be helpful in locating more information about electrical design and installation. They also provide recommendations and support.

National Electrical Contractors Association (NECA)
3 Bethesda Metro Center, Suite 1100
Bethesda, Maryland 20814
Telephone: 800-888-6322
www.necanet.org
NECA is comprised of more than 4,000 electrical contractors from the U.S. and abroad. NECA services are designed for contractors who are involved in Standard Industrial Code 1731 (electrical work — specialty contractors) and some of those involved in SIC 1623 (utility work, also referred to as "outside" or "line" work.)

National Electrical Manufacturers Association (NEMA)
1300 North 17th Street, Suite 1847
Rosslyn, VA 22209
Telephone: 703-841-3200
www.nema.org
NEMA has been developing standards for the electrical manufacturing industry since 1926 and is today one of leading standards development associations. It contributes to an orderly marketplace and helps to ensure public safety.

National Fire Protection Association (NFPA)
1 Batterymarch Park
Quincy, MA 02269-9904
Telephone: 800-344-3555
www.nfpa.org
The *National Electrical Code*® is available from the NFPA.

NFPA 70: *National Electrical Code*® (NEC®) —The original code document was developed in 1897 as a result of the united efforts of various insurance, electrical, architectural, and allied interests. The NEC® code is revised and updated every three years. All electrical installations should be done in accordance with NEC® and local ordinances.

NFPA 72: National Fire Alarm Code® —This standard covers all aspects of the installation, maintenance, and use of fire alarm systems.

NFPA 780: Installation of Lightning Protection Systems Code — This code covers lightning protection requirements for ordinary structures, miscellaneous structures, and special occupancies. It does not cover explosives-manufacturing structures and electric utility systems.

Underwriters Laboratories, Inc. (UL)
333 Pfingsten Road
Northbrook, Illinois 60062
Telephone: 847-272-8800
www.ul.com
UL is the leading third-party certification organization in the United States and the largest in North America. As a not-for-profit product safety testing and certification organization, UL has been evaluating products in the interest of public safety since 1894.

International Electrotechnical Commission (IEC)
3, rue de Varembé
P.O. Box 131
CH - 1211 Geneva 20
Switzerland
Telephone: 011 41 22 919 0211
www.iec.ch
The IEC is a worldwide organization that prepares and publishes international standards for all electrical, electronic and related technologies. Membership consists of more than 50 participating countries, including all the world's major nations and a growing number of industrializing countries.

The Institute of Electrical and Electronic Engineers (IEEE)
345 East 47th Street
New York, NY 10017-2394
Telephone: 212-705-7900
www.ieeeusa.org
The IEEE is the world's largest technical professional society. Founded in 1884 by a handful of practitioners of electrical science, it now includes electronic, computer engineering and computer science professionals. IEEE sponsors technical conferences, symposia, local chapter meetings and educational programs.

Illuminating Engineering Society of North America (IESNA)
120 Wall Street, 17th Floor
New York, NY 10005–4001
Telephone: 212-248-5000
www.iesna.org
IESNA is dedicated to the field of lighting design and application, and publishes handbooks, design guides, and recommended practices.

Note: Building Officials and Code Administrators International, Inc. (BOCA) provides numerous model codes, including the National Building Code, National Fire Prevention Code and the National Energy Conservation Code. These codes and the *National Electrical Code*® are available through BOCA (**www.bocai.org**).

The *International One- and Two-Family Dwelling Code* (formerly the CABO *One and Two Family Dwelling Code*) is now maintained and available through the International Code Council. BOCA, ICBO and SBCCI, which founded CABO, established the International Code Council and incorporated CABO into the ICC in November 1997. The *International One- and Two-Family Dwelling Code* (IOTFDC) is available from any of these four organizations.

(See "Understanding Building Codes & Other Standards" at the beginning of this book for information on contacting these organizations.)

Ed. Note: Comments and recommendations within this chapter are not intended as a definitive resource for a given project. Contractors must rely on the project documents and any applicable code requirements pertaining to their own particular location.

Residential Service — Underground and Overhead

Industry Standards

Means Graphic Construction Standards
(R.S. Means Co., Inc.)

Residential Service

A residential service includes all of the materials and equipment necessary to deliver electrical power from the utility supply lines to the distribution system within the residence. The electrical service may be brought to the residence by overhead or underground supply lines. Residential service equipment consists of four basic components: a service drop conductor (for overhead service) or a service lateral conductor (for underground service); metering equipment; overcurrent protection; and a distribution panel.

The service entrance, which connects the residence directly to the utility supply lines, is run either overhead or underground. (See **Figures 16.1-16.3**.) In overhead services, the connecting cable runs from the utility pole to a bracket (sometimes called a "weatherhead") installed on the building. This aerial cable, called the service drop, is installed and maintained by the utility company. In underground services, the connection between the utility pole and residence may be run from either a utility pole or a utility-owned underground supply line. Although overhead service is the most commonly used system for residential installations, underground service, or "Underground Residential Distribution," is steadily increasing in popularity.

Residential service layouts vary widely, depending on voltage and amperage rating and the type of residence being served. In most cases, residential service is 100A, but 200A systems are being installed with increasing frequency to accommodate the many convenience appliances in today's homes. The increase in installation cost of 200A service over that of 100A service is about 30%. A typical overhead service is comprised of the following components and equipment: service head; service lateral, which consists of type SE cable or PVC, EMT, or rigid steel pipe with individual conductors; meter box (sometimes supplied by the utility); LB fitting, which is used to gain entrance from outside the dwelling to the distribution panel inside; distribution panel, with a 100A, 150A, or 200A main breaker and space for 20, 30, or 42 circuits 110/208V single-phase; ground rod and bare copper cable for the grounding system; and branch circuit breakers of 15A to 60A double-pole.

The layout for a typical underground system consists of service lateral conductors made of URD (underground residential distribution) direct burial cable, PVC pipe with individual conductors made of URD direct burial cable, PVC pipe with individual cables, or galvanized steel pipe with individual cables. In cases where URD cable is used, an approved protective sleeve must be installed where the cable is exposed at each end of the service lateral conductor (between the ground and connection to the supply line on the utility pole and between finish grade and the meter socket on the dwelling). The layout for a typical underground system is the same as that for an overhead system in all other respects.

Through Roof Service Installation

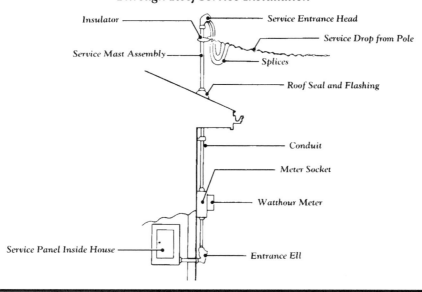

R.S. Means Co., Inc., *Means Graphic Construction Standards*

Figure 16.1

Underground Installation Requirements

Comments

The International Code Council has assumed responsibility for the development and maintenance of the CABO One and Two Family Dwelling Code. The 1998 International One- and Two-Family Dwelling Code replaces the CABO OTFDC © 1995, with 1996/1997 amendments. Chapter 43 of the 1998 IOTFDC covers wiring methods for services, feeders and branch circuits for electrical power and distribution. It includes information about topics such as allowable applications for wiring methods, aboveground/underground installation requirements, general installation and support requirements for wiring methods, and minimum cover requirements.

See the Introduction to this chapter for information on where to obtain the IOTFDC.

For underground installation of conduit and cable, refer to Figures 16.2, 16.3, 16.4, and 16.5. Rigid nonmetallic conduit, such as PVC Schedule 40 conduit and fittings, should be buried at least 18" (460 mm) deep. Conductors under residential driveways follow the same rules (a minimum of 18" deep). If an overcurrent device is used, the burial depth can be reduced to 12" (305 mm).

Some codes require a concrete jacket on underground installations of 220 or more volts.

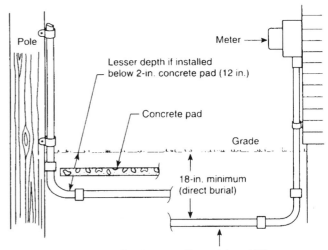

Rigid nonmetallic conduit and fittings may be directly buried in earth at a depth not less than 18 in. See Section 347-2(g) and Section 710-4(b), where circuits exceed 600 volts.

PVC rigid nonmetallic conduit buried in compliance with Section 300-5 and installed in accordance with Section 300-5(a).

Courtesy of NFPA, *National Electrical Code® Handbook [Figure 300-4]*

Figure 16.2

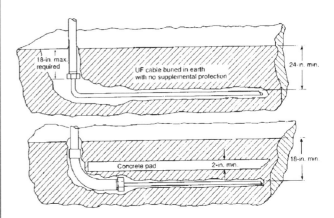

Type UF cable buried in compliance with Table 300-5. Note the protective bushing where the cable is used with metal conduit.

Courtesy of NFPA, *National Electrical Code® Handbook [Figure 300-9]*

Figure 16.3

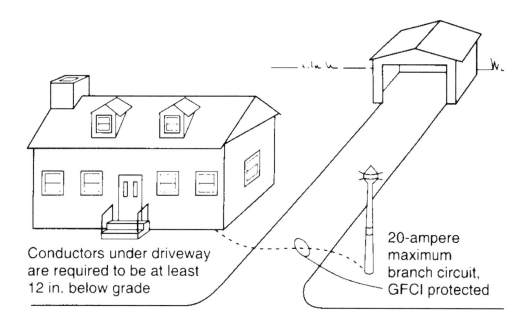

Conductors under driveway
are required to be at least
12 in. below grade

20-ampere
maximum
branch circuit,
GFCI protected

A 20-ampere, GFCI-protected residential branch circuit is permitted to be installed with a minimum burial depth of 12 inches beneath a residential driveway and outdoor parking areas used only for dwelling-related purposes.

Courtesy of NFPA, *National Electrical Code® Handbook [Figure 300-5]*

Figure 16.4

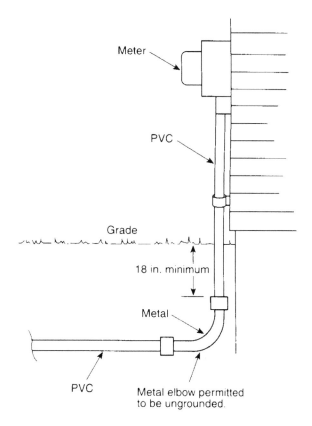

Meter

PVC

Grade

18 in. minimum

Metal

PVC

Metal elbow permitted
to be ungrounded.

An application of Section 250-32, Exception, which permits the metal elbow to be ungrounded, provided it is isolated from possible contact by a minimum cover of 18 inches to any part of the elbow. For other than service raceways, see companion Section 250-33, Exception No. 4.

Courtesy of NFPA, *National Electrical Code® Handbook [Figure 300-6]*

Figure 16.5

Overhead Service Drop

Industry Standards
Electrical Estimating Methods
(R.S. Means Company, Inc.)

Poles and *overhead routing* represent the most conventional method of distributing power and communication cables. Many cables are built and rated for aerial service. Some cables include "strength members" to carry the tensions of the stretched cables. Still other types of cable, such as service drops and telephone lines, will be supported by a steel messenger wire. Note: Code requirements may dictate certain minimum heights for suspended cable.

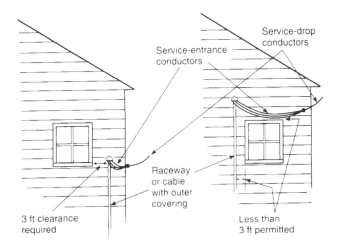

Required dimensions for service conductors located alongside a window and service conductors above the top level of a window designed to be opened.

Courtesy of NFPA, *National Electrical Code® Handbook [Figure 230-5]*

Figure 16.6

Comments

Service conductors without an outer jacket shall have a clearance at least 3' (0.9 mm) from windows. (See Figures 16.6 - 16.8.) For above roof installation, conductors shall have a vertical clearance between 18" and 8' above the roof surface, depending on the slope of the roof.

The hole for a line pole is usually made with an auger machine. After the pole is set, crushed limestone or similar fill is placed and compacted around the pole. In some areas, poles will need lightning rods and grounding. Don't forget to look for these requirements on the drawings.

Comments

Chapter 41 of the 1998 International One- and Two-Family Dwelling Code, which replaces the CABO One and Two Family Dwelling Code, covers service conductors and equipment for the control and protection of services and their installation requirements. Section 4104 addresses overhead service-drop and service conductor installation and includes requirements for clearance from building openings and roofs, vertical clearances, point of attachment, means of attachment, and supports.

Clearance from Buildings
NFPA 70: National Electrical Code®
230-24. Clearances.

(a) Above Roofs. Conductors shall have a vertical clearance of not less than 8 ft (2.44 m) above the roof surface. The vertical clearance above the roof level shall be maintained for a distance not less than 3 ft (914 mm) in all directions from the edge of the roof. (See **Figure 16.7**.)

Exception No. 1: The area above a roof surface subject to pedestrian or vehicular traffic shall have a vertical clearance from the roof surface in accordance with the clearance requirements of Section 230-24(b).

Exception No. 2: Where the voltage between conductors does not exceed 300 and the roof has a slope of not less than 4 in. (102 mm) in 12 in. (305 mm), a reduction in clearance of 3 ft (914 mm) shall be permitted.

Exception No. 3: Where the voltage between conductors does not exceed 300, a reduction in clearance above only the overhanging portion of the roof to not less than 18 in. (457 mm) shall be permitted if (1) not more than 6 ft (1.83 m)

of service-drop conductors, 4 ft (1.22 m) horizontally, pass above the roof overhang, and (2) they are terminated at a through-the-roof raceway or approved support.

Exception No. 4: The requirement for maintaining the vertical clearance 3 ft (914 mm) from the edge of the roof shall not apply to the final conductor span where the service-drop is attached to the side of a building.

230-9. Clearance from Building Openings. Service conductors installed as open conductors or multiconductor cable without an overall outer jacket shall have a clearance of not less than 3 ft (914 mm) from windows that are designed to be opened, doors, porches, balconies, ladders, stairs, fire escapes, or similar locations.

Exception: Conductors run above the top level of a window shall be permitted to be less than the 3 ft (914 mm) requirement above.

Overhead service conductors shall not be installed beneath openings through which materials may be moved, such as openings in farm and commercial buildings, and shall not be installed where they will obstruct entrance to these building openings.

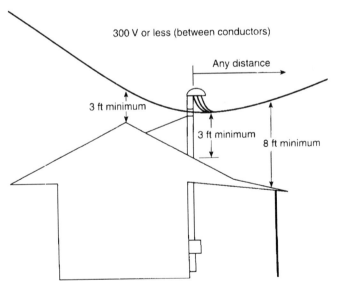

Exception No. 2 applies to steeply sloped roofs that are less likely to be walked on. These roofs have a slope of not less than 4 inches in 8 inches. On such roofs, the vertical clearance of overhead conductors may be reduced from 8 ft. to 3 ft. There are no restrictions on the length of the conductors over the roof or the horizontal distance over the roof.

Courtesy of NFPA, *National Electrical Code® Handbook [Figure 230-6(b)]*

Figure 16.7

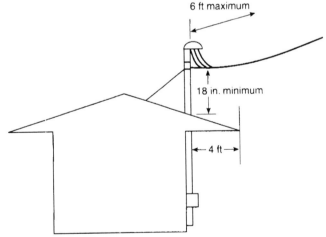

Exception No. 3 permits service conductor clearances to be reduced 18" for through-the-roof raceways passing through the overhanging portion, provided that not more then 6' of conductors pass over 4' of roof service, measured horizontally. This applies to flat or sloped roofs that are easily waled on (less then 4" in 12").

Courtesy of NFPA, *National Electrical Code® Handbook [Figure 230-6(c)]*

Figure 16.8

Work Space in Front of Equipment

NFPA 70: National Electrical Code®
110-34. Work Space and Guarding.

(a) **Working Space.** The minimum clear working space in the direction of access to live parts of electrical equipment such as switchboards, control panels, switches, circuit breakers, motor controllers, relays, and similar equipment shall not be less than specified in Table 110-34(a) [see **Figure 16.9**] unless otherwise specified in this Code. Distances shall be measured from the live parts, if such are exposed, or from the enclosure front or opening if such are enclosed.

Where the "Conditions" are as follows:

1. Exposed live parts on one side and no live or grounded parts on the other side of the working space or exposed live parts on both sides effectively guarded by suitable wood or other insulating materials. Insulated wire or insulated busbars operating at not over 300 volts shall not be considered live parts.

2. Exposed live parts on one side and grounded parts on the other side. Concrete, brick, or tile walls will be considered as grounded surfaces.

3. Exposed live parts on both sides of the work space (not guarded as provided in Condition 1) with the operator between.

Exception: Working space shall not be required in back of equipment such as dead-front switchboards or control assemblies where there are no renewable or adjustable parts (such as fuses or switches) on the back and where all connections are accessible from locations other than the back. Where rear access is required to work on de-energized parts on the back of enclosed equipment, a minimum working space of 30 in. (762 mm) horizontally shall be provided.

Minimum Depth of Clear Working Space at Electrical Equipment

Nominal Voltage to Ground	Conditions (feet)		
	1	2	3
	(feet)	(feet)	(feet)
601-2500	3	4	5
2501-9000	4	5	6
9001-25,000	5	6	9
25,001-75 kV	6	8	10
Above 75 kV	8	10	12

For SI units: 1 ft = 0.3048 m.

Courtesy of NFPA, *National Electrical Code® Handbook* [Table 110-34(a)]

Figure 16.9

Service Equipment — General

Comments

Service equipment in general includes service entrance transformers, either pad- or pole-mounted, installed near the service entrance. Fuses, circuit breakers, and panelboards are used to protect the branch circuits from short circuits or overloads.

Number of Services, Disconnects

NFPA 70: National Electrical Code®
230-2 Number of Services.

(a) **Number.** A building or other structure served shall be supplied by only one service.

(b) **Identification.** Where a building or structure is supplied by more than one service, or any combination of branch circuits, feeders, and services, a permanent plaque or directory shall be installed at each service disconnect location denoting all other services, feeders, and branch circuits supplying that building or structure and the area served by each.

Ed. Note: The Code cross references Section 230-2(b) and Section 225-8(d). Exception No. 2 in Section 225-8(d) states that "this identification shall not be required for branch circuits installed from a dwelling unit to a second building or structure."

230-62 Service Equipment—Enclosed or Guarded.
Energized parts of service equipment shall be enclosed as specified in (a) below, or guarded as specified in (b).

(a) Enclosed. Energized parts shall be enclosed so that they will not be exposed to accidental contact or guarded as in (b).

(b) Guard. Energized parts that are not enclosed shall be installed on a switchboard, panelboard, or control board and guard in accordance with Section 110-17 guarding of live parts (600 volts, nominal, or less) and Section 110-18 arcing parts.

230-64 Working Space. Sufficient working space shall be provided in the vicinity of the service equipment to permit safe operation, inspection, and repairs. In no case shall this be less than that specified by Section 110-6 conductor sizes.

230-66 Marking. Service equipment rated at 600 volts or less shall be marked to identify it as being suitable for use as service equipment. Individual meter socket enclosures shall not be considered service equipment.

Service Equipment — Disconnecting Means

230-70 General. Means shall be provided to disconnect all conductors in a building or other structure from the service-entrance conductors.

(a) Location. The service disconnecting means shall be installed at a readily accessible location either outside of a building or structure, or inside nearest the point of entrance of the service conductors.

Service disconnecting means shall not be installed in bathrooms.

(b) Marking. Each service disconnecting means shall be permanently marked to identify it as a service disconnecting means.

(c) Suitable for Use. Each service disconnection means shall be suitable for the prevailing conditions. Service equipment installed in hazardous (classified) locations shall comply with the requirements of Articles 500 through 517.

Ed. Note: Articles 500 – 517 pertain to special occupancies in classified locations, including hazardous locations, commercial garages, and health care facilities.

230-71 Maximum Number of Disconnects.
(a) General. The service disconnecting means for each service permitted by Section 230-2 ("Number of Services"), or for each set of service-entrance conductors permitted by Section 230-40 ("Number of Service - Entrance Conductor Sets"), Exception No. 1, shall consist of not more than six switches or six circuit breakers mounted in a single enclosure, in a group of separate enclosures, or in or on a switchboard. There shall be no more than six disconnects per service grouped in any one location.

(b) Single-Pole Units. Two or three single-pole switches or breakers, capable of individual operation, shall be permitted on multiwire circuits, one pole for each ungrounded conductor, as one multiple disconnect, provided they are equipped with "handle ties" or a "master handle" to disconnect all conductors of the service with no more than six operations of the hand.

(FPN): See Section 384-16(a) for service equipment in panelboards, and see Section 430-95 for service equipment in motor control centers.

Ed. Note: (FPN) denotes fine print note.

230-74 Simultaneous Opening of Poles. Each service disconnect shall simultaneously disconnect all ungrounded service conductors that it controls from the premises wiring system.

230-82 Equipment Connected to the Supply Side of Service Disconnect. Equipment shall not be connected to the supply side of the service disconnecting means.

Exception No. 5: Taps used only to supply load management devices, circuits for emergency systems, stand-by power systems, fire pump equipment, and fire and sprinkler alarms if provided with service equipment and installed in accordance with requirements for service-entrance conductors.

230-83 Transfer Equipment. Transfer equipment, including transfer switches, shall operate such that all ungrounded conductors of one source of supply are disconnected before any ungrounded conductors of the second source are connected.

Service Conductors & Grounding

Industry Standards
Plan Reading & Material Takeoff
(R.S. Means Co., Inc.)

Conductors and Grounding

A *conductor* is a wire or metal bar with a low resistance to the flow of electricity. *Grounding* is accomplished by a conductor connected between electrical equipment, or between a circuit and the earth. Wire is the most common material used to conduct current from the electrical source to electrical use. Wire is made of either copper or aluminum conductors with an insulating jacket, and is available in a variety of voltage ratings and insulating materials. Wire is installed within raceways, such as conduit or flexible metallic conduit (sometimes referred to as *Greenfield* or *flex*). *Flexible metallic conduit* is a single strip of aluminum or galvanized steel, spiral-wound and interlocked to provide a circular cross section of high strength and flexibility for the protection of the wire within. Other products similar to flex are covered with a liquid-tight plastic covering; they are used where protection from liquids is required.

Other types of conductors include armored cable (BX & MC), a fabricated assembly of cable with a metal enclosure similar in appearance to flex. Nonmetallic sheathed cable (Romex) is factory-constructed of two, three, or four insulated conductors enclosed in an outer sheath of plastic or fibrous material. It is available with or without a bare ground wire made of copper or aluminum conductors.

Special wires such as those used in low-voltage control wiring, signals, and telecommunications are also available for the performance required by the specific application.

In addition to the wire itself, special connectors or terminations at the end of each wire are required to complete the application. Various fasteners such as staples, clips, and flex fittings are also necessary.

Comments

Chapter 41 of the 1998 International One- and Two-Family Dwelling Code, which replaces the CABO One and Two Family Dwelling Code, covers service conductors and equipment for the control and protection of services and their installation requirements. Section 4101 provides general requirements, including the number of services, other conductors in the raceway or cable, raceway seal, service disconnect requirements, and maximum number of disconnects.

All service disconnects must be accessible at all times. Section 4105 addresses the installation of service-entrance conductors, including insulation and protection (from moisture and physical damage), wiring methods and terminations. Note that Chapter 43 of the IOTFDC addresses wiring methods.

Deteriorating Agents
NFPA 70: National Electrical Code®

110-11. Deteriorating Agents. Unless identified for use in the operating environment, no conductors or equipment shall be located in damp or wet locations; where exposed to gases, fumes, vapors, liquids, or other agents having a deteriorating effect on the conductors or equipment; nor where exposed to excessive temperatures.

(FPN No. 1): See Section 300-6 for protection against corrosion.

(FPN No. 2): Some cleaning and lubricating compounds can cause severe deterioration of many plastic materials used for insulating and structural applications in equipment.

Equipment approved for use in dry locations only shall be protected against permanent damage from the weather during building construction.

Conductor Identification

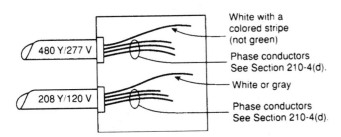

480 Y/277 V

208 Y/120 V

White with a colored stripe (not green)

Phase conductors See Section 210-4(d).

White or gray

Phase conductors See Section 210-4(d).

Grounded conductors of different systems in the same enclosure.

Courtesy of NFPA, *National Electrical Code® Handbook [Figure 210-4]*

Figure 16.10

Load Centers & Panelboards

NFPA 70: National Electrical Code®
Panelboards

384-14 Lighting and Appliance Branch-Circuit Panelboard. For the purposes of this article, a lighting and appliance branch-circuit panelboard is one having more than 10 percent of its overcurrent devices rated 30 amperes or less, for which neutral connections are provided.

384-15 Number of Overcurrent Devices on One Panelboard. Not more than 42 overcurrent devices (other than those provided for in the mains) of a lighting and appliance branch-circuit panelboard shall be installed in any one cabinet or cutout box.

A lighting and appliance branch-circuit panelboard shall be provided with physical means to prevent the installation of more overcurrent devices than that number for which the panelboard was designed, rated, and approved.

For the purposes of this article, a 2-pole circuit breaker shall be considered two overcurrent devices: a 3-pole circuit breaker shall be considered three overcurrent devices.

384-16 Overcurrent Protection.

(a) Lighting and Appliance Branch-Circuit Panelboard Individually Protected. Each lighting and appliance branch-circuit panelboard shall be individually protected on the supply side by not more than two main circuit breakers or two sets of fuses having a combined rating not greater than that of the panelboard.

(c) Continuous Load. The total load on any overcurrent device located in a panelboard shall not exceed 80 percent of its rating where, in normal operation, the load will continue for three hours or more.

(f) Back-Fed Devices. Plug-in-type overcurrent protection devices or plug-in-type main lug assemblies that are back fed shall be secured in place by an additional fastener that requires other than a pull to release the device from the mounting means on the panel.

384-18 Enclosure. Panelboards shall be mounted in cabinets, cutout boxes, or enclosures designed for the purpose and shall be dead front.

384-20 Grounding of Panelboards. Panelboard cabinets and panelboard frames, if of metal, shall be in physical contact with each other and shall be grounded in accordance with Article 250 or Section 384-3(c). Where the panelboard is used with nonmetallic raceway or cable or where separate grounding conductors are provided, a terminal bar for the grounding conductors shall be secured inside the cabinet. The terminal bar shall be bonded to the cabinet and panelboard frame, if of metal, otherwise it shall be connected to the grounding conductor that is run with the conductors feeding the panelboard.

Ed. Note: For space requirements around electrical equipment (600V, nominal, or less), see **Figure 16.11**. *Also refer to* **Figure 16.9** *in the section, "Work Space in Front of Equipment," earlier in this chapter.*

For additional information about circuit breakers, provided by Underwriters' Laboratories Inc., see "Circuit Breakers — Interchanging in Foreign Panels," later in this chapter.

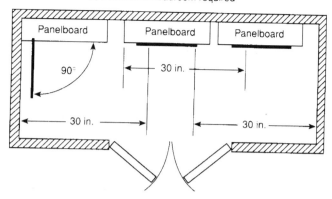

The 30-inch-wide front working space is not required to be directly centered on the electrical equipment where it can be assured that the space is sufficient for safe operation and maintenance of such equipment.

Courtesy of NFPA, *National Electrical Code® Handbook [Figure 110-9]*

Figure 16.11

Lightning Surge Arresters

Comments

Depending on local code, lightning protection may be required for special types of facilities, such as structures that store explosives, playgrounds, and aircraft fields. Generally, lightning protection is not required for residential structures unless specified by local code or in the project documents.

Industry Standard
Electrical Estimating Methods
(R.S. Means, Co., Inc.)

Lightning Protection

Lightning protection for the rooftops of buildings is achieved by a series of lightning rods or air terminals joined together by either copper or aluminum cable. The cable size is determined by the height of the building. The lightning cable system is connected through a downlead to a ground rod that is a minimum of 2' below grade and 1-1/2 to 3' out from the foundation wall. By code, all metal bodies on the roof that are located within six feet of a lightning conductor must be bonded to the lightning protection system.

One of the basic components of a lightning grounding system is the air terminal. These are manufactured in either copper or aluminum. The most common sizes used are 3/8" diameter copper at 10" high for roofs under 75' high. For roofs over 75', a 1/2" diameter by 12" high terminal is most common. For aluminum air terminals, a 1/2" diameter by 12" high is used for roofs under 75', and a 5/8" diameter by 12" high is used for heights over 75'. Air terminals are usually mounted in the perimeter parapet wall and include a masonry cable anchor base. A wide range of configurations is available from manufacturers for mounting air terminals to different roof surfaces. Most do not vary significantly in price.

Cable for main conductor use is calculated in pounds per 1,000'; it is available on 500' spools. Conductors are manufactured in copper and aluminum. The industry standard Class I minimum weight for copper is 187 lbs. per 1000' when used on a roof of less than 75' high, and Class II minimum weight for copper is 375 lbs. per 1000' for structures over 75' high. The main conductor for Class I aluminum cable is 95 lbs. per 1000' for structures over 75' high. Connections to main grounding conductor cable are accomplished in one of three ways: clamping, heat or exothermic welding, or brazing.

National Electrical Code® Handbook
Ed. Note: The following excerpt contains NFPA commentary by recognized experts in the field of safety, along with the National Electrical Code® *in numbered paragraphs.*

280-1. Scope. This article covers general requirements, installation requirements and connection requirements for surge arresters installed on premises wiring systems.

280-2. Definition. A surge arrester is a protective device for limiting surge voltages by discharging or bypassing surge current, and it also prevents continued flow of follow current while remaining capable of repeating these functions.

280-3. Number Required. Where used at a point on a circuit, a surge arrester shall be connected to each ungrounded conductor. A single installation of such surge arresters shall be permitted to protect a number of interconnected circuits, provided that no circuit is exposed to surges while disconnected from the surge arresters.

280-4. Surge Arrester Selection.
(a) On Circuits of Less than 1000 Volts. The rating of the surge arrester shall be equal to or greater than the maximum continuous phase-to-ground power frequency voltage available at the point of application.

Surge arresters installed on circuits of less than 1000 volts shall be listed for the purpose.

280-11. Location. Surge arresters shall be permitted to be located indoors or outdoors and shall be made inaccessible to unqualified persons.

Exception: Surge arresters listed for installation in accessible locations.

280-12. Routing of Surge Arrester Connections. The conductor used to connect the surge arrester to line or bus and to ground shall not be any longer than necessary and shall avoid unnecessary bends.

NFPA commentary: Arrester conductors should be as short and be run as straight as practicable, avoiding any sharp bends and turns, which would increase the impedance. High-frequency currents, such as those common to lightning discharges, tend to reduce the effectiveness of a grounding conductor.

Comments
A service surge arrester (SSA) is recommended in all geographical locations where lightning is a common occurrence.

Grounding Electrode
Industry Standards
Electrical Estimating Methods
(R.S. Means Co., Inc.)
Grounding
In most distribution systems, one conductor of the supply is grounded. This conductor is called the "neutral wire." In addition, the N.E.C. requires that a grounding conductor be supplied to connect non-current-carrying, conductive parts to ground. This distinction between the "grounded conductor" and the "grounding conductor" is important.

Grounding protects persons from injury in the event of an insulation failure within equipment. It also stabilizes the voltage with respect to ground and prevents surface potentials between equipment — which could harm both people and equipment (in a hospital, for example).

Lightning protection systems are a separate concern but are closely related to grounding in intent and practice. Lightning poses two kinds of danger. The first is the lightning strike itself. This can damage structures and distribution systems by passing a very high current for a brief time — causing heat, fire, and/or equipment failure. The second danger is from induced voltages in lines running close to the lightning's path. These pulses can be very high and can damage electrical equipment or cause injury to people.

In both systems, it is essential that a good, low-resistance ground path be provided. This can be accomplished via the use of ground rods, a ground grid, or attachment to metal pipes in contact with the earth (such as water pipes). Note: In communities where plastic water pipes are used between the street main and a building, this grounding method is not suitable — even though copper pipes may be used for the building's interior.

Connections between ground wires and pipes, conduits, or boxes are often made with cable clamps. For residential and light commercial applications, grounding is typically accomplished using the configuration shown in **Figure 16.12**.

Comments

Chapter 41 of the 1998 International One- and Two-Family Dwelling Code, which replaces the CABO One and Two Family Dwelling Code, addresses service conductors and equipment for the control and protection of services and their installation requirements. Section 4110 covers the installation of grounding electrode conductors or their enclosures. Section 4111 provides requirements for connections to the grounding electrode.

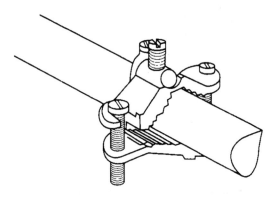

A listed ground clamp generally used with No. 8 through No. 4 grounding electrode conductors. Exothermic welds are also acceptable. Kits are commercially available for this purpose.

Courtesy of NFPA, *National Electrical Code® Handbook [Figure 250-47]*

Figure 16.12

NFPA 70: National Electrical Code®
Grounding Electrode

250-51. Effective Grounding Path. The path to ground from circuits, equipment, and metal enclosures for conductors shall (1) be permanent and electrically continuous; (2) have capacity to conduct safely any fault current likely to be imposed on it; and (3) have sufficiently low impedance to limit the voltage to ground and to facilitate the operation of the circuit protective devices.

The earth shall not be used as the sole equipment grounding conductor.

250-53. Grounding Path to Grounding Electrode at Services.
(a) Grounding Electrode Conductor. A grounding electrode conductor shall be used to connect the equipment grounding conductors, the service-equipment enclosures, and, where the system is grounded, the grounded service conductor to the grounding electrode.

250-94. Size of Alternating-Current Grounding Electrode Conductor. The size of the grounding electrode conductor of a grounded or ungrounded ac system shall not be less than given in Table 250-94 (see **Figure 16.13**).

Exception:

    a. Where connected to made electrodes as in Section 250-83(c) or (d), that portion of the grounding electrode conductor that is the sole connection to the grounding electrode shall not be required to be larger than No. 6 copper wire or No. 4 aluminum wire.

    b. Where connected to a concrete-encased electrode as in Section 250-81(c), that portion of the grounding electrode conductor that is the sole connection to the grounding electrode shall not be required to be larger than No. 4 copper wire.

    c. Where connected to a ground ring as in Section 250-81(d), that portion of the grounding electrode conductor that is the sole connection to the grounding electrode shall not be required to be larger than the conductor used for the ground ring.

Grounding Electrode Conductor for AC Systems

Size of Largest Service-Entrance Conductor or Equivalent Area for Parallel Conductors		Size of Grounding Electrode Conductor	
Copper	Aluminum or Copper-Clad Aluminum	Copper	Aluminum or Copper-Clad Aluminum*
2 or smaller	1/0 or smaller	8	6
1 or 1/0	2/0 or 3/0	6	4
2/0 or 3/0	4/0 or 250 kcmil	4	2
Over 3/0 thru 350 kcmil	Over 250 kcmil thru 500 kcmil	2	1/0
Over 350 kcmil thru 600 kcmil	Over 500 kcmil thru 900 kcmil	1/0	3/0
Over 600 kcmil thru 1100 kcmil	Over 900 kcmil thru 1750 kcmil	2/0	4/0
Over 1100 kcmil	Over 1750 kcmil	3/0	250 kcmil

Courtesy of National Fire Protection Association, *National Electrical Code® Handbook [Table 250-94]*

Figure 16.13

Switches

Comments

Switches are devices used to turn an electric circuit on and off. Circuit breakers control power to branch circuits. Snap switches are used primarily for lighting.

National Electrical Code® Handbook

Ed. Note: The following excerpt contains NFPA commentary by recognized experts in the field of electrical safety, along with the National Electrical Code® *in numbered paragraphs.*

Installation of Switches

380-1. Scope. The provisions of this article shall apply to all switches, switching devices, and circuit breakers where used as switches.

380-2. Switch Connections.
(a) Three-Way and Four-Way Switches. Three-way and four-way switches shall be so wired that all switching is done only in the ungrounded circuit conductor. Where in metal raceways or metal-jacketed cables, wiring between switches and outlets shall be in accordance with Section 300-20(a).

Exception: Switch loops shall not require a grounded conductor.

380-10. Mounting of Snap Switches.
(a) Surface-type. Snap switches used with open wiring on insulators shall be mounted on insulating material that will separate the conductors at least 1/2 inch (12.7 mm) from the surface wired over.

(b) Box mounted. Flush-type snap switches mounted in boxes that are set back of the wall surface as permitted in Section 370-20 shall be installed so that the extension plaster ears are seated against the surface of the wall. Flush-type snap switches mounted in boxes that are flush with the wall surface or project therefrom shall be so installed that the mounting yoke or strap of the switch is seated against the box.

NFPA commentary: Cooperation is necessary among the building trades (carpenters, dry-wall installers, plasterers, etc.) in order for electricians to properly set device boxes flush with the finish surface, thereby ensuring a secure seating of the switch yoke and permitting the maximum projection of switch handles through the installed switch plate.

380-11. Circuit Breakers as Switches. A hand-operable circuit breaker equipped with a lever or handle, or a power-operated circuit breaker capable of being opened by hand in the event of a power failure, shall be permitted to serve

517

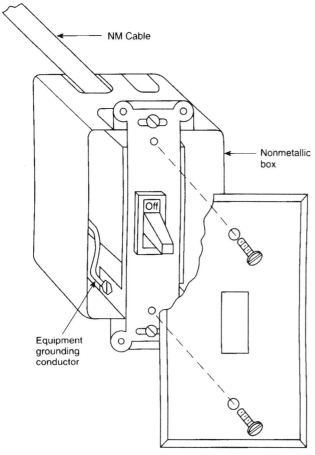

The effective grounding of metal faceplates can be accomplished by connecting the equipment grounding conductor provided with the wiring method to a grounding terminal on a metal yoke or strap.

Courtesy of NFPA, *National Electrical Code® Handbook [Figure 380-1]*

Figure 16.14

as a switch if it has the required number of poles. Note: See provisions contained in Section 240-81 and Section 240-83.

NFPA commentary: Circuit breakers capable of being hand-operated are required to clearly indicate whether they are in the open, "off," or closed, "on," position.

See Section 240-83(d) for marking (SWD) for circuit breakers used as switches for 120V and 277V fluorescent lighting circuits. Also see Section 380-7.

380-12. Grounding of Enclosures. Metal enclosures for switches or circuit breakers shall be grounded as specified in Article 250. Where nonmetallic enclosures are used with metal raceways or metal-jacketed cables, provisions shall be made for grounding continuity. Metal face plates for snap switches shall be effectively grounded where used with a wiring method that includes or provides an equipment ground.

Ed. Note: For additional information on switches, see IOTFDC, section 4501.

Wiring Devices — Receptacles and Caps

Industry Standards

Means Graphic Construction Standards
(R.S. Means Co.,Inc.)

Receptacles provide a convenient means of connecting portable power equipment and electrical appliances to the electrical source. These devices are available in voltage ratings of 125, 208, 250, 277, 347, 480, and 600 volts and in amperage ratings ranging from 10 to 400 amps. Receptacles are classified as either the grounded or ungrounded type. Because of the dangers of fire and shock associated with all electrical installations, care should be exercised in determining the proper size and type of receptacle and in following installation guidelines, as well as local, state, and national codes.

In accordance with the *National Electrical Code®*, all receptacles rated at 15 and 20 amps must be classified as the grounding type. The only exception to this regulation applies to the replacement of outlets that are installed in existing ungrounded systems. Installing a grounded receptacle as a replacement in such an ungrounded system may cause a false sense of safety and security. Because of the great variation of voltage and amperage combinations and the *National Electrical Code®* rule that calls for specific voltage and current ratings for all grounding-type receptacles, standard configurations have been adopted by NEMA (National Electrical Manufacturers Association). This standardization also prevents low-voltage caps (plugs) from being inserted into high-voltage receptacles. Configurations for general purpose, grounding-type receptacles and caps appear in the tables included in this section.

Receptacles are connected to the wiring leads in several ways, depending on the set-up of the particular receptacle or its amperage rating. Some receptacles with 15- and 20-amp ratings are equipped with terminal screws to which the lead wire is attached. After the end of the wire is stripped of its covering, it is wrapped clockwise around the terminal screw, which is then securely tightened to form a mechanical connection. Another common type of 15- and 20-amp receptacle provides a pressure-lock connection in place of the terminal screws. With this type of receptacle, the stripped end of the wire is pushed into a recessed pressure-locking contact that grips the wire to form a permanent locking connection. Receptacles rated at 30 amps and higher are equipped with set screws to form wire-to-device connections.

Several grades of receptacles exist to assure that the proper capacity and durability requirements for their use are met. Residential-grade receptacles can be installed in structures located only in noncommercial areas; specification-grade receptacles are used in office and industrial locations. Hospital-grade receptacles, which are labeled "Hospital Grade" and contain a green dot on the face of the outlet, must be able to withstand more severe damage tests than conventional receptacles.

Another safety rating required for receptacles is the ground-fault type, or GFI, which is specified by code for installations in bathrooms, attached garages, construction sites, and outdoor locations. These receptacles are equipped with a safety switch set of 5 milliamps to prevent accidental shock and with a reset button to restore power when a ground condition has been cleared.

All receptacles must be housed in some type of specified enclosure, which is determined by the installation procedure. Outdoor installations require cast weatherproof boxes and matching weathertight covers. Commercial and industrial receptacle enclosures often consist of a 4" square box with a raised cover. In residential and office situations, where a permanent outlet must be inconspicuous, recessed single-gang boxes may be used. The covers for all receptacle enclosures are usually manufactured from metal or plastic materials.

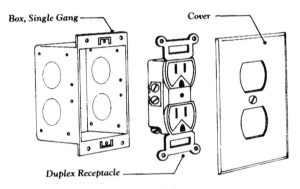

Receptacle, Including Box and Cover

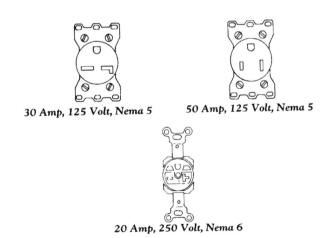

30 Amp, 125 Volt, Nema 5   *50 Amp, 125 Volt, Nema 5*

20 Amp, 250 Volt, Nema 6

Receptacles

R.S. Means, Co., Inc., *Means Graphic Construction Standards*

Figure 16.15

Receptacle Outlets
National Electrical Code® Handbook

Ed. Note: The following excerpt contains NFPA commentary by recognized experts in the field of electrical safety, along with the National Electrical Code® *in numbered paragraphs.*

Receptacles
210-52. Dwelling Unit Receptacle Outlets.
(a) General-Purpose. In every kitchen, family room, dining room, living room , parlor, library, den, sun room, bedroom, recreation room, or similar room, or area of dwelling units, receptacle outlets shall be installed so that no point along the floor line in any wall space is more than 6 feet (1.83m), measured horizontally, from an outlet in that space, including any wall space 2 feet or more (610 mm or more) in width and the wall space occupied by fixed panels in exterior walls, but excluding sliding panels in exterior walls. The wall space afforded by fixed room dividers, such as freestanding bar-type counters or railings, shall be included in the 6-foot (1.83m) measurement.

As used in this section, a "wall space" shall be considered a wall unbroken along the floor line by doorways, fireplaces, and similar openings. Each wall space 2 feet (610 mm) or more wide shall be treated individually and separately from other wall spaces within the room. A wall space shall be permitted to include two or more walls of a room (around corner) where unbroken at the floor line. (See **Figure 16.16.**)

Receptacle outlets shall, insofar as practicable, be spaced equal distances apart. Receptacle outlets in floors shall not be counted as part of the required number of receptacle outlets unless located within 18 in. (457 mm) of the wall.

The receptacle outlets required by this section shall be in addition to any receptacle that is part of any lighting fixture or appliance, located within cabinets or cupboards, or located over 5-1/2 ft (1.68 m) above the floor.

NFPA commentary: Receptacles are required to be located so that no "point" in any wall space is more than 6 ft from a receptacle. This rule intends that an appliance or lamp with a flexible cord attached may be placed anywhere in the room and be within 6 ft of a receptacle, thus eliminating the need for extension cords.

A "wallspace" is a wall unbroken along the floor line by doorways, fireplaces, archways, and similar openings and may include two or more walls of a room (around corners, as illustrated in Figure 210-24. (See **Figure 16.16.**)

Fixed room dividers, such as bar-type counters and railings, are to be included in the 6-ft measurement. Fixed panels in exterior walls are counted as regular wall space, and a floor-type receptacle close to the wall can be used to meet the required spacing. Isolated, individual wall spaces 2 ft or more in width are considered usable for the location of a lamp or appliance, and a receptacle outlet is required to be provided.

519

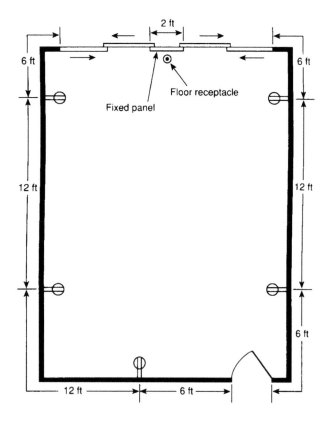

2 ft

6 ft   6 ft

Floor receptacle

Fixed panel

12 ft   12 ft

6 ft

12 ft   6 ft

Plan view of the location of receptacles in a typical room.

Courtesy of NFPA, *National Electrical Code® Handbook [Figure 210-24]*

Figure 16.16

Exception: Permanently installed electric baseboard heaters equipped with factory-installed receptacle outlets or outlets provided as a separate assembly by the manufacturer shall be permitted as the required outlet or outlets for the wall space utilized by such permanently installed heaters. Such receptacle outlets shall not be connected to the heat circuits.

(FPN): Listed baseboard heaters include instructions that may not permit their installation below receptacle outlets.

NFPA commentary: According to listing instructions [see Section 110-3(b)], permanent electric baseboard heaters are not permitted to be located beneath wall receptacles. Where the receptacle is a part of the heater, cords of appliances or lamps are less apt to be exposed to the heating elements, as might occur should they fall into convector slots.

(b) Small Appliances.

(1) In the kitchen, pantry, breakfast room, dining room, or similar area of a dwelling unit, the two or more 20-ampere small appliance branch circuits required by Section 220-4(b) shall serve all receptacle outlets, covered by Sections 210-52(a) and (c) and receptacle outlets for refrigeration equipment.

(2) The two or more small appliance branch circuits specified in (b) (1) above shall have no other outlets.

Exception No. 1: A receptacle installed solely for the electrical supply to and support of an electric clock in any of the rooms specified above.

Exception No. 2: Receptacles installed to provide power for supplemental equipment and lighting on gas-fired ranges, ovens or counter-mounted cooking units.

Exception No. 3: Receptacles installed in the kitchen to serve countertop surfaces shall be supplied by not less than two small appliance branch circuits, either or both of which shall also be permitted to supply receptacle outlets in the kitchen and other rooms specified in Section 210-52(b)(1). Additional small appliance branch circuits shall be permitted to supply receptacle outlets in the kitchen and other rooms specified in Section 210-52(b)(1).

(c) Countertops. In kitchens and dining rooms of dwelling units, receptacle outlets for counter spaces shall be installed in accordance with (1) through (5) below.

NFPA commentary: This section was rewritten for the 1996 *Code*. Dwelling unit receptacles serving countertop spaces in kitchens, dining areas, and similar rooms are required to be

1. Installed in each wall space wider than 12 in.

2. Spaced so that no point along the wall line is more than 24 in. from a receptacle

3. Installed not more than 18 in. above the countertop

4. Installed in a position other than face up

5. Installed at each countertop island and peninsular countertop meeting minimum dimensions

6. Accessible for use and not blocked by appliances occupying dedicated space or fastened in place

7. Fed from two or more of the required 20-ampere small-appliance branch circuits

8. GFCI protected according to 210-8(a)(6)

Receptacles installed in a face-up position in a countertop could collect crumbs, liquids, and other debris, resulting in a potential fire or shock hazard and, therefore, are not allowed.

(1) **Wall counter space.** A receptacle outlet shall be installed at each wall counter space 12 in. (305 mm) or wider. Receptacle outlets shall be installed so that no point along the wall line is more than 24 in. (610 mm), measured horizontally from a receptacle outlet in that space.

(2) **Island counter spaces.** At least one receptacle outlet shall be installed at each island counter space with a long dimension of 24 in. (610 mm) or greater and a short dimension of 12 in. (305 mm) or greater.

(3) Peninsular counter space. At least one receptacle outlet shall be installed at each peninsular counter space with a long dimension of 24 in. (610 mm) or greater and a short dimension of 12 in. (305 mm) or greater. A peninsular countertop is measured from the connecting edge.

(4) Separate spaces. Countertop spaces separated by range tops, refrigerators, or sinks shall be considered as separate countertop spaces in applying the requirements of 4401.5.1, 4401.5.2 and 4401.5.3 above.

(5) Receptacle outlet location. Receptacle outlets shall be located not more than 18 in. (458 mm) above the countertop. Receptacle outlets shall not be installed in a face-up position in the work surfaces or countertops. Receptacle outlets rendered not readily accessible by appliances fastened in place or appliances occupying dedicated space shall not be considered as these required outlets.

Exception: Where acceptable to the authority having jurisdiction and to meet the special conditions as specified in a or b below, receptacle outlets shall be permitted to be mounted not more than 12 in. (305 mm) below the countertop. Receptacles mounted below the countertop in accordance with this exception shall not be located where the countertop extends more than 6 in. (153 mm) beyond its support base.

   a. Construction for the physically impaired.

   b. Where island or peninsular counter space construction precludes practical mounting above the countertop.

(d) Bathrooms. In dwelling units, at least one wall receptacle outlet shall be installed in bathrooms adjacent to each basin location. Bathroom receptacle outlets shall be supplied by at least one 20-ampere branch circuit. Such circuits shall have no other outlets. See Section 210-8(a)(1).

Receptacle outlets shall not be installed in a face-up position in the work surfaces or countertops in a bathroom basin location.

NFPA commentary: New in the 1996 *Code,* bathroom receptacle outlets are required to be supplied from a 20-ampere circuit with no other outlets. However, this circuit is permitted to supply the required receptacles in more than one bathroom. According to 210-8(a)(1), as required in the past, all 125-volt single-phase, 15-ampere and 20-ampere receptacles installed in bathroom areas are also required to be protected by a GFCI.

In bathrooms of a dwelling unit, one wall receptacle is required to be installed adjacent to the wash basin and is required in addition to any receptacle that may be part of any lighting fixture or medicine cabinet. Where there is more than one basin, a receptacle outlet is required adjacent to each basin location. Where the basins are in close proximity, one receptacle outlet installed between the two basins may satisfy this requirement. See Section 410-57(c). See Figure 210-9 for typical electrical layout of a bathroom.

(e) Outdoor Outlets. For a one-family dwelling and each unit of a two-family dwelling that is at grade level, at least one receptacle outlet accessible at grade level and not more than 6 ft, 6 in. (1.98 m) above grade shall be installed at the front and back of the dwelling. See Section 210-8(a)(3).

(f) Laundry Areas. In dwelling units, at least one receptacle outlet shall be installed for the laundry.

Exception No. 1: In a dwelling unit that is an apartment or living area or in a multifamily building where laundry facilities are provided on the premises that are available to all building occupants, a laundry receptacle shall not be required.

Exception No. 2: In other than one-family dwellings where laundry facilities are not to be installed or permitted, a laundry receptacle shall not be required.

(g) Basement and Garages. For a one-family dwelling, at least one receptacle outlet, in addition to any provided for laundry equipment, shall be installed in each basement and in each attached garage, and in each detached garage with electric power. See Sections 218-8(a)(2) and (a)(4).

NFPA commentary: In a one-family dwelling, it is mandatory to install a receptacle in a basement (in addition to the laundry receptacle), in each attached garage, and in each detached garage with electric power. Section 210-8(a)(4) requires receptacles in unfinished basements to be protected by a GFCI. Section 210-8(a)(2) requires receptacles installed in garages to be protected by a GFCI. If no electric power is provided, it is not mandatory to install a receptacle in detached garages.

(h) Hallways. In dwelling units, hallways of 10 ft (3.05 m) or more in length shall have at least one receptacle outlet.

As used in this subsection, the hall length shall be considered the length along the centerline of the hall without passing through a doorway.

NFPA commentary: This is intended to minimize strain or damage to cords and receptacles. The requirement is for dwelling unit receptacles and is not applicable to common hallways of hotels, motels, apartment buildings, condominiums, etc.

IOTFDC — 1998 (formerly CABO)

Comments

Chapter 45 of the 1998 International One- and Two-Family Dwelling Code, which replaces the CABO One and Two Family Dwelling Code, addresses devices and lighting fixtures, including switches, receptacles, fixtures and fixture installation, and track lighting.

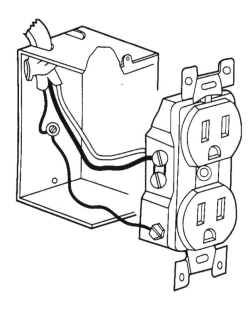

Grounding conductors may be attached to a box by a variety of methods, such as with a screw, as shown here, or with a grounding clip.

Courtesy of NFPA, *National Electrical Code® Handbook [Figure 250-46]*

Figure 16.17

Ground Fault Interrupter (GFI)

Comments

Any receptacle located in a potentially wet area, such as a bathroom, kitchen, laundry room, or basement, must have a ground-fault interrupter. This type of receptacle is designed to cut power instantly when it senses a false ground, such as a wet hand.

Chapter 44 of the 1998 International One- and Two-Family Dwelling Code, which replaces the CABO One and Two Family Dwelling Code, addresses power and lighting distribution. Section 4402 covers ground-fault circuit-interrupter protection.

Chapter 46 of the 1998 IOTFDC covers installation requirements for appliances and fixed heating equipment, including allowed disconnecting means.

NFPA 70: National Electrical Code®
210-8 Ground-Fault Circuit-Interrupter Protection for Personnel.

(a) **Dwelling Units.** All 125-volt, single-phase, 15- and 20-ampere receptacles installed in the locations specified below shall have ground-fault circuit-interrupter protection for personnel.

(1) Bathrooms.

(2) Garages and grade-level portions of unfinished accessory buildings used for storage or work areas.

Exception No. 1: Receptacles that are not readily accessible.

Exception No. 2: A single receptacle or a duplex receptacle for two appliances located within dedicated space for each appliance that in normal use is not easily moved from one place to another, and that is cord- and plug-connected in accordance with Section 400-7(a)(6), (a)(7), or (a)(8).

Receptacles installed under exceptions to Section 210-8(a)(2) shall not be considered as meeting the requirements of Section 210-52(g).

(3) Outdoors.

Exception: Receptacles that are not readily accessible and are supplied from a dedicated branch circuit for electric snow-melting or deicing equipment as covered in Article 426 shall be permitted to be installed without ground-fault circuit-interrupter protection for personnel.

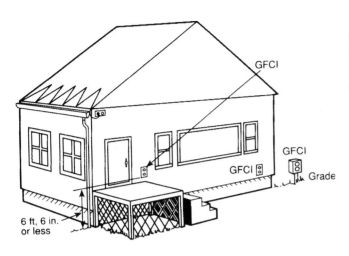

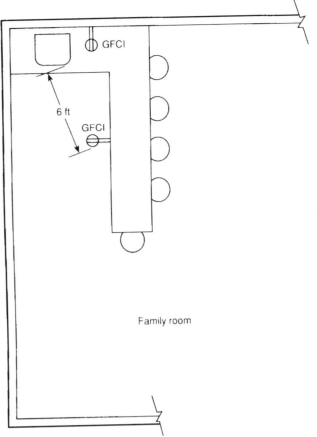

This dwelling unit has four outdoor receptacles. Three of these receptacles are considered to be at direct grade level access and must have GFCI protection for personnel. The fourth receptacle located adjacent to the gutter for the roof-mounted snow melting cable is not readily accessible and, therefore, is exempt from the GFCI requirements of Section 210-8(a)(3). However, this receptacle is covered by the requirements of Section 426-28, Equipment Protection. See also commentary following Section 210-52(e) and Section 410-57.

Courtesy of NFPA, *National Electrical Code® Handbook [Figure 210-12]*

Figure **16.18**

Receptacles within 6 feet of a wet bar sink are required to be GFCI protected.

Courtesy of NFPA, *National Electrical Code® Handbook [Figure 210-14]*

Figure **16.19**

(4) Crawl spaces. Where the crawl space is at or below grade level.

(5) Unfinished basements. For purposes of this section, unfinished basements not intended as habitable rooms and limited to storage areas, work areas, and the like.

Exception No. 1: Receptacles that are not readily accessible.

Exception No. 2: A single receptacle or a duplex receptacle for two appliances located within dedicated space for each appliance that in normal use is not easily moved from one place to another, and that is cord- and plug-connected in accordance with Section 400-7(a)(6), (a)(7), or (a)(8).

Receptacles installed under exceptions to Section 210-8(a)(5) shall not be considered as meeting the requirements of Section 210-52(g).

(6) Kitchens. Where the receptacles are installed to serve the countertop surfaces.

(7) Wet bar sinks. Where the receptacles are installed to serve the countertop surfaces and are located within 6 ft. (1.83 m) of the outside edge of the wet bar sink.

Smoke Detectors

Ed. Note: Smoke detector code requirements are largely focused on places where people sleep. The 1997 Uniform Building Code has smoke detector requirements for day-care or health-care facilities serving five or more people in Section 308.10. Information for hotels, apartments, or congregate living facilities housing 10 or more individuals may be found in Section 310.9. Location, power source and any special requirements are all covered.

NFPA 72: National Fire Alarm Code®
2-2 Basic Requirements

2-2.1.1.1 Smoke detectors shall be installed outside of each separate sleeping area in the immediate vicinity of the bedroom and on each additional story of the family living unit, including basements and excluding crawl spaces and unfinished attics. In new construction, a smoke detector also shall be installed in each sleeping room.

2-3 Power supplies.

2-3.1.2 There shall be a primary (main) and a secondary (standby) power source. For electrically powered household fire warning equipment, the primary (main) power source shall be ac; the secondary (standby) power source shall be a battery.

2-4 Equipment performance.

2-4.1 General. The failure of any nonreliable or short-life component that renders the detector inoperable shall be easily apparent to the occupant of the living unit without the need for test.

2-5 Installation.

2-5.2.1.1 Smoke detectors in rooms with ceiling slopes greater than one-foot rise per 8-feet (1 mm rise per 8 mm) horizontally shall be located at the high side of the room.

2-5.2.1.2 A smoke detector installed in a stairwell shall be so located as to assure that smoke rising in the stairwell cannot be prevented from reaching the detector by an intervening door or obstruction.

2-5.2.1.3 A smoke detector installed to detect a fire in the basement shall be located in close proximity to the stairway leading to the floor above.

2-5.2.1.4 The smoke detectors installed to comply with 2-2.1.1.1 on a story without a separate sleeping area shall be located in close proximity to the stairway leading to the floor above.

Comments

In some locations, smoke detectors must be installed by specialty contractors, depending on the project specifications. There are also differences in local requirements for wiring and the use of local, battery-only smoke detectors.

Ed Note: See Chapter 13 for information on fire extinguishers, and Chapter 14 for fire protection (sprinkler) systems.

Lighting Outlets

Industry Standard
Means Electrical Estimating Methods
(R.S. Means Co., Inc.)
Outlet Boxes

Outlet boxes made of steel or plastic are used to hold wiring devices, such as switches and receptacles. They are also used as a mount for lighting fixtures. Some outlet boxes are ready for flush mounting; others require a plaster frame. Some have plain knockouts for pipe up to 1-1/4", while others have built-in brackets for Romex or BX wire. The capacity of outlet boxes ranges from one to six devices. They may have brackets for direct stud mounting or plaster ears for mounting in existing walls.

National Electrical Code® Handbook

Ed. Note: The following excerpt contains NFPA commentary by recognized experts in the field of safety, along with the National Electrical Code® *in numbered paragraphs.*

210-70. Lighting Outlets Required. Lighting outlets shall be installed where specified in Sections 210-70(a), (b), and (c) below.

(a) Dwelling Unit(s). At least one wall switch-controlled lighting shall be installed in every habitable room; in bathrooms, hallways, stairways, attached garages, and detached garages with electric power; and at the exterior side of outdoor entrances or exits. A vehicle door in a garage shall not be considered as an outdoor entrance or exit.

At least one lighting outlet controlled by a light switch located at the point of entry to the attic, underfloor space, utility room, and basement shall be installed where these spaces are used for storage or contain equipment requiring servicing. The lighting outlet shall be provided at or near the equipment requiring servicing.

Where lighting outlets are installed in interior stairways, there shall be a wall switch at each floor level to control the lighting outlet where the difference between floor levels is six steps or more.

NFPA commentary: It is not permitted to switch a receptacle as a lighting outlet on a small-appliance branch circuit. It is permitted to switch a receptacle as a lighting outlet (in the dining room, for example) supplied by a branch circuit other than a small-appliance branch circuit.

Exception No. 1: In habitable rooms, other than kitchens and bathrooms, one or more receptacles controlled by a wall switch shall be permitted in lieu of lighting outlets.

Exception No. 2: In hallways, stairways, and at outdoor entrances, remote, central, or automatic control of lighting shall be permitted.

Exception No. 3: Lighting outlets shall be permitted to be controlled by occupancy sensors that are (1) in addition to wall switches, or (2) located at a customary wall switch location and equipped with a manual override that will allow the sensor to function as a wall switch.

(b) Guest Rooms. At least one wall switch-controlled lighting outlet or wall switch-controlled receptacle shall be installed in guest rooms in hotels, motels, or similar occupancies.

(c) Other Locations. At least one wall switch-controlled lighting outlet shall be installed at or near equipment requiring servicing such as heating, air-conditioning, and refrigeration equipment in attics or underfloor spaces. The wall switch shall be located at the point of entry to the attic or underfloor space.

NFPA commentary: This section points out that adequate lighting and proper control and location of switching is as essential to the safety of occupants of dwelling unit(s), hotels, motels, etc., as are proper wiring requirements. Proper illumination ensures safe movement for persons of all ages, thus many accidents are avoided.

Installation of lighting outlets in attics, under floor spaces or crawl areas, and in utility rooms or basements is required "only" where these spaces are used for storage (e.g., holiday decorations and luggage) or where such spaces contain equipment requiring servicing (e.g., air-handling units, cooling and heating equipment, water pumps and sump pumps).

Remote, central, or automatic control of lighting for hallways, stairways, and outdoor entrances is practical in multifamily dwellings where it is desirable to use time clocks or to locate switches where they may not be intentionally or inadvertently turned to the "off" position.

Although the requirement calls for a switched lighting outlet at outdoor entrances and exits, it does not prohibit a single lighting outlet, if suitably located, from serving more than one door.

A wall-switch-controlled lighting outlet is required in the kitchen and bathroom. A receptacle outlet controlled by a wall switch is not permitted to serve as a lighting outlet in these rooms. Occupancy sensors are permitted to be used for switching these lighting outlets, provided they are equipped with a manual override or used in addition to regular switches.

Lighting Fixtures

Comments

The most important thing to remember when doing electrical work is to turn off power to the area or device you are working on. Always confirm that the power is off by testing the circuit with a neon circuit tester. Restore power only when your work is completed. Following are some additional tips:

- *When choosing a light fixture, consider the weight of the fixture, height of the fixture above the floor, and location of the fixture relative to the placement of furniture in the room.*
- *Remember this rule of thumb: If a light fixture is high, it will light a wide area. If it is low, it will light a smaller area.*

Exact fixture placement should be established before any work begins, with sign-off from the owner, to avoid disputes and cost overruns from having to relocate fixtures, patch and touch up finishes. Responsibility for any related cutting, patching, and touch-up should also be determined before the electrical work begins.

Chapter 44 of the 1998 International One- and Two-Family Dwelling Code, which replaces the CABO One and Two Family Dwelling Code, addresses power and lighting distribution. Sections 4503 and 4504 cover fixtures and fixture installation, respectively.

NFPA 70: National Electrical Code®
410-4 Fixtures in Specific Locations.

(a) Wet and Damp Locations. Fixtures installed in wet or damp locations shall be so installed that water cannot enter or accumulate in wiring compartments, lampholders, or other electrical parts. All fixtures installed in wet locations shall be marked, "Suitable for Wet Locations." All fixtures installed in damp locations shall be marked, "Suitable for Wet Locations" or "Suitable for Damp Locations."

Installations underground or in concrete slabs or masonry in direct contact with the earth, and locations subject to saturation with water or other liquids, such as locations exposed to weather and unprotected, vehicle washing areas, and like locations, shall be considered to be wet locations with respect to the above requirement.

Interior locations protected from weather but subject to moderate degrees of moisture, such as some basements, some barns, some cold-storage warehouses and the like, the partially protected locations under canopies, marquees, roofed open porches, and the like, shall be considered to be damp locations with respect to the above requirement.

(d) Above Bathtubs. No parts of cord-connected fixtures, hanging fixtures, lighting track, pendants, or ceiling fans shall be located within a zone measured 3 ft. (914 mm) horizontally and 8 ft. (2.44 m) vertically from the top of the bathtub rim. This zone is all encompassing and includes the zone directly over the tub. (See **Figure 16.20**.)

410-5 Fixtures Near Combustible Material. Fixtures shall be so constructed, or installed, or equipped with shades or guards that combustible material will not be subjected to temperatures in excess of 90°C (194°F).

410-6 Fixtures Over Combustible Material. Lampholders installed over highly combustible material shall be of the unswitched type. Unless an individual switch is provided for each fixture, lampholders shall be located at least 8 ft. (2.44 m) above the floor, or shall be so located or guarded that the lamps cannot be readily removed or damaged.

410-8 Fixtures in Clothes Closets.
(a) Definition.
Storage Space: Storage space shall be defined as a volume bounded by the sides and back closet walls and planes extending from the closet floor vertically to a height of 6 ft. (1.83 m) or the highest clothes-hanging rod and parallel to

the walls at a horizontal distance of 24 in. (610 mm) from the sides and back of the closet walls respectively, and continuing vertically to the closet ceiling parallel to the walls at a horizontal distance of 12 in. (305 mm) or the width of the shelf, whichever is greater.

For a closet that permits access to both sides of a hanging rod, the storage space shall include the volume below the highest rod extending 12 in. (305 mm) on either side of the rod on a plane horizontal to the floor extending the entire length of the rod.

(b) Fixture Types Permitted. Listed fixtures of the following types shall be permitted to be installed in a closet:

(1) A surface-mounted or recessed incandescent fixture with a completely enclosed lamp.

(2) A surface-mounted or recessed fluorescent fixture.

(c) Fixture Types Not Permitted. Incandescent fixtures with open or partially enclosed lamps and pendant fixtures or lampholders shall not be permitted.

(d) Location. Fixtures in clothes closets shall be permitted to be installed as follows:

(1) Surface-mounted incandescent fixtures installed on the wall above the door or on the ceiling, provided there is a minimum clearance of 12 in. (305 mm) between the fixture and the nearest point of a storage space.

(2) Surface-mounted fluorescent fixtures installed on the wall above the door or on the ceiling, provided there is a minimum clearance of 6 in. (152 mm) between the fixture and the nearest point of a storage space.

(3) Recessed incandescent fixtures with a completely enclosed lamp installed in the wall or the ceiling, provided there is a minimum clearance of 6 in. (152 mm) between the fixture and the nearest point of a storage space.

(4) Recessed fluorescent fixtures installed in the wall or on the ceiling, provided there is a minimum clearance of 6 in. (152 mm) between the fixture and the nearest point of a storage space.

410-9 Space for Cove Lighting. Coves shall have adequate space and shall be so located that lamps and equipment can be properly installed and maintained.

410-10 Space for Conductors. Canopies and outlet boxes taken together shall provide adequate space so that fixture conductors and their connecting devices can be properly installed.

410-13 Covering of Combustible Material at Outlet Boxes. Any combustible wall or ceiling finish exposed between the edge of a fixture canopy or pan and an outlet box shall be covered with noncombustible material.

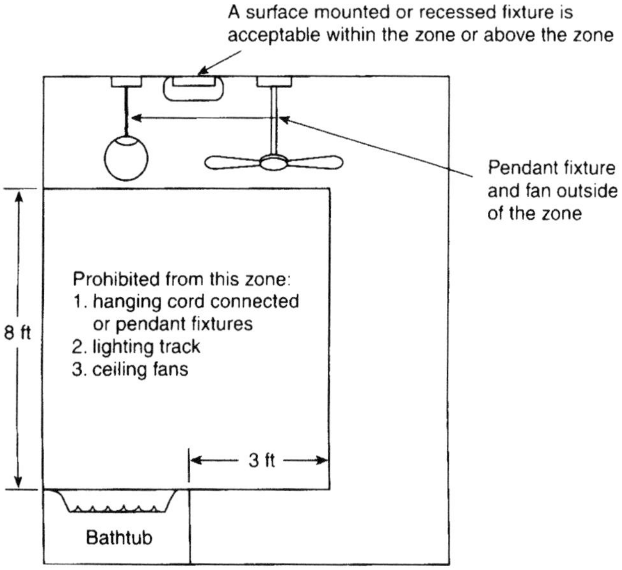

A surface mounted or recessed fixture is acceptable within the zone or above the zone

Pendant fixture and fan outside of the zone

Prohibited from this zone:
1. hanging cord connected or pendant fixtures
2. lighting track
3. ceiling fans

8 ft

3 ft

Bathtub

Fixtures and fans located near bathtubs.

Courtesy of NFPA, *National Electrical Code® Handbook [Figure 410-1]*

Figure 16.20

410-16 Means of Support.

(a) Outlet Boxes. Where the outlet box or fitting will provide adequate support, a fixture shall be attached thereto or be supported as required by Section 370-23 for boxes. A fixture that weighs more than 50 lb. (22.7 kg) shall be supported independently of the outlet box.

(b) Inspection. Fixtures shall be so installed that the connections between the fixture conductors and the circuit conductors can be inspected without requiring the disconnection of any part of the wiring.

(c) Suspended Ceilings. Framing members of suspended ceiling systems used to support fixtures shall be securely fastened to each other and shall be securely attached to the building structure at appropriate intervals. Fixtures shall be securely fastened to the ceiling framing member by mechanical means, such as bolts, screws, or rivets. Clips identified for use with the type of ceiling framing member(s) and fixture(s) shall also be permitted.

(d) Fixture Studs. Fixture studs that are not a part of outlet boxes, hickeys, tripods, and crowfeet shall be made of steel, malleable iron, or other material suitable for the application.

(e) Insulating Joints. Insulating joints that are not designed to be mounted with screws or bolts shall have an exterior metal casing, insulated from both screw connections.

(f) Raceway Fittings. Raceway fittings used to support lighting fixture(s) shall be capable of supporting the weight of the complete fixture assembly and lamp(s).

(h) Trees. Outdoor lighting fixtures and associated equipment shall be permitted to be supported by trees.

410-20 Equipment Grounding Conductor Attachment.

Fixtures with exposed metal parts shall be provided with a means for connecting an equipment grounding conductor for such fixtures.

Supporting Ceiling Fans

National Electrical Code® Handbook

Ed. Note: The following excerpt contains NFPA commentary by recognized experts in the field of safety, along with the National Electrical Code® *in numbered paragraphs.*

422-18. Support of Ceiling Fans

(a) Ceiling Fans 35 lb (15.88 kg) or Less. Listed ceiling fans that do not exceed 35 lb. (15.88 kg) in weight, with or without accessories, shall be permitted to be supported by outlet boxes identified for such use and supported in accordance with Sections 370-23 and 370-27.

Ed. Note: See also **Figure 16.20**.

NFPA commentary: Section 370-27 does not permit standard-type boxes to support ceiling fans unless provided with supplemental support (see **Figure 16.21**). However, Section 422-18(a) permits boxes identified for fan support to be used to support listed ceiling fans that do not exceed 35 pounds (see **Figure 16.22**).

(b) Ceiling Fans Exceeding 35 Lb. (15.88 kg). Listed ceiling fans exceeding 35 lb. (15.88 kg) in weight, with or without accessories, shall be supported independently of the outlet box. See Section 370-23.

NFPA commentary: This new subsection requires listed fans exceeding 35 pounds in weight, with or without accessories, to be supported independently from the outlet box. (See **Figure 16.21**.) Additionally, Section 370-23 requires boxes to be rigid and securely fastened in place.

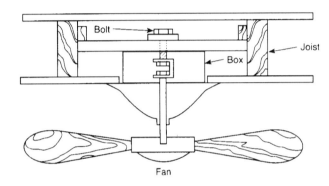

Ceiling fan supported without depending on box for sole support.

Courtesy of NFPA, *National Electrical Code® Handbook [Figure 370-8]*

Figure 16.21

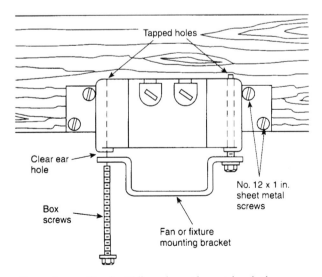

Supporting a ceiling fan 35 lbs. or less with special outlet box.

Courtesy of NFPA, *National Electrical Code® Handbook [Figure 422-2]*

Figure 16.22

Conductors: Wire/Cable

Industry Standards

Means Graphic Construction Standards
(R.S. Means, Co., Inc.)

Electrical conductors are the means by which current flows in an electrical distribution system. The primary elements of the distribution system are wires and cables, which are classified and rated by such variables as their diametric size, type of insulated covering, and current-carrying capacity. Basically, wires and cables are comprised of the conductor itself, either copper or aluminum, and usually some type of insulated covering. The most comprehensive source of detailed information on wire and cable material is the *National Electrical Code®*, which provides guidelines and data on all aspects of wire and cable, including their characteristics, allowable operating temperatures, ampacities, and application provisions.

The only difference between wire and cable is that of size, because their function and material composition are the same. When the circular mils area of a round cross-sectional conductor is #6 AWG or larger, it is referred to as cable; when the cross-sectional area is #8 AWG or smaller, it is called wire. Confusion often arises in the size designations of small round cross-sectional conductors as established by the American Wire Gauge system (AWG), because the AWG numbers increase as the wire size decreases, and, conversely, the AWG numbers decrease as the wire size increases. For example, #6 AWG conductor is larger than #12 AWG conductor and smaller than #1 AWG conductor. This AWG numbering system is maintained to #0 AWG, more commonly designated #1/0 AWG, when a different numeric designation is employed for conductors. Beginning with #1/0 AWG, the designation numbers increase with the increase in the size of the cable to the largest AWG rating of #0000, or #4/0. For example, a cable sized at #3/0 is larger than a cable sized at #2/0. For very heavy cables larger than #4/0 AWG, the designation changes again to kcmil, or thousand circular mils. With this designation system, the kcmil number increases with the increase in cable size; for example, 500 kcmil cable is larger or heavier than cable sized at 300 kcmil. The reason for the corresponding increase of designation number and cable size is that the circular mil is an artificial area measurement which represents the square of the cable diameter measured in mils, or thousandths of an inch. For example, a solid conductor of 1/2", or 500 mils, in diameter is sized at 250,000 circular mils in area, or 250 kcmil.

Most current-carrying conductors are covered with some type of insulated covering which protects them from physical damage and provides an obvious safety function. Insulation also serves as a shield against heat and moisture and prevents arcing and short circuits. Wire and cable insulation is rated by voltage, with the most commonly used ratings of 250, 600, 1,000, 3,000, 5,000, and 15,000 volts.

The conductor or current carrying component of a wire or cable is manufactured from copper or aluminum. These two materials are used because they possess the low resistance required for efficient electrical conduction. Generally, larger aluminum conductors are necessary to meet the same ampacity needs of copper conductors. Copper, because it is less resistant than aluminum and possesses other advantageous properties, is the more commonly employed material of the two, especially for smaller wires and cables. Because aluminum costs and weighs less than copper, it is most often used in larger size cables. Difficulties may arise when aluminum is employed, however, as aluminum cold flow characteristics when under pressure may cause joints to loosen. Also, aluminum conductor is prone to rapid oxidation if exposed to the air. Because the oxide which forms on the surface of the wire or cable is not conductive, it creates high resistance to the electrical flow and must be removed and prevented from reforming. Experience and skilled craftsmanship have reduced the risk of aluminum conductor oxidation, but many states have banned the use of aluminum conductors in branch wiring to prevent unskilled homeowners from installing them. The *National Electrical Code®* provides charts and other sources of information on the ampacities of aluminum and the corresponding ampacities for copper conductors.

Conductor Sizing & Overcurrent Protection

Comments

Use of correct wire gauges for given applications is crucial to prevent overload, malfunction of current protection devices (such as fuses or circuit breakers), and risk of fire. **Figure 16.23** *provides NEC's correct wire gauges for various circuit ratings, and overcurrent protection requirements, as well as maximum loads for different current ratings.*

Chapter 42 of the 1998 International One- and Two-Family Dwelling Code, which replaces the CABO One and Two Family Dwelling Code, addresses branch circuits and feeder requirements. Section 4205 covers required overcurrent protection for branch circuits and feeders that serve less than 100 percent of the total dwelling unit load. Note that Chapter 41 addresses feeder circuits that serve 100 percent of the dwelling unit load.

Summary of Branch-Circuit Requirements

Table 210-24.	Summary of Branch-Circuit Requirements				
Circuit Rating	**15 Amp**	**20 Amp**	**30 Amp**	**40 Amp**	**50 Amp**
Conductors: (Min. Size) Circuit Wires*	14	12	10	8	6
Taps	14	14	14	12	12
Fixture Wires and Cords			Refer to Section 240-4		
Overcurrent Protection	**15 Amp**	**20 Amp**	**30 Amp**	**40 Amp**	**50 Amp**
Outlet Devices: Lampholders Permitted	Any Type	Any Type	Heavy Duty	Heavy Duty	Heavy Duty
Receptacle Rating**	15 Max. Amp	15 or 20 Amp	30 Amp	40 or 50 Amp	50 Amp
Maximum Load	**15 Amp**	**20 Amp**	**30 Amp**	**40 Amp**	**50 Amp**
Permissible Load	Refer to Section 210-23(a)	Refer to Section 210-23(a)	Refer to Section 210-23(b)	Refer to Section 210-23(c)	Refer to Section 210-23(c)

*These gauges are for copper conductors.

**For receptacle rating of cord-connected electric-discharge lighting fixtures. See Section 410-30(c).

Courtesy of National Fire Protection Association, *National Electrical Code® Handbook*

Figure 16.23

Maximum Number of Wires (Insulation Noted) for Various Conduit Sizes

Table below lists maximum number of conductors for various sized conduit using THW, TW or THWN insulations.

Copper Wire Size	1/2"			3/4"			1"			1-1/4"			1-1/2"			2"			2-1/2"		
	TW	THW	THWN	TW	THW	THWN	TW	THW	THWN	TW	THW	THWN	TW	THW	THWN	TW	THW	THWN	TW	THW	THWN
#14	9	6	13	15	10	24	25	16	39	44	29	69	60	40	94	99	65	154	142	93	
#12	7	4	10	12	8	18	19	13	29	35	24	51	47	32	70	78	53	114	111	76	164
#10	5	4	6	9	6	11	15	11	18	26	19	32	36	26	44	60	43	73	85	61	104
#8	2	1	3	4	3	5	7	5	9	12	10	16	17	13	22	28	22	36	40	32	51
#6		1	1		2	4		4	6		7	11		10	15		16	26		23	37
#4		1	1		1	2		3	4		5	7		7	9		12	16		17	22
#3		1	1		1	1		2	3		4	6		6	8		10	13		15	19
#2		1	1		1	1		2	3		4	5		5	7		9	11		13	16
#1					1	1		1	1		3	3		4	5		6	8		9	12
1/0					1	1		1	1		2	3		3	4		5	7		8	10
2/0					1	1		1	1		1	2		3	3		5	6		7	8
3/0					1	1		1	1		1	1		2	3		4	5		6	7
4/0						1		1	1		1	1		1	2		3	4		5	6
250 kcmil								1	1		1	1		1	1		2	3		4	4
300								1	1		1	1		1	1		2	3		3	4
350									1		1	1		1	1		1	2		3	3

R.S. Means Co., Inc., *Electrical Estimating Methods*

Figure 16.24

Minimum Copper and Aluminum Wire Size Allowed for Various Types of Insulation

Minimum Wire Sizes

Amperes	Copper THW THWN or XHHW	Copper THHN XHHW *	Aluminum THW XHHW	Aluminum THHN XHHW *
15A	#14	#14	#12	#12
20	#12	#12		
25			#10	#10
30	#10	#10		
40			#8	
45				#8
50	#8		#6	
55		#8		
60				#6
65	#6		#4	
75		#6	#3	#4
85	#4			#3
90			#2	
95		#4		
100	#3		#1	#2
110		#3		
115	#2			#1
120			1/0	
130	#1	#2		
135			2/0	1/0
150	1/0	#1		2/0
155			3/0	
170		1/0		
175	2/0			3/0
180			4/0	

Amperes	Copper THW THWN or XHHW	Copper THHN XHHW *	Aluminum THW XHHW	Aluminum THHN XHHW *
195		2/0		
200	3/0			
205			250kcmil	4/0
225		3/0		
230	4/0		300kcmil	250kcmil
250			350kcmil	
255	250kcmil			300kcmil
260		4/0		
270			400kcmil	
280				350kcmil
285	300kcmil			
290		250kcmil		
305				400kcmil
310	350kcmil		500kcmil	
320		300kcmil		
335	400kcmil			
340			600kcmil	
350		350kcmil		
375				500kcmil
380	500kcmil	400kcmil	700kcmil	
385				
420	600kcmil		750kcmil	600kcmil
430		500kcmil		700kcmil
435				
475		600kcmil		750kcmil

*Dry Locations Only

Notes:
1. Size #14 to 4/0 is in AWG units (American Wire Gauge).
2. Size 250 to 750 is in kcmil units (Thousand Circular Mils).
3. Use next higher ampere value if exact value is not listed in table.
4. For loads that operate continuously increase ampere value by 25% to obtain proper wire size.

R.S. Means Co., Inc., *1999 Electrical Cost Data*

Figure 16.25

Maximum Circuit Length (approximate) for Various Power Requirements Assuming THW, Copper Wire @ 75° C, Based Upon a 4% Voltage Drop

Maximum Circuit Length: Table R161-120 indicates typical maximum installed length a circuit can have and still maintain an adequate voltage level at the point of use. The circuit length is similar to the conduit length.

If the circuit length for an ampere load and a copper wire size exceeds the length obtained from Table R161-120, use the next largest wire size to compensate voltage drop.

Example: A 130 ampere load at 480 volts, 3 phase, 3 wire with No. 1 wire can be run a maximum of 555 L.F. and provide satisfactory operation. If the same load is to be wired at the end of a 625 L.F. circuit, then a larger wire must be used.

Amperes	Wire Size	Maximum Circuit Length in Feet				
		2 Wire, 1 Phase		3 Wire, 3 Phase		
		120V	240V	240V	480V	600V
15	14*	50	105	120	240	300
	14	50	100	120	235	295
20	12*	60	125	145	290	360
	12	60	120	140	280	350
30	10*	65	130	155	305	380
	10	65	130	150	300	375
50	8	60	125	145	285	355
65	6	75	150	175	345	435
85	4	90	185	210	425	530
115	2	110	215	250	500	620
130	1	120	240	275	555	690
150	1/0	130	260	305	605	760
175	2/0	140	285	330	655	820
200	3/0	155	315	360	725	904
230	4/0	170	345	395	795	990
255	250	185	365	420	845	1055
285	300	195	395	455	910	1140
310	350	210	420	485	975	1220
380	500	245	490	565	1130	1415

*Solid Conductor

Note: The circuit length is the one-way distance between the origin and the load.

R.S. Means Co., Inc., 1999 *Electrical Cost Data*

Figure 16.26

Boxes & Fittings

Industry Standards

Plan Reading & Material Takeoff
(R.S. Means Co., Inc.)

A box is used in electrical wiring at each junction point, outlet, or switch. Boxes provide access to electrical connections and serve as a mounting for fixtures or switches. They may also be used as pull points for wire in long runs or conduits. A wiring device can be defined as a mechanism that controls but does not consume electricity, such as a switch or receptacle.

Boxes often require accessories such as plaster rings, covers, and various fasteners to support them. Boxes are constructed of galvanized or coated steel, or high-density plastic.

Wiring devices, in addition to receptacles and switches, include pilot lights, relays, low-voltage transformers, and a variety of specialized controls and finish wall plates.

Figure 16.27 shows the *NEC*® correct application of a grounding clip in a box.

Comments

Chapter 44 of the 1998 International One- and Two-Family Dwelling Code, *which replaces the CABO* One and Two Family Dwelling Code, *addresses power and lighting distribution. Sections 4405 and 4406 cover the installation of boxes, conduit bodies and fittings.*

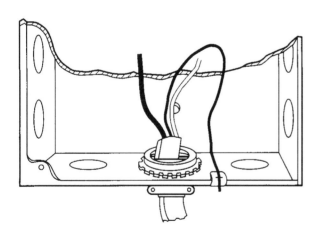

An application of a grounding clip.

Courtesy of NFPA, *National Electrical Code*® Handbook [Figure 250-45]

Figure 16.27

Industry Standards

Electrical Cost Data
(R.S. Means Co., Inc.)

Standard Electrical Enclosure Types: NEMA Enclosures

Ed. Note: NEMA Types 1 and 3R are used for residential and light commercial applications.

Electrical enclosures serve two basic purposes; they protect people from accidental contact with enclosed electrical devices and connections, and they protect the enclosed devices and connections from specified external conditions. The National Electrical Manufacturers Association (NEMA) has established the following standards. Because these descriptions are not intended to be complete representations of NEMA listings, consultation of NEMA literature is advised for detailed information.

The following definitions and descriptions pertain to NONHAZARDOUS locations.

NEMA   Type 1: General purpose enclosures intended for use indoors, primarily to prevent accidental contact of personnel with the enclosed equipment in areas that do not involve unusual conditions.

NEMA   Type 2: Dripproof indoor enclosures intended to protect the enclosed equipment against dripping noncorrosive liquids and falling dirt.

NEMA   Type 3: Dustproof, raintight and sleet-resistant (ice-resistant) enclosures intended for use outdoors to protect the enclosed equipment against wind-blown dust, rain, sleet, and external ice formation.

NEMA   Type 3R: Rainproof and sleet-resistant (ice-resistant) enclosures which are intended for use outdoors to protect the enclosed equipment against rain. These enclosures are constructed so that the accumulation and melting of sleet (ice) will not damage the enclosure and its internal mechanisms.

NEMA   Type 3S: Enclosures intended for outdoor use to provide limited protection against wind-blown dust, rain, and sleet (ice) to allow operation of external mechanisms when ice-laden.

NEMA   Type 4: Watertight and dust-tight enclosures intended for use indoors and out — to protect the enclosed equipment against splashing water, seepage of water, falling or hose-directed water, and severe external condensation.

NEMA   Type 4X: Watertight, dust-tight, and corrosion-resistant indoor and outdoor enclosures featuring the same provisions as Type 4 enclosures, plus corrosion resistance.

NEMA Type 5: Indoor enclosures intended primarily to provide limited protection against dust and falling dirt.

NEMA Type 6: Enclosures intended for indoor and outdoor use — primarily to provide limited protection against the entry of water during occasional temporary submersion at a limited depth.

NEMA Type 6R: Enclosures intended for indoor and outdoor use — primarily to provide limited protection against the entry of water during prolonged submersion at a limited depth.

NEMA Type 11: Enclosures intended for indoor use — primarily to provide, by means of oil immersion, limited protection to enclosed equipment against the corrosive effects of liquids and gases.

NEMA Type 12: Dust-tight and driptight indoor enclosures intended for use indoors in industrial locations to protect the enclosed equipment against fibers, flyings, lint, dust, and dirt, as well as light splashing, seepage, dripping and external condensation of noncorrosive liquids.

NEMA Type 13: Oil-tight and dust-tight indoor enclosures intended primarily to house pilot devices, such as limit switches, foot switches, push buttons, selector switches, and pilot lights, and to protect these devices against lint and dust, seepage, external condensation, and sprayed water, oil, and noncorrosive coolant.

The following definitions and descriptions pertain to HAZARDOUS, or CLASSIFIED, locations:

NEMA Type 7: Enclosures intended to use in indoor locations classified as Class 1, Groups A, B, C, or D, defined in the *National Electrical Code®*.

NEMA Type 9: Enclosures intended for use in indoor locations classified as Class 2, Groups E, F, or G, as defined in the *National Electrical Code®*.

Branch Circuits

Comments

Branch circuits contain any combination of receptacles, switches, and lighting outlets.

National Electrical Code® Handbook

Ed. Note: The following excerpt contains NFPA commentary by recognized experts in the field of safety, along with the National Electrical Code® *in numbered paragraphs.*

210-19. Conductors—Minimum Ampacity and Size.
(a) General. Branch-circuit conductors shall have an ampacity not less than the maximum load to be served. In addition, conductors of multioutlet branch circuits supplying receptacles for cord- and plug-connected portable loads shall have an ampacity of not less than the rating of the branch circuit. Cable assemblies where the neutral conductor is smaller than the ungrounded conductors shall be so marked.

NFPA commentary: Only multioutlet branch-circuit conductors supplying receptacles for cord- and plug-connected portable loads are required to have an ampacity not less than the rating of the circuit (the rating of the overcurrent device per Section 210-3), because the loading of such circuits is unpredictable.

(FPN No. 1): See Section 310-15 for ampacity ratings of conductors.

(FPN No. 2): See Part B of Article 430 for minimum rating of motor branch-circuit conductors.

(FPN No. 3): See Section 310-10 for temperature limitation of conductors.

(FPN No. 4): Conductors for branch circuits as defined in Article 100, sized to prevent a voltage drop exceeding 3 percent at the farthest outlet of power, heating, and lighting loads, or combinations of such loads and where the maximum total voltage drop on both feeders and branch circuits to the farthest outlet does not exceed 5 percent, will provide reasonable efficiency of operation. See Section 215-2 for voltage drop on feeder conductors.

NFPA commentary: Improper voltage is a major source of trouble and inefficient operation in electrical equipment. Both overvoltage and undervoltage reduce the capability and reliability of motors, lighting sources, heaters, and solid-state equipment. Sample voltage-drop calculations may be found in the commentary following Section 215-2, FPN No. 3, and in Chapter 9, Table 9.

(b) Household Ranges and Cooking Appliances. Branch-circuit conductors supplying household ranges, wall-mounted ovens, counter-mounted cooking units, and other household cooking appliances shall have an ampacity not less than the rating of the branch circuit and not less than the maximum load to be served. For ranges of 8-3/4 kW or more rating, the minimum branch-circuit rating shall be 40 amperes.

NFPA commentary: A minimum 40-ampere branch-circuit rating would be as follows:

No. 8 AWG copper, Type TW = 40 amperes

or

No. 6 AWG aluminum, Type TW = 40 amperes

See Table 310-16 for other applications.

210-20. Overcurrent Protection. Branch-circuit conductors and equipment shall be protected by overcurrent protective devices having a rating or setting (1) not exceeding that specified in Section 240-3 for conductors; (2) not exceeding that specified in the applicable articles referenced in Section 240-2 for equipment; and (3) as provided for outlet devices in Section 210-21.

Exception No. 1: Tap conductors as permitted in Section 210-19(c) shall be permitted to be protected by the branch-circuit overcurrent device.

Exception No. 2: Fixture wires and cords as permitted in Section 240-4.

(FPN): See Section 240-1 for the purpose of overcurrent protection and Sections 210-22 and 220-3 for continuous loads.

210-21. Outlet Devices. Outlet devices shall have an ampere rating not less than the load to be served and shall comply with (a) and (b) below.

(a) Lampholders. Where connected to a branch circuit having a rating in excess of 20 amperes, lampholders shall be of the heavy-duty type. A heavy-duty lampholder shall have a rating of not less than 660 watts if of the medium type and not less than 750 watts if of any other type.

(b) Receptacles.
(1) A single receptacle installed on an individual branch circuit shall have an ampere rating of not less than that of the branch-circuit.

Exception No. 1: Where installed in accordance with Section 430-81(c).

Exception No. 2: A receptacle installed exclusively for the use of a cord- and plug-connected arc welder shall be permitted to have an ampere rating not less than the minimum branch-circuit conductor ampacity determined by Section 630-11(a) for ac transformer and dc rectifier arc welders, and Section 630-21(a) for motor-generator arc welders.

(FPN): See definition of "Receptacle" in Article 100.

(2) Where connected to a branch circuit supplying two or more receptacles or outlets, a receptacle shall not supply a total cord- and plug-connected load in excess of the maximum specified in Table 210-21(b)(2).

(3) Where connected to a branch circuit supplying two or more receptacles or outlets, receptacle ratings shall conform to the values listed in Table 210-21 (b)(3), or where larger than 50 amperes, the receptacle rating shall not be less than the branch-circuit rating.

NFPA commentary: A single receptacle installed on an individual branch circuit is required to have an ampere rating of not less than that of the branch circuit. For example, a single receptacle on a 20-ampere branch circuit must be rated

at 20 amperes; however, two or more 15-ampere receptacles are permitted on a 20-ampere general-purpose branch circuit. New in the 1996 *Code*, this requirement does not apply to some specific types of cord- and plug-connected welders.

(4) The ampere rating of a range receptacle shall be permitted to be based on a single range demand load specified in Table 220-19.

Branch-Circuit Requirements

422-4. Branch-Circuit Rating. This section specifies sizes of branch circuits capable of carrying appliance current without over-heating under the conditions specified. This section shall not apply to conductors that form an integral part of an appliance.

NFPA commentary: Conductors that form integral parts of appliances are tested as part of the listing or labeling process.

(a) Individual Circuits. The rating of an individual branch circuit shall not be less than the marked rating of the appliance or the marked rating of an appliance having combined loads as provided in Section 422-32.

Exception No. 1: For motor-operated appliances not having a marked rating, the branch-circuit size shall be in accordance with Part B of Article 430.

Exception No. 2: For an appliance, other than a motor-operated appliance, that is continuously loaded, the branch-circuit rating shall not be less than 125 percent of the marked rating; or not less than 100 percent if the branch-circuit device and its assembly are listed for continuous loading at 100 percent of its rating.

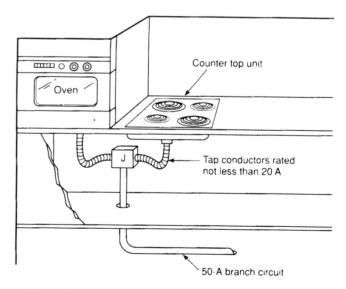

Tap conductors are permitted to be sized smaller than the branch-circuit conductors but are to be no longer than necessary for servicing.

Courtesy of NFPA, *National Electrical Code® Handbook [Figure 210-23]*

Figure 16.28

Exception No. 3: Branch circuits for household cooking appliances shall be permitted to be in accordance with Table 220-19.

NFPA commentary: If a labeled or listed appliance is provided with installation instructions from the manufacturer, the branch-circuit size is not permitted to be less than the minimum size stated in the installation instructions.

(b) Circuits Supplying Two or More Loads. For branch circuit supplying appliance and other loads, the rating shall be determined in accordance with Section 210-23.

422-5. Branch-Circuit Overcurrent Protection. Branch circuits shall be protected in accordance with Section 240-3.

If a protective device rating is marked on an appliance, the branch-circuit overcurrent device rating shall not exceed the protective device rating marked on the appliance.

Circuit Breakers — Interchanging in Foreign Panels
Industry Standards
The Code Authority
(Underwriters Laboratories Inc.)

Ed. Note: Underwriters Laboratories, Inc. publishes The Code Authority, *a newsletter for the code community. In a column called "Questions and Answers," UL engineers answer questions concerning UL and its operations, or inquiries about UL Standards and how they coincide with installation codes (such as the NEC®) and various building codes. Send questions to Bob Pollock, Editor, UL, 333 Pfingsten Rd., Northbrook, IL 60062.*

Q. I've seen UL Classified circuit breakers from one manufacturer used in panelboards/load centers built by other manufacturers. Is this acceptable? In other instances, UL Lists circuit breakers. When does UL Classify rather than List circuit breakers?

A. UL has a program wherein circuit breakers are Classified for use in specific listed panelboards. This program could make it possible for you to see one manufacturer's Classified circuit breaker in another manufacturer's panelboard. The appearance of the UL Classified Product marking on a circuit breaker is evidence of compliance with this UL program covering expected applications of the circuit breaker. A list of compatible panelboards, including manufacturers and model numbers is required to be issued with a Classified breaker — and the Classified breakers are to be used only with those itemized compatible panelboards. The use of the UL Classified Product marking instead of the UL Listing Mark was chosen for products in this program to draw attention to the need for the installer to check the specific instructions provided with the circuit breaker for panelboard suitability.

Following is a summary of UL's Classified circuit breaker program:

A) UL Classified molded-case circuit breakers are subjected to the identical testing and evaluation programs used for Listed molded-case circuit breakers as described in UL 489, Molded-Case Circuit Breakers and Circuit-Breaker Enclosures. The Classified breakers must have the same ratings as the breakers they may replace.

B) UL Classified molded-case circuit breakers are evaluated in specific panelboards in accordance with UL 67, Panelboards. The identical testing and evaluation requirements are used to evaluate listed molded-case circuit breakers that are identified on the listed panelboard markings.

There continue to be questions about the use of Classified circuit breakers in series-rated systems. Markings identify the limitation of Classified circuit breakers for systems having an available fault current not exceeding 10 kA — emphasizing that Classified circuit breakers are not for use in series-rated systems. Classified circuit breakers are not for installation where markings, such as those required by Section 110-22 of the NEC®, identify the application as a series-rated system.

UL Classified Circuit Breaker Label

This Classified label assures you the breaker is UL-accepted for all panelboards listed.

Courtesy of Underwriters Laboratories, Inc. (UL)

Figure 16.29

Bonding

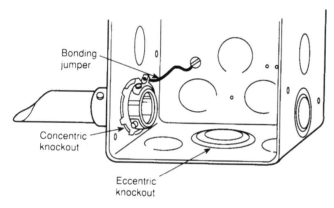

Bonding jumper

Concentric knockout

Eccentric knockout

A bonding jumper installed around a concentric or eccentric knockout is usually required.

Courtesy of NFPA, *National Electrical Code® Handbook [Figure 100-3]*

Figure 16.30

Safety Switches

Industry Standards

Means Graphic Construction Standards
(R.S. Means Co., Inc.)

A safety switch provides a manual method of disconnecting power, from electrical equipment, which cannot be overridden by automatic controls. If the switch is fused, it provides branch circuit protection. The safety switch itself is mounted inside a sheet metal or cast iron enclosure and controlled by a handle connected to the mechanism and located on the outside of the enclosure. The switch mechanism is manufactured as either single- or double-break type, in knife-blade or butt-contact format. Because these switches usually conduct large amounts of power, the enclosure doors are designed so that they cannot be opened if the switch handle is set in the "up" or "on" position.

Safety switches are manufactured in general-duty and heavy-duty grades and in both fused and unfused types. General-duty switches are available in two-and three-pole design for up to 240 volts, with ratings of 30, 60, 100, 200, 400, and 600 amps. Heavy-duty switches are also manufactured in two- and three-pole formats, with voltage ratings of 250 and 600 volts and amperage ratings of 30, 60, 100, 200, 400, 600, 800, and 1,200 amps.

During installation, line side power is connected to the terminal lugs, which are located at the top of the switch before the blade mechanism. Power to a piece of electrical equipment is tapped off the load side of the switch before the blade mechanism. Accidental feeding of the load terminals, which would cause the blades of the switch to become "hot," even when the switch is in the open position, can be avoided by following precisely correct line and load installation rules.

The enclosures for safety switches are classified by the NEMA according to their particular interior or exterior safety function. Several of the NEMA enclosure types classified for interior use include NEMA 1, NEMA 2, NEMA 7, AND NEMA 12. The NEMA 1 enclosure type is intended for indoor use where no unusual service conditions exist. Its primary function is to protect personnel from accidental contact with live electrical equipment. NEMA 2 is designed with a drip-proof housing to protect the enclosed equipment against falling dirt and noncorrosive liquids. NEMA 7 is used to protect equipment in hazardous locations where indoor atmospheres containing volatile gas and vapors may cause explosion. This type of switch enclosure is marked to show the class and group letter designation. NEMA 12, which is designed for indoor industrial use, features dust- and drip-tight seals. Because it contains no conduit openings or knockouts, access may be gained only through field-installed holes with oil resistant gaskets. An additional safety features of this type of enclosure is that a special tool is required to open its cover.

Safety Switches

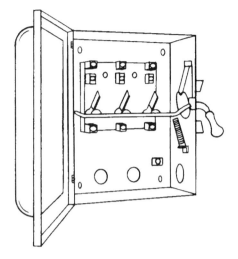

NEMA 1, Non-fusible, 600 Volt

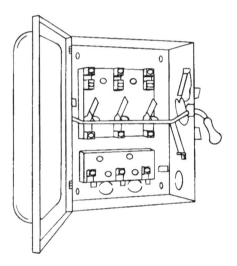

NEMA 1, Fusible, 600 Volt

R.S. Means Co., Inc., *Means Graphic Construction Standards*

Figure 16.31

Two commonly used exterior NEMA enclosure classifications include NEMA 3 and NEMA 3R. NEMA 3 is a rain-tight, dust-tight, and ice-resistant enclosure that protects equipment from penetration by water, ice, and wind-blown dust. NEMA 3R is designed to protect against rain, sleet, and snow. This type of enclosure is also equipped with a conduit hub to assure weathertight connections for conduits, which are fed into the top of the unit.

Appliance Installation

Comments

Chapter 46 of the 1998 IOTFDC covers installation requirements for appliances and fixed heating equipment, including allowed disconnecting means. Section 4601 provides general requirements.

Electrical clothes dryers typically require a 240-volt (30 amps), two-pole receptacle. Electric cooking ranges require a 240-volt (50 amps) receptacle.

NFPA 70: National Electrical Code®
Installation of Appliances

422-6. General. All appliances shall be installed in an approved manner.

422-7. Central Heating Equipment. Central heating equipment other than fixed electric space-heating equipment shall be supplied by an individual branch circuit.

Exception: Auxiliary equipment such as a pump, valve, humidifier, or electrostatic air cleaner directly associated with the heating equipment shall be permitted to be connected to the same branch circuit.

422-8. Flexible Cords.

(a) **Heater Cords.** All cord- and plug-connected smoothing irons and electrically heated appliances that are rated at more than 50 watts and produce temperatures in excess of 121°C (250°F) on surfaces with which the cord is likely to be in contact shall be provided with one of the types of approved heater cords listed in Table 400-4.

(b) **Other Heating Appliances.** All other cord- and plug-connected electrically heated appliances shall be connected with one of the approved types of cord listed in Table 400-4, selected in accordance with the usage specified in that table.

(c) **Other Appliances.** Flexible cord shall be permitted (1) for connection of appliances to facilitate their frequent interchange or to prevent the transmission of noise or vibration or (2) to facilitate the removal or disconnection of appliances that are fastened in place, where the fastening means and mechanical connections are specifically designed to permit ready removal for maintenance or repair, and the appliance is intended or identified for flexible cord connection.

(d) **Specific Appliances.**

(1) Electrically operated kitchen waste disposers shall be permitted to be cord- and plug-connected with a flexible cord identified for the purpose, terminated with a grounding-type attachment plug where all of the following conditions are met:

    a. The length of the cord shall not be less than 18 inches (457 mm) and not over 36 inches (914 mm).

    b. Receptacles shall be located to avoid physical damage to the flexible cord.

    c. The receptacle shall be accessible.

(2) Built-in dishwashers and trash compactors shall be permitted to be cord-and-plug connected with a flexible cord identified for the purpose, terminated with a grounding-type attachment plug where all of the following conditions are met:

    a. The length of the cord shall be 3 ft to 4 ft (0.914 m to 1.22 m).

    b. Receptacles shall be located to avoid physical damage to the flexible cord.

    c. The receptacle shall be located in the space occupied by the appliance or adjacent thereto.

    d. The receptacle shall be accessible.

Exception: Listed kitchen waste disposers, dishwashers, and trash compactors protected by a system of double insulation, or its equivalent, shall not be required to be grounded. Where such a system is employed, the equipment shall be distinctively marked.

422-25. Unit Switch(es) as Disconnecting Means. A unit switch(es) with a marked "off" position that is a part of an appliance and disconnects all ungrounded conductors shall be permitted as the disconnecting means required by this article where other means for disconnection are provided in the following types of occupancies:

(b) **Two-Family Dwellings.** In two-family dwellings, the other disconnecting means shall be permitted either inside or outside of the dwelling unit in which the appliance is installed. In this case, an individual switch or circuit breaker for the dwelling unit shall be permitted and shall also be permitted to control lamps and other appliances.

(c) **One-Family Dwellings.** In one-family dwellings, the service disconnecting means shall be permitted to be the other disconnecting means.

422-28 Overcurrent Protection

(f) **Electric Heating Appliances Employing Resistance-type Heating Elements Rated More than 48 Amperes.** Electric heating appliances employing resistance-type heating elements rated more than 48 amperes shall have the heating elements subdivided. Each subdivided load shall not exceed 48 amperes and shall be protected at not more than 60 amperes.

These supplementary overcurrent protective devices shall be (1) factory-installed within or on the heater enclosure or provided as a separate assembly by the heater manufacturer; (2) accessible, but need not be readily accessible; and (3) suitable branch-circuit protection.

The main conductors supplying these overcurrent protective devices shall be considered branch-circuit conductors.

Exception No. 1: Household-type appliances with surface heating elements as covered in Section 422-28(b) and commercial-type heating appliances as covered in Section 422-28(d).

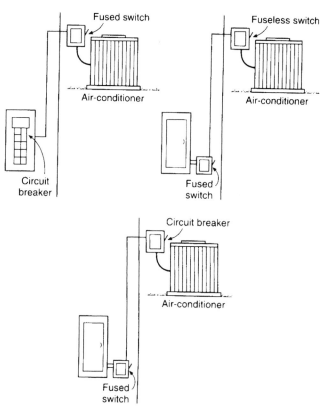

Three correct alternate wiring configurations satisfying a nameplate that specifies fuses. The equipment is intended to be protected by fuses only.

Courtesy of NFPA, *National Electrical Code® Handbook [Figure 440-1]*

Figure 16.32

424-19 Control and Protection of Fixed Electric Space-Heating Equipment

(a) **Heating Equipment with Supplementary Overcurrent Protection.** The disconnecting means for fixed electric space heating equipment with supplementary overcurrent protection shall be within sight from the supplementary overcurrent protective device(s), on the supply side of these devices, if fuses, and, in addition, shall comply with either (1) or (2) below.

(1) **Heater Containing No Motor Rated Over 1/8 Horsepower.** The above disconnecting means or unit switches complying with Section 424-19(c) shall be permitted to serve as the required disconnecting means for both the motor controller(s) and heater under either item a or b below.

    a. The disconnecting means provided is also within sight from the motor controller(s) and the heater; or

    b. The disconnecting means provided shall be capable of being locked in the open position.

(2) **Heater Containing a Motor(s) Rated Over 1/8 Horsepower.** The above disconnecting means shall be permitted to serve as the required disconnecting means for both the motor controller(s) and heater by one of the means specified in items a through d below.

    a. Where the disconnecting means is also in sight from the motor controller(s) and the heater.

    b. Where the disconnecting means is not within sight from the heater, a separate disconnecting means shall be installed, or the disconnecting means shall be capable of being locked in the open position, or unit switches complying with Section 424-19(c) shall be emitted.

    c. Where the disconnecting means is not within sight from the motor controller location, a disconnecting means complying with Section 430-102 shall be provided.

    d. Where the motor is not in sight from the motor controller location, Section 430-102(b) shall apply.

BIBLIOGRAPHY

Chapter 1 Asphalt

Asphalt Institute, P.O. Box 14055, Lexington, KY 40512-4053, (Telephone: 606-288-4960), Internet Web site: www.asphaltinstitute.org.

Horsley, F. William, ed. *Means Graphic Construction Standards*. Kingston, MA: R.S. Means Co., Inc., 1986.

National Asphalt Pavement Association, 5100 Forbes Blvd., Lanham, MD 20706-4413, (Telephone: 301-731-4748), Internet Web site: www.hotmix.org.

Chapter 2 Concrete

Brantley, L. Reed, and Ruth T. Brantley. *Building Materials Technology, Structural Performance & Environmental Impact*. New York: The McGraw-Hill Companies, 1996. Reprinted by permission of publisher.

DelPico, Wayne J. *Plan Reading & Material Takeoff*. Kingston, MA: R.S. Means Co., Inc., 1994.

Emmons, Peter H. *Concrete Repair and Maintenance Illustrated*. Kingston, MA: R.S. Means Co., Inc., 1994.

Figures 2.10 and 2.16 reprinted with permission of Portland Cement Association, 5420 Old Orchard Road, Skokie, IL 60077-1083, (Telephone: 847-966-6200), Internet Web site: www.portcement.org.

Figure 2.19, Copyright ASTM. Reprinted with permission.

Figure 2.23, Copyright Home Planners, LLC, 3275 West Ina Road, #110, Tucson, AZ 85741 (800-322-6797).

Olin, Harold B., J.L. Schmidt, W.H. Lewis. Revised by H.L. Simmons. *Construction Principles, Materials, and Methods, Sixth Edition*. New York: Van Nostrand Reinhold, 1995; John Wiley & Sons, Inc, 1998. Reprinted by permission of John Wiley & Sons, Inc.

Reprinted with permission of the Wire Reinforcement Institute, 301 East Sandusky Street, Findlay, OH 45840 (Telephone: 419-425-9473).

Reproduced from the 1997 edition of the *Uniform Building Code*™, copyright © 1997, with the permission of the publisher, the International Conference of Building Officials.

Although the International Conference of Building Officials, Inc. (ICBO) has granted permission for reproduction of sections contained within the *Uniform Building Code*™ in conjunction with this publication, ICBO assumes no responsibility for the accuracy or the completion of summaries provided herein.

Reproduced from the 1997 edition of the *UBC Field Inspection Workbook*, copyright © 1997, with the permission of the publisher, the International Conference of Building Officials.

Although the International Conference of Building Officials, Inc. (ICBO) has granted permission for reproduction of sections contained within the *UBC Field Inspection Workbook* in conjunction with this publication, ICBO assumes no responsibility for the accuracy or the completion of summaries provided herein.

Chapter 3 Masonry

American Concrete Institute. *ACI Manual of Concrete Practice*. Farmington Hill, MI: American Concrete Institute.

Mortar Specifications reprinted with permission of the American Society of Testing and Materials (ASTM).

Copyright 1998, International Code Council, Inc. — *International One- and Two-Family Dwelling Code*, 5203 Leesburg Pike, Suite 708, Falls Church, Virginia 22041.

Horsley, F. William, ed. *Means Graphic Construction Standards*. Kingston, MA: R.S. Means Co., Inc., 1986.

Reproduced from the 1997 edition of the *Uniform Building Code*™, copyright © 1997, with the permission of the publisher, the International Conference of Building Officials.

Although the International Conference of Building Officials, Inc. (ICBO) has granted permission for reproduction of sections contained within the *Uniform Building Code*™ in conjunction with this publication, ICBO assumes no responsibility for the accuracy or the completion of summaries provided herein.

Chapter 4 Metal Framing

Allen, Don. "A Real Stud...Is A Steel Stud, A Description of Steel Framing Members." In *Steelman's: How-To Guide and Resource Catalog for Residential Steel Framing*. Alexandria, VA: L.D. Marketing Communications, January/February 1998.

Allen, Don. "How to Design Steel Framed Walls." In *Steelman's: How-To Guide and Resource Catalog for Residential Steel Framing*. Alexandria, VA: L.D. Marketing Communications, January/February 1998.

Ballast, David Kent. *Handbook of Construction Tolerances*. New York: The McGraw-Hill Companies, 1994. Reprinted by permission of publisher.

Copyright© 1998, International Code Council, Inc. — *International One- and Two-Family Dwelling Code*, 5203 Leesburg Pike, Suite 708, Falls Church, Virginia 22041.

Horsley, F. William, ed. *Means Graphic Construction Standards*. Kingston, MA: R.S. Means Co., Inc., 1986.

Simpson Strong-Tie Connectors. *Simpson Catalog on Light Gauge Steel Construction, Catalog C-S96-R*. Pleasanton, CA: Simpson Strong-Tie Connectors, 1997.

Steel in Residential Construction Advisory Group. *Residential Construction Guidelines.* Publication No. RG–934a. Washington, D.C.: American Iron and Steel Advisory Group, June 1993.

United States Gypsum Company. *Gypsum Construction Handbook, 4th edition.* Chicago, IL: United States Gypsum Company, 1992.

Chapter 5 Wood Framing

Adaptive Environments Center, Inc. and R.S. Means Engineering Staff. *ADA Compliance Pricing Guide.* Kingston, MA: R.S. Means Company, Inc., 1994.

American Institute of Timber Construction. *Timber Construction Manual, Second Edition.* New York: John Wiley & Sons, Inc., 1974. Reprinted by permission of John Wiley & Sons, Inc.

APA — The Engineered Wood Association. *Build Strong Walls with Plywood and OSB.* Tacoma, WA: APA — The Engineered Wood Association, June 1997.

APA — The Engineered Wood Association. *Introduction to Lateral Design.* Tacoma, WA: APA — The Engineered Wood Association, December 1997.

Ballast, David Kent. *Handbook of Construction Tolerances.* New York: The McGraw-Hill Companies, 1994. Reprinted by permission of publisher.

DelPico, Wayne J. *Plan Reading & Material Takeoff.* Kingston, MA: R.S. Means Co., Inc., 1994.

Horsley, F. William, ed. *Means Graphic Construction Standards.* Kingston, MA: R.S. Means Co., Inc., 1986.

Reproduced from the 1997 edition of the *Uniform Building Code*™, copyright © 1997, with the permission of the publisher, the International Conference of Building Officials.

Although the International Conference of Building Officials, Inc. (ICBO) has granted permission for reproduction of sections contained within the *Uniform Building Code*™ in conjunction with this publication, ICBO assumes no responsibility for the accuracy or the completion of summaries provided herein.

Reproduced with permission from American Wood Preservers Institute, www.awpi.org.

Simpson, Scot. *Basics for Builders: Framing & Rough Carpentry.* Kingston, MA: R.S. Means Co., Inc., 1991.

Utterback, David. *Common Roof-Framing Errors.* WWPA Reprint Series: from *The Journal of Light Construction,* Richmond, VT: Builderburg Partners, Ltd., 1995; Portland, OR: Western Wood Products Association, 1997.

Utterback, David. *Field Guide to Common Framing Errors.* WWPA Reprint Series: from *The Journal of Light Construction,* Richmond, VT: Builderburg Partners, Ltd., 1991; Portland, OR: Western Wood Products Association, 1997.

Wagner, John. *House Framing.* Upper Saddle River, NJ: Creative Homeowner Press®, 1998.

Western Wood Products Association. *Guide to Understanding WWPA Stamps and Quality Control Identification.* Portland, OR: Western Wood Products Association, 1997.

Western Wood Products Association. *Notching & Boring Guide for Floor Joists & Stud Walls in Conventional Light-Frame Construction.* Portland, OR: Western Wood Products Association, 1997.

Chapter 6 Finish Carpentry & Cabinetry

Adaptive Environments Center, Inc. and R.S. Means Engineering Staff. *ADA Compliance Pricing Guide*. Kingston, MA: R.S. Means Company, Inc., 1994.

Architectural Woodwork Institute. *Architectural Woodwork Quality Standards Illustrated, 7th edition*. Reston, VA: Architectural Woodwork Institute, 1997.

Horsley, F. William, ed. *Means Graphic Construction Standards*. Kingston, MA: R.S. Means Co., Inc., 1986.

Stoeppelwerth, Walter W. and Darrell L. Lewis. *Kitchen & Bathroom Installation Manual, Volume I*. Hackettstown, NJ: National Kitchen & Bath Association, 1996.

Woodwork Institute of California. *WIC Manual of Millwork*. W. Sacramento, CA: Woodwork Institute of California, 1992 with 1995/1996 amendments.

Chapter 7 Insulation & Vapor Retarders

Figure 7.1 reprinted with permission of Home Planners, LLC, 3275 West Ina Road, #110, Tucson, AZ 85741 (Telephone: 800-322-6797), Internet Web site: www.homeplanners.com.

Herbert, Robert D., III. *Roofing: Design Criteria, Options, Selection*. Kingston, MA: R.S. Means Co., Inc., 1989.

Olin, Harold B., J.L. Schmidt, W.H. Lewis. Revised by H.L. Simmons. *Construction Principles, Materials, and Methods, Sixth Edition*. New York: Van Nostrand Reinhold, 1995; John Wiley & Sons, Inc, 1998. Reprinted by permission of John Wiley & Sons, Inc.

Reprinted with permission from the National Insulation Association (NIA), 99 Canal Center Plaza, Suite 222, Alexandria, VA 22314 (Telephone: 703-683-6422), Internet Web site: www.insulation.org.

Reprinted with permission from the Insulation Contractors Association of America (ICAA), 1321 Duke Street, #303, Alexandria, VA 22314 (Telephone: 703-739-0356), Internet Web Site: www.insulate.org.

Reproduced from the 1997 edition of the *Uniform Building Code*™, copyright © 1997, with the permission of the publisher, the International Conference of Building Officials.

Although the International Conference of Building Officials, Inc. (ICBO) has granted permission for reproduction of sections contained within the *Uniform Building Code*™ in conjunction with this publication, ICBO assumes no responsibility for the accuracy or the completion of summaries provided herein.

R.S. Means Company, Inc. *Exterior Home Improvement Costs*, Sixth Edition. Kingston, MA: R.S. Means Company, Inc., 1998.

R.S. Means Co., Inc. *Assemblies Cost Data*. Kingston, MA: R.S. Means Co., Inc., 1999.

Wagner, John. *House Framing*. Upper Saddle River, NJ: Creative Homeowner Press®, 1998.

Chapter 8 Roofing, Siding & Moisture Protection

Brantley, L. Reed, and Ruth T. Brantley. *Building Materials Technology, Structural Performance & Environmental Impact*. New York: The McGraw-Hill Companies, 1996. Reprinted by permission of publisher.

DelPico, Wayne J. *Plan Reading & Material Takeoff*. Kingston, MA: R.S. Means Company, Inc., 1994.

Figure 8.54, EIFS illustration (for 1998 catalogue), is reprinted with permission from the United States Gypsum Company, 125 South Franklin Street, Chicago, IL 60606-4678 (Telephone: 312-606-4000).

Gorman, et al. *Plaster and Drywall Systems Manual*, Third Edition. Anaheim, CA: BNI Publications, Inc., 1988.

Herbert, Robert D. III. *Roofing: Design Criteria, Options, Selection*. Kingston, MA: R.S. Means Co., Inc., 1989.

Horsley, F. William, ed. *Means Graphic Construction Standards*. Kingston, MA: R.S. Means Co., Inc., 1986.

National Roofing Contractors Association. *NRCA Roofing & Waterproofing Manual, Fourth Edition*. Rosemont, IL: National Roofing Contractors Association, 1995.

Olin, Harold B., J.L. Schmidt, W.H. Lewis. Revised by H.L. Simmons. *Construction Principles, Materials, and Methods, Sixth Edition*. New York: Van Nostrand Reinhold, 1995; John Wiley & Sons, Inc, 1998. Reprinted by permission of John Wiley & Sons, Inc.

Reproduced from the 1997 edition of the *Uniform Building Code*™, copyright © 1997, with the permission of the publisher, the International Conference of Building Officials.

Although the International Conference of Building Officials, Inc. (ICBO) has granted permission for reproduction of sections contained within the *Uniform Building Code*™ in conjunction with this publication, ICBO assumes no responsibility for the accuracy or the completion of summaries provided herein.

Reprinted from the SMACNA *Architectural Sheet Metal Manual*, Fifth Edition, Copyright© 1993, with permission.

Reprinted with permission from the Cedar Shake & Shingle Bureau, P.O. Box 1178, Sumass, Washington 98295 (Telephone: 604-462-8961), Internet Web site: www.cedarbureau.org.

Reprinted with permission from the Brick Industry Association (BIA), 11490 Commerce Park Drive, Reston, VA 20191 (Telephone: 703-620-0010), Internet Web site: bia.org.

Reprinted with permission from the Western Red Cedar Lumber Association, 1200 – 555 Burrard Street, Vancouver, BC V7X 1S7 (Telephone: 604-684-0266), Internet Web site: www.wrcla.org.

Rose, James J. *Cracking in Portland Cement Plaster*. Woodland Hills, CA: Plastering Information Bureau.

Scharff, Robert et al. *Roofing Handbook*. New York: The McGraw-Hill Companies, 1996. Reprinted by permission of publisher.

Reprinted with permission from the United States Gypsum Company. *Gypsum Construction Handbook*, 4th edition. Chicago, IL: United States Gypsum Company, 1992.

Chapter 9 Windows & Doors

Adaptive Environments Center, Inc. and R.S. Means Engineering Staff. *ADA Compliance Pricing Guide*. Kingston, MA: R.S. Means Company, Inc., 1994.

Bateman, Robert. *Nail-On Windows*. Mill Valley, CA: DTA, Inc., 1995.

Bentil, Kweku K. *Fundamentals of the Construction Process*. Kingston, MA: R.S. Means Co., Inc., 1989.

California Association of Window Manufacturers. *Standard Practices for Installation of Windows (CAWM 400-95)*. Santa Ana, CA: California Association of Window Manufacturers, August 31, 1995.

California Association of Window Manufacturers. *Standard Practices for Installation of Sliding Glass Doors (410-97)*. Santa Ana, CA: California Association of Window Manufacturers, August 15, 1997.

DelPico, Wayne J. *Plan Reading & Material Takeoff*. Kingston, MA: R.S. Means Company, Inc., 1994.

Gorman, et al. *Plaster and Drywall Systems Manual*, Third Edition. Anaheim, CA: BNI Publications, Inc., 1988.

National Wood Window & Door Association. *Specifiers Guide to Wood Windows and Doors*. Des Plaines, IL: National Wood Window & Door Association, 1997.

Olin, Harold B., J.L. Schmidt, W.H. Lewis. Revised by H.L. Simmons. *Construction Principles, Materials, and Methods, Sixth Edition*. New York: Van Nostrand Reinhold, 1995; John Wiley & Sons, Inc, 1998. Reprinted by permission of John Wiley & Sons, Inc.

Reproduced from the 1997 edition of the *Uniform Building Code*™, copyright © 1997, with the permission of the publisher, the International Conference of Building Officials.

Although the International Conference of Building Officials, Inc. (ICBO) has granted permission for reproduction of sections contained within the *Uniform Building Code*™ in conjunction with this publication, ICBO assumes no responsibility for the accuracy or the completion of summaries provided herein.

United States Aluminum — Commercial Products Group. *Architectural Aluminum Entrances, Storefronts, and Window Walls*. Waxahachie, TX: United States Aluminum — Commercial Products Group, March, 1997.

Woodwork Institute of California. *WIC Manual of Millwork*. W. Sacramento, CA: Woodwork Institute of California, 1992 with 1995/1996 amendments.

Chapter 10 Drywall & Ceramic Tile

DelPico, Wayne J. *Plan Reading & Material Takeoff*. Kingston, MA: R.S. Means Company, Inc., 1994.

Germer, Jerry. *Bathrooms*. Upper Saddle River, NJ: Creative Homeowner Press®, 1995.

Gorman, et al. *Plaster and Drywall Systems Manual*, Third Edition. Anaheim, CA: BNI Publications, Inc., 1988.

Horsley, F. William, ed. *Means Graphic Construction Standards*. Kingston, MA: R.S. Means Co, Inc., 1986.

Olin, Harold B., J.L. Schmidt, W.H. Lewis. Revised by H.L. Simmons. *Construction Principles, Materials, and Methods, Sixth Edition*. New York: Van Nostrand Reinhold, 1995; John Wiley & Sons, Inc, 1998. Reprinted by permission of John Wiley & Sons, Inc.

Reproduced from the 1997 edition of the *Uniform Building Code*™, copyright © 1997, with the permission of the publisher, the International Conference of Building Officials.

Although the International Conference of Building Officials, Inc. (ICBO) has granted permission for reproduction of sections contained within the *Uniform Building Code*™ in conjunction with this publication, ICBO assumes no responsibility for the accuracy or the completion of summaries provided herein.

Reproduced from the 1997 edition of the *UBC Field Inspection Workbook*, copyright © 1997, with the permission of the publisher, the International Conference of Building Officials.

Although the International Conference of Building Officials, Inc. (ICBO) has granted permission for reproduction of sections contained within the *UBC Field Inspection Workbook* in conjunction with this publication, ICBO assumes no responsibility for the accuracy or the completion of summaries provided herein.

Stoeppelwerth, Walter W. and Darrell L. Lewis. *Kitchen & Bathroom Installation Manual, Volume I*. Hackettstown, NJ: National Kitchen & Bath Association, 1996.

Tile Council of America, Inc. *1998 Handbook for Ceramic Tile Installation*. Clemson, S.C.: Tile Council of America, Inc., 1998.

United States Gypsum Company. *Gypsum Construction Handbook, 4th edition*. Chicago, IL: United States Gypsum Company, 1992.

Chapter 11 Floor Covering & Acoustical Ceilings

Ballast, David Kent. *Handbook of Construction Tolerances*. New York: The McGraw-Hill Companies, 1994. Reprinted by permission of publisher.

Bentil, Kweku K. *Fundamentals of the Construction Process*. Kingston, MA: R.S. Means Co., Inc., 1989.

Brantley, L. Reed, and Ruth T. Brantley. *Building Materials Technology, Structural Performance & Environmental Impact*. New York: The McGraw-Hill Companies, 1996. Reprinted by permission of publisher.

Excerpted with permission from *Hardwood Floors: Laying, Sanding, and Finishing*, by Don Bollinger. Copyright© 1990 by The Taunton Press, Inc. All rights reserved.

Illustrations in Figures 11.4 and 11.5 reprinted with permission from SH_2A, Inc., Architects, 1718 Third Street, Suite 201, Sacramento, CA 95814 (Telephone: 916-441-0686).

Olin, Harold B., J.L. Schmidt, W.H. Lewis. Revised by H.L. Simmons. *Construction Principles, Materials, and Methods, Sixth Edition*. New York: Van Nostrand Reinhold, 1995; John Wiley & Sons, Inc, 1998. Reprinted by permission of John Wiley & Sons, Inc.

Reproduced from the 1997 edition of the *Uniform Building Code*™, copyright © 1997, with the permission of the publisher, the International Conference of Building Officials.

Although the International Conference of Building Officials, Inc. (ICBO) has granted permission for reproduction of sections contained within the *Uniform Building Code*™ in conjunction with this publication, ICBO assumes no responsibility for the accuracy or the completion of summaries provided herein.

Reprinted with permission from National Wood Flooring Association, 16388 Westwoods Business Park, Ellisville, MO 63021 (Telephone: 314-391-5161), Internet Web site: www.woodfloors.org.

Reprinted by permission of the National Oak Flooring Manufacturers Association, 22 North Front Street, Suite 660, Memphis, TN 38103 (Telephone: 901-526-5016), Internet Web site: www.nofma.org.

Chapter 12 Painting & Wallcovering

Bentil, Kweku K. *Fundamentals of the Construction Process*. Kingston, MA: R.S. Means Co., Inc., 1989.

Excerpts from PDCA P5-94, PDCA P4-94, and PDCA P1-92 are reprinted with permission from Painting and Decorating Contractors of America, 3913 Old Lee Highway, Suite 3313, Fairfax, VA 22030-2433 (Telephone: 703-359-0826), Internet Web site: www.pdca.com.

Farren, Carol E. *Planning & Managing Interior Projects*. R.S. Means Company, Inc., 1988.

NAHB Research Center. *Builders Guide to Paints and Coatings*. Upper Marlboro, MD: NAHB Research Center, 1993.

National Wood Window & Door Association. *Specifiers Guide to Wood Windows & Doors*. Des Plaines, IL: National Wood Window & Door Association, 1997.

Reprinted with permission from the Paint & Decorating Retailers Association, 403 Axminister Drive, St. Louis, MO 63026 (Telephone: 314-326-2636), Internet Web site: info@pdra.org.

Woodwork Institute of California. *WIC Manual of Millwork*. W. Sacramento, CA: Woodwork Institute of California, 1992 with 1995/1996 amendments.

Chapter 13 Specialties

Adaptive Environments Center, Inc. and R.S. Means Engineering Staff. *ADA Compliance Pricing Guide*. Kingston, MA: R.S. Means Company, Inc., 1994.

Reproduced from the 1997 edition of the *Uniform Building Code*™, copyright © 1997, with the permission of the publisher, the International Conference of Building Officials.

Although the International Conference of Building Officials, Inc. (ICBO) has granted permission for reproduction of sections contained within the *Uniform Building Code*™ in conjunction with this publication, ICBO assumes no responsibility for the accuracy or the completion of summaries provided herein.

Chapter 14 Plumbing

Adaptive Environments Center, Inc. and R.S. Means Engineering Staff. *ADA Compliance Pricing Guide*. Kingston, MA: R.S. Means Company, Inc., 1994.

Bentil, Kweku K. *Fundamentals of the Construction Process*. Kingston, MA: R.S. Means Co., Inc., 1989.

Copyright© 1998, *International One- and Two-Family Dwelling Code*, 5203 Leesburg Pike, Suite 708, Falls Church, Virginia 22041.

Copyright© 1997, International Code Council, Inc., Falls Church, Virginia. *International Plumbing Code*. Reprinted with permission of the author. All rights reserved.

Galeno, Joesph J. and Sheldon T. Greene. *Means Plumbing Estimating Methods*. Kingston, MA: R.S. Means Company, Inc., 1991.

Reproduced from the 1997 edition of the *Uniform Building Code*™, copyright © 1997, with the permission of the publisher, the International Conference of Building Officials.

Although the International Conference of Building Officials, Inc. (ICBO) has granted permission for reproduction of sections contained within the *Uniform Building Code*™ in conjunction with this publication, ICBO assumes no responsibility for the accuracy or the completion of summaries provided herein.

R.S. Means Company, Inc. *Plumbing Cost Data*. Kingston, MA: R.S. Means Company, Inc., 1999.

Reproduced from the *Uniform Plumbing Code*™, copyright 1997, with permission of the publisher, International Association of Plumbing and Mechanical Officials (IAPMO), 20001 East Walnut Drive South, Walnut, CA 91789 (Telephone: 909-595-8449), Internet Web site: www.iapmo.org.

Reprinted with permission from NFPA 13D, *Installation of Sprinkler Systems in One- and Two-Family Dwellings and Manufactured Homes*, copyright© 1996, National Fire Protection Association, Quincy, MA 02269. This reprinted material is not the complete and official position of the National Fire Protection Association, on the referenced subject which is represented only by the standard in its entirety.

Reprinted with permission from NFPA 54, *National Fuel Gas Code*, copyright© 1996, National Fire Protection Association, Quincy, MA 02269. This reprinted material is not the complete and official position of the National Fire Protection Association, on the referenced subject which is represented only by the standard in its entirety.

Chapter 15 HVAC

Copyright 1998, International Code Council, Inc. — *International One- and Two-Family Dwelling Code*, 5203 Leesburg Pike, Suite 708, Falls Church, Virginia 22041.

Figure 15.10 (Table R157-020), reprinted from the *1999 Means Mechanical Cost Data*, with permission from the publisher, R.S. Means Company, Inc., 63 Smiths Lane, Kingston, MA 02364 (Telephone: 800-334-3509).

Horsley, F. William, ed. *Means Graphic Construction Standards*. Kingston, MA: R.S. Means Co, Inc., 1986.

Reprinted from the *SMACNA Architectural Sheet Metal Manual, Fifth Edition*, Copyrighted 1993, with permission.

Reproduced from the 1997 edition of the *Uniform Mechanical Code*™, copyright © 1997, with the permission of the publisher, the International Conference of Building Officials.

Although the International Conference of Building Officials, Inc. (ICBO) has granted permission for reproduction of sections contained within the *Uniform Mechanical Code*™ in conjunction with this publication, ICBO assumes no responsibility for the accuracy or the completion of summaries provided herein.

Reprinted with permission from NFPA 54, *National Fuel Gas Code*, Copyright© 1996, National Fire Protection Association, Quincy, MA 02269. This reprinted material is not the complete and official position of the National Fire Protection Association, on the referenced subject which is represented only by the standard in its entirety.

Reproduced from the *Uniform Plumbing Code*™, copyright 1997, with permission of the publisher, International Association of Plumbing and Mechanical Officials (IAPMO), 20001 East Walnut Drive South, Walnut, CA 91789 (Telephone: 909-595-8449), Internet Web site: www.iapmo.org.

Rowe, William H., III. *HVAC: Design Criteria, Options, Selection, Second Edition*. Kingston, MA: R.S. Means Company, Inc., 1994.

Chapter 16 Electrical

DeLong, Paul H. and John H. Chiang, eds. *Electrical Estimating Methods, Second Edition*. Kingston, MA: R.S. Means Company, Inc., 1995.

DelPico, Wayne J. *Plan Reading & Material Takeoff*. Kingston, MA: R.S. Means Company, Inc., 1994.

Horsley, F. William, ed. *Means Graphic Construction Standards*. Kingston, MA: R.S. Means Co, Inc., 1986.

Reproduced from the December 1995 issue of *The Code Authority*, copyright © 1995, with permission of the publisher, Underwriters Laboratories, Inc., 333 Pfingsten Road, IL 60062 (Telephone: 847-272-8800).

Portions reprinted with permission from NFPA 70-1996, the *National Electrical Code® Handbook*, Seventh Edition, copyright© 1995, National Fire Protection Association, Quincy, MA 02269. This reprinted material is not the complete and official position of the National Fire Protection Association, on the referenced subject which is represented only by the standard in its entirety.

Reprinted with permission from NFPA 70-1996, the *National Electrical Code®*, copyright© 1995, National Fire Protection Association, Quincy, MA 02269. This reprinted material is not the complete and official position of the National Fire Protection Association, on the referenced subject which is represented only by the standard in its entirety.

National Electrical Code® and *NEC®* are registered trademarks of the National Fire Protection Association, Inc., Quincy, MA 02269.

Reprinted with permission from NFPA 72, *National Fire Alarm Code*, copyright© 1996, National Fire Protection Association, Quincy, MA 02269. This reprinted material is not the complete and official position of the National Fire Protection Association, on the referenced subject which is represented only by the standard in its entirety.

R.S. Means Co., Inc. *Electrical Cost Data*. Kingston, MA: R.S. Means Co., Inc., 1999.

INDEX

Z

Your Complete Code Resource

ICBO offers a complete line of building and construction codes and related technical products.

The **1997 *Uniform Building Code*™** (UBC) is the most widely adopted model building code in the world with complete regulations covering all major aspects of building design and construction. The **1997 *Uniform Mechanical Code*™** (UMC) provides a complete set of requirements for the design, construction, installation and maintenance of heating, ventilating, cooling and refrigeration systems, and incinerators. The ***Handbook to the Uniform Building Code*™** and the ***Handbook to the Uniform Mechanical Code*™** are completely detailed and illustrated commentaries on the 1997 UBC and UMC, tracing historical background and rationale and clarifying the application and intent of the provisions.